Charles T. Brues

Psyche - A Journal of Entomology

Volume xxx - 1923

Charles T. Brues

Psyche - A Journal of Entomology
Volume xxx - 1923

ISBN/EAN: 9783741178153

Manufactured in Europe, USA, Canada, Australia, Japa

Cover: Foto ©berggeist007 / pixelio.de

Manufactured and distributed by brebook publishing software
(www.brebook.com)

Charles T. Brues

Psyche - A Journal of Entomology

PSYCHE

A Journal of Entomology

Volume XXX

1923

EDITED BY CHARLES T. BRUES

Published by the Cambridge Entomological Club, Bussey Institution, Forest Hills, Boston 30, Mass., U. S. A.

Printed by The St. Albans Messenger Company
St. Albans, Vermont

PSYCHE

VOL. XXX. FEBRUARY 1923 No. 1

THE OCCURENCE OF *MUSCINA PASCUORUM* MEIGEN IN NORTH AMERICA IN 1922.[1]

(Presented Dec. 26, 1922, at the Boston meeting of the Entomological Society of America.)

BY CHARLES W. JOHNSON.

Boston Society of Natural History.

The increase and spread of this European fly in such numbers and over so wide an area, before its presence was actually discovered, was a great surprise, especially to the dipterist. The first specimens to come under my observation were received on October 10, among some Diptera collected by Dr. W. M. Wheeler, at Colebrook, Connecticut. The three specimens were taken, August 10, 18 and 21. A few days later I received a box of flies from Mr. K. F. Chamberlain, of Cornwall Bridge, Conn., and among them was a specimen collected August 6, the earliest record I have for the species. Mr. R. T. Webber found among the material collected at the Bound Brook nurseries, N. J., a specimen taken September 1. Professor C. T. Brues observed it in numbers both in his house and about a neighboring cider mill at Petersham, Mass., October 8. Mr. F. H. Walker collected two specimens at Marblehead, Mass., October 15. A few days later I received five specimens from Mrs. Ella L. Horr of the Worcester Natural History Society. Mrs. Horr said they were abundant in the cupola of the building and that the janitor said they were there in September, but that she did not happen to go there until about October 21. I wrote her that the fly was new to me and that I should like very much to have some more specimens. No males had been seen and I was doubtful in which of two European species to place it. On October 25, Mrs. Horr wrote to me that she had sent some to Washington and on the 26th sent me 51 specimens. I wrote to Dr. J. M. Aldrich in regard to the matter and on November 1 he replied as follows "It is *Muscina pascuorum* Meigen. I have compared it with European specimens determined by several authorities, and hence there is no doubt of what it is."

On October 27 I took two specimens on the window at my home in Brookline and on the 31st I received several specimens from Mrs. L. C. Marshall. of East Walpole, who said they were abundant in her house. On November 1, Dr. G. M. Allen captured a specimen in his house in Cambridge. On the 3d Dr. F. T. Lewis brought in seven specimens taken at Waban, Newton, and on the same date Dr. J. A. Cushman collected a specimen at Sharon. On the 7th a specimen was taken on a window at the Boston Society of Natural History, and on the 8th Dr. Lewis took a specimen at the Harvard Medical School, Boston. Thes single specimens indicate that they were by no means common in the city. On the 7th Dr. Cushman collected at Sharon nine specimens, among which was a male, the first I had seen. Dr Cushman then made three collections at Sharon, which are interesting in showing the relative proportion of this and the other species that normally frequent houses in the autumn.

November 12, 46 *Muscina pascuorum* (all females), 30 *M. assimilis*, 19 *Pollenia rudis*, 10 *Phormia regina*, 1 *Cynomyia cadavorina*. and 1 *Musca domestica*.

November 16, 22 *M. pascuorum*, 12 *M. assimilis*, 15 *P rudis*, and 2 *P. regina*.

November 26, 13 *M. pascuorum*, 11 *P. rudis*, and 5 *P. regina*

Another interesting series showing the relative abundanc of this species was made by Mr. F. H. Walker in the attic of a summer cottage at Asbury Grove, Mass. November 9, he collected 275 *Muscina pascuorum* (2 males), 21 *Pollenia rudis*, 15 *Phormia regina*, and 1 *M. assimilis*. Mr. Walker says: "I could have obtained thousands from neighboring cottages. The skylight from which I obtained these flies measured 22 by 36 inches."

The following additional records show how abundant and generally distributed the species is throughout eastern Massachusetts On November 10 Mr. M. T. Smulyan took a specimen at Melrose Highlands; on the 11th Mr. A. P. Morse captured a number at Ipswich; and on the 12th at Wellesley. On the 13th Mr. W. L. Maxcy reported it as abundant in his house at Still-water. On the 14th I caught the second male on a window in Brookline, and on the same date Mr. R. T. Webber reported it from Dover, and Mr. G. W. Barber from Arlington. On the 15th Miss Margaret Hayden collected it at Ashland; on the 18th Mr. C. V. Blackburn obtained it at Stoneham; on the 19th Mr. L. W. Jenkins secured it at Putnamville. On the 30th Mr. S. N. F. Sanford caught a specimen at Fall River, and on Dec. 2 Dr. G. M. Allen captured two at Cohasset.

Correspondence, together with a note published in Science (November 24), has further added to our knowledge of its distribution. Under date of November 14, Dr. W. E. Britton, of the Connecticut Agricultural Experiment Station, New Haven, writes: "We have noticed a number of large-sized flies around the windows and have killed some of them. We paid little attention to the species, but there are now some dead ones around the place and I will have some of them relaxed, pinned, and sent to you." I received the flies, November 21 and they were all *M. pascuorum*. Dr. H. T. Fernald, of Amherst, Mass., writes, "Answering your letter of Nov. 17, I may say that we have noticed a species of Muscina on our windows this fall and took specimens first on Oct. 12, though they were present considerably before that date. We are referring it to *Muscina pabulorum* Meig. I should be very glad to know whether we are on the right track." Under date of November 28, Dr. Fernald again writes: "Many thanks for your letter of Nov. 27. It has been reasonably abundant here, and was certainly present for at least a week or ten days before we thought of taking and actually dating a specimen. I have not heard of it from any other part of the state mainly because nobody appears to pay any attention to flies which show up on house windows."

In a letter from Dr. O. A. Johannsen of Ithaca, N. Y., dated November 24, he says:—

"I saw your note in Science this evening with regard to *Muscina pascuorum* and hasten to state that in Ithaca we have just discovered a new Muscina. Tuesday of this week I caught a fly in my laboratory which looked like *M. stabulans* but with black legs. As I was busy with other things I thought no more about it until the next day when Mr. Raymond C. Shannon came in with a fly which he asked me to look at. He realized that it was not one of the two species of Muscinas which were prevalent here. Mr. Shannon has been taking this species in Ithaca now for several days and he told me that there is one (either in his own or in the University collection, I have forgotten which) which was caught here in September. We tried to identify it and reached the conclusion that it was either *pabulorum* or *pascuorum.*"

Later Mr. Shannon wrote: "My captures of *Muscina pascuorum* consist of nine females and one male, collected from September 5 to November 22. "On December 16 Jos. C. Ouellet, C. S. V. of Outremont, Quebec, writes:—"I have just received from Father Ducharme of Rigaud College, a specimen which closely resembles *Muscina pascuorum.* I am mailing you the specimen today." The specimen was received on the 20th and proved to be a male of that species and the most northern record.

Over 450 specimens have come under my observation and of these only ten were males. A natural inference is, that this is probably due to their having been discovered so late in the season, and that it is usually the female that comes into the houses to hibernate. On the other hand it was not until November 7 that I saw a male, after over 90 specimens had been seen, and Dr. Wheeler informs me that the specimens he collected in August were taken on flowers.

I can find very little in literature pertaining to the habits of this species. Schiner (Fauna Austriaca, I, 597) says that "Bremi found the larvæ in *Agaricus citrinus.*" On making some inquiry regarding the fungi found in the vicinity of Boston, Miss Jennie F. Conant, Secretary of the Boston Mycologial Club, informed me that this is the same as *Amanita citrina*, common to both

Europe and North America. It is found from August to early November, and some of the members of the Club say that it was quite common this year. Charles McIlvaine (One thousand American Fungi, p.7. 1900) considers it only a form of *A. phalloides.* Miss Conant also reported a number of other species of Amanita, including *A. phalloides,* as being common, and as early as July. If *Muscina pascuorum* is strictly fungicolous, the abundance of these fungi might account for the rapid increase of this fly during the autumn.

The wide distribution that this fly has attained in this country before being discovered, makes it difficult to ascertain where the species was actually introduced. The pre ence of the fly in Connecticut and New Jersey at least two months before being observed in the vicinity of Boston, is an indication that it was probably introduced somewhere near New York City, sometime prior to the present year (1922). This theory is strengthened by the usual or apparently natural line of dispersal of species in a northerly or northeasterly direction, as followed by most of the introduced species; *e. g.*, elm beetle, asparagus beetles, leopard moth, gipsy moth, etc.

Its present distribution would indicate a still wider dispersal if all records were available. Its habit of entering houses would also induce it to enter railroad cars and thus be rapidly and widely transported over the country, a factor that probably partly accounts for its sudden and wide-spread appearance. It promises to be as great a nuisance to housekeepers as the cluster fly (*Pollenia rudis*) which often enters houses in great numbers in the autumn. The last living specimen of *Muscina pascuorum* was received from Dr. Lewis, Waban, Mass., December 14. It will probably continue to appear in lesser numbers during the warm days throughout the winter and spring. A study of its habits and dispersal during the coming year will prove very interesting.

TWO NEW BEMBECIDS (HYMENOPTERA) FROM THE CHANNEL ISLANDS, CALIFORNIA.

By Chas. L. Fox, San Fransico, Cal.

Bembix hamata sp. nov.

Male: Black; labrum, mandibles except apex, broad base and narrow lateral margins; clypeus; lower part of frons between antennal bases (angled dorsally); scape below; broad anterior orbits much shortened above; very narrow posterior orbits, abbreviated above and much shortened below at lower fourth of eye from mandibles; fascia on the first tergite reduced to small subovate lateral spots; narrow undulate fascia on tergites 2-6, usually narrowly interrupted medially, except that on 6 which is continuous and strongly notched on posterior border; small spot on each side apical area of ultimate tergite, sometimes wanting, lateral spots of sternites 2-5, sometimes very small ones on 6, an apical wedge shaped stripe on femora above, longer on anterior pair, tibiæ except black stripe on posterior surface and tarsi, all dull greenish yellow, the tarsi having a rusty tinge. Segments 7-9 of flagellum sub-spinose on posterior border; segments 9-11 bearing large open flat depressions, the ultimate segment a trifle longer than the preceding, only slightly curved, almost as broad at the roundedly truncate apex as at the base; intermediate femora below irregularly serrate-dentate; second sternite bearing a median hooked process distinctly higher than its basal length, much as in *foxi*, the sixth bearing a prominent oblique process narrowed and more produced posteriorly than in *nubilipennis;* this sternite also bearing a similar pair of rounded lateral processes or ridges; seventh sternite with a prominent median carina. Inner margins of the eyes nearly parallel. Flagellum tinged with fulvous below. Wings hyaline, veins dark brown. Head, thorax, median segment, base of abdomen, coxæ, trochanters and femora clothed with dense long pale pubescence, becoming longer and white beneath, the rest of the abdomen shorter-pubescent.

Genital stipites shaped much as in *comata* as shown by Parker (fig. 163) but the inner margin more arcuated before the apical notch, the hairs longer and confined to the inner half of the surface and the basal suture oblique for its whole length, as in Parkers' figure 169. Length 18-20 mm.

Both in the Handlirsch and Parker keys this species runs to *nubilipennis* from which it differs in the size and shape of the body (being very robust) and in the absence of maculation on the thorax, pattern of maculation on the tergites and sternites, color and maculation of the legs, spinose character of the segments of the flagellum, serrate dentations of the intermediate femora, the longer and more dense pale pubescence and the form of the male stipites. In general appearance this species somewhat resembles *amœna*, principally on account of the robustness of the body and the pattern of maculation on the tergites, but from which it can readily be distinguished by the character of the processes on the second and sixth sternites, absence of maculation on the thorax, the much shorter apical spurs on the intermediate tibiæ and the form of the stipites. Like the related species this shows some variation in the yellow marking; two specimens have small spots on the tegulæ and one a larger spot at the inferior angle of the prothorax.

Described from twelve males taken by Mr. E. P. Van Duzee on San Miguel Island, Santa Barbara County, California, May 20, 1919.

Holotype, male, No. 928, Mus. Calif. Acad. Sci.; paratypes in the collection of the Academy and in that of the author.

Type locality; San Miguel Island, Calif.

Bembix hamata subsp., **lucida** subsp. nov.

Male: Black; labrum, mandibles except apex and very narroe base; clypeus, lower part of frons between antennal bases (angled dorsally); anterior orbits, much shortened above, narrow posterior orbits slightly shortened above and below almost reaching base of mandibles; posterior edge of tubercles continued in a narrow stripe down the sides of the prothorax; tegulæ except apex; fascia on first tergite, very widely interrupted medially, shortened to large elongated lateral spots; fasciæ on tergites 2-5, continous and undulate on anterior border, deeply notched on posterior, that on sixth covering entire tergite except narrow posterior edge; large quadrate spot on apex of ultimate tergite, emarginate anteriorly; lateral spots on sternites 2-6; femora distally above and below; anterior tibiæ except broad stripe below and narrow one above, intermediate and posterior except short stripe below, and tarsi, all greenish yellow. The markings of head and femora below are more of a greenish white (in the species yellow). The segments of the flagellum have the same characters and color as in the species; the intermediate femora are more strictly dentate than in the species. The second sternite bears a large median hooked process (not so high as in the species), and the sixth a shorter and more acute median process and less prominent lateral ridges; seventh with a prominent median carina. The characters of the eyes and pubescence are the same as in the species.

This subspecies can readily be distinguished from the typical form of the species by the maculations on the head, thorax and abdomen and the general clearer color.

Described from one male taken by Mr. E. P. Van Duzee on Santa Cruz Island, Santa Barbara County, California, May 18, 1919.

Holotype, male, No. 929 Mus. Calif. Acad. Sci.

Type locality; Santa Cruz Island, California.

A SINGULAR HABIT OF SAWFLY LARVÆ

By W. M. Wheeler and W. M. Mann.

The following casual observations made in two widely separated South American localities seem worth recording as we have been unable to find any published account of similar behavior among the larvæ of New World sawflies.

July 16, 1920, the attention of the senior author was attracted to a very conspicuous, compact mass of sawfly larvæ crawling like a hugh slug over the short grass and sandy soil along the side of a trail through the jungle near Kartabo, British Guiana. The mass was about ten inches long, four inches broad and two inches thick in the middle. It was elongate elliptical and rather pointed at each end and retained its shape and size unaltered as it progressed like a single organism over the substratum. It consisted of about 200 larvæ, each an inch long and of a deep metallic blue color (Fig. 1). Further investigation of of this singular mass was cut short by a heavy tropical shower. A number of the larvæ were hastily thrown into a vial of alcohol. Although the senior author hoped to find the larvæ in the same locality under conditions more favorable for study, they were not again encountered either by him or by any of the other workers at the Tropical Laboratory.

The junior author had occasion to study a migrating mass of the same or of a closely related sawfly larva during February 1922, on the forest trail between the Mission and the edge of the pampa, near Cavinas on the Rio Beni, in Bolivia. The mass which he encountered was about a foot long, three or four inches broad at the middle, narrowed in front and behind and thickest in the middle. It, too, consisted of more than a hundred dark metallic blue larvæ of the same size as those observed by the senior author. The mass was also moving along as a compact unit and from a distance looked like a gigantic Planarian. When a pair of forceps was thrust into the midst of the larvæ and a number of them thrown out to the side, those in front and behind slowed up, appeared to be disturbed and jerked from side to side. The ejected individuals immediately headed for the mass and crawled into it and the whole, thus redintegrated, then quickened its pace and was soon moving along as before.

Fig. 1. Sawfly larvae from Kartabo, British Guiana. X 1⅔

Mr. S. A. Rohwer kindly examined a number of the larvæ taken at Kartabo and reported as follows: "I regret that I am unable to help you very much with the identification of these specimens. We know so little about the larvæ of exotic sawflies and especially about those from South America. The only thing I can do is to guess as to the group to which your specimens belong. They remind me very much of the larva of Perga, and as this group is not represented in South America, but is replaced by another subfamily, I venture to suggest that your specimens belong to the family Perreyidæ, subfamily Syzygoniidæ (Philomastiginæ of my classification of 1910). I imagine that the crawling larvæ you saw were in their last feeding stage and were looking for a place for pupation. I should also imagine that they had fed gregariously and that they would cocoon gregariously. Perhaps their cocoons will resemble those of the Australian genus

Perga or those of the subfamily Argiinæ; that is, they would have a single, more or less impervious cocoon surrounded by a loosely woven, reticulate, outer cocoon which would be covered with long hair."

Such literature as we have been able to consult on the habits of the Australian saw-flies of the genus Perga proves to be very interesting in connection with the South American larvæ referred by Mr. Rohwer to the family Perryidæ. Froggatt (1891, 1901 and 1918) has published notes on the larval habits of several species of Perga. Concerning one of them, the "steel-blue saw-fly", *P. dorsalis* Leach, he says (1918): "The gregarious larvæ feed at night, and rest during the day, clustered together in an oval mass, on the stem of the gum-tree upon which they are feeding. When disturbed, they exude a sticky yellow substance from the mouth, at the same time raising the tip of the body, and tapping it down on the foliage. The leaves are devoured from the top of the young gum trees; and when the larvæ are full fed, they crawl down the stem to pupate. I have found them fully developed in the middle of April; but when they descend from their resting place, they wander about over the grass for several days before they finally select a place in which to pupate, generally the softer soil against a tree-trunk. Into this they burrow to a depth of three or four inches, massing their large, oval cocoons in rows, one against the other. I watched several large swarms feeding upon the Peppermint-gums (*Eucalyptus novæ-angliæ*) at our Experiment Station at Uralla, and afterwards in their erratic wanderings over the grass; and marked down their final resting place and dug up the cocoons. At Binalong, in April, I observed two large swarms marching in massed formation; the heads of the hind rows always rested upon those in front as they moved along steadily together. Every now and then, the front rank came to a dead stop, when they all rested for three or four minutes; then a number began raising up and tapping down the tip of the abdomen, whereupon the whole band took up the motion; the leading ranks made a fresh start, and all moved along again. In the largest band, I counted two hundred and fifty caterpillars."

Social tendencies are revealed not only by the Perga larvæ and pupæ, but also in the extraordinary protection of the young larvæ by the mother saw-fly. Lewis (1836) long ago described this behavior in *P. lewisi* Westwood of Tasmania, and Froggatt (1901), who says that this is "the commonest sawfly about Sydney on bloodwood" (*Eucalyptus corymbosa*), records his own observations as follows: "The female makes a double slit on the upper surface of the leaf generally among the young growth, in which she inserts a double row of elongate eggs, which, as they swell form a regular blister, but the most remarkable fact in the life history of this insect is the care she takes after laying her eggs. Nearly all insects after the eggs are laid leave them to their fate, but Lewis' saw-fly not only stands guard over them until they are hatched but further looks after the helpless grubs for some time after they have commenced feeding. She straddles the eggs with her wings half opened, the tip of her abdomen turned up, and with her jaws open, makes a slight buzzing sound if meddled with; if you pick her up, she never attempts to fly, but crawls back to her post, reminding one of an old hen protecting her chicks. The grubs when full grown are slightly under 1½ inches in length, general colour dull brown to dirty yellow, covered with short brown hairs, the last abdominal segment yellow. When full grown they crawl into the ground and form the typical form of cocoon, generally in regular rows."

LITERATURE.

1836. *Lewis, R. H.* Case of Maternal Attendance on the Larva by an Insect of the Tribe of Terebrantia, belonging to the genus Perga, observed at Hobarton, Tasmania. Trans. Ent. Soc. London 1, 1836, pp. 232-234.

1891. *Froggatt, W. W.* Notes on the Life-history of Certain Saw-flies (Genus Perga) with Description of a New Species. Proc. Linn. Soc. New South Wales 5, 1891, pp. 283-288.

1901. ....The Pear and Cherry Slug (*Eriocampa limacina* Retz), generally known as *Selandria cerasi*, with Notes on Australian Sawflies. Agric. Gazette N. S. Wales 1901, pp. 1-11, 4 pls.

1918. .... Notes on Australian Sawflies (Tenthredinidæ). Proc. Linn. Soc. N. S. Wales 43, 1918, pp. 668-726.

TWO NEW ANTS FROM BOLIVIA

(Results of the Mulford Biological Exploration.—Entomology.)

BY WM M. MANN.

BUREAU OF ENTOMOLOGY, U. S. DEPARTMENT OF AGRICULTURE.

Among the material collected in Bolivia and so far studied, two ants are of especial interest. One belongs to an aberrant undescribed genus of "driver ant" (Dorylinæ) and the other is a Ponerine species very similar to *Probolomyrmex filiformis* Mayr known from workers described in 1901, from Port Elizabeth, Cape Colony. The latter is an example of discontinuous distribution, such as is frequently found among the Ponerine ants, but it is the first case in its subfamily of a South African and South American relationship.

Subfamily Dorylinæ

Leptanilloides gen. nov.

Worker.—Small, slender, monomorphic. Head elongate, subquadrate, anterior portion of front rather strongly impressed. Clypeus short. Frontal carinæ very short, fused between the antennæ, separated anteriorly and bordering the antennal fossæ. Cheeks with a strong carina, which projects forward as a blunt tooth. Mandibles with distinct basal and apical portions separated by a rounded angle. Eyes absent. Antennæ 12-jointed, stout, scape short, funiculus moderately thickened distally, joints submoniliform. Thorax long, slender and flattened; mesoëpinotum compressed laterally; promesonotal impression strong; mesoëpinotal impression obsolete. Epinotum unarmed. Petiole subcylindrical, not pedunculate. Postpetiole shorter and broader than the petiole. Gaster long and slender, the three segments visible from above separated by strong constrictions. Legs, long spines of anterior tibiæ very strongly pectinate, those of middle tibiæ small, of the posterior pair moderately pectinate. Claws simple.

Genotype.—Leptanilloides biconstricta, new species.

Leptanilloides biconstricta sp. nov. (Fig. 1)

Worker.—Length 1.80-2 mm.

Head subquadrate, very slightly narrowed behind, more than twice as long as broad, sides nearly straight and parallel; occipital corners rounded, border feebly concave. Mandibles slender; their blades edentate. Anterior border of clypeus straight. Antennæ stout, scapes clavate, extending about three-eighths the distance to occipital borders; first funicular joint rounded, broader and longer than the second; joints 2-10 slightly transverse, gradually increasing in size toward apex; terminal joint about as long as the two preceding together. Thorax and epinotum elongate, slender, flat above; pronotum from above broadest at humeri, with sides feebly convex; mesoëpinotum seen from above, quadrate, two and a half times as long as broad, with nearly straight sides; epinotal declivity very short and rounding into the basal portion. Petiolar node from above a little longer and two-thirds as broad as the post petiole, very slightly narrowed from front to rear and with straight sides; in profile slightly convex above, the ventral outline convex at anterior half and concave behind, projected anteriorly as a blunt cone. Postpetiole in profile rather strongly convex beneath, feebly above; from above a little longer than broad, feebly broadened from front to rear, with straight anterior and posterior borders and nearly straight sides. First gastric segment a little longer than the second or third. Legs long, the femora swollen and the tibiæ enlarged apically.

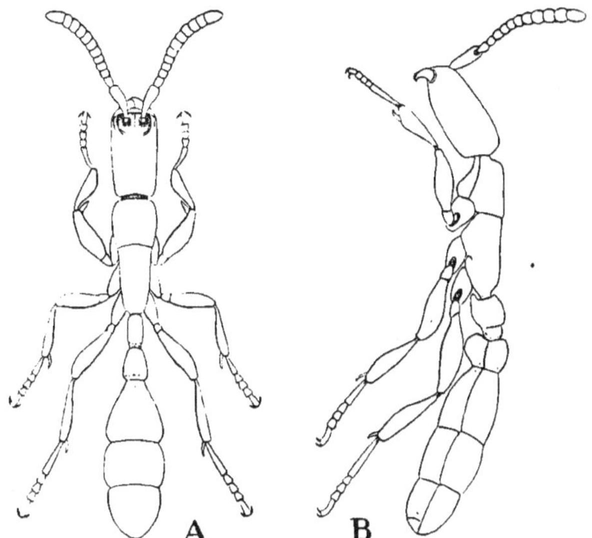

Fig. 1. Worker *Leptanilloides biconstricta* gen. nov. et sp. nov. A, dorsal, B, profile view.

Shining; head with abundant, separated, coarse, punctures; thorax and abdomen with much finer and sparser punctures. Head, body and appendges with abundant, rather coarse, short and erect, brownish hairs.

Color brownish red.

Type-Locality.—Tumupasa, Bolivia.

Cotypes.—Cat. No. 25905, U. S. N. M.

Described from a small series of workers, taken with callows, but without sexual or immature phases, from beneath a deeply embedded stone near a stream.

In general habitus this is very similar to *Leptanilla*, but the structure of the head associates it more closely with *Eciton*, from which it is distinct in the form of the frontal lamellæ, the form of the gaster and in not being polymorphic.

Subfamily Ponerinæ.

Probolomyrmex? boliviensis sp. nov. (Fig. 2).

Female.—(deälated) Length 2.8 mm.

Head about one and one-half times as long as broad, with slightly convex sides, rounded occipital angles and straight border; vertex and posterior portion of head broadly and evenly rounded, anterior part projected as a thick plate, broader than long and truncated in front, completely covering the mandibles. Clypeus on the anterior truncated portion, triangular, not sharply defined. Mandibles small and rather slender, blades rounding into the basal portions, with two indistinct and blunt teeth. Maxillary palpi 3-jointed, the first and second joints subequal in length and together as long as the third. Labial palp small, apparently 2-jointed. Frontal area rather large, feebly impressed. Frontal lamellæ fused into a high, thin plate, strongly convex in profile; behind separated and very short. Antennal insertions near front margin of head, bordered by a fine carina. Antennæ 12-jointed, scape extending about four-fifths the distance to occipital corners; funiculus evenly enlarged distally, without club; first funicular joint longer than broad; joints 2-10 transverse; terminal as long as the three preceding joints together. Eyes small, little convex, situated at middle of sides. Ocelli small. Thorax long and rather narrow, moderately convex above and at sides, humeri broadly rounded Mesonotum one and one-third times as long as broad. Scutellum longer than broad, rounded behind, with feeble impressions at middle of sides. Epinotum with feebly convex base and nearly flat declivity, bluntly dentate at angle. Petiole elongate nodiform; from above, twice as long as broad, with the posterior margin concave at middle and subdentiform at sides; in profile longer than broad and nearly twice as thick behind as in front, its ventral outline bisinuate, with a blunt antero-ventral tooth; posterior surface strongly concave. Gaster slender, strongly constricted between the first and second segments, first segment narrowed in front, shorter than the second, remaining segments small, directed downward. Sting well developed and strong.

Legs long, rather slender, tibial spines coarse, those on posterior pair strongly pectinate.

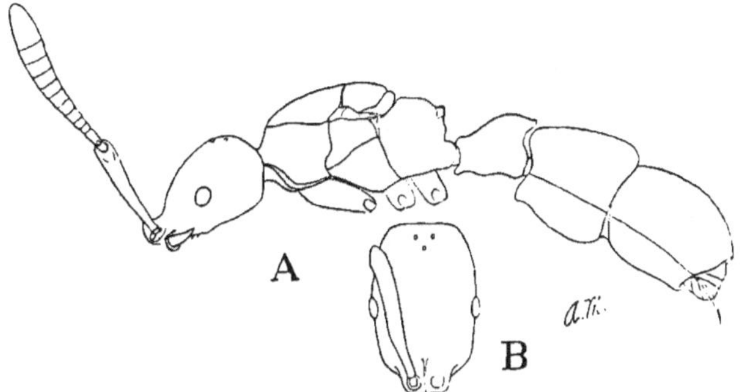

(Fig. 2. Female *Probolomyrmex? boliviensis* sp. nov. A, profile view; B, head, dorsal view)

Opaque, finely, densely reticulate and in addition with rather coarse, foveolate punctures, especially prominent on the front of head, epinotum and gaster. Pubescence white, very fine, closely appressed, moderately abundant, more so on gaster and appendages.

Brownish red, appendages brownish yellow.

Type-locality.—Rurrenabaque, Bolivia.

Type.—Cat. No. 25906, U. S. N. M.

Described from a unique female found beneath a stone, near a small colony of *Ponera* sp.

In *Probolomyrmex boliviensis* the posterior segments of the gaster are much smaller, the antero-ventral petiolar spine is rounded and points forward and the epinotum is dentate rather than angulate, characters different from those in *P. filiformis* Mayr, but I can find no difference of generic value that would separate the two. In the worker of *filiformis* Mayr the posterior gastric segments are larger, the antero-ventral petiolar spine is lamellate and directed backward and the epinotum is angulate, instead of dentate. Perhaps when the female of *filiformis* or the worker of *boliviensis* is discovered it will be necessary to separate the two species generically, but the female of the latter resembles *filiformis* so closely, even to the curious Platythyrea-like sculpture, that had it been taken in South Africa, instead of South America, one would be tempted to regard it merely as the female of Mayr's species.

A NEW GENUS OF MYRMECOPHILOUS PHORIDÆ, WITH NOTES ON SOME RELATED FORMS.[1,2]

By Charles T. Brues.

Among the insects obtained by Dr. William M. Mann while a member of the Mulford Exploration in South America, are several species of wingless and subapterous Phoridæ. With the exception of a single species, all were taken in the nests of ants and are undoubtedly myrmecophilous. One, which proves to represent a new genus, occurs with Tranopelta, a hypogæic ant not hitherto known to harbor any phorid myrmecophiles, while the others are ecitophiles previously described from other parts of the South American continent.

The type of the new species is deposited in the United States National Museum.

Tranopeltoxenos gen. nov. (Fig. 1).

Entirely wingless. Head seen from above wide, twice as broad as long; antennæ widely separated, nearly round, their cavities separated; arista very short and thick, indistinctly pubescent; palpi strongly bristled; front with a series of six small, slightly proclinate, bristles along the anterior margin between the antennæ, and with eight macrochætæ disposed in two transverse rows; of these, the anterior row curves forward medially, with its lateral bristle behind the eye and the posterior row lies close to the occipital margin. Eyes very small; ocelli

[1]Results Mulford Biological Exploration.—Entomology.

[2]Contribution from the Entomological Laboratory of the Bussey Institution, Harvard University. No. 215.

absent. Proboscis short, stout, heavily chitinized and porrect. Thorax very short on its dorsal surface (as indicated by a pair of humeral and posterior-lateral macrochætæ) but when the abdomen is bent down, exposing the posterior slope, it is seen to be nearly as long as the head. Abdomen large, ovate, fully twice as wide as the head and broadest at the third segment behind which it tapers obliquely; second to fifth segments each with a row of six long, but not very stout bristles extending across the disc near the middle; sixth with a denser fringe along the margin; sides of all the segments each with several additional bristles. First six segements heavily chitinized, without any membranous borders; following three segments tubular. Abdomen above moderately convex, below flat, so that in cross-section it is very strongly depressed. Legs rather short and stout; four posterior tibiæ ciliate on the edge.

Type: *T. manni* sp. nov.

This insect is quite unique and I cannot place it in any of the described genera in spite of the fact that these are already very numerous. There is no indication of any gland opening on the fifth abdominal segment and the abdomen is heavily chitinized over its entire dorsal surface. It resembles Chonocephalus Wandolleck, but the form of the abdomen is very different, the palpi are very densely bristled, and both the cephalic and thoracic chætotoxy disagree. Chonocephalus, also, so far as is known, is not myrmecophilous.

Tranopeltoxenus manni sp. nov. (Fig. 1).

♀. Length 1.5 mm. Head and its appendages, thorax and legs, pale yellow; first five abdominal segments black or piceous, the sixth segment fuscous, the extrusible ones beyond whitish. Head above covered with sparse, appressed black hairs and at the sides anteriorly below the antennæ with a row of bristly hairs. Bristles of palpi dense, as long as the width of the palpus. Antennæ rather small, the arista but little longer than the diameter of the third joint. Post-antennal bristles rather stout, parallel, proclinate; inner bristles of lower frontal row rather weak, set far apart, just above the antenna; bristles of upper row very large and curving backward very strongly. Second to fifth abdominal segments of about equal length, the third wider than the second; third and fourth narrower, the base of the fifth only two-thirds as wide as the second; sixth small; seventh to ninth fleshy, completely retractile. Transverse row of bristles

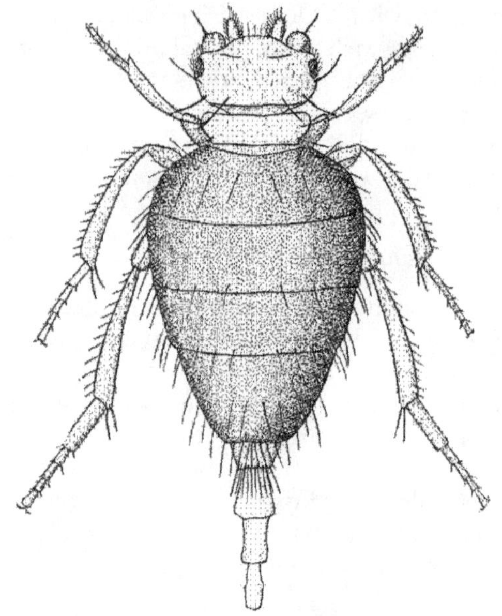

Fig. 1. *Tranopeltoxenos manni* sp. nov. ♀

on second segment placed before the middle, those of the third behind the middle, of the fourth and fifth some distance before the apex; sixth with a dense fringe at the apex.

Described from two specimens, taken in a nest of *Tranopelta gilva*, var. *amblyops* by Dr. W. M. Mann during December 1921 at Tumupasa, Bolivia. Type No. 25904, United States National Museum.

Acontistoptera brasiliensis Schmitz

Zool. Jahrb , Abth. f. Syst. vol. 37, p. 527 (1914)

Dr. Mann obtained this species on two occasions, once at Tumupasa, Bolivia (December 1921) with *Eciton cæcum* and again at Covendo, Bolivia, with the same ant. The type was found with *E. predator* in Santa Catarina, Brazil.

There is a slight disagreement between these specimens and Schmitz's original description, but I think this is undoubtedly due to the poor condition of the type which according to its describer is defective and glued to a card The mesonotum bears a pair of marcochætæ on the disc in front of the pair shown in the original figure; so that there are two pairs of dorso-centrals instead of one. Also the abdomen bears a very small basal plate, elongate oval in form which is no doubt a vestige of the second tergite which is so large in most of the related genera. The three known species of Acontistoptera may be distinguished quite readily by the form of the thorax which is more or less triangular in all, but varies in width and length. Thus in *A. melanderi* Brues from Texas it is considerably longer than broad, in *A. mexicana* Malloch from Mexico, nearly twice as long as broad and narrowed almost to a point at the base of the scutellum, while in the present species the length scarcely exceeds the width.

Ecitomyia comes Schmitz.

Zool. Jahrb. Abth. f. Syst., vol. 37, p 524 (*Ecitophora*)

This species is represented by two series, one taken with *Eciton burchelli* at Huachi, Bolivia and the other with *E. cæcum* at the mouth of the Rio Madidi, Bolivia (January 1922).

The specimens all agree exactly with Schmitz's original description and figures, but have no ocelli, and I feel quite positive that the hyaline spots referred to as ocelli are really the points where bristles have been broken off. Compared with *Ecitomyia wheeleri* Brues, *E. comes* may be readily recognized by the complete absence of the second chitinous plate (third tergite) on the abdomen and by the more heavily bristled wings.

Puliciphora venata Aldrich

Trans. Entom Soc. London, p. 436 (1896) (*Phora*).

Brues. Trans. Amer. Entom. Soc., vol. 29, p. 382 (1903). (*Pachyneurella*)

Brues. Bull. Wisconsin Nat. Hist. Soc., vol. 12, p. 142 (1915)

I cannot distinguish a series of females taken at Espia, Rio Bopi, Bolivia from the West Indian form. Dr. Mann's specimens were attracted to masses of old cheese that had been abandoned by the expedition. A number of others in my collection from Grenada, B. W. I. were similarly trapped in jars containing chicken bones to which I found them attracted in great numbers.

THE PROBABLE OCCURRENCE OF PARTHENOGENESIS IN *OCHTHIPHILA POLYSTIGMA*. (DIPTERA)

By A. H. Sturtevant, New York City.

A total of 68 living specimens of *Ochthiphila polystigma* Meigen (one of the Ochthiphilinæ, a subfamily included among the Acalypterate Diptera) was examined between August 23 and September 30, 1922. All were females; and there is no possibility that the males were found but not recognized as belonging to this species, since during that period no other member of the genus was taken. With the exception of a single female belonging to an apparently undescribed genus, the only other members of the subfamily Ochthiphilinæ taken belonged to the very different genus Leucopis, and here both sexes were found. Eleven of the *O. polystigma* females were dissected, and three more were fixed and sectioned. In none of these was any trace of sperm found. I was during this time making a comparative study of the structure of the internal reproductive organs of the females of all the Acalypteræ, and was thus in a position to know how and where to look for sperm. It is safe to say that none was present. Yet several of these females contained what appeared to be fully formed eggs—in fact in a number of cases there was an egg already in the uterus. Such females, evidently laying eggs but without sperm present, were found as early as August 23 and as late as the middle of September. At both times there were also found females with ovaries still small—these again being without sperm. It seems clear thus that the results are not due to the collecting having been done either at the beginning of a generation, before males had emerged or at the end of one, after the males had mated and died.

In addition to the live females just discussed, I have examined the pinned material in my own collection, in the collection of the American Museum of Natural History, in that of the United States National Museum, and in that of Prof. J. M. Aldrich. All the specimens of *O. polystigma* found in these collections were again females. The data thus obtained (including the live specimens examined) are summarized in Table I.

Table I. Distribution of *Ochthiphila polystigma* Meigen

State or Province	Number of females	Months in which taken
New Hampshire	1	?
Ontario	7	May—?
Massachusetts	89	June—Sept
Connecticut	3	May
New York[1]	4	Sept.
New Jersey	1	Sept.
Pennsylvania[1]	8	Oct.
Maryland	3	Apr.—Aug.
Indiana	10	July—Aug.
Illinois	3	June
Wisconsin	1	July
South Dakota	1	June
Manitoba	2	July
Utah	2	July
Holland	2	June
Total	137	Apr.—Oct.

[1]Two of the specimens from New York and all of those from Pennsylvania were taken by Dr. F. Schrader, and have not been seen by me. Dr. Schrader states that all were females.

In the collections of Prof. Aldrich and of the U. S. National Museum are specimens of four other species of Ochthiphila, identified by Coquillett and by Aldrich. These all include males, as will appear from Table II (which also includes 6 European specimens from my own collection). In all four species the males have large conspicuous external claspers, and could not possibly be mistaken for females. This indicates that the failure to find males of *O. polystigma* is not due to failure to recognize them as males.

Table II Relative abundance of the sexes in Ochthiphila.

Species	♀	♂
O. aridella Fallén	11	11
O. elegans Panzer	12	5
O. geniculata Zetterstedt	1	1
O. juncorum Fallén	5	9

A case very similar to the one just described occurs in *Lonchoptera furcata* Fallén. It was found by de Meijere (1906) that nearly all individuals of this species were females, and that these did not have sperm in their receptacles. In other European species, such as *L. lutea* Panzer, both sexes occur in nearly equal numbers, and sperm is present in the receptacles. The extreme scarcity of males has been confirmed by Lundbeck (1916) for the European *L. furcata*, and by Aldrich (1918) for the American forms, which apparently belong to the same species. Aldrich was able to find only two American males of the genus (one from Ontario and one from Colorado), though he recorded 2652 females.

I have myself collected numerous American specimens of Lonchoptera, and have examined the material in the American Museum of Natural History. Table III shows the result of this study. The five males that appear in the table, and two of the California females as well, appear to belong to a distinct species; all the others (except perhaps the Colorado female) are almost certainly *L. furcata*. I have several times obtained eggs from females of this species, and these have hatched into larvæ; but in no case have I been able to rear these larvæ, nor have I been able to be sure that the mothers did not contain sperm—though it is extremely unlikely that sperm was present. This observation makes it probable, however, that Lonchoptera reproduces by adult parthenogenesis, rather than by pedogenesis.

Table III. Relative abundance of the sexes in Lonchoptera.

State or Province	♀	♂
New Hampshire	1	0
Vermont	1	0
Massachusetts	53	0
New York	403	0
New Jersey	53	0
Ontario	1	0
Pennsylvania	1	0
District of Columbia	1	0
North Carolina	2	0
Wisconsin	1	0
Colorado	1	0
Santa Clara Co., California	426	0
Monterey Co., California	23	4
Truckee, California	344	1
Total	1311	5

Parthenogenesis has been described in the Chironomid genera Chironomus, Corynoneura, and Tanytarsus by Grimm (1870) Johannsen (1912), Goetghebuer (1913), Edwards (1919), and others. Eggs are produced in some cases by the larvæ, in others by the pupæ, and in still others by the imagines. In all cases in which imagines have been produced by parthenogenetic (including pedogenetic) lines, these have been females and have bred parthenogenetically if at all. Males are known to occur in these genera, and in one case even in a species that reproduces parthenogenetically; but in no case are males reported as arising from larvæ known to have been produced by parthenogenesis.

The first case of parthenogenesis recorded among the Diptera was that of the Cecidomyiid, Miastor, discovered by

Wagner (1863). In this case it is the larvæ that reproduce parthenogenetically. Imagines are not often produced, but when they do appear both sexes are found (Meinert 1864, Wagner 1865, Kahle 1908). Kahle states that there is a significant excess of females, and Felt (1911) describes only the female, though he does not state that males were absent. It is not known whether the imagines breed at all, or not; Kahle states that he did not observe copulation. It does not appear to have been entirely proven that the males arise from larvæ that have been produced by pedogenesis, though most students of Miastor have apparently taken this for granted without making cultures from isolated larvæ.

Parker (1922) has reported a probable case of pedogenesis in the blow-fly, *Calliphora erythrocephala* Meigen, with the production of male and female imagines in something like equal numbers from isolated individual larvæ. Since the actual production of eggs or larvæ was not observed to go on in Parker's larvæ, and since Lowne (1892) and others have dissected large numbers of larvæ of this species without finding mature eggs or larvæ in them, it seems best to withhold judgment for the present as to the occurrence of pedogenesis in Calliphora, as Parker himself indicates.

LITERATURE CITED.

Aldrich, J. M. 1918. Notes on Diptera. Psyche 25; 30-35.

Edwards, F. W. 1919. Some Parthenogenetic Chironomidæ. Ann. Mag. Nat. Hist. 3; 222-228.

Felt, E. P. 1911. *Miastor americana.* An account of pedogenesis. New York State Mus. Bull. 147; 82-104.

Goetghebuer, M. 1913. Un cas de parthénogenèse observé chez un Diptère Tendipédide (*Corynoneura celeripes*). Bull. Acad. Roy. Belg. 1913; 231-233.

Grimm, O. 1870. Die ungeschlechtliche Fortpflanzung einer Chironomus-Art und deren Entwicklung aus dem unbefruchteten Ei. Mém. Acad. Imp. Sci. St. Pétersbourg ser. 7, tome 15.

Johannsen, O. A. 1912. Parthenogenesis and Pædogenesis in Tanytarsus. Maine Agr. Exp. Sta. Bull. 187; 3-4.

Kahle, W. 1908. Die Pädogenesis der Cecidomyiden. Zoologica, Bd. 21. Heft. 55. 80 pp., 6 plates.

Lowne, B. T. 1892-1895. The Anatomy, Physiology, Morphology, and Development of the Blow-fly. London. 2 vols., 778 pp

Lundbeck, W. 1916. Lonchoptera. Diptera Danica 5; 1-18.

de Meijere, J. C. H. 1906. Die Lonchopteren des paläarktischen Gebietes. Tijd. v. Ent. 49; 44-98.

Meinert, F. 1864 Weitere Erläuterungen über die von Prof. Nic. Wagner beschriebene Insectenlarve, welche sich durch Sprossenbildung vermehrt. Zeits. wiss. Zool. 14; 394-399.

Parker, G. H. 1922. Possible Pedogenesis in the Blow-fly *Calliphora erythrocephala*. Psyche 29; 127-131.

Wagner, N. 1863. Beitrag zur Lehre von der Fortpflanzung der Insect enlarven. Zeits. wiss. Zool. 13; 513-527.

Wagner, N. 1865. Ueber die viviparen Gallmückenlarven. Zeits. wiss. Zool. 15; 106-117.

PHORTICOLEA BOLIVIÆ, A NEW MYRMECOPHILOUS COCKROACH FROM SOUTH AMERICA.

(Results Mulford Biological Exploration.—Entomology).

By A. N. Caudell.

Bureau of Entomology, U. S. Department of Agriculture, Washington, D. C.

Among the insects collected in Bolivia by Dr. Wm. M. Mann, entomologist with the Mulford Expedition to South America in 1921-1922, was an apparently undescribed myrmecophilous cockroach belonging to the genus *Phorticolea* of Bolivar. Although only males were collected there seems to be no doubt that this generic assignment is correct, as the specimens agree in every essential with the characters given for *Phorticolea*. The size and locality of the new species here described indicate specific distinctness from *testacea*, the type and only described species of *Phorticolea*, though the very brief diagnosis of the latter makes comparative characterization impossible.

Phorticolea boliviae sp. nov.

Description.—Adult male, the opposite sex unknown. General color reddish brown, laterally somewhat darker. Head yellowish with black eyes; vertex evenly convex, not quite concealed beneath the pronotal disk; eyes lateral, subreniform, strongly fasceted and almost or quite three times as long vertically as broad; interocular space fully twice as great as the vertical length of one of the eyes; labial palpus with the terminal segment large, thick, fusiform, about two and one half times as long as the median width and a little more than twice as long as the preceeding segment, which is triangular in shape. Antenna approximately as long as the insect itself and consisting of at least thirty segments[1]; first segment noticeably longer than broad and flattened basally; second and third segments subquadrate, each being about, or a little more than half as long and scarcely

[1]One specimen only of the three examined has both antennae apparently complete and here consists of thirty segments. The other two specimens have the antennae more or less mutilated.

as thick as the basal one; fourth to fourteenth segments transverse, the fourth to the eleventh or twelfth being two or more times as broad as long, the more basal ones especially broad; fifteenth and sixteenth segments subquadrate and the succeeding ones longer than wide, those towards the apex being twice as long as broad, some of them slightly more.

Pronotum about twice as broad as long, broadly rounded anteriorly, truncate posteriorly, the lateral angles rounded and slightly produced posteriorly, as are also those of the meso- and metathorax, which segments are subequal with each other in length and together barely as long as the pronotum. Organs of flight entirely absent. Legs stout; femora fusiform, broad and flattened, the anterior pair somewhat smaller than the others, the intermediate pair about three times as long as the greatest width and the posterior ones a little stouter, being about two and one half times as long as broad; anterior femora armed beneath with a series of fine setiform hairs, the intermediate and posterior ones armed beneath on both margins with a few very minute spinules in the apical portion, so small as to be scarcely noticeable under moderate magnification, a subapical one on each margin being decidedly larger; all the femora have an apical calcar on the cephalic geniculation; tibiæ strongly spinose above, the spines in three series, and beneath with mostly finer hair-like spinules, a couple of larger ones in the cephalic margin of the intermediate and posterior ones; tarsi slender, the posterior metatarsus barely shorter than the combined length of the rest of the segments; arolia present, of medium size.

Abdomen anteriorly about as broad as the posterior width of the metanotum, abruptly narrowing posteriorly and scarcely as long as the combined lengths of the three thoracic segments; there are seven dorsal segments visible exclusive of the supraanal plate; lateral margins straight, the posterio-lateral angles sharp and moderately produced posteriorly; the posterior margins of the segments are subtruncate, that of the one preceeding the supraanal plate concave near each side opposite the insertion of the cerci; supraanal plate somewhat more than twice as broad as long, rather narrowly rounded apically; subgenital plate broad and rounded apically; cerci short and very broad, tapering from near the base, about twice as long as the greatest width, apically pointed and without distinct segmentation; styles simple, about two thirds as long as the cerci, subcylindrical in shape, rather bluntly pointed apically and the whole organ about four times as long as the basal width.

The entire insect is beset with short pile, the lateral margins of the abdominal segments, supraanal plate, cerci, styles and legs with stout setæ instead of pilose hairs.

Measurements.—Length, entire insect from front of head to tip of abdomen, about 2.7 mm.; pronotum 1 mm.; posterior femora, 1 mm.; posterior tibia, .8 mm.; posterior tarsus, .7 mm.; posterior metatarsus, .3 mm. Width pronotum posteriorly, 1.8 mm.; metanotum posteriorly, 2.1 mm.; posterior femora medially, .3 mm.

Type locality.—Cachuela Esperanza, Beni, Bolivia.

Described from three males collected in March, 1922, by Dr. Wm. M. Mann in the joint nests of *Crematogaster limata var. parabiotica* Forel *and Camponotus (Myrmothrix) femoratus* Fabr.

Type and paratypes in U. S. National Museum. Catalogue No. 25757, U. S. N. M.

VERBENAPIS - A CORRECTION.

In Psyche, vol. 29, p. 162 (August 1922) the name of the genus of bees, Verbenapis is misspelled. Although the error is quite obvious, Professor Cockerell has reminded me that it might receive the attention of nomenclaturists unless corrected. [Editor.]

A FOSSIL GENUS OF DINAPSIDÆ FROM BALTIC AMBER (HYMENOPTERA)

Contribution from the Entomological Laboratory of the Bussey Institution, Harvard University, No. 22C.

By Charles T. Brues.

A small lot of amber insects which I have had for a number of years contains a very extraordinary hymenopterous insect. Several times I have attempted to locate it in one of the recognized families of the order, but I have never been satisfied with the result. It has also been shown to a number of entomologists, none of whom were willing to express any positive opinion concerning its relationships. Several weeks ago it was sent to the hymenopterists of the United States National Museum with a request that they examine it, and I soon received a note from Mr. R. A. Cushman calling my attention to a paper by Dr. James Waterston just received in the current October number of the Annals and Magazine of Natural History wherein he describes an almost exactly similar living insect from South Africa. For the African form Waterston has proposed the genus Dinapsis which he makes the type of a new family, Dinapsidæ. He regards Dinapsis as more closely related to Megalyra than to any known Hymenoptera and from an examination of the fossil insect it seems that he is quite justified in expressing this opinion. Dinapsis is known only from the female, while the amber species is represented only by the male, but the two differ so clearly in wing venation and in the structure of the head and thorax that they cannot be regarded as congeneric. As the amber insect throws much light on the relationship of Dinapsis, it seems appropriate to describe it immediately after the appearance of Waterston's paper.

Fortunately, the fossil specis is beautifully preserved and I able to give a quite complete description.

Prodinapsis gen. nov.

♂. General form and size similar to Dinapsis Waterston. Head slightly broader than the thorax, obliquely narrowed behind the eyes which are large and pubescent; occipital margin raised, carinate; posterior orbits with a narrow groove; ocelli in a large triangle; vertex with a fine, but clearly impressed median line. Antennæ 14-jointed, filiform, inserted near the clypeus. Mouthparts not visible. Mesonotum about twice as broad as long; without parapsidal furrows but with a deep, complete, crenulate median furrow; inner angles of axillæ not meeting, their edges margined by deeply crenulate grooves and their inner angles connected by a crenulate groove. Propodeum coarsely reticulated and apparently without the more prominent longitudinal carinæ present in Dinapsis. Four anterior legs slender, the hind pair stout, with the femora somewhat swollen and the tibiæ enlarged apically; tibial spurs very small;hind coxæ very large; tarsal claws very small and slender, simple. Abdomen as long as the thorax, elongate oval, with seven nearly equal segments; claspers prominent, projecting downwards and curved forwards, obtusely pointed. Venter convex, the sternites almost as wide as the tergites. Fore wing with a small elongate stigma; subcostal cell broad; radial vein short, curved, leaving the cell widely open; basal half of cubitus present, but the transverse cuoiti and recurrent nervure are wanting; two closed discoidal cells; basal cells indistinctly separated as the separating vein is very weak and delicate; nervulus interstitial.

Type: *P. succinalis* sp. nov.

Prodinapsis differs ro m D.napsis most strikingly in having the radial cell inocmplfete, in lacking the transverse cubitus and in possessing two discoidal cells. Also the orbital groove is narrower and the axillæ do not meet at their inner angles.

Prodinapsis succinalis sp. nov. (Fig. 1).

♂. Length 2.7 mm. Probably with the head and mesonotum black, the remainder of the thorax dark brown, the abdomen light brown and the legs piceous on the femora and tibiæ; wings hyaline and antennæ with no trace of annulation. Head coarsely shagreened, about one-half wider than long; temples two thirds as broad as the eye, occipital groove distinctly crenulate; posterior ocelli two-thirds as far from the eye as from one another. Antennæ (Fig. 1c) slightly longer than the head and thorax; scape stout, curved; pedicel globose or but little elongated; flagellar joints of about equal length, all long and slender (probably the basal joints are slightly longer, but they cannot be viewed exactly in the proper plane). Mesonotum and scutellum shagreened; posterior edge of mesonotum straight, the suture not crenulate. Pleuræ and coxæ smooth or finely granulate; mesopleura with a crenulate line along the anterior and posterior edges. Abdominal segments of nearly

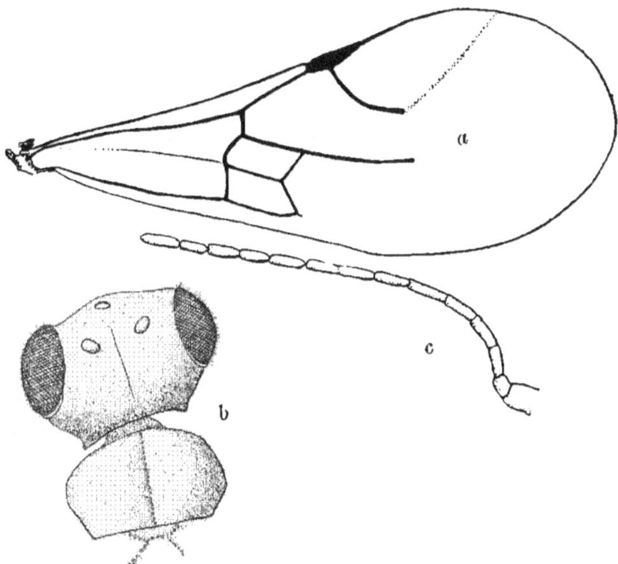

Fig. 1. *Prodinapsis succinalis* sp. nov. A, wing; B, head and anterior portion of thorax, C, antennae

equal length, the second and also the first slightly, but not very noticeably, longer than the others; the posterior edges of the segments sinuous and slightly incised medially. Claspers almost as long as the dorsal length of the sixth segment. Wings ample, the margins with the usual short fringe of hairs, but none of the veins appear to be bristly as in Dinapsis. Venation (Fig. 1a) rather pale brown, but very distinct, the veins terminating abruptly as indicated; weak apical section of radial vein very indistinct and visible only in certain lights.

Type in the Amber collection of the Zoological Museum of the University of Königsberg.

Taken together the two genera exhibit a much closer affinity to Megalyra than is evident from a knowledge of either Dinapsis or Prodinapsis alone. In fact the neuration of Prodinapsis is almost identical to that of Megalyra except that the basal cells are separated by a very heavy vein in the latter and the apical part of the radius, although not vein-like, is indicated by a much more evident thickening. That the unknown female may be provided with a long ovipositor is also probable. The short and complete radial cell and absence of discoidal cells in Dinapsis give the wing a very different appearance, but the almost exactly similar, yet strikingly characteristic cephalic thoracic and abdominal structure, shows Dinapsis and Prodinapsis to be very closely related. On account of this similarity to Megalyra, it seems very doubtful whether the Dinapsidæ can be retained as a family distinct from the Megalyridæ since the differences are of a very minor nature. In both groups the head, antennæ, medially grooved mesonotum, scutellum with separated axillæ, oval sessile abdomen with more or less equal segments, long thread-like ovipositor and wing venation agree closely in form and structure; only the size is different, for Megalyra is a large insect and the other two genera are very small.

The actual relationship of the three genera is rather difficult to elucidate, since as already stated Megalyra and Prodinapsis have almost identical wings while Prodinapsis and Dinapsis are almost identical in bodily characters, but each with a wing type that cannot be derived one from the other, nor can both be derived from that of Megalyra. If the three are closely related, as seems undoubted, the ancestral form must have had a body like Dinapsis or Prodinapsis and wings with a marginal, cubital, two basal and two discoidal cells. Such an insect must have been more or less Oryssoid in many somatic and venational characters although perhaps only superficially similar. The median thoracic suture so pronounced in Dinapsis and Prodinapsis occurs elsewhere, so far as I am aware, only in certain Ceraphronidæ, Scelionidæ and Belytidæ of the Serphoid series where it may or may not be associated with the paired parapsidal furrows, although a few Bethylidæ and the Ampulicidæ have a median pronotal (not mesonotal) furrow. In Megalyra it is prominent and undoubtedly homologous to the one in Dinapsis.

Recent Books.

In these lists are included titles relating entirely or directly to insects, as well as books in the related fields of biology which are of immediate interest to the Entomologist.

Folsom, J. W. Entomology, with Special Reference to its Ecological Aspects. pp. 502, extensively illustrated. P. Blakiston's Son & Co. Philadelphia, 1922. A third edition of this well known and useful text, containing much new material, and needing no introduction to American entomologists.

Parker, G. H. Taste, Smell and Allied Senses in the Vertebrates. pp. 192, illustrated. J. B. Lippincott Co., Philadelphia $2.50. Relates specifically to the vertebrates from the standpoint of both anatomy and physiology and presents material that the entomologist will find very useful.

Rousseau, E. Les larves et nymphes aquatiques des insectes d'Europe. vol. 1, pp. xx 967, 344 figures. J. Lebèque, Brussels. The first volume includes the Rhynchota neuropteroids and Trichoptera. A very complete and well illustrated compendium on the biology, morphology and classification of the aquatic members of these groups, with extensive bibliographical references.

Bouvier, E. L. THE PHYSIC LIFE OF INSECTS. English translation by L. O. Howard, pp. XVI†377 New York, The Century Co.

Dr. Howard has made available to the English-reading public, in a most excellent translation, Bouvier's highly entertaining and stimulating treatment of insect-behavior.

Lavier, Geo. LES PARASITES DES INVERTÉBRÉS HÉMATOPHAGES; PARASITES QUI LEUR SONT PROPRE; PARASITES QU'ILS TRANSMETTENT AUX VERTÉBRÉS. 218 pp. illus. Paris, Vigot Frères, 1921.

A very complete account of the microparasites of blood-sucking insects and of their relations to disease in man and other vertebrates.

PROCEEDINGS OF THE CAMBRIDGE ENTOMOLOGICAL CLUB.

March 14, 1922, Mr. C. W. Johnson showed a collection of New England Hippoboscidæ and gave an account of their habits, classification and distribution. See vol. 39, Nos. 4-6.

Mr. W. J. Clench showed the milkweed beetles *Tetraopes tetraophthalmus* and *canteriator* and a supposed hybrid between them.

Prof. W. M. Wheeler told about a mass of saw-fly larvæ, which he had observed in South America, moving slowly through the wet grass like a single animal. Mr. C. W. Johnson called attention to a similar habit in the dipterous genus Sciara in which the larvæ cluster together in a long narrow mass which moves along like a worm. See vol. 29, Nos. 4-6.

April 11, 1922. Mr. F. Waldo Dodge showed a collection of over a hundred species of the coleopterous family Tenebrionidæ. He also gave an account of the common species of Coccinella, illustrated by drawings.

Several members discussed the food-habits of Dragon-flies. Mr. Frost said that while collecting he had been protected from mosquitoes by Dragon-flies as long as he remained in sunshine. Mr. Dodge described the catching of Cicindela by Dragon-flies; he said the beetle could defend itself by standing on end and offering only its head and mandibles to attack.

Mr. Roland Hussey gave an account of the hemipterous bugs of the genus Triatoma. See Psyche Vol. 29 No. 3.

Mr. C. W. Johnson described a Tipula from Mt. Washington in which the venation of the wings differed on the two sides in ways previously considered characteristic of different species.

The committee on public lectures reported that six lectures had been given as follows:

February 18. L. O. Howard. On the work of the Bureau of Entomology with special reference to the Gipsy Moth and other injurious insects of local interest. February 25. Wm. T. M. Forbes. On the Butterflies and Moths. March 4. J. Chester Bradley. On Some Habits of Wasps and their relatives. March 11. C. T. Brues. On Mosquitoes and other insects as carriers of disease. March 18. Miss Edith M. Patch. On the Seven Lives of an Elm Aphis, *Erisoma lanigerum*. March 25. J. H. Emerton. On the Spiders, their structure, habits and relations to Insects.

The lectures were fully illustrated by lantern slides and by the new motion-pictures of insects of the Society for Visual Education. Audiences of about one hundred persons attended and paid half the expense of the course, the rest being met by subscription among members of the Club.

May 9, 1922 Prof. W. M. Wheeler read a paper on the distribution of the genus Formica in the tropics. See Psyche Vol. 29 Nos. 4.

Mr. C. W. Johnson described two new dipterous flies from Mt. Desert, Maine and other New England localities.

Mr. R. H. Howe, Jr., remarked on recent collections of Dragon-flies, especially the formerly rare *Williamsonia lintneri*, several of which have lately been taken near Boston.

Miss Butler exhibited an unidentified larva found in Michigan in considerable numbers among eggs of Tabannus flies on leaves of *Typha latifolia*.

June 13, 1922 Mr. Denton showed May-flies found in great numbers near ponds and collected by handfuls beneath the hood of his automobile.

Mr. C. A. Frost showed recently collected Coleoptera.

Prof. Brues gave some notes on food plants of the Colorado potato-beetle, especially *Solanum rostratum*.

Prof. W. M. Wheeler showed some wingless Hymenoptera of the genus Scleroderma from Texas which feed on soft larvæ of any kind, raise a brood in a month's time and can be kept in confinement. It has winged and wingless forms of both sexes and appears to be an attractive subject for genetic studies

September 12, 1922 Mr. O. E. Plath gave an account of his observations on Bumblebees begun in 1921 and continued through the summer of 1922, during which time thirty-seven colonies were kept in boxes and watched through the season. In most of the nests Atherophagus beetles were found, sometimes attached to the feet or antennæ of bees. Chelifers were found in considerable numbers in one nest. The parasitic bees, Psithyrus, were found in several nests and new observations made on their habits and relations to their hosts. See vol. 29, Nos. 4-6.

October 10, 1922 the list of members was read and corrected. The death was announced of Laurence R. Reynolds, Vice-president of the Club, and a well known student of the Coleoptera. He had been on a collecting trip to the West Indies and Venezuela from which he returned in poor health and died in Boston, October 9. Mr. C. W. Johnson gave an account of his summer collecting at Mt. Desert in June and again in September and at the Rangeley Lakes, Maine. Mr. Johnson also discussed a collection of insects made by Owen Bryant in Vermont near Mt. Mansfield. Mr. J. H. Emerton spoke of his collecting in July in eastern Maine where successful photographs were made of the webs of *Theridion zelotypum,* a spruce-forest spider, and where *Leinyphia nearctica* had been found in a bog at South Gouldsboro fifty miles farther south than any previous record.

November 14. 1922 Dr. J. W. Chapman, who had returned from six years residence in the Phillippines, read a paper by himself and Prof. Wheeler on the mating of ants of the genus *Diacamma* of which no winged females are known. See vol. 29, Nos. 4-6. Dr. Chapman afterwards showed some lantern slides and gave an account of the country near Dumaguete where he had been living.

Mr. C. W. Johnson gave an account of the recent occurrence in large numbers of the European fly *Muscina pascuorum* which had been reported at various places in the eastern United States. See vol. 30, No. 1.

Prof. C. R. Crosby of Cornell University told about the Extension Entomological work in New York State by which entomologists of the State College of Agriculture are kept in touch with farmers, information in regard to injurious insects collected and remedies recommended.

December 12, 1922 Dr. Alice M. Boring of Wellesley College read a paper on the chromosomes in the germ cells of the two varieties of the frog-hopper, *Monecphora bicincta.* No differences were found.

PSYCHE

A JOURNAL OF ENTOMOLOGY

ESTABLISHED IN 1874

VOL. XXX APRIL, 1923 NO. 2

CONTENTS

CAMBRIDGE ENTOMOLOGICAL CLUB

PSYCHE is published bi-monthly, the issues appearing in February, April, June, August, October and December. Subscription price, per year, payable in advance: $2.00 to subscribers in the United States, Canada or Mexico; foreign postage, 15 cents extra. Single copies, 40 cents.

Cheques and remittances should be addressed to Treasurer, Cambridge Entomological Club, Bussey Institution, Forest Hills, Boston 30, Mass.

Orders for back volumes, missing numbers, notices of change of address, etc., should be sent to Cambridge Entomological Club, Bussey Institution, Forest Hills, Boston 30, Mass.

IMPORTANT NOTICE TO CONTRIBUTORS.

Manuscripts intended for publication, books intended for review, and other editorial matter, should be addressed to Professor C. T. Brues, Bussey Institution, Forest Hills, Boston 30, Mass.

Authors contributing articles over 8 printed pages in length will be required to bear a part of the extra, expense for additional pages. This expense will be that of typesetting only, which is about $2.00 per page. The actual cost of preparing cuts for all illustrations must be borne by contributors: the expense for full page plates from line drawings is approximately $5.00 each, and for full page half-tones, $7.50 each; smaller sizes in proportion.

AUTHOR'S SEPARATES.

Reprints of articles may be secured by authors, if they are ordered before, or at the time proofs are received for corrections. The cost of these will be furnished by the Editor on application.

Entered as second-class mail matter at the Post Office at Boston, Mass. Acceptance for mailing at special rate of postage provided in Section 1103, Act of October 3, 1917, authorized on June 29, 1918.

PSYCHE

VOL. XXX. APRIL 1923 No. 2

OBSERVATIONS ON THE FEEDING HABITS OF ROBBER FLIES. PART I.

PROCTACANTHUS RUFUS WILL. AND *P. BREVIPENNIS* WIED.

BY S. W. BROMLEY.

Massachusetts Agricultural College, Amherst, Mass.

One of the characteristic insects of the sandy plains along the Quinnipiac river in southern Connecticut during the hot sunny days of July is the large and handsomely-colored robber-fly, *Proctacanthus rufus* Will. Its rusty-orange abdomen and swift, undulating flight as it starts up in advance of the collector make it very conspicuous. The frequency with which one is seen bearing away some large insect that it has captured invites attention to what particular species are being taken.

The flies are very active and hard to approach, taking wing at the slightest movement and flying long distances before again alighting. In fact, the only times that they are at all easily captured is when they are encumbered with prey, and even then they are very wary and when disturbed carry such large prey as *Polistes* several rods before they again settle down. Because of these habits, it was very exasperating to stalk an individual over the hot sands only to have the specimen take flight just as the net was poised for the stroke.

Of the prey taken, all were of the order Hymenoptera. I did not see them attack species of any other order, although it is probable that they would capture Hymenoptera-resembling Diptera if opportunity offered. No attention was paid by them to the Lepidoptera and Odonata that occasionally drifted over the sands.

For aid in determining the species recorded, both from *P. rufus* and *P. brevipennis*, I wish especially to thank Dr. W. E. Britton of the Conn. Exp. Station who allowed me access to the Station collection, and to Dr. H. T. Fernald for the use of the Massachusetts Experiment Station collection.

The insects taken from *P. rufus* are as follows:

Sex of Fly		Date	Locality	Prey
1.	♀	July 2, '22	Hampden, Conn.	*Vespa vidua* Sauss. (queen)
2.	♀	"	"	*Polistes variatus* Cresson. (worker)
3.	♀	"	"	*Apis mellifera* L. (worker)
4.	♀	July 8, '22	"	*Polistes pallipes* LePel. (worker)
5.	♀	"	"	" "
6.	♂	"	"	*Apis mellifera* L. (worker)
7.	♀	"	"	"
8.	♀	"	"	"
9.	♂	"	"	"
10.	♀	"	"	"
11.	♀	"	"	"
12.	♂	"	"	"
13.	♀	"	"	"
14.	♀	"	"	"
15.	♀	"	"	"
16.	♀	"	"	*Pompiloides tropicus* L. ♀
17.	♀	July 16, '22	Wallingford, Conn.	*Apis mellifera* L. (worker)
18.	♀	"	"	"
19.	♀	"	"	"
20.	♂	"	"	*Polistes pallipes* LePel. (worker)
21.	♀	"	"	*Microbembex monodonta* Say. ♀
22.	♂	"	"	*Tiphia inornata* Say. ♀
23.	♀	"	"	"
24.	♂	"	"	*Elis interrupta* Say. ♂
25.	♂	"	"	*Amblyteles rufiventris* Brullé.
26.	♂	"	"	*Hemipogonius* sp? ♀

Summarized Table of Prey

Hymenoptera.

14	*Apis mellifera* L.	1	*Elis interrupta* Say.
3	*Polistes pallipes* Le Pel.	1	*Pompiloides tropicus* L.
2	*Tiphia inornata* Say.	1	*Hemipogonius* sp?
1	*Vespa vidua* Sauss.	1	*Microbembex monodonta* Say.
1	*Polistes variatus* Cresson.	1	*Amblyteles rufiventris* Brullé.

From this may be seen that over 50% of the prey taken from the flies consisted of honey-bee workers. The explanation of the presence of so many bees in such an uninviting environment as these sand areas is this: beyond the western edges of the fields where I made these observations were banks of sumac to and from which the bees were continually streaming, many taking their course over the sand plains not more than ten or fifteen feet from the ground. It was from these that the robber-flies took heavy toll. Where the flies were most abundant I often saw one sweep upward and grasp a bee, only to fly so far with its prey as I approached that I was unable to locate it and obtain the record.

Several honey-bees that were taken from the flies were afterwards dissected and examined by Mr. R. E. Snodgrass of the Bureau of Entomology, with whom I was staying at the time, and myself. A specimen that the fly had dropped because it had consumed all parts possible was found to be nothing but an empty shell. Nearly all of the digestive, nervous, and muscular systems had been dissolved, probably by the introduction of an enzyme, and sucked out. The poison sac was intact, as was the tracheal system and all chitinized portions. A bit of the small intestine and unrecognizable pieces of other organs remained in the body cavity, but most of the internal structures were gone. Examination of others in different stages of consumption showed the muscle tissue of the thorax reduced to a shredded mass and the muscles and brain in the head-capsule disintegrated. Whether or not this was accomplished by an enzyme secreted by the salivary glands, I do not know. Further work might determine this point.

An interesting point noted in watching the flies was the fact that although *Psammocharids* were the predominating and most conspicuous hymenopterous insects flying over the plains, the flies seemed to have trouble in capturing these. I watched them dart at these wasps on several occasions but the wasps eluded them by dropping to the ground and running through clumps of bunch-grass. They are occasionally captured, however, and I was able to take the flies preying upon *Psammo-*

charids in two instances, as shown by the list, but I never had the good fortune of seeing any in the act of capturing the wasps.

Females of *P. rufus* were watched for oviposition habits. No attempts were seen to be made, but empty pupa cases were seen protruding from the sand. These, because of their size, were evidently of this species, indicating the underground life of the immature stages.

Recently, through the kindness of Mr. Nathan Banks, I was allowed to examine the collection at the M. C. Z. where two records of this species with prey were obtained.

♀ *P. rufus*: prey, *Polistes* sp? Woods Hole, Mass., VII,19, 1893. A. P. Morse, Coll.

♀ *P. rufus*: prey, *Bremus* sp? ♂ West Springfield, Mass., VII, 26, 1915. H. E. Smith, Coll.

Proctacanthus rufus seems to be restricted to sandy areas such as those above mentioned and I have never taken it in the fields and pastures frequented by *P. philadelphicus* except those in the immediate vicinity of the sand areas. That the insect is not more widely spread is a fortunate thing for bee-keepers.

Another Asilid found in the same sandy areas as the above but less conspicuous and active is *Proctacanthus brevipennis* Wied. This belongs to the same genus but is smaller and more of the color of the sand on which it alights. I found it to be far less abundant than its larger relative in the area studied.

It will be seen from the list of prey that the type of insects captured by this species is quite different from that taken by by the last. Here half the species recorded were specimens of the beetle *Anomala lucicola* Fab. which is common on the sand fields and captured during flight, as is the case of all prey taken.

The list of insects taken from *P. brevipennis* is as follows:

Sex of Fly		Date	Locality	Prey
1.	♀	July 8, '22	Hampden, Conn.	*Anomala lucicola* Fab.
2.	♀	"	"	"
3.	♀	July 16,'22	Wallingford, Conn.	*Formica fusca* var? ♂
4.	♀	"	"	*Anomala lucicola* Fab.
5.	♀	"	"	*Zelus exsanguis* Stal. ♀
6.	♂	July 23,'22	"	*Sarcophaga* sp?

Summarized Table of Prey.

Coleoptera	Diptera
3 *Anomala lucicola* Fab.	1 *Sarcophaga* sp?
Hymenoptera	Hemiptera
1 *Formica fusca* var?	1 *Zelus exsanguis* Stal.

McAtee and Banks in their paper on the Asilidae of the District of Columbia (Proc. Ent. Soc. Washington, vol. 22. p. 26) record *P. brevipennis* as feeding upon *Anomala* sp. This fly evidently has a predilection for this genus of beetles.

Most of the prey from both species were taken from females, as one would naturally expect to be the case in predacious insects, for they are larger and more powerful than the males and require more stored-up energy for the discharge of of their sexual functions.

NOTES ON THE DIPTEROUS FAMILY CYRTIDÆ.

By F. R. Cole.

Stanford University, California.

In 1919 the writer published a revision of the Cyrtidæ of North America (Trans. American Ent. Soc., XLV, 1-79). There are some mistakes and omissions in this paper which should be corrected and some notes have accumulated on various species of the group.

Eulonchus marginatus O. S. There are two specimens of this apparently rare species in the collection of the California Academy of Sciences, taken at Sobre Vista, Sonoma Co., Cal., May 8 (Kusche).

Ocnæa helluo O. S. A specimen taken at College Station, Texas, was sent to the writer by Mr. H. J. Reinhard. It is 12.5 mm. in length and answers the original description in most respects; it differs in that all the longitudinal veins reach the wing margin. In each wing there is an adventitous cross-vein in cell M-3, one in cell 1st R-5 in one wing and one in cell R-1 in both wings (see fig. 1).

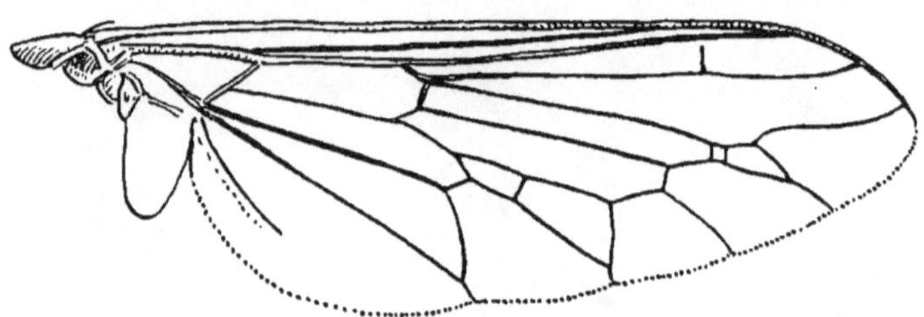

Fig. 1. *Ocnæa helluo* O. S., wing.

Acrocera liturata Will. The writer has one specimen taken at Los Gatos, Cal., June 20, 1917. This is a female with very little black at the base of the scutellum. There is more yellow on the abdomen than in the typical description. The species is evidently quite variable in coloration. Length 3 mm.

Acrocera hubbardi Cole. There are several specimens of this species in the collection of the Calif. Acad. of Sciences and most of them are typical. Specimens taken at Crystal Lakes, San Mateo Co., Cal., June 25, 1916 (E. P. Van Duzee) have the scutellum entirely black and less yellow on the abdomen than in the typical specimens; vein R-1 is brown, the rest of the wing veins yellow, including the costa, the membrane hyaline. Other specimens were taken at Sisson, July 25 (E. P. Van Duzee), Santa Cruz, June 8 (Giffard) and Oakland, August, 1905 (E. P. Van Duzee), all in California.

Ogcodes albicinctus Cole new name for *O. marginatus* Cole which is preoccupied by *O. marginatus* Meigen, a synonym of *O. pallipes* Latreille. The length, omitted in the original description, is 4-4.5 mm. A series of specimens received from Mr. B. C. Cain, taken at Brentwood Lodge, Bear Lake Co., Idaho, July 17, 1920, probably belong here but are not quite typical, the pile of the thorax not being unusually long; the femora are yellow on less than the apical third. The genitalia are distinct from *O. costatus*, but no males of *melampus* were available for comparison.

Ogcodes albiventris Johnson. There is a male specimen in the collection of the Cal. Acad. of Sciences, taken at Livermore, Cal., August 1904 (F. X. Williams). The abdomen is largely white; the first segment of the abdomen has a large basal black spot, separated from the posterior margin by the white border; the second, third and fourth tergites have a narrow, transverse black band at the base and one of about equal size near the posterior margin, a black mark connects the bands on the second and third segments; the fifth segment has a narrow anterior and posterior black margin, the latter interrupted in the middle and not quite reaching the posterior margin. The venter differs from the typical description in having a basal black band on sternites 1, 4 and 5, a small round spot on each side on the second and third sternites. The length is 5.25 mm. The sex of the type is not given and the differences in color may be due to a difference in sex.

Ogcodes rufoabdominalis Cole. The length was omitted in the original description and should be 4.25-5.5 mm. Specimens of this species were kindly loaned by Mr. McAtee from the collection of the U. S. Biological Survey. The black on the abdomen of one male was reduced to a basal triangle on the second, third and fourth tergites, the incisures yellowish; there was a basal blackish brown band on the second sternite. Two males were taken at Bear River, Utah, June 17, 1915 (A. K. Fisher) and one at the same place July 11, 1915 by A. W. Wetmore. One female I make a neotype and describe below.

Female. The black color more suffused, the general color amber, with markings indistinct. Like the male in most respects, the wings larger and more infuscated. The squamæ faintly infuscated. The tarsi blackish brown. Length 5 mm.

Neotype, female, in the collection of the U. S. Biological Survey, taken at the mouth of the Bear River, Utah, July 11, 1915 (A. W. Wetmore).

This species is related to *Ogcodes varius* Latreille, judging from a specimen of *O. varius* in the writer's collection from the sandy steppes of Hungary.

Ogcodes pallidipennis Loew. One small specimen, 3 mm. in length, taken by the writer in Mill Creek Canyon, San Bernardino Co. Cal. The specimen was sitting on a rock in the bright sunlight.

The length of *Ogcodes borealis* Cole and *O. niger* Cole was omitted in the original description; it is about 5 mm. in both species.

NEW SPECIES OF NORTH AMERICAN CYRTIDAE

By Charles W. Johnson.

Boston Society of Natural History.

Acrocera stansburyi sp. nov.

♂ ♀ Head black, occiput with whitish tomentum, antennæ yellow. Thorax yellow with three broad narrowly separated black stripes (in two specimens, male and female, the stripes are fused, forming a large trilobed mark), the dorsal stripe is truncate behind at a line corresponding with the base of the wings, the lateral stripes are truncate in front at about the middle of the dorsal stripe, becoming gradually narrower behind and reaching the post-alar callosities, tomentum whitish, pleura on the upper half yellow, with large, irregular, black spots, which are connected with the black of the lower half, humeri and post-alar callosities whitish, scutellum yellow, metanotum black. Abdomen yellow, the second segment is margined anteriorly with black expanding centrally and forming a dorsal triangle, a small dorsal triangle is also present at the base of the third and the fourth, with a small spot usually present on the side of the third, in one specimen there is a narrow margin similar to that on the second segment, ventral segments blackish margined with yellow. Legs white, coxæ yellow, tips of the tarsi and claws black. Wings hyaline, venation as in *O. liturata* Will., squamæ white, halteres yellow. Length, 3mm.

Eight specimens, Stansbury Island, Great Salt Lake, Utah, July 13, 1913 (Hagan and Titus). Holotype and three paratypes in the author's collection. Two paratypes in the collection of Mr. H. R. Hagan, one in the Museum of Comparative Zoology, and one in the U. S. National Museum.

I had referred this to *A. liturata*, but it is evidently quite different, as indicated by the thoracic and abdominal markings and the color of the scutellum. At the request of Mr. Hagon I am dedicating it to Howard Stansbury, who made and elaborate survey of Great Salt Lake and vicinity in 1849 and 1850.

Ocnaea auripilosa sp. nov.

♀ Head black, eyes hairy, antennæ brown, second joint about one half the length of the first (third joint wanting). Thorax, including the pleura and scutellum honey-yellow, shining and covered with quite thick yellow pile, humeri prominent and lighter than the disc of the thorax, behind the shoulder is a whitish stigma, narrowly margined with black, sternum black. Abdomen bright orange-yellow, with short golden pile; the segments have the following blue-black markings,—a spot in the middle of the first, a triangle at the base of the second and third, a square occupying the middle half of the fifth and all of the sixth segment except a narrow margin, venter yellow. Legs yellow with yellow pile, tips of the tarsi dark brown, claws black. Wings hyaline, veins yellow, squamæ white margined with black and fringed with yellow hairs; the first posterior cell is closed and petiolate. Length 11mm., the abdomen is about double the width of the thorax.

One specimen, Tucson, Arizona, March 16, 1916 (J. F. Tucker). Type in the author's collection. It agrees somewhat with *O. micans* Erichson, but its yellow not "fuscous" color, the blue-black abdominal markings and larger size separate it from that species.

Ogocodes vittatus sp. nov.

♀ Head black, antennæ dark brown. Thorax reddish brown, with three broad black stripes, the lateral stripes abbreviated anteriorly and the dorsal stripe obsolete posteriorly, humeri, post-alar callosities, metanotum, and upper parts of the pleura yellow, a blackish spot in front of the base of the wing, and the lower part of the pleura shining black, scutellum black, the base brownish on the sides. Abdomen black, shining, with the posterior margins of the segments narrowly edged with yellow, venter yellow. Legs brownish, the knees yellow, the posterior tibiæ and tarsi black. Wings and squamæ light brown, veins dark brown, knobs of the halteres blackish, stems yellow. Length 4.5mm.

One specimen, Middlesex County, New Jersey, May 19, (Harry B. Weiss). Type in the author's collection. This is readily separated from all the described species by its striped thorax.

The Zoological Record.

The attention of Entomologists thoughout the world is called to the fact that, beginning with the Volume for 1922, the preparation of the "Insecta" part of the "Zoological Record," is being undertaken by the Imperial Bureau of Entomology. In order that the Record may be as complete as it is possible to make it, all authors of entomological papers, especially of systematic ones, are requested to send separata of their papers to the Bureau. These are particularly desired in cases where the original journal is one that is not primarily devoted to entomology All separata should be addressed to:—

The Assistant Director,
Imperial Bureau of Entomology,
41, *Queen's Gate,*
London, S. W. 7,
England.

NORTH AMERICAN DIXIDÆ.

By O. A. Johannsen.

Cornell Universty, Ithaca, N. Y.

Some years ago I published a key to the species of Dixa (Bull. New York State Museum, 68:431, 1903) based largely on the color characters given in the descriptions. Through the kindness of Mr. Nathan Banks I have recently had the opportunity to compare my specimens with the Loew types in the Museum of Comparative Zoology at Cambridge, and now offer a new table which includes three new species.

A study of a series of specimens collected at the same time and place, having similar color characters, and an identical type of hypopyguim, therefore presumably one species, shows that the venation of the wings in this genus is subject to some variation, for which allowance must be made in identification. The length of the fork of the media is particularly variable. In one wing of one of the type specimens of *D. fusca* Lw. the petiole and the fork are nearly subequal in length while in the other wing of this specimen and in both wings of the second specimen the petiole is noticeably longer than the anterior branch of the fork. In *D. cornuta* described below, a species having a very characteristically formed clasper, the variation in the proportions is even greater.

Key to species of Dixa.

a. Costal half of the wing distinctly smoky; a dark spot at the apex of Cu 2; proboscis and scutellum yellow; knob of halteres black. D. C. . . . . . . *marginata* Lw.

aa. Costal part of the wing not distinctly differentiated in color.

b. Tips of the hind tibiæ noticeably enlarged, deep black, sharply contrasting with the remainder of the member; wing veins with clouded margins; proboscis black; halteres yellowish; scutellum fuscous testaceous; terminal clasper segment tapering, mesal process of the basal segment simple, elongate.(fig. 2)Me., Mass., N.Y, *clavata* Lw.

bb. Tips of hind tibiæ not so sharply differentiated.

c. Petiole of R2+3 (measured on a straight line from its base to base of fork), less than 3/8 as long as R3; proboscis, scutellum, and knob of the halteres yellow; crossvein of wing very feebly clouded; r-m crossvein slightly distad of the base of R4+5. N. Y., *terna* Lw.

cc. With other characters.

d. Wing with one or more spots.

e. The space between the bases of the cubitus and anal vein, between the branches of the cubitus, and the basal part of the anal lobe infuscated; terminal clasper segment triangular, mesal process of basal segment forked (fig. 1), *californica* n. sp.

ee. With but a single, rather distinct spot on the wing.

f. Petiole of R 2+3 and R3 subequal in length, wing spot very distinct, veins strongly marked; proboscis and scutellum blackish; halteres sordidly yellow; terminal clasper segment not tapering, truncate apically, mesal process of basal segment forked (fig 6). Me., N. Y. *centralis* Lw.

ff. Petiole shorter; proboscis, scutellum, and halteres yellow, N. J.; Md. . . . *notata* Lw.

dd. Wing spot very indistinct or wanting.

e. The r-m crossvein is situated slightly proximad of the base of R4+5 thus intersecting the petiole of the radial sector; Sc endsopposite the base of Rs. St. Vincent Is. *calvula* Will.

ee. The r-m crossvein is situated at or slightly distad of the base of R4+5 thus connecting this vein with the media.

f. Dorsum of the thorax yellowish with thoracic darker stripes which may be more or less confluent; palpi dark.

g. Proboscis yellow; scutellum and halteres blackish; wing veins strongly marked, subcosta ends opposite to base of Rs; thoracic stripes black and more or less confluent, large part of the pleura yellow. Texas *venosa* Lw.

gg. Proboscis dark; scutellum yellowish; wing veins not unusually pronounced; intervals between the thoracic stripes yellow.

h. Fore basitarsus about 2/3 as long as the tibia; Sc ends proximad of the base of Rs; knob of the halteres dark; basal segment of the clasper of the male with a black, ventrad projecting, and much curved mesal process (fig. 4). N. Y. . . *cornuta* n. sp.

hh. Fore basitarsus about 3/4 as long as the tibia.

i. Apical segment of the clasper of the male fully as broad beyond the middle as at the base (fig. 3); Sc ends about opposite the base of Rs; distance between the crossveins measured on the media usually not exceeding 1/2 the length of the m-cu crossvein. N.Y., N. C., Cal. . . *modesta* Joh.

ii. Apical segment of the clasper tapering (fig.7); Sc ends distinctly proximad of the base of Rs; distance between the crossveins about equal to the length of the m-cu crossvein. N. Y. . . . . *similis* n. sp.

ff. Dorsum of the thorax as well as the upper part of the pleura, black; proboscis, halteres and scutellum dark; Sc ends opposite the base of the radial sector. N. Y. . . . . *fusca* Lw.

Dixa californica sp. nov.

Male. Head black, proboscis, palpi, and flagellum of antennæ brown, basal antennal segments light brownish. Dorsum of the thorax and upper part of the pleura, yellow; dorsal stripes rich dark brown, nearly confluent, laterals anteriorly, median one posteriorly abbreviated; scutellum, metanotum, and larger part of pleura brown. Abodmen black; the mesal process of the basal clasper segment forked; the apical segment in ventro-lateral aspect more or less triangular, apically with acute angle, mesally with a number of stout black setæ (fig. 1).

Legs yellowish brown, becoming darker towards their extremities; tips of femora and of tibiæ darker; coxæ yellow; fore barsitarsus nearly 7/8 as long as the tibia. Wings grayish hyaline, a distinct cloud covering the r-m crossvein extending up on the petiole of R2+3; space between the petiole of the cubitus and the anal vein, between the branches of the cubitus, and basal part of the anal angle more or less infuscated; veins yellowish brown; Sc ends opposite the base of Rs, petiole of R2+3 (measured on a straight line from its base to base of fork) .64 as long as R3, petiole of the media measured from the crossvein 1.3 as long as M1+2, the distance between the cross veins 2/3 as long as the m-cu crossvein. Halteres brownish with yellow peduncle. Length 2.5 mm. Type in my collection. Stanford University, Cal., March.

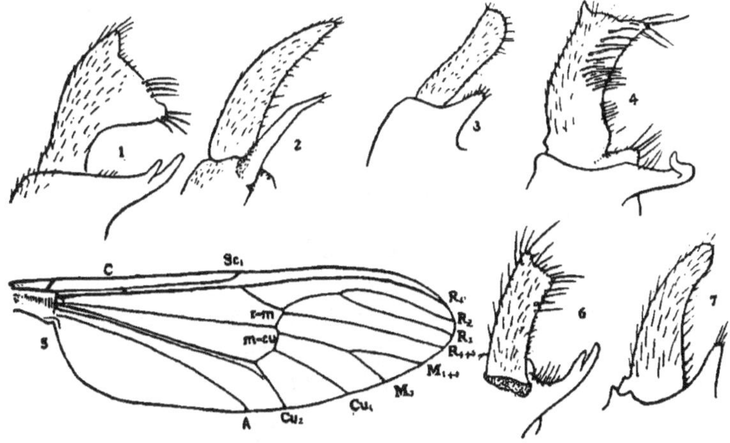

Fig. 1. Claspers of males. Figs. 1, 3, 7 are in ventro-lateral aspect; 2, 4, 6 in ventral aspect. 1. *D. californica.* 2. *D. clavata.* 3. *D. modesta.* 4. *D. cornuta.* 6. *D. centralis.* 7. *D. Similis.* 5. Wing of male *D. modesta.*

Dixa cornuta sp. nov.

Male. Head, including proboscis, palpi and antennæ, brown, front shining. Thorax, including scutellum, brownish yellow, with three dull, dark brown lines, the middle one divided by a hair line, the laterals abbreviated anteriorly; metanotum and sternopleura pale brown. Abdomen blackish; the basal segment of the clasper yellow, moderately swollen, with a black, elongate, ventrad projecting and much curved mesal horn-like process; terminal segment of clasper viewed from the ventral side elongate as shown in fig. 4 with rows of ventro-mesal black spines; when viewed from the side, quadrangular, shaped somewhat like that of *D. californica* (fig. 1) but with the mesal angle much truncated and more spinous. Legs brownish yellow, extreme tips of tibiæ and of tarsi darker, the hind tibiæ distinctly swollen at tip; fore basitarsus about 2/3 as long as the corresponding tibia. Wings hyaline, very faintly cinereous, veins yellowish, crossveins not clouded; Sc ends slightly before base of Rs; petiole of R2+3 (measured on a straight line from its base to base of fork) about 0.4 as long as R3; petiole of the media measured from the crossvein, about 1.12 as long as M1+2. Halteres dark with yellow peduncle. Length 2.5 mm. Holotype in my collection. McLean, N. Y. October.

Female. In coloring like the male. Allotype in my collection. Ithaca, N. Y. August.

Paratypes from Ithaca, N. Y., October, and from Orono, Me., June. In the Cornell University Collection and in the Museum of Comparative Zoology, Cambridge, Mass.

The coloring is rather constant, except in teneral specimens. In the paratypes the venation is rather variable. The ratio measurement, as defined above for the radius, ranges from .36 to .50 in male specimens while the ratio measurements of the media ranges between 1.12 and 2.1. The distance between the bases of the crossveins measured along the media, is in most cases nearly equal to the length of the m-cu crossvein. The fore tibia-tarsus ratio ranges between .61 and .71, with an average of .65.

Dixa modesta Joh.

Too hastily, in the Entomological News (14:302), I declared this species to be the same as *D. clavula* Will. A careful examination of a co-type specimen of Williston's species shows *modesta* to be quite distinct, as indicated sufficiently in the key. To my original description may be added that Sc ends about opposite or slightly beyond, or at most but slightly proximad of the base of the radial sector (fig. 5); the petiole of R2+3 (measured in a straight line) is about .55 as long as R3; the petiole of the media, measured from the crossvein, about equal to M1+2; the distance between crossveins along the media less than 1/2 as long as the m-cu crossvein. In the western specimen there is a very faint suggestion of a cloud on the r-m crossvein. The fore basitarsus is about 3/4 as long as the tibia. The basal clasper segment is somewhat enlarged, mesal process short with some stout apical setæ; apical segment broadest beyond the middle when viewed from the side, thence tapering to the tip; viewed more ventrally the sides are more or less parallel (fig. 3).

Specimens from Ithaca N. Y., April, May; Black Mts., N. C. May; and S. Jacinto Pk., Cal., August. Type in my collection.

Dixa similis sp. nov.

Closely resembling *D. modesta,* differing chiefly in the characters given in the key.

Male. Head including proboscis, palpi, and antennæ, brown; front shining. Thorax including scutellum, yellow, with three dull dark brown stripes, the middle one divided by a hair line, the laterals abbreviated anteriorly; metanotum and lower part of the pleura brown. Abdomen brown, including the globose basal segment of the clasper whose mesal process is simple and provided with a few stout apical setæ (fig. 7); terminal segment rather tapering when viewed more or less from the side. Legs yellow, tarsi and tips of hind tibiæ a little darker; fore basitarsus about 3/4 as long as the corresponding tibia. Wings hyaline, very faintly cinereous, veins yellowish, crossvein not clouded; Sc ends in the costa at least the length of the r-m crossvein proximad of the base of the radial sector, the distance between the crossveins measured along the media about equal to the length of the m-cu cross vein; petiole of R2+3 (measured in a straight line from its base to the base of the fork) about .55 as long as R3; petiole of the media measured from the cross-vein about 1.25 as long as M1+2. Halteres yellow. Ienght, 2.5 mm. Holotype in my collection. Ithaca, N. Y., August.

Female. In coloring like the male. Allotype in my collection. Ithaca, N. Y., August.

Paratypes collected at the same time and place in the Cornell University collection and in the Museum of Comparative Zoology at Cambridge, Mass. The radius ratio in the paratype specimens varies from .44 to .66, the media ratio from 0.8 to 1.3.

TWO NEW SPECIES OF PHORIDÆ FROM BALTIC AMBER.[1]

By Charles T. Brues.

Some years ago, while examining a small series of amber-insects, now in the collections of the museum of the University of Königsberg, I chanced upon a beautifully preserved specimen of the family Phoridæ. This species, which is described below as *Dohrinphora transita* is in a small piece of amber together with an hymenopterous insect representing an undescribed genus of Bethylidæ. A second species included in the same lot proves also to be new.

The occurence of Phoridæ in Baltic amber was noted many years ago by Behrendt[2] and soon afterwards Loew[3] mentioned the existence of eleven species of this family in amber that had passed through his hands. Much more recently the present writer[4] has described two species from the Miocene shales of Florissant Colorado. In 1909 Meunier[5] described and figured a number of species from amber. Unfortunately, it is very difficult to recognize his species as the descriptions are based to a great extent upon characters not generally used, and many important diagnostic characters are not included. In spite of these difficulties I am quite certain that the two species described below are different from any of those dealt with by Meunier.

The first one differs from all previously known species by the presence of a broad, flattened enlargement before the tip of the third longitudinal wing vein, a character which seems to form a transition between the recent species of Hypocera and those of the more generalized genera with forked third vein, since a number of species of Hypocera show a very similar swelling at the tip of the third vein. They lack the second vein, however, which is present in the fossil species.

[1]Contribution from the Entomological Laboratory of the Bussey Institution, Harvard University, No. 219.

[2]Organische Reste im Bernstein, vol. 1, p. 57 (1845).

[3]Ueber den Bernstein und die Bernsteinfauna, Progr. Königl. Realsch. Meseritz, 1850, pp. 1-44.

[4]Bull. American Mus. Nat. Hist. vol. 24 pp. 273-275.

[5]Monographie der Leptiden und Phoriden des Bernsteins, Jahrb. Königl. Preuss. Geolo, Landesanst., vol. 30, pp. 64-90, 5 pls.

Dohrniphora transita sp. nov.

Sex? Length 3 mm. A stout species with well developed bristles on the hind legs. Two median supra-antennal bristles reclinate, strong, but rather short and divergent. Lower row of four frontal bristles forming a straight transverse line, the bases of the lateral bristles close to the lower angles of the front. Next row forming a curved line, all four bristles equidistant. Upper transverse row normal. Post-ocular cilia strong, not enlarged below. Antennæ rather small, round; arista short and very slender. Mesonotum with a single pair of dorso-central macrochætæ; scutellum with a pair of small lateral bristles and also two stronger bristles on the hind margin. Abdomen completely clouded, so that its structure cannot be observed. Anterior tibiæ each with a single bristle at the middle on the front side; middle tibiæ each with a similar one at the basal third, and also perhaps just before the tip which is not visible. Hind femora stout, fringed with short hairs along the lower edge. Hind tibia with a strong bristle at the end of the basal third; a pair at the middle, one of these bristles on the outer and the other one on the hind side; also with two shorter bristles just before the tip, and, so far as can be seen, with at least one stout spur. Costal vein not extending beyond the middle of the wing, its cilia delicate and very long, although most of the cilia have been broken off in the single specimen before me. First vein very long, its tip twice as far removed from the mediastinal vein as from the apex of the third vein; on its basal two-thirds it runs almost parallel to the costa, bending sharply forwards apically to meet the costa. Second vein short, the angle of furcation very close to the tip of the third vein. Third vein with a large, oval spot or swelling extending from the fork halfway to the apex of the vein; although this spot scarcely extends over the anterior edge of the vein, it is broadened out behind into a strong bow. Fourth vein straight, except at base, where it is weakly curved; originating opposite the fork of the third; fifth vein almost parallel to the fourth, slightly bent forward on its basal third; sixth and seventh veins present, straight.

Similar in size to *Dohrniphora ablata* Meunier, but the antennæ are small and the apical half of the anterior tibia bears no bristles, while the apical swelling on the third wing-vein described above will serve to distinguish it immediately.

Dohrniphora loewi sp. nov.

♂. Length 2 mm. Apparently brown in color, with the legs light brown; head and abdomen above more or less blackened. All frontal bristles reclinate, strong, but not greatly lengthened. Post-ocular cilia small and densely placed. Antennæ rather small, the third joint globular, almost bare, and only a little shorter than the width of the head. Palpi clouded, their apical bristles which are clearly to be seen, however, are strongly developed and densely placed. Front apparently at least as high as broad, perhaps higher, slightly convex. Cheeks each with a single downwardly directed bristle. Mesonotum bearing only a few fine hairs, as long as wide and strongly convex, on each side with four marginal bristles, of which two lie before and two behind the insertion of the wing; only one pair of dorsocentral macrochætæ present. Scutellum with four marginal bristles of which the anterior pair are slightly weaker. Abdomen one-third longer than the head and thorax together, uniformly narrowed toward the tip; second and sixth segments elongated, the second without tufts of hairs at the sides. Seventh segment, seen from above, furnished with a row of short bristles along the posterior margin. Hypopygium small. Legs not thickened; the hind femora broadened, but without distinct hairs on the lower margin. Front tarsi distinctly thickened, the second and third joints each quadrate; front tibiæ with a single large bristle on the outer side just before the middle. Middle tibiæ with a pair of strong bristles at the basal third; hind tibiæ each with only a single bristle at the basal third and with two apical spurs of which the inner one is much more strongly developed. Wings apparently entirely hyaline; costal vein only one third as long as the wing, thickened toward the apex, with very fine cilia that are visible only under considerable magnification; first vein very long, its tip three times as far from the mediastinal vein as from the tip of the third vein; second vein entering the costa at a point equidistant from the tips of the first and third veins; fourth vein almost straight, reaching the margin far before the wing-tip: fifth vein almost stright, entering the margin far beyond the wing tip; sixth vein with a sigmoid flexure; seventh vein obsolete.

Type, No. B243, imbedded in a piece of amber with a specimen of an ant.

The present species resembles two amber forms described by Meunier (*op. cit.*) but appears to be quite distinct; from "*Phora*"[1] *inclusa* Meun. it differs in having two basal bristles on the middle tibiæ and by being much larger, 2 mm. instead of 1 mm. From *D. concinna* Meun. It differs by the presence of a large bristle near the base of the front tibia and by having only one preapical bristle on the hind tibia.

[1]Whether this species is a Dohrniphora or Paraspiniphora cannot be determined, as the apical portion of the middle tibiae are not visible in the type, according to Meunier's description.

NEW SPECIES OF NORTH AMERICAN DOLICHOPODIDÆ.

By M. C. Van Duzee.

Buffalo, N. Y.

Nothosympycnus luteipes sp. nov.

Male: length 2 mm. Face very narrow, white. Front dark blue, shining. Antennæ black or brown; third joint rather large, oval; arista twice as long as the antennæ, pointed at tip. Lateral and inferior orbital cilia whitish.

Dorsum of thorax brown, shining, still a little dulled with brown pollen; scutellum blue. Abdomen with the first, second, sides of third segment and the venter yellow; dorsum of third segment, the apical segments and the hypopygium blackish with green reflections; appendages of the hypopygium wholly black, except the yellow penis.

All coxæ and the posterior edge of the pleuræ yellow; coxæ without black hair or bristles, except the erect bristle on outer surface of hind ones. All femora and fore and middle tibiæ yellowish, tips of hind femora and the hind tibiæ more brown or black, still the base and lower edge of the tibiæ are yellowish. Fore tarsi (fig. 4) yellow, blackened from the tip of the third joint; first joint about as long as wide, second as long as the two following joints taken together, fourth distinctly shorter than third and slightly longer than fifth. Middle tarsi (fig. 5) black from the tip of the first joint, which is about as long as the remaining four taken together; tip of first joint with two and basal half of second joint with three long, slender, crooked hairs; second joint a little widened on basal half; third joint as long as second, fourth slightly shorter, fifth still shorter. Hind tarsi wholly blackish, shorter than their tibiæ, first joint shorter than second. Calypters and halteres yellow, the former with black cilia.

Wings brownish gray, narrowed to the root; last section of fifth vein nearly four times the length of the cross-vein.

Described from two males taken at Bar Harbor, Me., July 22, 1914, by C. W. Johnson.

This is almost like *frontalis* Loew, except in the formation of the tarsi, *frontalis* having the fourth joint of fore tarsi much longer than the third. The middle tarsi of *frontalis* also have the first joint longer than the remaining four taken together, and the second about twice as long as the third.

Campsicnemus wheeleri sp. nov.

Male: Length 2 mm. Face brown, narrow, the eyes nearly touching on upper part, wider below. Palpi and proboscis black. Front black with slight blue reflections. Antennæ black; third joint somewhat conical in outline, about as long as wide; arista basal, twice as long as the antenna. Orbital cilia black above, brownish below.

Dorsum of thorax shining black, slightly dulled with brown pollen; humeri and pleuræ green, the latter with brown pollen; scutellum blue. Abdomen green with purple reflections on the center of the dorsum. Hypopygium small, mostly concealed.

Coxæ blackish, anterior pair more yellowish apically, with black hair on the front surface. Femora and tibiæ brownish yellow; fore and middle femora slightly thickened. Fore tibiæ blackish at base and tip, with two very small bristles above and one below; middle and hind tibiæ darkened apically;middle ones widened and bent as in figure 1; the tip, when viewed from above, is enlarged, blackish, with two yellow spots on the edge (fig. 2). Middle tarsi black, formed as in figures 1 & 2, the first joint is narrowed in the middle when viewed from the side and is enlarged near the apex, terminating in a thumb-like tip; when viewed from above it is slightly tapering, not narrowed in the middle. Last four joints of middle tarsi of nearly equal length and about as long as the first, still the fifth is slightly shorter and has three long hairs at tip. Fore tarsi brown, first joint as long as the three following taken together, third and fifth of nearly equal length second slightly longer and fourth shorter than third. Hind tarsi brown, first and second joints of equal length, the following joints of slightly decreasing length. Calypters, their cilia and the halteres brown.

Wings tinged with brownish; third and fourth veins parallel beyond the cross-vein, widely separated; last section of fourth vein with a faint brown spot at its basal fourth; last section of fifth being twice as long as the cross-vein; anal angle prominent.

A female which probably belongs with this species differs in the thorax having purple reflections; legs plain and a little more yellow; middle and hind basitarsi yellow with a black tip; calypters and knobs of halteres more yellowish, the former with black cilia; middle tibiæ with two bristles below and several on upper surface. wings with the spot at basal fourth of the last section of fourth vein very conspicuous.

Described from one pair taken in Maine; the holotype, male, was taken at Machias, July 20, 1909, and the allotype a female at Bar Harbor, August 4, 1918; both were taken by C. W. Johnson. He sent them to me with the name *wheeleri* attached but had never described them.

This is very much like *œdipus* Wheeler, but this form has the legs more yellowish; the middle tibiæ of the male of a little different shape; the middle basitarsus contracted in the middle, more enlarged apically, and not ending in a point; their third and fourth joints are also nearly twice as long as in *œdipus*; the brown spot on the fourth vein of the wing is very indistinct in this form. The females of the two species are probably difficult to separate.

Hercostmus costalis sp. nov.

Male: Length 3 mm.; of wing the same. Face of moderate width, silvery white. Front thickly covered with white pollen, so as to conceal the ground color when viewed obliquely.

Antennæ wholly black; third joint not as long as wide, somewhat pointed at tip, arista nearly basal. Lateral and inferior orbital cilia whitish, about five to six of the upper cilia on each side black.

Thorax and abdomen green with bronze reflections; mesonotum dulled with gray or brownish gray, pleuræ with white pollen; abdomen with white pollen on the sides. Hypopygium (fig. 3) black; its lamellæ somewhat angulated and deeply notched at tip, yellow with the edge narrowly black, fringed with bristles which are deep black in color, some of them flattened, and a little enlarged at tip; there appear to be two pairs of inner appendages, one blackish and the other yellow.

Coxæ and femora black; tips of coxæ and narrow tips and the base of all femora yellow, the yellow at base of hind femora sometimes nearly reaches their middle. Middle and hind femora each with one preapical bristle. Tibiæ yellow, posterior pair with their tips blackened for nearly one third their length; fore tibiæ with only two or three slender bristles on upper surface. Fore and middle tarsi black from the tip of the first joints; anterior pair about as long as their tibiæ, their joints in the proportion of 24-8-6-4-6; hind tarsi wholly black, first joint scarcely as long as second. Calypters and halteres yellow, the former with black cilia.

Wings slightly grayish; costa considerably enlarged at tip of first vein, this enlargement tapers quite rapidly at first, more gradually afterwards and extends nearly to the tip; third and fourth veins converge from the cross-vein to their tips, where they are about half as far apart as at the cross-vein; last section of the fifth vein about one and a third times as long as the cross-vein; anal angle rather prominent, its margin nearly parallel with the sixth vein.

Described from four males; I took one at Toronto, Ont., July 4, 1911, one at Port Credit, Ont., July 14, 1918 and one at Ridgeway, Ont., June 22, 1919; the other was taken by J. S. Rogers, at Floodwood, Schoolcraft Co., Mich., July 11, 1915, this is in the collectiom of Dr. J. M. Aldrich.

Holotype in the author's collection and taken at Toronto, Ont.

Diaphorus spinitalus sp. nov.

Male: Length 3 mm. Face wide, shining green, only slightly dulled with brownish pollen. Palpi rather small, dark yellow; proboscis black. Antennæ black, third joint small, rounded, arista apical. Lower orbits nearly bare, below the head there are a few white bristles.

Thorax and abdomen green with coppery reflections; scutellum with one pair of large bristles and a pair of hairs on the margin. Hypopygium and its appendages small, black, the bristles at tip short.

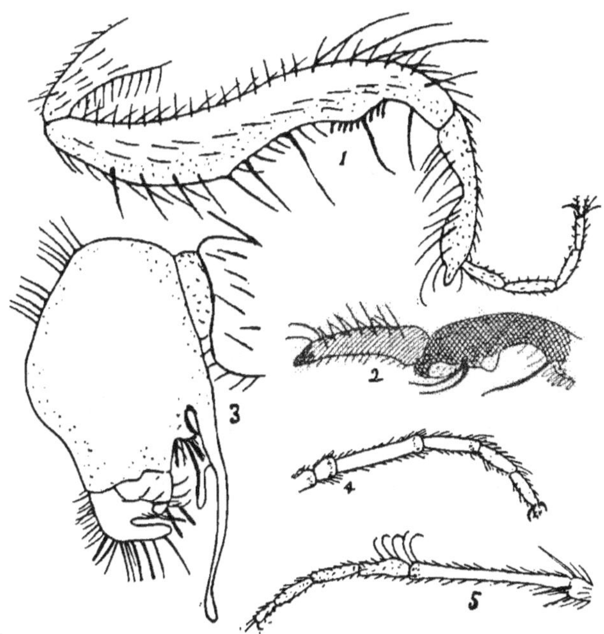

Fig. 1, *Campsicnemus wheeleri* sp. nov., middle tibia and tarsus; fig. 2, tip of middle tibia and basitarsus of the same, viewed from the side; fig. 3, *Hercostomus costalis* sp. nov., hypopygium; fig. 4, *Nothosympycnus luteipes* sp. nov., fore tarsus· fig. 5, middle tarsus of the same.

Coxæ, legs and feet black, fore and middle knees yellowish. Fore coxæ with white hairs on their anterior surface. Joints of fore tarsi as 21-12-9-3-7; those of hind tarsi as 19-13-8-6-6; first joint of hind tarsi with an erect bristle below near the base, which is about as long as the diameter of the joint. Pulvilli of fore tarsi slightly enlarged.

Wings grayish; first vein reaches two-fifths of the distance to the tip of the second; third and fourth veins nearly parallel, fourth ending just before the apex of the wing; last section of fifth vein nearly twice as long as the cross-vein, which is near the middle of the wing.

Described from one male taken by E. P. Van Duzee, at Strawberry Valley, Eldorado Co., California, August 15, 1912. Type in the California Academy of Sciences.

Diaphorus spinifer Malloch.

Chrysotuss pinifer, Bull. Ill. State Lab. of Nat. Hist., Vol. X, p. 238.

The pulvilli of the fore tarsi are somewhat enlarged in this species and it has very small bristles at the tip of the abdomen, these points together with its slender form are enough to place this in the genus Diaphorus, especially as that will bring it near the species described above, which differs from it in having the bristles at the tip of the abdomen larger, the bristle on the hind tarsi smaller, and the palpi much smaller, those of *spinifer* being each as large as the face, or nearly so. *Simplex* Ald. also has a large bristle below at base of hind tarsi, but in that species the third and fourth veins are much bent.

I have taken *spinifer* in Erie Co., N. Y., in August; Ft. Erie, Ont., July; Alpine, San Diego Co., Calif., April; Sacramento, Calif., June; Dr. Aldrich took it at Lewiston, Idaho. It was described from Illinois.

Dolichopus uliginosus sp. nov.

Male: Length 4.7 mm.; of wing 4 mm. Face rather narrow, yellowish. Front shining green. Antennæ wholly black; third joint about as long as wide, scarcely pointed at tip. Orbital cilia black with the four lowest ones on each side yellow.

Thorax shining blue-green with violet reflections; pleuræ slightly dulled with gray pollen. Abdomen shining green with black incisures and with white pollen on its sides. Hypopygium and its lamellæ black, the latter somewhat triangular in outline and about as wide as long.

Coxæ, legs and feet black. Fore coxæ with black hairs on their anterior surface. Middle and hind femora each with one preapical bristle, the latter ciliated on lower inner edge with long black hairs, which appear nearly white in certain lights, the longest of these hairs scarcely as long as the width of the femora. Hind tibiæ with brown pollen on inner surface, which is conspicuous when viewed obliquely, they are distinctly thickened almost from their base. Middle tibiæ with one large bristle just beyond the middle on their lower surface. Anterior tarsi scarcely as long as their tibiæ, the first joint as long as the remaining four taken together, fifth as long as second, fourth joint the shortest. Middle tarsi as long as their tibiæ, the first joint without a bristle above. Calypters yellow with black cilia. Knob of the halteres yellow, their stem brown.

Wings grayish; costa with a slight knot-like enlargement at tip of first vein; fourth vein a little bent just before the middle of its last section; hind margin of wing scarcely indented at tip of fifth vein; anal angle of wings rounded, not prominent, the hind margin being nearly evenly rounded.

Described from one male taken at the Biological Station at Nanaimo, B. C., June 23, 1920, by E. P. Van Duzee. Type in the California Academy of Sciences.

This would run in the table of species in the Bulletin U. S. National Museum No. 116, p. 11, couplet 8, of group C, to *deterus* Loew; it very much like that species in the form of the hypopyginal lamellæ and structure of the legs and feet, but differs in having only four or five of the lower orbital cilia yellow, in *deterus* the lower orbital cilia are grayish white, not yellow and the pale cilia reach above the middle of the eye.

Dolichopus interjectus sp. nov.

Male: Length 4 mm.; of wing 3.5 mm. Face rather narrow, silvery white. Front shining green. Antennæ wholly black; third joint a little longer than wide, obtusely pointed at tip. Lower half of the orbital cilia whitish.

Thorax dark shining green; pleuræ with whitish pollen. Abdomen green with slight bronze reflections. Hypopygium black with green reflections; its lamellæ of moderate size, somewhat oval in outline, whitish with rather wide black border on apical margin, which is jagged and bristly, upper edge fringed with a few short black hairs.

Coxæ, legs and feet black; fore and middle trochanters and all knees yellow. Fore coxæ covered with black hairs on their anterior surface. Middle and hind femora each with one preapical bristle, the latter nearly bare below. Hind tibiæ slightly thickened, more so at tip. Fore tarsi about one and a fourth times as long as their tibiæ, first joint fully as long as the following three taken together, fifth nearly as long as the second, fourth the shortest. Middle tibiæ with one large bristle below at apical third. Middle tarsi about equal to their tibiæ in length, their first joint without a bristle above. Calypters and halteres yellow, the latter with whitish cilia.

Wings grayish, tinged with brown in front of third vein; costa with a small knot-like enlargement at tip of first vein; last section of fourth vein a little bent before its middle; hind margin of wing not indented at tip of fifth vein; anal angle of wing prominent.

Female; Agrees with the male, except that the face is wider and the white is scarcely silvery; third antennal joint not longer than wide; cilia of the calypters about half black; the costa not enlarged at tip of first vein.

Described from two males and one female, taken in Powell Co., Montana, by A. L. Melander. Holotype and allotype in the collection of A. L. Melander.

This would run to *formosus* in the table of species in the U. S. National Museum Bulletin 116, page 11, couplet 5, in group C, but differs from that species in having the hypopygial lamellæ jagged at apex and fringed with short hairs above, *formosus* has the lamellæ fringed above with longer hairs and their apical margin is not at all jagged, the black border is broader in this form than it is in *formosus*. The wing in *interjectus* has a distinct enlargement at tip of first vein and the anal angle is more prominent than in *formosus*.

The female runs in the table of species in the Bulletin, page 28, couplet 23, to *nigrimanus*, but it differs in having the fore tarsus fully as long as the tibiæ, while in *nigrimanus* they are scarcely as long as the tibiæ.

Dolichopus perplexus nom. nov.

Dolichopus misellus Melander, Canadian Entomologist, vol. xxxii, p. 130, 1900. U. S. National Museum Bulletin 116, page 229, 1921. *Dolichopus melanderi* Becker, Zool-Boten. Gellschaft, Wien, vol. xiii, No. i, page 15, 1921.

Dr. Becker in the American portion of his monograph of the Dolichopodidæ gives the name *melanderi* to *Dolichopus misellus* Melander, as that name was preoccupied by *Dolichopus misellus* Bohem., 1851, but as that name is also preoccupied by the publication of the description of a *Dolichopus melanderi* VanDuzee, Cole & Aldrich, in March, 1921 (U. S. National Museum Bulletin 116, page 70, I would propose the name *perplexus* for this form.

Psilopus longitalus sp. nov.

Male; Length 5 mm. Face bare; fore coxæ and all femora and tibiæ yellow; all tarsi plain with only short hairs and bristles, except the fore basitarsus which has three long slender bristles; middle tibiæ with only minute scattering bristles, which are scarcely as long as the diameter of the tibiæ.

Face bare, blue-green with white pollen. Front shining blue with the upper corners green. Antennæ black; its second joint with a bristle above which is twice as long as the short third joint; arista as long as the height of the head. Lateral and inferior orbital cilia white.

Thorax, scutellum and basal half of first abdominal segment blue, the remainder of the abdomen green with bronze reflections, its incisions black. Bristles of the thorax and abdomen rather short. Hypopygium and its appendages black, formed about as in *sipho* and *furcatus*.

Fore coxæ wholly yellow with yellow hair and two black bristles; middle and hind coxæ and their trochanters black with white hairs and black bristles; femora and tibiæ yellow, posterior tibiæ scarcely blackened at extreme tip. All femora with long yellow hairs below and about three small black bristles near the tip. Anterior tibiæ with four long black bristles on lower posterior edge; middle pair with only very short, scattering bristles; hind tibæ without bristles. Fore basitarsi equal to their tibiæ in length, and with three long slender bristles on posterior surface, they are yellow with the extreme tip black; last four joints taken together scarcely as long as the first. Middle tarsi with the first joint nearly one and one fourth times as long as their tibiæ, black from the extreme tip of first joint; last four joints taken together about half as long as the first. Hind tarsi black, plain, first joint a little more yellowish and longer than the remaining four joints taken together. Calypters and halteres yellow, the former black with tip and cilia.

Wings with two brown cross-bands connected on the costal edge as far back as the third vein, the basal band covers the cross-vein but does not reach back of the fifth vein; anterior branch of the fourth vein at right angles to the fourth vein and with the upper bend also a right angle but still it is a little rounded, it ends close to the tip of the third vein.

Female: The bristle on upper edge of second antennal joint twice as long as the third joint; the first joint of fore and middle tarsi is nearly as long as their tibiæ and shorter than the remaining four joints taken together; the anterior branch of the fourth vein of the wing bends backward a little, its upper bend is nearly a right angle and only a little rounded.

Described from one male and eleven females taken at Winnfield, La., July 14, 1918, by G. R. Pilate.

Holotype and allotype in the collection of Prof. James Hine.

This differs from*elegantulus* Becker from Brazil (Zool -Botan. Gesellschaft, Wien, Vol. xiii, part i, p. 294) in having three long slender bristles on the first joint of fore tarsi, while *elegantulus* has only one long bristle on the fore basitarsus; this species is also larger.

This form belongs to the group with *sipho* Say, *scaber* Loew, and *furcatus* VanDuzee, but differs in there being only very small bristles on the middle tibiæ, it differs from the first two in not having a row of bristles below on middle tibiæ. It also has the first joint of fore and middle tarsi longer than any of the other species. The female differs from that of *sipho* in having the bristles on upper edge of the first antennal joint longer; in *sipho* the anterior branch of fourth vein is much more bent backward and its upper bend is much more broadly rounded, not at all a right angle.

NOTES ON *SINEA DIADEMA* (FABR.); HEMIPTERA

By Geo. W. Barber.

Bureau of Entomology, U. S. Dept. of Agriculture.

During the month of September the blossoms of goldenrod are visited by myriads of insects, many of which are attracted there for the food that may be obtained from the flowers. But all is not fortunate, sometimes, for the unwary fly or bee, especially when *Phymata erosa* (Linn.) and spiders such as *Misumena vatia* await them. These, by means of the color with which nature has favored them, are all but indistinguishable from the blossoms. Other predators not so fortunately endowed are frequently present on the flowers, that must for them be excellent hunting grounds. Among these is *Sinea diadema* (Fabr.) one of the most common species of the Reduviidæ, which though not of particularly ferocious appearance to our eyes, must seem sufficiently so to the insect that it attacks.

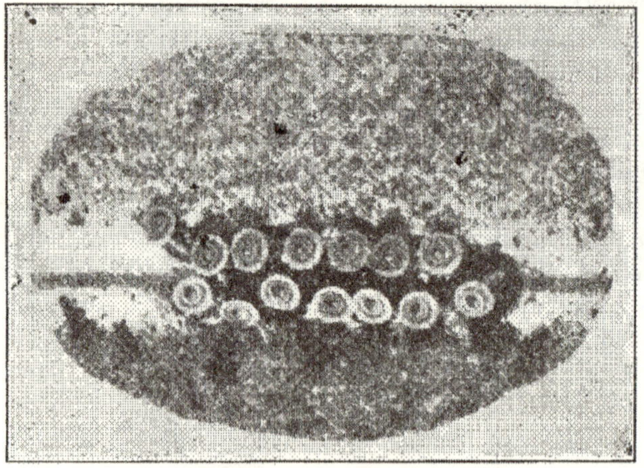

Fig. 1. *Sinea diadema* (Fabr.) Egg-mass enlarged six diameters.

Eggs of this species may be readily obtained by confining the adults in salve boxes. They are deposited usually in small masses, the individual eggs upright and arranged in two rows. As thus seen under magnification they are very beautiful, the structures of the cap and the collar-like extension of the chorion, which extends outwards from the new laid egg, appearing like delicate lace.

The first instar nymph is a most grotesque little insect with a very large head powerful beak and large, strong front femora provided with numerous stout, sharp spines. The armature is admirably designed for a predatory habit, the head and thorax being covered with plates of very stout, smooth, black chitin against which, we are pleased to believe, a much larger insect might struggle without effect, once it is in the grasp of powerful front femora. Young nymphs that I confined wasted no time on covering themselves with litter and soon became all but indistinguishable. Here again the insect is found superbly fitted for its habit, for on the thorax it bears four sharp, stout spines, than which no structure, perhaps, would better serve for retaining the litter with which it covers itself.

The egg of this species has been described by Ashmead (1895—Insect Life VII p. 321) and Heideman (1911—Proc. Ent. Soc. Wash. XIII p. 135) and the young nymph by Ashmead. Since I intend to display illustrations, I have enlarged these excellent descriptions somewhat.

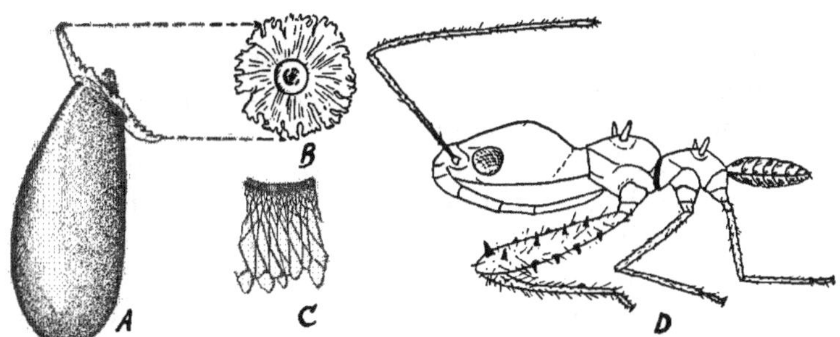

Fig. 2. *Sinea diadema* (Fabr.) A—egg, lateral view; B—egg, dorsal view of the cap and the extension of the chorion; C—Detail structure of the extension of the chorion; D—first instar nymph, lateral view; E—egg mass.

Egg. Length 1.3 mm.; width .6 mm.; diameter of extension of chorion .8 mm. Color brown, minutely granulated, somewhat shining; central area of cap brown, outer rim brown with minute, regular, white reticulations; extension of the chorion white with dark lines, brown towards the inner edge; shape, subilliptical, narrowed towards the cap; central area of the cap raised, cone-like, bluntly rounded at the tip, composed of several scales which fail to meet at the tip; outer rim of the cap flat with minute, regular reticulations; extension of the chorion on the same plane with the outer rim of the cap in new laid eggs, after hatching or drying bending upwards or downwards, squamose, minutely so towards the inner border, gradually coarser outwards, edge sinuate; chorial processes numerous, elongate, club-shaped, within the extension of the chorion.

First Instar Nymph. Length 1.8 mm.; Color dark brown to black, the antennæ, except the basal half of the first segment, the apical half of the middle and posterior tibiæ and all the tarsi brownish; eyes red; body smooth, shining, plates of the head and thorax strong and heavy, closely united; head oblong, as long as the thorax, wider and elevated behind the eyes, then depressed and narrowing into a neck of moderate length; antennæ cylindrical, 4-jointed, as long as or slightly longer than the body, first and last joints subequal, second and third united less than the first, minutely and sparsely ciliate, the basal joint less so, hairs light brown; beak very stout at base, gradually narrowing, attaining the front coxæ; pro and mesothorax each provided with a stout spine each side the median line, as long as one fourth the length of the prothorax and separated by about their own length, directed upwards; anterior legs with very stout femora, enlarged towards the apex, with several stout, sharp spines arranged in rows, those towards the apex larger, each with a hair arising from the apex, sparsely pilose, the hairs long; tibiæ slender with three blunt spines beneath, more densely pilose than the femora; middle and posterior legs somewhat shorter and more slender, moderately pilose; abdomen short, somewhat more than half the length of the thorax, rounded, somewhat flattened, the edges moderately undulated and sparsely fringed with tufts of hairs.

NEW SAW-FLIES, HYMENOPTERA, FROM OREGON.[1]

BY ALEX. D. MACGILLIVRAY.

The following new species constitute a part of a collection that has been in hand for several years. The collection was received from Professor A. L. Lovett of the Oregon Agricultural College, Corvallis, Oregon.

Macremphytus lovetti sp. nov.

Female. Body black with the four distal segments of the antennæ, the labrum, the tegulæ, the protibiæ and protarsi, the mesotibiæ and mesotarsi, the metatrochanters, and the metatarsi, white; antennæ with the three proximal segments and part of the fourth, the head except the clypeal suture and the postocellar area, the thorax except the margins of the lobes of the mesonotum and the mesoscutellum, the proximal two-thirds of the metatibiæ, and the abdomen except the saw guides, rufous; antennæ flattened, first and second segments of the flagellum subequal; clypeus roundly emarginate; ocellar basin small, irregular; saw-guides with the dorsal margin straight, the ventral convex, obliquely convexly rounded at apex; wings yellowish, costa reddish, proximal half of stigma white, veins black. Length, 14 mm.

Habitat:—Rock Creek, Corvallis, Oregon; A. L. Lovett' collector. This beautiful large species is similar to *varianus* Norton, but easily separated by the difference in color. It gives me pleasure to name this species after its collector, Professor A. L. Lovett.

Hemitaxonus dediticius sp. nov.

Male. Body black with the labrum, tegulæ, coxæ, and trochanters, white; the legs beyond the trochanters, abdominal segment two for the most part and all of segments three and four, rufous; the clypeus roundly emarginate; antennæ

[1]Contributions from the Entomological Laboratories of the University of Illinois. No. 75.

with the first segment of the flagellum slightly longer than the second; ocellar basin distinct, concave; the median fovea pit-like; ocellar and interocellar furrows indicated; vertical furrows distinct; head and thorax finely punctate; wings hyaline, spinulæ distinct, veins, costa, and stigma brownish. Length, 6.5 mm.

Habitat:—Corvallis, Oregon; G. F. Moznette, collector. This species is entirely different in coloration from the eastern *dubitalus* Norton.

Taxonus inclinatus sp. nov.

Male. Body black with the labrum, line on collar, tegulæ, and a fine line on the caudal margin of the abdominal segments, white; the legs beyond the trochanters except an elongate spot on the proximal part of the upper side of the profemora and mesofemora and the tarsi of all the legs more or less, rufous; the clypeus roundly emarginate; antennæ short, the first segment of the flagellum nearly twice as long as the second, the second and third subequal; ocellar basin shallow, divided into two parts, not extending to the median ocellus; ocellar and interocellar furrows deep, the latter extending to and around the median ocellus; the wings hyaline, the veins and stigma uniformly colored. Length, 6.5 mm.

Habitat:—Corvallis, Oregon; received from A. L. Lovett, Hardman collector. This species runs to *nigrasoma* Norton from which its color and structure will readily separate it.

Monophadnoides contortus sp. nov.

Female. Body black with the knees and the tibiæ, except the underside and distal portion of the mesotibiæ and metatibiæ, and more or less of the proximal part of the tarsal segments, white; clypeus truncate; antennæ with the first segment of the flagellum longer than the second, the second longer than the third; head polished, the ocellar basin deep, also with a basin around the median ocellus; ocellar furrow deep, interrupted at middle; the collar and tegulæ black; the saw-guides finger-shaped, bluntly pointed at middle of apex; wings hyaline, veins including costa brown, caudal half of stigma paler. Length, 6 mm.

Habitat:—Corvallis, Oregon; received from A. L. Lovett, Ballard collector. The interrupted interocellar furrow will serve for the indentification of this species.

Monophadnoides corytus sp. nov.

Male. Body black with the prothoracic legs beyond the middle of the femora, the knees of the other legs and beyond to apex, pale; clypeus truncate; antennæ with the first segment of the flagellum distinctly longer than either of the subequal second or third; head and thorax setiferous; ocellar basin almost wanting; median ocellus surrounded by a depressed area connecting with the distinct interocellar furrow; ocellar furrow almost wanting; vertical furrows deep, not reaching caudal aspect of head; wings dusky, spinulæ distinct, veins and costa brownish, stigma with cephalic half brown, caudal half paler. Length, 5 mm.

Habitat:—Corvallis, Oregon; A. L. Lovett, collector. This species can be differentiated from the preceeding by the form of the ocellar furrow.

Monophadnus aeratus sp. nov.

Male. Body black and densly covered with white setæ, protibiæ and mesotibiæ, metatibiæ except black ring at apex, and proximal half of the metabasitarsis, white; clypeus convex, truncate; antennæ with segments of the flagellum swollen, the third and fourth subequal, the second longer than the third, and the first much longer than the second; lateral fovea wanting; ocellar basin deep concavity; reaching half way to the median ocellus, area below median ocellus flat and finely punctate; vertical furrows deep, bipunctiform; ocellar furrow prominent, interocellar furrow extending to the median ocellus; scutellum flat impunctate; wings smoky, larger veins black, smaller brownish, stigma of two colors. Length, 6 mm.

Habitat:—Corvallis, Oregon; received from A. L. Lovett, collected by Godding. This species is related to *planus* and *bipunctatus*.

Monophadnus ruscullus sp. nov.

Male. Body black without any pale marks; clypeus uniformly convex, truncate; antennæ with the first segment of the flagellum subequal or slightly shorter than the second, the second slightly longer than the third; the lateral foveæ wanting; ventral ends of the antennal furrows subpunctiform, with a minute median fovea; front flat adjacent to the median ocellus; ocellar, vertical, and interocellar furrows distinct, the latter surrounding the dorsal portion of the median ocellus; head polished; wings smoky, the veins and the stigma black. Length, 5 mm.

Habitat:—Mary's Peak, Corvallis, Oregon; received from A. L. Lovett, Middlekauff collector. The coloration and structure of the head is very different from that of *tiliæ* Norton.

Periclista electa sp. nov.

Male. Body black with the distal half of the femora, the tibiæ, and the tarsi, shading between yellow and rufous; the clypeus shallowly circularly emarginate; head closely finely roughened; lateral fovea wanting; median fovea indefinite; ocellar basin scarcely defined, frontal crest thin, shelving; vertical furrows punctiform, ocellar furrow wanting, interocellar furrow linear; head not depressed about the median ocellus; thorax polished, setiferous; abdomen with caudal margins of segments with a fine pale margin; wings hyaline, veins and stigma brown. Length, 6 mm.

Habitat:—Corvallis, Oregon; received from A. L. Lovett. This species is related to *media* Norton and its allies.

Hylotoma onerosa sp. nov.

Female. Body black with the labrum, clypeus, mandibles, flagellum of antennæ, legs beyond the apices of the coxæ, and the abdomen beyond the basal plates, rufous; head and thorax setiferous; setæ white; clypeus angularly emarginate; supraclypeal area with ventral portion elevated with declivous sides, dorsal portion with an angular depression, median fovea in dorsal part, not distant from median ocellus, depression extending almost to median ocellus; antennal, vertical, ocellar, and interocellar furrows obsolete; head and thorax polished; mesocutellum flat; saw-guides greatly swollen, convex on lateral and ventral portions; distal portion obliquely truncated, joining ventral portion in a rounded ridge; wings yellowish, costa colored like membrane, stigma and veins brownish. Length, 10 mm.

Habitat:— Moscow, Idaho, J. M. Aldrich, collector; Revelstoke, British Columbia; R. C. Osborn, collector; Male collected in Okanogan County, Washington, by C. W. Sutton, is evidently the same.

This species is similar to *clavicornis* Fabricius.

TWO NEW MISSISSIPPI ANTS OF THE SUBGENUS COLOBOPSIS.

By M. R. Smith.

Mississippi State Plant Board, A. & M. College, Mississippi.

The subgenus *Colobopsis* is a division of the genus *Camponotus*. It includes those ants the major workers and females of which have anteriorly truncated heads. The truncated area may be concave or blunt, in either case the sides are always marginate and well defined. The characters mentioned are so distinct that one has no difficulty in assigning ants of this type to the proper genus.

The subgenus *Colobopsis* in North America seems to have very few species, most of the known forms having been described by Dr. W. M. Wheeler in a paper published in 1904.[1] In this paper the following species are recorded as occuring in North America, namely: *Colobopsis impressus* Roger, *Colobopsis pylartes* Wheeler, *Colobopsis abditus* var. *etiolatus* Wheeler. Since that time Dr. Wheeler has described and added another variety to the known North American forms, this species being *Colobopsis pylartes* var. *hunteri*.

Because of the fact that these ants nest in galls, twigs of trees and the stems of plants they are seldom taken by collectors. This partly accounts for the few known forms. Their habits are also imperfectly known.

In Mississippi three distinct species of *Colobopsis* have been taken, two of which are being described as new in this paper. The writer would feel somewhat hesitant about describing these as new if Dr. Wheeler had not examined the specimens and reviewed the descriptions. The third species of *Colobopsis* found in Mississippi is one that can be assigned to *C. impressus*. All three of these forms are very distinct and it is impossible

[1]The American Ants of the Subgenus Colobopsis; Bulletin American Museum Natural History Vol. 20, Article 10, pp. 139-158.

for one to confuse them. *C. impressus,* which has a head with distinctly parallel sides, can easily be distinguished from the other two species both of which have heads with the sides diverging anteriorly.

In this section of the state *C. pylartes fraxinicola* and *C. mississippiensis* nest in the twigs of white ash, *Fraxinus americana* Linn. and are rather common species, particularly the latter, which can be found in the twigs of ash with very little effort. Without doubt these species must feed to a large extent if not altogether, on the honey dew excreted by aphids, scale insects, etc. for the writer has on a number of occasions seen the workers lapping up this substance from the leaves of trees and plants. *C. mississippiensis* seems to breed here thruout the winter. Nests examined at various dates during the season always contained eggs and larvæ. Since the winters in Mississippi are rather mild and the ants are well protected from exposure, this is to be expected.

The writer is very grateful to Dr. W. M. Wheeler for examining the specimens described here and for reviewing the technical descriptions. To Professor R. W. Harned the writer wishes to express his appreciation for encouragement given in the study of these and other Mississippi ants and for the generous allotment of time for such work.

Colobopsis mississippiensis sp. nov.

Soldier. Length, 4.5—5mm.

Head subcylindrical, from above rectangular, longer than broad, sides divergent anteriorly, occipital border convex, anterior truncated surface deeply concave, its edges sharply marginate along the sides but less so in the clypeal region. Mandibles small, with flattened ventral surfaces, 4-toothed with a short toothless proximal portion to the blade. Clypeus on the truncated surface about one and a half times longer than broad, upper portion on the truncated area more divergent than the lower portion. There is a distinct median keel running the full length of the clypeus. On the front, carinæ far apart, with sides converging anteriorly. Eyes moderate, oblong, convex. Antennal scapes curved, slender at the base, gradually enlarging toward their tips. All the funicular joints except the first subequal, first joint almost equal to the next two in length. Thorax robust, pronotum about as broad as long, convex. Meso-epinotal constriction distinct but not deep. Epinotal base and declivity meeting in such a way as to form a decided angle. Petiole low, convex and rounded in front and above, flattened behind, the posterior dorsal edge of the node faintly impressed in the middle but not excised or emarginate. Gaster oblong. Legs short, femora compressed, anterior pair distinctly dilated.

Mandibles and anterior two thirds of head subopaque, the former obscurely longitudinally rugose, the latter coarsely and irregularly reticulate—rugose, with punctate interrugal spaces. On the cheeks and front the sculpture gradually passes over into umbilicately punctate, shallow and scattered foveolæ.

Cheeks and anterior dorsal surface of the head with short, erect, blunt yellowish hairs. There are a few short hairs on the tips of the scapes and femora. Vertex of the head and dorsl and sternal sides of the gaster with longer, erect, whitish hairs.

Anterior two thirds of head including antennæ reddish brown, posterior portion of head blackish brown; thorax and appendages brown; abdomen black.

Worker. Length 3.5-4 mm.

Head longer than broad, a little broader behind than in front, occipital borders and cheeks convex. Mandibles small, 4-toothed. Clypeus nearly square, medianly keeled. Frontal carinæ converging anteriorly. Antennæ proportionately longer than in the soldier; scapes flattened, gradually enlarging toward their tips. Thorax similar to that of the soldier with the exception of the epinotum whose basal surface meets the declivity in such a manner as to form a sharp angle. Petiole low, robust, with convex anterior and superior surfaces, the posterior dorsal edge of node centrally impressed as in the soldier; posterior surface flat. Gaster oblong. Legs as in the soldier.

Body and appendages shining, distinctly shagreened, the head and thorax more coarsely than the gaster; the cheeks and upper surface of the head with scattered punctures.

Head, legs and gaster covered with delicate white appressed hairs. Clypeus, front, vertex, tips of scapes and femora with a few long, scattered, hairs.

Dark brown; head almost black, gaster black, thorax and appendages lighter than either.

The specimens on which these descriptions are based were taken at Starkville, Mississippi, on January 7th, 1922, in the twigs of white ash, *Fraxinus americana* Linn.

This seems to be a very common species of *Colobopsis* in Mississippi. In every instance observed it has been found nesting in the twigs of white ash. The ants mine out all of the soft portion of the twigs forming longitudinal galleries within the axes of the stems. The galleries may be from a few inches to over a foot in length. The young are reared within these galleries. Small entrance holes in diameter about the size of the soldiers' heads lead from the outside of the twigs to the galleries within. There may be from one to several entrance holes to a nest. No soldiers have been observed using their heads to block these holes as has been noticed in other species of the genus. The female must undoubtedly construct her nest alone and rear the first brood to maturity unaided, as the writer has on a number of occasions found dead or live queens alone in small galleries.

Colobopsis mississippiensis was so named because it is the most common species of the genus in Mississippi. It is very easily recognized by the deeply concave, truncated surface of the head. The sides of the truncated area are very sharp and well defined, except in the dorsal clypeal region. The head of this species when viewed from above has sides that are distinctly divergent anteriorly with the anterior area of the head very concave or hollowed out. This species seems to be somewhat variable in color. In some specimens the soldiers have abdomens with the basal segment yellowish, in others there is a faint yellowish band on the anterior portion of the second segment, in still others there is a combination of the two. There is variation in the color of the head and thorax, some specimens being much lighter than others. The writer hesitates to assign these speicmens to varieties based on color, especially in view of the fact that he has not seen material from many localities.

Colobopsis pylartes fraxinicola subsp. nov.

Soldier. Length, 4.5-5 mm.

Head subcylindrical, viewed from above only slightly longer than broad, noticeably wider in front than behind, with inflated cheeks; occipital border straight or faintly convex. Anterior truncated surface oblique, border blunt on sides of face and mandibles, on the clypeal and adjacent region the truncated passes into the dorsal surface thru a rounded angle. Mandibles with blunter ventral margins than those of *mississippiensis*, blade with 4 distinct teeth and a toothless proximal basal portion. Clypeus projecting above surface of truncated area, broader or more divergent above than below. Eyes, frontal carinæ and antennæ as in *mississippiensis*. Thorax short, robust. Meso-epinotal constriction distinct and pronounced. The angle formed by the junction of the basal surface of the epinotum and the declivity distinct. Petiole low, robust, with convex anterior and superior surfaces and flat posterior surface; the posterior margin of the superior surface deeply excised or emarginate. Gaster and legs as in *mississippiensis*.

Mandibles and anterior half of head subopaque, the former obscurely longitudinally rugose-punctate, the latter regularly and coarsely reticulate-rugose with punctate interrugal spaces. On the cheeks and front the sculpture gradually passes over into umbilicately punctate, shallow, scattered foveolæ. Posterior half of the head and the remainder of body shining, finely shagreened.

Hairs yellowish short, erect and obtuse on the cheeks, longer and more tapering on front and vertex. Gaster above and below with scattered tapering hairs. There are a few short hairs at the tips of the scapes and femora.

Anterior half of head light yellowish, posterior half of head including antennæ dark brown, thorax and appendages brown, abdomen black, with base of first and second segment tinged with yellow.

Worker. Length, 3-3.5 mm.

Head longer than broad, broader behind than in front, with convex occipital border and somewhat less convex sides. Mandibles small, 4 toothed. Clypeus convex, almost square and not noticeably keeled. Antennal scapes flattened, gradually tapering from base to tip. Thorax very deeply constricted at the junction of meso-epinotum. The base of the epinotum in profile appears flattened and forms with the declivity a distinct angle. Petiole low, robust, with convex anterior and superior surfaces, the posterior margin of the latter deeply excised to form two distinct lateral teeth, the posterior surface of the petiole flattened. Gaster oblong. Legs similar to those of the soldier.

Body and appendages shining, distinctly shagreened, the head and thorax more coarsely than the gaster, the cheeks and upper surfaces of the head with scattered punctures.

Head, legs and gaster sparsely covered with delicate, white, appressed hairs. Clypeus, front, vertex, tips of antennæ and femora and the gastric segments with a few scattered and longer hairs.

Dark brown; head darker, mandibles, cheeks and appendages light brown, gaster black.

The ants on which these descriptions are based were collected at Starkville, Mississippi, on January 11, 1922. Like *mississippiensis* this subspecies has a fondness for nesting in white ash but has also been taken by Mr. Andrew Fleming at

Sibley, Mississippi from the twigs of elder. The nesting habits of the two seem to be about the same. Besides the localities mentioned the writer has specimens from Columbus and A. & M. College.

The soldier of this subspecies can be recognized by its peculiarly blunt head, the truncated area of which is oblique in profile. The clypeus on the truncated area projects above the surface very noticeably and it much broader above than below. The punctation and sculpturing on the anterior portion of the head is regular and distinct. When the head of the soldier is viewed from above it appears rectangular, very little broader than long, with divergent sides and inflated cheeks.

The workers can be distinguished by the very deep constriction at the meso-epinotum and by the prominent 2-toothed petiole, both of which are very different from those of *mississippiensis.*

The color in *fraxinicola* is variable as in the preceeding species, some specimens being very dark while others are lighter and have more yellow on the base of the gaster and the second segment.

THE VARIETIES OF *MONECPHORA BICINCTA* FROM THE POINT OF VIEW OF A CYTOLOGIST.

ALICE M. BORING.

Wellesley College.

A curious case of distribution in *Monecphora bicincta* and its variety *ignipecta* was called to my attention by Mr. A. P. Morse in the summer of 1921. Since then I have been studying the chromosomes of these forms to see whether a study of the internal cell phenomena would throw any light on their relationship.

In Psyche for February 1921 (vol. 28), Mr. Morse describes the case. The normal range of *Monecphora bicincta* var. *bicincta*, the form with red bands on its wings, is from southern New Jersey south, while the normal range of *Monecphora bicincta* var. *ignipecta*, the common black form, is from southern New Jersey north. Mr. Morse found a number of the variety *bicincta* near Norridgewock, Maine, while the variety *ignipecta* was taken in all other localities around. It is possible that that particular spot is subject to some peculiar environmental conditions which may have caused the banded form to appear there, but it does not seem likely that this aberrant colony could be due to environmental causes, when its environment, at least as far as general climatic conditions are involved, was apparently more like that of the nearby black colonies than of the other banded colonies in the south. What is the genetic status of these two forms? They apparently breed true within their range of distribution, since such aberrant groups as described by Mr. Morse are not frequent. They must then be genetically stable and according to present-day genetical theories there should be some physical basis for their phenotypic differences. Is the change from one to the other great enough to involve a visible cytological differentiation or is it a mutation in one gene of one chromosome as in the races of Drosophila and therefore not visible by present cytological methods?

The *Monecphora bicincta* var. *bicincta* material was very kindly sent to me at Woods Hole, Mass., in July, 1921, by Mr. Z. P. Metcalf and Mr. C. O. Eddy of the North Carolina Agricultural Experiment Station. The *M. bicincta* var. *ignipecta* material was collected at Wellesley, Mass., partly by Mr. Morse and partly by myself. I could not find Monecphora at Woods Hole, so trusted to obtaining it in September at Wellesley, as it was reported to be a late summer form. But the only specimens found as late as September 15 were females and they had laid their eggs and were much shrivelled in appearance. The material finally studied was collected in July, 1922 at Wellesley. A careful watch was kept from July 1 on for the first forms to appear. The first individual was taken on July 14. By July 21 the species was abundant. They appeared just as their food plant, the bunch-grass, was attaining its full growth. In looking over a field of the grass, one could pick out the Monecphora as conspicuous black specks clinging to the grass at various distances from the ground. I did not find any nymphs in their frothy masses of spittle on these plants although I carefully examined the young tufts of grass for some time before the adults appeared. In the *Monecphora bicincta* var. *bicincta* material sent me from North Carolina, the nymphs were on the roots of the food plants. These nymphs were not reared to assure their identity, but they were surrounded by a typical mass of white exudate and those old enough to contain mature sperm cells showed the same cytological conditions as the adults. Probably an examination of the roots of the young bunch-grass around Wellesley in early July, would show the habits of *Monecphora bicincta* var. *ignipecta* to be similar.

The cytological study of the chromosomes of these two varieties reveals them to be identical. This was tested by camera lucida drawings placed side by side. The spermatogonial number is 19, the primary spermatocyte 10, and the secondary spermatocyte 9 and 10. They are like other species of Cercopidæ studied (Boring '13 and Boring & Fogler '15) in having an X chromosome which divides in the second spermatocyte division. The chromosomes have the same absolute size in the two varieties and show the same relative size differences within the group, 2 largest, 5 medium and 3 smaller (including X). These size differences are not clean-cut enough to be always certain but they are usually discernible in the primary spermatocytes.

Applying these facts to taxonomy, we can say that the cytology of *Monecphora bicincta* var. *bicincta* and var. *ignipecta* corroborates their close relationship. In some insects, as shown by the researches of McClung, Robertson and others on the grasshoppers the chromosome number is not a function of the species or genus but of the family. All species of the Acrididæ have 23 chromosomes and all species of the Tettigidæ have 27. A few apparent exceptions have proved to be due to fusion or breaking of certain chromosomes. The generic and specific differences are expressed in differences in chromosome size and arrangement within the given number. The degree of chromosome similarity has been found to correspond directly to the nearness of taxonomic relationship. But so far among the Cercopidæ studied each species has its own specific chromosome number so that the identity of number in the two varieties of *Monecphora bicincta* would substantiate their classification as varieties of the same species instead of as separate species. *Philænus lineatus* has 15 as reduced number of chromosomes, while *Philænus leucophthalmus* (*spumarius*) has 12; *Aphrophora parallela* has 15 while *Aphrophora quadrinotata* has 14 and *Aphrophora spumaria* (European form) has 12; *Lepyronia quadrangularis* has 11; *Clastoptera obtusa* has 8, while *Clastoptera proteus* has 7; but *Monecphora bicincta* has 10 and *Monecphora ignipecta* also has 10. The change from one to the other is not great enough to involve a visible change in chromosomes.

In two other species of Cercopidæ the cytological study of varietal forms has been recorded; *Philænus leucophthalmus* (*spumarius*) collected from goldenrod and wild sunflower at Woods Hole and the European form, *Aphrophora spumaria*, collected from grass sweepings in a meadow at Eisenach (Boring, Biol. Bull. vol. 24.). In neither case were the varieties accurately identified and named, but a wide range of color and distinctness of marking was observed and the testes preserved from individuals representing these differences. These specimens of Philænus were sent to Mr. Van Duzee at the time, 1912, and identified by him as all belonging to the species *Philænus leucophthalmus* (*spumarius*). From a study of Mr. Van Duzee's Catalogue of the Hemiptera, 1917, I find many varieties of *P. leucophthalmus* recorded. The names of some of these are clearly descriptive of the somatic characters which were conspicuous in the Woods Hole material which I studied cytologically. The chromosome group in all these varietal forms was identical, the same situation as in the two varieties of *Monecphora bicincta.* There is therefore cytological evidence for the present systematic classification of the varieties of *Philænus leucophthalmus* and of *Monecphora bicincta* as varieties instead of as separate species. In the Cercopidæ specific differences seem to be correlated with difference in number of chromosomes while varietal differences do not seem to be expressed in visible differences of any sort in the chrosomomes.

Those few specimens of the southern banded form of *Monecphora bicincta* at Norridgewock, Maine, raise other interesting questions, especially as to which was the original form. Evidently the banded form was the first one described. If it is the older, has the black form arisen from it as a result of suffusion? If so, what caused the return to the banded condition in those few specimens at Norridgewock? Can this be explained as a genetic reversion due to the chance recombination of genes? On the other hand, the black form may be the original which occasionally throws off banded mutants, those once thrown off in the south having firmly established themselves, those in Norridgewock being recent mutants. These questions are of course not to be answered by cytological methods. Experimental breeding would answer some. The cytologist must content himself with establishing these two varieties of *Monecphora bicincta* as belonging within one species.

PROCEEDINGS OF THE CAMBRIDGE ENTOMOLOGICAL CLUB.

The annual meeting was held January 9, 1923. The report of the secretary shows that ten meetings were held in 1922 with an average attendance of seventeen persons. Four members were elected, one resigned and two died. A club seal was adopted and is now used on the cover of Psyche. A course of six lectures on insects was given in Febuary and March, a report of which is in the record of the April meeting (Psyche vol.XXX No. 1, Feb. 1923).

The treasurer's report shows that the Club's income was increased by $124.55 from the sale of back numbers of Psyche so that all expenses of the year were paid.

The following officers for 1923 were nominated and elected.

President	A. P. Morse	Executive Committee	C. W. Johnson
Vice President	R. Heber Howe		O. E. Plath
Secretary	J. H. Emerton		Miss Priscilla Butler
Treasurer	Fred H. Walker		
		Editor of Psyche	C. T. Brues.

Dr. C. S. Ludlow of the Army Medical Museum, Washington, D. C. was elected a member.

The retiring president, W. M. Wheeler, addressed the club on the relations of some Hemiptera and Diptera with ants. In most cases this relation is that of scavengers, the dipterous larvæ living among the ant larvæ and eating their excrement. Certain fly larvæ coil around ant larvæ near the head and eat food from a pouch in which is it placed by the worker ants. Some adult flies take food directly from the anus of ant larvæ. Other flies hover over adult ants and take food as it passes from the mouth of one ant to another. The hemipterous Ptilocerus has unde the abdomen a spot covered with brilliant orange hairs from which comes a secretion attractive to ants. The Ptilocerus stands near moving ants and offers them this secretion which has a narcotic effect. If sufficient is taken the ant soon becomes helpless and the soft parts are eaten by the Ptilocerus.

Miss Butler exhibited her collecting coat made of canvas, without collar or sleeves, containing 47 pockets of various sizes and shapes.

C. W. Johnson described a honey bee with a single eye in the center of the head in place of the usual pair, which was shown by Mr. Du Porte of MacDonald College, Canada at the recent meeting of the Entomological Society of America.

At the Febuary meeting, C. T. Brues gave an account of a new, minute hymenopterous insect from Sumatra. It has wide and thin mandibles, concave on the inner side like a pair of clam shells and a long abdominal appendage which may be either an ovipositor or a male copulatary organ.

C. W. Johnson told of various new discoveries among the Diptera, especially in the family Syrphidæ which he had latley reviewed with Mr. Curran of Ottawa.

J. H. Emerton exhibited on the screen a large number of lantern slides of spiders and cobwebs including examples of all the principal families represented in New England.

C. V. Blackburn exhibited some butterfly jewelry of original designs made in Italy.

PSYCHE

A JOURNAL OF ENTOMOLOGY

ESTABLISHED IN 1874

VOL. XXX JUNE-AUGUST, 1923 NOS. 3-4

CONTENTS

CAMBRIDGE ENTOMOLOGICAL CLUB

PSYCHE is published bi-monthly, the issues appearing in February, April, June, August, October and December. Subscription price, per year, payable in advance: $2.00 to subscribers in the United States, Canada or Mexico; foreign postage, 15 cents extra. Single copies, 40 cents.

Cheques and remittances should be addressed to Treasurer, Cambridge Entomological Club, Bussey Institution, Forest Hills, Boston 30, Mass.

Orders for back volumes, missing numbers, notices of change of address, etc., should be sent to Cambridge Entomological Club, Bussey Institution, Forest Hills, Boston 30, Mass.

IMPORTANT NOTICE TO CONTRIBUTORS.

Manuscripts intended for publication, books intended for review, and other editorial matter, should be addressed to Professor C. T. Brues, Bussey Institution, Forest Hills, Boston 30, Mass.

Authors contributing articles over 8 printed pages in length will be required to bear a part of the extra, expense for additional pages. This expense will be that of typesetting only, which is about $2.00 per page. The actual cost of preparing cuts for all illustrations must be borne by contributors: the expense for full page plates from line drawings is approximately $5.00 each, and for full page half-tones, $7.50 each; smaller sizes in proportion.

AUTHOR'S SEPARATES.

Reprints of articles may be secured by authors, if they are ordered before, or at the time proofs are received for corrections. The cost of these will be furnished by the Editor on application.

Entered as second-class mail matter at the Post Office at Boston, Mass. Acceptance for mailing at special rate of postage provided in Section 1103, Act of October 3, 1917, authorized on June 29, 1918.

PSYCHE

VOL. XXX. JUNE-AUGUST 1923 Nos. 3-4

OCCURRENCE, LIFE-CYCLE, AND MAINTENANCE, UNDER ARTIFICIAL CONDITIONS, OF *MIASTOR*.

By Reginald G. Harris

From the Laboràtoire d'évolution des êtres organisés, Paris, Prof. Caullery, Director.

The genus *Miastor* is extremely interesting for several reasons. It was in this genus that paedogenesis was discovered by Nicholas Wagner in 1861. Though at first Wagner misinterpreted the phenomenon which he observed, and though his observations were doubted, subsequent investigation has demonstrated the fact of paedogenesis as well as the occurrence of polymorphism in this genus. But investigations upon *Miastor* have been limited, due to some extent at least, to the lack of a suitable method of maintaining the larvæ of this genus in the laboratory. Now that a method, which will be discussed later, has been found, it seems to the writer desirable to make a short resume of the occurrence of Miastor, its life cycle, and polymorphism among the larvæ of the genus.

Occurrence of Miastor.

Miastor larvæ were first observed underneath the bark of decaying trees. I have found them in France under the bark of decaying oak, chestnut, and birch logs, and in edible mushrooms.

Other observers have found *Miastor* larvæ in many kinds of decomposing wood and in fermenting beet pulp. It may be safely concluded that their occurrence is fairly widespread in decaying logs and that they are sometimes present in other vegetable matter. Their habitat is not limited to Europe. In America Felt[1] found *Miastor* larvæ in 1910 under the partially decayed inner bark of chestnut rails.

In such environments *Miastor* larvæ usually occur in characteristic, compact, white colonial masses, a colony often containing a hundred or more individuals in close contact with each other. Among *Miastor* larvæ occurring in mushrooms I have not observed colonial arrangement. Here yellow or yellowish white larvæ are found singly although a single plant may contain many larvæ directly beneath the superficial cell-layers of the stalk or between the gills of the umbrella.

The Life-Cycle of Miastor.

Pædogenetic reproduction maintains in this genus during the autumn, winter, and spring, until the early summer, at which time pupæ occur, producing, after metamorphosis, male and female imagines. (The occurrence of pupæ, however, is not limited to the early summer. I have found them in nature in October, and in the same material pupæ continued to arise in the laboratory during the early winter. Though these were kept in conditions as natural as possible, at room-temperature, none of the pupæ has as yet given adults, though the usual period required for this metamorphosis in Miastor is about five days. Some of the pupæ have been destroyed by mould. It would seem that others, apparently in good condition, are in diapose.) The copulation of the adult flies results in the fertilization of the eggs which develop outside the mother into typical pædogenetic larvæ, and the cycle is complete.

Pædogenesis in *Miastor* is realized as follows: The ovaries of a typical pædogenetic larva produce eggs varying in number in different individuals, types and species. The development of larvæ from the eggs occurs within the body-cavity of the mother. The embryos continue to develop at the expense of the fat-bodies, muscles and surrounding tissues of the mother larva until

[1]Felt, E. P. Miastor americana, an account of Pedogenesis. Bull. New York State, 1911 vol. 147, pp. 82ff.

a suitable growth is attained. The embryos seem to be suitably developed, and are usually active for several days previous to their escape. At the time of escape, the larva, while not full grown, is well formed, active, and capable of continuing its existence. The time required for a typical pædogenetic generation is about two weeks, though the period varies with indivuals and environmental conditions. White pædogenetic larvæ produce four to ten or more embryos.

Polymorphism in Miastor Larvæ.

In all species of *Miastor* larvæ, which I have observed, there occur three distinct larval forms. Two are pædogenetic: viz. white and yellow pædogenetic larvæ, while the third is incapable of pædogenetic reproduction; it is the pupa-larva.

(1) *Typical white pædogenetic larvæ.*
The body of the larva contains fourteen segments. In the first or head-segment are the mouth opening and two antennæ. The mouth parts are arranged for sucking. The second and third segments contain the optic ganglia, and the third segment two eyes. In typical pædogenetic larvæ the eyes usually touch each other at their convex surfaces. The brain is in the fourth and fifth segments. Dorsal and partially posterior to it is the brain fat body. The salivary glands are in the fifth and sixth segments on either side of the œsophagus, their ducts opening in the mouth cavity. The œsophagus extends posteriorly from the mouth and opens into the intestine in the fifth segment. In this region the intestine enlarges and folds, forming two blind appendices, which are in turn divided into two parts each. The digestive tube continues to enlarge slightly until it reaches the region of the tenth segment where it narrows into the rectum which is not functional in later stages. The intestine contains a peritropic membrane for inclosing undigested food. Four tubes of Malpighi extend anteriorly from the region of the twelfth to the tenth segment. The anus is in the fourteenth segment. Here are also two symmetrical anal flaps which are easily visible when protruded. The larva contains well developed fat-bodies,

filling much of the body-cavity from the sixth to the fourteenth segments. The two ovaries occur in the region of the tenth segments, and are closely connected anteriorly with fat-bodies.

There are small chitinous points, arranged in four or more rows, extending around the larva between each segment from 2 to 14. Six chitinous hooks terminate the larva in the last segment.

There are two tracheal trunks on each side of the body, one laterally ventral, one dorsal. These have numerous cross branches, viz., one large branch connecting the two dorsal trunks in each segment from 6 to 13. From each of these branches two other minute branches extend posteriorly in each segment. Numerous branches and sub branches proceed from the ventral trunks. The dorsal and ventral trunks are connected in each segment from 6 to 13, another branch opening to the exterior on each side thus forming eight pairs of stigmata. There being no protruding spiracles it would seem difficult for the larvæ to remain long submerged. However, larvæ remain alive for long periods of time, a fortnight or more, when completely submerged in water under a cover-glass.

A series of large ganglia occur ventral to the digestive tube·

Locomotion results from stretching each segment and then contracting it, the process extending anteriorly. The rows of chitinous points prevent the larvæ from slipping.

The size of larvæ varies with species, individuals, cultures and age. New born pædogenetic larvæ of *Miastor metraloas,* average 1.35 x 0.16 mm, while pædogenetic mother-larvæ attain a length of from 3 to 4 mm.

2) *Yellow pædogenetic larvæ.*
Yellow forms (wanderers) are similar in general structure to white pædogenetic forms. They are extremely active. The body is usually slimmer, and the fat bodies less heavily developed than in white pædogenetic larvæ. The yellow pigment seems to occur for the most part in the fat-bodies. The eyes are noticeably larger than in other Miastor larval forms, and approach closely along their surfaces.

Yellow larvæ usually produce but a single embryo in the species (*Miastor metraloas*?) which I found in decaying wood. Yellow larvæ (undescribed) occuring in mushrooms, however, produce a large number of embryos. I have frequently observed twenty embryos in a mother-larva.

Neither the role of, nor the incentive factor producing, yellow forms is clear.

In active yellow larvæ I have observed a jumping locomotion. This seems to occur as a result of the larva bending its body until the anal chitinous hooks catch against the chitinous points of the second or third segment. Extension of the segments then tightens the tension which finally breaks with a snap resulting in a jump. The yellow forms are extremely active, and may often be seen lifting their heads and much of their bodies straight into the air.

3) *Pupa-larvæ.*

Larvæ which will metamorphose into pupæ are immediately distinguishable from other forms by means of three characteristic differences, though in general their structure is similar to that of white and yellow pædogenetic forms.

a) In newly born living pupa-larvæ the imaginal discs are visible. These occur laterally in the third, fourth and fifth segments. They are not present in pædogenetic forms.

b) The spathula sternalis, a structure typical of Cecidomyid larvæ, occurs ventrally in the third segment of the pupa-larvæ of *Miastor*. It is not visible in newly born living pupa-larvæ, but after four or five days becomes clearly visible, due to a yellowish coloration which later changes to orange and dark brown. The shape of this structure differs with various species. Its function is not understood.

c) The eyes of pupa-larvæ do not touch as in pædogenetic forms but are usually clearly separated.

The fat-bodies of pupa-larvæ are extremely well developed. The larvæ are active up to the time of pupation, unlike pædogenetic larvæ which of necessity become inactive with the progressive destruction of their muscles, due to the development of the embryos.

In *Miastor* as in all cyclorrhaphous diptera, the pupa is formed within the last larval skin. After the pupa-larva comes to rest the color of its skin changes from white to yellow, later to orange red and dark brown.

Under optimum conditions a period of about five days is required for the metamorphosis of pupæ into imagines.

The causes which lead to the occurrence of the various types of larvæ within a single species of *Miastor* are not known. I have observed all the various types occurring side by side in nature and in the laboratory. Springer's[2] belief that the yellow forms and pupa-larvæ are produced by the action of light upon typical pædogenetic mothers does not seem tenable, since I have observed all types occurring in the laboratory in cultures reared in the dark as well as in those reared in the light.

Method of Culture in the Laboratory.

In order to carry on investigations concerning the factors regulating the life-cycle of *Miastor* and those causing polymorphism among the larvæ of a single species, it seemed immediately desirable to find a suitable artificial medium in which cultures might be reared in the laboratory under controlled conditions. With this in view I attempted to rear *Miastor* larvæ on various media, finally meeting with success on a mushroom bouillon-agar innoculated with yeast.

The mushroom bouillon is made by taking equal parts by weight of mushrooms and water. The mushrooms are boiled in the water for 20-30 minutes. At the end of this time the mushrooms are withdrawn from the bouillon to which is added sufficient agar to make 4 per cent of the bouillon weight. The whole is heated until the agar is dissolved, when it is poured into small mouthed stock bottles stoppered with cotton, and sterilized; in this way the culture medium may be kept indefinitely. When it is needed for use, the medium is liquified in a hot water-bath and while still hot poured into culture dishes, and allowed to

[2]Springer, Fritz. Polymorphismus bei den Larven von *Miastor metraloas.* Zool. Jahrb Abth. f. Anst. vol. 40 p. 57 (1917).

harden. For mass cultures of pædogenetic larvæ I have found petri dishes very suitable for culture containers. Since they allow but little loss by evaporation, the water of condensation falling back upon the culture medium, the medium remains moist, suitable for the reproduction of the yeast and the growth of the larvæ for some time. Larvæ may be more easily removed for examination from cultures reared in petri dishes than from those maintained in deep containers. Very small petri dishes may be used for individual cultures.

After the agar has hardened, a little powdered yeast is sprinkled over its surface, to which the larvæ are transferred. Cultures are then placed in the incubator at 20-22 degrees Centrigrade.

I have employed this culture medium for *Miastor* larvæ of various species, and have observed in colonies reared in this way all the larval forms occurring under natural conditions.

It seems then that a method has been found for rearing cultures of *Miastor* larvæ in the laboratory under conditions which may be easily regulated. This method should be suitable for maintaining cultures of a pædogenetic insect in the laboratory for class work as well as for carrying on investigations concerning the factors influencing the life-cycle and the polymorphism of the larvæ of *Miastor*.

THE GENUS CYRTOPOGON (DIPTERA; ASILIDÆ)[1]

By A. L. Melander.

In the elaboration of Osten Sacken's table of Cyrtopogon given in Back's 1909 study of Robber-flies thirty species are included. This genus is particularly well represented in the Pacific States and several new forms have been discovered by western collectors since the publication of Back's review. Accordingly the following indentification table is appropriate to bring to date our knowledge of this group of especially interesting flies. References are given in the table to those species described since Back's paper was published.

Many of the species of Cyrtopogon exhibit sex dimorphism. This is particularly the case with those species having red antennæ. At times the males and females look quite unlike. The males present easy recognition characters in their elaborate and brilliant sex attire, but sometimes the more modest appearing females of several species resemble each other so closely as to be differentiated with difficulty.

The characters used in the table are for the most part reasonably constant. There is some individual variation in the color of the legs and of the hairs of face, hypopleuræ, scutellum, abdomen and legs, and in the extent of interruption of the abdominal fasciæ. Where such variations have been sufficient to cause doubt in interpreting the table, cross-references have been introduced for more accurate guidance. Types of the new species are in the writer's collection.

Key to the Species of Cyrtopogon.

1. Scutellum convex, generally long-pilose, usually shining or with touch of pollen at base, rarely pollinose among the species with long arista. . . . . 2.
   Scutellum flattened and uniformly and quite densely pollinose; antennæ black. . . . . 32.

[1]Contribution from the Zoology Laboratory of the State College of Washington.

2. Third antennal joint red; mystax largely white or yellow;. (if halteres are blackish and face has white hairs, see *longimanus*; if large species with base of abdomen densely pilose, see *dasyllis*) . . . . 3.
   Third antennal joint black. . . . . 11.
3. Tibiæ and tarsi more or less reddish. . 4.
   Legs black; claws white with black tip. . . . . 10.
4. Pile of scutellum and hypopleuræ white; apex of femora reddish; mystax mostly white; pile of tibiæ and pleuræ very long. (Can., N. H., Ct., N. Y., Mass., Va., N. C. *marginalis* Lw.
   Pile of scutellum black; of hypopleuræ more or less black; femora black; western species. . . . . . 5.
5. Front tibiæ and tarsi of male silvery pilose on posterior side; wings hyaline. . . . . 6.
   Legs not silvery, but sometimes with yellowish white hairs fringing tarsi; pile of male abdomen more or less tufted; wings with light clouding about veins, anterior crossvein near base of discal cell. . . . . 7.
6. Male: front tibiæ with fine white silky pile on outer side, becoming longer and denser apically; front tarsi with silvery hairs on anterior side of joints 2-5 in addition to the silvery hairs on posterior side; abdominal segments 1, 2 with pale yellow pile, longer on sides, remaining segments with very short hair, yellowish on 3, black on rest, segments 2-5 white-fasciate, interrupted on 4, 5. (Col.) *pulcher* Back
   Male: front tibiæ with moderately long silvery pile posteriorly, short yellow pile anteriorly; front tarsi with yellow hairs on anterior side of first two joints; abdomen with reddish yellow pile forming dense apical bands on segments 1-4, segments 2-4 silvery fasciate. (Alta.) (Can. Ent. liv. 278, 1922) . . . . . *albitarsis* Curran.
7. Pile of abdomen yellow or fulvous at least on first segment, tip of male abdomen blue-black, segments 2-4 with complete fasciæ, sometimes hidden by dense pile in male; basal half of claws reddish. . . . . 8.

Male abdomen with lateral tufts of black not fulvous hair, female with less tufted black and white pile, abdomen with interrupted white pollinose fasciæ; claws black, front tarsi of male very long. (Or.) (Proc.Cal. Acad. Sc., 1919, 233) . . . . *perspicax* Cole

8. Male abdomen with black tuft on sides of second segment, a dorsal pollinose vitta on segments 2-5, female abdomen with lateral pile pale yellow and almost entirely confined to basal two segments; male front tibiæ with white pubescence toward tip, tarsi yellow with brush of yellowish-white hairs along entire outer face and with black bristles inside, tarsi of female reddish; central hairs of face mixed black and white. (Wash.) . . *glarealis*, n. sp.

Male abdomen with dense fulvous pile arranged in tufted bands across segments 2-4, no dorsal vitta, yellow pile of female abdomen continuing on third segment. . . . 9.

9. Segments 5-7 of male abdomen with dense tufts of short black velvet pile; front tibiæ and tarsi without brush on posterior side, bristles black, some white pile on extensor face of male tarsus; female with tarsal joints tipped with black and with center hairs of face white. (Cal., Wash.) . . . . *aurifex* O. S.

Segments 5-7 of male abdomen not tufted; posterior edge of front tibiæ and tarsi of male with uniform brush of white hairs containing white bristles; female with yellowish tarsi and with central hairs of face yellow. (Or., Id.) (Proc. Cal. Acad. Sc. 1919, 230.) . . . . . *auratus* Cole

10. Thorax white-gray pollinose, markings nearly obsolete; wings hyaline; face and front heavily coated with cinereous pollen. Male unknown. (Cal.) . . . . . *cretaceus* O. S.

Thorax of male black, of female brown and gray; wings of male black, of female subfuscous; male front tarsi very long, silvery on extensor side, hind tibiæ and tarsi silvery pilose. (Cal., Or., Wash.) . . . . *princeps* O. S.

11. Style nearly as long as third joint of antennæ; wings with distinct dark spots on furcations and crossveins; scutellum often dusted. . . . . 12.

Style evidently shorter than third joint of antennæ. . . . 15.

12. Thorax compressed gibbous, the undivided median stripe bearing a strong mane of long black pile and setiform hairs; scutellum margined with long black setæ; costal and marginal cells hyaline; halteres black. (Wash.) . . . . *maculosis* Coq.

Thorax convex as usual, with erect black pile but no mane; scutellar bristles less developed; middle dorsal stripe geminate. . . . . 13.

13. Costa fringed with uniform close hairs; pile of face tipped with white; halteres black. (Cal., Or., Wash., B. C.) *nebulo* O. S.

Costa with only microscopic hair; white tips of facial hairs less evident; costal and marginal cells brown apically. 14.

14. Halteres black; a single spot in first basal cell at origin of third vein. (Id., Wash.) . . . . . . *punctipennis*, n. sp.

Halteres yellowish; first basal cell with two blackish spots near middle. (Wash., Or.) . . . . *varipennis* Coq.

15. Abdomen with dense erect pile forming a bright yellow band across middle part, and black at tip. . . . . 16.

Abdomen not densely clothed but sometimes with lateral or parted tufts of pile in male. . . . . 18.

16. Style short and thick, almost square; wings hyaline; anterior crossvein near base of discal cell; anterior tibiæ and front tarsi with dense white pile on extensor face; yellow pile of abdomen confined to basal three segments. (Wash.) . . . . *semitarius*. n. sp.

Style longer than wide; anterior crossvein near middle of discal cell; hairs of legs black aside from the fulvous recumbent pubescence on inside of front tibiæ. . . . 17.

17. Wings of male with large black sharply limited spot; all hairs of head black; yellow hairs of abdomen confined to segments 2-4 (Col., Id.) . . . . *dasyllis* Will.

Wings with dark spot more suffused; hairs of face and beard yellow; yellow hairs of abdomen extending on fifth segment. (Wash., Or., Id., Cal., N. Y.) .*dasylloides* Will.

18. At least hind tibiæ in part reddish, usually anterior pairs also more or less reddish. . . . . 19.
Legs entirely black, sometimes hind tibiæ with dark castaneous tinge. . . . . 27.

19. Wings of male with two large black marks; vertex little excavated and heavily deep golden pollinose; mesonotum deep golden pollinose, the four corners shining; mystax golden; abdomen with yellow lateral tufts; segments 2-5 with broadly interrupted posterior fasciæ. Wings of female infuscated over apical part and over end of anal cell; color of pile and pollen less deep. Anterior crossvein near middle of discal cell. (N. H., Minn., N. M., Col., Wyo., Id., Or., Wash.) . . . . *bimacula* Walk.
Wings not bimaculate; vertex more evidently excavated; 20.

20. Abodmen of male with a large tergal patch of dense fulvous tomentum; hypopleural hairs white.(Ont.) *vulneratus*,n. sp.
Abdomen without such mark of fulvous tomentum. . 21.

21. Male front tarsi with recumbent silvery pile, last two joints of middle tarsi of male with disk of black hairs; gray pruinose marks of abdomen very small and located at hind angles of the segments. (If male front tarsi silvery but middle tarsi without disk, see *tacomæ*.) . . . . . . 22.
Front tarsi without silvery recumbent hairs and middle tarsi without black disk. . . . . 25.

22. Silvery hairs of male front tarsi parted; black disk of middle tarsi confined to last two joints. . . . . 23.
Silvery hairs of front tarsi not parted, beginning on second joint; short black hairs on third joint of middle tarsi beginning the disk; pulvilli dark brown. . . . . 24.

23. First two segments of abdomen with white pile on sides, in male contrasting with black pile on remainder; front metatarsi of male not silvery above, but densely beset on both sides below with black bristles; pulvilli whitish. (Cal., N. M., Wyo., Col.) . . . . . . *callipedilus* Lw.
Abdomen with black pile over all; front metatarsi of male silvery above and not spinose beneath; pulvilli brown. (Cal.) . . . . *cymballista* O. S.

24\. Scutellum and most of thorax shining; pile of abdomen yellow and black. (B. C. ,Alta., Wash.) (Can. Ent. 1922, 277) . . . . *willistoni* Curran.

Base of scutellum and much of thorax brown pollinose; pile of abdomen yellow. (N. M., Utah, Id., Col., Neb.) . . . . *plausor* O. S.

25\. Gray pruinose marks of abdomen confined to hind angles of segments; pile of face deep golden; pile of hypopleuræ yellow, of abdomen yellow except at end; tibiæ abruptly black on apical half. (N. S., Queb., Ont., N. H., Mass., N. Y., Ct., N. J., N. C., Fla., Ill.) (If legs are entirely dark chestnut, see *alleni*) . . *falto* Walk.

Gray pruinose marks following hind margins of abdominal segments; pile of face whitish, black on sides; hind tibiæ not black apically. . . . . 26.

26\. Hairs of hypopleuræ black; abdominal fasciæ narrowly interrupted, sometimes entire in female; pile of abdomen mainly black. (Col., N. M., Cal., Id., Wash., B. C.) . . . . *montanus* Lw.

Hairs of hypopleuræ white; abdominal fasciæ entire; pile of abdomen white Male unknown. (Cal., N. M., Or.) . . . . *leucozona* Lw.

27\. Middle segments of abdomen with complete fasciæ; male front tarsi elongate, tarsal hairs chiefly white, long on upper side of basal three joints of hind pair, tarsal hairs of female chiefly black; hypopleural hairs black; halteres blackish brown; extensor hairs of hind tibiæ white. (Cal., Wash., B. C.) (If hind tibiæ are dark chestnut color, see *montanus*) . . . . *longimanus* Lw.

Fasciæ of abdomen interrupted, sometimes reduced to lateral spots; crossveins, etc., usually clouded. . . . . 28.

28\. Fasciæ broader than long, following the hind margins; front tarsi of male slender . . . . 29.

Fasciæ confined to hind angles of segments. . . . . . 30.

29\. Front tibiæ and tarsi of male with not dense white pilef which does not conceal the ground-color; hind tarsi o, male darker than others; claws broadly yellowish; humeri subshining. (Mont.) . . . . *rufotarsus* Back.

Front tibiæ and tarsi of male with appressed silvery pile concealing the ground-color at least of tarsus; middle tarsi darkest; claws black the base reddish; humeri and adjacent region of thorax heavily silvery-white pruinose. (Wash.) . . . . *tacomæ* n. sp.

30. Front tarsi of male with single row of silvery pile from very base; last two joints of middle tarsi with the flat disk of black pile longer than broad; pile of abdomen yellowish white at base, black apically. (Wash., Or.) (If front metatarsi of male are not silvery, see *Willistoni*) . . . . *præpes* Will.

Front and middle tarsi of male not ornamented. . . . . 31.

31. Scutellum with long black pile; mystax and hypopleuræ pile black; pleuræ shining above; notal pattern including mark like a tuning-fork. (N. H., N. Y., N. C.) *lyratus* O .S.

Scutellum with short white pile; mystax partly white, hypopleural pile white; pleuræ densely white pruinose. (N. H., N. C.) . . . . *alleni* Back.

32. Abdomen with pollinose markings at least of segments 2-4 extending from side to side. . . . . 33.

Abdominal fasciæ interrupted, sometimes subinterrupted, that of first segment sometimes entire. . . . 39.

33. Greater part of middle segments of abdomen covered with gray pollen and the front angles polished; hypopleural pile white. . . . . 34.

Greater part of abdominal segments shining, or if largely pollinose the pollen extending along the sides so that the front angles are not polished. . . . . 36.

34. Pollen denuded in circular spot in middle of each tergite; tibiæ with many white bristles, male with brushes of white hair on front side of middle tibiæ below knee and on front side of middle metatarsi. (Wash.) . . . *ablautoides*, n. sp.

Middle of tergites pollinose, or if shining not forming a central round spot; white hairs of legs evenly distributed. . . . . 35.

35. Hypopleural pile black; hairs of hypopygium yellowish white; mystax white; abdomen of both sexes gray except front angles of segments; tibial bristles white except those at tips and on front side of first pair. (Cal.) . . *rattus* O. S.
Hypopleural pile white; hypopygial hairs black above; mystax white and black; anterior half of male abdominal segments shining; tibial bristles black, a few pale ones on extensor side of hind tibiæ of female. (Wash.) . . . . *cæsius*, n. sp.

36. Face convex below but not gibbous, facial pile dense and white; tibiæ reddish at base; male abdomen broad, with sides and posterior margins pollinose, female abdomen narrow, anterior margins of segments 2-4 sometimes also pollinose. (Or., Wash.) (Proc. Cal. Acad. Sc. 1919, 230) . . . . *anomalus* Cole.
Face more gibbous, its pile largely or wholly black. . . 37.

37. Legs largely brownish red; geminate stripe of thorax distinct and complete; pollen of abdomen confined to posterior and side margins of segments; style one-third the third antennal joint; scutellum without bristles; face and front brownish gray. (Ks., Col., N. M.) . . *profusus* O. S.
Legs black; scutellum with black bristles. (If scutellum with only marginal pile, see *nugator* female if facial hairs all black, or *cæsius* male if facial hairs white.) . . 38.

38. Abdominal fasciæ extending along posterior edge of segments; stripes of thorax very distinct. (Cal.) *evidens* O. S.
Abdominal fasciæ extending along anterior margin of segments 2-6 but not reaching sides, posterior angles with spots of white pollen; stripes of thorax indistinct; style one-tenth the third antennal joint. (Cal.) *cerussatus* O. S.

39. Legs in part reddish; mystax black. . . . . 40.
Legs black, rarely the knees alone brownish. . . . . . 41.

40. Hypopleural pile whitish; mystax rather sparse; wings hyaline; mesonotum largely gray. (Ariz.) . *tibialis* . Coq.
Hypopleural pile black; mystax dense; wings brownish apically, crossveins clouded; mesonotum largely brown. (Or.) . . . . *dubius* Will.

41. Bases and hind angles of abdominal segments pruinose, sides of first segment pruinose; anterior crossvein beyond middle of discal cell; mystax and hypopleural hairs mainly black; thorax largely gray, marks diffuse, pleura bear of pile, scutellar margin with strong bristles. (Cal.) . . . . *nigricolor* Coq.
No fasciæ at base of segments; scutellum more or less pilose; thorax darker. 42.

42. Hypopleural pile wholly or in large part white. . . . . 43.
Hypopleural pile wholly black. . . . . 47.

43. Pleuræ with polished spot beneath wings; tibial bristles white; first abdominal segment with entire fascia. (N. S., Mass., N. Y. Md. Va.) . . . . . . *lutatius* Walk.
Pleuræ wholly pollinose and with some fine pile; tibial bristles mainly or entirely black; fascia of first segment of abdomen interrupted. . . . . 44.

44. Scutellar pile pale yellow, wings hyaline; facial pile mixed white and black. (Or.) (Proc. Cal. Acad. Sc. 1921, 255) *thompsoni* Cole
Scutellar pile black. . . . . 45.

45. Scutellar pile abundant; wings dark, especially in male; facial pile white in male, black in female. (Or.) (Proc. Cal. Acad. Sc. 1919, 233) . . . . *infuscatus* Cole.
Scutellar pile sparse and marginal; facial pile black. . . 46.

46. Tarsal claws yellowish with black tip; wings hyaline; median stripes as distinct as the blackish lateral spot. (Cal., Or., Wash., Id.) . . . . *nugator* O. S.
Tarsal claws reddish at base, otherwise black; wings brownish hyaline; median geminate stripe of mesonotum abbreviated posteriorly and less distinct than the rich dark brown lateral spot. (Cal. Or.) . . . . *rejectus* O. S.

47. Front and face broad, cinereous; notal marks often feeble. (Cal., Or., Wash.) . . . . *sudator* O. S.
Front and face relatively narrow, brownish; notal stripes coalescing, dark brown. (Cal., Ariz., N. M., Id.) *positivus* O.S.

Cyrtopogon ablautoides, new species

Male.—Length 11 mm. Head cinereous pollinose, frontal hairs whitish, becoming black at orbits, hair of center of face dense and white with slight yellowish tinge, of sides and beneath black, hairs of occiput abundant, silvery, nearly white, antennæ slender, the style one-fourth as long as third joint, its basal segment scarcely visible. Thorax dusted with yellowish-gray pollen, the geminate stripe interrupted one-third the distance in front of scutellum, lateral stripes nearly obsolete, slightly darkened in front of suture and a weaker indication behind, three strong lateral presutural bristles, four intraalar, post-alar callosities with four black bristles; hairs of notum white in front, a few blackish hairs intermixed behind, scutellum flat, brownish-gray pollinose, disc with erect white pile, margin with white pile, about six black setæ, pleuræ gray pollinose with yellowish tinge on mesopleura which also bears long white pile, trichostical hairs yellowish-white. Abdomen with shining or subshining anterior margins to the segments the posterior margins white pruinose, a central subshining black spot on each of segments two, three and four, sides of segments two, three and four subshining except posteriorly, the first three segments bearing dense lateral tufts of whitish yellow hair, hair of remaining segments sparse short and white, hypopygium small and subshining black. Legs dusted, femora with whitish pile, front tibiæ bristly, the bristles of extensor face stout and black, of posterior face strong and yellow, of interior face fine and setiform, flexor surface golden pubescent; middle tibiæ with dense cluster of white pile at two-fifths its length on anterior face, bristles mainly whitish, similar tuft of white pile on front face of middle metatarsus; bristles of hind tibiæ whitish and black mixed, claws black, pulvilli alutaceous. Halteres with pale yellow knob, calypteres yellow; wings hyaline, veins narrow and black, anterior crossvein at two-fifths length of discal cell, anal cell closed or narrowly opened at margin.

Female.—Apical segments of abdomen shining black.

Types.—Mabton, Washington, May 3, 1911 (Melander). Paratypes from Lind, Wash. May and June (F. W. Carlson),

Columbia River near Trinidad, Washington, May 1, 1919 and Wenatchee, Washington, April 12, (Melander). Four males and six females. The species presents a curious superficial resemblance to *Ablatus mimus* O. S. with which it is associated in the sandy desert region.

Cyrtopogon caesius, new species

Male.—Length 9 mm. Related to *C. rattus* O. S. Head heavily whitish pruinose, vertical hairs white and black mixed, facial hairs similar but longer, the black hairs predominating below, occipital pile abundant, white and very fine, third antennal joint long and slender, the arista not very distinct, quite as thick as end of third joint and in length about one-fourth the latter, its basal joint undeveloped. Thorax heavily pollinose, its pile rather short sparse and black, three black lateral bristles and a cluster of about three postalar, four intraalar bristles, median geminate stripe black, lateral stripe interrupted at the suture so as to form a broad presutural blackish round spot and an indefinite broad postsutural stripe, front margin and humeri grayish-white; scutellum flat, white pruinose, its margin with black setiform hairs and white pile; pleuræ uniformly white pollinose, pectus with fine white pile, trichostical hairs dense and white. First abdominal segment entirely white pruinose, second and third segments with narrow white band on front margin and broad white band on hind margin, the intervening space shining black, remaining segments shining black, the hind margin broadly white pruinose, the white bands do not encroach forward on the sides of the tergites; hypopygium scarcely widening at termination of the abdomen, lateral valves cupuliform; hairs of abdomen long tufted and white at side margins of basal three segments, largely short and black on remaining segments, under side of hypopygium with yellow hairs, tuft of grayish hairs at apex of venter. Legs entirely black, femora and posterior tibiæ white pilose, front tibiæ with black pile on front face, dense yellow pubescence on inner face and loose comb of black setiform hairs on both outer and flexor surfaces and another comb of black bristles on forward face, setiform hairs of middle tibiæ long and black, of hind tibiæ almost bristle-like, forming rows on extensor and anterior faces, claws black, pulvilli alutaceous. Halteres of each specimen with rosy knob, calypteres yellowish; wings hyaline, veins black, anterior cross-vein at one-third the length of the discal cell, anal cell open as widely as the length of anterior crossvein or less.

Female.—White hairs predominating on vertex and upper part of face, marginal bristles of scutellum stronger, white pruinosity of abdomen more extended, the second third and fourth segments with shining narrow base, expanding as an anterior quadrate shining spot at side margin, remainder of segment white pruinose, posterior segments similarly colored except that the lateral expanse of shining area is more triangular, seventh and eight segments polished black. Tibial bristles stronger.

Types.—South slope of Mount Adams, Washington, July 24, 1921. (Melander). Two males, seven females, taken at an elevation of 4000 feet.

Crytopogon glarealis, new species

Male.—Length 14 mm. Head with golden tomentum, upper hairs rather sparse and black, mystax black, the lowermost hairs mixed with golden, beard white, third antennal joint reddish-yellow, style black and one-fifth the length of the third joint. Mesonotum with fulvous pollen, middle stripes very indistinct, humeri and postalar callosities shining, pollen denuded on posterior half of thorax except a quadrate spot next to scutellum, scutellum convex and shining except for a touch of pollen at middle of base, notal hairs sparse and black, scutellar hairs mostly black, not dense, no marginal bristles; pleuræ uniformly dusted with brown-gray pollen, meso and sternopleuræ pilose, hypopleural hairs black. the lowermost brown. Abdomen mostly polished, segments two to four with yellowish posterior fasciæ, the tomentum extending along middle of segments two, three, four and anterior two-thirds of segment five as a dorsal vitta, pile of abdomen entirely black, short, tufted on sides of second segment; base of hypopygium with stubby black setæ, lateral valves with two terminal prongs. Coxæ pollinose, the front pair with white hairs; femora shining black, flexor hairs yellowish, dorsal hairs mainly black and inconspicuous; tibiæ reddish brown, hairs black except towards apex of front pair where they are whitish, bristles strong, abundant and black; anterior tarsi yellow, hind tarsi reddish, the front pair with brush of yellowish-white hairs covering outside face, inside face with conspicuous black bristles, a few black bristles on flexor face of metatarsus, bristles of posterior tarsi heavy, numerous and black; basal half of claws yellow, apical half black, pulvilli white. Knob of halteres pale yellow. Wings sub-hyaline,a slight brownish tinge at furcations, anterior crossvein at basal third of the discal cell which is nearly four times as long as broad.

Female.—Prescutellar dusted area more extensive, dorsal stripe wanting on abdomen, pile of abdomen yellowish, longest on sides of basal segments. All tarsi reddish, almost no whitish hair on front tibiæ and tarsi, bristles of front tarsi stronger than in male.

Types.—Wolf Fork of Touchet River in the Blue Mountains of southeastern Washington, Three specimens, July 12-20, 1922. (V. Argo).

Cyrtopogon punctipennis, new species.

Male.—Length 7.5 mm. Closely resembling *C. nebulo* O. S. but without fimbriate costa. Vertex and face black with slight violaceous tinge, thinly overlaid with white pollen, more distinct along facial boundaries, pile of front fine dense and black, of face longer and more abundant, the individual hairs tipped with whitish, third antennal joint tapering, the arista nearly equal in length, slender with first segment distinct, occiput with light bluish tinge, orbits white pollinose, hairs very fine abundant and hairy. Thorax bluish-black in ground-color, median stripe of white pollen extending from neck to scutellum, dorso-central stripes of white pollen broadening behind, lateral and posterior margins largely blue pollinose, when viewed from in front the notum shows four silvery spots, the posterior ones on the suture,

the anterior ones half way to the front margin; pile abundant and black, three fine lateral bristles; scutellum convex, shining blue-black, its silky pile long and white, no bristles, pleuræ uniformly and lightly cinereous dusted, ground-color blue-black, pile of pectus white, trichostichal hairs white and black mixed. Abdomen shining blue-black, extreme posterior corners of segments white pruinose, pile rather sparse short and pale, becoming darker in back, hypopygium very small, sunken, venter with bluish-gray pile, the hairs very dense on apical third. Legs entirely blue-black, front coxæ with abundant whitish pile, hairs of femora pale at base, front tibiæ with a row of very long bluish hairs on posterior edge, these hairs continuing on first three tarsal joints, hind tibiæ brown pubescent within, claws black, pulvilli brownish. Halteres black, calypteres alutaceous; wings lightly infumated, paler along portions of the first three veins, marked with distinct blackish spots at the bases of submarginal cells and of first and second posterior cells, the last two spots sometimes thickened and extending basally to the cross-veins, costa blackish from end of first vein to tip of wing.

Female.—Hairs somewhat shorter, notum more heavily pollinose so as to appear brownish in general color, median bisected stripe almost black; scutellum brownish pollinose, with about eight marginal setiform hairs; front legs marked with a prominent comb of hairs.

Types.—Moscow Mountain, Idaho, various dates from May to October (Melander); Pullman Washington; Goodnoe Hills, Washington (A. C. Burrill).

Cyrtopogon semitarius, new species.

Male.—Length 15 mm. Resembling *dasyllis.* Upper part of head black with abundant black hair, facial hair mainly white, along oral margin black, beard fine and white, palpal hairs black, antennæ black, style deformed, as wide as long, blunt, apically with a concavity in which the minute terminal joint is inserted. Thorax largely shining, a very narrow indistinct median line of grayish-brown dust, a mark of similar dust bearing the supra-alar bristles and a less extended similar mark above humeri, posterior half of mesonotum and scutellum shining black; hairs of thorax abundant, erect and black, of scutellum dense and black, no bristles; pleuræ with very faint touch of dust, mostly shining, black pile on meso, sterno, and hypopleuræ, the later dense and long. Basal three segments of abdomen uniformly and densly clothed with long pale yellow hair, apical half of abdomen shining and provided with dense short black pile, tip of hypopygium with a few yellow hairs; pile of venter entirely black. Coxæ and femora shining black, posterior tibiæ dark castaneous, tarsi reddish; pile of front face of front coxæ white, of exterior face of hind coxæ yellowish white; pile of femora mostly black, that of posterior face of front femora white, femoral bristles black; pile of extensor face of anterior tibiæ abundant and white, of entire hind tibiæ black, inner face of front tibiæ with fulvous pubescence, middle tibiæ with lateral black bristles, hind tibiæ with rows of black bristles, particularly on extensor, anterior and apical half of flexor faces; basal half of claws reddish, apical half black. Stem of halteres black, knob pale yellow. Wings hyaline, veins black, anterior crossvein at basal fifth of discal cell, the discal cell nearly five times as long as wide.

Holotype.—Alta Vista, Mt. Rainier, Wash., July 29, 1922 (Melander).

The specimen was taken from its vantage position on one of the ghost trees on the Alta Vista ridge. The structure of its style is unique but is probably not the result of a deformity, since the two antennæ are alike.

Cyrtopogon tacomae, new species.

Closely related to *C. rufotarsus* Back. Ground-color entirely black, thorax beautifully marked with silvery white pattern, extensor face of front tibiæ and tarsi of male densely covered with appressed silvery-white hairs, middle legs normal, anterior and extensor faces of hind tibiæ of male with white hairs, front and hind tarsi sometimes fuscous.

Male.—Length 10 mm. Antennæ black, third joint broadening underneath, thickest at two-thirds its length, style one-fourth as long as the third joint; front and face heavily silvery-gray, occiput subshining, more whitish at orbits, facial gibbosity nearly hemispherical, its central hairs long and silvery-white, mystax entirely black, beard largely white, frontal hairs long, delicate, not abundant, black. Thorax viewed from above presenting the following pattern in dark brown pollen: a bisected median stripe contiguous with a presutural round spot, and the entire postsutural area except postalar callosities and a narrow triangle in front of the convex shining scutellum, —this brown picture changing to shining black when viewed from behind; viewed from in front the anterior portion of the mesonotum is silvery-white pruinose, but from above a posthumeral area appears subshining black; all hairs of thorax black; pleuræ subshining lightly coated with brownish dust, but whitish pruinose above front coxæ, on upper sternopleura and narrowly along posterior part of mesopleura. Abdomen polished black with slight violaceous tinge, lightly dusted on apical segments, hypopygium polished, interrupted silvery-white fasciæ along posterior part of segments 2-6, narrowly leaving the hind margin on segments 2, 3 but attaining the hind edge on segments 4-6, the marks of the sixth segment less distinct, all hairs of abdomen black, those at sides of first three segments long and almost tufted. The silvery hairs of front tarsi cover the ground-color; the middle tarsi are always black, the front and hind ones sometimes are brown but usually are quite black; inner face of front tibiæ and metatarsi densely coated with glistening fulvous depressed short pubescence, similar fulvous pubescence extends along posterior face of hind tibiæ; pulvilli and basal third of claws brown. Halteres with yellowish knob; wings with brownish tinge and with brownish markings occupying the root, auxiliary cell, furcation of veins, crossveins, and forming an oblique band along first section of third vein, the anterior crossvein at basal fifth of discal cell.

Female.—Larger by one or two millimeters. Front largly lightly dusted with brown, face and central hairs less pure white.

Tarsi usually black, sometimes reddish, lacking the silvery ornamentation of the male. Notal picture more definite, humeri appearing subshining only when viewed from above, posthumeral spot of male appearing silvery-white, a quadrate prescutellar area emitting two anterior extensions pruinose, base of scutellum lightly pruinose; whitish pruinosity of pleuræ more extended, the entire mesopleura except central brown spot pruinose,pile of sides of prothorax and of sternopleura white. Hairs at base of abdomen pale yellow and less conspicuous, sides of first segment also with pruinosity, sixth and following segments entirely shining black. Wing markings less distinct, auxiliary cells hyaline.

Types.—Mount Rainier, Washington, various places in the natural parks visited at about 5000-6000 feet elevation. In all over ninety specimens were secured, including four collected by Dr. Aldrich. The flies were observed alighting on stones in the sunny pathways and were encountered in Paradise Park, Van Trump Park, and Indian Henry Hunting Ground, on Alta Vista, Mt. Ararat, and Crystal Mountain.

A grant from the Elizabeth Thomspon Science fund for the purpose of studying the alpine insects of Mount Rainier made possible the securing of much of the type material. Paratypes have been deposited in the National Museum, the Canadian National Museum, the Museum of Comparative Zoology of Harvard and the Philadelphia Academy of Science.

Cyrtopogon vulneratus, new species.

Male.—Length 10 mm. Readily distinct in having a large spot of heavy fulvous tomentum beginning at middle of second segment of abdomen and reaching to hind margin of fifth. Front and face thickly clothed with pale golden tomentum, a denuded spot between antennæ and front ocellus, facial hairs yellow, mystax black, frontal hairs sparse, fine and black; upper occiput rather lightly dusted with dull yellow pollen, brighter along orbits, a denuded spot underneath each ocellus, hairs sparse and black, lower occiput with brighter yellow dust, beard silky delicate and white; antennæ black, basal joints equal, hairs few and black, third joint slightly longer than basal joints together, style acuminate, one-eigth the length of the third joint. Pronotum shining black, a median inverted trianglar mark and a subhumeral spot of golden pollen, sides with tuft of white pile; mesonotum tomentose except postalar callosities and adjacent area, median geminate stripe light brown, interrupted a short distance behind suture, the usual broad lateral stripe consisting of a vaguely rounded mark on each side of suture, humeri golden, front part of mesonotum golden-gray, rear middle part cinereous; notal hairs short, sparse and black, lateral bristles black; scutellum convex, shining black, a touch of yellow pollen at base, no discal hairs, marginal hairs sparse and black; pleuræ lightly cinereous, more golden above, pteropleura shining, trichostichal hairs white. Abdomen slender, shining, sides of first segment with tufted white pile, of second segment with looser white hairs, third and fourth segment with short fulvous hairs; fifth, sixth and seventh segments and hypopygium with black hairs, posterior margins of second to fifth segments laterally golden tomentose, hypopygium globose, wider than termination of abdomen; venter black, hairs yellow. Femora black, tibiæ and tarsi reddish except apex, hairs largely whitish, bristles black, two strong yellow bristles near middle of anterior face of hind femora, inner face of front and hind tibiæ with close deep golden pubescence, claws black with brown base. Halteres and calypteres yellow, wings broad and hyaline, veins piceous, yellowish at base, a very faint cloud over crossveins, anterior crossvein at one-fifth length of discal cell, anal cell briefly open.

Holotype.—Coniston, Ontario, 27, July (H. S. Parish).

NOTES ON A NEW ENGLAND ARADID.

By Geo. W. Barber.

Bureau of Entomology, U. S. Dept. of Agriculture.

Among the species of the very interesting family *Aradidæ* that occur in New England is *Aradus 4-lineatus* Say.* It is not uncommon, being found beneath the bark of dead trees, particularly old stumps and logs where the fungus on which it feeds grows abundantly. On this fungus the eggs are laid and the young feed.

Fig. 1. *Aradus 4-lineatus* Say. From left to right, adult female, adult male, full-grown nymphs.

The eggs are closely cemented to the fungus and those which I have seen, always laid singly, oviposition continuing for some time. During 1920 one female in a cage deposited 13 eggs from May 16 to June 2 In 1922 eggs were obatined from June 14 to June 18. In all, ten eggs hatched in from 16 to 18 days the average incubation period being 17.8 days. Six first instar nymphs moulted in fron 8 to 13 days, the average length of the first instar being 11.1 days. Males that I confined in cages lived from 28 to 30 days, females from 14 to 35 days.

*Determined by H. M. Parshley.

Lugger, in the 6th. Rep. Div. Ent. Minnesota. St. Exp. Sta. 1900 p. 40 described the egg of an *Aradid*, probably *Aradus robustus* Uhl. as follows; "the eggs glistening white in color are deposited under the bark."

Heidman, 1911—Proc. Ent. Soc. Wash. XIII p. 134 described the egg of an *Aradid, Neuroctenus simplex* as ;"Egg about 1mm. long 5mm. wide; laid in a heap numbering from 20 to 60 or more. Chorion whitish, irregular, coarse, hexagonal; no apical cap; the chorial processes seem to be wanting."

The egg of *Aradus* 4-*lineatus* Say is quite different in structure and the habit of oviposition is dissimilar. It differs in structure particularly in the flattened ventral surface and in possessing both a distinct cap and chorial processes, altho the latter are very minute and inconspicuous. The habit of oviposition differs in that all those which I have seen are deposited singly as previously mentioned.

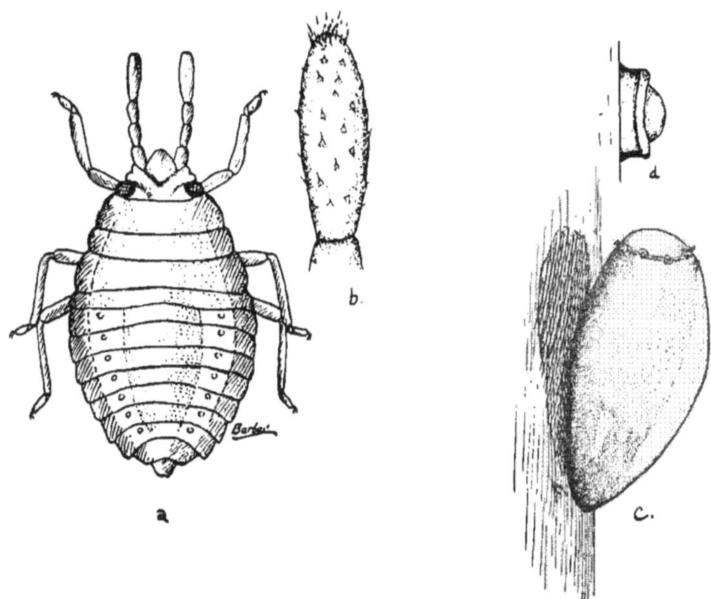

Fig. 2. *Aradus 4 lineatus* Say. a, first instar nymph; b, apical joint of antennæ of first instar nymph; c, egg, viewed laterally; d, corial process of egg.

THE EGG.

Length 1.2 mm.; width at middle .8 mm.; thickness at middle .425 mm.

Color, light red, smooth, moderately shining; viewed dorsally oval, narrowing towards the cap; flattened ventrally for a half to three fourths of its surface where it adheres to the fungus, the cap somewhat raised; cap not prominent, chorial processes ten in number, placed in a circle about the cap, minute, cup-shaped, raised but little above the chorion, a white hemispherical protuberance sometimes protrudes from the apex.

THE FIRST INSTAR NYMPH.

Length 1.2 mm.; width .7 mm. Color light red, the legs lighter, nearly cream color, femura lighter red, apical joint of antennæ and eyes dark; general aspect of body flattened; head with a groove rising before each eye, curving towards the Posterior line of the head, which it nearly attains, and somewhat towards the median line; eyes moderately prominent; beak scarcely reaching the anterior edge of the third ventral segment; antennæ one third the length of the body, 4-jointed, apical joint widest, as long as the third and fourth together, minutely and sparsely tuberculate, apically bearing a few very minute hairs; thorax slightly wider than eyes; abdomen evenly rounded at the sides, a third longer than the thorax and somewhat broader; edge of the thorax and abdomen foliaceous.

ON THE WING-VENATION OF INSECTS

By Aug. Lameere.

Translated by Austin M. Brues

The admirable method discovered by Comstock and Needham,[1] of showing homologies in the wing neuration of various types of insects does not allow us, unfortunately, to discover veins which have disappeared during the course of evolution. It is absolutely necessary to make a study of fossil forms in order to complete the ontogenetic data by means of information derived from the connections and topography of the veins in ancestral types which no longer exist.

No living insect possesses neuration as complete as that of many fossils from the coal measures; the result is that Comstock's[2] scheme of the fundamental primitive neuration is inexact, for it is based on living Perlids. To take this scheme as a basis of comparison leads to confusing entirely different veins under the same heading. That is what has happened notably with the Ephemerids and Odonata, of which the neuration does not seem to me to have been well understood.

We know that ontogentic study shows two tracheæ penetrating the wing; the ramifications of the anterior trachea correspond to the costal, sub-costal, radial, and median nervures; those of the posterior trachea correspond to the cubital and the three anal nervures.

The radial nervure presents two branches: the radial, strictly speaking, and its sector.

In the wings of the Ephemerids, the Odonata, and the Protohemiptera from the coal measures, the median nervure forks, not far from the base of the wing, into two branches which I have termed the anterior median and the posterior median[3]; that is to say the median has exactly the same configuration as the radial, so that the posterior median can be considered as the sector of the anertior median. The comparison of the form of the median

[1]Sur la nervation alaire des Insectes. Bull. Class. des Sci. Acad. Roy. Belgique, 1922 pp. 38-149.

with that of the radial follows, if it is assumed that the radial is a high nervure while its sector is a low nervure; then the anterior median is a high nervure, the posterior a low nervure.

The sector of the median is missing in the Perlids and consequently does not figure in Comstock's scheme. I have shown that this nervure is very short and that it rejoins the cubital, or rather that it is completely lost in all the Orthoptera (*sensu latissimo*, including the Perlids); Tillyard has also shown that the same thing happens to the sector of the median (which he calls M^5) in the Holometabola.[4]

The cubital nervure has a configuration exactly like that of the radial and median; even nearer the base of the wing than does the median, it divides into two branches, an upper anterior, which I have called anterior cubital, and a lower posterior, the the posterior cubital, which is in a way the sector of the cubital.

Thus radial, median, and cubital show an identical form among the primitive insects, consisting of an upper vein followed by a lower sector.

Now we may ask if the same plan does not apply to the other nervures.

The costal is a high nervure, the sub-costal a low nervure, although the sub-costal appears not to be a branch of the costal, but arises directly behind the costal from the anterior tracheal (trunk) of the wing, it seems to me that we must admit that the sub-costal is the sector of the costal.

In the living insects only three anal nervures are found; but an examination of the fossils from the coal measures shows that there are apparently many more, for they are branched. I distinguish a first upper anal, a second lower anal, a third upper anal followed frequently by lower branches. I believe that we find but two anal nervures, the so-called second anal being the sector of the first.

The wing thus contains six (principal) nervures, three forming the anterior group: the costal, the radial, the median; and three belonging to the posterior group: the cubital, a first anal (1A) which we may call the *penultimate*, and a second anal

(3A) which we may call the *ultimate*; each of these six nervures is high and has a low sector.

Consequently we return, in the oldest insects known, to that regular alternation of high nervures and low nervures included in Adolph's old hypothesis. We can even use the nomenclature of J. Redtenbacher, accepted by C. Brongniart, numbering the nervures from I to XII, the odd numbers designating the primary nervures and the even numbers their sectors.

To adapt these ideas to the nomenclature of Comstock and Needhan, which is today universally accepted, I propose to designate all the sectors by the names of their respective nervures. adding to these names the prefix *sub*.

Then we shall have in the first group: the costal, high (C or I), with the sub-costal, low (Sc or II): the radial, high (R or III) with the sub-radial, low (Sr or IV): the median, high (M or V), with the sub-median, low (Sm or VI) and, in the second group: the cubital, high (Cu or VII), with the sub-cubital, low (Scu or VIII): the penultimate, high (P or IX), with the sub-penultimate, low (Sp or X): the ultimate, high (U or XI), with the sub-ultimate, low (Su or XII).

The sub-radial, the median, the sub-median, the cubital and the sub-cubital are each forked twice in the primitive insects, giving two limbs and four branches; we have then, adapting the the data to the accepted nomenclature: Sr^1, Sr^2, Sr^3, Sr^4,; M^1, M^2, M^3, M^4, Sm^1, Sm^2, Sm^3, Sm^4; Cu^1, Cu^2, Cu^3, Cu^4; Scu^1, Scu^2, Scu^3, Scu^4.

The general evolution of insect wings is characterized by a lengthening which is concurrent with a diminution of the breadth; this phenomenon has been accompanied by the disappearance of certain longitudinal nervures; but these are not the same nervures which have disappeared if we consider the two great groups of Pterygota; a misunderstanding of this fact has caused a regrettable confusion.

With all the insects whose embryogeny has caused them to be called Ectoblastic[5]—that is to say the Paurometabola (*sensu latissimo*, the Orthoptera) and the Holometabola,—we have made mention of them above,—the sub-median as is reduced to a very short nervure rejoining the cubital, or perhaps as is more frequently the case, it aborts completely. What is called the median in the Pterygota (M^1, M^2, M^3 M^4) is then really our own median, that is to say the upper anterior branch of the third nervure of the first group, and there is no change in the terminology.

As for the Endoblastic Pterygota (Subulicornia and Rhynchota) more primitive than the Ecoblastic forms, it is entirely otherwise. Here the neuration is complete, or rather if the longitudinal nervures disappear it is never the sub-median alone, but very often the anterior median and also the anterior cubital, the narrowing of the wing ordinarily involving the spaces adjacent to the sub-median. This I shall have to show by palæontology, for the ontogeny of living forms not only has been insufficient to show this peculiarity, but has at the same time led zoologists to form totally erroneous homologies.

It is in the Ephemeroptera of the group Spilapteridæ from the coal measures that we meet with the most complete neuration; this suits our scheme completely (e. g. Lamproptilia Ch. Brongn.) in certain genera, however, the anterior median and anterior cubital may be simple; that is, not branched.

Everyone agrees in considering the Stephanian genus *Triplosoba* Handl. (Blanchardia Ch. Brongn.), type of the Protephemeroidea, as the precursor of the real Ephemeroidea, which are found already in the Permian; the neuration is the same as that of the Spilapteridæ, in which the anterior median and cubital are represented by a simple nervure (*e. g.*, Apopappus Handl.); but there are adventitious sectors in the sub-radial, sub-median, and sub-cubital spaces; the sub-median is simply forked, and between its branches is an adventitious sector.[7]

Now if we compare the wing of the Ephemeroids of the Permian, Secondary, Tertiary and the present day to that of Triplosoba, the configuration and connections show at once that the lower nervures considered by Comstock as M^1 and M^2 with the adventitious sectors between, correspond to Sr^1 and Sr^4 of Triplosoba, that is to say, the sector of the radial has been wrongly considered a branch of the median, because of the fact that the latter is reunited at the base, which, from a morphological standpoint, is of only relative importance; it is seen that Comstock's M^3 and M^4, with the adventitious sector between, are Sm^1 and Sm^4; that Cu^1 and Cu^2, low nervures, with the adventitious sector between, are Scu^1 and Scu^4; that 1A, high, is P; 2A, low, is Sp; 3A, high, is U.

The high nervures M and Cu, which are present and simple in Triplosoba, are missing between Sr^4 and Sm^1, in some cases, between Sm^4 and Scu^1 in others; we may consider that they have disappeared, in consequence of the narrowing of the wing, a change which becomes very marked with the Protereismidæ of the Permian.[8]

It is very interesting to show the Sm and its branches are high in the *Ephemeroidea*, while these nervures are low in *Triplosoba*, which brings back the regular alternation of high and low nervures broken up by the disappearance of the adjacent high nervures *M* and *Cu*.

The wings of the Ephemeroidea differ from those of the Protephemeroidea by the reunion of the median with the sector of the radial near the base of the wing, by the disappearance of the anterior high median and cubital, the sub-median and sub-cubital alone remaining, the sub-median having become a high nervure.

Following the conclusion of a work by Miss Morgan[9] Comstock agreed that in the Ephemeroidea the radial sector is represented by a small trachea arising from the radial, not far from the extremity of the wing; he considered as belonging to the sector of the radial the two final added sectors situated in the space which I have called sub-radial, and in which it makes a median space. These authors tried to discover in the wing of the Ephemeroidea the sector of the radial which they did not see, taking it for a branch of the median, and they sought the solution in a comparison with the wing of the Odonata.

None of Miss Morgan's drawings seem to me convincing; the numerous preparations of young larvæ of Ephemeroidea of different genera *Baëtis, Clœon, Leptophlebia, Cœnis*) made at the Overmeire biological station by Mr. Paul Brien, student-assistant, have shown us nothing which recalls anything of the singular arrangement existing among the Odonata of the group Anisoptera. We have not seen the small sector trachea described by Miss Morgan; supposing that it really does exist, it has only the value of an adventitious trachea, the only value which can also be attributed to the famous trachea which, according to Comstock and Needham, represented the sector of the radial in the Odonata.

Tillyard, to whom we are indebted for so many fine works on living and fossil insects, recently confirmed the opinion that the subnodal sector of de Selys-Longchamps among the Libellulidæ is the sector of the radial crossing the median nervure.[10] I was for a long time persuaded that this nervure, absent in the Zygoptera, as Tillyard has shown [11] is an additional simple nervure serving in the Anisoptera to close up the sub-radial space which was enlarged during the course of evolution; this nervure, which may be called the secant (S), is a physiological realization of what exists in the Neuroptera, where the enlarged sub-radial space is closed by a supplementary branch of the radial sector.

Tillyard's conclusion is that the neuration of the Odonata can be interpreted only by palæontology.

Here is the reply which I believe I can support, using as a basis what we have learned from the evolution of neuration in the Ephemeroidea, and what the evolution of the Odonatoptera shows us.

In the Odonata, the nervures which all present-day entomologists consider as M^1, M^2, Ms and M^3 are with me the four branches of the sector of the radial, Sr^1, Sr^2, Sr^3, Sr^4, the sector of the radial being, as in the Ephemeroidea, reunited at the base of the median; the upper anterior median (*M*) is represented alone by the high nervure at present designated by the symbol M^4; the posterior median (*Sm*) is absent; the anterior cubital (*Cu*) has disappeared, as in the Ephemeroidea; the nervure considered as Cu^1, low nervure, is the sector of the cubical (*Scu*); the nervure considered as Cu^2, upper nervure, is the first anal or penultimate (P), reunited at the base of the sub-cubital, the nervure 1*A* of current usage, high, is the third anal or ultimate (*U*), partly attached to the penultimate.

The neuration of the wing of the Libellulidæ would not be exactly similar to that of the Ephemeroidea, contrary to what has been considered heretofore, and the comparison which has been made with that of Ectoblastic insects is rather lame.

The evolution of fossil Odonatoptera, which I have been able to study at the Paris Museum, will show us this.

In the Dictyoneuridæ of the coal measures the primitive neuration is complete and typical, but very often the anterior median and anterior cubital are simple (as in the genus *Stenodictya* Ch. Brongn.)

Dictyoptilus Ch. Brongn., of the Stephanien, has a more elongated wing; the median is contiguous to the radial at the base of the wing, which gives a small pre-costal space,—all characters which are accentuated in the Protodonata[1].

These last have the median confused with the radial at the base of the wing, and the radial sector arises from the median, as in the Ephemeroidea.

Let us now consider *Meganeura Monyi* of Ch. Brongniart, the giant Libellulid of Commentry, and compare its neuration, on one hand with that of Dictoptilus, on the other hand with that of the Odonata, the nervures being for the latter designated according to their current names.[2]

In Meganeura, we see, leaving the common trunk which leads to the radial, a nervure which soon divides into a lower anterior and an upper posterior nervure; the first (Brongniart'sV) corresponds evidently to the radial sector in *Dictyoptilus*, and it divides, as in the latter; into two low nervures Brongniart's IV and V) in which we recognize, on one hand, $M^{1\ 2}$ Ms; on the other, M^3, of the Odonata; the second (Brongniart's VII) is the median in *Dictyoptilus*, which is reunited to the radial at the base of the latter's sector; this median is divided into a high nervure, the anterior median, in which we recognize M^4 of the

[1]See the fine photographic reproductions of the wing of *Dictyoptilus* (*Cockerelliella*) *sepultus* F. Meun, published by Boule in the Annales de Paleontologie, vo. 7, pl. 7, figs. 4, 4a.

[2]The figure of the wings of *Meganeura monyi* in the work of Brongniart (Pl. 42) is correct; in Handlirsch the fore wing is in part inaccurate.

Odanta, and a low nervure, the posterior median; this last the Odonata, and a low nervure, the posterior median; this last is missing in the Odonata, which have retained only the upper anterior median.

From the base of the wing of *Meganeura*, a little behind the radio-median trunk arises a long, winding, simple nerve (Brongniart's VIII) which is very low; comparison with Dictyoptilus shows that it must be the posterior cubital (Scu), as the anterior upper cubital which approaches very near to the posterior median in *Dictyoptilus* is evidently absent. It is certain that this nervure Scu is represented in the Odonata by the low nervure at present known as Cu^1.

Still a third nervure leaves the base of the wing of Meganeura; it is parallel to the posterior cubital and is high (Brongniart's IX); almost on the level at which the radial detaches itself from its sector and from the median, this high nervure gives rise to a low nervure (Brongniart's X); we now have the first and second anal, the penultimate nervure with its sector, and this nervure corresponds to Cu^2 of the Odonata.

We know that in the Odonata a trachea gives rise to Cu^1 and Cu^2, these nervures proceeding from a common trunk, and another trachea furnishes the nervure designated as 1A; this last attaches itself very near the base of the wing to the common trunk of Cu^1 and Cu^2, and then becomes independent.

We have the same thing with Meganeura and even probably with Dictyoptilus; no attention has been paid to it, because Ch. Brongniart has neither seen nor figured anything, except in Meganeura; between the base of the wing and the level of the division of the penultimate into P and Sp, there exists an oblique nervure which attaches the cubital again to the last nervure arising from the base of the wing. [1]It is evidently a case of an anastomosis between the cubital and the penultimate, the latter proceeding thus from the cubital, as in the Odonata. So the last nervure which leaves the base of the wing in *Meganeura* is

[1]This oblique nervure is immediately recognizable in the photographic reproduction of a wing-fragment of Meganeura, given by Bolton (Quart. Journ. Geol. Soc., vol. 70 (1914), pl. 18, fig. 1) and in that of another Meganeura published by Boule (Ann. de Paleont, vol. 4 (1909) pl. 17, fig. 2); E. H. Sellards has figured it in *Typus permianus* (American Journ. Sci., vol. 23 (1907), p. 250, fig. 1, p. 252, fig. 2.

only the ultimate; it corresponds to 1A in the Odonata, and, just as with the latter, it is attached along a certain length to the nervure which precedes it, supporting the secondary nervures which are opposite in direction to those which are supported by the sector of the penultimate. The Protodonata also seem to have three anal nervures, *P*, and *Sp* and *U*, *U* rejoining the common trunk of *P* and *Sp* after this has left *Scu*.

In the Odonata, on account of the attenuation of the base of the wing, the attachment of the sub-cubital and penultimate extends farther than in the Protodonata, the sub-penultimate is missing, and the ultimate is attached in part to the portion common to *Scu* and *P*.

The essential differentiation between the Protodonata and Dictyoptilus lies in the reunion of the median to the base of the radial and the disappearance of the anterior cubital; the Odonata are derived from the Protodonata by the suppression of the posterior median and of the sector of the penultimate nervure.

It remains for us only to inspect the neuration of the Rhynchota. Is what we call the median in Endoblastic insects the nervure *Sm* of the Subulicornia or rather the nervure M of the Ectoblastic insects? The study of existing forms does not permit us to decide. Let us then have recourse to palæontology.

The numerous Protohemiptera of the coal measures[12] offer a complete wing-neuration; but in all the anterior median is simple, and the anterior cubital is ordinarily so.

The real Hemiptera, Rhynchota which undoubtedly descend from the Protohemiptera and of which a representative is known in the Stephanian, have a forked median and cubital, and the two branches of these are ramified. It is sufficient to consider the neuration of the permian genera Scytinoptera and Prosbole, in Handlirsch's Atlas to be presuaded that with neither the Homoptera nor the Heteroptera is there an anterior median or an anterior cubital, that the position of these nervures is occupied by a great empty space and that the two forked nervures are the sector of the median and the sector of the cubital.

The evolution of neuration in the Hemiptera thus takes

place in the same way as with the Ephemeroptera, a new proof that the Endoblastic insects may be placed opposite to the Ectoblastic in classification.

Conclusion.

The scheme of primordial wing neuration worked out by Comstock is useful only for Ectoblastic insects, which have lost the posterior branch of the median nervure, and that since their appearance in the coal measures.

The Endoblastic forms, Subulicornia and Rhynchota have, for the most part, in the coal measures, a complete neuration conforming to a scheme in which six low nervures alternate with six high nervures; those between in which the wings do not agree with this type, notably all the forms which have persisted beyond the Permian, have lost other longitudinal nervures than the Ectoblasts.

The Ephemeroptera, the Protodonata, the Odonata, and the Hemiptera do not possess the anterior branch of the cubital nervure; the Ephemeroptera and Hemiptera lack also the anterior branch of the median nervure; the Protodonata, as well as the Odonata, have retained this, but the Odonata have lost the posterior branch of the median nervure.

REFERENCES

1. Comstock, J. H. & J. G. Needham. The Wings of Insects. American Naturalist, vol. 32, p. 43 (1918).
2. Comstock, J. H. The Wings of Insects. Ithaca. (1918).
3. Lameere, A. Revision sommaire des Insectes fossiles du Stephanien de Commentry. Bull. Mus. Paris, p. 141.
4. Tillyard, R. J. The Panorpid Complex, Part 3. The Wing-venation. Proc. Linn. Soc. New South Wales, vol. 44, p. 533 (1919).
5. Lameere, A. La vie des Insectes aux temps primaires. Rev. gén. Sci., vol. 29, p 5 (1918).
6. Lameere, A. Paléodictyoptères et Subulicornes. Bull. Soc. Entom. France p. 101 (1917).
7. Lameere, A. Etude sur l'Evolution des Ephemères. Bull. Soc. Zool. France, vol. 42, p. 41 (1917).
8. Sellards, E. H. Types of Permian Insects. II. Plectoptera. American Journ. Sci., vol. 23, p. 345.
9. Morgan, A. H. Homologies in the Wing-viens of May-flies. Ann. Entom. Soc. America, vol. 5, p. 89 (1912).
10. Tillyard, R. J. New Researches upon the Problem of the Wing-venation of Odonata. Entom. News, vol. 33, p. 45 (1922).
11. Tillyard, R. J. On the Development of the Wing-venation in Zygopterous Dragonflies, with Special Reference to Calopterygidae. Proc. Linn. Soc. New South Wales, vol. 40, p. 212(1915).
12. Lameere, A. Note sur les Insectes houillers de Commentry. Bull. Soc. Zool. France, vol. 42, p. 27 (1917).

BOOK REVIEW

"Les Termites. Partie Générale." by E. Hegh. Bruxelles, September 1922. published by Imprimerie Industrielle & Financière (Société Anonyme), 4 rue de Berlaimont, Bruxelles. Price $6.00. 756 pp., 460 figs. Review by ALFRED EMERSON, Department of Zoology, University of Pittsburgh.

Mr. Hegh has done a remarkable piece of work in the gathering of information and the arranging of facts which have been brought together in this large book (756 pages) profusely illustrated with the best drawings and photographs which have been published on termites.

It is a compilation, but a compilation of such thoroughness that one has no hesitation in pronouncing it as valuable to students of termites and to entomologists in general as new extended observations on the insects would be. Although termites (Isoptera) constitute one of the smaller orders, there being a little over 1000 species described and a bibliography of a little more than 1200 titles, the gathering of all the important biological material is an enormous task.

Everything known at the present time concerning the biology of this fascinating group of social insects is dealt with; their geographical distribution; their caste system and the function of the various castes in all the groups of termites; their nourishment and modes of obtaining it; their nests, the classification and construction of the nest; their predaceous enemies, parasites, termitophiles, and associates; their influence on vegetation and physiography; the utilization of termites as food by man; these and many other subjects are dealt with in a most thorough manner. An extended bibliography is added with a list of the African species.

The economic problems are not emphasized although many photographs of their damage are given and their feeding habits are discussed at great length. Methods of control are not discussed. It is a monograph on the biology of this group. Of course the errors made by the various students of termites have been prepetuated in various parts, each statement, however, being ascribed to the authority. As a whole the information given represents the viewpoint of the modern investigators and observers of termites.

This book should be in every entomological library and undoubtedly will be the best reference and source book on this order of insects yet written and likely to be written for many years.

CAMBRIDGE ENTOMOLOGICAL CLUB

A regular meeting of the Club is held on the second Tuesday of each month (July, August and September excepted) at 7.45 p. m. at the Bussey Institution, Forest Hills, Boston. The Bussey Institution is one block from the Forest Hills station of both the elevated street cars and the N. Y., N. H. & H. R. R. Entomologists visiting Boston are cordially invited to attend.

PSYCHE

A JOURNAL OF ENTOMOLOGY

ESTABLISHED IN 1874

VOL. XXX OCTOBER 1923 No. 5

CONTENTS

CAMBRIDGE ENTOMOLOGICAL CLUB

PSYCHE is published bi-monthly, the issues appearing in February, April, June, August, October and December. Subscription price, per year, payable in advance: $2.00 to subscribers in the United States, Canada or Mexico; foreign postage, 15 cents extra. Single copies, 40 cents.

Cheques and remittances should be addressed to Treasurer, Cambridge Entomological Club, Bussey Institution, Forest Hills, Boston 30, Mass.

Orders for back volumes, missing numbers, notices of change of address, etc., should be sent to Cambridge Entomological Club, Bussey Institution, Forest Hills, Boston 30, Mass.

IMPORTANT NOTICE TO CONTRIBUTORS.

Manuscripts intended for publication, books intended for review, and other editorial matter, should be addressed to Professor C. T. Brues, Bussey Institution, Forest Hills, Boston 30, Mass.

Authors contributing articles over 8 printed pages in length will be required to bear a part of the extra, expense for additional pages. This expense will be that of typesetting only, which is about $2.00 per page. The actual cost of preparing cuts for all illustrations must be borne by contributors: the expense for full page plates from line drawings is approximately $5.00 each, and for full page half-tones, $7.50 each; smaller sizes in proportion.

AUTHOR'S SEPARATES.

Reprints of articles may be secured by authors, if they are ordered before, or at the time proofs are received for corrections. The cost of these will be furnished by the Editor on application.

Entered as second-class mail matter at the Post Office at Boston, Mass. Acceptance for mailing at special rate of postage provided in Section 1103, Act of October 3, 1917, authorized on June 29, 1918.

PSYCHE

VOL. XXX. OCTOBER 1923 No. 5

THE GENUS LASIOPOGON (DIPTERA, ASILIDÆ)[1]

By A. L. Melander.

State College, Pullman, Wash.

The genus *Lasiopogon* is represented in the western states by several common species, some of which are undescribed. As characters separating these species are not difficult to discern the following table is presented in order to bring to date our knowledge of the species of this genus. If male specimens are available identification is facilitated, since distinctive characters are offered by the genitalia.

The species of *Lasiopogon* and *Cyrtopogon* have the face strongly gibbose, thus forming a natural group in the Dasypogoninæ. At first sight they appear to intergrade, but the two genera are quite distinct in several characters. The species of *Lasiopogon* are browner in general color, and have the abdomen nearly parallel-sided. They possess a vertical row of setæ on the hypopleuræ, lack the short first segment of the arista, and have the anal cell closed just within the margin. *Cyrtopogon* presents a more tapering abdomen, usually more pilose, the hypopleuræ with patch of fine pile, the trichostichal hairs, in place of bristles, the basal joint of the arista usually distinct, and the anal cell usually narrowly open. The male genitalia are different in the two genera; in *Lasiopogon* the lateral valves are most prominent, the lower valves being undeveloped, the dorsal side is deeply emarginate and furnished with a distinctive fringe; in *Cyrtopogaon* the lower valves are usually large and there is no dorsal fringe of setæ.

The species of *Lasiopogon* known from North America are separable on the characters given in the following key. Most of the species appear to be western in their distribution. The

[1] Contribution from the Zoology Laboratory of the State College of Washington.

structure of the hypopygium affords the most reliable distinctions for identifying the species, and fortunately can be easily discerned without relaxing.

Key to the Neartic Species of Lasiopogon.

1. Bristles of body and legs wholly or in part whitish; mystax white; abdomen rather dull..........................2.
   Bristles black (not including the long straggling white setiform hairs sometimes present on underside of femora)...5.
2. Legs entirely black, coated with gray pollen.............3.
   Front tibiæ with basal two-thirds and middle tibiæ with base yellowish; median and lateral stripes of thorax brownish median stripe very feebly divided by a paler line; abdomen dusted with blackish brown, hind margins gray. (Ariz.)...........................*arizonensis* Schaeffer
3. Abodmen sericeous with short and long white pile; hypopygium with yellow fringe at base above; thorax bivittate on dorsocentral rows. (on sand, Pacific Coast).........4.
   Abdomen less pilose, base of segments rufous; thorax with four nearly median brown vittæ. (Nebr.).*quadrivittata* Jones
4. Lateral valves of hypopygium emarginate at apex and with a rectangular corner at end of upper edge; bristles typically wholly whitish; scutellum lightly dusted with fulvous. (Cal.)..................................*arenicola* O. S.
   Valves with rounded apex and with a broadly obtuse upper corner; lateral bristles of thorax black; scutellum cinereous-dusted. (Wash.)...................*actius*, n. sp.
5. Mystax wholly or in large part white..................6.
   Mystax wholly black.................................9.
6. Tibiæ and tarsi and sometimes femora also, reddish brown; wings lightly infumated; abodmen shining black, only hind angles of segments pruinose. (on low damp ground, Mass., N. J.) *terricola* Johnson.
   Legs wholly black in ground color; wings quite hyaline..7.
7. Large robust species measuring 12 mm.; abdominal segments marked with two anterior semicircular blackish

spots, the gray of hind margins extending triangularly between them; heavily pollinose and quite pilose. (Wash.) *ripicola*, n. sp.

Small species of 7 to 9 mm.............................8.

8. Nearly bare species; abdominal segments with narrow white pruinose fascia along hind margin; thorax trivittate with brown. (Wash.).......*trivittatus*, n. sp.

A great deal of white pile on body; the paler hind portion of abdominal segments extending forward along the middle; thorax bivittate. (Cal.)..........*drabicola* Cole.

9. Tibiæ and tarsi reddish-brown; wings quite infumated; halteres with black spot on knob; abdomen dull, the posterior two-fifths of each segment with gray fascia. (mountain species, Wash.) ....*fumipennis*, n. sp.

Legs black in ground-color; wings nearly hyaline........10.

10. Thorax evittate; hypopygial valves polished; small species, 6 to 8 mm...11.

Thorax vittate..12.

11. Mesonotum uniformly brown pollinose; hypopygial valves twice as long as wide, with strong projection below near base, dorsal fringe black. (Wash.).....*delicatulus*, n. sp.

Mesonotum brownish gray pollinose; valves short, very convex, almost hemispherical, dorsal fringe reddish. (Mass. to Col.)......................*opaculus* Loew.

12. General color gray pollinose; hypopygial valves cinereous, about three times as long as wide, without basal prong or swelling. (on stones about streams, Or., Wash.) *cinereus* Cole

General color brownish pollinose; hypopygial valves polished, or of *tetragrammus* grayish-brown pruinose.........13.

13. Space between intermediate and lateral stripes of thorax polished black; ovipositor white pilose; about four conspicuous bristles across each abdominal segment. (Can., N. H.) ....*tetragrammus* Loew

Thorax without shining stripes; no transverse rows of bristles on abdominal segments. (western species)......14.

14. Hypopygium greatly enlarged, wider than abdomen, its valves nearly as broad as long, with basal swelling below; abdomen largely polished.........................15.
    Hypopygium not wider than abdomen, its valves about twice as long as wide, with strong tooth on inner edge toward base; abdomen dull. (Wash.).*monticola*, n. sp.
15. Thorax narrowly vittate; anterior crossvein beyond middle of discal cell. (Cal., Or.).............*bivittatus* Loew
    A narrow median dark line extending down the center paler stripe between the broad principal vittæ; anterior crossvein before middle of discal cell. (Id., Wash.) *aldrichii*, n. sp.

Lasiopogon actius, sp. nov.

Male.—Length 7-9 mm. Front and upper occiput dusted with brownish, face with white, hairs of upper part of head and of antennæ whitish with yellowish tinge; style three-fifths as long as third antennal joint. Notum rather closely pollinose, changing in color according to incidence of light, dorsocentral vittæ distinct, dark brown, curved, the broad undivided middle stripe yellowish brown, sides fulvous brown, connecting with the dorsocentral vittæ behind the gray humeri; scutellum, postalar callosities and a vitta extending forward from each callosity cinereous; hairs and bristles of mesonotal disk and of scutellar margin yellowish, lateral bristles stout and black; pleuræ cinereous, the mesopleura brownish, hairs of meso-, sterno- and hypopleuræ pale. Abdomen quite dull, first segment gray, 2-7 segments marked with paired basal semicircular brown spots and apical gray band, vestiture abundant and whitish; hypopygium slightly wider than abdomen, dorsal piece centrally polished, not emarginate, fringe fulvous becoming almost golden laterally, valves lightly dusted and with abundant yellowish hair, curved, over twice as long as wide and parallel-sided as seen obliquely from above, their apex rounded and furnished with short blackish hairs, base below strongly widening and then narrowed at attachment; venter cinereous, the coating thinner posteriorly. Legs gray dusted, hairs and femoral bristles whitish, bristles of tibiæ black and whitish mixed, of tarsi black, claws reddish, tipped with black. Halteres with pale yellow knob, wings hyaline, veins blackish, crossvein a little before middle of discal cell.

Female.—Third antennal joint even shorter, the style two-thirds or three-fourths the length of the third joint; ovipositor shining black, the terminal rosette consisting of long black hooks.

Types.—Sixteen specimens, collected on the dry sands of the seabeach near Seaview and Nahcotta, Washington, May to July. (Melander). The species is closely related to *L. arenicola,* but that species has a less patterned thorax, subshining scutellum and abdomen, wholly pale bristles, yellow rosette on ovipositor and a different construction to the hypopygium. The lateral valves of *arenicola* are squared off at the end and even emarginate, the dorsal fringe is golden, and the dorsal piece is polished.

Lasiopogon aldrichii, sp. nov.

Male.—Length 8 mm. Entirely black, the halteres yellow, calypteres yellowish, front brownish-gray pollinose, the pollen of face slightly more yellowish, mystax black, hairs of face and lower occiput cinereous pollinose with long silky white pile; style thick, one-half as long as third joint of antenna. The usual pair of anteriorly diverging stripes of mesonotum distinct and blackish, the immediate brownish stripe medially bisected by a distinct blackish line, lateral stripes vaguely represented by darkenings above root of wings; bristles and sparse hairs black; scutellum dusted at base, its hairs and bristles black; pleuræ dull gray pollinose; the hypopleural fringe consisting of a single row of long black bristles. Major portion of abdomen polished black, the hind margins of the individual segments grayish-pollinose, lateral hairs whitish, becoming black on posterior segments; genitalia large, forming a club-like globular termination to the abdomen, hairs rather short and black, the lateral valves strongly convex, nearly quadrate, the apical edge crenulate-truncate, lower basal angle not toothed but with an umbo, dorsal incision deep and U-shaped, the marginal fringes black, the hairs obliquely crossed; venter uniformly dark grayish-pollinose, subshining, the short sparse hairs pale. Legs entirely black, the coxæ pollinose and concolorous with pleuræ, remainder of legs shining, very lightly dusted, the hairs and bristles black except the fine pile at base of femora beneath, pulvilli fuscous. Wings lightly infumated, veins black, anterior crossvein slightly before middle of discal cell.

Female.—Pile of lower occiput more sordid white; lateral whitish hairs of abdomen shorter and confined to basal segment, ovipositor highly polished, short-conical, the ventral keel brown.

Types.—Male and female, Moscow Mountains, Idaho, June 29, 1918 (Melander). Sixty paratypes from same locality (Melander) and from the Blue Mountains of southeastern Washington (Piper and Melander) and Nahcotta, Washington (Melander). The two specimens from Nahcotta, male and female are indistinguishable from the others, notwithstanding their totally different provenience. These specimens have been taken on almost every visit to Moscow Mountain. They occur along the trails and frequent rocks on the summit. It is a pleasure to dedicate this species in honor of Dr. J. M. Aldrich, and in memory of the many trips we have made together to this interesting collecting ground. The species is evidently very closely related to *L. bivittatus* Lw. but is constant in showing the bisected median stripe of the thorax.

Lasiopogon delicatulus, sp. nov.

Male.—Length 6 mm. Ground color entirely black, halteres yellow, the root of wing and the calypteres light brownish. Vertex dusted with dull yellowish-gray, face almost silvery, mystax and rather sparse facial hairs white, upper occiput brownish dusted, lower occiput becoming whitish, the lower hairs short silky and white, hairs and bristles of upper part of head short and black, style scarcely one-half the length of the broad third joint of antenna. Thorax brownish-pollinose, the dorsocentral stripes only vaguely indicated, middle stripe not divided, bristles black, scutellum completely dusted, bare except for the few marginal hairs; lower pleuræ becoming grayish-blue, hypopleural fringe consisting of about five black setæ. Abdomen slender, mostly shining, the hind margin of the segments narrowly whitish and with thinner cinereous pollen extending across the posterior two-fifths of each segment and also triangularly filling the extreme sides, first segment entirely cinereous pollinose, hairs very sparse, short and whitish; hypopygium of same diameter as abdomen, the lateral valves curved, two and one-half times as long as the width of the apical half, abruptly broader on basal half so as to form rectangular projection at middle beneath, apex of valves rounded, hairs rather sparse long and black, dorsal notch broad and deep, fringe of each side with black hairs; venter uniformly grayish dusted, its hairs fine, short, sparse and whitish. Legs entirely black, lightly dusted, the coxae cinereous, the hairs of femora and coxæ white, of tibiæ and tarsi black, bristles strong and black, pulvilli piceous. Wings hyaline, veins black, anterior crossvein a little before middle of discal cell.

Female.—Hairs of face in large part black, the polished ovipositor as long as sixth segment, blunt, ventral keel castaneous.

Types.—Mount Rainier, Washington. Six specimens from Alta Vista, Crystal Mountain, and Van Trump Park, July and August, 1922 (Melander).

The collection of these specimens was largely made possible through a grant from the Elizabeth Thompson Science Fund for a study of the alpine insect fauna of Mt. Rainier.

Lasiopogon fumipennis, sp. nov.

Female.—Length 8 mm. Black in ground-color, heavily dusted. Upper part of head brownish, hairs short, sparse, fine and black, face cinereous, pile long, abundant and black, pile of lower occiput fine dense and white; style one-third the length of the third joint of antenna. Mesonotum thickly brown-pollinose, dorsocentral vittæ widely separated, moderately narrow and brown, median stripe not divided; humeri and pleuræ cinereous, no pile, four black setæ in hypopleural row, no dorsocentral bristles, two prealar black bristles, anterior part of notum with scattered minute appressed black setulæ, no hairs; scutellum brownish gray pollinose, its sparse marginal hairs black. Posterior two-fifths of abdominal segments cinereous pollinose, anterior portion nearly black and subshining, first segment alone with outstanding hairs which on the hind margin are setiform and black and white mixed, remainder of abdomen with minute black setulæ; ovipositor polished black, nearly as long as sixth and seventh segments combined, the ventral keel castaneous. Legs black, very lightly dusted, the posterior tibiæ with brownish tinge, hairs of femora very short, sparse and whitish, of tibiæ black, bristles black, two preapical extensor bristles on front femur, one on anterior face of middle femur, an imperfect row along upper front face of hind femur, under side of femora with about three straggling long white setiform hairs. Pulvilli alutaceous; wings infumated, veins black, anterior crossvein at middle of discal cell; halteres yellow, the upper side of knob with distinct black center, calypteres yellow.

Types.—Paradise Park, Mount Rainier, Washington, Aug. 1921 (Melander). Two paratypes, same locality and south slope of Mount Adams, Washington. (Melander).

Lasiopogon monticola, sp. nov.

Male.—Length 9 mm. General color brownish-gray due to heavy coat of pollen, vertex and upper occiput dusted with brown, face cinereous brown, mystax entirely black, hairs of lower occiput fine silky and white, of upper occiput black; style two-fifths the length of third antennal joint, thorax marked only with the narrow dorsocentral brown stripes which diverge anteriorally, median space not bisected, bristles black, two lateral bristles in front of suture, about five on postalar callus, about five presutural dorsocentrals; scutellum margined with about eight black bristles in addition to interspaced black hairs, bare on disc; six bristles in hypopleural row, mostly black, four black hairs at posterior margin of mesopleura. Anterior half of abdominal segments piceous, posterior half cinereous brown, hairs white, becoming black at apex, five black bristles in lateral row of first segment; hypopygium globose black shining, somewhat wider than termination of abdomen, the dorsal incision very broad, its fringe black, lateral valves very broad, less than twice as long as wide, truncate at apex, the lower margin with very strong tooth, hairs coarse and black, venter concolorous with posterior portions of tergites, its hairs fine and whitish. Hairs of femora white in large part, the outer half of femora with about five extensor setæ, the upper front face of hind femora setose; tarsi concolorous with remainder of legs, claws piceous with black apex, pulvilli alutaceous. Halteres and calypteres yellowish; wings lightly cinereous, veins black, anterior crossvein slightly before middle of discal cell.

Female.—Ovipositor short, ventral keel black, hairs of abdomen short and mostly black.

Types.—Mount Adams, Washington, July 24, 1921 (Melander). Other localities, Moscow Mountain, Idaho, and Mount Rainier, Washington. Thirty specimens.

Lasiopogon ripicola, sp. nov.

Male.—Length 10 mm. Dull brownish-gray, heavily pollinose and rather densely pilose species, upper part of head alutaceous, with abundance of black hairs but no bristles, face whitish, the dense hairs nearly white with slightly yellowish tinge, with a few black hairs intermixed on upper portion, lower occiput heavily white pilose, antennal hairs black, third joint compressed cylindrical, slightly more than twice the length of the acuminate style. Dorsum of thorax brownish-gray, the dorsocentral vittæ widely separated, dark brown and rather narrow, bearing about six very fine black setæ of which three are presutural, humeri cinereous, lateral markings very indistinct, three prealar bristles; scutellum dark cinereous, the apical fine bristles black and hairs white; pleuræ cinereous with faint yellow tinge, mesopleura with black hairs behind, sternopleura with fine white hairs, hypopleural fringe consisting of a few white and black bristle-like hairs. Abdomen not shining, the segments dark brown with apical two-fifths cinereous, the brown color intensified as two semicircular spots, the gray color extending forward triangularly between the brown markings, pile conspicuous and whitish, long on sides of second and third segments, sides of first segment with a cluster of black bristles in addition to the pile; hypopygium larger than diameter of end of abdomen, black, subshining, mainly black-hairy, dorsal fringe transverse and black, declivous beneath fringe and not emarginate but with strong central broad projection, lateral valves spoon-shaped, the inferior margin entire, without tooth below but with slight basal umbo, venter uniformly gray pollinose and with an abundance of fine whitish hairs. Legs coated with gray pollen, front femora with two preapical extensor bristles, hind femora with a complete row of black bristles along upper anterior face, bristles of tibiæ and tarsi black, hairs of legs abundant, fine and white, pulvilli alutaceous. Wings hyaline, veins black, anterior cross-vein at two-fifths the length of the discal cell, halteres yellow, the base brown, calypteres and fringe yellow.

Female.—Facial hairs more yellowish, ovipositor black polished, short, carina usually black.

Types.—Wawawai, Washington, May 20, 1911 (Melander) Eighteen paratypes from same locality and from Wilbur, and Yakima (Jenne) Wash. Most of the specimens were taken in the month of April.

Lasiopogon trivittatus, sp. nov.

Female.—Length 7 mm. Entirely black in ground color, the halteres and calypteres pale fuscous, the carina of the ovipositor castaneous, upper part of head yellowish-gray, bristles and hairs black, face whitish, its hairs nearly white with slightly yellowish tinge, lower pile of occiput fine and white. Thorax thickly coated with cinereous pollen, the dorsocentral stripes full brown, a median stripe of similar brown color and supraalar indications of lighter brown; bristles prominent and black, a strong presutural dorsocentral present, scattered black setulæ on anterior portion of mesonotum; scutellum densely cinereous, bare except for black marginal bristles and setula; pleuræ heavily coated with cinereous, almost pruinose, a slight tinge of yellowish developed beneath root of wing. Abdomen scarcely at all shining, first segment wholly cinereous, second to seventh segments fulvous over greater portion, the posterior margins narrowly cinereous, the gray color extending forward at the sides to merge into the fulvous, no long pile, hairs appressed, whitish, becoming black on posterior segments, ovipositor slightly longer than seventh segment, polished, blunt, but little tapering; venter heavily cinereous pollinose. Legs densely coated with gray pollen, femora with a few whitish long bristle-like hairs beneath, no coating of pile but the short hairs of femora and under side of tibiæ white, hairs of remainder of tibiæ and of tarsi and bristles black, pulvilli brownish. Wings nearly hyaline, veins blackish, anterior crossvein slightly before middle of discal cell.

Holotype.—Gold Creek, Montana, July 29, 1918 (Melander.)

OBSERVATIONS ON THE SO-CALLED TRUMPETER IN BUMBLEBEE COLONIES.[1]

By O. E. Plath,

College of Liberal Arts, Boston University.

About 250 years ago, the Dutch painter Goedart (1685) published a comprehensive treatise[2] on insects, volume 2 of which contains a unique and probably the oldest account of the life-history and habits of bumblebees. The account seems to be based almost entirely on the author's own observations, and is of interest chiefly because of its many naive anthropomorphisms. Thus, for example, Goedart (pp. 242-245) states that the members of a bumblebee colony, besides keeping a "king" like the honeybees, also have another individual among them which mounts to the top of the nest each morning about 7 A. M., and, like the bugler in the army, calls his companions to work by rapidly vibrating his wings, thereby producing a noise not unlike that of a drum. This performance, according to Goedart (p. 245), lasted for about a quarter of an hour each morning, and was observed repeatedly, not only by him, but also by others. About seventy-five years later, Goedart's (1685) observation was confirmed by the French Abbé Noël de Pluche (1764)[3], but de Pluche (p. 185) found that the "drummer", or "trumpeter", which he had under observation, called his companions to work at 7.30 A. M., instead of 7.

No one seems to have questioned this fantastic story until 1742 (about 75 years after the story originated), when the great French engineer and entomologist, Réaumur (pp. 1-30), published his observations on bumblebees. Although this famous scientist had a large number of bumblebee colonies under observation, he was unable to discover any such behavior as that described

[1]Contributions from the Entomological Laboratory of the Bussey Institution, Harvard University, No. 225.

[2]The first edition of this work appeared from 1662-1669, both in Dutch and in Latin. It was later also translated into English (1682) and French (1700).

[3]According to Sladen (1912, p. 48), other editions of this work appeared as early as 1732. Translations into English (by Samuel Humphreys (1740), German (1746), and Spanish (1754), made this comprehensive work accessible to a large number of readers outside of France.

by the earlier observers, and therefore came to the conclusion that Goedart's (1685) "trumpeter" story was a fable. Réaumur's (p. 30) opinion in this matter naturally carried much weight, being accepted by such eminent entomologists as Kirby and Spence (1818, p. 384), and dealt the bumblebee "trumpeter" a blow which was effective for almost 150 years, when Goedart's (1685) story was again revived by the well-known Austrian bumblebee student Hoffer (1881, 1882-83).

Being acquainted with the contradictory claims of Goedart (1685) and Réaumur (1742), Hoffer (1882-83, p. 23) tried for a number of years to find a "trumpeter" among the numerous bumblebee colonies which he had under observation, but his efforts were unsuccessful until the summer of 1881. On July 7 of that year, Hoffer (p. 23) obtained a strong colony of *Bremus* (*Bombus*) *ruderatus* which he placed in a window facing southeast. Early the following morning, Hoffer's (p. 24) attention was suddenly attracted by a peculiar humming in the new colony, and, upon investigating, he found that the sound was produced by one of the larger bees which was perched on the waxen envelope of the nest and was vigorously, but uniformly vibrating her wings. Overjoyed at having rediscovered the long-sought "trumpeter," Hoffer (p. 25) roused his wife and children, and later also called in the neighbors, to witness the interesting performance. However, Hoffer's (1882-83) "trumpeter", or "trumpeterette" as she ought to be called, evidently was somewhat of a slave-driver, and rather persistent, as compared with those of Goedart (1685) and de Pluche (1764), for "with painful regularity" she called her companions to work every morning shortly after three o'clock, and continued her "trumpeting" for about an hour. Hoffer (p. 25) now became interested to know what would happen if he removed the "trumpeter" from the colony, and, on doing so, found that thereafter the "trumpeting" was performed by another member of the colony, although about an hour later than before. As the colony grew smaller toward the end of the summer, the activities of the "trumpeter" became more and more irregular. This, and the fact that one of his former students claimed to have heard a "trumpeter" in a colony of *Bremus lapidarius*, led Hoffer (1882-83, pp. 25, 26) to the conclusion that only *Bremus ruderatus*, and perhaps some other "hypogeic" species, have "trumpeters," but only while the colonies are strong.

Hoffer's (1882-83) confirmation again brought Goedart's (1685) "trumpeter" story into good repute among biologists for a period of more than twenty years. With apparently the single exception of Pérez (1889), it was accepted—in most cases after personal verification—by Firtsch (cf. Hoffer, 1882-83, p. 25), Kristof (1883), Härter (1890), Sharp (1899), Marshall (1902), and Bengtsson (1903). Pérez (p. 117), while not in the least doubting the general correctness of Hoffer's (1882-83) observations, rejected the latter's interpretation by pointing out (1) that there is little sense in having a "trumpeter" unless he be the first one to rise, and (2) that the sound produced by the "trumpeter" is of no use whatever, as far as rousing the colony is concerned, since (according to Pérez) bumblebees, like honeybees and ants, are completely deaf. Pèrez (1889) then offers his own explanation. After expressing the opinion that the bumblebee "trumpeter" fulfills no social function, and that the "trumpeting" is probably done for his own benefit, Pérez (p. 117) suggests that the "trumpeters" in bumblebee colonies, like the so-called ventilators among honeybees, are newly-hatched individuals which are training their wing muscles for the long flights which they will soon make. However, as we have already seen, Péréz' (1889) theory, although more plausible than that of Goedart (1685), seems to have made little or no impression upon contemporary biologists.

Fourteen years after the publication of this theory, a third interpretation was offered by the well-known German bee student von Buttel-Reepen (1903, 1907). Unlike Pérez (1889), this author suggested that the bumblebee "trumpeter" has the same social function as the ventilators in the honeybee colony,[4]

[4]Since writing the above, I have discovered that a similar explanation was offered by Mr. J. Angus in a letter to Messrs. A. S. Packard and F. W. Putnam (cf. Packard (1868), 35 years before von Buttel-Reepen published his interpretation. Mr. Angus' letter partly reads as follows: "I have found the males [of *Bremus* (*Bombus*) *vagans*] plentiful near our garden fence, with a hole such as would be made by a mouse. They seem to be quite numerous. I was attracted to it by the noise they were making in fanning at the opening. I counted at one time as many as seven thus employed, and the sound could be heard several yards off. Several males were at rest, but mostly on the wing, when they would make a dash among the fanners, and all would scatter and sport around. The workers seem to be of a uniform size, and fully as large as the males. I think the object of the fanning was to introduce air into the nest, as is done by the Honey-bees."

namely, to reduce the temperature, or to expel moisture or bad odors from the nest. Similar conclusions were reached by the Norwegian biologist Lie-Pettersen (1906). This new interpretation was accepted—in some cases after extensive experimentation—by Stierlin (1906), Wagner (1907), Gundermann (1908), Lindhard (1912), and Sladen (1912).

However, within the last decade, Goedart's (1685) "trumpeter" story has found another adherent in Bachmann (1915, 1916). What is more, Bachman (1915) has discovered that the bumblebee "trumpeter", in addition to rousing the members of the colony in the morning, also attends to the "curfew" in the evening. This latter perfomance, Bachmann (1915, p. 87) describes as follows: "Um ½ 9 Uhr begann der Hummeltrompeter sein Abendlied. Es war ein längerer Ton, unterbrochen von einem Triller ähnlich wie wenn ein Tier im Kästchen fliegen würde. Der Trompeter schlug aber nur, auf der Wabe stehend, die Flügel."

The activity of the bumblebee "trumpeter" in the morning is described very vividly by Bachmann (1916, p. 103) in the following words: "Genau um 6 Uhr erhebt sich ein Summen im Nest, das ununterbrochen 2 Minuten dauert. Ich musste gleich an den Hummeltrompeter denken, den Hoffer in einem Nest von *Bombus ruderatus* entdeckt hat. Dreimal setzt mein Musikant an, bis es lebendig wird und ein Tierchen zum Abflug erscheint. Um 6.26 bringt ein geschäftiges Weibchen eine grosse Larve geschleppt und der Trompeter übt unentwegt seine Kunst. Zuerst in gleicher Tonlage summend, werden, wenn es länger dauert, die Schwebungen höher und tiefer, vibrierend, dann stossweise wie das Geräusch des Wagnerschen Hammers oder bei der Entladung elektrischer Funken, endlich wie ein langsamer Trommelwirbel, bis der Ton etwas höher wird und dann langsam erstirbt.

"Mitunter höre ich deutlich die Flügel schlagen und meine dabei, es fliege eine Hummel nahe am Kopf vorüber. Dieses Wecken dauert von 6.44 bis 7.06, also 22 Minuten ohne Unterbrechung and ohne die geringste Störung meinerseits. Bis ½ 8 Uhr höre ich noch dreimal einen kürzeren Ruf. Dann kriechen gleich 3 Hummeln auf einmal aus dem Nestloch, nachdem mit Körbchen beladene im Tor vorher einpassiert waren und der Betrieb in der Hummelburg kommt in regen Gang."

These two passages would not have been written, had Bachmann (1915, 1916) paid more attention to the literature of the preceding decade. As we have already seen, Bachmann's (1915, 1916) assertions were contradicted years before, by statements published by several authors, notably von Buttel-Reepen (1903), Lie-Pettersen (1906), Wagner (1907), Lindhard (1912), and Sladen (1912). To these may be added certain observations and experiments of my own.

During the summers of 1921 and 1922, I had under observation about sixty Bremus (Bombus) colonies belonging to ten[5] of our thirteen New England species, and have frequently had occasion to observe the behavior which gave rise to the "trumpeter" story. That the fanning of these so-called trumpeters has to do with ventilation of the nest, and not with rousing the colony, or the exercising of wing muscles, may be demonstrated very easily by exposing a bumblebee colony to the rays of the sun, a fact which was first pointed out by Lie-Pettersen (1906) and Wagner (1907). The conclusions which these two authors reached are corroborated by the following observations which were made during the summer of 1921.

Of the thirteen colonies which I had under observation during that summer, eleven were kept in windows facing south and the remaining two in a window which faced north. Like Lie-Pettersen (p. 18), I found that on every warm day, especially if the weather was sultry, one or more workers in each of the colonies on the south side of the building mounted to the top of the nest and began to fan shortly after the rays of the sun reached the nest-boxes. In a colony of *Bremus impatiens*, consisting of about 125 individuals, the number of fanning workers sometimes even increased to more than a dozen. As soon as the sun receded from their nest-box, these "trumpeters" discontinued their work, one after another, and crawled back into the nest.

[5]*Bremus affinis, bimaculatus, fervidus, impatiens, pennsylvanicus, perplexus, separatus, ternarius, terricola*, and *vagans*.

While this restless activity was in progress on the south side of the building, not a single bee, as a rule, was engaged in "trumpeting" in the two colonies which were kept on the north side, although one of the latter—also belonging to *Bremus impatiens*—consisted of more than 450 workers. The exposure to the hot midday sun evidently did not agree with the bees, for the colonies on the south side of the building did not thrive nearly so well as those on the north side, and during the following summer all of my bumblebee colonies were therefore kept in shady situations.

While "trumpeting" in a bumblebee colony is most pronounced when the nest is exposed to the rays of the sun on a hot day, it may, as is indicated by the observations of Goedart (1685), de Pluche (1764), Hoffer (1882-83), Bengtsson (1903), and Bachmann (1915, 1916), also take place in the morning and evening, in fact, as Wagner (1907) has pointed out, at any time of the day. Thus, for example, I have occasionally found one or two workers fanning at various hours during the night, even if the temperature outside was less than 70°. In this case, as has been suggested by von Buttel-Reepen (1903), fanning no doubt has to do with the expulsion of moisture or disagreeable odors from the nest.

Neither is it true, as Hoffer (1882-83), von Buttel-Reepen (1903), and Sladen (1912) assume, that "trumpeting" is resorted to only by species which have subterranean nests. Wagner (1907) found that *Bremus muscorum*, a European species which usually nests on the surface of the ground, resorts to fanning when the temperature of the nest gets too high, and this, as will be seen later, is also true of *Bremus fervidus* in this country.

As already stated, Hoffer (1882-83) believed that small Bremus colonies have no "trumpeter." Wagner (1907) and Lindhard (1912), on the other hand, claim that small colonies also resort to fanning. In order to determine which one of these claims is correct, the following experiment was performed. At 2 P. M., on June 3, 1922, I exposed the next-box of a small colony (1 queen and 2 workers) of *Bremus impatiens* to the rays of the sun. Three minutes later, one of the workers crawled to the top of the nest and began to fan, and within another minute, the remaining worker and the queen appeared and assisted in this activity.

Later in the summer, an experiment was also carried out to test Pérez' (1889) theory, according to which the so-called bumblebee trumpeters are newly emerged individuals which are exercising their wing muscles. On August 14th, at 1.30 P. M., I removed the board which shaded the nest of a queenless colony of *Bremus fervidus* so that the nest-box was exposed to the sun. The result was as follows: At 1.34, a worker appeared on top of the nest, and after crawling about a few seconds, began to fan vigorously. By 1.36 two more workers were engaged in this work, and by 1.38, the number of "trumpeters" had increased to six. All of these "trumpeters", as the hardened pollen lump on the thorax showed[6], were old bees which had done considerable foraging. *Bremus fervidus* usually nests on the surface of the ground, and hence this experiment incidentally also shows that Hoffer (1882-83), von Buttel-Reepen (1903), and Sladen (1912) are wrong in assuming that only "subterranean" species have "trumpeters."

Summary and Conclusions.

1. The so-called trumpeters in bumblebee colonies are bees which are engaged in ventilating the nest.
2. This ventilation is brought about by a rapid vibration of the wings and may take place at any time during the day or night.
3. Species which nest on the surface of the ground likewise make use of this method of ventilating their nests.
4. Ventilation by fanning is also resorted to by small bumblebee colonies.
5. Pérez' theory, according to which the so-called trumpeters in bumblebee colonies are newly emerged individuals which are exercising their wing muscles, is not founded upon facts.

Literature Cited.

Bachmann, M. 1915. Biologische Beobachtungen an Hummeln. Mitteil. Münch. Ent. Gessellsch., Vol. 6, pp. 71-112.
1916. Beobachtungen vor dem Hummelnest. Ent. Zeitschr. Frankfurt a. M., Vol. 29, pp. 89-90, 93-94, 98-99, 103-104; Vol. 30, pp. 1-3.

[6]The source of these pollen lumps will be discussed in connection with another paper.

Bengtsson, S. 1903. Studier och iakttagelser öfver Humlor. Ark. Zool., Vol. 1, pp. 197-222.

Buttel-Reepen, H. von 1903. Die stammesgeschichtliche Entstehung des Bienenstaates, sowie Beiträge zur Lebensweise der solitären und sozialen Bienen (Hummeln, Meliponen, etc.). Georg Thieme, Leipzig.

1907. Zur Psychobiologie der Hummeln I. Biol. Centralbl., Vol. 27, pp. 579-613.

Goedartius, J. 1685. De Insectis, in Methodum Redactus; cum Notularum Additione. London. Vol. 2, pp. 233-249.

Gundermann, E. 1908. Einige Beobachtungen an Hummelnestern. Ent. Wochenbl., Vol. 25, pp. 30-31, 35-36.

Härter, R. 1890. Biologische Beobachtungen an Hummeln. 27 Bericht. Oberhess. Gesellsch. Natur-u. Heilkunde pp. 59-75.

Hoffer, E. 1881. Biologische Beobachtungen an Hummeln und Schmarotzerhummeln. Mitth. Naturw. Ver. Steiermark, Vol. 18, pp. 68-92.

1882-83. Die Hummeln Steiermarks. Lebensgeschichte und Beschreibung derselben. Leuschner & Lubensky, Graz.

Humphreys, S. 1740. Spectacle de la Nature: or Nature Display'd. R. Francklin, C. Davis, and J. Pemberton. London.

Kirby, W. and Spence, W. 1818. An Introduction to Entomology: or Elements of the Natural History of Insects. Longman, Hurst, Rees, Orme, and Brown, London. Vol. 2.

Kristof, L. 1883. Eigene Beobachtungen über das Leben einheimischer Hummeln verbunden mit einer Besprechung der darüber von Prof. Dr. E. Hoffer im 31. und 32. Jahres-Berichte der steierm. Landes-Oberrealschule (1882-83) veröffentlichten Monographie. Mitth. Naturw. Ver. Steiermark, pp. LXIV-LXXIV.

Lie-Pettersen, O. J. 1906. Neue Beiträge zur Biologie der norwegischen Hummeln. Bergens Mus. Aarb., pp. 1-43.

Lindhard, E. 1912. Humlebien som Husdyr. Spredte Træk af nogle danske Humlebiarters Biologi. Tidsskr. Landbrugets Planteavl, Vol. 19, pp. 335-352, 4 figs.

Marshall, W. 1902. Allgemeines über den Insektenstaat. Hummeln und Meliponen. Hochschul-Vorträge. Seele & Co., Leipzig. Heft 27 u. 28, pp. 1-42.

Packard, A. S. Jr. 1868. The Home of the Bees. Amer. Naturalist, Vol. 1, pp. 364-378, 596-606, pl. 10 and 4 figs.

Pérez, J. 1889. Les Abeilles. Paris (After Wagner).

Pluche, A. N. de 1764. Le Spectacle de la Nature. Chez les Freres Estienne. Paris, Vol. 1.

Réaumur, R. A. de 1742. Memoires pour servir a l'histoire des insectes. L'imprimerie Royale, Paris. Vol. 6, pp. 1-30, pls. 1-4.

Sharp, D. 1899. Insects. Part II. The Cambridge Natural History. Macmillan and Co., London. Vol. 6.

Sladen, F. W. L. 1912. The Bumble-bee, Its Life-History and how to Domesticate it. Macmillan and Co., London.

Stierlin, R. 1906. Über das Leben der Hummeln. Mitt. Naturw. Ges. Winterthur, Vol. 6, pp. 130-144.

Wagner, W. 1907. Psycho-biologische Untersuchungen an Hummeln mit Bezugnahme auf die Frage der Geselligkeit im Tierreiche. Zoologica, Vol. 19, pp. 1-239, 1 pl., 136 figs.

A NOTE ON A RECENTLY INTRODUCED LEAFHOPPER.

By Geo. W. Barber,

Bureau of Entomology, U. S. Dept. of Agriculture.

On July 21, 1919 the writer took a single specimen of *Allygus mixtus* Fabr. on the trunk of a beech tree at Medford, Mass. This specimen was determined by Messrs. Sanders and DeLong and a note of its occurence published by them (8). The species was also noticed in a local list published by the writer (9).

During the season of 1920 over forty specimens of the insect were taken from the same tree, the occurence ranging from July 16 to September 3. No specimens other than these were seen. Hundreds of specimens were taken from this tree during 1921, and a few near by and in adjoining towns from the middle of July to the middle of September.

So far as these collecting records go it would seem that this insect was rapidly gaining a foothold in this locality, at least one thriving colony having become well established. However, during 1922 only two specimens were captured and but one of these on the tree mentioned heretofore.

This species is not uncommon in Europe and northern Africa where it occurs quite generally as the following distribution record by Oshanin (6) will show; Sweden, Germany, England France, Spain, Italy, Austria, Hungary, Roumania, Algeria, Tunis, Finland, and Russia. Specimens from Germany are in the writer's collections. It is a common species in England according to Buckton (4), and Edwards (5) records that it feeds on the oak. So far, the writer has not taken the insect from oak in Massachusetts but the young have not been observed.

Allygus mixtus was originally described by Fabricius (1) in the genus *Cicada*. Subsequent writers placed the species in the genera *Jassus* and *Thamnotettix* until Scott (3) described the genus *Allygus*. This name had been proposed by Fieber (2) but it seems that he had given no description of it.

Three species assigned to *Allygus* now occur in the fauna of the United States;

Allygus gutturosus (Ball) (7) originally described as *Thamnotettix* from California.

Allygus modestus Fieb an European species discovered in New Jersey by Mr. H. B. Weiss and recorded by Sanders and DeLong (8).

Allygus mixtus Fabr.

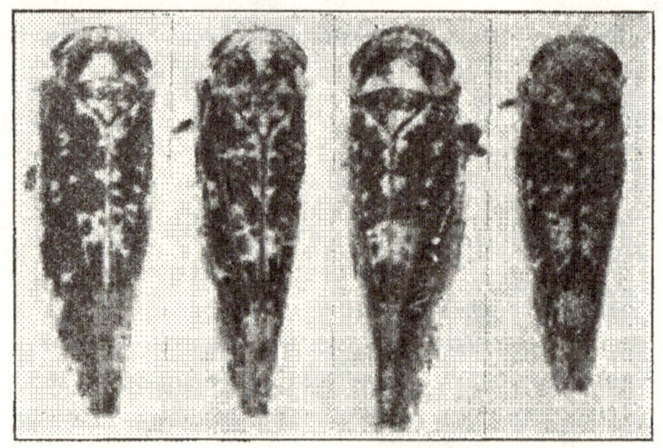

Fig. 1. *Allygus mixtus* Fab., Adults.

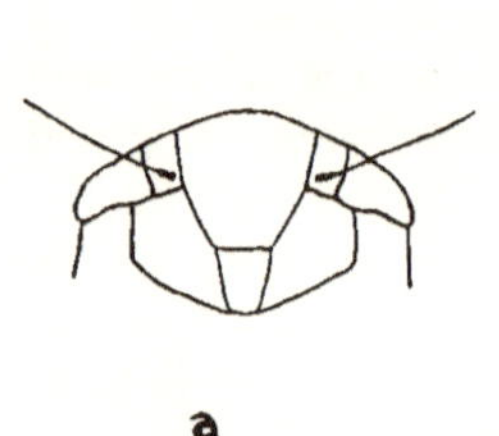

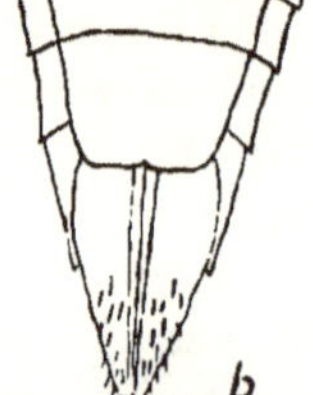

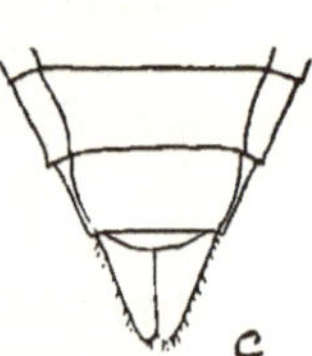

Fig. 2. *Allygus mixtus* Fabr., a-face; b-female genitalia; c-male genitalia.

Literature referred to

1. 1803—Fabricius, Syst. Rhyng., p. 86.
2. 1872—Fieber, Kat. der Europ, Cicad., p. 13.
3. 1875—Scott, Ent. Month. Mag. XII, p. 171.
4. 1891—Buckton, on. Brit. Cic. II, p. 71.

5. 1896—Edwards, Hemip. Homop. Brit. Isds., p. 166.
6. 1906—Oshanin, Verz. Paläark. Hemip. II, p. 137.
7. 1910—Ball. Canadian Ent. XLII, p. 307.
8. 1920—Sanders and DeLong, Pennsylvania Bur. Plant Ind., Tech. Bull. No. 1, p. 18.
9. 1920—Barber, Psyche XXVII, p. 149.

FLOWER VISITS OF INSECTS

By Charles Robertson

Carlinville, Illinois.

In the study of the pollination of flowers by insects (6) a good many observations have been made which relate primarily to the habits of insects and only indirectly, if at all, to the elucidation of insect flowers. It is proposed here to consider the data from the standpoint of the insects.

The flower groups adopted are divided into a social set, whose flowers are in heads, spikes or close umbels, so that insects pass from one to another without taking wing or climbing, and a non-social set. The latter contains 54.4 per cent of the flowers, and is divided into Ma, long-tongued bee flowers, including 11 adapted to birds, hawk-moths and butterflies, and Mi, short-tongued bee flowers, including six fly flowers. The social set includes Mas, long-tongued bee flowers; Mis, short-tongued bee flowers; and Pol, visited by miscellaneous short-tongued insects.

The insect visits were first distributed under Müller's flower classes. These were then divided into non-social and social sets and the visits were distributed again under them. Of 9 cases, maxima under Hb fell under non-social Hb in 6. In 27 other cases, however, maxima under B, AB, or A always fell under the social sets.

The percentages for each class and color and the visits observed are:

	Non-social		Social			Total	Colors		
	Ma	Mi	Mas	Mis	Pol		Red	White	Yellow
Local Flora	28.3	27.9	16.4	22.0	5.1	540	29.2	39.6	31.1
Flowers observed	30.2	24.2	18.7	21.5	5.2	437	30.2	39.1	30.6
Before July	28.9	32.3	11.0	22.9	4.6	235	26.3	44.6	28.9
After June	30.5	15.2	28.2	19.0	6.8	262	34.3	33.5	32.0
Pollinating visits	7.5	13.3	20.4	39.8	18.7	13971	16.8	51.3	31.7
Non-pollinating visits	41.1	9.5	31.3	10.9	7.0	852	46.3	33.3	20.3

Percentages of visits to red flowers are given for the Berlin Garden and Low Germany (Loew **2,3**) and the Alps (Müller **5**,512-23). The percentages of red flowers observed are for the Alps 41.6 and Berlin Garden 48.2. In 31 cases, all except Sphingidæ, the percentage of local visits to red ranges from 5.4 to 51.3 less, or an average of 24. The term *preference,* as used here, means only that the percentage of visits is greater than the percentage of flowers observed. For each group the percentages of flowers visited as well as the visits were distributed under each flower class. Usually these are much alike, so that the percentages of flowers visited are not mentioned except when they are quite different from the visits.

The flowers were also divided into an early group containing 235 plants, 142 blooming, and 33 observed, before July, and a late group containing 262 plants, 144 blooming, and 58 observed, after June. In the case of 60 plants the visits observed before July and after June were referred to each group. Of these 60 plants 13 are not native. Visits to these groups were first distributed under Müller's classes. Before July there are maxima under B, AB, including Po, and A. After June there is a slight increase in Hb, including O and F, and a marked increase in B′.

The visits to these groups were also distributed under the new classes. The early group shows maxima of the simplest flowers, non-social Mi, and white colors. These along with Mis decrease in the late group, which shows maxima of Ma and red, and a great increase in Mas. The specialization of the late group is marked by the increase of the social flowers from 38.7 to 54.1 per cent.

When B′ as an element of the flora changes from 8.0 to 28.2 per cent, the maxima of the insect groups change from the four other dominant classes to B′. The only exceptions are the ruby-throated and the Non-aculeata. The maxima of the same insects, when distributed into early and late sets of the new categories, in 62.8 per cent of the cases, fall under the same flower groups.

The Bombidæ, Euceridæ, Anthophoroidea, Dasygastræ and long-tongued bees in general change from Ma to Mas, due to the fact that Mas is not well represented in the early flora.

Apis mellifera, the Ceratinidæ and Bombyliidæ change from Mis to Mas. Early there is greater contrast between Ma and Mis than late between Mas and Mis. Consequently these mid-tongued insects are excluded from a considerable number of early Ma, while they can reach the nectar of most of the late Mas. A like change in Melectoidea and Andrenidæ is owing to the fact that the late ones have longer tongues.

Bees.

Apis mellifera.—Of 196 visits, 30.1 per cent are to Mis, 27.0 to Mas, 43.3 to white, 65.3 to social flowers and 28.3 to Compositæ. Of its pollen visits 36.7 per cent, while of its nectar visits 29.0, are under yellow. Red shows: local 24.4, Low Germany 47.3, Berlin Garden 55.0 and the Alps 60.7. Before July the hive-bee prefers Mis; after June, Mas, Mis and Pol. The maxima shift from AB 33.3 to B′ 44.7, Mis 32.2 to Mas 43.8.

An introduced domesticated insect, it is the most important single obstacle in the way of the anthecologist. It occupies an intermediate position between long-tongued and short-tongued bees, though it makes more visits to flowers preferred by the latter. On account of its abundance and long flight it makes more legitimate visits than any other insect, except *Bombus americanorum.*

It shows inferiority to several indigenous bees, *Bombus, Melissodes, Megachile, Calliopsis andreniformis*, in its inability to utilize some complicated flowers like *Desmodium*, but this is somewhat offset by its ingenuity in extracting pollen from *Dicentra cucullaria.*

Bombinæ.—Of 717 visits to 273 flowers, 39.4 per cent are to Ma, 31.9 to Mas, 41.1 to red, 10.0 to Labiatæ, 10.6 to Leguminosæ and 25.2 to Compositæ. Visits to red are: Low Germany 61.5, Berlin Garden 63.7 and Alps 64.7. Four prefer Ma, four Mas, seven red and one yellow.

Loew (**2**, 87) states that since male bumblebees have shorter tongues than the workers, the relations holding for the females and workers do not apply to them, and that therefore they prefer flowers of class B′. This is not dependent upon the difference in the length of the proboscis, but is largely a phenological matter connected with the late flight of the workers, after May 13, still later flight of the males, after July 4, and the late blooming of B′ which is really a phenological class. The males only resemble bees in general in preferring B′ in their late visits. The percentage of visits to B′ after June is for the females 32.1, workers 38.1, and males 57.6. So that under the same conditions all three forms prefer B′. The females show a maximum under Ma, 47.3, while the workers and males show maxima under Mas, 43.5 and 57.8.

Seven species, forming 4 per cent of the long-tongued bees, make 23 per cent of the long-tongued bee visits, the average being 102. *Bombus americanorum* makes 227 visits, the highest number for any visitor. Bumblebees are the characteristic visitors of long-tongued bee flowers and have probably had more influence in producing such flowers than all other bees together. They make 39 per cent of the visits to Ma, the highest specialized of non-social flowers.

Psithyrus.—Of 47 visits to 39 flowers, 61.7 per cent are to Mas, 87.2 to social flowers, 42.5 to Compositæ, 14.9 to Labiatæ and 12.7 to Leguminosæ.

Loew (2, 103) says: "the habit possessed by female bumblebees of chiefly seeking out hymenopterid flowers, while the males give preference to social flowers, is exaggerated in the parasitic genus *Psithyrus*, which constitutes a small side-branch of the group. The species of this genus consequently prefer dark-colored flowers even more than do the short-tongued species of *Bombus.*"

The European visits for the females show 34.3 more in percentage of visits to Hb than to B′, while the local visits show only 6.0 more. In the local species the apparent preference for red flowers is not a consequence of a preference for Hb or of any difference in the visits of the males, for, while the males show 33.3 more in percentage of visits to B′ than the females do, they also show 15.1 more in percentage of visits to red. Local visits to red are 55.3 per cent, in the Berlin Garden 71.5, Low Germany 74.0 and the Alps 77.8. The visits of the males which fly late, do not differ from those of the females as much as the late visits of the females differ from the early ones. Visits to red show: females 51.5, males 66.6; females before July 71.4, after June 36.3.

Bombidæ.—Before July the Bombidæ prefer Ma and red; after June, Mas, red and yellow. They show less preference for B′ than does any other considerable group of long-tongued bees. The maxima shift from Hb 59.8 to B′ 42.0, Ma 50.8 to Mas 48.6. Visits to yellow change from 19.6 to 34.0.

Apygidial Scopulipedes.—These show every indication of great age: the fragmentary nature and the marked structural differences of the still existing groups, as well as their wide and discontinuous distribution. Müller says that the maxillary palps of *Bombus*, etc. are aborted as a result of specialization of the proboscis, lengthening of the glossa and labial palps (4,57). But it is evidently a mark of age, for many Pygidialia have the proboscis as long and even more highly specialized, but retain the primitive number of six joints. It seems that the Apygidialia were the primitive long-tongued bees and had most to do with the origin of the earliest long-tongued bee flowers. The specialized genera of Pygidialia are characterized by long tongues, rapid flight, rather short seasons, often oligolectic and more peculiar habits, just as would be expected of later developed competitors.

Anthophoridæ.—Of 75 visits to 56 flowers, 66.6 per cent are to Ma, 22.6 to Mas, 54.6 to red, 21.3 to Labiatæ, 16.0 to Leguminosæ and 10.6 each to Polemoniales and Personales.

Euceridæ (521 visits to 202 flowers).—These prefer Mas, which shows 31.6 per cent of the flowers visited and 54.7 per cent of the visits, red 39.9 and yellow 35.7, 10.5 per cent of the visits being to Labiatæ and 40.8 to Compositæ. Twenty prefer Mas, 11 Ma, 19 red, 11 yellow, two white. Before July they prefer Ma, Mas and red; after June, Mas, yellow and red. The group is a late one. The maxima shift from Hb 60.3 to B′ 51.8, Ma 48.4 to Mas 66.2, red 42.8 to yellow 41.0.

Emphoridæ.—Of 14 visits to 11 flowers, 57.1 per cent are to Ma, 35.7 to Mas, 57.1 to red, 42.8 to white, 28.5 to Polemoniales and 21.4 to Compositæ.

Anthophoroidea.—Of the 610 visits of the last three families, 50.3 per cent are to Mas, 42.′ to red, 32.4 to yellow, 11.6 to

Labiatæ and 35.7 to Compositæ. Before July they prefer Ma, Mas and red; after June, Mas, red and yellow. The maxima shift from Hb 68.9 to B′ 49.0, Ma 56.1 to Mas 64.4.

Xylocopidæ.—The single species, *Xylocopa virginica*, near its northern limit here, is rare and its visits few. It seems to prefer Mas and red.

Ceratinidæ.—Of 194 visits to 162 flowers, 33.5 per cent are to Mis, 27.8 to Mi, 21.1 to Mas, 47.4 to white and 24.7 to Compositæ. The visits of the males differ remarkably from those of. the females and under similar conditions. The females show Mi 22.4, Mas 30.4, Mis 23.2 and red 32.5. The males show Mi 42.8, Mas 3.0, Mis 40.8 and red 14.2. In their visits they resemble the Halictidæ and *Apis mellifera.* Before July they prefer Mis, Mi, Pol, and white; after June, Mas, Mis and red. The maxima shift from AB 28.4 to B′ 55.2, Mis 35.3 to Mas 52.2, white 50.7 to red 37.3.

Melectoidea (ex. Nomadidæ; 209 visits to 72 flowers).—These prefer Mas 67.9, Mis 25.8 and yellow 41.1. Fifteen prefer Mas, five Mis, one Ma, ten yellow, six red, six white. Of the visits of Epeolidæ 15.6 per cent are to Labiatæ and 58.5 to Compositæ.

Nomadidæ.—Of 272 visits to 108 flowers 48.5 per cent are to Mis, 31.9 to Mi, 51.1 to white, 36.3 to yellow, 14.7 to Compositæ, 14.3 to *Salix* and 11.7 to Rosaceæ. Being inquilines at least principally of Andrenidæ they are associated with them in time and place and naturally show similar flower visits. Sixteen prefer Mis, four Mi, two Mas, 14 white, nine yellow.

Melectoidea.—Of the 481 visits, 38.6 per cent are to Mis, 33.4 to Mas, 41.7 to white and 38.4 to yellow. The Nomadidæ make only 17 visits after June, and the other Melectoidea make only five visits before July, so that their differences are largely phenological. Before July they prefer Mis, Mi, yellow and white; after June, Mas, Mis and yellow. The maxima shift from AB 32.6 to B′ 58.9, Mis 45.7 to Mas 66.0, white 50.5 to yellow 39.6.

Megachilinæ.—The Megachilini (331 visits to 151 flowers) prefer Mas, Mis, red 40.1 and yellow 33.3. The flowers visited show Mas 33.1, Mis 26.4, while the visits show Mas 53.8, Mis 16.1. Visits to red in Low Germany are 67.0 per cent and the Berlin Garden 74.0.

Of 110 visits of *Cœlioxys* to 62 flowers, 54.5 per cent are to Mas, 28.1 to Mis and 36.3 to yellow. Loew (2,264) calls it an oligotrope of red colors, but it shows 30.0 under red compared with 60.0 in the Berlin Garden and 66.0 in Low Germany. Of visits to red the females show 42.2 and the males 28.9.

Nineteen species of Megachilinæ prefer Mas, three Ma, 11 red, nine yellow and two white. Of their visits 12.8 per cent are to Labiatæ, 17.5 to Leguminosæ and 39.5 to Compositæ. The maximum changes from Hb 50.3 before July to B′ 42.0 after June.

Osmiinæ.—Of 295 visits to 138 flowers, 27.7 per cent are to Ma, 27.4 to Mi, 48.1 to white, 15.2 to Leguminosæ, 11.1 to Rosaceæ and 10.3 to Polemoniales. Seven prefer Mi, 41.8 per cent of visits, 5 Ma 66.6, 5 Mas 41.3, 3 Mis 57.1, 13 white 52.6, 5 red 43.3, 2 yellow 66.6. Local visits to red are 27.4 per cent, Berlin Garden 65.0 and Low Germany 77.2. Visits to Mas show for the females 22.6, for the males 6.2. Before July the Osmiinæ prefer Ma, Mas, Mi, white and red; after June, Mas, Mis, white and yellow. The maxima shift from Hb 43.7 to B′ 48.9, Mi 32.8 to Mas 57.4.

Anthidiini.—Of 9 visits to 8 flowers, 88.8 per cent are to Mas, 44.4 to red and 33.3 to yellow. Visits to red in Low Germany are 72.7 and in the Berlin Garden 87.0.

Stelidini.—Of 17 visits to 16 flowers, 76.4 per cent are to Mis, 58.8 to white, 41.1 to yellow, 58.8 to Compositæ. In the Berlin Garden 41.6 per cent of the visits were to red.

Dasygastræ.—Of 812 visits made by the last four groups, 40.8 per cent are to Mas, 33.3 to red, 10.3 to Labiatæ, 15.6 to Leguminosæ and 30.7 to Compositæ. Of the visits of the nest-makers 18.2 per cent are to Mis, 34.1 to red and 61.9 to social flowers; while of the visits of the inquilines 34.6 per cent are to Mis, 35.6 to yellow and 90.4 to social flowers. Before July (Osmiinæ 256 visits, Megachilinæ 133) they prefer Mas and red; after June (Osmiinæ 47, Megachilinæ 389) Mas, yellow and red. The maxima shift from Hb 44.8 to B′ 43.4, Ma 27.2 to Mas 57.2, white 43.3 to red 36.4.

Müller (4,55) says: "More than nine-tenths of the flowers visited by bees with abdominal brushes are such as are adapted to dust the ventral surface of the bee with pollen (*Echium*, Papilionaceæ, Compositæ, etc.) without any action of the tarsal brushes. More rarely, bees with abdominal brushes may be seen feeding on flowers whose pollen gets applied to their backs; in such cases the bee makes use of its tarsal brushes to sweep off the pollen from the parts where it has fallen into the abdominal brushes." Considering the composition of the flora Müller's statement shows about what these bees would be expected to do without preference. Of 243 local flowers visited for pollen by long-tongued bees in general, only 11.1 per cent require the use of the tarsal brushes. Of 146 visited for pollen by the Dasygastræ, 5.2 per cent require the use of the tarsal brushes. It is not easy to separate such flowers, because the Dasygastræ often reverse on nototribe flowers so as to receive the pollen on their undersides, as in the case of *Linaria vulgaris*, *Pentstemon*, *Impatiens* and *Pinguicula*. They also reverse on some species of *Gerardia* and *Viola*, but these flowers compel them to turn head downwards. On tubular flowers with included anthers they collect the pollen which adheres to their tongues, *Lithospermum canescens*, *Verbena stricta*.

Compared with other groups the Dasygastræ show a marked predilection for sternotribe flowers, 47.5 per cent of thei pollen visits. They do not equal the Euceridæ in their prefercrence for Compositæ or antipathy to nototribe flowers.

Müller (4,55) further says: "There can be little doubt therefore that the bees with abdominal brushes have adapted themselves to the flowers which were fitted to dust their ventral surfaces (Papilionaceæ, Compositæ, *Echium*, etc.), and the contrary view, that these flowers have become adapted to the bees, is untenable, for the flowers are visited and fertilized by other and far more numerous insects." The Dasygastræ and Papilionaceæ have July maxima. There are several sternotribe flowers of which these bees are the most important and almost exclusive visitors.

Panurgidæ.—Of 141 visits to 84 flowers, 44.6 per cent are to Mas, 31.9 to Mis, 50.3 to yellow and 60.2 to Compositæ.

Red shows 31.3 per cent of the flowers visited and 19.8 per cent of the visits. Yellow shows 33.7 per cent of the flowers. Nine prefer Mas, five Mis, two Mi, ten yellow, four white and two red. Before July they prefer Mas, Pol and red; after June, Mas, Mis and yellow. The maxima shift from Hb 35.7 to B′ 66.6, red 39.2 to yellow 55.8. The heterotropy is given in **7**, 172-3.

Halictidæ (ex. Sphecodini).—Of 1840 visits to 287 flowers, 41.8 per cent are to Mis, 28.5 to Mi, 51.3 to white, 33.4 to yellow and 21.6 to Compositæ. Mis shows 30.3 per cent of the flowers visited. Visits of females show Mi 30.8, Mas 13.4; of males, Mi 10.0, Mas 27.1. Visits to red are 15.2 per cent, Low Germany 35.6 and Berlin Garden 38.0.

Loew (**2**,71) calls Halictidæ males oligotropes of B′. The males begin to fly about June 4 and are limited mainly to flowers observed after June, when the Halictidæ in general make a smaller percentage of visits to B′ than any other short-tongued bees, except *Prosopis*. The percentage of visits to B′ after June is for the females 36.3, while that for the males is 39. The females make pollen visits to many deep tubed Compositæ on which the males do not occur.

Sphecodini.—Of 111 visits to 57 flowers, 54.9 per cent are to Mis, 33.3 to Pol, 63.9 to white, 35.1 to yellow, 27.9 to Umbelliferæ, 18.9 to Compositæ, and 10.8 to Labiatæ. Visits to red are 0.9 per cent, in Low Germany 26.7.

Halictidæ.—Of 1951 visits of the Halictidæ in general, 42.5 per cent are to Mis, 27.5 to Mi, 52.0 to white and 33.5 to yellow. Of 165 non-pollinating visits, 53.7 per cent are to Ma, 37.5 to Mas and 52.1 to red. Forty prefer Mis, six Pol, six Mi, three Mas, 38 white, 17 yellow and only one red. Before July they prefer Mis, Pol, Mi, yellow and white; after June, Mis, Pol and white. The maximum shifts from AB 37.2 to B′ 37.6.

Andrenidæ.—Of 585 visits to 133 flowers, 59.6 per cent are to Mis, 54.4 to white, 40.0 to yellow, 18.6 to Rosaceæ, 15.7 to *Salix,* 12.8 to Umbelliferæ and 11.4 to Compositæ. Mis shows 37.5 per cent of the flowers visited. Red shows 5.4 per cent of local visits, in Low Germany 26.0 and Berlin Garden 46.7. Thirty-seven prefer Mis, four Mas, four Ma, four Mi, 28 white,

19 yellow and four red. Before July they prefer Mis, Pol, white and yellow; after June, Mis, Mas and yellow. The maxima shift from AB 50.5 to B′ 86.2, Mis 60.7 to Mas 50.0, white 56.9 to yellow 56.8.

Prosopididæ.—Of 166 visits to 74 flowers, 61.4 per cent are to Mis, 24.7 to Pol, 68.6 to white, 34.9 to Umbelliferæ, 16.8 to Compositæ and 12.6 to Rosaceæ. Visits to red are 0.6 per cent, Berlin Garden 32.5, Low Germany 36.7. Eight prefer Mis, and one Mi. Before July they prefer Mis, Pol, white and yellow; after June, Mis, Pol and white. The maximum shifts from A 40.5 to B′ 31.2.

Colletidæ.—Of 140 visits to 89 flowers, 52.1 per cent are to Mis, 15.0 to Pol, 50.0 to white, 39.2 to yellow, 14.2 to Umbelliferæ and 37.1 to Compositæ. Seven prefer Mis, four Mi, three Mas, seven white, five yellow and three red. Under Mas the females show 22.0 per cent, while the males show only 8.6. Before July there is a maximum of 34.3 under B, after June it changes to 58.7 under B′.

Long-tongued Bees.—Of 3061 visits to 370 flowers, 37.7 per cent are to Mas, 22.1 to Mis, 34.0 to red, 31.4 to yellow, 10.5 to Leguminosæ and 30.3 to Compositæ. Of the flowers visited and visits Ma shows 32.4 and 23.6, while Mas shows 22.4 and 37.7. Visits to red in the Berlin Garden are 60.4, in the Alps 63.3. Seventy prefer Mas, 31 Ma, 11 Mi, 60 red, 43 white, 43 yellow. Before July they prefer Mas, Ma, Mis and red; after June, Mas, Mis, yellow and red. Visits after June show the preferences probably better than the general visits because the majority of long-tongued bees are late. The maxima shift from Hb 43.0 to B′ 46.9, Ma 31.5 to Mas 56.9, white 43.5 to red 37.8.

Of the visits of the polyleges 32.5 per cent are to Mas, 30.8 to Ma and 37.0 to red; of the inquilines 38.4 to Mas, 36.3 to Mis, 35.8 to yellow and 40.4 to white; of the oligoleges 68.2 to Mas, 45.5 to yellow and 36.2 to red. The polyleges show the highest percentages to Ma and red, the oligoleges to Mas and yellow, and the inquilines to Mis and white. The oligoleges show the highest percentage of visits to social flowers, 86.0, and the polyleges to non-social 43.9. Forty-two prefer non-social flowers. Non-pollinating visits (66) show for Ma 68.1, Mas 28.7

and red 56.0. The long-tongued bee visits show gains over the short-tongued of 19.6 for Ma, 23.8 for Mas and 22.1 for red.

Short-tongued Bees.—Of 3002 visits to 305 flowers, 46.7 per cent are to Mis, 24.4 to Mi, 10.8 to Pol, 52.1 to white, 35.8 to yellow, 10.8 to Umbelliferæ and 21.9 to Compositæ. Of the flowers visited Mis shows 29.1 per cent and Mi 32.1. Ninety-seven prefer Mis, 20 Mas, 18 Mi, 6 Pol, 4 Ma, 87 white, 53 yellow and ten red. Visits to red are 11.9 per cent, Berlin Garden 34.3, Alps 36.2. There is a preference for Mas after June. The maximum changes from AB 39.1 to B′ 44.1. Of the visits of the polyleges (*Prosopis* excluded) 44.6 per cent are to Mis, 27.9 to Mi, 9.3 to Pol, 52.8 to white, 33.3 to yellow; of the oligoleges 49.7 to Mis, 31.7 to Mas, 7.1 to Pol, 55.3 to yellow; of the inquilines 58.7 to Mis, 29.3 to Pol, 62.7 to white and 36.5 to yellow. Their preference for Mi connects the short-tongued bees pretty definitely with the origin of these most primitive entomophilous flowers.

The short-tongued bees, compared with the long-tongued, show preferences for Mi 12.4, Mis 24.6, Pol 6.4, white 17.6 and yellow 4.4. Non-pollinating visits (192) show under Ma 56.7, Mas 38.5 and red 53.6.

Bees, Total (6063 visits to 417 flowers).—Of bee visits 34.2 per cent are to Mis, 25.7 to Mas, 43.2 to white and 33.5 to yellow, 127 preferring Mis, 93 Mas, 35 Ma, 29 Mi, 6 Pol, 130 white, 96 yellow and 70 red. Visits to red are 23.1 per cent, Berlin Garden 55.4 and the Alps 57.1. As might be expected, bee visits coincide more nearly with the observed flora than the visits of any other group of anthophilous insects.

Before July the bees prefer Mis, after June they prefer Mas. The change in the maximum from Mis 38.1 to Mas 45.2 results from the combination of the short-tongued bees which predominate early with the long-tongued bees which predominate late. The maximum shifts from AB 29.9 to B′ 45.7.

The polyleges (*Prosopis* excluded) make 73.3 per cent of the total bee visits. They show the highest percentages of visits to Ma 16.9, Mi 21.0, red 24.6 and white 44.6, the oligoleges to Mas 50.0 and yellow 50.4, and the inquilines to Mis 39.9 and Pol 8.5.

Of the visits of bees 13.9 per cent are to Ma and these are 81.6 per cent of the total visits to that class. Bees show the highest percentages of visits to flowers of all classes, except Pol, and to all colors, Ma 81.6, Mi 59.7, Mas 54.7, Mis 37.3, red 59.7, white 36.6, yellow 45.9. They are 22.9 per cent of the insects observed and make 43.3 per cent of the visits.

According to the general visits the long-tongued bees show a preference for Mas 19.0, for Mis 0.6. In the case of 61 flowers on which the individuals were taken as they came, they showed a gain over visits for Ma 8.9 and Mas 15.4. The short-tongued bee visits show a preference for Mis 25.2, Pol 5.6 and Mi 0.2. The individuals show a gain over visits for Mis, 33.1. So the characteristic differences between long-tongued and short-tongued bees are better indicated by counting the individuals than by counting the visits.

Literature Cited.

1. Knuth, P. Handbook of flower pollination. **1**:1-382. (1906). Transl. of Handbuch der Blütenbiologie. 1898.
2. Loew, E. Beobachtungen über den Blumenbesuch von Insekten an Freilandpflanzen des Botanischen Gartens zu Berlin. Jahrb. K. bot. Gart. Berlin. **3**:69-118, 253-9. (1-94). 1884.
3. ....Weitere Beobachtungen u. s. w. Jahrb. k. bot. Gart. Berlin. **4**:93-178. 1886.
4. Müller, H. The fertilisation of flowers. (1883). Transl. of Die Befruchtung der Blumen. 1873.
5. ....Die Alpenblumen, ihre Befruchtung durch Insekten und ihre Anpassungen an dieselben. 1881.
6. Robertson, C. Flowers and insects. I-XXII. Botanical Gazette 1889-1923.
7. ....Synopsis of Panurgidæ. Psyche **29**:159-173 1922.

A NEW GENUS OF MAYFLIES FROM THE MIOCENE OF FLORISSANT, COLORADO.

BY T. D. A. COCKERELL.

University of Colorado, Boulder, Colo.

Among some fossil insects from Florissant kindly loaned by Director J. D. Figgins of the Colorado Museum of Natural History, I find a very fine Ephemerid belonging to the Siphlonuridæ* and apparently referable to an undescribed genus. Banks, in 1907, treated *Chirotonetes* and *Ameletus* of Eaton as synonyms of *Siphlonurus*. On this broad basis the fossil might also be referred to *Siphlonurus*; but more recent authors have recognized Eaton's segregates, and from this point of view *Siphlurites* forms a sufficiently valid genus. In the description, I have followed Tillyard's revised nomenclature†, but it should be understood that Tillyard's first and second cubitus are Comstock's first and second anals (following Miss Morgan); Tillyard's media is Comstock's cubitus, and Comstock's media is considered part of the radius. In Needham's key to the genera‡, *Siphlurites* runs out on p. 25 at ff, forming a third section as follows:

fff. The intercalaries between the first and second anal veins (of Needham and Comstock) represented by a pair of veins, the first simple, the second forking, from the first anal to the wing margin, and a third vein which bends and runs a long course parallel with the first anal, emitting below about nine simple veins to the margin . . . . *Siphlurites*.

Siphlurites new genus.

Anterior wings with costa somewhat arched basally, the costal area broadened, so that its depth is 1 mm., gradually decreasing apicad; transverse veins of costal area numerous

*Tillyard writes Siphluridae, but Eaton named the type genus *Siphlonurus* in 1868, and was not at liberty to alter it to *Siphlurus* in 1871.
†Transactions New Zealand Institute 54. (1923) p. 227.
‡Bull. 86, New York State Museum (1905) pp. 23-26.

in subbasal region, forming cells which are twice as high as long, but beyond they become widely spaced, forming cells which are much longer than high; subcosta in subbasal region very close to radius, gradually diverging from it, so that near middle of wing the subcosta is equally distant from costa and radius; radial sector with four very oblique branches, the first forking a little over 6 mm. from end, and including within the forks a supplementary longitudinal vein; the second and third branches of the radial sector originate close together, but the origin of the third, though delicate, is not obsolete; the fourth, arising about 7.6 mm. from end of wing, starts downward at nearly a right angle with the sector, and then bends distad; between it and the sector are three supplementary veins, the first long, the two lower shorter; media branching about 3.7 mm. from base of wing, the fork very acute, and between the branches a long supplementary vein, and near the margin four short very delicate supplementary veins, two above and two below the main supplement; cubitus with main (upper) part strong, slightly curved subapically, emitting about five cross veins to the strongly arched second cubitus, then two long veins (the second forked) to margin, then, beyond level of end of second cubitus, a vein which curves distad travelling to the margin parallel with the first cubitus, and emitting about nine oblique veins below. Hind wings developed, but the details cannot be made out. Type the following.

Siphlurites explanatus, sp. nov.

Length from front of head to end of abdomen 21 mm.; expanse 44 mm.; length of anterior wings 21 mm., the width about middle 7.7 mm.; eyes to base of wings 1.7 mm., the prothoracic region short and broad (it is considerably longer in *Ephemera howarthi*.) Head and thorax brown; wings hyaline, with pale brown veins; a slight suggestion of mottling along costa

Miocene shales of Florissant.

Scudder described five species of Ephemerid nymphs from Florissant; so far as can be seen, they suggest the genera *Ephe-*

merella, Hexagenia, Potamanthus and *Bactis*. Two species have been described from adults. *Ephemera exsucca* Scudd. has an expanse of only 16 mm.; *E. howarthi* Ckll has three strong tails, as in true *Ephemera*. In the somewhat arched costa and broad costal area *Siphlurites* agrees with *Cronicus anomalus* (Pictet) from Baltic amber, but is is otherwise quite different.

It is worthy of note that in the Permian *Protereisma* and *Protechma* of Sellards the first cubitus emits a couple of veins at very acute angles (not curved at base as the long branch of *Siphlurites*), and these proceed distad to the margin, subparallel with the first cubitus. Thus the special feature of *Siphlurites* may be regarded as primitive. The Permian insects constitute a distinct family Protereismatidæ, having the lower wings almost or quite as large as the upper.

UTAH VARIETIES OF A ROSE ROOT GALL WASP (HYMENOPTERA)[1]

By Allan R. Hubter.

Diplolepis radicum var. utahensis (Bassett)

Rhodites Utahensis Bassett, 1890, Trans. Amer. Ent. Soc., XVII, p. 62.

Diplolepis radicum utahensis Kinsey, 1922 (in part), Ind. Univ. Studies, 53, p. 68.

Female.—Differs from the female of variety *angustior* in the following characters; Parapsidal grooves more gradually convergent toward and more separated at the scutellum; med an groove distinctly but discontinuously indicated for one half the mesonotal length; anterior parallel lines not as distinct toward the pronotum; the smooth area on the scutellum is larger, more rugose, and connected to the mesonotum by a much wider isthmus; the transverse, rugose band across the mesopleura is considerably wider and less distinct in outline; the rufous area on the abdomen, dorso-basally, is larger and lighter; the areolet is a little smaller.

Male.—Differs from the male of variety *angustior* only in varietal characters as described for the female.

Gall.—Practically the same as the gall of *angustior*.

Range.—Utah: Thistle (Weld), Price (Kinsey). Probably occurs throughout the Colorado Plateau country of parts of Utah, Colorado, New Mexico, and Arizona.

Types.—Lost.

Diplolepis radicum var. angustior var. nov.

Diplolepis radicum utahensis Kinsey, 1922 (in part), Ind. Univ. Studies, 53, p. 68.

Female.—Differs from *utahensis* in the following characters: Parapsidal grooves make an abrupt curve in, and converge more closely at the scutellum; median groove is variable, from a mere indication at the scutellum to discontinuous indications for one-third of the mesonotal length, and is less distinct; an-

[1]Contribution from the Zoological Laboratories of Indiana University No. 195 (Entomological No. 4).

terior parallel lines more distinct toward the pronotum; the smooth area on the scutellum is smaller, more distinct in outline, not so rugose, and connected to the mesonotum by a narrower isthmus; the transverse, rugose band across the mesopleura is considerably narrower and more distinct in outline; the rufous area on the abdomen, dorso-basally, is smaller and darker; the areolet is a little larger.

Male.—Differs from the male of variety *utahensis* only in varietal characters as described for the female.

Gall.—Practically the same as the gall of *utahensis.*

Range.—Utah: Provo, Brigham (Kinsey). Probably confined to more northern Utah and adjacent Idaho.

Types.—A great many females, about forty galls. Holotype female, paratype females, males, and galls at The American Museum of Natural History; paratype adults and galls at the Museum of Comparative Zoology, the U. S. National Museum, the Philadelphia Academy, Stanford University, the California Academy, and the Kinsey collection. Labelled Provo, Utah; April 18, 1920; Kinsey collector.

The variety *utahensis* is found at Price, Utah, while variety *angustior* is found at Provo; the two localities are separated by only sixty miles, but Price is a thousand feet higher in elevation. The two varieties are so closely related that they have heretofore been considered the same; the relationship is so close that they are hardly separable on any one character, but they are easily distinguished by a combination of characters. The most distinctive characters are the transverse rugose band on the mesopleura, the size of the areolet, and the smooth area and isthmus on the scutellum.

It is interesting to note that all other Cynipidæ known from Utah have two very closely related varieties in a more northern and more southern faunal area; *utahenesis* has been the only exception, but now that *angustior* has been described, the rule holds without exception. *Plana*, another variety of the same species from southeastern Oregon, is almost as closely related to *utahensis* and *angustior*.

Dr. Kinsey of the Zoology Department of Indiana University has supervised this study.

CAMBRIDGE ENTOMOLOGICAL CLUB

A regular meeting of the Club is held on the second Tuesday of each month (July, August and September excepted) at 7.45 p. m. at the Bussey Institution, Forest Hills, Boston. The Bussey Institution is one block from the Forest Hills station of both the elevated street cars and the N. Y., N. H. & H. R. R. Entomologists visiting Boston are cordially invited to attend.

PSYCHE

A JOURNAL OF ENTOMOLOGY

ESTABLISHED IN 1874

VOL. XXX DECEMBER 1923 No. 6

CONTENTS

CAMBRIDGE ENTOMOLOGICAL CLUB

PSYCHE is published bi-monthly, the issues appearing in February, April, June, August, October and December. Subscription price, per year, payable in advance: $2.00 to subscribers in the United States, Canada or Mexico; foreign postage, 15 cents extra. Single copies, 40 cents.

Cheques and remittances should be addressed to Treasurer, Cambridge Entomological Club, Bussey Institution, Forest Hills, Boston 30, Mass.

Orders for back volumes, missing numbers, notices of change of address, etc., should be sent to Cambridge Entomological Club, Bussey Institution, Forest Hills, Boston 30, Mass.

IMPORTANT NOTICE TO CONTRIBUTORS.

Manuscripts intended for publication, books intended for review, and other editorial matter, should be addressed to Professor C. T. Brues, Bussey Institution, Forest Hills, Boston 30, Mass.

Authors contributing articles over 8 printed pages in length will be required to bear a part of the extra, expense for additional pages. This expense will be that of typesetting only, which is about $2.00 per page. The actual cost of preparing cuts for all illustrations must be borne by contributors: the expense for full page plates from line drawings is approximately $5.00 each, and for full page half-tones, $7.50 each; smaller sizes in proportion.

AUTHOR'S SEPARATES.

Reprints of articles may be secured by authors, if they are ordered before, or at the time proofs are received for corrections. The cost of these will be furnished by the Editor on application.

Entered as second-class mail matter at the Post Office at Boston, Mass. Acceptance for mailing at special rate of postage provided in Section 1103, Act of October 3, 1917, authorized on June 29, 1918.

PSYCHE

VOL. XXX. DECEMBER 1923 No. 6

ANTS OF THE GENERA MYOPIAS AND ACANTHOPONERA.[1]

BY WILLIAM MORTON WHEELER.

A recent study of the Australian ants collected some years ago by Mr. A. M. Lee and myself has led me to revise the Ponerine genera Myopias and Acanthoponera, two groups of more than usual interest on account of their singular geographical distribution. The former genus was established by Roger[2] more than 60 years ago for a Ceylonese ant, *M. amblyops,* which has not been taken since, although considerable thorough collecting has been done in India and Ceylon. A second species was brought to light in New Guinea by L. Biró and described in 1901 by Emery as *M. cribriceps*[3]. A third species has now been discovered by Mr. Lea in Tasmania and is described in the sequel. The highly vestigial eyes in the workers of these ants show that they are subterranean in habit, but they must be extremely rare, since a total of only eleven specimens has been seen. Their recorded distribution is so discontinuous that we may regard them as vanishing relicts of forms very close to the direct ancestors of Trapeziopelta, a genus represented by a number of species in the East Indies and New Guinea.

The distribution of Acanthoponera is even more interesting. It comprises two species in Australia, one in New Zealand and five in the Neotropical Region, from Chile, Argentina and Brazil to Central America and Mexico. All the American species occur in the southern portion of the range and the forms in Central America and Mexico are merely small varieties or subspecies which have strayed beyond the optimum environ-

[1]Contributions from the Entomological Laboratory of the Bussey Institution, Harvard University, No. 230.

[2]Berlin. Entom. Zeitschr. 5, 1861, p. 39.

[3]Termeszetr. Fuzet. 25, 1901, p. 156.

ment. The American forms, moreover, may be readily separated into two groups, one of which, including *A. mucronata* Roger, the type of the genus, and *goeldii* Forel, have tridentate claws and long epinotal spines, while the other, including the remaining species, *carinifrons* Mayr, *dentinodis* Mayr and *dolo* Roger, have, like the Australian forms, simple claws and a merely dentate epinotum. In my opinion, the latter group should be regarded as a distinct subgenus, for which I suggest the name **Anacanthoponera** subgen. nov., with *Ponera dolo* Roger as the type.

Few groups of ants resemble Acanthoponera in having an "antarctic" distribution. Perhaps the best example is the subgenus Notomyrmex of the genus Monomorium, which is represented by a number of species in Australia, New Caledonia, Lord Howe Island, Norfolk Island, New Zealand, a few in Patagonia and Chile and, according to Emery, also a few in Madagascar and East Africa. Mann's subgenus Fulakora, a group of species of the archaic genus Stigmatomma, with approximated frontal carinæ, may also be cited in this connection because it is represented in the East Indies, Solomon Islands, New Zealand, Argentina, Chile and Southern Brazil. The Chilean ants of the genus Lasiophanes, which are closely related to those of the genus Prolasius in New Zealand and of Melophorus in Australia afford another example. I might also cite the singular little hypogæic Ponerine ants of the genus Discothyrea, of which a few species occur in the East Indies, one in New Zealand, one of a closely allied genus, Prodiscothyrea, in Australia, a species recently discovered by Bruch in Argentina, one in Kamerun, one in Columbia and one which was described by Roger in 1863 from "North America", but which has never been taken since. Apart from its occurrence in Africa, the distribution of this genus is not unlike that of Iridomyrmex, though the latter is represented by many species in Australia and is absent from New Zealand, though occurring on Norfolk Island, in the Neotropical Region and as far north as our southern states. When we consult the fossil record, however, we find that the two genera last mentioned were represented by species of Bradyponera and Iridomyrmex respectively in the Baltic amber and this suggests that they were cosmopolitan groups, possibly of northern origin, which now survive in the tropics and mainly in the southern hemisphere. I maintain, therefore, that the same explanation may account for the present peculiar and restricted distribution of Acanthoponera, Notomyrmex and Fulakora, since these, too, may have had a northern Eurasian origin during Cretaceous or early Tertiary times. Mann has recently discovered in Bolivia a species of the archaic Ponerine genus Probolomyrmex (*P. boliviensis*)[1], previously known only from a species in South Africa (*P. filiformis* Mayr). These, too, in my opinion, may be isolated survivors of a group which had its origin in the northern hemisphere rather than on an antarctic land-mass or on a land-bridge between Africa and South America.

Genus **Myopias** Roger

Myopias tasmaniensis sp. nov.

(Fig. 1.)

Worker. Length 3.8-4 mm.

Head subrectangular, as broad as long, slightly narrower behind than in front, with nearly straight sides and feebly, broadly concave posterior border. Eyes very small and flat,

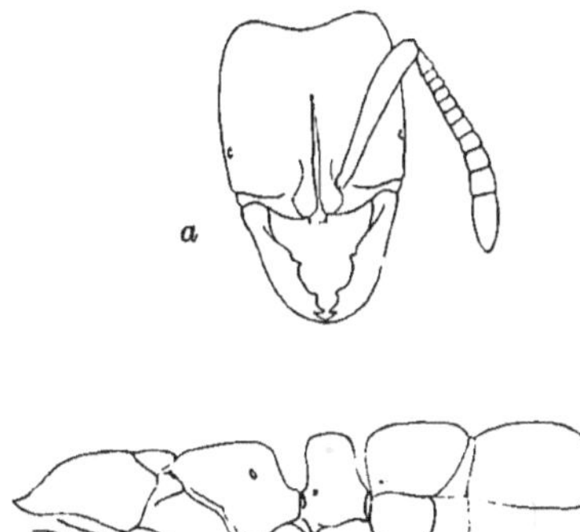

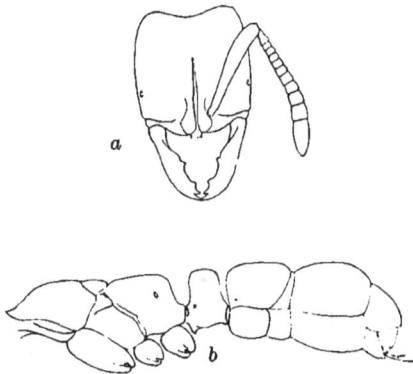

Fig. 1. *Myopias tasmaniensis* sp. nov. worker. *a*, head from above; *b*, thorax and abdomen in profile.

situated more than their own length from the posterior border of the clypeus, consisting of hardly more than 15 minute, crowded

[1]Psyche 30, 1923 p. 16, Fig. 2.

ommatidia. Mandibles long and narrow, convex and deflected, their external border straight in the middle, the apical border with four teeth (counting the terminal), the most basal small, acute and erect, near the middle of the border, the next somewhat larger and blunter and the preapical small and close to the terminal tooth. Clypeus very short, vertical, and transverse, above with a short, shelf-like, projecting, rectangular lobe immediately under the frontal carinæ. The latter with prominent, closely approximated lobes, their posterior continuations short and subparallel. Frontal groove deep and broad, extending back somewhat beyond the middle of the head. Antennal scapes reaching to within about twice the diameter of their tips from the posterior corners of the head; funiculi long, thickened distally, first joint about one and one-half times as long as broad, not as long as the three following joints together; these and the remaining joints, except the last, distinctly broader than long, the four terminal joints forming a distinct club. Thorax narrower than the head, with rather straight dorsal outline in profile, interrupted at the pronounced promesonotal and mesoëpinotal sutures; pronotum broader than long, somewhat rounded above and on the sides; mesonotum transversely elliptical, nearly twice as broad as long; epinotum subcuboidal, the base straight and distinctly longer than the abrupt declivity with which it forms a rounded rectangle, the declivity flat, not marginate on the sides or above. Petiole subcuboidal, higher and somewhat broader than long, rounded above; in dorsal view trapezoidal, narrower in front than behind, with straight sides and very feebly concave anterior and posterior borders, its ventral surface anteriorly with a small, blunt, lamellate tooth. Postpetiole broader than long, nearly half again as broad as the petiole, truncated in front and marked off by a strong constriction from the broader and more rounded first gastric segment, which is about one and one-third times as broad as long. Remaining segments very small. Sting well-developed. Legs long and rather stout; middle and hind tibiæ each with a well developed spur, the one on the hind tibiæ larger.

Very smooth and shining; mandibles with a few scattered punctures; clypeus transversely rugulose; cheeks finely punctate; upper surface of head, thorax, petiole, postpetiole and first gastric segment rather coarsely punctate, the punctures being smallest and most numerous on the head, largest and least numerous on the thorax and node and intermediate in size and density on the postpetiole and gaster. Legs rather finely and indistinctly punctulate.

Hairs yellow, sparse, erect or suberect, longest on the gaster; short, abundant and subappressed on the appendages. Pubescence long, distinct only on the dorsal surface of the head.

Deep ferruginous brown; clypeus and borders of mandibles darker; legs paler, dull brownish yellow.

Described from two specimens taken by Mr. A. M. Lea at Hobart, Tasmania.

This species seems to be very close to the two other known species of the genus. It differs from *amblyops* in possessing an additional tooth on the mandibles, from *cribriceps* in having a shorter head and petiole and smaller eyes, and from both in having a small rectangular shelf-like lobe which projects from the upper part of the clypeus immediately under and between the lobes of the frontal carinæ. This last character is of peculiar significance since a similar though longer rectangular projection is one of the peculiarities of Trapeziopelta Mayr, a genus in other respects very closely related to Myopias, as Emery has remarked. One might, indeed, go so far as to regard Trapeziopelta as a subgenus of Myopias.

Genus **Acanthoponera** Mayr

Acanthoponera (*Anacanthoponera*) *imbellis* Emery

(Fig. 2.)

Acanthoponera imbellis Emery, Ann. Soc. Ent. Belg. 39, 1895, p. 346 ☿; Gen. Insect. Ponerinæ 1911, p. 36 ☿; Forel, Ark. Zool. 9, 1915, p. 10 ☿.

The typical form of this species was originally described from Kamerunga, Queensland, but seems to be widely distributed in Australia. Forel has recorded it from Adelaide, South Australia (E. Mjöberg), and I have seen specimens taken by Mr. A. M. Lea at Port Lincoln and Gawler in the same commonwealth. Emery gives the length of the type specimen as 2.75 mm. My specimens are somewhat larger (3.2 mm.) and Forel's measured 3-3.2 mm. The petiole when viewed from above is decidedly broader than long, the postpetiole and gaster are decidedly shining, the former densely punctate, with super-

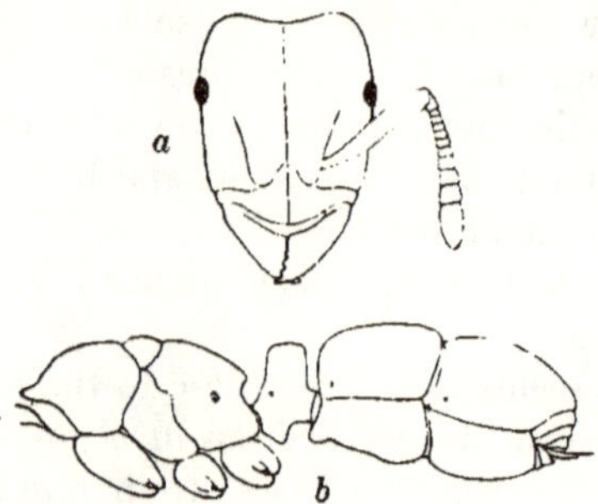

Fig. 2. *Acanthoponera* (*Anacanthoponera*) *imbellis* Emery, worker. *a*, head from above *b*, thorax and abdomen in profile.

imposed, scattered, larger punctures, or foveolæ, which have sharp anterior borders so that they are somewhat "eingestochen", to use a German expression. The color appears to be rather variable, the gaster being sometimes dark brown like the head or like both the head and thorax, sometimes paler brown with only the head dark.

Var. *hilaris* Forel.

Ectatomma (*Acanthoponera*) *imbellis* var. *hilare* Forel, Ann. Soc. Belg. 39, 1895, p. 421 ☿.

Acanthoponera imbellis var. *hilaris* Emery, Gen. Insect. Ponerinæ 1911, p. 10 ☿.

According to Forel, this variety, taken at Mackay, Queensland (Gilbert Turner), is larger than the type (3.6 mm.) and differs in sculpture as follows: "Abdomen densely punctate and subopaque. All the remainder densely and finely reticulate-punctate and opaque. Moreover, the front is coarsely longitudinally rugose, while the other portions of the head, the thorax and petiole are covered with dense, superimposed foveolæ, in part reticulate or transformed into rugæ."

A single specimen taken at Sydney, New South Wales (A. M. Lea) agrees with this description.

Var. *scabra* var. nov.

Worker. Length 2.5-3 mm.

Differing from the typical *imbellis* and the preceding variety in having the petiolar node distinctly longer in proportion to its width. The sculpture of the head, thorax and petiole is coarser and the postpetiole and base of the first gastric segment, though feebly shining, are longitudinally reticulate-rugulose. The color is dark brown, with the mandibles, antennæ and legs brownish or reddish yellow. One specimen has the postpetiole and gaster paler and more reddish than the head and thorax.

Described from three workers taken by Mr. A. M. Lea at Sydney, New South Wales.

Acanthoponera (Anacanthoponera) leæ sp. nov.

(Fig. 3.)

Worker. Length 4 mm.

Head subrectangular, a little longer than broad and very slightly narrower in front than behind, the posterior border

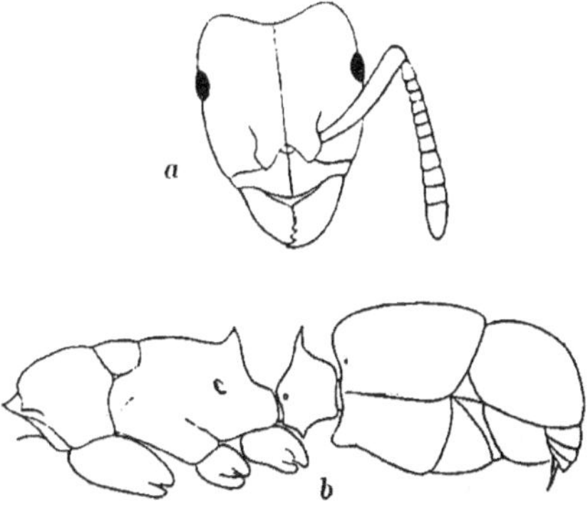

Fig. 3. *Acanthoponera (Anacanthoponera) leæ* sp. nov. worker. *a*, head, from above; *b*, thorax and abdomen in profile.

rather deeply and broadly concave, the sides feebly and evenly convex, the median longitudinal costa, or carina, extending back over the front and vertex, very pronounced. Eyes rather small, moderately convex, their anterior orbits just behind the median transverse diameter of the head. Mandibles large and broad, their external border rather straight in the middle, the terminal border with only three distinct large apical teeth, the more basal denticles appearing as mere undulations. Clypeus sharply carinate, its anterior border entire, broadly rounded and depressed; frontal area short and indistinct, with a median carina continuous with those of the clypeus and dorsal surface of the head; frontal carinæ separated as in *imbellis*, subparallel, scarcely reaching to the level of the anterior orbits, bordering a depressed area on each side for the accomodation of the antennæ. Scapes of the latter reaching somewhat beyond the eyes; funicular joints 2-7 subequal, transverse but less so than in *imbellis*, the three terminal joints forming an indistinct club, the last joint somewhat longer than the two preceding subequal joints together. Thorax in profile feebly rounded above, slightly more convex and broadest in the region of the pronotum, which is transversely subrectangular, with distinctly dentate anterior corners, the teeth being nearly as long as the width of their bases. Promesonotal suture subangular, distinct but not strongly impressed; mesoëpinotal suture obsolete. Mesonotum short, broader than long, somewhat semicircular. Epinotum with nearly straight base which is distinctly longer than the abrupt, slightly concave declivity, the lateral angles between the two surfaces forming stout, broad, rather acute and erect teeth. The declivity is longitudinally grooved in the middle but not marginate on the sides below. Petiolar node cuneate in profile, about one and one-half times as high as long, narrowed above, its summit produced in the middle as a short, stout, erect spine; seen from above the node is somewhat hexagonal, broader than long, the median transverse diameter corresponding with the narrowed, transverse summit. At the anteroventral end of the petiole there is an acute, backwardly directed tooth. Postpetiole very large, longer than broad, narrowed in front, where its anterior surface is abruptly truncated and concave, its sides convex, its anteroventral edge with a transverse tubercle. Gaster small and short, much smaller than the postpetiole, the first segment convex above, semicircular, scarcely longer than broad, enveloping the remaining segments which are very small and together form a downwardly directed cone. Sting small. Legs rather long and stout; tarsal claws simple.

Opaque; mandibles somewhat shining, finely striate and coarsely punctate, the striæ and punctures more numerous near the apical border. Clypeus finely and indistinctly punctate-rugulose. Head between and behind the frontal carinæ coarsely and divergently longitudinally rugose, with coarse punctures, or foveolæ in the interrugal spaces; sides of head with the rows of foveolæ more distinct. Thorax, petiole, postpetiole and first gastric segment coarsely rugose and foveolate, the rugæ vermiculate and reticulate on the pronotum and petiole, longitudinal on the mesoëpinotum, including the epinotal declivity, mesopleuræ, postpetiole and first gastric segment, most sharply on the two latter regions. Terminal gastric segments smoother and somewhat shining; scapes and legs subopaque, densely punctate.

Hairs yellow, fine, uneven, rather abundant and rather short, erect or suberect on the body; the appendages covered with abundant, fine, rather appressed hairs with fewer, interspersed, long, erect hairs.

Deep castaneous brown; mandibles, scapes, tip of gaster and legs, excluding the coxæ, yellowish brown; apical borders of mandibles and median carina of head black.

Described from two specimens taken by Mr. A. M. Lea in the National Park, near Sydney, New South Wales.

This very distinct species is interesting because, unlike the other known Australasian species of the genus, it approaches the Neotropical *mucronata* in the armature of the petiole.

Acanthoponera (*Anacanthoponera*) *brouni* Forel

Acanthoponera brownii Forel, Mitteil. Schweiz. Ent. Zeitschr. 8, 1892, p. 330 ☿; Emery, Gen. Insect. Ponerinæ 1911, p. 36 ☿.
Acanthoponera brounii Forel, Trans. New Zealand Inst. 37, 1904, p. 353 ☿.

This species was described from specimens taken by Major Thos. Broun at Drury, near Auckland, New Zealand. Forel originally spelled the gentleman's name "Brown" and named the species "brownii" but corrected the error in 1904. Emery in the "Genera Insectorum" questions the advisability of this procedure. I can only record my conviction that such obvious taxonomic blunders should be corrected and not propagated indefinitely in the literature in a spirit of silly pedantry.

Subsp. *kirki* subsp. nov.

(Fig. 4.)

Worker. Length 2.3-3 mm.

Smaller than the typical form of the species, which measures 3.2-3.5 mm. The head is not coarsely but very finely and indistinctly rugulose. The declivity of the epinotum is strongly concave, its lateral marginations enlarged above to form blunt but distinct teeth. The color differs from that of the type as

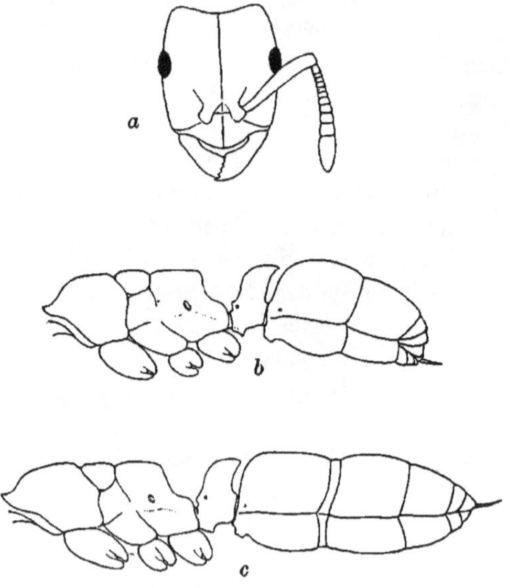

Fig 4. *Acanthoponera* (*Anacanthoponera*) *brouni* Forel subsp. ***kirki*** **subsp. nov.** *a*, **head** of worker from above; *b*, thorax and abdomen of same in profile; *c*, thorax and abdomen of ergatomorphic female in profile.

follows; Body ferruginous red; mandibles, clypeus, mesonotum and gaster brownish yellow; dorsal surface of epinotum, the petiole and posterior borders of postpetiole and gastric segments dark brown; coxæ and legs pale yellow, knees and tarsi reddish.

Female. Length 3.2 mm.

Wingless and ergatomorphic, differing from the worker only in its slightly larger size, in possessing small ocelli, in having the marginations of the epinotal declivity more rounded and less dentate above and in the larger abdomen, the postpetiole and first gastric segment especially being more voluminous. The color of the body is also different, the pronotum being darker then the meso- and epinotum, the petiole, postpetiole and gaster reddish brown like the pronotum, with the posterior borders of the segments brownish yellow. The anterior is somewhat paler than the posterior half ot the head.

Described from numerous workers and a single female which I took Sept. 5, 1914 from a single colony, comprising about 100 individuals in the Waitakari Forest, near Auckland, New Zealand. The ants were nesting under a dead branch of one of the huge kaori trees (*Agathis australis*), which was lying on an exposed root of the tree from which it had fallen. When first disturbed the workers were quite active but on being touched curled up and "feigned death". Similar behavior was observed by Hetschko in the Brazilian *A. dentinodis*, according to Mayr. The single female, described above, was evidently the mother queen of the colony, which had a number of small larvæ. These resembled the larvæ of Ectatomma in being smooth, that is nontuberculate, and in being covered with dense, soft hairs. The subspecies is dedicated to Prof. H. B. Kirk of Victoria University, Wellington, the memory of whose kindness during my sojourn in New Zealand I shall always cherish.

The occurence of a single ergatomorphic female as the mother queen of *kirki* is of interest, because so few females of Acanthoponera have been taken, and because in the Neotropical *dentinodis*, *dolo* and *mucronata* all the recorded individuals were of the typical winged type. But Emery in 1906 found two individuals like the workers but with more voluminous abdomens among specimens of the Chilean *carinifrons*. One of these, with the larger abdomen, was paler in color than the workers, with higher petiole and more pubescent legs and gaster. He regarded this individual as an ergatoid female and the other as a form transitional to the normal worker. That he was correct in his assumption is shown by the foregoing observations on *kirki*. Whether such ergatomorphic females ever co-exist with winged forms in the same species or colony will have to be determined by future observations.

I insert here a list of the American species and varieties of Acanthoponera with their synonymy and known distribution:

Acanthoponera (*Anacanthoponera*) *carinifrons* (Mayr)

Heteroponera carinifrons Mayr, Verh. zool. bot. Ges. Wien 37, 1887, p. 533 ♀; Dalla Torre, Cat. Hymen. 7, 1893, p. 43 ☿.

Acanthoponera carinifrons Emery, Ann. Soc. Ent. Belg. 39, 1895, p. 347 ☿; Bull. Soc. Ent. Ital. 37, 1906, p. 112 ☿ ♀; Gen. Insect. Ponerinæ 1911, p. 36 ♀ ♀.

Type locality: Valdivia, Chile.

Chile: Coipué, San Vicente (F. Silvestri); Corral (R. Thaxter, my collection).

Acanthoponera (*Anacanthoponera*) *dentinodis* Mayr.

Ectatomma (*Acanthoponera*) *dentinode* Mayr, Verh. zool. bot. Ges. Wien 37, 1887, p. 541 ☿ ♀ ♂; Emery, Bull. Soc. Ent. Ital. 26, 1894, p. 143, 144 ☿.

Ectatomma dentinode Dalla Torre, Cat. Hymen. 7, 1893, p. 24 ☿ ♀ ♂.

Acanthoponera dentinodis Emery, Gen. Insect. Ponerinæ 1911, 0p. 36, ☿ ♀ ♂.

Type locality: Santa Catharina, Brazil (Hetschko).

Bolivia (L. Balzan); Brazil: Novo Friburgo.

Var. *inermis* Emery.

Ectatomma (*Acanthoponera*) *dentinode* var. *inerme* Emery, Bull. Soc. Ent. Ital. 26, 1894, p. 143 ♀.

Acanthoponera dentinodis var. *inermis* Emery, Gen. Insect. Ponerinæ 1911, p. 36 ♀.
Type locality: Rio de Janeiro, Brazil.

Var. *panamensis* Forel.

Ectatomma (*Acanthoponera*) *dentinode* Forel var. *panamense* Forel, Biol. Centr. Amer. Hymen. 3, 1899-1900, p. 9 ☿.
Acanthoponera dentinodis var. *panamensis* Emery, Gen. Insect. Ponerinæ 1911, p. 36 ☿.
Type locality: Volcan de Chiriqui, 3000 ft., Panama (Champion).

Acanthoponera (*Anacanthoponera*) *dolo* (Roger).

Ponera dolo Roger, Berlin. Ent. Zeitschr. 4, 1860, p. 293 ☿ ♀.
Ectatomma (*Acanthoponera*) *dolo* Mayr, Verh. zool. bot. Ges. Wien 12, 1862, p. 733; *ibid.* 37, 1887, p. 540.
Ectatomma dolo Dalla Torre, Cat. Hymen. 7, 1893, p. 24 ☿.
Acanthoponera dolo Emery, Bull. Soc. Ent. Ital. 37, 1906, p. 112 ☿; Forel Verh. zool. bot. Ges. Wien 1908, p. 342 ☿; Emery, Gen. Insect. Ponerinæ 1911, p. 36 ☿ ♀; Forel, Ann. Soc. Ent. Belg. 56, 1912, p. 34 ☿; Bruch, Revist. Mus. La Plata 19, 1914, p. 214 ☿ ♀; Gallardo, An. Mus. Nac. Hist. Nat. Buenos Aires 30, 1918, p. 18 ☿ ♀; Luederwaldt, Notas Myrmecologicas, São Paulo, 1918, p. 6.
Type locality: Brazil (Schaum and von Olfers).
Brazil: Bella Vista, Paraná (F. Silvestri); São Paulo (von Ihering); Prov. Rio Janeiro (Goeldi); Ilha de S. Sebastião, Alto da Serra, Salto Grande, Ituverava, São Paulo (H. Luederwaldt).
Argentina: Puerto Piray, Misiones (F. Silvestri).

Var. *aurea* Forel.

Acanthoponera dolo var. *aurea* Forel, Bull. Soc. Vaud. Sc. Nat. 49, 1913, p. 203 ☿ ♂; Bruch, Revist, Mus. La Plata 19, 1914, p. 214 ☿; Gallardo, An. Mus. Nac. Hist. Nat. Buenos Aires 30, 1918, p. 20 ☿ ♂. Fig. 1.
Type locality: Misiones, Argentina (C. Bruch).

Var. *schwebeli* Luederwaldt.

Acanthoponera dolo var. *schwebeli* Luederwaldt, Revist. Mus. Paul. 1918, p. 51 ☿; German transl. São Paulo 1920, p. 3 ☿; Notas Myrmecologicas, São Paulo 1918, p. 6.
Type locality: Alto da Serra, São Paulo, Brazil (E. Schwebel)

Acanthoponera goeldii Forel.

Acanthoponera goeldii Forel, Ann. Soc. Ent. Belg. 56, 1912, p. 34 ☿.
Type locality: Prov. Espiritu Santo, Brazil (Goeldi).

Subsp. *schwarzi* subsp. nov.

(Fig. 5.)

Worker. Length 4.5 mm.

Agreeing well with Forel's description of the type but smaller, with the petiolar spine as long as the epinotal spines and apparently directed somewhat more upward. The epinotal spines diverge and their downward deflection is feeble. There is no constriction between the postpetiole and gaster. The color seems to be paler, being brownish yellow, the postpetiole and

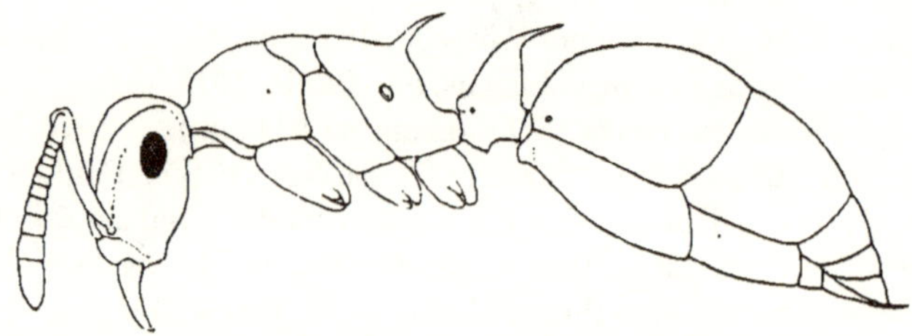

Fig. 5. *Acanthoponera goeldii* subsp. *schwarzi* subsp. nov. Worker, lateral aspect.

gaster lighter than the head and thorax (darker in the typical *goeldii*), as pale as the legs, only the overlapping posterior borders of the segments brown. Judging from the description of *goeldii*, the sculpture of the head, thorax and petiole is finer and more indistinct and the postpetiole and gaster are not aciculate, but very finely and superficially punctulate. Pubescence on these latter regions conspicuously long. The frontal carinæ with their accompanying scrobes extend to the posterior corners of the head and there curve downward and forward to terminate under the eyes, as in the typical *goeldii*.

Described from a single specimen found running on a cacao tree at Trece Aguas, Alta Vera Paz, Guatemala by Messrs. E. A. Schwarz and H. S. Barber.

This may be a distinct species, but as I have seen no specimens of the typical *goeldii*, with the description of which it agrees in quite a number of characters, it may stand provisionally as a subspecies.

Acanthoponera mucronata (Roger).

Ponera mucronata Roger, Berlin. Ent. Zeitschr. 4, 1860, p. 299 ☿ ♀.

Ectatomma (Acanthoponera) mucronatum Mayr. Verh. zool. bot. Ges. Wien 12, 1862. p. 962; *ibid.* 37, 1887, p. 540; Emery, Bull. Soc. Ent. Ital. 26, 1894, p. 143 ♀; Forel, Biol. Centr. Amer. Hymen. 3, 1899-1900, p. 9 ☿ ♀.

Ectatomma mucronatum Dalla Torre, Cat. Hymen. 7, 1893, p. 25 ☿ ♀.

Acanthoponera mucronata Emery, Gen. Insect. Ponerinæ 1911, p. 36 ☿ ♀. Pl. 2, Fig. 2; Forel, Ann. Soc. Ent. Belg. 56, 1912, p. 34 ☿; Luederwaldt, Notas Myrmecologicas, São Paulo 1918, p. 6. Type locality: Brazil (von Olfers).

Brazil: Matto do Governo, São Paulo (H. Luederwaldt); Corcovado, near Rio de Janeiro (A. Müller); Matto Grosso.

Var. *minor* Forel.

Ectatomma (Acanthoponera) mucronatum var. *minor* Forel, Biol. Centr. Amer. Hymen. 3, 1899-1900, p. 9 ☿.

Acanthoponera mucronata var. *minor* Emery, Bull. Soc. Ent. Ital. 28, 1896, p. 33 ☿; Gen. Insect. Ponerinæ 1911, p. 36 ☿. Type locality: Teapa en Tabasco, Mexico (H. H. Smith). Costa Rica: Suerre (A. Alfaro).

Var. *wagneri* Santschi.

Acanthoponera mucronata var. *wagneri* Santschi, Bull. Soc. Vaud Sc. Nat. 54, 1921, p. 84 ☿.

Type locality: Banderas, 55 km. north of Icaño, Chaco de Santiago del Estero, Argentina (E. R. Wagner).

The following key may serve for the identification of the workers of the various forms of Acanthoponera mentioned in this paper:

1. Claws tridentate; epinotum armed with spines; petiole terminating above and behind in a spine; constriction between postpetiole and gaster feeble or absent (subgen. *Acanthoponera* sens. str.) 2
   Claws simple: epinotum at most dentate or subdentate; petiole (except in *A. leæ*) unarmed or merely with a median tooth or projection behind; constriction between postpetiole and gaster well-developed. (subgen. *Anacanthoponera* subgen. nov.) ....6.
2. Frontal carinæ and adjacent scrobes extending around the posterior corners of the head and terminating under the eyes; funicular joints 2-5 at least twice as broad as long; epinotal spines curved downward..............3.
   Frontal carinæ and scrobes terminating at posterior corners of head; scapes more slender, funicular joints 2-5 somewhat broader than long...........................4.
3. Petiolar spine shorter than the epinotal spines; constriction between postpetiole and first gastric segment distinct; these segments aciculate, subopaque. Length 4.9-5 mm. (Brazil)............................... *goeldii* Forel.
   Petiolar spine as long as the epinotal spines; constriction between postpetiole and first gastric segment absent; these segments shining, finely punctate. Length 4.5 mm. (Guatemala)................subsp. *schwarzi* subsp. nov.
4. Epinotal spines curved inwards. Length 8 mm.; female 10 mm. Postpetiole and first gastric segment punctate-rugulose, subopaque. (Brazil).....*mucronata* (Roger.)
   Length 6 mm. or less.............................5.

5. Anterior corners of pronotum angular; epinotal spines straight and divergent; postpetiole and gaster shining and sparsely punctate. Length 6 mm. (Argentina). var. *wagneri* Santschi.
   Anterior corners of pronotum more rounded; petiolar spine somewhat more erect. Length 5.3mm. (Mexico). var. *minor* Forel.
6. Australasian species; dark brown......................7.
   Neotropical species; black, brownish yellow, or brownish red.. ....12.
7. Petiole armed with an erect spine above; anterior corners of pronotum dentate. Length 4 mm. (New South Wales). *leæ* sp. nov.
   Petiole unarmed, anterior corners of pronotum rounded. Length less than 4 mm............................8.
8. Petiolar node concave behind, the posterior border of its summit distinctly produced backwards...............9.
   Petiolar node truncated behind, its posterior border not produced......................................10.
9. Larger (3.2-3.5 mm.); head coarsely rugose; epinotum scarcely dentate (New Zealand).......*brouni* Forel.
   Smaller (2.3-3 mm.); head finely and distinctly rugose; epinotum more distinctly dentate; legs paler. (New Zealand)...................subsp. *kirki* subsp. nov.
10. Front of head rather finely rugose; postpetiole and gaster shining, punctate and sparsely foveolate. Length 2.75-3.2 mm. (Queensland; South Australia).*imbellis* Emery.
   Front of head more coarsely rugose; postpetiole and gaster subopaque....................................11.
11. Postpetiole and gaster densely punctate. Length 3.6 mm. (Queensland; South Australia)....var. *hilaris* Forel.
   Postpetiole and first gastric segment longitudinally reticulate-rugose. Stature smaller (2.5-3mm.). (New South Wales)........................var. *scabra* var. nov.
12. Black; petiole without a distinct tooth on its posterior border. Length 3.3-3.7 mm. (Chile)..*carinifrons* Mayr.
   Brownish yellow or brownish red; petiole usually armed with a distinct tooth or projection.....................13.

13. Frontal carinæ as long as the antennal scapes...........14.
Frontal carinæ much shorter, reaching only to the level of of the eyes...................................16.
14. Sculpture coarse. Length 3-4.2 mm. (Brazil, Bolivia), ...*dentinodis* Mayr.
Sculpture finer...................................15.
15. Petiolar tooth reduced to a mere convexity (Brazil). var. *inermis* Emery.
Petiolar tooth distinct; pubescence more abundant; color deeper. (Panama)..............var. *panamensis* Forel.
16. Teeth of epinotum and petiole distinct..................17.
Teeth of epinotum and petiole absent. (Brazil)............. *dolo* var. *schwebeli* Luederwaldt.
17. Larger (5-5.5 mm.); anterior surface of petiolar node more rounded; legs with numerous suberect hairs (Brazil, Argentina)..............................*dolo* Roger.
Smaller (4.5) mm.; anterior surface of petiolar node more angular in profile above; thorax less convex; legs only with appressed or subappressed hairs; pubescence more brilliant and golden (Argentina).....var. *aurea* Forel.

NOTES ON THE EGG-EATING HABIT OF BUMBLEBEES.[1]

By O. E. Plath,

College of Liberal Arts, Boston University.

Among the older treatises on the biology of bumblebees, that of the Swiss biologist Huber (1802) occupies a preëminent position, partly because it is more comprehensive than those of earlier workers, but chiefly on account of the many new observations which are described by the author. Among other things, Huber (pp. 259-260) relates that, while engaged in egg-laying, the bumblebee queen is frequently molested by the workers who try to steal the newly-laid eggs in order to "drink the milky juice", and that the queen repels such offenders with great fury. About eighty years later, Huber's (1802) account was confirmed by the well-known Austrian bumblebee student Hoffer (1882-83), and a few years later also by Härter (1890, pp. 62-65). Hoffer (I, pp. 12-14) describes this interesting phase in the life-history of the bumblebee colony as follows: "While engaged in egg-laying, the queen usually is severely molested by the workers and the so-called small queens (and if she be one of the latter, even by the old queen), while the males, although coming into close proximity, do not cause the slightest trouble. In the case of *B. lapidarius*, I frequently observed small queens, or also common workers, force their heads between the cell-wall and the dorsal side of the abdomen of the egg-laying individual in the attempt to snatch the freshly-laid eggs from the cell******, an endeavor in which they frequently succeeded to the great vexation of the egg-laying queen.*******

"The proper number of eggs having been laid, the queen quickly withdraws her abdomen from the cell, and turning about quickly, first of all drives away the most obtrusive workers and other females, and closes the cell with wax*******; if the remaining individuals approach too close, she quickly makes an example by seizing the boldest individual with her legs and mandibles and engaging in a rough and tumble fight with her for a few moments, during which both individuals sometimes tumble

[1]Contributions from the Entomological Laboratory of the Bussey Institution, Harvard University. No. 232.

to the floor over the other members of the colony. She then leaves the individual which has been chastized, and frequently severely bitten in this manner, and quickly returns to the cell to protect it against the onslaughts of others; occasionally, however, she is already too late, for some of the more active individuals have meanwhile opened it [the cell], and have taken out several eggs and devoured them.

"Punishment is almost always meted out only with the legs and mandibles, and the [chastized] individual, conscious of her guilt, does not even attempt to defend herself, all of her efforts being directed toward a hasty escape. This punishment sometimes is so severe that the poor creature is seriously wounded or even killed.*****.

"When, after such interruptions, the egg-laying queen has again returned to the cell,******she opens the latter with her mandibles and lays more eggs******, molested in the same manner as before*****; egg-laying completed, she remains near the newly-laid eggs for several hours. *******

"The attacks of the other individuals become less and less frequent, and finally cease altogether; and these same little insects which previously tried their very best to destroy the newly-laid eggs, now become attentive guardians and devoted nurses of their embryo brothers and sisters; they keep them warm and provide with tender solicitude for their nourishment."

Some twenty years after the publication of this description, the Russian psycho-biologist Wagner (1907) published a comprehensive treatise on bumblebees, in which he denies the correctness of Hoffer's (1882-83) observation, because Wagner (p. 90) found that whenever he opened an egg-cell in one of his bumblebee colonies, the workers invariably repaired the damage without molesting the eggs[2]. Only once did Wagner (pp. 90; 111-112)

[2]In regard to these experiments of Wagner (p. 90), it may be stated that more than a century before it was discovered by Huber (1802) that bumblebee workers seldom show a desire to rob eggs after the latter are a day old. Huber (p. 260) says: "It seems that the old eggs are less sought after by the workers than those which are newly-laid; indeed I have seldom seen workers attack them the second day.

"I once tried to offer them old eggs just as they were attacking the fresh ones; they carefully closed up the first without attempting to eat them."

It seems probable therefore that the eggs which Wagner (p. 90) used in his experiments were not newly-laid eggs.

observe that an egg was sucked dry by a worker, but he believes that this was entirely due to the fact that the egg was accidentally injured, and that the worker, after having tasted the sweet juice, found the latter suitable as food. "If", says Wagner (p. 88), "this affair [the fight for the eggs] took place in the manner described by the author, bumblebee colonies could never become as populous as they actually are, since the eggs would be inevitably destroyed by one of the workers as soon as the queen takes up the pursuit of other obtrusive workers; this [the destruction of the eggs] naturally takes considerably less time than is required for a rough and tumble fight****, and for rolling about on the floor******. During such encounters not only one, but five 'batches of eggs' can be despoiled." Wagner (pp. 88-89) therefore comes to the conclusion that Hoffer (1882-83) permitted himself to be deceived by the usual excitement among the members of a bumblebee colony when the latter is exposed to light.

Opposed to this negative evidence of Wagner (1907), we have the further positive evidence of Sladen (1912, pp. 51-52) who states that this fight for the eggs may be witnessed in the case of *Bremus (Bombus) lapidarius* and *Bremus terrestris* at the time the male and queen eggs are laid[3], a statement which, as I have shown recently (1922a, p. 28), also applies to one—if not all—of our American species.

We now come to the more difficult task of interpreting this race-suicidal habit of bumblebees. After describing this unnatural (from the human standpoint) practice of bumblebee society with considerable detail, Huber (pp. 260-261) gives way to the following reflexions: "What is to be thought of Nature, when she seems to give to insects the faculty of destroying their own species, when she permits hivebees to kill their males, and gives bumblebees the right and the desire to devour the newly-laid eggs?

[3]That "the fight for the eggs" probably occurs only at this period of the life-history of bumblebee colonies, is corroborated by my own observations (1922a, p. 28), and partly also by these of Harter (1890) and Lindhard (1912). Although I had about fifty incipient bumblebee colonies under close observation during the summers of 1922 (cf. 1923) and 1923, I failed to find any trace of such habit in the colonies during this period of their development.

"Would it not seem natural to conclude that she wishes to bring about total destruction? However, the species are conserved, the colonies multiply, the laws are not changed; on the contrary, it seems that is it by the sacrifice of a few that the conservation of the species is assured. Special observations show us that the hivebees only kill their males when the latter have become useless to their colony; they [the males] would consume a large quantity of provisions which the bees need for nourishment during the winter; and Nature prefers the conservation of the industrious ones to that of the males which no longer render any service after the time of reproduction.

"As for the pillage of the eggs of bumblebees, one must seek the cause further.

"It doesn't seem of any usefulness to the colony itself; for the eggs which are subject to the gluttony of the workers are as much the eggs of the workers as eggs of males and females.

"But perhaps the Author of nature wished to diminish the number of 'mellivores' in that way.

"The bumblebees are the largest insects that feed on honey; and if their number trebled or quadrupled, other insects would not find any nourishment, and perhaps their species would be destroyed.

"This argument will have more force, if we notice with what care Nature has put limits on too great a population of bumblebees. These insects have several kinds of enemies; among others a pseudomoth and a big white caterpillar which feed on their wax, their pupæ, and sometimes themselves; they are even burdened with a numerous family of lice which attach themselves to their thorax, and which they carry off with them in the air."

Although describing the egg-eating habit of bumblebees in great detail, Hoffer (1882-83) offers no explanation of this habit. However, a few years later, the well-known French bee student Pérez (1889), who was much interested in the observations of Hoffer (1882-83), ventured to discuss this interesting question. After quoting a large part of Hoffer's (I, pp. 12-14) description, Pérez (p. 110 ff.) goes on to say: "But this return to better feelings [on the part of the workers] cannot make us forget the wildness of the instinct which carried them away at a certain instant. That is one of the most astonishing habits among those which we owe to the observations of Hoffer, and one of the most inexplicable which the biology of bumblebees presents. That the egg-laying queen energetically defends her offspring, is such an ordinary and natural act that it cannot surprise us. As for the acquired instinct [of destroying the eggs], that is the natural consequence of the momentary cannibalism of the disappeared ones [instincts] when the indifferent mother abandoned her eggs to the voracity of her first-born. But why this fratricidal instinct, this passing madness, which for an instant interrupts and somewhat mars the upright and honest life of bumblebees? Indeed, in the case of the hivebee, we sometimes see the workers destroy, and without doubt also devour the eggs. But that only happens at a time when honey is abundant in the flowers, when the care of storing up as many provisions as possible, obliges them to sacrifice these objects of such tender solicitude ***. Here [in the case of bumblebees] the guilty ones have no such excuse. We are actually confronted with a case of plain gluttony. A freshly-laid egg is undoubtedly a delicacy which gives off an irresistable fragrance. That is perhaps all that we need to see in this habit; an imperfection of the social instinct which selection has not succeeded in correcting. The necessity of restricting too great a multiplication of the colony, cannot be entertained for a moment [as a possible explanation]. Here, as in the case of the hivebee, and elsewhere, a large population means riches and power. And if nature wished to moderate the increase, she had—without speaking of parasites—a much more simple and less savage means; that of restricting*****the number of eggs in the ovaries of the queen.

"That is not all. If we suppose that a restriction in the number of eggs is advantageous—which in some way would justify the fratricidal instinct of the workers—, of what use is the instinct of the mother which impels her to defend her eggs, an instinct which is diametrically opposed to the first? Why two instincts, not only contrary, but even contradictory? And if we accept that the voracity of the workers requires a corrective that the maternal instinct of the queen be from that time useful to the species, we must agree that its adaptation is very defective. It would be better that the mother, less impetuous, would not leave the cell for an instant and would not engage in a fight with the agressors. Not a single egg would be lost, and the covetousness of the evil-intentioned ones would not be satisfied. How are we to unravel this chaos? I give it up, as far as I am concerned. We delude ourselves, I believe, in wishing to seek perfection everywhere in nature, and under all conditions. Let us recognize that all is not for the best in the realm of the bumblebees anymore than in other realms."

Twenty-three years after the publication of this rather pessimistic speculation of Pérez (1889), another explanation was suggested by the late F. W. L. Sladen (1912).

After having given a detailed description of this strange habit of bumblebees in the first part (pp. 51-52) of his admirable treatise on bumblebees, Sladen (p. 257) says: "I think that the strange race-suicidal habit the *lapidarius* workers have of attempting to devour their mother's new-laid eggs is associated with the parasitism of *Psithyrus*. It is natural to suppose that workers that attempt to devour the eggs of their *Psithyrus* step-mother perpetuate their egg-devouring instinct through their sons that they sometimes succeed in rearing. In support of this view it is interesting to note that in nests of *B. latreillellus*, a species that is not preyed upon by any species of *Psithyrus*, I have never seen the queen's eggs molested by the workers."

As I have already pointed out elsewhere (1922a, p. 28), this explanation does not seem very plausible. It is a well-known fact that ants, even those belonging to species which are not molested by parasitic ants, frequently eat their own eggs (cf. Wheeler, 1910, p. 332). Moreover, I have frequently seen the workers of *Bremus fervidus* eat their mothers' eggs, and this species (cf. Plath, 1922b) probably does not suffer any species of *Psithyrus* to breed in its nests, a view which is supported by a large number of records (10 by Putnam (1864), "a large number" by Franklin (1912-13), and 33 by the writer) of *fervidus* nests, none of which were victimized by a Psithyrus.

In the same year in which Sladen (1912) published his work, another explanation was offered by the Danish biologist

Lindhard (1912). After quoting a part of Hoffer's (1882-83) description and giving a brief resume of Pérez' (1889) explanation, Lindhard (pp. 347-349) describes his own observations as follows:

"The *lapidarius* nest which is shown in Fig. 4 was without any wax covering or any other roof during the warm weather from the 10, to the 20-22, of August. When the lid of the box was opened and a glass plate removed, one could see all that took place in the nest. The bees did not let themselves be disturbed by the light[4]. Each evening, from about 4 o'clock until 7, egg-laying could be observed. Besides the old queen, as a rule, 2-4 large workers laid eggs, each one in her low, poorly-formed wax-cell. Generally there were 2-3 such small pots in use at the same time*****. The egg-laying workers were very uneasy, but did not bother one another very much, and only seemed to be shoving each other about in order to get a chance to lay eggs. If one succeeded in shoving another away from the cell, she, as a rule, took the other one's place. They [the workers] could also be seen shoving the queen about while she was engaged in egg-laying, but I did not see any worker try to take her eggs. Once she ran from one cell to another without closing the eggs, but a small worker went over at once and closed the cell without touching an egg. The queen however seemed nervous and jealous when one of the small females [workers] tried to lay eggs near her. I saw her one day shove a female [worker] away from a cell, carefully examine the eggs in the cell throw out three of them, bite the fourth one to pieces, and, after having chewed it together with a little pollen, lay it on top of a cell of a queen larva. The three other eggs were turned over and examined by two small workers and were dragged away.

"That was another explanation! Those were the unfertilized eggs which were used as food for the young queen larvæ.

"In the bumblebee colony the army of workers comes first[5], in constantly increasing numbers, the individuals of each new batch being larger than those of the preceding one. The last

[4]This contradicts one of Wagner's (1907, pp. 88-89) assertions to which reference was made in the earlier part of this paper.

[5]This, as I have shown recently (1923, p. 332), is not always the case.

large workers or small queens in several species approach the old queen in size, and more or less of them lay eggs which are normally unfertilized. After these come the males, frequently in a large, homogeneous batch; but after this, the production of males in nests with a strong queen is very small. The young queens come forth 6-10 days after the males, and the production of queens continues as long as the old queen and the workers are in full strength, even if there are produced at the same time some workers and males. The number of large, egg-laying workers in a strong colony is now quite considerable. They lay only male eggs, and if all their eggs hatched, the number of males would be steadily increasing and would be many times as large as the number of young queens. But this is not the case; so there must therefore be some other use for these eggs, and, it seems, they must be used for food, and only those larvæ which receive such an extra albumen-rich food, become queens.

"If this theory is correct, *Bombus* and *Psithyrus* species are more closely related to each other than is generally believed. *Psithyrus* is accused of feeding its larvæ with the eggs of bumblebees and all of its own fertilized eggs become queens."

This explanation, in my opinion, seems to be the most plausible, and is very suggestive. If Lindhard's (1912) hypothesis is correct, we have here a similar state of affairs as in the case of certain ants (cf. Wheeler, 1910, p. 332) where the destruction of eggs insures the preservation of the species.

In this connection a few words may be said in regard to the food of hivebee larvæ. Dr. E. F. Phillips (1921, p. 111) has the following to say on this subject: "The feeding of the larvæ is one of the most ardently disputed questions in bee activity. The chief controversy arises over the source of the food, some authors claiming that it is a secretion of glands, while others maintain that it is regurgitated from the ventriculus." It seems that none of the investigators whom Dr. Phillips (pp. 111-116) mentions, have considered the possibility that the so-called royal jelly with which hivebees feed their queen larvæ may, at least in part, consist of malaxated eggs[c], a surmise which is

[c]That hivebees sometimes destroy eggs is asserted by Pérez (1899) in one of the preceding extracts.

further suggested by the similarity in color between this food-paste of hivebees and their eggs.

LITERATURE CITED.

Franklin, H. J. 1912-13. The Bombidæ of the New World. Trans. Amer. Ent. Soc., Vol. 38, pp. 177-486, Vol. 39, pp. 73-200, pls. 1-22.

Härter, R. 1890. Biologische Beobachtungen an Hummeln. 27. Bericht Oberhess. Gesellsch. Natur—u. Heilkunde, pp. 59-75.

Hoffer, E. 1882-83. Die Hummeln Steiermarks. Lebensgeschichte und Beschreibung derselben. Leuschner & Lubensky, Graz.

Huber, P. 1802. Observations on several Species of the Genus Apis, known by the Name of Humble-bees, and called Bombinatrices by Linnæus. Trans. Linn. Soc. London, Vol. 6, pp. 214-298, pls. 25-27.

Lindhard, E. 1912. Humlebien som Husdyr. Spredte Træk of nogle danske Humlebiarters Biologi. Tidsskr. Landbrugets Planteavl, Vol. 19, pp. 335-352, 4 figs.

Pérez, J. 1899. Les Abeilles. Paris (After Wagner).

Phillips, E. F. 1921. Beekeeping. The Macmillian Company, New York.

Plath, O. E. 1922a. Notes on Psithyrus, With Records of Two New American Hosts. Biol. Bull., Vol. 43, pp. 23-44, pl. 1.

1922b. A Unique Method of Defense of *Bremus* (*Bombus*) *fervidus* Fabricius. Psyche, Vol. 29, pp. 180-187.

1923. Breeding Experiments With Confined *Bremus* (*Bombus*) Queens. Biol. Bull., Vol. 45, pp. 325-341.

Putnam, F. W. 1864. Notes on the Habits of Some Species of Humble Bees. Proc. Essex Inst., Salem, Mass., Vol. 4, pp. 98-105.

Sladen, F. W. L. 1912. The Humble-bee, Its Life-History and how to Domesticate it. Macmillan & Co., London.

Wagner, W. 1907. Psycho-biologische Untersuchungen an Hummeln mit Bezugnahme auf die Frage der Geselligkeit im Tierreiche. Zoologica, Vol. 19, pp. 1-239, 1 pl., 136 figs.

Wheeler, W. M. 1910. Ants, their Structure, Development, and Behavior. Columbia University Press.

NOTES ON THE CAPE COD BROOD OF PERIODICAL CICADA DURING 1923.

By Donald S. Lacroix.

Massachusetts Agricultural Experiment Station.

The Cape Cod brood of *Tibicen septendecim* L. has been one watched with great interest since the early colonial days of Massachusetts, and it was during those days that it first came to the attention of the colonists who were then settling in and around Plymouth.

Early this year (1923) Dr. H. T. Fernald of the Massachusetts Agricultural College called my attention to the fact that the Periodical Cicada was due to appear on the Cape this season, and he asked me to observe the brood, to get some idea of its range and abundance.

The first record I obtained was on June 13th when Dr. H. J. Franklin of the Cranberry Experiment Station at East Wareham, gave me several specimens of *T. septendecim* which had been given to him the day before. The gentleman who brought them in said that he found them in abundance near Pocasset, Mass., in the town of Bourne.

On June 15th I went to that territory and struck into the woods for a distance of a half mile when I came into the infested area. This was one mile east of Monument Beach (a part of Bourne). It may be interesting to note at this point that part of this territory had been burned over by a tremendous forest fire on May 23rd-26th (inclusive), 1923, and that the brood appeared first in the burned area. On reaching this territory I met Mr. Lumbert who owns a considerable amount of land there. He told me that the Cicadas had been out for about two weeks (making the first appearance on or about June 1st). Examination of the burned area showed "chimneys" all over the ground, some of them partially charred, indicating that they had probably been constructed prior to the invasion of the forest fire. In many cases the chimneys were very numerous, one to a square foot of ground where they were thickest.

The "active pupæ" were emerging until about June 22d, the height of the emergence apparently coming from about the 16th to the 19th. At this time, during the evenings, tremendous swarms of immature forms came out of the ground and ascended any upright object within range. Mr. Lumbert claimed to have seen several nymphs come out of a single chimney during this time. He also told me he had found active pupæ in the spring, about 18 inches below the surface of the ground. The adults were usually all on the wing by the morning following nymphal emergence.

On June 20th my attention was called to another part of the brood in Plymouth, between that place and Manomet on a ridge known locally as The Pine Hills. On the same date, I received reports of Cicadas infesting territory from Falmouth east to Osterville; and on Wing's Neck, which is a part of Bourne extending westward into the waters of Buzzards Bay. On June 21st two specimens were taken in East Wareham near the State Cranberry Bog.

The area of infestation of the Cape Cod brood for 1923 may be described as follows:

Town of Plymouth.—From the southern end of the village (Plymouth proper) southeast to Manomet and west from there to Great South Pond; a second area around the northern end of Great Herring Pond.

Town of Wareham.—Eastern corner.

Town of Bourne.—The whole town more or less, the heaviest infestation occurring on the south side of the Cape Cod canal from Bourne High School eastward to Sagamore and southward to Bourne-Falmouth town line, and westward to within one mile of the Coast line of Buzzards Bay except at Wings Neck, where the infestation came to the water's edge.

Town of Falmouth.—Whole town except from Falmouth village to Woods Hole where only a few specimens were taken after full emergence had taken place to the northward.

Town of Sandwich.—Whole town except a strip one to two miles wide along Cape Cod Bay.

Town of Mashpee.—Whole town.

Town of Barnstable.—Southern half of town.

Town of Yarmouth.—Whole town except a strip about one to one and a half miles wide along Cape Cod Bay.

The heaviest infestations were in the Plymouth Pine Hills central and southern part of Bourne, northern, central and eastern Falmouth, Mashpee, southern Barnstable, central Sandwich and central Yarmouth.

Individual, lone specimens were taken at East Wareham, Ellisville (southeastern Plymouth), Woods Hole, Harwich, and Carver indicating, possibly, the former existence of parts of this brood in those sections. Fishermen from Woods Hole said that Cicadas could frequently be found floating in the ocean south of the Falmouth shore. I obtained no record of any on the Islands. (Nantucket or Marthas Vineyard).

Older inhabitants of the village of East Wareham tell me that they remember two broods previously when the insect was abundant in the village.

Mr. Lumbert of Monument Beach called my attention to a "big green beetle" which was preying on adult Cicadas and I asked him to collect some for me if he found more. This he did, and I found that it was the Calosoma beetle, *C. sycophanta* L. Later, in company with Prof. W. H. Sawyer, of the Department of Biology, Bates College, I took several Calosomas in the act of capturing Cicadas.

The order of emergence for this brood, as nearly as I can make out, is as follows: 1st week in June at Bourne; 2nd week in June at Falmouth, Mashpee, Sandwich, Yarmouth, Barnstable, and Plymouth (south of village); 3rd week in June at Plymouth (north of Great Herring Pond).

In driving through the infested territories south and east of the Cape Cod Canal, on July 11th, I found that by far the greatest damage done by this brood of *T. septendecim* L. occurs in the eastern part of the town of Falmouth, around the village of Waquoit. Here the insect has deposited its eggs in practically every suitable plant, including ferns, false indigo and goldenrod. Almost every oak from one to twenty feet high has dead and dying twigs hanging from it in abundance. In several cases I saw oaks twelve feet high and three or four inches through at the base with foliage entirely brown, and much of the youngest growth already drooping. A list of plants attacked is herewith submitted. I suspect many more could be added to the list by other observers, but the following have come to my attention: *Aster* spp. (Wild Asters), *Baptisia tinctoria* (False indigo), *Linaria canadensis*, *Myrica asplenifolia* (Sweet Fern), *Prunus serotina* (Black Cherry), (*Prunus cuneata*) (Plum), *Pteris auilina* (Common Brake), *Pyrus Malus* (Apple), *Quercus illcifolia* (Scrub Oak) and *Quercus rubra* (Red Oak), *Robinia Pseudo-Acacia* (Locust), *Solidago* spp. (Goldenrod), *Vaccinium* spp. (Blueberry and huckleberry), *Viburnum cassinoides*, *Vitis* sp. (Grape).

Quercus ilicifolia (scrub-oak) is the favorite host for oviposition in every case, but lack of room on the oaks, and lack of oaks have driven the females to laying in practically any woody plant available.

One of the interesting points in this season's occurrence of the Cicada, is the uneven emergence through the whole brood; often sections of the brood but a few miles distant from one another emerging at different times. Another interesting feature is the "patchy" occurrence throughout the area of infestation. Some places are heavily infested and others within the suspected area are practically free from the insect, although the same host plants and the same soil conditions exist in both cases. The digging of the Cape Cod Canal has disrupted part of the brood, as no Cicadas could be found within 100-500 feet of the canal banks.

About July 1st dead Cicadas could be picked up frequently in the infested area and by July 11th, dead and dying Cicadas could be found in abundance. By the middle of July very few living specimens could be found in Bourne, but the section of the brood around Great Herring Pond was still in full operation.

STUDIES IN ASILIDÆ (DIPTERA)[1]

By A. L. Melander.

Pullman, Washington.

While the June-August issue of Psyche, containing a review of the genus *Cyrtopogon*, was in preparation a similar study by C. Howard Curran appeared in the Canadian Entomologist, April to October. In the paper in Psyche I described seven new species of *Cyrtopogon*, and Curran's paper included twelve new species. This curious coincidence in the selection of a genus for review might have resulted in unfortunate additions to synonymy, but such is not the case, for among the nineteen new species described neither Curran nor myself chanced upon the same forms.

Two reflections are pertinent in this connection. First, there should be some clearing house where investigators could report their intended activities and thus be notified if the field is preempted. Possibly the National Research Council will in time function in this capacity for all America, or better for all nationalities. With reference to my own studies twice before have other workers independently selected the same groups for review, referring to Malloch's Agromyzidæ and to Cresson's Sciomyzidæ, which papers were in the printers' hands coincidentally with manuscripts of mine. Second, the fact that two workers discover nineteen new species in a well-known genus of an eagerly sought family without conflicting with each other shows that much more is still to be done in systematic dipterology than we are wont to realize.

With regard to the two new genera described by Curran both have a slender, tapering, third antennal joint with long style. *Comantella* was established for two species, *cristata* Coquillett and *fallei* Back, hitherto assigned to *Cophura*, and because *fallei* was regarded as the same as *Cyrtopogon maculosis* Coquillett the last-named species was designated as the genotype.

[1]Contribution from the Zoology Laboratory of the State College of Washington.

I have nineteen specimens of *Cyrtopogon maculosis,* in none of which is there a trace of the curved claw-like spur at the apex of the front tibiæ. I also have another specimen, almost indistinguishable from the others, which has the spur strongly developed. This last specimen I refer to *fallei* in the genus *Comantella. C. fallei* has the fork of the third vein located before the posterior crossvein and the anterior crossvein at nearly three-fourths the length of the discal cell. Its bristles are stronger, the pygidium longer and the thoracic gibbosity more compressed than in *maculosis,* which has the anterior crossvein at the middle of the discal cell and the fork of the third vein opposite the end of this cell. *Maculosis* is referable to Curran's new genus *Eucyrtopogon.* The genotype of *Comantella* is therefore *fallei* Back, synonym *maculosis* Curran, not Coquillett. Instead of being a highly variable character the terminal claw-like spur maintains its dignity as an "atavic index" to the two main subdivisions of both the Dasypogoninæ and the Laphrinæ.

Key to the North American Species of Cophura.

Wings dark; abdomen and legs more or less reddish......2.
Wings more or less hyaline; abdomen black or blue-black, with pollinose spots..........................4.

2\. Three deep black stripes on notum, the middle one geminate; wings uniformly brown; abdomen reddish-yellow. (Mex.) ....*sodalis* O. S.
Thoracic stripes brownish; wings in part clear toward apex....................................3.

3\. Legs black, the knees, base of tibiæ and part of tarsi yellow; abdomen brown-black, the hind margins of segments narrowly reddish. (Mex.)....*humilis* Will.
Legs reddish, anterior femora darkened on outer posterior side; abdomen red, laterally white pruinose. (Tex.) ....*bella* Lw.

4\. Pollinose marks of abdomen large, extending along sides and more or less across front part of segments; tibiæ reddish.....................................5.

Lateral pollinose marks of abdomen not extending across front part of segments . . . . 7.

5. Wings clouded on crossveins and furcations, base of second submarginal cell truncate and with a spur of a vein . . . . . 6.
Wings hyaline, no spur at fork of third vein, anal cell closed and petiolate. (Cal.) . . . . *clausa* Coq.

6. Anal cell open. (Cal.) . . . . *trunca* Coq.
Anal cell closed in the margin; lateral pollinose marks of abdomen each with central black shining spot. (Cal.) . . . . *highlandica* Cole.

7. Legs red; oral and trichostical bristles black. (Wash., Or., Wyo. . . . . *brevicornis* Will.
Legs entirely black . . . . 8.

8. Oral bristles black . . . . 9.
Oral hairs white . . . . 10.

9. Crossveins and furcations tinged with brown; pruinosity of thorax brownish, bristles pale, scutellar margin narrowly black and with six pale hairs; abdominal segments scarcely pruinose at base. (Wash., Or.). . *scitula* Will.
Wings clear hyaline; pruinosity of thorax grayish, bristles black, scutellar margin broadly black and with two short black setæ; abdominal segments with basal pruinose fascia. (Id.) . . . . *melanochæta*, n. sp.

10. Wings tinged with brown; mesonotum marked with brown broad geminate median stripe and lateral spots. (Mex.) . . . . *pulchella* Will.
Wings nearly or wholly hyaline; mesonotal pattern nearly obsolete . . . . 11.

11. Mesonotum nearly bare; pygidium white-pruinose. (Ariz.) . . . . *fur* Will.
Mesonotum whitish pilose; pygidium polished. (*cyrtopogona* Cole) (B. C., Wash., Or.) . . . . *albosetosa* Hine.

The genus *Cophura* has been heterotypic, serving to combine various species that run to it in the keys, without regard to their phylogeny. The separation of *Comantella* helps to unify the group, but it is still diverse. The species are considered rare, only the type material being known of most of its forms. I have taken *brevicornis* near Spokane, in the Olympic Peninsula and near Mount Adams, in Washington; at Portland, Oregon; and in the Yellowstone Park. I have also taken *scitula* at Portland, Oregon, and *albosetosa* at Yakima, Washington. The preceeding key differentiates the species assigned to *Cophura*.

Cophura melanochaeta, new species.

Male.—Length 6.5 mm. Black, head and thorax cinereous pollinose, abdomen marked with silvery pruinose fasciæ on segments 2-5 and round pruinose spots on hind angles of segments 1-5. Facial hairs sparse, white, oral bristles strong and black, a row of black setulæ along frontal orbits, occipital hairs and setæ white; basal joints of antennæ rounded, with strong black inferior setæ, third joint widest beyond middle, three times the length of either basal joint, the style three-jointed, including its apical peg-like joint as long as a basal joint of the antennæ. Mesonotum with dense pollen, darker gray in center, its vestiture short black recumbent setulæ, lateral bristles black, base of scutellum heavily light-gray pollinose, only two short black apical setæ, middle of metanotum lightly pollinose. Abdominal hairs inconspicuous, pale, those at base of the small pygidium dark; ventral segments mostly shining black, each gray-fasciate at base and apex. Leg bristles black, hairs pale, inside of distal half of hind tibiæ and of basal two joints of hind tarsi thickly yellow pubescent. Halteres yellow; wings entirely hyaline, veins black, clear-cut, fork of third vein a little beyond discal cell, anterior crossvein slightly beyond middle of discal cell, anal cell open.

Female.—Length 10 mm.

A pair taken at Waha, Idaho, 12 Aug. 1923; another female, Moscow Mt., Idaho, Jul. 8.

Key to the Species of Metapogon.

Legs in part reddish; wings more or less clouded on crossveins..2.

Legs black, at most knees reddish; wings n6t marked about crossveins; antennæ black...........................4.

2. Antennæ black; anterior crossvein at middle of discal cell; pluræ with golden spots. (Cal.)........*pictus* Cole.
   Base of antennæ yellow; anterior crossvein beyond middle of discal cell.. ....3.
3. Abdomen with large triangular pollinose marks; bristles yellow; femora reddish. (Cal.)..........*gilvipes* Coq.
   Abdomen polished, with gray pruinose spots at base of segments 2-6; bristles black; femora black except knees. (N. Mex.)..........................*punctipennis* Coq.
4. Mainly black, abdomen with small pruinose spots; wings of male white on basal half, lightly infumated apically, of female uniformly lightly infumated; mystax stiff and black. (Wash., Id., Or., Cal.)...........*setiger* Cole.
   Body mainly cinereous, base of abdominal segments black; wings hyaline; mystax white. (Wash.)..*albulus*, n. sp.

Metapogon albulus, new species

Male.—Length 7 mm. Black, entirely and heavily coated with silvery gray pruinosity, leaving only the bases of abdominal segments showing black. Bristles of face and front white, ocellar bristles black; third antennal joint widest at three-fifths its length, the style almost microscopic, setæ below basal joints of antennæ black; beard sparse and white, upper part of occiput bare except for the row of white setæ. Bristles of anterior part of thorax white, of posterior part black, four or five stout bristles in dorsocentral row, posthumeral bristle present, white, two supraalar bristles, scutellum with two marginal bristles, otherwise bare, two to five hypopleural setæ, pleuræ devoid of pile except on prothorax. Pile and setæ at sides of first abdominal segment white, remaining segments with very sparse short white hairs, base of segments two to five very narrowly devoid of pruinosity, hypopygium small black and inserted in the end of the cylindrical abdomen, its hairs pale and rather sparse; venter entirely glaucous. Legs black, the coxæ alone pruinose, knees very narrowly yellowish, femora with a few small white flexor bristles, bristles of tibiæ white except those at apex, tarsal bristles black, claws black, pulvilli brownish, hairs of legs sparse short and white. Halteres yellow; wings almost hyaline, veins dark brown, becoming paler at root, hind margin closely fringed with fine hair, anterior crossvein at two-fifths the length of the discal cell, anal cell open.

Female.—Bases of abdominal segments two to six with broader black fasciæ, seventh segment lightly black, venter with triangular black denuded marks increasing in size posteriorly, the sixth segment entirely black, some of tibial bristles blackish.

Types.—Six specimens Pullman, Washington, and Collins, Idaho (C. V. Piper) July and August. Type in collection of State College of Washington.

Key to Species of Dioctria.

Femora wholly black, the tibiæ alone sometimes reddish...2.
Femora and rest of legs wholly or largely yellow or red; mystax pale.....................................11.

2. Mystax fulvous and dense; body brilliant greenish black. (Cal.)............................*resplendens* Lw.
Mystax generally black, rarely white, if fulvous not dense; body less brilliantly metallic.........................3.

3. Third joint of antennæ one and one-half times the length of the two basal joints together and cylindrical (*Banksi* Johns.).......................................4.
Third joint of antennæ subequal to basal joints together. ..5.

4. Legs wholly black. (Va.)............*Banksi* Johns., s.str.
All tibiæ reddish on basal half. (Va.)..var. *tibialis* Banks

5. Legs wholly black......................................6.
Tibiæ more or less reddish-yellow...................9.

6. Wings yellowish on basal half, blackish on apical half. (Cal.)..................................*parvula* Coq.
Base of wings not markedly yellowish.................7.

7. Upper plate of hypopygium wide, with two broad lobes; fulvous coat of mesopleura extending along upper edge only. (Eastern U. S., doubtful if in West)..*albius* Walk.
Upper plate of hypopygium narrow, pronged but not with flat lobes...8.

8. Upper plate divided into two long tapering parts ending in a knob-like enlargement, with a tooth on inner surface and a pencil of yellow hair on outer edge (N. Y.; N. Car.) . . . . *brevis* Banks
Upper plate a slender finger-like undivided projection about four times as long as wide and with parallel sides, lateral arms short and heavy. (Cal.; Wash.) *media* Banks
9. Tibiæ except tips reddish-yellow; notum heavily coated with fulvous, abdomen metallic violaceous; large species, 11-13 mm . . . . 10.
Only base of tibiæ yellowish; mesopleural pollen extending down along posterior edge; face of male silvery, of female golden; 7-9 mm. (Wash., Id.,; doubtful if East) . . . . *sackeni*, form *rivalis* new
10. Mesopleural pollen along upper edge only; face of both sexes brassy. (Cal., Wash.) . . . . *nitida* Will.
Mesopleura with dense fulvous pollen and pile extending down along posterior edge; face of male silvery. (Cal.) . . . . *doanei*, n. sp.
11. Abdomen wholly black; femora with black line above.. . . 12.
Abdomen in part reddish, at least with lateral spot or incisures reddish; femora wholly yellow; thorax polished black . . . . 14.
12. Mesonotum densely coated with golden pollen; wings largely yellow. (Ida., Wash., Or.; if eastern in distribution, probably dimorphic form of *albius* Walk.) . . . . *sackeni* Will.
Mesonotum thinly coated with yellow pollen, leaving two narrow black lines . . . . 13.
13. Face silvery, mystax white; wings hyaline. (Eur.; Mass.) . . . . *baumhaueri* Mg.
Face golden, mystax yellow; wings dark. (Cal.) *vera* Back
14. Coxæ black; abdomen reddish, first four segments more or less black; arista one-sixth the third antennal joint; wings blackish. (Cal.) . . . . *rubida* Coq.
Coxæ yellow; style one-fourth to one-half the third antennal joint; wings lighter; hind metatarsus swollen, equal to next three joints in length . . . . 15.

15. A yellowish pollinose stripe extending from base of wings to front coxæ; abdomen dull rufous, segments with indistinct black near middle; arista one-fourth the third antennal joint. (Cal.) . . . . *pleuralis* Banks.
    Pollinose spot above front coxa disconnected; arista longer . . . . 16.
16. Abdomen largely dull reddish; legs reddish. (Cal., Col.) . . . . *pusio* O. S.
    Abdomen largely black, legs pale yellow. 17
17. Abdomen black and yellow banded. (Or. Wash.) . . . . *vertebrata* Cole
    Abdomen narrowly fasciate with reddish and with red spot on sides of second segment. (Wash.) . . . . *henshawi* Johnson

Dioctria doanei, new species.

Male.—Length 14 mm. Robust, black, abdomen bronzed, tibiæ luteous, vestiture dense, yellow. Face silvery, mystax black, vertex and occiput golden, hairs yellow; antennæ elongate, black, third joint a little longer than the basal two together. Thorax coated with fulvous pollen, especially pronounced on posthumeral areas, scutellum black, lateral bristles of notum fine and yellow; meso- and sternopleuræ largely polished. Anterior part of abdominal segments 2-4 sunken, pile of apical segments appressed, deep golden, becoming almost reddish beneath pygidium. Legs strong, hind femora robust, coxæ, femora, tips of tibiæ, and tarsi black, bristles of tibiæ and tarsi reddish, pulvilli brown, claws black. Wings strongly and uniformly infumated, discal cell widened apically, anterior crossvein before its middle and fork of third vein just beyond its end, sixth vein curving forward, anal cell narrowly open; halteres yellow.

Two specimens collected by Professor R. W. Doane at Pasadena, California, June 6, 1895. Type in collection of the State College of Washington. The dense pilosity and constricted abdominal segments suggest *Dicolonus*, but the head is different, the vertex being deep-set and the face flat.

Dioctria sackeni, new form **rivalis.**

Male.—Length 7 mm. Basal half of wings smoky hyaline, distal half merging into blackish; legs black, the anterior knees and the basal half of hind tibiæ reddish yellow. Face entirely silvery, mystax, hairs of front, of antennæ and of upper occiput black, vertex with scant fulvous coating and not golden. Coating of mesonotum fulvous and not heavy, hairs black; the golden patch in front of wing connected with the more silvery patch on upper sternopleura. The appressed hairs on posterior half of abdomen black, not golden as in form *Sackeni*; dorsal plate of hypopygium continued posteriorly as two long narrow clavate processes, each tipped without by a closed cluster of black bristles and bearing on inner side of knob a pronounced parallel-sided prong, long black hairs on ventral lip and on stout lateral valves. In *Sackeni* hairs fringing the ventral lip are brown.

Female.—Length 8 mm. Face deep golden. Wings uniformly blackish. Legs black.

Morphotypes.—Priest Lake, Idaho, Aug. 1920; Coeur d'Alene, Moscow Mt., Avon, Id.; Big Fork, Mont.; Friday Harbor, Quilcene, Wash.; Nelson, B. C. (Melander): Stuart Island, Wash. (H. S. Davis); Wolf Fork of Touchet River, Wash. (V. Argo). Thirty-two specimens.

Late one afternoon while collecting insects at Priest Lake, Idaho, I noticed many specimens of a *Dioctria* running over the foliage of some alder bushes growing near the water's edge. On mounting the captured specimens there were found to be seven males of *D. Sackeni*, four males of the present black form and nine black females. The only interpretation is that *Sackeni* is dimorphic in the male sex. I have also taken the lighter colored male of *Sackeni* together with the dark female at Nelson, B. C.

Light-colored males, similar to *D. Sackeni*, have been found associated with the dark *albius* in several places in the East. Dr. Back ventured the opinion that *Sackeni*, therefore, might prove to be the same as *albius*, but the recent note by Banks that the Eastern reddish males have genitalia of the *albius* structure suggests that male dimorphism in *Dioctria* is probably extended to several species. The Pennsylvania female with hyaline wings recorded by Johnson in Psyche, 1918, p. 103, as undoubtedly belonging to *Sackeni*, is more likely a distinct species.

Neopogon salinus, new species.

Male.—Length 9 mm. Entirely densely covered with whitish-gray pollen, abdomen incompletely fasciate with blackish-gray. Antennæ cinereous, the style three-fourths the length of the third joint, mystax, hairs and postvertical row of bristles white. Hairs of mesonotum short and white, slightly longer on sides, scutellum bare; a few hairs on propleuræ, pleuræ otherwise bare, about eight setiform hairs in hypopleural row. First, fourth and eighth abdominal segments almost wholly whitish-gray, remaining segments with transverse blackish-gray marking, pile and bristles at sides of first segment white, hypopygium small, silvery, and white pilose, the hood-like covering pink and penicillate below, venter white-gray, bare at base, last four segments with double brush of yellowish-white hairs directed to the middle and covering a subshining space. Legs as heavily coated as body, nearly bare of hairs, bristles mainly white, claws, empodia and some of tarsal bristles black, pulvilli white. Halteres whitish yellow. Wings hyaline, with very faint yellowish tone, veins black, yellowish at base, neuration normal.

Female.—Length 10 mm. Darkened markings of abdomen present on second to sixth segments, ovipositor, *i. e.* eighth ventral segment, shining beneath, tarsal bristles all white.

Types.—Six specimens collected by Dr. J. M. Aldrich at Great Salt Lake, Utah, July 31, 1908. Type, allotype and two paratypes returned to the Aldrich collection. The species runs to *N. Coquilletti* in Bezzi's table (Ann. Hung. Mus. 8. 147-153, 1910) but that species has the abdomen colored as in the familiar *N. trifasciatus*, with a strong white band on fourth segment, the second and third segments dull black, and the fifth, sixth and seventh segments shining black.

Nicocles punctipennis, new species

Length 12 to 13 mm. Black species, with hyaline wings marked with dark spots around the discal cell and with brownish clouds at the tips of the veins. Fifth segment of male about twice as wide as deep, its front border and the sixth segment silvery. Last three segments of the female abdomen respectively with a pair of gray pruinose triangles, a pair of squares, and entirely gray pruinose. Hind tarsi of male silvery within. Antennal style one-third the length of the third joint. Three strong lateral presutural bristles, two supra-alar, two or three postalar.

Male.—Face, front and occiput gray-white pruinose; facial hairs fine, white, comparatively dense, extending to the antennæ, long below, bristles of mystax yellowish, oral, ocellar, and postocular bristles yellowish brown; beard and palpal hairs white; face nearly square, and but little convex. Antennæ black, the basal segments subequal, and provided with white hairs, the second segment with a conspicuous light brown bristle below, the third segment nearly twice as long as the basal joints together, slender, cylindrical, little tapering, three times as long as the thick style. Upper side of the thorax with an irregular gray-brown pattern, showing gray, however, on the narrow median entire stripe, on each side of which is a narrow line, abbreviated posteriorly and on the humeri, scutellum, a large square prescutellar spot, with a triangular space on each side, and a curved sutural stripe extending up above the root of each wing. This sutural stripe does not continue across the notum, but stops on the row of dorsocentral bristles, where it connects with gray horns from the anterior angles of the prescutellar spot. The brown color is not uniform, and is darkest as an interrupted vitta crossing the interior end of the gray sutural stripe. The oval center of the prescutellar spot is denuded and shows the polished black ground color of the thorax. Mesonotal hairs very fine, and rather sparse and long, pale yellowish, the posterior bristles pale, with brownish base: disc of the scutellum with white hairs, the margin with two cruciate bristles. Pleuræ and coxæ gray pruinose, the center of the mesopleuræ alone brownish; trichostichal hairs long, numerous, and whitish;

halteres black, their stem brown. Abdomen flat, shining black except for the gray lateral margins of the basal three and a half segments, and the silvery tip, which occupies the whole of the last segment and the anterior part of the fifth. On this segment the silvery band is broadly emarginate behind, so that it occupies but one-fourth of the segment at the middle, and then curves down to the hind angles; this segment is but little more than twice as broad as deep. The vestiture of the abdomen consists of very sparse, appressed, golden hairs and longer erect white hairs growing from black pittings on the gray lateral marks. The venter is gray, speckled with brown at the root of each hair. Legs with appressed whitish pubescence and with yellowish bristles, the inner side of the hind tarsi and of the end of the hind tibiæ with dense silvery hairs, anterior tibiæ rufous, rest of legs black in ground color. Wings hyaline, but with dark brown spots located at the very root, on the crossveins, bordering the ends of the veins at the wing-tip, and across the wing at the base of the discal cell as a much interrupted band, broadest and darkest in the marginal cell. The hyaline anal cell is closed in the margin, the posterior cells all open, and the fork of the third vein is broken at the base of the second submarginal cell, and there provided with a spur.

Female.—Differs in that the gray covering is less pure, but sullied with brown on the face, front, pleural sclerites and venter. The end of the abdomen lacks the silvery pruinosity, but instead, the fifth segment has lateral gray triangles, the sixth is gray except for a median stripe, and the seventh is completely gray. The pubescence of the legs is duller and there is none of the silvery ornamentation.

Types.—Male, Wawawai, Washington, May 1, 1909 (Wm. M. Mann). Two females from same locality, April 10 and 23, and two from Wallula, Washington, April, 1923 (P. G. Putnam.) A female paratype collected by E. L. Jenne, at North Yakima, Washington, September 18, 1903, is in the collection of the Washington State College.

This large and distinct species can be quickly recognized in the male by the concave silvery mark on the fifth abdominal segment, and in the female by the spotting of the wings as well as by the maculation of the abdomen. In Coquillett's key (page 385, Back monograph, 1909) it goes to the last couplet, but does not conform with either *argentatus* or *æmulator*. The recently described *N. utahensis* Banks likewise goes to the last couplet of the key but differs from the present species in weaker chætotaxy, blacker thorax, and, apparently, much smaller size.

A NOTE ON THE NESTING HABITS OF *TACHYTES DISTINCTUS* Sm.

By Phil Rau.

St. Louis, Missouri

A bank at Creve Coeur Lake, composed of sand and soil, contained in a space of six by twelve feet, five nests of this species, on August 16, 1922. All of these domiciles had been established in burrows or openings made by other creatures or objects. Two nests were within the burrows made by rodents, one in an opening left in the soil by a disintegrating root, one in a crack in the bank, and the last in an opening made by a half buried sheet of tin. The mother wasp in each case gained access to her nest by these openings, which were unmodified and quite inconspicuous.

A careful study of these mothers revealed that it is the habit of these wasps to approach the opening by flight, accompanied by a noisy hum that resembles somewhat that of a horse-fly. She drops into her tunnel without preliminary search, or a pause at the doorway, but in a very businesslike manner she plunges in, remains a moment, then flies out and dashes off again. The same quickness characterises her movements, whether she is empty-handed or burdened with prey.

The prey is always a long-horned grasshopper of the species *Orchelimum vulgare* Harr[1]. It is carried on the under side of her body, held in position by her legs, and despite the fact that its size equals or sometimes exceeds her own, she has no difficulty in managing it, and is not even compelled to readjust it before entering the burrow. She does not experience the difficulty that many wasps do in entering the burrow with a large parcel, since the openings are always large.

The activities of one mother were watched closely, during which time she brought in four grasshoppers after hunts of 65, 55, 32 and 33 minutes respectively, and she took from three to five minutes each time to store them after she entered the burrow.

[1]The wasp was identified by Mr. S. A. Rohwer, and the hopper by Mr. A. N. Caudell.

An effort was made to excavate the burrows but the sandy soil was friable and in only one was the terminus successfully reached. This was the burrow under the sheet of tin; this sheet lay horizontally about ten inches under the surface of the soil, and by shoveling off this soil the sheet was removed and the tunnel exposed. It was found that her own gallery began about four inches from where she entered the opening beneath the tin. The tunnel ran horizontally and the tin served as its roof, leaving a miniature trench when the sheet was lifted; this trench ran in the shape of a quarter circle for about four inches, where it entered the ground and continued as a straight burrow for an additional distance of six inches, never at any point going down more than ¾ inch below the plane of the first portion. The diameter of the burrow of her own making was approximately ½ inch. One grasshopper was found at the end of the burrow. It lived about a day after its disinterment.

The most interesting feature about the nesting habits of this species is that, though they utilize the old burrows of other creatures, they use them only as a vestibule; but once under cover they dig their own tunnel in a way well becoming to industrious creatures. They do not, like certain other wasps, use ready made burrows for nesting purposes, but only use that site to conceal their nests from prying eyes, where they can work unhindered. My observations on the habits of this species would be incomplete if I failed to note the very interesting and significant characteristic, its ability to find out and utilize the beginnings of burrows, and thus gain safety and save labor.

Williams (Kans. Univ. Sci. Bull 8:194-197, 1913) finds that the entrance to a burrow of this wasp had a circular mound resembling "somewhat the appearance of a mud tube such as are made by crayfish." May this not actually have been a crayfish burrow that *Tachytes* used as a vestibule to her own tunnel? Williams also finds in Kansas, that the cells are strung along the main shaft in an irregular manner, and in twenty cells that he opened, fifty six acridians were found. Fifty one of these belonged to the tribe *Melanopli*, and the other five being *Ageneotettix deorum* and *Orphuella speciosa*.

WILLIAMSONIA LINTNERI (HAGEN), ITS HISTORY AND DISTRIBUTION

By R. Heber Howe, Jr.

Belmont, Mass.

A male of this unique species was supposedly figured, without name or description, in 1854 (Emmons, DeKay's Agric. N. Y. 5: Pl. 15.f.1) though the plate is inaccurate as to wing venation (triangle with cross vein) pattern of abdominal markings, and the superior abdominal appendages are shown as distinctly furcate. I feel confident that it was not intended for a figure of this insect. The species was first thought definitely referred to, but not described, by Hagen in 1867 (Stett. ent. Zeit. 28:91) under the title of *Diplax vacua*,—evidently based on two females collected in 1860, one at Lake Winnipeg and one from the Saskatchewan river (in litt. Hagen) by Robert Kellicott. Later in 1878 (Bull. Acad. Belg. (2) 45:187) Hagen described what he thought to be the same species from material collected at Center, (now Karner) N. Y., naming the insect *Cordulia lintneri*. The type, a male (No. 2840) was taken on May 27 (1874?), and a female (No. 2839) paratype on May 21 (1874?) by Dr. J. A. Lintner. In a later paper by Hagen (Psyche 5: 371-373. 1890) he again fully described the species, and figured (Pl. 1. fs. 10-17) both sexes, recording at the same time the two females taken by Kellicott which he had formerly named *Diplax vacua*, but here calls *Libellula vacua* and which he considered identical. He made however a significant remark that "It is very interesting that this apparently arctic species is found in eastern New York." In this article Hagen refers to four males and four females as taken by Dr. Lintner, but Dr. E. P. Felt writes me under date of October 17, 1922 that "Knowing what I do of Doctor Lintner, I doubt very much if he ever had four males and four females of this species, though I am unable to explain the significance of the numeral 4 preceding the sign for the male. I am inclined to think it must be a subnumber, though apparently Hagen published his record and allowed it to suggest at least four individual males and four individual females. This data as we may infer from Hagen's letter was in manuscript for some time and he doubtless transcribed the labels just as they were and later forgot to call attention to the erroneous construction likely to be placed upon the numeral just before the sex sign or the possibility of any such thing may have escaped his attention." As the label reads V 27 4♂ is it not likely that it meant May 27, 1874, a date that would fit in well with the other facts? In 1895 (Journ. N. Y. Ent. Soc. 3:46) Dr. P. P. Calvert placed the species in the genus *Somatochlora*, and in 1907 (Cat. Coll. Selys 17:36) Martin referred it to *Dorocordulia*, and figures (f42) the male abdominal appendages from a photograph sent him of the type by Dr. E. P. Felt. In 1913 (Bull. Brooklyn Ent. Soc. 8:93-96) Mr. Wm. T. Davis proposed for the species a new genus *Williamsonia*, and figured the wings of a female found in the collection of the American Museum of Natural History, New York taken by John A. Grossback on May 4? at Paterson, N. J.

The two females from Manitoba are not *Williamsonia lintneri* (Hagen), but represent a different species, *Williamsonia fletcheri* Will. (Can. Ent. 55:96. 1923). The two specimens collected by Mr. C. H. Young at Mer Bleue, near Ottawa, Canada (48th Ann. Report Ent. Soc. Ont. 25:1915), and specimens collected last May at the same location are also *Williamsonia fletcheri* though somewhat intermediate and less distinct from *W. lintneri* than the Manitoba specimens which would have supplied better and more characteristic type material. In my opinion it would have been more appropriate to revive the nomen nudum *vacua* already applied to the species rather than propose a new name. The discovery of the two species explains the supposed two curious distributional "lakes" that have heretofore been attributed to *Williamsonia lintneri*, the distribution of which is now made clear.

2839. ♂. Center, N. Y. May 27, '?4, "a sandy pine woods region" (J. A. Lintner). Coll. State Mus., Albany, N. Y.. Bull. Acad. Belg. (2) vol. 45, p. 187 (1878).

2840. ♀. Center, N. Y. May 21, '?4, (J. A. Lintner) Coll. Mus. Comp. Zool., ibid.

♀. Paterson, N. J. May 4, ??, "recorded 1908" (J. A. Crossbeek) Coll. Amer. Mus. Nat. Hist., Bull. Brooklyn Ent. Soc. vol. 8, p. 93, 1913.

♂ ♀ ♀. Concord, Mass. (E. L. Peirson) Coll. ♂Howe, Ent. News, vol. 26, p. 238, 1915, Coll. ♀Acad. Nat. Sci., Proc. Thoreau Mus. Nat. Hist. vol. 1, p. 41, 1915, ♀, destroyed.

♂. Framingham, Mass. May 6, 1911 (C. A. Frost) Coll. Boston Soc. Nat. Hist., Mem. Thoreau Mus. Nat. Hist. vol. S, 1921.

♀. Dedham, Mass. May 20, 1912, "in low swampy woodland near Wigwam ice pond" (C. W. Johnson). Coll. Boston Soc. Nat. Hist., Ent. News, vol. 26, p. 238, 1915 and Proc. Thoreau Mus. Nat. Hist., vol. 1, p. 41, 1915.

♂. Sherborn, Mass. April 30, 1913, "taken in an opening in a scrubby woodland adjoining a wet meadow", (E. J. Smith), Coll. Smith, Psyche, vol. 24, p. 48, 1917.

♀ ♀. Blue Hills, Milton, Mass. May 13, 1916, "both localities were hilly, rocky and covered with at hick growth of oak, birch and little maple. There was also quite a bit of under-brush. *Both* streams drained a marsh. That is, they were both outlets for swamps, but in both cases the swamps were small. The streams, themselves, were more or less swift; their water was of that peculiar type, containing a large percentage of organic matter in solution," (W. J. Clench) Coll. Mus. Comp. Zool., Boston Soc. Nat. Hist., Mem. Thoreau Mus. Nat. Hist. vol. II, pt. 4, p. 53, 1919.

♂. Hopkinton, Mass. May 21, 1916. (C. A. Frost) Coll. Howe, ibid. sup. 8, 1921.

♂. Concord, Mass. May 20, 1918 (R. W. Howe, Jr.) Coll. Howe.

♂. Concord, Mass. June 1, 1919. (R. H. Howe, Jr.) Coll. Thoreau Mus. Nat. Hist., Concord, Mass.

♀. Middleton, Mass. May 29, 1920. (F. H. Walker) Coll. Peabody Museum, Salem, Mass., Mem. Thoreau Mus. Nat. Hist., vol. II. sup. 8, 1921.

♂. Stony Brook, West Roxbury, Mass. May 6, 1922. (W. J. Clench) Coll. Williamson; Hammonds Pond, Brookline, Mass., May 7, 1922 (R. H. Howe, Jr.) Coll. Howe.

♀. Rumford, R. I. May 11, 1922, "near Ten Mile River and Central Pond in "the shadow of Pine and Hemlock woods.... in low growth of scrub mostly oak.....swampy with sphagnum and skunk cabbage growth, also checkerberry and other boreal life." (E. D. Keith) Coll. Howe.

♂ ♀ ♀. Stony Brook, West Roxbury, Mass. May 13, 1922, "were flying in the vicinity of a small pond, one of them on a hillside some distance from the water. This pond is a permanent one, surrounded by low land that is covered with water in the spring, and along one side is a bog with sphagnum and Drosera," (Students, Bussey Institution) Coll. Mus. Comp. Zool. Cambridge, Mass. ♀. Bos. Soc. Nat. Hist., ♀. Howe.

♂. High Rock, Summer Hill, Stoneham, Mass. April, 1, 1923, "in roadway and on rocks," (C. V. Blackburn), Coll. Howe.

♀. Bear Hill, Stoneham, Mass. April 20, 1923, (C. V. Blackburn) Coll. Howe.

♀. Bear Hill, Stoneham, Mass. May 5, 1923, (C. V. Blackburn) Coll. P. Garman, Conn. Agric. Expt. Station, New Haven, Conn.

The dates, as will be seen, range from April 1, to June 4, and undoubtedly the reason *W. lintneri* has been overlooked is because of its flight season when collectors are not alive to the presence of Odonata in the field. My own observations of the species bears out the above field notes of other collectors. I always find it a woodland species inhabiting the heighborhood of cold bogs and brook runs, and it alights generally on stones. The orange ring on each abdominal segment makes the insect particularly easy of identification in the field. Its larva is unknown.

NOTES ON THE NESTS OF ODYNERUS (ANCISTROCERUS) BIRENINACULATUS SAUSSURE.

By Charles W. Johnson.

Boston Society of Natural History.

Early in May, 1923, Mr. F. E. Zeissig, of Ware, Mass., brought me four nests of this interesting solitary wasp. The nests are irregular lumps of coarse hardened clay, built around small twigs, the leaves of the tree or shrub being sometimes imbedded in the clay. The cells are near the center, arranged somewhat radially and with a thin silky lining. The nest is figured by Viereck in the Hymenoptera of Connecticut, plate 4, figure 1.

Having secured this wasp only from nests, and as species of parasitic Diptera (Bombyliidæ) have been obtained from the nests of solitary wasps, I placed each nest in a separate jar and numbered these as the wasps began to emerge. Althouth irregular in form the nests varied but little in size, nests numbers 1 and 2 having a diameter of about 40 mm. and numbers 3 and 4 a diameter of about 35 mm.

Nest No. 1. Two males emerged May 14, gnawing their way through the hard dry clay; on the 15th to 18th one and two males appeared each day, until the 19th when four males and one female emerged; on the 26th another female appeared, and on the 28th two, making a total of 13 males and 4 females. The specimens emerged through 13 openings in the nest.

Nest No. 2. One male appeared May 15, three on the 17th and one on the 21st. On the 22d one female emerged and on the 23d an ichneumon parasite, *Acroricnus junceus* Cress., female. On the 24th two females emerged and on the 25th four, a total of 5 males, 7 females, and a parasite. They issued through six openings.

Nest No. 3. Two males emerged on May 21 and two on the 22d, one female on the 24th, one on the 25th, two on the 26th, and four on the 27th, a total of 4 males and 8 females. They emerged through nine openings.

Nest No. 4. The parasite, *A. junceus* (female), emerged on May 22, two male wasps on the 23d, one on the 24th, one female on the 27th, and two on the 28th, a total of 3 males, 3 females and one parasite. These emerged through seven openings.

The presence of a parasite in nest No. 4 can hardly account for so few wasps, for nest No. 2, with a parasite, had the same number of wasps as nest No. 3. *A. junceus* has also been bred from the potter wasp (*Eumenes* sp.) and from *Odynerus tigris* Sauss.

PROCEEDINGS OF THE CAMBRIDGE ENTOMOLOGICAL CLUB.

At the meeting of March, 1923, Prof. C. T. Brues showed some new photographs of insects in amber and gave a review of the present knowledge of amber insects and fossil insects in general. See Scientific Monthly vol. 17, pp. 289-304, (1923.)

Mr. Emerton exhibited his outfit for collecting spiders.

At the April meeting, Dr. J. W. Chapman gave a lecture on the animals of the Philippine Islands where he has lived for the past six years.

Mr. A. P. Morse told about his entomological experiences in Nebraska where, for several summers, he has been observing the grasshoppers that eat wheat and corn and also the binder-twine with which the grain is tied up.

At the meeting in May, Mr. O. E. Plath read a paper on the various theories in regard to the humming of bumblebees at the entrance to the nest. This was noticed as far back as 1665 and at first interpreted as a call to the other bees. Observation, however, has shown that its object is to ventilate the nest. See Psyche, vol. 30, pp. 146-154, (1923.)

Mr. R. F. Hussey described the development of the sucking mouthparts of the Hemiptera.

At the June meeting, Miss E. P. Butler described the development of pseudopodia on the first abdominal segment of several insects. These at first resemble the rudimentary legs but at an early stage their growth stops, they become enveloped by the growing parts around them and are eventually absorbed.

Prof. W. M. Wheeler gave an account of a recent visit to the Panama Canal Zone and the Galapagos Islands, referring especially to the large associations of insects that live in the hollow stems of various tropical trees.

PSYCHE

INDEX TO VOL. XXX. 1923.

INDEX TO AUTHORS.

INDEX TO SUBJECTS

All new genera, new species and new names are printed in Small Capital Letters.

PSYCHE

A Journal of Entomology

Volume XXXI

1924

EDITED BY CHARLES T. BRUES

Published by the Cambridge Entomological Club, Bussey Institution, Forest Hills, Boston 30, Mass., U. S. A.

Printed by The St. Albans Messenger Company
St. Albans, Vermont.

PSYCHE

A JOURNAL OF ENTOMOLOGY

ESTABLISHED IN 1874

VOL. XXXI FEBRUARY 1924 No. 1

CONTENTS

PSYCHE is published bi-monthly, the issues appearing in February, April, June, August, October and December. Subscription price, per year, payable in advance: $2.00 to subscribers in the United States, Canada or Mexico; foreign postage, 15 cents extra. Single copies, 40 cents.

Cheques and remittances should be addressed to Treasurer, Cambridge Entomological Club, Bussey Institution, Forest Hills, Boston 30, Mass.

Orders for back volumes, missing numbers, notices of change of address, etc., should be sent to Cambridge Entomological Club, Bussey Institution, Forest Hills, Boston 30, Mass.

IMPORTANT NOTICE TO CONTRIBUTORS.

Manuscripts intended for publication, books intended for review, and other editorial matter, should be addressed to Professor C. T. Brues, Bussey Institution, Forest Hills, Boston 30, Mass.

Authors contributing articles over 8 printed pages in length will be required to bear a part of the extra, expense for additional pages. This expense will be that of typesetting only, which is about $2.00 per page. The actual cost of preparing cuts for all illustrations must be borne by contributors: the expense for full page plates from line drawings is approximately $5.00 each, and for full page half-tones, $7.50 each; smaller sizes in proportion.

AUTHOR'S SEPARATES.

Reprints of articles may be secured by authors, if they are ordered before, or at the time proofs are received for corrections. The cost of these will be furnished by the Editor on application.

Entered as second-class mail matter at the Post Office at Boston, Mass. Acceptance for mailing at special rate of postage provided in Section 1103, Act of October 3, 1917, authorized on June 29, 1918.

PSYCHE

VOL. XXXI. FEBRUARY 1924 No. 1

EARLY HISTORY OF THE CAMBRIDGE ENTOMOLOGICAL CLUB.

BY J. H. EMERTON.

Before the year 1874 the entomologists around Boston had been accustomed to meet as a section of the Boston Society of Natural History,[1] but some of them had ambitious plans in their minds: they wanted to publish a journal, to meet outside of Boston and to have members from all over the country, so a new society was planned and as a large proportion of the members lived in Cambridge, the society was formed there.

January 9, 1874, at the house of H. A. Hagen, Putnam Street, Cambridge, the following persons met and agreed to form the Cambridge Entomological Club:

E. P. Austin	J. H. Emerton	H. K. Morrison
Edw. Burgess	H. A. Hagen	J. C. Munro
G. R. Crotch	S. Henshaw	A. S. Packard
Geo. Dimmock	B. P. Mann	E. A. Schwarz
	S. H. Scudder	

During the year a large number of members were elected, among them

H. G. Hubbard	F. G. Sanborn	F. C. Bowditch
C. R. Osten-Sacken	G. D. Smith	L. Trouvelot
Roland Thaxter	P. S. Sprague	S. W. Williston
C. P. Whitney	Holmes Hinkley	F. Blanchard

The only officer thought necessary was a secretary, and B. P. Mann was elected to this office. Meetings were held at

[1]In January 1864 members of the Boston Society of Natural History organized the Harris Entomological Club which formed the nucleus of the Section of Entomology which was organized Nov. 25, 1866 and continued to hold meetings until 1886. Its proceedings are reported in the published proceedings of the B. S. N. H.

Mann's residence, 19 Follen St., in a little building in the yard nicknamed the "entomologicon," and the proceedings were much the same as at meetings of the Club to-day.

At the fourth meeting, April 10, 1874, it was voted to publish an entomological journal for which Scudder furnished the name, "Psyche." B. P. Mann was appointed editor, and the first part, of four pages, was issued in time for the next meeting on May 8. H. K. Morrison was appointed committee on excursions, and one was held at Waverly on May 7.

At the sixth meeting, June 12, it was voted to hold the July meeting on Mt. Washington, and the August meeting at Hartford, Conn., in connection with the American Association for the Advancement of Science.

Fig. 1. Camp of the Cambridge Entomological Club on Mount Washington, July 1874, rom a drawing by J. H. Emerton.

The seventh meeting, July 8, was held on Mt. Washington in a camp quarter of a mile below the Halfway House and far enough into the woods to be out of sight of the road. Eight persons were present at the business session:

W. B. Allen
E. P. Austin
F. Blanchard
Geo. Dimmock
G. M. Dimmock (father of George)
R. W. Greenleaf
B. P. Mann
H. K. Morrison

The party was joined later by J. H. Emerton and J. C. Munro.

The eighth meeting, August 14, 1874, at Hartford, Conn. was attended by Messrs. Austin, Dimmock and Mann, and they were joined by C. J. S. Bethune, S. S. Haldeman, J. L. Leconte, J. G. Morris, J. A. Lintner, C. V. Riley, Wm. Saunders, and other wellknown entomologists of the time. At the meeting of September 11, The Entomological Club of the American Association for the Advancement of Science was organized to continue such meetings.

In the following year, July, 1875, another field meeting was held on Mt. Washington, this time with 24 persons—6 of them members of the Club, 18 guests: 10 of them men, 14, women. The August meeting was again with the American Association at Detroit, Mich.

In 1877, the Club was incorporated, a constitution and by-laws were adopted, and the membership revised, after which there were 24 resident members and 23 non-resident; a by-law defined a resident member as one who lived where he could attend meetings and get home the same night. The average attendance at meetings was for the first year 11.1; second year, 11.8; third year, 7.4 The first volume of "Psyche" was finished in 1877 with a deficit of $128.39; the running expenses of the Club in 1877 having been only $3.00.

The first meeting of the executive committee was on March 17, 1877, when it was proposed to start the collection of a publication fund of $2000. A circular was sent out in which was the following statement of the Club's objects:

> "While the headquarters of the Club are in Cambridge and its welfare would redound particularly to the credit of that city, its membership extends over the whole of North America and its advantages are offered with entire liberality to all the entomologists of the country, as far as practicable. There is but one other incorporated entomological society in the United States—The American Entomological Society in Philadelphia—and none other that is actually engaged at the present time in work of general interest."

June 13, 1879, a contract was made with Geo. Dimmock to publish Vol. 3 of "Psyche," beginning in 1880. By February, 1881, the resident membership had fallen to 16, while the non-reisdent had increased to 59. In December, 1882, the secretary, Mr. Dimmock, offers in "Psyche" to present at meetings papers by non-resident members and to send them on request reports of meetings. Books from the Club's library were sent to distant members on payment of postage, but little use was made of these facilities. In 1882 the average attendance at meetings fell to 5.2 and in 1884 to 4.

The loss on Vol. 3 of "Psyche" was $252.60, which was paid by Mr. Dimmock, and a vote of thanks passed by the Club.

In 1887 Mann moved away from Cambridge and the Club's library was taken to the Boston Society of Natural History. "Psyche" was not published between 1886 and 1888 for want of an editor, but it was taken up again by Scudder, who had built his new study in his garden and invited the Club in 1888 to meet and keep its library there.

The main interests of the Club at this time were the publication of "Psyche" and the membership of entomologists all over the country, and the meetings of local members were small. Presidents were elected from prominent entomologists in distant places, their principal duty being to furnish an address at the end of their term. W. H. Ashmead of Washington was president in 1893 and T. M. Bean of Laggan in the Rocky Mountains in 1894.

By 1895 Scudder's health began to fail and meetings were held at Henshaw's house in Cambridge or Hayward's in Boston, usually with small attendance. The annual meeting of 1903 was adjourned from month to month for want of a quorum, and the election took place only in April.

The original members of the Club had now nearly all given up an active part in its work. Austin, Dimmock, Mann, Morrison and Schwarz had moved away from Cambridge, Scudder was sick, and Hagen had died.

At this time a new set of men came into the Club. While the Cambridge Club had been spending its strength in spreading its influence all over the continent, the local entomologists had formed another organization, the Harris Club.[2] In 1895, W. L. W. Field became a member of the Cambridge Club and soon after was elected secretary; he was also a member of the Harris Club and arranged the union of these two organizations and at the meeting of December 26, 1902, the entire Harris Club was nominated for membrship.

March 13, 1903, at a meeting with three members present, Bowditch, Field and Hayward, 39 members of the Harris Club were elected. Many of these soon disappeared, but among them were a dozen active members for many years, some to the present day,—among them:

P. G. Bolster	W. F. Low	A. C. Sampson
H. K. Burrison	John Lowell	F. Sheriff
W. D. Denton	H. H. Newcomb	L. W. Swett
H. H. Kirkland	J. H. Rogers	A. G. Weeks

December 26, 1902, S. Henshaw was elected editor of "Psyche."

Meetings were held at the house of the Boston Society of Natural History and the annual meeting of 1903 (adjourned since January) was held on April 10, with 18 members present. During this year C. W. Johnson and C. V. Blackburn were elected members. A committee, Messrs. Bolster, Field, Henshaw and Johnson, was appointed to take charge of "Psyche." Scudder's sickness had gone so far that it was necessary to remove the Club's library from his house, and having no other place to keep the books, the Club voted to give to the Boston Society of Natural History any books it might need and to sell the rest. Some of these were sold by auction at Club meetings by H. H. Newcomb and the proceeds used toward the expenses of "Psyche." Meetings were held at the Boston Society of Natural History, at J. H. Emerton's room at 194 Clarendon St., and at the Appalachian Club's rooms in the Tremont

[2]The Harris Club (which has no relation to the Harris Entomological Club of 1866) was organized November 24, 1899 at 35 Court St., Boston in the office of H. H. Newcomb. W. L. W. Field was elected secretary and continued in office until the union with the Cambridge Entomological Club in 1903. The records of the Club are deposited in the library of the Boston Society of Natural History.

Building, and in emergencies at H. H. Newcomb's office, 35 Court Street, with attendance of 12 to 13. December 6, 1904 a meeting was held at Wm. Denton's in Wellesley to see his butterflies, with attendance of 12 members and 5 guests.

In 1904 to 1908 exhibitions of insects, open to the public, were held at the rooms of the Appalachian Club. The exhibition of November, 1908, included the following:

H. H. Newcomb, *Papilia turnus* and *glaucus* with intermediate forms.

A. P. Morse, Grasshoppers, showing methods of egg-laying.

W. L. W. Field, North American Sphingidæ.

F. B. Low, Gipsy moth, Browntail, etc.

W. M. Wheeler, 85 species of Ants of New England.

J. H. Emerton, Collection of 200 New England Spiders.

Emerton & Swett, Collection of Lepidoptera.

January 19, 1909, the amended by-laws, which had been in preparation for a long time, were adopted.

March, 1909, the last of the books from the Club's library were sold, and the old record books deposited with the Boston Society of Natural History.

December, 1909, the Club entertained the entomologists attending the meeting of the American Association for the Advancement of Science at a smoker at the Grundmann Studios, Clarendon Street.

At the annual meeting, January, 1910, the retiring president, P. G. Bolster, read a paper on the history of the Club.

C. T. Brues was elected a member of the Club October 19, 1909, and editor of "Psyche" at the annual meeting, January, 1910. At the same meeting W. M. Wheeler was elected president, and at the meeting of February, 1910, the Club voted to hold its meetings at the Bussey Institution. This brings us to another period in the Club's life familiar enough to the present members, and so my story ends.

THE BIOLOGY OF *TRICHOPODA PENNIPES* FAB. (DIPTERA, TACHINIDÆ),

A PARASITE OF THE COMMON SQUASH BUG.*

By Harlan N. Worthley.

Massachusetts Agricultural Experiment Station, Amherst, Mass.

PART I.

INTRODUCTION.

The common squash bug, *Anasa tristis* de Geer, is an ever-present and often troublesome pest in Massachusetts, and has been a subject for investigation at the Massachusetts Agricultural Experiment Station for the past three years. While studying the life history and habits of this pest, the writer discovered abundant evidence of the presence and activity of the parasite *Trichopoda pennipes.* A review of the literature showed that comparatively little is known of the life history and habits of this beneficial fly. Much to the surprise of the writer, in view of his own observations, it was found that some authors have even intimated that little good is derived by mankind from the work of this supposedly beneficial species.

Failure of the written records to substantiate observations of the writer furnished the initial stimulus to a study of the habits of the fly, the object of this study being to discover the exact relationship existing between parasite and host. A portion of the following account is the result of these studies.

During the course of the work it was found necessary to confine adults of both sexes in the same cage to induce mating. Some difficulty was experienced at first in determining the sex

*Thesis submitted for the degree of Master of Science at the Massachusetts Agricultural College, and published with the consent of the Director of the Graduate School. The writer takes this opportunity to express his thanks to Dr. H. T. Fernald, whose kindly interest has made the present study possible, and who has criticized, to their benefit, the drawings accompanying the paper; to Dr. G. C. Crampton, under whose supervision the morphological study has been carried on, for aid in matters of technic and the interpretation of parts; and to Dr. C. P. Alexander for assistance with the literature of dipterology.

of living flies, without undue handling, and this led to a study of the external anatomy of the species, the primary aim being the discovery of secondary sexual characters that might be readily recognized.

The scope of this investigation has gradually increased, and in this paper takes the form of an exposition of the external morphological characters of the species. These characters are here designated according to the most widely accepted view of leading workers in insect morphology, and thereby do violence to the terminology in common use among taxonomic workers. This is perhaps unfortunate, but it is unavoidable, if morphological accuracy is to be maintained.

SYNONYMY.

The species was first described by Fabricius (1794)[1] as *Musca pennipes*, from material secured from the "Carolinas." His subsequently described *Thereva hirtipes* (1805, p. 219.9), *Thereva pennipes* (1805, p. 219.8), and *Ocyptera ciliata* (1805, p. 315.9) have proved to be synonyms. His *Dictya pennipes* (1805, p. 327.5) is a change of genus from *Musca*. Other synonyms are *Phasia jugatoria* Say (1829), and *Trichopoda flavicornis* and *T. haitensis* of Robineau-Desvoidy (1830). The genus Trichopoda was erected by Latreille (1829), and both Wiedemann (1830) and Robineau-Desvoidy (1830) soon placed the *Musca pennipes* of Fabricius in this genus. The *T. pyrrhogaster* and *T. ciliata* of Wiedemann (1830) have since fallen as synonyms, Brauer and Bergenstamm (1891) showing that these were but females of the species. The complete synonymy, so far as can be determined by the writer, is included in the bibliography at the end of this paper.

GEOGRAPHICAL DISTRIBUTION

The genus *Trichopoda* belongs to the New World fauna. *T. pennipes* has a wide distribution in both North and South America and among the adjacent islands, according to Townsend

[1]Dates in parenthesis refer to the bibliography.

(1893), who records it from Argentina, Brazil, Mexico, San Domingo and Jamaica, and in the United States from New England to Florida, along the coast of the Gulf of Mexico to Texas, and in California. He speaks of it also from Michigan, Illinois, Indiana, and Iowa. It is essentially a lowland form, being most abundant within its range at elevations of five hundred feet or less. Aldrich (1915) states that the species "appears to occur from Argentina north to about the latitute of Kansas, and further north to the eastward, but not in the northwest." Records of its capture in St. Vincent, Porto Rico, and other islands of the West Indies are given in Aldrich's Catalogue (1905). Wilson (1923) adds St. Croix, of the Virgin Islands group, to this list.

HOSTS.

The first record of the life history of *Trichopoda pennipes* appears to be a note by Packard (1875) of a Tachina fly parasitic upon the squash bug (*Anasa tristis* de Geer, Hemiptera, Coreidæ.) While the species is not mentioned, the description points quite conslusively to *T. pennipes.* A. J. Cook (1889) records the insect by name and gives an account of its habit of parasitizing the squash bug. Later authors recording it as a parasite of the squash bug were Coquillett (1897), Chittenden (1899), and Weed and Conradi (1902). For a number of years no other host was known, but Morrill (1910) recorded a rearing of *T. pennipes* from the Northern Leaf-footed Plant Bug (*Leptoglossus oppositus*, Hemiptera, Coreidæ). Jones (1918) records it as an enemy of the Southern Green Plant Bug or Pumpkin Bug (*Nezara viridula*, Hemiptera, Pentatomidæ), and Watson (1918) also records this host in Florida, Drake (1920) also reared this parasitic fly in Florida from the Green Soldier Bug (*Acrosternum hilaris*, Hemiptera, Pentomidæ), the Green Stink-bug (*Acrosternum pennsylvanicum*) and a large Coreid, *Archimerus calcarator.* He also noted eggs on *Acanthocephala femorata* and *A. declivis.* Wilson (1923), in collecting *Nezara viridula* on the Island of St. Croix, found 93 per cent of the specimens parasitized by *T. pennipes.*

Mr. H. J. Reinhard, entomologist of the Texas Agricultural Experiment Station and a specialist in Tachinidæ, says in correspondence with the writer that in Texas *T. pennipes* is parasitic upon *Nezara viridula* and *Leptoglossus phyllopus*. He adds, "I have observed adults depositing eggs on the adult Harlequin Bug (*Murgantia histrionica*, Hemiptera, Pentatomidæ) but have never been able to obtain any emergence of the parasite."

In Massachusetts this beneficial insect is important as an enemy of the squash bug, and in the following pages it is treated in its relation to this host.

Methods employed.

The following account of the life history and habits of *Trichopoda pennipes* has been taken from field and laboratory records compiled by the writer during an investigation of the squash bug. Collections of the bugs in the field furnished parasitized material for breeding purposes and also indicated the percentage of infestation. In the laboratory the parasitized bugs were kept in breeding cages containing small potted squash plants. The cages used were devised at this Station, and are so built as to afford a maximum of light. A vertically-sliding pane of glass comprises the door, and this, together with a hinged glass top, allows all corners of the cage to be readily observed from the outside. The sides and back of the cage may be covered with fine-mesh cloth screening, or with copper wire cloth. During this investigation, the cages rested on pieces of slate covered with an inch of soil, to provide normal conditions for pupation of the parasite.

LIFE HISTORY.

The Egg. The female fly lays its eggs upon the body wall of the host, to which the eggs are firmly attached. The great majority of the eggs are found on the sides of the abdomen and thorax, although they are sometimes seen fastened to the upper surface of the body and the head, and rarely to the antennæ and legs.

The length of time necessary for the hatching of the egg was found to be in the neighborhood of thirty hours. To prove this point eggs were removed from the body of a bug as soon as laid, a moistened camel's hair brush proving to be excellent for this purpose, and were isolated in vials. After twenty-four hours the mouth-hooks of each young maggot could be seen rasping away at the inner surface of the egg-shell, and in thirty hours the larva was found protruding from the hole it had scraped in the floor of its prison. Eggs removed from the body surfaces of bugs thirty hours after oviposition were found to be empty, a hole in the bottom of each, and a corresponding hole in the chitin of the host, testifying to the penetration of the parasite.

The Larva. As stated above, the larva, upon hatching, penetrates the bottom of the egg-shell and burrows directly through the body-wall of the host, regardless of the thickness of chitin at that particular point.

Sufficient dissections of parasitized squash bugs have not been made to enable the writer to state accurately the habits of the parasite within its host, or the number of larval instars. Individuals of three different instars have been observed, and it is probable that there are four in all, as has been stated by Townsend (1908, p. 98) for certain other Tachinid parasites. Dissections seem to show that the larvæ while young live in the general body-cavity, no derangement of organs being apparent in these dissections. As the larvæ approach maturity, however, they gradually consume the fat body and those organs contained in the abdomen of the host, which was seen to be practically hollow in some adult squash bugs from which parasites had just emerged.

Upon the completion of growth, which requires approximately sixteen days, the larva forces its way out at the posterior end of the body of the host, which is still alive, and drops to the ground. This is not the case with the second generation larvæ, which appear to remain within the body of the host throughout the winter, completing their growth when the latter become active in the spring. The host dies within a day or two of the emergence of the parasite. Emergence through the side of the body, as recorded by Weed and Conradi (1902), has not been observed.

The Puparium. Within a few hours of the time the mature larva quits the host, it burrows into the soil to a depth of one to two inches, and there pupates within the last larval skin, which forms the puparium. The pupa, then, falls in the first class as defined by Thompson (1910, p. 284), and probably has a rapid early development. Dissections of the puparia have not been made, and thus the appearance of the pupa and its rate of development are unknown. The pupal period of the spring generation is approximately a month in length, while that of the summer generation lasts from thirteen to nineteen days.

The Adult. The flies are able to take wing within a few seconds following emergence, and have been observed to mate within twenty-four hours. The length of time which then ensues before oviposition commences is not known, nor has the average number of eggs laid per female been determined. One fly laid thirty-nine eggs in twenty-four hours, and another, when captured in the field, contained over one hundred eggs.

In the cages, honey-water on sponges failed to attract the flies. They were captured in the field from the flowers of Wild Carrot (*Daucus carota*) and Meadow Sweet (*Spiræa salicifolia*) and would feed from these flowers in the cages. The writer did not learn of Townsend's (1908, p. 110) method of feeding, using dry sugar and sponges moistened with water, until too late to use it in the breeding work.

The behavior of caged females toward the bugs confined with them was interesting to observe. The urge to lay eggs did not appear to be constant. At times the flies would walk about among the bugs, with apparent friendliness, and would even crawl over them without making a menacing movement. At other times a fly would dart at a bug and alight upon its back, and the writer would focus his attention in the expectation that an egg would be laid. The fly would turn this way and that upon the unresponsive host, as if trying to decide where to place the egg, but after a few seconds would walk off, as if having changed its mind, leaving no egg behind. When oviposition actually took place, the act was accomplished with great rapidity, the fly seeming scarcely to come to rest upon its host. That no such speed was necessary could be seen in the lack of interest displayed by the victim, which neither resisted the attack of the fly nor tried to dislodge the egg.

Relation Between Parasite and Host.

Various observers have noted the parasitic habit of *Trichopoda pennipes* and have speculated upon the amount of benefit derived from its activities. Thus Dr. A. S. Packard (1875) says, "The larvæ are very large, one specimen only occurring in the body of the *Coreus,* which seems apparently healthy, and performs its sexual functions in spite of the presence of so large a parasite." Chittenden (1899) observes that "Although these flies appeared soon after the advent of the bugs and in considerable abundance, they seemed to accomplish little in the direction of reducing the numbers of their host.—The parasitized individuals were not noticed to die much earlier than those which succumbed to natural causes." Weed and Conradi (1902)

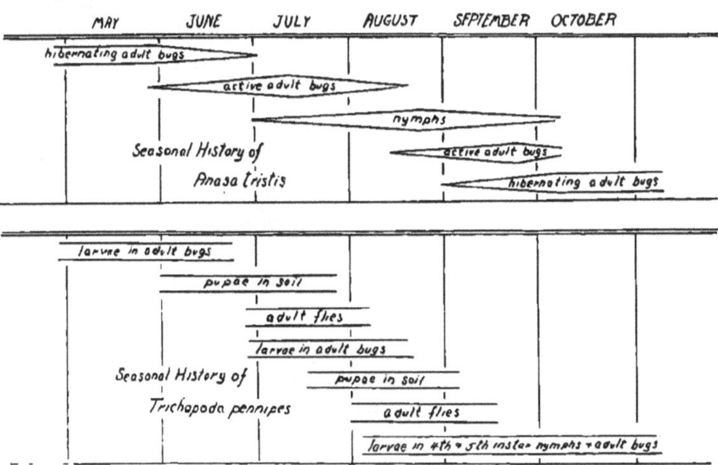

Fig. 1. Relation of *Trichopoda pennipes* to its host, *Anasa tristis,* Amherst, Massachusetts, 1922. Worthley (1923).

also mention the continued egg-laying of parasitized squash bugs. Drake (1920) in his notes on *T. pennipes* as a parasite of the Southern Green Stink-bug mentions percentages of parasitism ranging from 31 to 80 per cent.

About Amherst, Massachusetts, *Trichopoda pennipes* appears to have two full generations each year (Worthley, 1923). A single adult captured in October may indicate a partial third generation, but it is thought more probable that this was a laggard individual of the second generation.

The emergence and pupation of second generation larvæ in the fall was not observed in the cages, and it therefore appears that the parasite passes the winter as a larva within the body of the hibernating host. Development of these larvæ is completed in the spring, emergence from the host and pupation occurring during June and July. This emergence is shortly followed by the death of the host, which, in all cases so far observed, has not been able to commence egg-laying.

Pupæ developing from these overwintered larvæ begin to yield flies in late June. At this time only adult squash bugs are available, and upon these the flies deposit their eggs. These bugs are individuals which escaped parasitism the previous fall, and have lived to mate and lay eggs. Many of them are actively engaged in oviposition when attacked by the parasite, and these can often complete their egg-laying before the activities of the maggots become fatal. One female squash bug laid a cluster of viable eggs just six days previous to her death from parasitism, showing that the metabolism of the host is not seriously unbalanced until late in the development of the parasite. It is this apparent slight effect of parasitism on the egg-laying bugs which has caused investigators to question the efficiency of the parastism of *T. pennipes*.

While parasitized egg-laying squash bugs may be permitted to complete a practically normal existence, as has been shown above, the parasite itself may not be so well favored. Thus adult bugs begin to disappear from the fields about the middle of July, having completed the normal span of life. Parasite flies are actively laying eggs at this time, and often deposit them upon bugs which are destined to die before the parasitic larvæ have attained full growth. In such cases the parasite cannot complete its development, and perishes with its host.

Larvæ which have been more fortunately situated mature and pass on to the pupa stage during the latter part of July and early August. When these pupæ yield adult flies during August and the first part of September, many young squash bugs have become adult, and more have reached the fourth and fifth instars. Upon these bugs the parasite lays its eggs, and it is in this generation that the work of the fly is seen to be effective beyond question, since no parasitized bug appears to live to sexual maturity. Many nymphs (counts have shown about 50 per cent) die before becoming adult, and those which reach the adult state and pass the winter safely in hibernation, are subsequently killed by the parasite before laying eggs.

No parasites appear to reach maturity in nymphs which die. In this regard the egg-laying flies seem unable to discriminate closely between nymphs which are sufficiently developed to support the parasite maggots and those which contain too little substance. However, the flies seem to realize that their progeny will find too little nourishment in nymphs younger than the fourth instar, since third instar nymphs were rarely molested in the cages, and parasitized third instar nymphs were not collected in the field.

It was interesting to note that occasionally a nymph would escape parasitism by molting, leaving an unhatched parasite egg on the molted skin. This does not account for any great loss, however, since the egg of the parasite hatches in thirty hours, while the fourth and fifth instars of the squash bug require about six days and sixteen days respectively for their completion.

But one parasite has ever been observed to issue from one host. Several maggots have been observed to enter one host, but this has always seemed to result in the early death of the host and of the parasites within.

Collections of squash bugs in the fall give no indication of the true percentage of parasitism, since many nymphs die, and others slough off the empty egg-shells of the parasite with their molted nymphal skins. In midsummer, however, collections of overwintered adult bugs have indicated a parasitism as high as 80 per cent. There is no reason to suppose that the percentage of parasitism may not often run as high among the older nymphs and new adult squash bugs in the fall. Thus it would seem that the activities of *Trichopoda pennipes* furnish an exceedingly important natural check upon the increase of *Anasa tristis*.

Summary

Trichopoda pennipes is a parasitic fly belonging to the family Tachinidæ. The species enjoys a wide distribution in the lowlands of North and South America and the adjacent islands, and has been recorded as attacking several species of insects belonging to the hemipterous families Coreidæ and Pentatomidæ. Among these hosts is the common squash bug, which in Massachusetts is the principal host, and possibly the only one attacked by the fly.

The investigations recorded in this paper indicate that in Massachusetts this parasite passes through two full generations annually. Adults of the first generation deposit their eggs on egg-laying adult squash bugs, during July. Those of the second generation attack the older nymphs and new adult bugs in August and September. Collections of squash bugs have indicated a parasitism of eighty per cent. Squash bugs which are parasitized in the fall apparently do not live to sexual maturity, and thus an important natural check is placed upon the increase of the squash bug.

NOTES ON *MUSCINA PASCUORUM* MEIGEN DURING 1923.

By Charles W. Johnson.

Boston Society of Natural History.

The sudden occurrence, and in great numbers, of *Mucina pascuorum* in North America in 1922, was recorded by the writer in Psyche, Vol. 30, p. 1-5, Feb., 1923.

Early in 1923 very few specimens were seen. Mr. A. P. Morse took a specimen Jan. 18 at Wellesley, Mass. The most interesting recorded is that from Bridgeton, N. J., where Mr. F. M. Schott captured a specimen under bark, Feb. 11. This, so far, is the most southern record for the species. Specimens were also taken under bark, at Annandale, N. J. March 7, by parties scouting for Gypsy Moth eggs. The locality is about 20 miles west of Bound Brook, where it was previously recorded. A specimen was taken in a window at Brookline, Mass., March 3. Having stated to Mr. F. W. Walker that it would be interesting to see how the fly had stood the winter, Mr. Walker visited the locality where they were so abundant, and in a letter says:—"I am sending a box of flies taken April 10, 1923, at Asbury Grove, Hamilton, Mass., on the same skylight that I collected from Nov. 9, 1922. A few scattering ones were taken on other windows." The box contained 125 *M. pascuorum*, 93 *Pollenia rudis*, 7 *Phormia regina* and 6 *Muscina assimilis*.

None were observed during the late spring and summer, but early in September, Mr. L. W. Swett, brought me a number of flies that had accumulated in the globe of an arc light at the Glen House, at the foot of Mt. Washington, N. H. Among these was one *M. pascuorum* the most northern record for New England. A few specimens were received from Attleboro, Mass., Oct. 14 and Worcester, Nov. 2. Two were collected on windows at Brookline, Oct. 28 and Nov. 4 and one on a window in Boston Dec. 3. Mr. Walker informs me that appararently the fly was not seen at Asbury Grove this fall.

The scarcity of this fly during 1923 in comparison with its abundance in 1922 is undoubtedly due to the very dry weather during the late summer and fall. Owing to the drouth there was comparatively little fungi. As this species is said, by European authors, to frequent *Amanita citrina*, the paucity of fungi during the late summer and early autumn would, also, probably account for the scarcity of the fly. It seems an interesting problem;— if the hibernating females lay eggs in the spring and the larvæ live on fungi, on what does the female lay her eggs, when there are practically no fungi in the early spring?

I hope, during the coming season if possible, to make some experiments relative to the breeding habits of this fly and information regarding its further distribution will be greatly appreciated.

NOTES ON CUBAN ANTS.

WM. M. MANN.

Bureau of Entomology, U. S. Department of Agriculture.

In a small collection of ants from Cuba sent by Mr. S. C. Bruner, of the experimental station at Santiago de las Vegas, and collected by him and Mr. C. H. Ballou, are two undescribed species of the genus *Macromischa*. This increases the number of known Cuban species to sixteen, and I think it probable that future collectors will find still more of these interesting ants, the species of which appear to be very local in distribution and difficult to find.

In addition to the descriptions of these I have listed for distributional data several other species of interest.

Macromischa (Macromischa) bruneri, new species.

Worker. Length 2.75 mm.

Head a little longer than broad, as broad in front as behind, with slightly convex sides, broadly rounded corners and nearly straight occipital border. Clypeus convex, obtusely carinate at middle, straight at anterior border. Antennal scapes nearly attaining occipital corners; funicular joints 3-8 transverse, club rather strong. Thorax rather robust, without sutures above; sides of prothorax evenly rounded. Epinotal spines nearly approximate at base, not very acuminate, about as long as the epinotal declivity. Petiolar peduncle slender, about as long as the node, which is longer than high, rounded above, and seen from above twice as long as broad. Postpetiole twice as broad as petiole, as long as broad and only slightly broader behind than in front. Femora slender basally, swollen at middle and narrowed apically, with the flexor border rather strongly concave. Tibiæ strongly incrassate.

Moderately shining. Mandibles sparsely striate and with several coarse punctures. Head, thorax and epinotum densely punctate and subreticulately striate, the latter strongest on pronotum; petiolar pedicel subtly punctate, nodes of petiole and postpetiole smooth above, obliquely striate at sides. Gaster and appendages finely punctate.

Pilosity pale yellow, fine and erect, rather sparse on head, body and appendages.

Brownish red, the gaster darker and the legs lighter than the rest.

Sierra Maestra, July, 1902, Alt. 4500-5000 ft.

Type. Cat. No. 26497 U. S. N. M.

Described from four workers.

M. bruneri is most closely related to *M. affinis* Mann, and like it, superficially resembles a Tetramorium. It differs from *affinis* in its smaller size, the much shorter epinotal spines (in *affinis* these are fully as long as the petiolar pedicel), in the petiolar node rising less abruptly from the pedicel and in sculpture and coloration.

Macromischa (Macromischa) violacea, new species.

Worker. Length 4.5 mm.

Head, excluding mandibles, one-sixth longer than broad, sides very slightly convex, posterior corners broadly rounded, border nearly straight. Mandibles with five rather strong teeth. Clypeus nearly flat, its anterior border straight at middle. Eyes large and convex, situated at middle of sides of head. Antennal scapes not quite attaining occipital corners; funicular joints 2-8 scarcely broader than long; club shorter than remainder of funiculus. Thorax and epinotum very robust, as broad in front as behind and only feebly and narrowly constricted at sides between pro- and mesothorax; no sutures discernible. Epinotal spines moderately thick, slightly curved, shorter than their distance apart at base. Peduncle of petiole nearly twice as long as the node, which rises from it abruptly and, in profile, is higher than long, with nearly straight anterior and posterior surfaces and slightly convex dorsum, and from above transversely suboval. Postpetiole campanulate and broader than long. Femora and tibiæ rather strongly incrassate.

Shining throughout. Mandibles coarsely striate. Head and thorax with fine, widely separated longitudinal wavy carinulæ, discernible above only in certain lights, stronger on pleuræ; head, body and appendages rather finely punctate and with erect, whitish hairs that are longer and stiffer on the legs.

Color black, head and thorax with strong violaceous reflections.

Sierra Maestra, July, 1922. Alt. 600-900 m.

Cotypes. Cat. No. 26498 U. S. N. M.

Described from two workers.

This is a very distinct species, resembling *M. scabripes* Mann somewhat in form and in having the femora minutely tuberculate, but differing strongly in sculpture and color and in its larger size and stouter thorax.

The violaceous reflection of the tegument is unusually strong, even for a *Macromischa*.

Macromischa (Macromischa) affinis Mann

Sierra Maestra, July, 1923. Alt. 3000-3500 ft.

A single worker in the collection is considerably darker than those in the type series, with the head and thorax dark, reddish brown and only the bases of the femora pale, otherwise agreeing exactly.

Macromischa (Croesomyrmex) wheeleri Mann

Vinales, April

Three workers.

Macromischa (Croesomyrmex) poeyi Wheeler

Worker. Length 5.5 mm. (Fig. 1.)

Head longer than broad, strongly narrowed from behind eyes to occipital border which has an elevated margin. Clypeus convex, carinate at middle, shallowly concave at middle of anterior border. Antennæ very slender, their scapes surpassing occipital corners by one-third of their length; first funicular joint shorter than the second and third together, second joint about two and one-half times as long as broad, remaining joints gradually increasing in length toward apex, club long and slender. Prothorax with a transverse, subquadrate "neck"; sides of mesothorax angulately expanded behind the middle. Epinotum unarmed, its base three times as long as broad and nearly four times as long as the declivity; in profile shallowly concave. Petiole very long and slender, its node low and rounded above

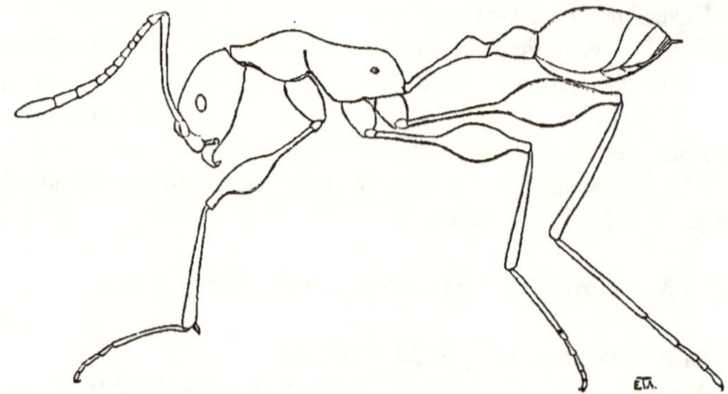

Fig. 1. *Macromischa Cræsomyrmex poeyi* Wheeler. Worker.

and a little more than half as long as pedicel; from above, the node is scarcely thicker than the pedicel, about four times as long as broad and with straight sides. Postpetiole elongate, campanulate. Legs long and very slender, except the apical three-eighths of femora which are very strongly swollen.

Thorax and epinotum shining, with moderately strong and irregular rugæ which are transverse on dorsum, subconcentric on mesonotal and longitudinal on epinotal pleuræ; head, petiole, gaster and appendages more shining, and finely punctate.

Stiff, blunt, erect, brownish hairs, abundant on head and body; finer and pointed on legs; erect hairs lacking on antennæ which bear fine and shorter semirecumbent hairs.

Thorax, epinotum and basal portion of femora reddish brown, the remainder black.

Vinales, April.

Described from one worker. The species was described from a specimen in the Gundlach collection in Havana under a sealed glass and Wheeler's description differs only in the shape of the postpetiole, described as broad as long, and in the sculpture of the thorax, described as finely and densely punctate, points which probably could not be made out with a hand lens at some distance from the specimen.

In addition to the unusual structure of the femora, the elongate head, narrowed behind, resembling that of some of the Aphænogasters, is distinctive.

Myrmelachista rogeri Ern. André.

Sierra Maestra, Alt. 3000-3500 ft. July.

Prenolepis gibberosa Roger.

Sierra Maestra, July. Alt. 2900-3500 ft.

This is evidently widely distributed in the higher, wooded portions of Cuba.

Camponotus (Myrmeurynota) gilviventris Roger.

Nagua, Oriente, July.

Colobopsis (Manniella) sphaericus Roger var. **sphaeralis** Roger.

Sierra Maestra, Alt. 3000-3500 ft. July.

NOTES UPON SURCOUF'S TREATMENT OF THE TABANIDÆ IN THE GENERA INSECTORUM AND UPON ENDERLEIN'S PROPOSED NEW CLASSIFICATION OF THIS FAMILY.[1]

By J. Bequaert.

The Tabanidæ are a family of Diptera of considerable economic importance. They are universal in their distribution and extremely numerous in species, over 2,100 forms having been described thus far. The great majority of these bite and suck the blood of vertebrates and thus become at times very troublesome to man and his domestic animals, in addition to being actual or potential carriers of infectious diseases. Surcouf's review of the family in Wytsman's "Genera Insectorum" (Brussels, 1921, 205 pp., 5 Pls.) must therefore be greeted with satisfaction. Only those who have attempted work along similar lines can fully appreciate the amount of painstaking drudgery and first-hand knowledge involved to make such compilations of real value. Considered as a whole, Surcouf's revision is as satisfactory as it could have been made within a reasonable limit of time and it is far from my intention to present herewith unfavorable criticism. My remarks are merely prompted by the ever increasing interest these flies are assuming for medical and veterinary entomology, so that Surcouf's work is likely to be perused as a source of information by many students with little or no entomological training. It seems therefore necessary to call attention to certain omissions and errors which might easily lead astray the non-specialist.

In the introductory part Surcouf deals with the external morphology and adds certain details of internal anatomy: his researches upon the structure of the ocelli and the genitalia are presented as original work. An account of the habits of the adults, oviposition, larval and pupal stages, and enemies follows. This is supplemented by some original observations in an appendix (pp. 186-194) and also by notes under the several genera.

[1]Contribution from the Department of Tropical Medicine of Harvard University Medical School.

Nevertheless the treatment of the bionomics is very inadequate and hardly does justice to our present knowledge. Thus it is stated that "the habits of *Goniops* are unknown" (p. 105), although the life-history of that genus has been worked out by W. R. Walton (Ent. News, XIX, 1908, pp. 464-465, Pl. XXII) and W. L. McAtee (Proc. Ent. Soc. Washington, XIII, 1911, pp. 21-29, Pls. I-III). Incidentally it may be mentioned that Surcouf's supposition that *Goniops* lives as an external parasite "after the fashion of *Hippobosca*" is a mere surmise not backed by any observation and highly improbable. To return to the bionomics of the family, W. Marchand has fortunately published a recent and very full account of "The Early Stages of Tabanidæ" (Monogr. of the Rockefeller Institute, New York, No. 13, 1920, 204 pp., 15 Pls.), in which the student will find all needed information. In his discussion of the parasitary specificity of tabanids (pp. 189-190), Surcouf mentions that, while most of the blood-sucking species attack mammals, *Tabanus crocodilinus* Austen and other African forms bite crocodiles and that he has himself taken a *Tabanus* in the Sahara on *Varanus griseus*. Still more remarkable, however, is the behavior of *Tabanus albipectus* Bigot, which, according to Fryer's observations in the Seychelles (Austen, Bull. Ent. Research, XI, 1920, p. 45), attacks sea-turtles, biting them between the plates of the neck.

It would be fastidious to list the errors of dates and pages which I have noticed in the bibliography, but the student should be warned against trusting the references indiscriminately.

REMARKS UPON THE GENERA

Surcouf is extremely conservative in his taxonomic treatment, since, with few exceptions, he accepts only genera that have been in use for a long time among students of the group. He retains the division into two subfamilies, Tabaninæ and Pangoniinæ, proposed more than fifty years ago by H. Lœw (Die Dipteren-Fauna Südafrika's, I, 1860, pp. 14 and 31). *Thaumastocera* Grünberg he places at the end of the family as a genus of doubtful affinities, but, on account of the absence of tibial spurs, it certainly comes in the Tabaninæ, a group which, moreover, contains several other forms with well-developed ocelli. Surcouf admits 43 genera, of which *Baikalia* (p. 39; monotypic for *B. vaillanti* Surcouf), *Guyona* (p. 141; monotypic for *Pangonia mesembrinoides* Surcouf, 1908),[1] *Brodenia* (p. 160; monotypic for *B. cinerea* Surcouf), and *Lesneus* (p. 161; monotypic for *L. canescens* Surcouf) are proposed for the first time. Unfortunately two of these new generic names are preoccupied: *Baikalia* Surcouf (not *Baicalia* v. Martens, 1876) I propose to replace by *Surcoufiella*, new name, and *Brodenia* Surcouf (not *Brodenia* Gedoelst, 1913) by *Braunsiomyia*, new name. The only species of the last-named genus, *Braunsiomyia cinerea* (Surcouf) was discovered on the sandy beach at Port Elizabeth (Algoa Bay), Cape Colony, by that enthusiastic South African entomologist Dr. H. Brauns.

Walker's subdivisions of *Pangonius* and most of Ad. Lutz' generic creations among South American tabanids are not accepted by Surcouf and many of those proposed by Ad. Lutz are not even enumerated. There are, however, a number of other generic names published previous to 1920, which have been overlooked by Surcouf and in some other cases the names he uses are obsolete or wrongly spelled.

Hexatoma Meigen, 1820 (p. 26). This name is preoccupied by *Hexatoma* Latreille, 1809, and should be replaced by *Heptatoma* Meigen, 1803, which, moreover, has many years priority.

Chrysozona Meigen, 1800 (p. 28). I cannot agree with those who claim that this name should replace *Hæmatopota* Meigen, 1803. I have recently examined an original copy, now at the Library of the American Museum of Natural History, of Meigen's pamphlet "Nouvelle Classification des Insectes Diptères" (Paris, 1800) and find that this work merely gives short generic descriptions without mentioning any species, so that these so-called genera having no genotypes should be regarded as *nomina nuda*, and therefore without nomenclatorial standing.

Lepidoselaga Osten Sacken, 1876 (p. 43). There is no sufficient reason why this amended form should be preferred to the original *Lepiselaga* Macquart, 1838.

[1]*Guyona* does not appear to be generically distinct from *Orgizomyia*, as will be shown in a subsequent paper.

Dorcalæmus Austen, 1910 (p. 112). This name was originally spelled *Dorcalœmus.*

Cœnoprosopon Ricardo, 1915 (p. 132). The original spelling of this name is *Cænoprosopon.*

Diclisa (p. 112) as characterized by Surcouf is not *Diclisa* Schiner, 1867, which has as genotype *Pangonia incompleta* Macquart and is evidently a synonym of *Scione* Walker, 1850. Surcouf's genus *Diclisa* appears to correspond to Enderlein's (1922) *Rhinotriclista* and *Triclista.*

Cadicera Macquart, 1855 (p. 106). As shown by Austen (Bull. Ent. Research, XI, 2, 1920, p. 140), this name should be replaced by the earlier *Phara* Walker, 1850.

Diatomineura Rondani, 1863 (p. 129). Brèthes (Bull. Soc. Ent. France, 1914, p. 59) and Austen (Bull. Ent. Research, XI, 2, 1920, p. 139) have shown that this is a synonym of the earlier *Osca* Walker (Insecta Saundersiana, Dipt., I, 1850, p. 10).

Orgyzomyia Grünberg, 1906 (p. 139). The correct spelling is *Orgizomyia.*

Pelecorrhynchus Macquart, 1850 (p. 110). This name was originally spelled *Pelecorhynchus.*

The following generic names are not listed by Surcouf:

Acanthocerella Brèthes, An. Mus. Nac. Buenos Aires, XX, 1910, p. 475. Monotypic for *A. boliviensis* Brèthes, 1910. South America.

Amphichlorops Ad. Lutz, Mem. Inst. Osw. Cruz, VI, 1914, p. 166. Type: *Tabanus flavus* Wiedemann, 1828. South America.

Anacampta Schiner, Verh. Zool. Bot. Ges. Wien, XVII, 1867, p. 305. Without description or species. Evidently an error for *Apocampta* Schiner.

Catachlorops Ad. Lutz, Mem. Inst. Osw. Cruz, VI, 1914, p. 166. Type: *Dichelacera fuscipennis* Macquart, 1847. South America.

Chelotabanus Ad. Lutz, Mem. Inst. Osw. Cruz, VI,1914, p. 166. Type: *Tabanus fuscus* Wiedemann, 1819. South America.

Chlorotabanus Ad. Lutz, Mem. Inst. Osw. Cruz, VI, 1914, p. 167. Type: *Tabanus mexicanus* Linnæus, 1767. North and South America.

Cœnura Bigot, Ann. Soc. Ent. France, (3) V, 1857, p. 286. Monotypic for *C. longicauda* Bigot, 1857. Chile. A number of species have been described, all of which have been omitted by Surcouf.

Cryptotylus Ad. Lutz, Mem. Inst. Osw. Cruz, VI, 1914, p. 166. No species mentioned. South America.

Cydistomyia Taylor, Proc. Linn. Soc. New South Wales, XLIV, 1919. p. 47. Monotypic for *C. doddi* Taylor, 1919. Queensland.

Dicladocera Ad. Lutz, Comm. Linhas Telegr. Estr. de Matto Grosso ao Amazonas, Ann. No. 8, Zool., Taban., 1912, p. 4. Monotypic for *Dicladocera unicolor* Ad. Lutz, 1912.

Dyspangonia Ad. Lutz, Revista Soc. Scientif. Sao Paulo, I, 1, 1905, p. 27. Type: *Pangonia fuscipennis* Wiedemann, 1828. This is a synonym of *Esenbeckia* Rondani.

Erephosis Bigot, Mém. Soc. Zool. France, IV, 1891, p. 414. Misspelling of *Erephopsis*.

Esenbackia Surcouf, Bull. Mus. Hist. Nat. Paris, XV, 1909, p. 257. Misspelling of *Esenbeckia*.

Gonisops Kertész, Catal. Tabanid., 1900, p. 25. Evidently a misspelling of *Goniops*.

Holococeria Ricardo, Arch. f. Naturgesch., LXXX, Abt. A, Heft 8, (1914) 1915, p. 128. A misspelling of *Holcoceria*.

Laphriopsis Ad. Lutz, Mem. Inst. Osw. Cruz, III, 1911, p. 71. An evident error for *Laphriomyia*.

Leptotabanus Ad. Lutz and A. Neiva, Mem. Inst. Osw. Cruz, VI, 1914, p. 72. The name is used in an enumeration of species for *Leptotabanus nigrovenosus* Ad. Lutz and A. Neiva, but I was unable to find a description of either genus or species.

Leucotabanus Ad. Lutz, Mem. Inst. Osw. Cruz, VI, 1914, p. 167. Type: *Tabanus leucaspis* Wiedemann, 1828. South America.

Macrocormus Ad. Lutz, Mem. Inst. Osw. Cruz, VI, 1914, p. 167. Type: *Tabanus sorbillans* Wiedemann, 1828. South America.

Melanotabanus Ad. Lutz and A. Neiva, Mem. Inst. Osw. Cruz, VI, 1914, p. 76. Monotypic for *M. fuliginosus* Ad. Lutz and A. Neiva, 1914. South America.

Metoponaplos Ricardo, Arch. f. Naturgesch., LXXX, Abt. A, Heft 8, (1914) 1915, p. 124. Type by original designation: *Pangonia parva* Walker, 1848. According to Enderlein (Mitt. Zool. Mus. Berlin, X, 2, 1922, p. 342), this is a synonym of *Scarphia* Walker, 1850, a view with which I fully concur.

Merycomyia Hine, Ohio Naturalist, XII, 1912, p. 515. Type by original designation: *Tabanus whitneyi* Johnson, 1904 (Syn.: *Merycomyia geminata* Hine, 1912). North America.

Neochrysops Walton, Proc. Ent. Soc. Washington, XX, 1918, p. 191. Monotypic for *N. globosus* Walton, 1918. North America.

Neotabanus Ad. Lutz, Mem. Inst. Osw. Cruz, VI, 1914, p. 167. Type: *Tabanus trilineatus* Latreille, 1814. South America. Ad. Lutz (Ibidem, p. 47) claims that his generic name has priority over *Neotabanus* Ricardo, 1911, but I have been unable to discover on what evidence this statement is based.

Orthostylus Ad. Lutz and A. Neiva, Mem. Inst. Osw. Cruz, VI, 1914, p. 74. Monotypic for *O. ambiguus* Ad. Lutz and A. Neiva, 1914. South America.

Palimmecomyia Taylor, Proc. Linn. Soc. New South Wales, XLII, 1917, p. 518. Monotypic for *P. celænospila* Taylor, 1917. Queensland.

Parasilvius Ferguson, Proc. Roy. Soc. Victoria, N. S., XXXIII, 1921, p. 8. Monotypic for *P. fulvus* Ferguson, 1921. Australia.

Phæomyia Ad. Lutz, Mem. Inst. Osw. Cruz, III, 1911, p. 83. Evidently a misspelling for *Phæoneura*.

Phæotabanus Ad. Lutz, Mem. Inst. Osw. Cruz, VI, 1914, p. 168. Type: *Tabanus litigiosus* Walker, 1850. South America.

Phibalomyia Taylor, Proc. Roy. Soc. Victoria, N. S., XXXII, 2, 1920, p. 165. New name for *Elaphromyia* Taylor (Proc. Linn. Soc. New South Wales, XLI, 1917, p. 749), not of Bigot, 1859. Monotypic for *Elaphromyia carteri* Taylor, 1917. Queensland.

Philorites Cockerell, Entomologist, XLI, 1908, p. 264. Monotypic for *P. johannseni* Cockerell, 1908. Fossil in the Eocene of Colorado.

Rhabdotylus Ad. Lutz, Mem. Inst. Osw. Cruz, VI, 1914, p. 166. Type: *Tabanus planiventris* Wiedemann, 1828. South America.

Pœcilosoma Ad. Lutz, Mem. Inst. Osw. Cruz, VI, 1914, p. 167. Type: *Tabanus quadripunctatus* Fabricius, 1805. South America.

Rhigioglossa Wiedemann, Aussereurop. Zweifl. Ins., I, 1828, p. 105. Used in the combination "*Rhigioglossa testacea*" as a synonym of *Rhinomyza edentula* Wiedemann, which thus will be its genotype. The name takes precedence over *Erodiorhynchus* Macquart, 1838, based upon the same species.

Rhynomyza Surcouf, Bull. Mus. Hist. Nat. Paris, XV, 1909, p. 260. Misspelling of *Rhinomyza.*

Stenotabanus Ad. Lutz, Mem. Inst. Osw. Cruz, VI, 1914, p. 167. Type: *Tabanus tæniotes* Wiedemann, 1828. South America.

Stictotabanus Ad. Lutz and A. Neiva, Mem. Inst. Osw. Cruz, VI, 1914, p. 72. The name is used in an enumeration of species for *Stictotabanus maculipennis* (Macquart). Since this is a described species the generic name has a standing in nomenclature, even though the genus has apparently not been hitherto defined.

In the case of the new generic names proposed by Ad. Lutz in Mem. Inst. Osw. Cruz, VI, 1914, pp. 166-168, the only published descriptions are contained in a key and are not accompanied by references to species. In a previous article by Lutz and Neiva, however, which appeared in the same volume (pp. 69-80), these new names have been used in enumerations of species and I have selected genotypes from among them. *Cryptotylus* alone has apparently not yet been used in connection with a specific name so that it still is a *nomen nudum.* Ad. Lutz also closes his article with the statement (p. 168) that it was published before (in 1913) in the Brazilian journal "Brazil Medico." I have been unable to discover whether his new generic names should therefore be properly dated from 1913, but it would appear that they were not used in connection with specific names previously to 1914. Many of Ad. Lutz' proposed genera have not been noticed in the Zoological Record.

The following additional genera of Tabanidæ are of more recent date:

Heterochrysops Kröber, Zool. Jahrb., Abt. f. Syst., XLIII, 1920, p. 55. For a number of Palaearctic species of *Chrysops*, none of which is designated as type. *Chrysops flavipes* Meigen, 1804, is herewith selected as such.

Neochrysops Szilády, Ann. Hist. Nat. Mus. Hungarici, XIX, 1922, p. 126. Type by original designation: *Neochrysops grandis* Szilády, 1922, Formosa. The name is preoccupied by *Neochrysops* Walton, 1918.[1] The genus, however, appears doubtfully distinct from *Chrysops* and need therefore not be renamed at present.

Silviochrysops Szilády, Ann. Hist. Nat. Mus. Hungarici, XIX, 1922, p. 126. Monotypic for *Silviochrysops flavescens* Szilády, 1922, Formosa.

Surcoufia Kröber, Arch. f. Naturgesch., LXXXVIII, Abt. A, Heft 8, 1922, p. 115. Monotypic for *Surcoufia paradoxa* Kröber, 1922, Northwest Africa.

Finally in a recent paper which will be considered in detail below, Enderlein has proposed a considerable number of new generic names. These it appears unnecessary to list at present, since their exact status is as yet uncertain.

Remarks Upon North American Species.

Among the misspellings of names, I mention only those of *Chrysops nigribimbo* Whitney (not *nigrilimbo*) and *Tabanus superjumentarius* Whitney (not *suberjumentarius*).

Tabanus lugubris Osten Sacken appears to belong properly in the genus *Snowiellus*, from examination of a specimen obtained at Tampa, Florida, by Mr. E. Bell.

Tabanus whitneyi Johnson belongs in the genus *Merycomyia*.

Tabanus mexicanus. The synonymy and distribution given by Surcouf under that name should be revised. As shown by F. Knab (Insecutor Inscitiæ Menstruus, IV, 1916, pp. 95-100), four species have been commonly confused under *mexicanus*:

[1] *Neochrysops* Bethune-Baker, Trans. Ent. Soc. London, (1922) 1923, p. 279, in Lepidoptera, is similarly preoccupied.

(1) *Tabanus mexicanus* Linnæus (Syn.: *T. olivaceus* de Geer and *T. punctatus* Fabricius). Mexico, Central America, Trinidad.

(2) *Tabanus inanis* Fabricius (Syn.: *T. ochroleucus* Meigen, *T. viridiflavus* Walker, and perhaps also *T. sulphureus* Palisot de Beauvois). South and Central America.

(3) *Tabanus flavus* Macquart. Southeastern United States: from New Jersey to Florida, Missouri and Louisiana. This name is unfortunately preoccupied by *Tabanus flavus* Wiedemann and no substitute appears to be available.

(4) *Tabanus luteoflavus* Bellardi (Syn.: *T. mexicanus* var. *limonus* Townsend). Mexico.

The following North American species have been omitted:

Chrysops calopterus Hine, Ohio Naturalist, VI, 1905, p. 392, ♀. Guatemala.

Chrysops hinei Daecke, Ent. News, XVIII, 1907, p. 143, ♀. New Jersey.

Chrysops parvulus Daecke, Ent. News, XVIII, 1907, p. 142, ♀. New Jersey.

Merycomyia geminata Hine, Ohio Naturalist, XII, 1912, p. 515, Pl. XXV, figs. 2 and 4, ♀ ♂. This is a synonym of *Merycomyia whitneyi* (Johnson).

Merycomyia mixta Hine, Ohio Naturalist, XII, 1912, p. 516, Pl. XXV, figs. 1 and 3, ♀. Georgia, North America.

Neochrysops globosus Walton, Proc. Ent. Soc. Washington, XX, 1918, p. 192, fig. I, ♀. Eastern United States (Maryland).

Silvius jonesi Cresson, Proc. Ac. Nat. Sc. Philadelphia, LXXI, 1919, p. 175, ♀ ♂. California.

Tabanus subniger Coquillett, Ent. News, XVII, 1906, p. 48, ♀. Illinois.

Tabanus atratus var. *fulvopilosus* Johnson, Psyche, XXVI, 1919, p. 164, ♀. Florida, New Jersey.

A number of additional species of *Tabanus* have been described by J. McDunnough in 1921 and 1922 (Canad. Entom., LIII, 1921, pp. 139-144 and LIV, 1922, p. 239), namely: *T. atrobasis*, *T. laniferus*, *T. metabolus*, *T. nudus*, *T. rupestris*, and *T. trepidus*; and this author has also reinstated *Tabanus calif-*

ornicus Marten and *T. hæmaphorus* Marten as valid species. More recently Hine (Canad. Entom., LV, 1923, pp. 143-146) has added *T. gracilipalpis* and *T. sexfasciatus.*

Including these, we obtain a total of 334 species of Tabanidæ known at present from America north of Panama. They are divided among the several genera as follows: *Apatolestes*, 1; *Chrysops*, 71; *Hæmatopota*, 3; *Corizoneura*, 4; *Diachlorus*, 1; *Diatomineura*, 4; *Dichelacera*, 6; *Rhinotriclista* (*Diclisa* of Surcouf), 1; *Erephopsis*, 2; *Esenbeckia*, 1; *Goniops*, 1; *Lepiselaga*, 1; *Merycomyia*, 2; *Neochrysops*, 1; "*Pangonius*,"[1] 18; *Pityocera*, 1; *Scione*, 2; *Silvius*, 4; *Snowiellus*, 2; *Stibasoma*, 2; and *Tabanus*, 206. Of these *Goniops*, *Merycomyia*, *Neochrysops*, and *Snowiellus* are restricted to the Nearctic region (north of Mexico).

It may still be mentioned that Surcouf (p. 130) erroneously quotes *Trichophthalma amœna* Bigot and *Hermoneura landbecki* Philippi among the synonyms of *Diatomineura latipalpis* (Macquart), having evidently followed in this Kertész (Cat. Dipt., III, 1908, p. 170). Both Bigot's and Philippi's descriptions refer, however, to a nemestrinid which should be known as *Eurygastromyia landbecki* (Philippi). See Lichtwardt, Deutsch. Ent. Zeitschr., 1910, p. 608.

Remarks Upon Ethiopian Species

Tabanus corax Lœw, Wien. Ent. Monatschr., VII, 1863, p. 10. Surcouf (p. 79) lists this as a doubtful synonym of *Tabanus pluto* Walker. Neave (Bull. Ent. Research, V, 1915, p. 308), however, has shown that Lœw's name should be used for *Tabanus xanthomelas* Austen, of which *T. leucaspis* v. d. Wulp (not of Wiedemann) is a synonym.

Tabanus alboventralis Newstead is recorded twice in the list (p. 59), the first time misspelled "*albiventralis.*" It is apparently a synonym of *T. sufis* Jænnicke.

[1]Whether there any true *Pangonius*, in the restricted sense, in North America appears extremely doubtful. The three species which I have examined, viz., *tranquilla* Osten Sacken, *rasa* Osten Sacken, and *fera* Williston present all the characters of Austen's genus *Buplex*, to which, I believe, they should be transferred.

Tabanus blanchardi Surcouf and *T. gabonensis* Macquart are still listed as distinct species, whereas they are now generally regarded as synonyms of *T. secedens* Walker.

Hæmatopota maculosifacies Austen is listed twice (p. 34); also erroneously as *maculifacies* Austen.

Pangonius brevis Austen (p. 127) belongs properly in the genus *Phara* (*Cadicera*).

Pangonius austeni J. Bequaert (p. 127). This name should be deleted from the list. As stated by Austen (Ann. Mag. Nat. Hist., (8) XI, 1913, pp. 560-562), it was based upon the male of *P. infuscus* Austen and the female of *Diatomineura neavei* Austen. I have convinced myself of the correctness of Major Austen's view after he has kindly compared some of my specimens with the types of these two species, during my recent visit at the British Museum.

Pangonius neavei J. Bequaert (p. 128) should also be dropped since it is not Austen's *Diatomineura neavei*, but was based on both sexes of *Corizoneura inornata* Austen, as I have recognized after comparison with the types.

In my paper on Congo tabanids, Rev. Zool. Afr., II, 1913, p. 222, I have also recorded a male *Chrysops fusca* and a female *C. distinctipennis*. As Major Austen has pointed out to me at the British Museum, both specimens belong to *Chrysops stigmaticalis* Lœw. On the other hand, *Diatomineura virgata* Austen, *Dorcalæmus candidolimbatus* Austen, and *D. compactus* Austen of the same paper were correctly identified.

I have noticed the following misspellings of names: *Hæmatopota heptogramma* for *H. heptagramma*; *H. hirsutitarsis* for *H. hirsutitarsus*; *Tabanus nyassæ* for *T. nyasæ*; and *T. wosnami* for *T. woosnami*.

The following Ethiopian species have been omitted:

Hæmatopota furva Austen, Bull. Ent. Research, III, 1912, p. 334, Pl. XI, fig. 7, ♀ ♂. Uganda and Kenya Colony.

Hæmatopota pertinens Austen, Ann. Mag. Hat. Hist., (8) I, 1908, p. 423, ♀. Nyasaland, Rhodesia, Northern Nigeria.

Hæmatopota picta Surcouf, Bull. Muséum Paris, XIV, 1908, p. 155, ♀. Abyssinia.

Hæmatopota schoutedeni (Surcouf) = *Chrysozona schoutedeni* Surcouf, Rev. Zool. Afric., I, 1911, p. 89, ♀. Belgian Congo.

Hinea distincta Ricardo, Arch. f. Naturgesch., LXXX, Abt. A, Heft 8, (1914) 1915, p. 126, ♀. Cameroon.

Diatomineura neavei Austen, Bull. Ent. Research, I, 1911, p. 279, ♀ ♂. Katanga.

Pangonius leucomelas Wiedemann, Aussereurop. Zweifl. Insekt., I, 1828, p. 90, ♀. Cape of Good Hope.

Pangonius oldii Austen, Ann. Mag. Nat. Hist., (8) I, 1908, p. 215, ♀ ♂. Nyasaland.

Tabanus zoulouensis (Bigot)=*Atylotus zoulouensis* Bigot, Mém. Soc. Zool. France, V, 1892, p. 647, ♀. Cape Colony.

Tabanus ugandæ "Ricardo" Surcouf, Bull. Muséum Paris, XIII, 1907, p. 41, has apparently not been described.

Silvius callosus Ricardo, Ann. South African Mus., XVII, 1920, p. 529, ♀ ♂. South Africa.

Silvius hirsutus Ricardo, Ann. South African Mus., XVII, 1920, p. 529, ♀ ♂. South Africa.

Professor J. S. Hine and I have recently completed a check-list of African Tabanidæ. We find that, after various additions and corrections, the total number of species at present described from the Ethiopian region is 422, divided among 23 genera as follows: *Adersia*, 1; *Aegophagamyia*, 1; *Braunsiomyia* (=*Brodenia*), 1; *Buplex*, 8; *Chrysops*, 30; *Dorcalæmus*, 6 (and 1 variety); *Hæmatopota* (including *Austenia*, *Holcoceria*, and *Parhæmatopota*), 118; *Hippocentrum*, 5; *Hinea*, 3; *Lesneus*, 1; *Nuceria* (=*Corizoneura*), 17; *Orgizomyia* (including *Guyona* and *Thriambeutes*), 4; *Osca* (=*Diatomineura*), 2 (and 1 variety); *Pangonius*, 35 (and 1 variety); *Phara* (=*Cadicera*), 15; *Pronopes*, 2; *Rhigioglossa* (=*Erodiorhynchus*), 1; *Rhinomyza*, 9; *Scarphia* (=*Metoponaplos*), 2; *Silvius* (including *Mesomyia*), 12; *Subpangonia*, 2; *Tabanus*, 145 (and 10 varieties); and *Thaumastocera*, 2. The Malagasy region possesses only 28 species, viz., *Aegophagamyia*, 2; *Bouvierella*, 12; *Chrysops*, 4; *Orgizomyia*, 1; *Rhinomyza*, 5; and *Tabanus*, 4. Of these genera *Adersia*, *Aegophagamyia*, *Bouvierella*, *Braunsiomyia*, *Dorcalæmus*,

Hinea, *Lesneus*, *Orgizomyia*, *Phara*, *Pronopes*, *Rhigioglossa*, *Scarphia*, *Subpangonia*, and *Thaumastocera* are precinctive.

* * *

The Tabanidæ are a very natural and remarkably uniform group of flies, and, whereas there has never been any doubt as to the limits of the family, its further subdivision is much more difficult.

Lœw's arrangement into two subfamilies has been generally adhered to and entomologists have been slow in recognizing the new generic divisions that have been proposed from time to time. This is clearly shown by the unsuccessful attempts at splitting up the extensive genus *Tabanus*, of which about 1150 species are known at present. In 1909, Ad. Lutz (Zool. Jahrb. Suppl., X, p. 624) proposed raising Lœw's subfamilies to the rank of major divisions. The Opisthacanthæ, with tibial spurs at the hind tibiæ, he divided into three subfamilies: Pangoniinæ, Silviinæ, and Chrysopinæ. The Opisthanoplæ, without tibial spurs, also formed three subfamilies: Diachlorinæ, Lepiselaginæ, and Tabaninæ. Among the Tabaninæ he further distinguished the Tabaninæ haplocceræ, with toothed third antennal joint, and the Tabaninæ schistoceræ, with branched third antennal joint. Ad. Lutz' subdivisions, however, have not all been very clearly defined and, as they were evidently based on a study of South American insects only, they have not been accepted by other entomologists.

Quite recently Enderlein has come forward with a much more pretentious scheme of classification, intended to be of universal application.[1] He also adopts Lœw's two major subdivisions of the family, for which he uses the names proposed by Ad. Lutz.

In the Opisthacanthæ he recognizes four subfamilies separable as follows:[2]

[1]G. Enderlein. Ein neues Tabanidensystem. Mitt. Zool. Mus. Berlin, X, 2, 1922, pp. 333-351.

[2]Throughout his key Enderlein uses the word "Fühlergeissel" for the third antennal segment and not for the terminal style, but I have corrected this oversight.

1. Antennal style four-jointed, rarely three-jointed (in one case all the joints fused) .... Silviinæ.
   Antennal style seven-jointed, rarely six-jointed .... 2.
2. Anal cell open .... Pelecorhynchinæ.
   Anal cell closed .... 3.
3. First posterior cell open, rarely closed just at the margin...... Melpiinæ.
   First posterior cell closed some distance before the margin .... Pangoniinæ.

The Opisthanoplæ he divides into five subfamilies:

1. Antennal style three-jointed, rarely two-jointed .... Hæmatopotinæ.
   Antennal style four-jointed .... 2.
2. Anal cell open; no ocelli .... Chasmiinæ.
   Anal cell closed, petiolate .... 3.
3. First antennal segment longer than thick; no ocelli .... Diachlorinæ.
   First antennal segment about as long as thick............ 4.
4. First posterior cell closed; ocelli always absent . . Bellardiinæ.
   First posterior cell open; ocelli sometimes present. Tabaninæ.

Enderlein accepts for the whole of the family Tabanidæ 131 genera, that is three times as many as Surcouf.[1] These are divided among his nine subfamilies as follows: Pelecorhynchinæ, 2; Melpiinæ, 17; Pangoniinæ, 22; Silviinæ, 25; Chasmiinæ, 2; Bellardiinæ, 5; Tabaninæ, 40; Diachlorinæ, 8; and Hæmatopotinæ, 10. According to this classification the North and Central American species would represent 27 genera, namely:

Melpiinæ: *Apatolestes, Osca* (*Diatomineura*), (and *Goniops*, which was not known to Enderlein).

Pangoniinæ: *Pangonius, Rhinotriclista, Scione, Pityocera, Fidena, Esenbeckia*, and *Ricardoa*.

Silviinæ; *Chrysops, Silvius*, (and *Neochrysops*, which was not known to Enderlein.)

Bellardiinæ: *Bellardia*.

[1]Quite recently (Deutsch. Ent. Zeitschr., 1923, pp. 544-545) Enderlein has briefly defined 21 additional new genera. Of these, *Anacimas* is based upon a North American species.

Tabaninæ: *Stibasoma, Dichelacera, Dasyommia, Selasoma, Snowiellus, Hybomitra, Therioplectes, Tabanus, Atylotus, Lepiselaga,* (and *Merycomyia,* which was not known to Enderlein).

Diachlorinæ: *Diachlorus.*

Hæmatopotinæ; *Hæmatopota.*

A commendable feature of Enderlein's work is the designation of genotypes, though in some cases they are manuscript names of as yet undescribed species. Unfortunately the author has evidently failed to inquire whether types had not been previously selected for some of the older genera. Since this is likely to cause some confusion in the future, I may point out some of the cases I have noticed.

Diachlorus Osten Sacken. The genotype is *Tabanus bicinctus* Fabricius, as designated by Coquillett (1910); not *Tabanus ferrugatus* Fabricius as given by Enderlein.

Dichelacera Macquart. The type of this genus is *Dichelacera unifasciata* Macquart, as designated by Coquillett (1910); Enderlein gives *Tabanus cervicornis* Fabricius.

Corizoneura Rondani. The type of this genus is *Tanyglossa æthiopica* Thunberg (Syn.: *Pangonia appendiculata* Macquart), as designated by Coquillett (1910) and again by Austen in 1920 (Bull. Ent. Research, XI, p. 139). Enderlein's genus *Corizoneura,* with *Pangonia angustata* Macquart as type, is entirely different and its characters seem to agree with those of *Buplex* Austen (Type: *Pangonia suavis* Lœw), a genus evidently overlooked by Enderlein.

Erephopsis Rondani. The genotype is *Pangonia fulvithorax* Wiedemann, as designated by Coquillett (1910). Enderlein gives *Tabanus guttatus* Donovan.

Lilæa Walker. *Pangonia lurida* Walker was designated as type by Coquillett (1910). Enderlein gives as such *Pangonia rœi* King.

Melpia Walker. *Pangonia fulvithorax* Wiedemann, is the genotype designated by Coquillett in 1910, which makes this generic name a strict synonym of *Erephopsis* Rondani. *Melpia* Enderlein, with *Melpia exeuns* Walker as type, if really generically distinct from *Erephopsis,* will need a new name.

Nemorius Rondani. Monotypic for *Chrysops vitripennis* Meigen, as originally proposed by Rondani. Enderlein gives *N. singularis* Meigen as type.

Nuceria Walker. *Pangonia longirostris* Hardwicke was designated as type by Coquillett in 1910. Enderlein gives as such *Tabanus rostratus* Linnæus.

Ommatiosteres Enderlein. Enderlein gives as type of this new genus *Pangonia bifasciata* Wiedemann, and places it in the Melpiinæ, which, according to his key, have the first posterior cell open. *P. bifasciata*, however, has been thus far placed among the *Pangonius* with the first posterior cell closed.

Pangonius Latreille. Latreille (1810) and Coquillett (1910) designated *Tabanus proboscideus* Fabricius, 1794 (=*Pangonia maculata* Fabricius, 1805) as the type. Enderlein gives as such *Tabanus marginatus* Fabricius, which was not among the species mentioned by Latreille when he originally proposed the genus.

Philoliche Wiedemann. Coquillett designated *Tabanus rostratus* Linnæus as type in 1910, so that *Nuceria* Enderlein (not of Walker) is an exact synonym of *Philoliche*. Enderlein's *Philoliche*, however, with *Tabanus angulatus* Fabricius as type, is entirely different.

Siridorhina Enderlein. This is an exact synonym of *Nuceria* Walker (not of Enderlein), since both have the same genotype: *Pangonia longirostris* Hardwicke. To judge from the characters given in Enderlein's key, both *Siridorhina* Enderlein and *Nuceria* Walker appear to equal *Corizoneura* Rondani and indeed Austen includes *Pangonia longirostris* Hardwicke in *Corizoneura* as defined by him in Bull. Ent. Research, XI, 1920, p. 139. The genus should be known as *Nuceria* Walker, since that name has several years priority.

In his introduction Enderlein mentions several genera whose descriptions were not accessible to him. There are, unfortunately, a number of others which have also been overlooked, for instance such a well-known type as *Goniops* Aldrich.

Enderlein's paper was issued as a preliminary account, pending the publication of a more comprehensive revision of the tabanid genera. Meanwhile it is difficult to judge of the validity or usefulness of the many subfamilies, tribes, and genera which he adopts, the more so since several of his new genera are based upon undescribed species. The real test as to whether these groups are natural divisions or merely based upon artificial combinations of characters will come when Enderlein attempts to classify all or at least the majority of the described species. Unless this test is satisfactorily met, it is difficult to see how Enderlein's work will not merely add to the intricacy of an already overburdened taxonomy.

NOTES ON SOME NEW ENGLAND PHORIDÆ (DIPTERA)[1]

By Charles T. Brues.

Among a small series of Phoridæ recently received for identification from Mr. C. W. Johnson there are two species of particular interest. One is a new species of Apocephalus, a genus known to develop as a parasite of ants, and the other a small wingless female of Puliciphora which appears during the winter months.

Apocephalus borealis sp. nov. (Fig. 1, a, b, c,)

♀. Length, including ovipositor 2.2 mm. Pale yellow, the central portion of the abdomen with an orange tinge and the legs pale brownish yellow; first segment of abdomen brownish, with pale hind margin; second segment with a brownish blotch at the middle of the lateral margin; third and fourth each with a

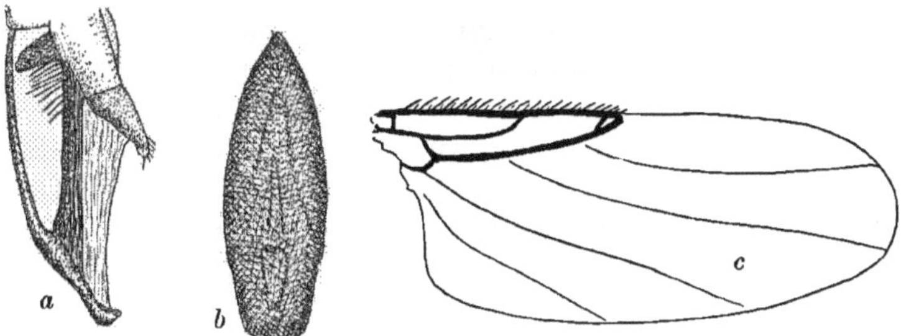

Fig 1. *Apocephalus borealis* sp. nov. a, apex of abdomen with ovipositor in lateral view; b, ovipositor in ventral view; c, wing.

larger darker spot; fifth entirely fuscous; sixth with the anterior angles brown; ovipositor brownish black, paler at tip, the membrane covering its upper side pale. Wings hyaline, venation pale fuscous. Front barely as high as wide; with only eight bristles below the ocelli; lowest row consisting of two reclinate

[1]Contribution from the Entomological Laboratory of the Bussey Institution Harvard University, No. 234.

post antennal ones and a lateral one next to the eye, median pair of the row above further apart than the post-antennals, this row curved upwards at the sides with the lateral bristle rather close to the eye margin and nearer to one of the median bristles than these are to one another. Ocellar row of four. All bristles strong, subequal. Median frontal suture distinct; lower half of front with scattered minute black bristles. Post-ocular cilia moderate, but the upper one on each side much enlarged. Antennæ pyriform, obtusely pointed, as long as the front; arista no longer than the third joint, very stout, especially at base, nearly bare. Palpi rather broad, weakly bristled; cheeks each with two downwardly directed macrochætæ. Mesonotum sub-shining, with one pair of dorsocentral marcrochætæ; scutellum with one pair of bristles, the lateral pair very minute, scarcely visible. Propleura with two slender bristles above the insertion of the coxa and two minute ones near the humeral angle; mesopleura bare. Front coxa with a noticeable stripe of minute bristles along the anterior edge; middle tibiæ not distinctly setulose; hind tibiæ with a line of very delicate, closely placed setulæ inside the posterior edge; all tarsi slender. Abdomen broad; second segment elongated, twice as broad as long, bare laterally; third to fifth segments gradually shorter, longer at the sides than along the median line; sixth longer and narrower, almost semicircular, with a few small marginal bristles medially at apex. Ovipositor of peculiar form; in dorsal view projecting beyond the sixth segment for a distance half the length of the abdomen; consisting of two chitinous pieces united at their apices, the upper one straight,issuing from the underside of the fifth and sixth segments and bearing below near the base a number of strong bristles; lower piece curved upward to meet the upper one and connected to it at the base by a large chitinous tooth originating at the extreme base of the upper piece. Viewed from the side (Fig. 1, A) the upper piece is seen to be nearly circular in section and the lower one greatly flattened; in ventral view (Fig. 1, B) the lower piece is spatulate, with truncate tip. Wing (Fig. 1, C) unusually narrow, costa not quite attaining the middle of the wing; first section of costa twice the length of the second; third very short, the minute second vein nearly perpendicular to the costa; fourth vein very slightly and evenly curved; fifth faintly bisinuate; sixth and seventh similarly sinuate; costal cilia rather long and set moderately close together.

Type from Salisbury Cove, Maine, July 17, 1913 (C. W. Johnson). It is deposited in the collection of the Boston Society of Natural History.

The distinguishing characteristics of this species may be indicated by the following tabular arrangement.

Key to the North American Species of Apocephalus (Females).

1. Front more than twice as wide as long, ovipositor narrowed to tip, without lateral enlargements....*wheeleri* Brues.
   Front quadrate or nearly so..........................2.
2. Costal vein much less than half the length of the broad wing, with long, sparse fringe; ovipositor broad, with acuminate apex..............................*spinicosta* Malloch.
   Costal vein about half the length of the wing, which is not unusually broad; costal fringe shorter and more dense 3.
3. Ovipositor, in dorsal view, swollen near base and apex, with a constriction between .... *coquilletti* Malloch.
   Ovipositor without lateral expansions, or with one at base only.......................................4.
4. Scutellum with two marginal bristles, ovipositor with widely separated dorsal and ventral valves; wing very narrow; front entirely yellow........*borealis* sp. nov..
   Scutellum with the second pair of bristles present, though smaller; ovipositor without separated valves, wing broader...5.
5. Ovipositor with very strong lateral expansions near base where it is three times as wide as at tip..*pergandei* Coquillet
   Ovipositor with weak expansions at base which is twice as wide as the tip.....................*similis* Malloch.

Two other North American species are known only in the male sex. *A. aridus* Malloch differs in having black halteres and a much more sparse costal fringe. *A. pictus* Malloch differs in having four subequal scutellar bristles and a black front.

Puliciphora glacialis Malloch

Proc. U. S. Nat. Mus., Washington, vol. 43, p. 507, figs. (1912).

Concerning the habits of this species there is appended to the original description of the minute wingless female, the remarkable note: " 'Active on the ice', Jan., 1874, Tyngsboro, Massachusetts (F. Blanchard)". As the genus Puliciphora and its relatives are typically tropical insects which extend only sparingly into temperate regions, I have been expectantly waiting for further information relating to this species. In the lot of Phoridæ containing the Apocephalus described above there is a single additional female specimen of *Puliciphora glacialis* found by Mr. C. A. Frost at Framingham, Mass. on March 23, 1907 while sifting for beetles. Reference to the Monthly Weather Review for March 1907, shows that there was an unprecedented warm period in the eastern states from March 21st to 23rd and that a maximum temperature of 76° was recorded at Framingham. Such temporary warm spells during the winter are, of course, the occasion for the appearance of most "winter" or "snow" insects, such as Boreus, Chionea, etc. So far as Chionea is concerned, its closest relatives seem to be inhabitants of cold climates (Pterochionea Alexander, of the nearctic region), and the same appears to hold true for most typical snow-insects.

The present species of Puliciphora is more darkly colored and the abdominal plates are much more heavily chitinized than is usual in the genus. Structurally, however, it seems to be quite typical, even to the presence of the slit-like gland opening on the fifth abdominal segment.

This habit is not unprecedented in the family for there are quite a number of species known, especially among those that frequent carrion which are often taken during the colder spring and fall months. Thus, Trupheoneura and Parastenophora include a number of autumnal forms some of which probably hibernate as adults.

A NEW SPECIES OF DIXA FROM CALIFORNIA.

By O. A. Johannsen.

Cornell University. Ithaca, N. Y.

The species described below was reared on May first, 1923, by Miss Alice M. Westfall from larvæ collected from the surface of a pool formed by the water from a leak in an irrigation pipe across the street eastward from the Claremont (Cal) high school. In the key published in Psyche (30: 52, 1923) the species will find a place in the couplet with *D. clavula* Will., but differs in having the point of intersection of the radio-median crossvein with the petiole of the radial sector less than one-fourth the length of the crossvein proximad of the base of R4+5 while in *clavula* the intersection lies almost the length of the crossvein proximad of this point. Moreover the basal segment of the clasper in the last mentioned species is distinctly globose.

Dixa aliciae sp. nov.

Male. Head, antennæ, proboscis and palpi brown, proboscis more yellowish below. Thorax including scutellum, yellow; mesonotum with three dull dark brown lines, the middle one divided by a hair line, the laterals abbreviated anteriorly; metanotum and sternopleura brown. Abdomen yellowish brown; basal segment of clasper not globose, its mesal process nearly as long as the terminal segment, straight, slender, parallel sided, the apical fourth still more slender and curved like a plow handle; terminal segment slightly clavate resembling that of *D. modesta* but with longer hairs, especially apically. Legs brownish yellow, extreme tips of femora and of tibiæ darkened, tips of hind tibiæ slightly swollen. Fore basitarsus broken in the only male specimen. Wings hyaline, veins brownish except the base of the radius which is more yellowish; a very faint suggestion of a cloud covers the radio-median crossvein while the petiole of the cubitus is margined posteriorly by a faint grayish line; the subcosta ends slightly distad of the base of the radial sector; petiole of R2+3, measured on a straight line from its base to the base of the fork, slightly more than half as long as R3; petiole of the media measured from the crossvein about an eighth its length longer than its anterior branch; the position of the radio-median crossvein as described above and nearly in line with the medio-cubital crossvein. Halteres yellow, the upper surface of the knob darkened. Length 2.75 mm. One specimen.

Female. Like the male in coloring. The petioles of both radial and medial forks relatively slightly shorter. Fore basitarsus 0.7 as long as the corresponding tibia. One specimen.

Slide mount of holotype and allotype in the Cornell University collection.

THE NAME OF THE LAC INSECTS

By T. D. A. Cockerell.

University of Colorado

The Monograph of the Tachardiinæ, by Mr. J. C. Chamberlin, recently published in Bulletin of Entomological Research, vol. XIV, is certainly a fine example of modern work on Coccidæ. It appears to exhaust the subject so far as the available materials permit, but of course many species remain to be discovered, and there is much to be done on the biology of all. Before it was published, I called the attention of Professor Ferris to the name *Laccifer* Oken, but he presumably had no access to Oken's work. I am indebted to Mr. C. D. Sherborn for a copy of Oken's account, in Lehrb. Naturg., III (1), 1815, p. 430. He proposes a genus *Laccifer*, for "*Chermes* or *Coccus lacca*." It is stated to be the source of the gum-lac, and to occur by the Ganges on *Mimosa cinerea* and *M. glauca*, plants now known as *Dichrostachys cinerea* (L.) Wight & Arn. and *Leucæna glauca* (L.) Benth. The old error of taking the male coccid for the adult female and some hymenopterous parasite for the adult female is repeated, but does not invalidate the name. I agree with Ferris that these peculiar insects deserve to rank as a family, and accordingly the following changes appear to be necessary:

Family Lacciferidæ (Tachardiidæ Ferris)
Subfamily Lacciferinæ (Tachardiinæ Ckll., pars.)
Laccifer albizziæ (Green, as *Tachardia*)
Laccifer meridionalis (Chamb., as *Tachardia*)
Laccifer greeni (Chamb., as *Tachardia*)
Laccifer fici (Green, as *Tachardia*)
Laccifer ebrachiatus (Chamb., as *Tachardia*)
Laccifer lacca (Kerr, as *Coccus*)
Laccifer conchiferatus (Green, as *Tachardia*)

It may be noted that according to the rules *Tachardina lobata* is to be credited to Green, as he not only published a full description, but gave the name and mentioned a difference from the

Philippine *T. minuta*. Also the combination *Tachardina albida* should not be credited to me, but to MacGillivray; I used the name *Tachardina* only in a subgeneric sense. Mr. Chamberlin indicates subgenera and then immediately uses the names in a generic sense, which is illogical; but it may be anticipated that the latter treatment will eventually prevail.

PSYCHE

A JOURNAL OF ENTOMOLOGY

ESTABLISHED IN 1874

VOL. XXXI APRIL 1924 No. 2

CONTENTS

CAMBRIDGE ENTOMOLOGICAL CLUB

PSYCHE is published bi-monthly, the issues appearing in February, April, June, August, October and December. Subscription price, per year, payable in advance: $2.00 to subscribers in the United States, Canada or Mexico; foreign postage, 15 cents extra. Single copies, 40 cents.

Cheques and remittances should be addressed to Treasurer, Cambridge Entomological Club, Bussey Institution, Forest Hills, Boston 30, Mass.

Orders for back volumes, missing numbers, notices of change of address, etc., should be sent to Cambridge Entomological Club, Bussey Institution, Forest Hills, Boston, 30, Mass.

IMPORTANT NOTICE TO CONTRIBUTORS.

Manuscripts intended for publication, books intended for review, and other editorial matter, should be addressed to Professor C. T. Brues, Bussey Institution, Forest Hills, Boston, 30 Mass.

Authors contributing articles over 8 printed pages in length will be required to bear a part of the extra expense, for additional pages. This expense will be that of typesetting only, which is about $2.00 per page. The actual cost of preparing cuts for all illustrations must be borne by contributors; the expense for full page plates from line drawings is approximately $5.00 each, and for full page half-tones, $7.50 each; smaller sizes in proportion.

AUTHOR'S SEPARATES.

Reprints of articles may be secured by authors, if they are ordered before, or at the time proofs are received for corrections. The cost of these will be furnished by the Editor on application.

Entered as second-class mail matter at the Post Office at Boston, Mass. Acceptance for mailing at special rate of postage provided in Section 1103, Act of October 3, 1917, authorized on June 29, 1918.

PSYCHE

VOL. XXXI. APRIL 1924 No. 2

A NEW SPECIES OF SCHIZASPIDIA (EUCHARIDÆ), WITH NOTES ON A EULOPHID ANT PARASITE.[1]

BY GEORGE C. WHEELER AND ESTHER HALL WHEELER.

Schizaspidia polyrhachicida new species

(Fig. 1.)

Female. Head small, three times as broad as long in dorsal view; but little narrower than the width of the thorax. Ocelli almost in a straight line, the outer ones less than an ocellus-diameter behind, the central one sunk in a grove which includes the antennal insertions. Head nearly twice wider than deep. Distance from ocellus to clypeus five-sevenths that from eye to eye. Malar line about equal to base of clypeus. Upper two-thirds of face striated vertically; those striæ nearest the antennal groove curved medially and continuous with transverse striæ below antennæ and also behind ocelli; those nearest the eyes continuous with transverse striæ on the vertex. Lower third of face smooth. Transverse striæ arising at either side of clypeus and passing backward across the genæ and then upward behind the eye. Clypeus smooth. Antennæ twelve-segmented, extending nearly to the metascutellum; first segment one-half, and second segment one-third the length of the third, which is one-third as wide as long; fourth three-fourths of third; remaining segments of equal length, about one-half of third. Labrum with eight digitiform processes on its anterior border. Mandibles long, falciform; the right one with two teeth at the inner base, the left with one larger tooth.

Thorax as long as wide dorsally, coarsely reticulate-rugose.

[1]Contribution from the Zoological Department in the Liberal Arts College, Syracuse University.

Prothorax extremely suppressed. Scutellar protuberance short, one-third the length of the scutellum, terminating in two short, asymmetrical prongs separated by a distance greater than their length. A wide reticulate-rugose channel extending from the base of the protuberance to the anterior border of the metascu-

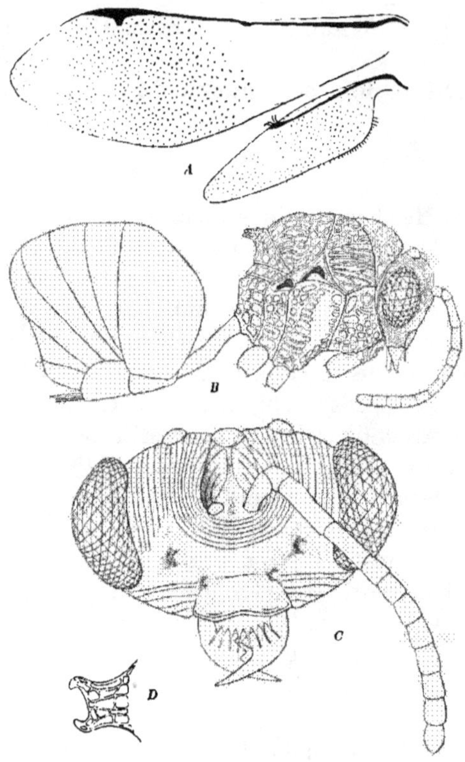

Fig. 1. *Schizaspidia polyrhachicida* n. sp. ♀. A, wings; B, lateral view; C, head in front view; D, metascutellar protuberance in dorsal view.

tum, where it is dilated into a deep pit surrounded by a ridge. Wings hyaline, reaching a little beyond the apex of the abdomen. Apical three-fifths of fore wing and entire hind wing finely hairy.

Hind wing with vein extending to hooks, which are four in number, and with a fringe of cilia on the posterior border. Tibial spurs simple.

Gaster nearly twice as long as broad dorsally. Petiole less than one-half the length of the gaster, almost as long as the hind femur (13:14), and extending from the base of the propodeum to the lower margin of the gaster. First gastric segment partly inclosing the two following segments. Ovipositor without barbs, exposed for one sixth of the length of the gaster.

Head and thorax aëneous, except antennæ and mandibles which are fulvous with fuscous inner borders. Legs fulvous, except dark brown metacoxæ. Abdomen dark brown with these exceptions: dorsal spot on pedicel and most of first segment of gaster fuscous, rest of pedicel fulvous.

Length: 3.5 mm. *Host.—Polyrhachis (Myrmhopla) dives* F. Smith.

Type Locality.—Manila, Philippine Islands. Described from two mature female pupæ found in cocoons of the host collected by McGregor. The ants are from Professor W. M. Wheeler's collection.

This species is near *S. tenuicornis* Ashmead, but is readily distinguishable from it by the pit on the metanotum. Mr. A. B. Gahan has very kindly compared a specimen with Ashmead's types in the United States National Museum.

The head of the parasitic pupa was at the anterior pole of the host cocoon, and its brilliant vermilion eyes were readily visible through the silken walls of the latter. The host pupa (phthisergate) had been almost completely drained of its contents, scarcely more than the exoskeleton remaining; this was pressed against the venter of the parasite.

This is the fourteenth species of *Schizaspidia* to be described, but only the third host record.[2] Mr. Curtis P. Clausen (1923) has recently shown what an interesting field of investigation the biology of this widely distributed genus affords. All the Eucharidæ, for that matter, probably have the same possibilities.

[2] *S. doddi* Bingham.—*Camponotus* sp. (Dodd, 1906).

S. ternucornis Ashmead.—*Camponotus herculeanus japonicus* May (Clausen, 1923).

So far as is known, they parasitize ants exclusively. We have been able to find host records for twenty-one species in thirteen genera. The life histories of *Orasema viridis* Ashmead (Wheeler, 1907), *Psilogaster fasciiventris* Brues (1919), and *Schizaspidia tenuicornis* Ashmead (Clausen, 1923) are known. All three have planidium larvæ in the first stage.

Catalogue of the Genus Schizaspidia Westwood.

caeruleiceps Cameron. ♂. Borneo: Kuching.
Schizaspidia cœruleiceps Cameron, Entomologist, vol. 42, p. 231 (1909).

caffra Westwood. ♂? Africa: Caffraria.
Schizaspidia caffra Westwood, Thesaur. Entom. Oxon., p. 152; plate 28, fig. 12 (1874). Dalla Torre, Cat. Hym., vol. 5, p. 363 (1898). Schmiedeknecht, Gen. Insect, fasc. 97, p. 76 (1909).

cyanea Walker. ♂. Moluccas: Amboina.
Schizaspidia cyanea Walker, Trans. Entom. Soc. London (3) vol. 1, p. 386 (1862). Dalla Torre, Cat. Hym. vol. 5, p. 363 (1898). Schmiedeknecht, Gen. Insect., fasc. 97, p. 76 (1909).

doddi Bingham. ♂. Queensland: Townsville.
Schizaspidia doddi Dodd, Trans. Entom. Soc. London, p. 123 (1906). Girault, Mem. Queensland Mus., vol. 4, p. 235 (1915).

furcifera Westwood. ♂? ♀? Asia: Eastern India and Bengal
Schizaspidia furcifer Westwood, Proc. Zool. Soc. London, vol. 3, p. 69 (1835).
Schizaspidia furcifera Westwood, Thesaur. Entom. Oxon., p. 151, plate 28, fig. 2 (1874). Kirby, Journ. Linn. Soc. London, Zool., vol. 20, p. 31 (1886). Dalla Torre, Cat. Hym., vol. 5, p. 364 (1898). Schmiedeknecht, Gen. Insect, fasc. 97, p. 76 (1909).

maculata Westwood. ♀. Brazil; Central Goyaz.
Schizaspidia (?) *maculata* Westwood, Thesaur. Entom. Oxon., p. 153, plate 28, fig. 1 (1874).

Orasema maculata Kirby, Journ. Linn. Soc. London, Zool., vol. 20, p. 29, plate 1, fig. 1 (1886). Dalla Torre, Cat. Hym., vol. 5, p. 361 (1898). Ashmead, Mem. Carnegie Mus., vol. 1, p. 469 (1904).

Schizaspidia maculata Schmiedeknecht, Gen. Insect., fasc. 97, p. 76, (1909).

murrayi Kirby. ♂. Tonga Islands: Tongatabu.

Schizaspidia murrayi Kirby, Ann. & Mag. Nat. Hist., (5) vol. 13, p. 403 (1884). Kirby, Journ. Linn. Soc. London, Zool., vol. 20, p. 37, (1886). Dalla Torre, Cat. Hym. Vol. 5, 364 (1898). Schmiedeknecht, Gen. Insect., fasc. 97, p. 76 (1909). Girault, Mem. Queensland Mus., vol. 4, p. 235 (1915).

polyrhachicida G. Wheeler & E. Wheeler. ♀. Philippine Islands: Manila.

Schizaspidia polyrhachicida G. Wheeler & E. Wheeler, Psyche, vol. 31, p. 49.

pretendens Walker. ♂. Brazil: Villa Nova.

Schizaspidia pretendens Walker, Trans. Entom. Soc. London, (3) vol. 1, p. 385 (1862). Dalla Torre, Cat. Hym., vol. 5, p. 364 (1898). Ashmead, Mem. Carnegie Mus., vol. 1, p. 469 (1904). Schiemdeknecht, Gen. Insect., fasc. 97, p. 76 (1909).

quinqueguttata Girault. ♂. Queensland: Gordonville (Cairns).

Schizaspidia quinqueguttata Girault, Mem. Queensland Mus., vol. 4, p. 235 (1915).

rudis Westwood. sex? South Australia: Angas.

Schizaspidia rudis Westwood, Thesaur. Entom. Oxon., p. 152, plate 28, fig. 5 (1874). Dalla Torre, Cat. Hym., vol. 5, p. 364 (1898). Schmiedeknecht, Gen. Insect., fasc. 97, p. 76 (1909). Girault, Mem. Queensland Mus., vol. 4, p. 235 (1915).

septentrionalis Brues. ♀. Arizona: Huachuca Mts.

Schizaspidia septentrionalis Brues, Bull. Wisconsin Nat. Hist. Soc., vol. 5, p. 104 (1907).

tenuicornis Ashmead. ♀ ♂. Japan: Northern Hondo and Hokkaido. Korea.

Schizaspidia tenuicornis Ashmead, Journ. New York Entom. Soc., vol. 12, p. 151 (1904). Clausen, Ann. Entom. Soc. America, vol. 16, p. 195-215 (1923).

trimaculata Cameron. ♀. Borneo: Kuching.

Schizaspidia trimaculata Cameron, Deutsch. Entom. Zeitschr., p. 205, (1909).

A EULOPHID ANT PARASITE

While examining a vial of ants (*Crematogaster acuta* Fabr.) collected by Professor W. M. Wheeler at Kartabo, British Guiana in the summer of 1920, we found that twenty-six of the larvæ were parasitized. In one instance, the parasites were pigmented pupæ, not, however, mature enough for identification. They were sent to Mr. A. B. Gahan, who reported as follows: "This is an Eulophid, apparently closely related to the genus *Paracrias* Ashmead, but I cannot identify it positively, even generically."

Of these twenth-six larvæ, twelve contained one parasite, thirteen contained two, while one contained four—a total of forty-one parasites, of which nineteen were larvæ and twenty-two were pupæ. Eleven host larvæ contained pupal parasites sufficiently developed for the sex to be evident: four contained one parasite (female); seven contained two—a male and a female in every case. With two parasites in one host, the heads of the former were at the caudal and of the latter. Of the four containing only one parasitic pupa, two had the heads directed towards the anterior end and two towards the posterior end of the host.

Figure 2 shows the mature pupæ referred to above—a male (length 2.0 mm.) on the right and a female (length 2.4 mm.)—with their ventral surfaces contiguous and occupying the greater part of the host's interior. The cloudy mass posterior to the pupæ is apparently a residue of host tissues, but probably also contains the meconia of the parasites.

The Eulophid larvæ are elongate, cylindrical, and entirely destitute of hairs. The button-like head is small, subterminal and elliptical in oral view. The conspicuous mandibles are falciform and sharp-pointed.

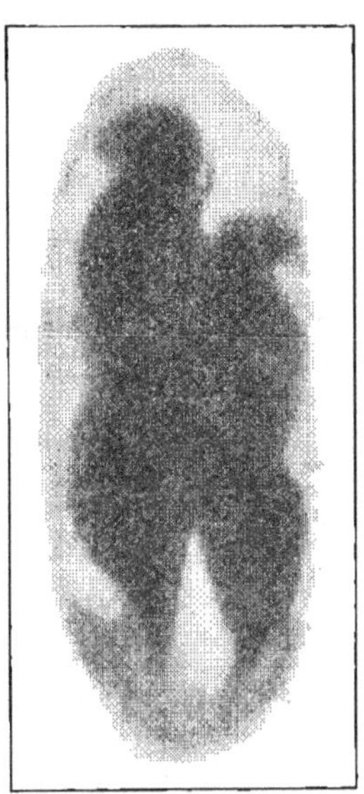

Fig. 2. Pupae of Eulophid parasite in larva of *Crematogaster acuta* Fabr.

This is, so far as we know, the only record of a Eulophid with an ant host. Although it cannot be stated definitely that the Eulophid is a primary parasite of the ant, it would seem that such is probably the case as none of the ant larvæ showed signs of parasitism by any other species.

Among the Chalcidoidea it is not unusual to find several parasites developing in a single host. In the Chalcididæ and Proctotrypidæ, where polyembryony occurs the number may reach a hundred, perhaps more. But this is not a case of polyembryony, for here both sexes occur within the same host individual. Whether all the parasites in a host larva are offspring of the same mother or whether two or more females have oviposited in one host (epiparasitism of Haviland) cannot, of course, be determined from our material. Among the Eucharidæ there are three records of this multiple parasitism:

Pseudochalcura gibbosa Provancher. (Host-*Camponotus herculeanus ligniperdus* var. *noveboracensis* Fitch.) "In one of the cocoons, ..., there were two pigmented and therefore nearly mature pupæ, lying face to face near the anterior pole while the remains of the ant pupa which they had consumed, were crowded against the black meconial spot at the posterior pole. The other cocoon contained four unpigmented pupæ." (Wheeler, 1907).

Rhipipallus affinis Bingham. (Host-*Odontomachus ruficeps coriaria* Mayr.)" . . . . .sometimes several from one cocoon." (Dodd, 1906).

Schizaspidia tenuicornis Ashmead. (Host-*Camponotus herculeanus japonicus* Mayr) "Occasionally two larvæ may be found on a single host pupa, and in such instances their position is symmetrical with reference to the body of the host." (Clausen 1923).

In all three of the above cases the host pupa is large and could easily provide nutriment for two, three or perhaps four parasites. But this is not true of the *Crematogsater* larvæ, which are only 2.8 millimeters long, and one might wonder whether on this ant multiple parasitism is generally successful.

LITERATURE CITED.

1919. Brues, C. T. Ann. Entom. Soc. America, vol. 12, pp. 13-21.

1923. Clausen, C. P. Ann. Entom. Soc. America, vol. 16, pp. 195-217.

1906. Dodd, F. P. Trans. Entom. Soc. London, pp. 119-132.

1907. Wheeler, W. M. Bull. American Mus. Nat. Hist., vol. 23, pp. 1-93.

THE BIOLOGY OF *TRICHOPODA PENNIPES* FAB. (DIPTERA, TACHINIDÆ), A PARASITE OF THE COMMON SQUASH BUG.*

By Harlan N. Worthley.

Massachusetts Agricultural Experiment Station, Amherst, Mass.

PART II.

MORPHOLOGY

In the study of the adult anatomy, pinned dried specimens were used. For the definition of the mouth parts, sclerites of the thorax, and the genitalia, however, it was found necessary to relax the parts and examine them in liquid. For this purpose, specimens were soaked for about an hour in a cold 10 per cent solution of caustic potash (boiling often causes distortion of the parts) washed in water and treated with weak acetic acid to stop the action of the caustic potash. They were then placed in 70 per cent alcohol.

The parts were examined under a Zeiss binocular microscope, at magnifications varying from sixteen to sixty-five diameters. Many structures were obscure except under the brightest illumination, and therefore most of the examinations were made in the rays from a powerful lamp. A Ford headlight was mounted on a ringstand and connected through a transformer with the ordinary one hundred and ten volt circuit. This lamp proved to be quite satisfactory, since it was placed on the desk at a distance of two feet from the binocular, allowing plenty of room to work. A lamp of this kind, focussed upon the microscope stage by means of the set-screw in the lamp, throws little light into the eyes and develops little heat, while the object under observation is brought into strong relief.

*The first portion of this article appeared in Psyche, vol. 31, pp. 7-16, February, 1924.

Adult.

The adult fly is about the size of the common house fly' but it is much more gay in appearance. It may be seen on sunny days hovering about squash plants, or resting with half-spread wings upon the foliage of squash and upon certain wild flowers as well. It is strikingly colored, with deep reddish brown eyes on a head marked with black, gold and silver. The thorax is golden in front, with four longitudinal black stripes, clear black behind, and gray at the sides. The abdomen is of a brilliant orange color, except at the extreme tip, which is darker. The conspicuous abdomen, and the fringe of feather-like setæ along the outer side of the hind tibiæ, immediately catch the eye of the observer, and serve to make this species one of the most striking among Tachinid flies.

A discussion of the adult anatomy is complicated by the diversity of terms which may be applied to the different structures. Taxonomists have applied names which, in many cases, are morphologically inaccurate, and morphologists themselves have differed both in the nomenclature and in the interpretation of parts. The source of the terms used in this paper is indicated in the text of the different sections, and in many cases duplicate names for the various structures are given in the list of abbreviations used in the figures.

Head. Pl. 1, figs. 1 and 2. In describing the head, the terms used are those of Peterson (1916), except the chætotaxy, which follows Coquillet (1897) and Walton (1909).

Viewed from in front, the head is elliptical in outline, and broader than deep (3.2 mm. by 2.4 mm.). Its most conspicuous feature is perhaps the frontal suture (fs),[2] which extends in a dark, shining, inverted U-shaped band from just above the insertion of the antennæ to a point midway between the vibrissæ (vib) and the curve of the compound eyes (ce), where it tapers out. Within the curve of the frontal suture lies the fronto-clypeus (fc), termed by Coquillett the "facial depression" and

[2]Letters in parenthesis are those used in labeling the figures, and are explained in the list of abbreviations preceding the plates at the end of this paper.

by Walton the "facial plate." The tentorial thickenings (tt) arising at each side near the oral margin and running upward nearly to the insertion of the antennæ, are easily seen, lying just within the facial or vibrissal ridges, which are not pronounced. The vertex (v) is all that portion of the head, viewed is the ocellar triangle, bearing on its raised surface three ocelli (oc). From the region of the ocelli to the frontal suture runs a median broad velvety-black band or "vitta" (mv), which is demarked from the rest of the vertex only by its color, which strongly contrasts with the golden-yellow tomentum of the lateral portions of the vertex. The genæ (ge) are those portions of the vertex lying below the ends of the frontal suture, and between the oral margin and the eyes. Their color is silvery-gray, which shades into the gold of the rest of the vertex above, and into the brownish-yellow of the fronto-clypeus.

Viewed from the side the head is quadrate in shape. The postgenæ (pge) are those regions behind the genæ and extending backward and upward along the curve of the compound eyes to a point midway between the oral margin and the ocellar triangle. The occiput is designated as that portion of the caudal aspect of the head extending from a line drawn midway across the occipital foramen upward to the vertex. The edge of this area can be seen from the side (ocp).

Chætotaxy of the Head. On either side of the median vitta is a row of frontal bristles (fb) which, since they bend inward across the vitta, may be called "transfrontals."[1]

On the ocellar triangle, just behind the anterior ocellus, lie the great ocellar pair (ob), while behind these, and passing between the two lateral ocelli, follow three or more pairs of "lesser ocellar" bristles, which in *T. pennipes* are very small.

[1]Here is one instance of the confusion of terms mentioned at the beginning of this paper. The area bearing the frontal bristles, although it has been called the "front" by taxonomists, is morphologically not the front at all, but the vertex. The true front, which lies below the antennae and is fused with the clypeus, also bears a double row of macrochaetae which, to one not a specialist, might readily be mistaken for the frontal bristles. The writer does not recommend here any reconciliation between the terms of the morphologists and the usage of the taxonomists, but merely wishes to point out the true relation of parts. To his mind, any attempt to modify the terminology other than by concerted action among taxonomic workers and morphologists would only result in "confusion worse confounded."

Behind the ocelli and on the edge of the occiput is a transverse row of four macrochætæ. The inner, larger pair are the postvertical bristles (pvt), and the smaller, outer ones, the inner vertical bristles (ivt). The outer verticals, present in some forms, are not represented in this species. The fronto-orbitals, which lie between the frontal bristles and the curve of the compound eyes, are also absent.

On the fronto-clypeus, disposed along each facial ridge, is a short row of facial bristles, the vibrissal row. The uppermost pair are the vibrissæ (vib) which in *T. pennipes* do not assume from the front, which lies between the compound eyes, and between these and the frontal suture. At the very top of the vertex their typical position immediately above the oral mragin, but are shifted upward to lie halfway between the oral margin and the tips of the antennæ. The smaller bristles accompanying the vibrissæ extend on either side in a single line along the oral margin to the region of the postgenæ, where they mingle with the silvery-white beard which depends from this region. A single row of short macrochætæ extends around the edge of the occiput from the inner vertical bristles downward to the region of the postgenæ. These are called the cilia of the posterior orbit (cpo).

Appendages of the Head.

Antennæ. The antennæ (ant) reach halfway between the base of the frontal suture and the oral margin. The first two segments are velvety-black in color, with a silvery sheen. The second segment bears a few macrochætæ. The third segment, which is much larger than the other two, is bean-shaped and varies from black to mouse-colored, with the base sometimes slightly tawny. This segment bears the arista (ar), a large bristle which is inserted on the outer edge about one third the distance from base to tip of the segment. The arista is practically bare, having but a few very tiny hairs near its base.

Proboscis. The proboscis (pb), usually folded well back in the oral cavity, is a very much modified structure, the parts of which it is very difficult to homologize with the mouth parts of generalized insects. The work of Peterson (1916) on the mouth parts of Diptera was very thorough, and his figures correct and intelligible, but since he derives his hypothetical dipterous mouth parts from a consideration of Orthoptera while Crampton (1921, p. 91) would evolve Diptera from ancestors like Mecoptera, the homologies of dipterous mouth parts still constitute a disputed question.

The membrane of the basiproboscis (bpb) is largely composed of the mentum and sub-mentum, according to Peterson. The maxillary palpi; (mxp) lie on this membrane in front. Above the maxillary palpi lie the exposed portions of the tormæ (to), and below lie the external plates of the stipes (st). The galeæ (ga) lie on the surface, and are continuous with the lower ends of the ental portions of the stipes. The large chitinous internal structure of the basiproboscis is the fulcrum (ful) and is composed of the basipharnyx, or united portions of the epipharynx and hypopharynx, and the ental portions of the tormæ. At the distal end of the basipharynx lies the hyoid (hy), which articulates with the distal portion of the hypopharynx as well, and through which passes the alimentary canal.

The mediproboscis (mpb) bears the chitinized plate, the theca (the), on its caudal aspect, and the hypopharynx (hyp) and labrum-epipharynx (lep) lie in a chitinized groove on the upper surface of the labium.

The distiproboscis (dpb) is composed of a pair of lobes or labella, which Peterson interprets as the paraglossæ (pg). Crampton, however, calls them the united labial palpi. Various other structures can be seen in the distiproboscis, such as a Y-shaped plate called the furca (fu) and the structures called pseudotrachæ (pst).

Thorax. Pl. I, figs. 3 and 4. The structure of the thorax in *Trichopoda pennipes* is typical of the order Diptera as a whole, in which the mesothorax, which is the only wing-bearing segment, is greatly enlarged and distorted, evidently for the purpose of accomodating the great wing muscles. The prothorax (P) is very small, and the metathorax, which bears the halteres(ha), is very much reduced.

In naming the sclerites of the thorax the terminology used by Young (1921), which is largely based on Crampton (1914), is employed.

The dorsal aspect of the thorax is completely covered by the notum of the mesothorax, as defined by Snodgrass (1909a), or the mesonotum. This is divided by two transverse sutures into three sclerites, the prescutum (psc^2), scutum (sc^2) and scutellum (sl^2). The prescutum, including the humeral calli (hc) is yellow in color, with four longitudinal bands of velvety-black. In the males the yellow coloration extends backward onto the scutum where it merges with the black of that sclerite. The scutellum of both sexes appears black to the naked eye, but under the binocular most specimens show a faint tinge of very dark orange. The scutum is produced laterally into an anterior wing process, the suralare (sur), and a posterior wing process, the adanale (ad). The scutellar bridge of Walton (sb) is seen as a lateral overlapping of the scutellum onto the scutum. Below this is the axillary cord (axc) of Snodgrass (1909a), which is produced to form the margin of the calypteres. A posttergite (pt^2) is demarked behind the scutellum. The pseudonotum or postnotum of Snodgrass, which he would recommend calling the "postscutellum", in this case is located ventrad of the scutellum, and cannot be seen from above. It is divided into a median plate, the meditergite (mt^2), and two pairs of lateral plates, the anapleurotergites ($aplt^2$) and the katapleurotergites ($kplt^2$). Mention may logically be made here of the character recently reported by Malloch (1923) for differentiating muscoid flies. In Malloch's own words, "It is invariably possible to distinguish between the Sarcophagidæ, Muscidæ and Calliphoridæ on one hand, and the Tachinidæ and Dexiidæ on the other, by the shape of the metanotum. In the last two this is biconvex in profile, there being a small but distinct convexity just below the scutellum which is absent in the other three families known to me." The use of the term "metanotum" by Malloch follows the usage of older taxonomic workers, and is morphologically inaccurate. It is really the meditergite (mt^2) of the postscutellum which is meant, and the "biconvexity" apparent in Tachinidæ and Dexiidæ is conditioned by the presence of the posttergite (pt^2), which, as a glance at the figure will show, lies just below the scutellum. An examination of figures 38, 39, 40 and 41 of Young bears out this point.

The pleural region of the mesothorax is pollinose gray in color, and is much distorted. The pleural suture, which in generalized insects runs a nearly straight course from the coxal cavity to the wing base, thus dividing the pleuron into an anterior episternum and a posterior epimeron, is here bent twice at right angles, so that while the two ends are nearly vertical, the middle is horizontal. In addition a portion of the anepisternum (aes^2) has been split off from the rest by a secondary invasion of membrane, and has become closely associated with the anepimeron or pteropleurite ($ptp.^2$) The katepisternum has fused with the sternum to form the sternopleurite (stp^2). It is the enlargement of this sclerite which has evidently caused the bending of the pleural suture, and has crowded the meropleurite (mep^2), which is composed of katepimeron plus meron, back against the pleuron of the metathorax.

The numerous small plates which lie in the membrane surrounding the base of the wing are very difficult to see, but are easily identified with those sclerites outlined by Crampton (1914) in his ground plan of a typical thoracic segment in winged insects. The tegula (tg) lies in the angle between the scutum and the anepisternum. The notale (n) is a detached portion of the scutum lying just above the base of the wing. The basalar plates are two in number, the anterior one (aba) not demarked from the posterior portion of the anepisternum, the posterior one (pba) very small and lying between it and the pleural wing process (wp). The subalar plates are two in number, the anterior one (asa) lying behind the wing process and above the pteropleurite, the posterior one (psa) which is much smaller lying just below a posterior lateral process of the scutum. These basalar and subalar plates are the pre and post paraptera of Snodgrass (1909a).

The tergum of the metathorax, or the metanotum (n^3) is reduced to a narrow band connecting the halteres (ha), and visible only at the sides where it is produced to form points of attachment for the abdomen. The pleuron of this segment is divided into metaepisternum (es^3) and metaepimeron (em^3). A spiracle (sp) is present just before the metaepisternum, as before the mesoepisternum. The region around the base of the haltere is so modified that it is impossible to tell whether pre and post alar bridges connect the metanotum with the metapleuron.

Some of the terms used above are different from those in common use among taxonomists. The mesoanepisternum (aes^2) has been called by dipterists the mesopleura. The mesosternopleurite (stp^2) is equivalent to the sternopleura of authors, while the meropleurite (mep^2) plus metapleuron plus metasternum equals the hypopleurite, so-called.

Chaetotaxy of the Thorax. The thorax of *T. pennipes* is not heavily armed with macrochætæ. However, representatives of most of the groups mentioned by Walton are present. Two humerals (hu) adorn each humeral callus. Posthumerals are wanting, as are anterior acrosticals. The anterior dorsocentral rows are represented by two very variable bristles (adc) placed near the hinder margin of the prescutum, while at each rear corner of this sclerite are borne two notopleural bristles (np). On each side, between the notopleurals and the anterior dorsocentrals, lies a single bristle, the presutural (psu).

On either side of the scutum a single bristle (sa) represents the supra-alar row, and another (ia) each intra-alar row. Two post alars (pa) are present, and each of the posterior dorsocentral (pdc) and posterior acrostical (pac) rows is represented by a single bristle. It will be seen that these last four bristles form a transverse row near the hind margin of the scutum. This is called the prescutellar row.

On the scutellum an anterior bristle and a posterior bristle mark the position of the marginal scutellar row (ms). The anterior bristle was seen to be accompanied by a smaller one in one or two specimens. No discal scutellars are present.

The mesoanepisternum bears a vertical row of bristles called the mesopleural row (mr), situated just before the membrane which divides it. Below the anterior spiracle are two bristles, one on the prothorax, the propleural bristle (pp), and one on the sternopleurite, which the writer has called the sub-stigmal bristle (ss). The sternopleurite bears typically two sterno-pleurals (stb), although a third was found to be present on some individuals. A curved row of three to five hypopleurals (hp) is located on the meropleurite. A single pteropleural bristle (ptb) was present in some specimens examined, while others bore as many as four.

Appendages of the Thorax.

Legs. Pl. I, fig. 4; Pl. II, figs. 7 and 8. The coxa (cx) is tawny in color, with a grayish bloom, while the trochanter (tr) and the proximal portion of the femur (fe) are yellowish. The distal portion of the femur and the tibia (tb) and tarsus (ta) are black. The claws are yellowish tipped with black, and are fringed with very fine light-colored hairs. There is a bristle-like empodium (ep) which, since it is a prolongation of a ventral plate, is a true empodium according to Crampton (1923). The pulvilli (pv) are buff-colored, and in the male are quite large and conspicuous. The first two pairs of legs display no features of particular interest. The tibiæ of the hind legs, however, exhibit on the outer side a peculiar row of black, feather-like setæ, which stand nearly erect, and the longest of which are at least one third the length of the tibia itself. This row is in reality double, since a row of smaller scales is appressed to the larger ones on the outside. The hind tibia also bears on its inner face a single bristle of a size noticeably larger than any of the surrounding hairs.

Wings. Pl. II, figs 5 and 6. The wings of the female are dusky, with the posterior margin sub-hyaline. Those of all the males examined bear a somewhat variable yellowish area in the forepart of the wing, the extent of which is indicated in figure 5. According to Coquillett (1897) this character is not constant.

The figure of the wing of the female (fig. 6) explains the venation of the wings, while the cells are labeled in the figure of the wing of the male. The chief point of interest in the wing venation of *T. pennipes* is that M_3 is bullate or weakened basally, making M_3 appear as a stub sticking up from Cu_1.

Abdomen. Pl. II, figs. 9-14. Pl. III, fig. 15. The abdomen in both sexes is of a bright orange color and is destitute of macrochætæ. It is sparsely clothed, however, with short black hairs. Seven pairs of spiracles (sp) are present, borne at the lateral margins of the tergites (t_1, t_2), etc.). Those of the sixth and seventh segments are hidden beneath the posterior edge of the fifth tergite (t_5). The tergites of the first and second segments are fused, the fusion being denoted by an area of weaker chitin, which is demarked in the figures by a pair of dotted lines between t_1 and t_2. The adventitious suture (as) in the first tergite, mentioned by Young, is readily seen.

The tip of the abdomen in the female is wholly black, this coloration including the fifth tergite and in some individuals extending further forward to include part of the fourth tergite. The terminal abdominal segments of the male in specimens examined by the writer were in no case wholly black, although t_5 and t_6 were darker than those preceding.

Genitalia.[1] Pl. II, figs. 13-14; Pl. III, fig. 15. In both sexes the segments beyond the fifth abdominal may truly be called genita segments. In the male these segments curve downward and come to lie beneath the fifth tergite. In the female those beyond the fifth are telescoped when at rest, being extended for oviposition.

In the male the fused tenth and eleventh tergites, which are ventral in position, act as a cover for the œdeagus (oe), being tucked beneath the edge of the fifth sternite (s_5) when at rest. When the œdagus is extruded, however, this flap lifts up, allowing the ninth sternite (s_9) to push forth. This latter segment is very much modified. Its fused cerci are median in position and form the œdagus, a very complicated structure which encloses the membranous penis. At the base of the œdagus are seen two pairs of lateral projections, called gonopophyses (go), the inner pair of which are hyaline. They are well-chitinized, however, feeling hard to the touch of a dissecting needle. At the base of the œdagus the ninth sternite is

[1]The writer has based his description of the genitalia largely on the condition of these structures in generalized insects. It is apparent that the study of a series of dipterous genitalia may reverse some of his decisions regarding the true character of the parts.

rather more heavily chitinized than elsewhere, resulting in the appearance of a chitinized box (chb) from which the ædeagus protrudes and on which the gonopophyses are borne. This chitinized box also bears a median dorsal hook-like projection, called by the writer the genital prong (gp). The styli of the ninth segment, which in some insects function as outer claspers, are here much reduced in size and are apparently non-functional, since when the genitalia are extruded they barely appear beyond the posterior edge of the eighth tergite. A peculiar structure, which the writer is at a loss to homologize with any genital appendage of generalized insects, appears in the "genital furca" (gf). This is a fork-like chitinized rod which lies between the sides of the ninth sternite, to which it is connected by muscles. It splits at the base of the œdagus, one arm extending to either side of the latter organ. Its function is quite evidently that of guiding the movements of the œdagus.

In the female the eighth segment is a narrow ring, bearing below the median ventral valve (vv) of the ovipositor and laterally the two inner valves (iv). Dorsally this segment seemed to bear a median dorsal valve (dv), but this may prove to be a modified portion of the ninth segment, which is supposed to bear the dorsal valve. This point could not be definitely determined from the dried material at the writer's disposal, even after soaking in caustic potash and gently extending the ovipositor by pushing from within by means of a blunt needle.

Secondary Sexual Characters. The foregoing account of the external anatomy of *Trichopoda pennipes* contains scattered references to certain differences which were apparent between the two sexes. These differences were constant in a series of eight males and seven females. Scarcely any difference in size could be noticed, the males averaging 8.6 mm. in length, the females 8 mm. Both the largest and the smallest were males, the one 10 mm. long, the other measuring 7 mm. To a certain extent the size of the adult fly is affected by the abundance of food available to the larva which preceded it, and when contained in keys for the identification of species may be found misleading.

Two characters were found by which the sex of living flies can be determined without undue handling. These are the ferrugineous spot in the wing of the male as against the evenly dusky wing of the female, and the black tip of the female abdomen as against the dark orange of that of the male.[1] A minor difference was in the size of the pulvilli, these being shorter than the last tarsal segment in the females, and inconspicuous. In the males the pulvilli were longer than the last tarsal segment, and quite broad and conspicuous. This is a character, however, that is not readily noticed unless a male and a female are examined at the same time, and it is therefore of little practical use, in a taxonomic sense.

EGG. Pl. III, fig. 16.

The eggs of *Trichopoda pennipes* vary in color from clear shining white to dirty gray, the coloration seeming not to depend on the age of the egg. The individual egg is ovate in outline, being slightly larger at one end. It is strongly convex, and is flattened on the side next the body surface of the host. This flattened surface is covered by a colorless cement, by which the egg is affixed to the body of the host. The egg measures .56 mm. in length by .37 mm. in breadth, and its greatest height is .25 mm. The surface of the chorion appears smooth except under high magnification, when it is seen to be faintly reticulate in tiny hexagons. The chorion is comparatively thick and "leathery", and remains rigid after hatching. The micropyle appears to be borne on a small papilla at the smaller end of the egg. Eggs which have hatched show a circular hole on the flattened side near the broader end. Since it is this flattened side which is pressed against the host, it is impossible to tell if an egg has hatched without first removing it from the body surface of the host.

LARVA. Pl. III, figs. 17 and 18.

The larva has not been examined in all instars. When fullgrown, it is a dead-white maggot, with black hook-like

[1]Drake (1920) published recognizable photographs of both sexes, but his designations are erroneous. Osten Sacken, in a foot-note to the work of Say (1829), also has confused the sexes.

rasping mouth parts (mh) and a pair of black anal stigmata. (ans) It is quite robust, and although its greatest circumference is about midway of its length, it can hardly be called fusiform, since it tapers away to a point in front, while the anal end is blunt. It is about 10 mm. long by 3.5 mm. in diameter, a surprising size when one considers that the adult host measures but 15 mm. in length.

The structure of the cephalo-pharnygeal skeleton, and the arrangement of the slits in the anal stigmata vary in the different species, and figures of these organs are therefore included in the plates. No sign of the parastomal sclerites mentioned by Banks (1912) as occurring in certain muscoid larvæ could be found in the cephalo-pharyngeal skeleton of *T. pennipes*.

PUPARIUM. Pl. III, figs. 19, 20, 21.

The pupa itself has not been observed. The puparium which encloses it, however, is of a deep reddish-black color, cylindrical in shape, and rounded at both ends. It is formed from the skin of the mature larva, and upon it the anal stigmata appear as twin tubercles at the posterior end. The puparia average about 7.5 mm. in length and 3.5 mm. in diameter. At the anterior end, before the emergence of the adult fly, a transverse split occurs, reaching backward nearly a quarter of the length of the puparium. The split then extends around the circumference, this resulting in the formation of two flaps which are pushed aside by the ptilinum of the emerging adult.

Some time after the examinations of the puparium had been finished by the writer, the work of Greene (1922) on the puparia of muscoid flies came to hand. The puparium of *T. pennipes* is there figured and discussed, and significant characters compared with those of the puparia of other species.

BIBLIOGRAPHY.

Aldrich, J. M.

1905. A catalogue of North American Diptera. Smithsonian Misc. Coll., vol. 16, no. 1444, p. 425.

1915. Collecting in Tachinidæ. Ann. Ent. Soc. America, vol. 8, p. 83. (Distribution of *T. pennipes.*)

Banks, Nathan.

1912. On the Structure of Certain Dipterous Larvæ, with Particular Reference to Those in Human Foods. U. S. Dept. Agric., Bur. Ent., Tech. Ser., Bull. 22.

Brauer, F. and Bergenstamm, J. E. V.

1891. Die Zweiflügler des Kaiserlichen Museums, vol. 5, p. 412 (calls *T. pennipes* the male, and *T. pyrrhogaster* and *T. ciliata* of Wiedemann the female).

Chittenden, F. H.

1899. Some Insects Injurious to Garden and Orchard Crops. U. S. Dept. Agric., Bur. Ent., Bull. 19, n. s., p. 26.

1902. Some Insects Injurious to Vegetable Crops. U. S. Dept. Agric., Bur. Ent., Bull. 33, n. s., p. 25.

1908. The Common Squash Bug. U. S. Dept. Agric., Bur. Ent., Circ. 39, 2nd ed. p. 9. (Mentions parasitism by *T. pennipes.*)

Cook, A. J.

1889. A squash Bug Parasite. 2nd Ann. Rept. Michigan Agric. Exp. Sta.—Rept. of Entomologist pp. 88-103. Also in Ann. Rept. of the Sec. of the Michigan State Bd. Agric., p. 151. (Gives first account of parasitism which names *T. pennipes.*)

Coquillett, D. W.

1897. Revision of the Tachinidæ of America North of Mexico. U. S. Dept. Agric., Bur. Ent., Tech. Ser. 7. (Gives key to species.)

Crampton, G. C.

1914. The Ground Plan of a Typical Thoracic Segment in Winged Insects. Zool. Anz., vol. 44, pp. 56-57.

1921. The Sclerites of the Head, and the Mouthparts of Certain Immature and Adult Insects. Ann. Ent. Soc. Amer. vol. 14, pp. 65-103, plates II-VIII.

1923. Preliminary note on the Terminology Applied to the Parts of an Insect's Leg. Canad. Ent., vol. 55, no. 6, p. 130.

Drake, Carl J.

1920. The Southern Green Stink Bug in Florida. In Quart. Bull. State Plant Bd. Florida, vol. 4, pp. 41-94. (Treats of *T. pennipes* on pp. 67-74, 87-88).

Fabricius, J. C.

1794. Entomologia Systematica. Vol. 4, p. 348. (Original description as *Musca pennipes.*)

1805. Systema Antliatorum. (p. 219.8, *Thereva pennipes*, p. 219.9, *Thereva hirtipes*; p. 315.9, *Ocyptera ciliata*, later declared synonyms; and p. 327.5, *Dictya pennipes*, change of genus from Musca.)

Giglio-Tos., B.

1896. Ditteri del Messico, pt. 3, Mem. Real. Accad. Sci., Torino, (2) vol. 44, p. 6 and 7. (*T. pyrrhogaster* and *T. pennipes.*)

Girault, A. A.

1904. *Anasa tristis* De Geer; History of Confined Adults. In Ent. News, Vol. XV, p. 335. (Records breeding *T. pennipes.*)

Greene, Chas. T.

1922. An illustrated Synopsis of the Puparia of 100 Muscoid Flies (Diptera). Proc. U. S. Nat. Mus. vol. 60, Art. 10, pp. 37, figs. 99.

Howard, L. O.
1904. Insect Book. Plate XV, figs 25. (Color illustration of *T. pennipes*, female.)

Jones, Thos. H.
1918. The Southern Green Plant Bug. U. S. Dept. Agric., Bull. 689, p. 22. (Records *T. pennipes* as parasitic upon *Nezara viridula*.)

Latreille, P. A.
1829. Cuvier's Regne Animale, vol. 5, p. 512. (Erection of genus Trichopoda.)

Malloch, J. R.
1923. A New Character for Differentiating the Families of Muscoidea. In Ent. News. vol. XXXIV, pp. 57-58.

Morrill, A. W.
1910. Plant Bugs Injurious to Cotton Bolls. U. S. Dept. Agric., Bull. 86, p. 92. (Reared *T. pennipes* from *Leptoglossus oppositus*.)

Osten Sacken, C. R.
1878. Catalogue of the Described Diptera of North America, 2nd edit. Smithsonian Misc. Coll., vol. 16, no. 270. (*T. pennipes*, p. 146.)

Packard, A. S.
1875. Tachina Parasite of the Squash Bug. In American Natural vol. 9, p. 513. (Evidently the earliest account of the habits of *T. pennipes*.)

Peterson, Alvah.
1916. The Head Capsule and Mouthparts of Diptera. Illinois Biol. Monog., vol. 3, No. 2, pp. 110; plate 25.

Robineau-Desvoidy, J. B.
1830. Essai sur les Myodaires. (P. 283.1, change of genus to Trichopoda; p. 284.2, *T. flavicornis*; and p. 285.7, T. *haitensis*, later declared synonyms.)

Say, Thomas.
1829. Description of North American Dipterous Insects. In Jour. Acad. Sci. Philadelphia vol. 6, p. 172. Complete Works, vol. 2, p. 364. (*Phasia jugatoria*, synonym of *T. pennipes.*)

Snodgrass, R. E.
1909a. The Thoracic Tergum of Insects. In Ent. News, vol. 20, pp. 97-103.
1909b. The Thorax of Insects and the Articulation of the Wings. In Proc. U. S. Nat. Mus., vol. 36, pp. 511-595, plates 40-69.

Thompson, W. R.
1910. Notes on the Pupation and Hibernation of Tachinid Parasites. Journ. Econ. Ent., vol. III, pp. 283-295.

Townsend, C. H. T.
1893. On the Geographic Range and Distribution of the Genus Trichopoda. Ent. News, vol. 4, pp. 69-71.
1897. On a Collection of Diptera from the Lowlands of Rio Nautla in the State of Vera Cruz. Ann. and Mag. Nat. Hist. (6), vol. 20, p. 279. (*Records T. pennipes.*)
1908. A Record of Results from Rearings and Dissections of Tachinidæ. U. S. Dept. Agric., Bur. Ent., Tech. Ser. 12, part VI.

Van der Wulp, F. M.
1888. Biologia Centrali-Americana. Dipt., Vol. 2, p. 434. *T. pennipes.*

Walton, W. R.
1909. An illustrated Glossary of Chætotaxy and Anatomical Terms used in Describing Diptera. Ent. News, vol. 20, pp. 307-319, plates XIII-XVI.

Watson, J. R.
1918. Insects of a Citrus Grove. Univ. of Florida Agric. Exp. Sta., Bull. 148, p. 261. (Records *T. pennipes* as parasitic upon *Nezara viridula.*)

Weed, C. M. and Conradi, A. F.
1902. The Squash Bug. New Hampshire Agric. Exp. Sta., Bull. 89. (An account of the parasitic habit of *T. pennipes.*)

Wiedemann, C. R. W.
1830. Aussereuropaische Zweiflugelige Insekten, vol. 2, (p. 272.6; *T. pyrrhogaster*; p. 273.8, *T. ciliata*; p. 274.9, *T. pennipes.*)

Williston, S. W.
1896. On the Diptera of St. Vincent (W. I.). Trans. Ent. Soc. London for 1896, p. 352. (Records *T. pennipes* from St. Vincent.)

Wilson, C. E.
1923. Insect Pests of Cotton in St. Croix and Means of Combating Them. Virgin Islands Agric. Exp. Sta., Bull. No. 3. (Record of *T. pennipes* on p. 14).

Worthley, H. N.
1923. The Squash Bug in Massachusetts. Jour Econ. Ent. vol. 16, p. 78. (Chart showing parallel seasonal histories of *T. pennipes* and *Anasa tristis.*)

Young, B. P.
1921. Attachment of the Abdomen to the Thorax in Diptera. Cornell Univ. Agric. Exp. Sta. Mem. 44, pp. 251-306, figs. 76.

Explanation of Figures.

Plate I.

Fig. 1. Head of male—front view.
Fig. 2. Head of male—side view, showing mouth parts.
Fig. 3. Dorsum of male thorax.
Fig. 4. Thorax of male—side view.

Plate II.

Fig. 5. Wing of male, showing extent of ferrugineous spot. Cells labeled.
Fig. 6. Wing of female. Veins labeled.
Fig. 7. Tibia of metathoracic leg, showing fringe of feather-barbed setæ.
Fig. 8. Terminal segments of tarsus of male.
Fig. 9. Abdomen of male—side view.
Fig. 10. Abdomen of female—side view.
Fig. 11. Abdomen of male—ventral view.
Fig. 12. Abdomen of female—ventral view.
Fig. 13. Male genitalia.
Fig. 14. Female genitalia.

Plate III

Fig. 15. Ninth abdominal sternite of male.
Fig. 16. Egg. a, outline from side; b, from top; c, showing hole in ventral surface after hatching.
Fig. 17. Mature larva.
Fig. 18. Cephalo-pharyngeal skeleton of larva. a and b, of second stage (?) larva, side and top views; c and d, mature of larva, side and top views.

Fig. 19. Puparium, from the top.
Fig. 20. Empty puparium, from the side.
Fig. 21. Anal stigmata of puparium.

Plate IV

Dorsal view of male fly.

Abbreviations

1st A —anal or 6th longitudinal vein
aba —anterior basalar plate
ad —adanale
adc —anterior dorso-central bristle
ae —oedagus
aes[2] —mesoanepisternum or mesopleura
aex —axillary excision
al —axillary lobe
ans —anal stigmata
ant —antenna
aplt[2] —anapleurotergite of post-scutellum
ar —arista
as —adventitious suture
asa —anterior subalar plate
AxC —axillary (or anal) cell
axc —axillary cord

bpb —basiproboscis
bu —button

C —costal vein
CC —costal cell
ce —compound eye
chb —chitinized box
cpo —cilia of posterior orbit
CuC —cubital (3rd basal or anal) cell
Cu_1C —3rd posterior cell
cx —coxa

dpb —distiproboscis
dv —dorsal valve (?) of ovipositor

em[3] —metaepimeron
ep —empodium
es[3] —metaepisternum

fb —frontal bristles
fc —fronto-clypeus (facial depression, facial plate)
fe —femur
fs —frontal suture
fu —furca
ful —fulcrum

ga —galea
ge —gena (cheek)
gf —genital furca
go —gonopophyses
gp —genital prong
ha —haltere
hc —humeral callus
hcv —humeral cross-vein
hp —hypopleural bristles
hu —humeral bristles
hy —hyoid
hyp —hypopharynx
hys —hypostomal sclerite

ia —intra-alar bristle
iv —inner valve of ovipositor
ivt —inner vertical bristle

kplt[2] —katapleurotergite of post-scutellum

lep —labrum-epipharynx
lp —lateral plate

M —media
m —medial (posterior)cross-vein
M_{1+2} —4th longitudinal vein
$M_{3+}Cu_1$ —5th longitudinal vein
MC —medial (2nd basal) cell
$1M_2C$ —discal cell
$2M_2C$ —2nd posterior cell

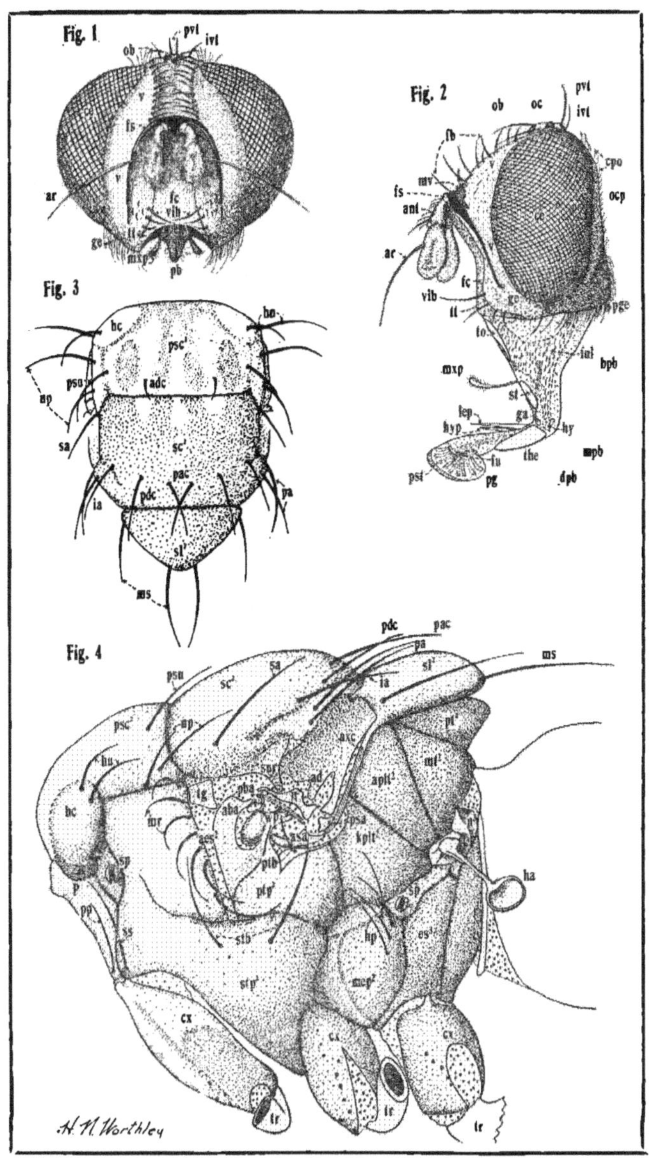

WORTHLEY—Biology of *Trichopoda pennipes*

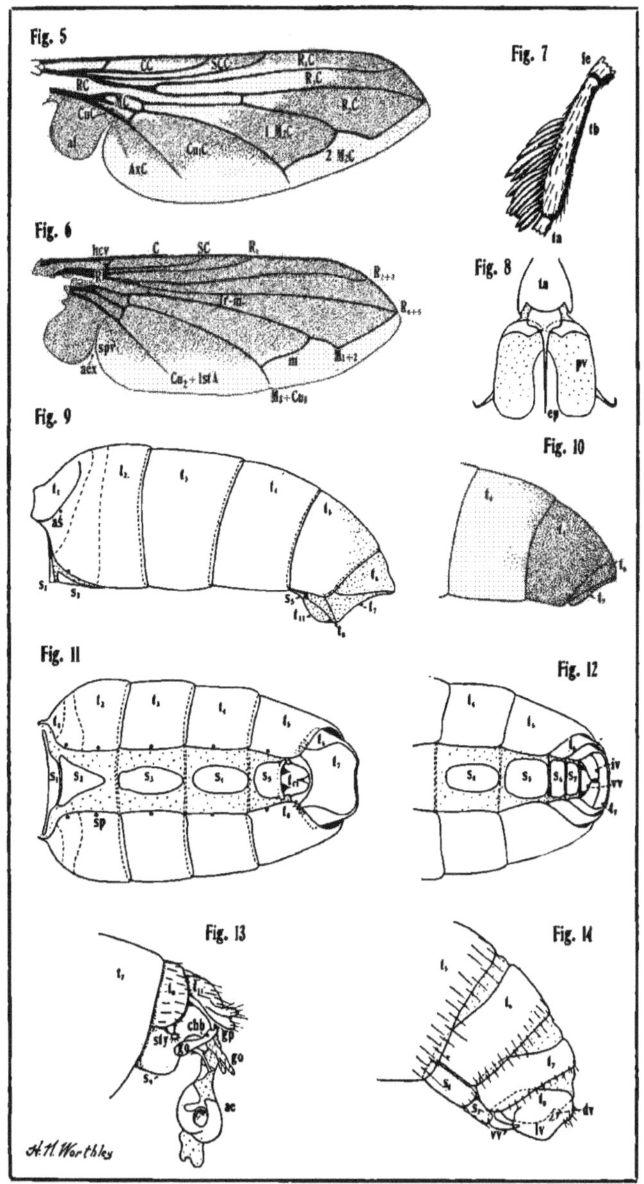

WORTHLEY—Biology of *Trichopoda pennipes*

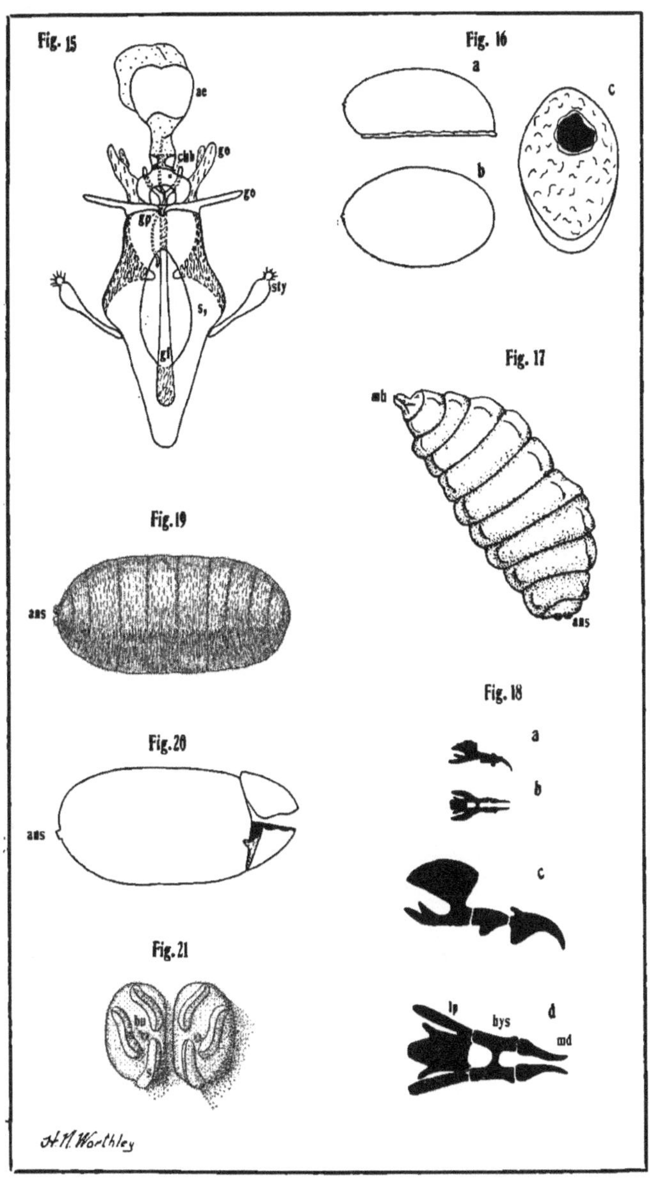

WORTHLEY—Biology of *Trichopoda pennipes*

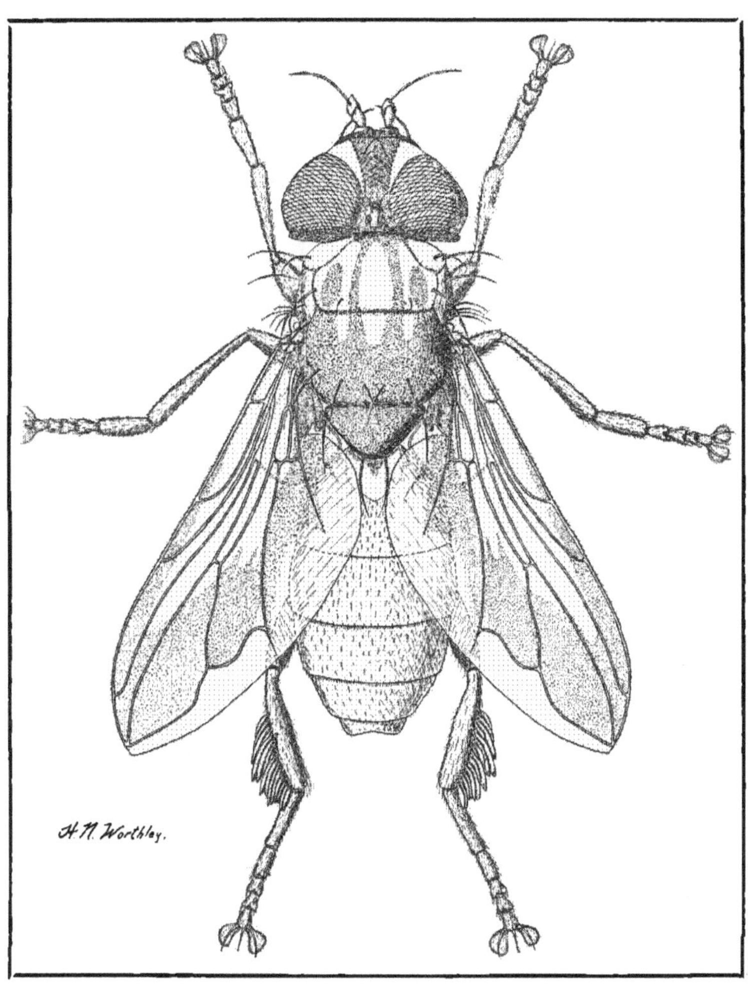

WORTHLEY—Biology of *Trichopoda pennipes*

md	—mandibles (great hooks) of larva
mep^2	—meropleurite
mh	—mouth hooks (or mandibles) of larva
mpb	—mediproboscis
mr	—mesopleural row
ms	—marginal scutellar bristles
mt^2	—meditergite of postscutellum
mv	—median vitta of vertex
mxp	—maxillary palpus
n	—notale
n^3	—metanotum
np	—notopleural bristles
ob	—ocellar bristles
oc	—ocelli
ocp	—occiput
P	—prothorax
pa	—postalar bristles
pac	—posterior acrostical bristle
pb	—proboscis
pba	—posterior basalar plate
pdc	—posterior dorso-central bristle
pg	—paraglossae
pge	—postgenae
pp	—propleural bristle
psa	—posterior subalar plate
psc^2	—mesoprescutum
pst	—pseudotrachae
psu	—presutural bristle
pt^2	—posttergite of mesoscutellum
ptb	—pteropleural bristle
ptp^2	—pteropleurite or mesoanepimeron
pv	—pulvillus
pvt	—posterior vertical bristles
R	—radius
R_1	—1st longitudinal vein
R_{2+3}	—2nd longitudinal vein
R_{4+5}	—3rd longitudinal vein
RC	—radial (1st basal)cell
R_1C	—marginal cell
R_2C	—submarginal cell
R_3C	—1st posterior or apical cell
r-m	—radio-medial (anterior) cross-vein
s	—slit
s_1, s_2, etc.	—abdominal sternites
sa	—supra-alar bristle
sb	—scutellar bridge
SC	—subcosta (auxiliary vein)
sc^2	—mesoscutum
SCC	—subcostal cell
sl^2	—mesoscutellum
sp	—spiracle
spv	—spurious vein
ss	—substigmal bristle
st	—stipes
stb	—sternopleural bristles
stp^2	—mesosternopleurite (sternopleura)
sty	—stylus
sur	—suralare
t_1, t_2, etc.	—abdominal tergites
ta	—tarsus
tb	—tibia
tg	—tegula
the	—theca
to	—tormae
tr	—trochanter
tt	—tentorial thickenings
v	—vertex
vib	—vibrissae
vv	—ventral valve of ovipositor
wp	—wing process

REVIEW OF THE DIPTEROUS FAMILY PIOPHILIDÆ.[1]

By A. L. Melander.

Pullman, Washington.

In 1917 in collaboration with Anthony Spuler I published a taxonomic study of the Piophilidæ in Bulletin 143 of the Washington Agricultural Experiment Station. This work was undertaken in order to facilitate identification in this group of insects many of which are of concern to man owing to their unsanitary habits of frequenting garbage. In the meantime additional collecting has brought to light several undescribed species which are herewith described together with some notes on the taxonomy of *Piophila* and a rectification of the identity of *P. pusilla*.

Key to the Species of Mycetaulus.

Thorax wholly reddish yellow, or almost entirely so; abdomen more or less blackened.. .... 2.
Body almost wholly black; wings uniformly subhyaline....... 7.
2. Occiput brownish; wings more than three times as long as broad; pectus, metanotum and an anterior spot on mesonotum sometimes blackish. (Can.; E. U. S) .... *longipennis* Loew
   Head yellowish or rufous; wings three times as long as wide.......... 3.
3. Anterior crossvein distinctly beyond middle of discal cell... 4.
   Anterior crossvein located near middle of discal cell....... 6.
4. Costal cell blackened; ocellar area concolorous with head... 5.
   Costal cell hyaline; ocellar area black (E. U. S.)............ *pulchellus* Banks
5. Costal area narrowly black from root of wing to tip, the apical spot excised in submarginal cell. (Or.)..*costalis*, n.sp.
   Costa not centrally blackened, the apical spot somewhat triangular. (Eur.; W. U. S.)........ *bipunctatus* Fallen

[1]Contribution from the Zoology Laboratory of the State College of Washington.

6. One dorsocentral bristle; cilia of calypteres white; wings uniformly subhyaline; front tibiæ yellowish; (W. U. S.) *testaceus*, n. sp.

   Two dorsocentrals; cilia of calypteres brown; wings with narrow clouding at apex; front tibiæ brown. (Wash.) *polypori*, n. sp.

7. Pleuræ, scutellum and end of abdomen reddish (Eur.) *analis* Meigen

   Pleuræ, scutellum and abdomen black, only prothorax and humeri yellowish; front yellow. (W. U. S.). *nigritellus*, n. sp.

Mycetaulus costalis, n. sp.

Male. Length 3 mm. Front reddish, occiput, face and cheeks testaceous, thorax luteous, abdomen black. Front tapering, slightly longer than width at anterior ocellus where it is twice as wide as at antennæ, posterior fronto-orbital strong. Notal hairs moderately scattering. Retracted genitalia black. Legs including coxæ mostly pale yellow, last tarsal joint dusky. Halteres white, calypteres dirty, with black fringe; wings mainly clear hyaline, costa, first vein and end of second and third veins black, remainder of veins yellowish, anterior edge of wing bordered with black which also borders the black tips of the second and third veins, costal cell wholly black, anterior crossvein about one-fourth the length of the posterior and located near two-thirds the length of the discal cell.

Holotype, North slope of Mt. Hood, Oregon, 29 July, 1921, at 3000 feet elevation.

Mycetaulus nigritellus, n. sp.

Male. Length 3 mm. Head bicolored, thorax and abdomen black, front legs partly black, wings uniformly but lightly brownish hyaline. Upper two-thirds of occiput black continuing forward on the ocellar triangle and as orbital stripes to the posterior fronto-orbital bristle, remainder of front luteous, face, cheeks and lower orbits pale yellow, lower setulæ indistinct, clypeus narrowly brown, antennæ luteous, the upper part of third joint brownish, arista blackish. Pectus and the part of the pleuræ above front coxæ brownish yellow, sometimes humeri brown, notal hairs minute and sparse, two strong sternopleurals. Base of abdomen subshining at sides, remainder of abdomen polished, genitalia small and retracted. Front coxæ whitish, basal half of front femora yellow, apical half black, ten flexor setæ, base of front tibiæ yellowish, remainder black, front metatarsi black, other joints yellowish, posterior legs yellowish, the hind femora distally slightly brown. Halteres, calypteres and fringe and root of wings whitish; wings rather pointed, veins brown, first posterior cell two-thirds as wide as submarginal on the costa, anterior crossvein at three-fifths the length of the discal cell and one-third as long as posterior crossvein.

Female. Front tarsi wholly black, the metatarsus somewhat thicker than the other joints; ovipositor terete.

Types. Lookout Mt., Priest Lake, Idaho, 20 August, 1919, paratypes, Lake McDonald, Glacier Park, Montana; Moscow Mt., Idaho; and Mt. Spokane, Washington; July-September: fifteen males and six females.

Mycetaulus polypori, n. sp.

Male. Length 3.5 mm. Head and thorax testaceous, abdomen blackish, legs mostly testaceous yellow, the distal part of front femora and tibiæ and the front tarsi blackish, wings narrowly blackened at apex. Antennæ pale yellow, arista brown, occipital black setulæ conspicuous; front wider than long and two-thirds as wide at lunule as at ocelli. Thoracic hairs fine and rather abundant, bristles long, two dorsocentrals. Base and apex of abdomen and venter yellowish brown, genitalia small, with spiral yellow filament. Front coxæ yellow, sometimes the front femora lack the darkening at the apex. Halteres white, calypteres yellowish white, the fringe brown; wings yellowish hyaline, auxiliary and first vein, distal end of second, third and fourth veins and apical part of costa blackish, remainder of veins yellowish, a narrow blackish cloud following the blackened portions of the veins at the apex of the wing, anterior crossvein at middle of discal cell and a little shorter than half the length of the posterior crossvein.

Types, twenty-six males and eleven females, in the vicinity of Longmire, Mt. Rainier, Washington, July, 1922. The specimens were taken disporting themselves on the underside of the shelf-fungus, *Polyporus*, growing on tree-trunks in the shady woods. They would not readily take to flight but were secured by suddenly blowing them into the net.

Mycetaulus testaceus, n. sp.

Male. Length 3.5 mm. Head and thorax entirely testaceous abdomen black, legs yellowish with the front tarsi and apical joints of posterior tarsi black; wings uniformly subhyaline. Occiput dull, its setulæ black; front wider than long, its setulæ fine and black. Hairs of mesonotum very fine and abundant, black, only the posterior dorsocentral developed; abdomen truncate at tip, genitalia small, without processes. Calypteres fringed with white hairs, halteres white; costa and first vein blackish, other veins yellowish at base, becoming darker distally, two apical sections of costa subequal, anterior crossvein very slightly beyond middle of discal cell, one-third as long as posterior crossvein.

Type, Moscow Mt., Idaho, 24 June 1919; two paratypes, Ilwaco, Washington, May and July.

The single dorsocentral bristle suggests *Piophila* were it not that the humeral and presutural bristles are strong as in *Mycetaulus*. Location in this genus is further indicated by the yellow body-color, two strong sternopleurals, long cephalic bristles and undoubted relationship to *M. polypori*.

Prochyliza brevicornis, n. sp.

Similar to *P. xanthostoma* in coloration except that the yellow of the face continues over the antennæ across the anterior part of the front. This yellow portion of the front curves down.

The second antennal joint is about one-half the length of the third. There are three or four black setæ on the lower part of the front coxæ.

This is the form mentioned in Bulletin 143 of the Washington State Agricultural Experiment Station, page 56, as superficially resembling *Piophila affinis*. Insamuch as I have taken seventeen specimens all constant in the correlation of characters given above the form may be given specific rank. The localities represented are Yellowstone Park, several places, Flathead Lake, Montana, and Chicago, Illinois; all captured in July or August.

P. xanthostoma has the front entirely black and plane or convex to the lunule. In only one specimen is there any yellow color above the antennæ. The second antennal joint is extremely variable but always is longer in proportion to the third joint than in this brachycerous form. The coxal setæ are present in the male but are undeveloped in the female. In *Piophila affinis* the venter of the male is shaggy with black hair, which is not the case in *Prochyliza*.

Subgenera of Piophila.

The genus *Piophila* was based on *P. casei* as genotype but the inclusion of many subsequently described species has caused it to become heterogeneous. In line with the present tendency to recognize finer distinctions Hendel in 1917 segregated the genus *Allopiophila* from the group, basing it entirely on chætotactic characters. *Piophila casei* and a few of its congeners are markedly different from the majority of the species left in *Piophila.* Removal of the species grouped with *P. casei* and the separation of those in *Allopiophila* makes it necessary to revive Lioy's name *Stearibia,* founded on *foveolata* Mg.=*nigriceps* Mg. As the size of bristles is quite variable the diagnostic characters have only relative and not absolute value. Hence it is premature to assign more than subgeneric rank to these names.

In order to show the relationships of the species of *Piophila* with reference to the divisions into subgenera and to facilitate identification of several new forms the following table is presented.

Five species not represented in my collection are omitted since their descriptions are too brief to show phyletic location in the key. The omitted species are: *P. concolor*, a red species probably a Cordylurid; *nitens*, perhaps a *Pseudodinia*; *senescens*, vaguely recorded by Macquart in 1851 as from North America and not since recognized, possibly not *Piophila* since it is gray pubescent; and the Greenland hairy species *pilosa* and *nigerrima*.

Key to the Subgenera and Species of Piophila.

Mesonotum finely scabrous, centrally not pubescent but with three rows of setulæ, one in the middle and one on each dorsocentral row; fronto-orbital, humeral, presutural and sternopleural bristles undeveloped; ocellar bristles small, widely distant and located opposite the front ocellus, the ocellar triangle differentiated as a shining space on the satiny front; vertical bristles small; mesopleuræ sparsely hairy; pygidium transverse, retracted within the fifth segment and asymmetrically excised toward the right side; cheeks more than half the eye-height; second and third joints of front tarsi subequal to metatarsus. Subgenus *Piophila* Fallen, *s. str.* Genotype and only American species, cosmopolitan. *casei* Linn.

Mesonotum smoothly polished and uniformly pubescent; ocellar bristles located behind the front ocellus; cheeks less than half the eye-height; sternopleural bristles usually present, though small; front metatarsi longer than two following joints together . . . . 2.

2 Fronto-orbital, humeral and presutural bristles minute or wanting; mesopleuræ usually sparsely hairy; pygidium retracted and cleft toward the right side, *i. e.* the sixth segment displaced: lower occiput black or blackish, with a pruinose vertical stripe below the eyes abruptly stopping in a vertical line on the cheeks. (if occiput is shining, front blackened on upper three fourths, legs mostly black, and antennæ dark above, see *Prochyliza brevicornis*, n. sp.) Genotype *P. nigriceps* Meig. Subgenus *Stearibia* Lioy. . . . . 3.

One or two fronto-orbitals, humeral and presutural bristles well developed; mesopleuræ bare; pygidium pendant and extending forward under abdomen, the sixth segment superior; back part of cheeks shining, no pollinose vertical stripe beneath the eyes. Genotype *P. luteata* Hal. Subgenus *Allopiophila* Hendel..........9.

3. Scutellum flattened and microscopically roughened; front entirely black and devoid of pubescence; veins thin and pale. (Eur.; N. Am.)................*nigriceps* Meigen.
   Scutellum convex and smooth; front more or less yellow or red..4.
4. Front coxæ yellow...............................5.
   Front coxæ entirely black; femora black except knees, front tibiæ blackish, their tarsi black.................8.
5. Venter of male heavily hairy; sixth abdominal segment large and convex; posterior legs in large part black; upper half of front black; hind metatarsi subequal to remaining joints together...........................6.
   Venter with short sparse hairs; sixth abdominal segment of male not strongly convex; hind metatarsi shorter than remaining joints together; front yellow quite to the vertex..7.
6. Halteres yellow. (Eur.; Mass., Ont., Wash.). *affinis* Meigen.
   Halteres tipped with black.(Wash.). *affinis*, var. *halterata* M.,S.
7. Posterior legs yellow: cheeks, antennæ, base of arista and mouthparts yellow (N. U. S., B. C.)..*privigna*, n., sp.
   Posterior legs in large part black; cheeks, antennæ, arista and mouthparts piceous. (Wash.)....*morator* n. sp.
8 Mouthparts, cheeks, face, half of front and antennæ yellowish; halteres entirely yellow. (Mont., Id., Wash.) *nigricoxa* M., S.
   Mouthparts, cheeks, face and antennæ black, anterior half of front deep reddish: halteres with blackened tip. (Ill.) .... *occipitalis* M., S.
9. Front coxæ yellow; yellow of front continuing as an M-shaped mark to vertex; at least posterior fronto-orbital strong...10.

Coxæ black; fronto-orbital weak ....14.

10. Wings hyaline, veins yellowish ....11.
Wings with dark apical cloud, veins brown; abdomen closely and finely scabrous. (Mont., Ida., Wash.) *liturata* M., S.

11. Sixth segment of male abdomen pruinose; cheeks one-third eye-height; base of arista brown; propleural bristle strong 12
Sixth segment shining; legs typically wholly yellow except tips of tarsi: cheeks less than one-third eye-height; arista black; propleural bristle weak. (Mont., Ida., Wash.) .... *xanthopoda* M., S.

12. Front legs black except coxæ and knees, posterior femora mostly black. (Mass., N. Y.) .... *oriens* M., S.
At least base of front femora yellow, posterior legs mostly yellow ....13.

13. Legs almost wholly yellow; lower occiput yellow. (Alaska) *setosa* M., S.
Front legs black beyond middle of femora, excepting knees; lower occiput largely black. (Eur.; Wash.) *pusilla* Meigen

14. Posterior femora and all tibiæ yellow, front metatarsi merging in color with remaining joints; front reddish toward antennæ. (Wyo., Mont., Ida., Wash., Cal.) *nitidissima* M., S.
All femora black except narrowly at knees, first joint of front tarsi yellow sharply contrasting with black remainder: front entirely black. (Ida., Wash.) *atrifrons* M., S.

Piophila morator, n. sp.

Male. Length 2.75 mm. Front testaceous, vertex, ocellar triangle, upper orbits and occiput piceous black, cheeks, face, mouthparts and antennæ brown, the antennæ appearing velvety with cinereous pubescence; a vertical gray pruinose stripe beneath eyes, cheeks at middle one-fourth the eye-height; base of arista brown, remainder black; interfrontal pubescence distinct but sparse and pale, bristles weak. Humeral, presutural and sternopleural bristles undeveloped, prothoracic bristle weak; hairs of meso- and sterno-pleuræ present, propleuræ heavily pruinose. Abdomen bluntly elliptical, ventral hairs short and sparse, pygidium retracted, cleft on right side. Front coxæ yellowish, posterior coxæ piceous, legs piceous except the yellowish knees and posterior tarsi. Halteres nearly white. Wings hyaline, veins pale.

Holotype, Pullman, Washington, May.

Piophila privigna, n. sp.

Male. Length 3 mm. Front light yellow up to the vertex, the small ocellar triangle and the uppermost orbits black, occiput shining black, its lower sides with a white pruinose stripe extending from the eyes to the oral margin, face, cheeks, mouthparts and antennæ light yellow, arista brown, paler at base; cheeks broad, at middle one-third and at pruinose stripe one-half the eye-height; interfrontal hairs sparse and yellow, ocellar and postvertical bristles small, no fronto-orbitals. Thorax polished black with bluish lustre, no humeral, presutural or sternopleural bristles, notal pubescence uniform, meso- and sternopleuræ with scattering hairs, scutellum convex, prothoracic bristle small, propleuræ heavily pruinose. Abdomen polished black with blue lustre, the sixth segment displaced so that the retracted pygidium appears cleft, ventral hairs short and sparse. Legs light yellow, the distal two-thirds of front femora black and the distal three-fourths of front tibiæ brown. Halteres whitish. Wings hyaline, veins pale yellow.

Female. Front tarsi black.

Types, four males and eight females; Woods Hole, and New Bedford (Hough) Mass.; Cold Spring Harbor, N. Y.; Chicago, Ill.; Sheridan (Metz), Wyo.; Potlatch, Ida.; Pullman, Colfax, Ilwaco, Wash.; Nelson, B. C.: July and August. This is the species recorded as *P. pusilla* in Bulletin of the Washington State Agricultural Experiment Station No. 143, p. 61., under which name the other specimens there listed have been distributed among collections. I have taken the real *pusilla* at Olympia, Wash.

NOTES ON PHORIDÆ FROM SOUTH AFRICA.[1]

BY CHARLES T. BRUES.

During the past summer I received from H. K. Munro, Border Entomologist of the Union of South Africa, a small collection of Phoridæ obtained by him in the Cape Province.

As he wishes to publish observations on the life-history of some of the species included, I am taking this opportunity to present descriptions of two new species and taxonomic notes on some of the others.

Hypocera vectabilis Brues.

Ann. Mus. Nat. Hungarici, vol. II, p. 1 (1913)

There are numerous specimens of both sexes agreeing in all particulars with this species originally described from Abyssinia. More recently Schmitz has described *Hypocera trinervis*[2] from Stanleyville, Congo, which he says is related to *H. vectabilis*, and which I cannot distinguish from his description. The single male was taken in a nest of *Sima æthiops* on *Barteria fistulosa* and Schmitz thinks that *trinervis* is probably myrmecophilous. The original specimens of *H. vectabilis* were reared from the bodies of dried beetles shipped from Abyssinia to the Hungarian National Museum in Buda-Pest.

Some of Mr. Munro's specimens were "bred from larvæ infesting fruits of *Solanum sodomeum*" at Prospect, Komgha, Cape Province, March-April 1923, and others were taken in his office during April and May.

Aphiochaeta picta Lehmann

There are two typical specimens (♂ ♀) collected by Dr. Munro at East London, July 26, 1922 and April 29, 1923. This common palæartic species is known also from America, but it has

[1]Contribution from the Entomological Laboratory of the Bussey Institution, Harvard University. No. 235.

[2]Deutsche entom. Zeits., 1915, p. 498.

not hitherto been reported from Africa (*cf.* Schmitz, Jaarb. Natuurhist. Genootsch., Limburg for 1914, pp. 108-109 (1915) and Brues (Bull. Wisconsin Nat. Hist. Soc., vol. 12, p. 126 (1915).

Aphiochaeta setifer, sp. nov.

♂. Length 1.5 mm. Head and thorax piceous, lower part of front and anterior part of mesonotum fuscous; abdomen black; antennæ fuscous; palpi pale yellowish: legs brownish yellow, the hind femora blackened at tips and their tibiæ with a black line above; hypopygium brownish, pruinose; wings hyaline, with a brownish tinge apically on the disc; venation dark brown. Front slightly but distinctly higher than wide; lower pair of post-antennal bristles very small, half as far apart as the upper pair which are nearly as large as the other frontal bristles and placed almost as far from one another as from the eye margin; bristles of lowest reclinate row with the inner one on a level with the upper post-antennal and one-third way toward the eye, the outer bristle very close to the eye and well above the inner one; upper row evenly spaced with the lateral one close to the eye, forming a slightly curved series across the upper third of the front; ocellar row of four bristles evenly spaced; ocellar triangle clearly elevated and delimited. Antennæ small, oval; arista as long as the eye. Palpi with four long and two short bristles. Proboscis very small. Post-ocular cilia strong, slightly enlarged below, cheek with a pair of strong bristles. Mesonotum highly shining, with one pair of dorsocentral bristles; scutellum with a single marginal pair. Abdomen dull, slightly pruinose; second segment elongated, with a couple of weak bristles at each side: fifth and sixth segments sparsely clothed with small black bristles. Hypopygium covered with minute bristles, but with no larger ones; apical lamella short. Ventral side of sixth segment bristly. Propleura along its posterior edge with a series of bristles, enlarged above and near the front coxa; mesopleura bare. Four anterior coxæ conspicuously bristly at tips; hind femora with a series of longer hairs below. Middle tibiæ with a line of seven or eight distinct but delicate setæ inside the posterior edge; hind tibia with a similar series of seven much larger ones, which are considerably longer than the width of the tibia, excepting the basal two which are much shorter. Costa barely less than four-ninths of the wing length, its bristles long (four times the width of the costal vein) and sparsely placed (five beyond the tip of the first vein); first section of costa slightly longer than the second and third together; third two-thirds the length of the second; second vein emerging from the third at a very acute angle; fourth vein faintly curved at base, straight beyond; fifth and sixth nearly straight; seventh weakly curved, well removed from the margin. Wing rather long and narrow. Halteres with black pedicel and light brown capitulum.

Type from Barberton, Cape Province, South Africa, May 22, 1913.

This species resembles the European *Aphiochæta fusco-halterata* Schmitz, but is at once distinguished by the large bristles on the hind tibiæ. It is similar to *A. decipiens* Wood (=*cilipes* Wood), but the bristling of the hypopygium will readily separate it from that species. It resembles *A. atrita* Brues from Java in color and many characters, but the ciliation of the hind tibia is very much stronger.

Puliciphora africana Brues (Fig. 1)

Ann. Mus. Nat. Hungarici, vol. 5, p. 410, fig. (1907)
Brues, Psyche, vol. 17, p. 36 (1910)

Numerous specimens of both sexes are referable to this species, described from females obtained at Kibosho, German

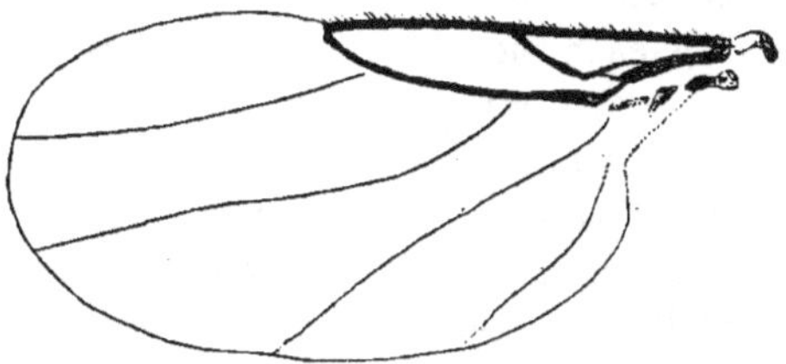

Fig. 1. *Puliciphora africana* ♂ wing.

East Africa. The several species of this quite cosmopolitan genus are extremely similar, and as they are attracted to and probably breed in old cheese, meat and other animal products, some have undoubtedly been widely spread by commerce particularly in the tropics.

To the original description of the female the following may be added from the well preserved specimens sent by Dr. Munro. There are four large divergent supra-antennal bristles, each longer than the diameter of the antenna; the lower pair are proclinate, the upper pair erect or slightly proclinate, set farther apart than the lower ones; above these are ten other bristles, one on each side of the front midway between the upper post-antennals and the eye, a median pair just below the ocelli, an ocellar row of six. The thorax bears six bristles, one at each anterior angle, one at each posterior angle and two very widely separated ones along the posterior margin. Pleura just below the posterior lateral bristle of the mesonotum with a very large bristle that projects laterally. In addition the head, thorax, abdominal plates and legs are rather densely clothed with fine black hairs.

Male. Considerably larger than the female, 1.7-1.8 mm. in length; wings large, approximately as long as the body. Head pale brownish, darker between the ocelli; thorax pale brown above, ochre yellow below; abdomen piceous above, whitish below, the hypopygium piceous, with brownish ventral lamella and pale dorsal one. Front with four supra-antennal bristles: the lower pair close together and clearly proclinate; the upper pair twice as far apart, strongly divergent and nearly porrect; above these there are 12 other bristles, a pair slightly above the post-antennals on each side of the front of which the lateral bristle is close to the eye and above the inner one, a pair just below the ocelli, and six forming a series of three pairs on the vertex above the ocelli. Post-ocular cilia much enlarged; cheek with a series of conspicuous forwardly directed bristles forming a line parallel with the lower eye-margin; palpus with about six moderate bristles; proboscis projecting, obtusely pointed, more slender than in the female. Third joint of antenna broadly ovate, as long as thick and less than half as long as the eye-height; arista apical, faintly pectinate, as long as the front coxa. Mesonotum with one pair of very widely separated dorsocentral bristles and four scutellar bristles of which the median (not lateral) pair is often much smaller. Abdomen clothed with minute, almost imperceptible bristly hairs, more distinct on the apical segment, and enlarged to form a very evident apical row along the posterior margin of the other segments; venter entirely membranous, without hairs or bristles. Central portion of hypopygium pyriform, with a slender, upturned stylet projecting from its tip; dorsal lamella attached at the middle of the middle lobe, with parallel sides, supplied with long sparse bristles; left side with a large plowshaped lamella; ventral middle-piece with a large upturned hook which is spinose inwardly near apex; right side above with a small triangular plate, the apex of which is drawn out into a small finger-shaped piece that bears two long bristles at its tip. Legs rather stout; anterior tibia without spur; others each with a single one; no very distinct tibial setulæ; hind metatarsus with six transverse bands of bristles. Wings with the costa extending distinctly beyond the middle, its bristles close-set, minute, scarcely longer than the diameter of the costal vein; first and second sections of costa equal; mediastinal vein distinct; fourth vein almost straight; fifth curved at base; sixth faintly bisinuate; seventh clearly indicated, close to the anal angle. Halteres very large, with pale stalk and dark-colored knob.

There are numerous specimens of both sexes bred from larvæ in a rotting stem of paw-paw (*Carica papaya*) at East London, Cape Province, February 2, 1922.

From the descriptions above it will be evident that the bristling of the front is different in the sexes, as the female has only one bristle lateral to and just above the post-antennal group of four. I have carefully examined a large number of the minute females and am certain that none of them show more than one bristle in this position.

ANOTHER "SNOW" PHORID (DIPTERA)

By Charles T. Brues.

Bussey Institution, Harvard University.

Since the preparation of the note in the last issue of Psyche (Notes on Some New England Phoridæ, vol. 31, p. 44, February 1924) I have received from Mr. C. W. Johnson specimens of another species of Phoridæ taken in midwinter in Maine.

These prove to be *Trupheoneura microcephala* Loew and strangely enough the five specimens which form the series are all males. They were collected together with some other "snow" insects at Woodland, near Caribou in Northern Maine by Mr. Olaf O. Nylander on December 1, 1917. Reference to the Monthly Weather Review for November and December of that year indicates that there was no warm spell at that time, nor at any time during either month. As the maximum temperature recorded for Maine during December was 47° (at Eastport on Dec. 9) it is evident that the flies were active at a considerably lower temperature in this more northerly inland section. Moreover, the presence of males strongly suggests that the species may even breed at this time of the year. Further south the same species (including the female) has been taken in the vicinity of Washington, D. C. on January 1, January 7 and March 29, according to Malloch (Proc. U. S. Nat. Mus., vol. 43, p. 422 (1912.)

FLOWER VISITS OF INSECTS II.[1]

BY CHARLES ROBERTSON.

Carlinville, Illinois.

HYMENOPTERA (ex. bees).

The lower Hymenoptera, 26 per cent of the visitors observed, make only 16.8 per cent of the visits. Of the 437 insect flowers observed, they occur on only 43 per cent, while the bees occur on 95.4 per cent. The only respect in which they resemble the bees and show more efficiency than the flies and Lepidoptera is in the thick proboscides composed of several appendages, so that on many flowers they are more apt to transfer pollen. The flowers showing the greatest numbers of these insects are *Cicuta maculata* 145, *Sium cicutæfolium* 95, and *Pastinaca sativa* 91, with exposed nectar, and *Pycnanthemum flexuosum* 89, and *Solidago canadensis* 81, with concealed nectar.

Of the visits of the lower Hymenoptera, 95.5 per cent are to social flowers, usually with epigynous nectaries. It is held here that these insects have produced no special flowers. They resort to highly specialized social flowers which have been modified by bees. They may have had some influence in further modifying these, especially in the case of fig flowers.

The ecology of lower Hymenoptera is associated with insects on which they are parasitic or with which they provision their nests. They are therefore most abundant in summer when all except Tenthredinidæ reach their maxima. They have no

[1]The first number was published in Psyche **30**: 158-69, 1923. In the table on page 158 the local flora should be 560, with percentages as follows: Ma 27.5, Mi 28.9, Mas 17.3, Mis 21.4, Pol 4.8, Red 29.4, White 39.8, Yellow 30.7. Of the 493 indigenous flowers the percentages are: Ma 25.9, Mi 29.6, Mas 17.0, Mis 22.7, Pol 4.6, Red 29.0, White 40.3, Yellow 30.6. On page 159, line 4, for "41.6" read "about 48". In line 32 "ruby-throated" came from an abortive attempt to shorten "ruby-throated humming-bird" to "ruby-throat." On page 167, line 24, for "seventy" read "seventy-three." Besides the tables mentioned there, each one of the 1288 visitors has its visits distributed under the classes and colors as shown in **3**, 173.

relation to flowers except to visit those which suit them and are in bloom when they fly. They make fewer non-pollinating visits than any other of the general groups.

Bembicidæ.—Of 99 visits of 10 species to 49 flowers, 39.3 per cent are to Mis, 32.3 to Mas, 28.2 to Pol, 52.5 to white, 34.5 to yellow, 37.3 to Compositæ, 20.2 to Labiatæ and 13.1 to Umbelliferæ. All visits are to social flowers.

Sphecidæ.—Of 377 visits of 16 species to 110 flowers, 43.2 per cent are to Mis, 27.8 to Mas, 27.3 to Pol, 53.3 to white, 33.4 to Compositæ, 14.8 to Labiatæ and 13.5 to Umbelliferæ. Pol. shows 15.4 per cent of the flowers visited.

Scoliidæ.—Of 133 visits of 7 species to 69 flowers, 45.8 per cent are to Mis, 29.3 to Pol, 20.3 to Mas, 61.6 to white, 31.5 to Compositæ, 15.7 to Labiatæ and 12.7 to Umbelliferæ. This and the two preceding are the only families of wasps showing more than 18.7 per cent of visits under Mas.

Eumenidæ.—Of 461 visits of 31 species to 109 flowers, 62.9 per cent are to Mis, 21.0 to Pol, 60.0 to white, 32.7 to yellow, 33.1 to Compositæ and 22.3 to Umbelliferæ.

Philanthidæ (including Cerceridæ).—Of 182 visits of 16 species to 63 flowers, 54.9 per cent are to Mis, 34.0 to Pol, 67.5 to white, 30.2 to Compositæ, 16.4 to Umbelliferæ and 12.6 to Labiatæ. Pol is 23.8 per cent of flowers visited.

Crabronidæ.—Of 253 visits of 27 species to 69 flowers, 49.4 per cent are to Mis, 44. 2 to Pol, 68.3 to white, 39.9 to Umbelliferæ and 26.8 to Compositæ. Pol shows 21.7 per cent of the flowers visited.

Vespidæ.—Of 182 visits of 8 species to 82 flowers, 56 per cent are to Mis, 26.3 to Pol, 59.3 to white, 39.5 to Compositæ and 13.7 to Umbelliferæ.

Chrysididæ.—Of 64 visits of 17 species to 35 flowers, 50 per cent are to Mis, 46.8 to Pol, 81.2 to white, 45.3 to Umbelliferæ and 25.0 to Compositæ. Of flowers visited, Mis shows 65.7 and Pol 31.4 per cent.

Larridæ.—Of 105 visits of 19 species to 42 flowers, 50.4 per cent are to Pol, 45.7 to Mis, 80.9 to white, 33.3 to Umbelliferæ, 20.0 to Compositæ and 16.2 to Labiatæ. Of the flowers visited, 57.1 per cent belong to Mis and 33.3 to Pol.

Tiphiidæ.—Of 19 visits of 4 species to 14 flowers, 52.6 per cent are to Pol, 42.1 to Mis, 64.4 to white, 31.5 to yellow, 78.9 to Umbelliferæ and 15.7 to Compositæ. Of flowers visited, 50 per cent belong to Mis, 42.8 to Pol and 42.8 to yellow.

Pompilidæ.—Of 188 visits of 33 species to 47 flowers, 58.5 per cent are to Pol, 36.7 to Mis, 70.7 to white, 39.3 to Umbelliferæ and 19.1 to Compositæ. Pol shows 36.1 per cent of the flowers and Mis 48.9

Nyssonidæ, Pemphredonidæ, Thynnidæ, Trypoxylonidæ, Bethylidæ, Myrmosidæ, Formicidæ male, Mutillidæ male.—Of 48 visits of 22 species to 20 flowers, 75 per cent are to Pol, 79.1 to white, 65.9 to Umbelliferæ and 10.6 to Compositæ. Pol shows 50 per cent of the flowers and Mis 40.0.

Wasps—Of 2111 visits of 210 species to 182 flowers, 49.5 per cent are to Mis, 34.4 to Pol, 63.5 to white, 30.0 to Compositæ, 24.8 to Umbelliferæ and 10.5 to Labiatæ. Of 825 visits of the Philanthidæ, Eumenidæ and Vespidæ, 59.6 per cent are to Mis. Of 677 visits of Crabronidæ and the last five groups, 51.8 per cent are to Pol. Of 574 visits before July, the wasps show 46.6 per cent to Mis, 39.3 to Pol, 54.7 to white and 37.6 to yellow, while of 1570 visits after June they show 50 per cent to Mis, 32.9 to Pol, 65.8 to white and 25.2 to yellow. The maximum shifts from A 35.1 to B' 36.7. Of the visits of Scoliidæ, Sphecidæ, Bembicidæ, Philanthidæ and Vespidæ, 13.9; of Eumenidæ, 22.3; and of Larridæ, Tiphiidæ, Pompilidæ, Crabronidæ, Nyssonidæ and Chrysididæ, 42.2 per cent are to Umbelliferæ. Of the visits of Scoliidæ, Sphecidæ, Bembicidæ, Philanthidæ and Larridæ, 15.2 per cent are to Labiatæ.

Ichneumonidæ.—Of 79 visits of 45 species to 35 flowers, 53.1 per cent are to Pol, 37.9 to Mis, 50.6 to yellow, 49.3 to white, 51.8 to Umbelliferæ and 30.3 to Compositæ. Of the flowers, 54.2 per cent are Mis, 28.5 Pol, 54.2 white and 45.7 yellow.

Braconidæ.—Of 58 visits of 33 species to 23 flowers, 51.7 per cent are to Pol, 32.7 to Mis, 58.8 to white, 41.3 to yellow, 53.3 to Umbelliferæ and 32.7 to Compositæ.

Chalcidoidea, Figitidæ, Evaniidæ.—Of 85 visits of 33 species to 25 flowers, 76.4 per cent are to Pol, 75.2 to white and 78.8 to Umbelliferæ.

Tenthredinidæ.—Of 27 visits of 14 species to 15 flowers, 59.2 per cent are to Mis, 33.3 to Pol, 70.3 to yellow, 40.7 to *Salix* and 11.1 to Umbelliferæ.

Non-aculeata.—Of 249 visits of 125 species to 62 flowers, 58.6 per cent are to Pol, 33.3 to Mis, 61.7 to white, 37.8 to yellow, 57.2 to Umbelliferæ and 20.8 to Compositæ. Before July 59.8 per cent of the visits are to yellow and 40.1 to white; after June 76.1 are to white and 23.0 to yellow. The maxima remain under A and Pol, but shift from yellow to white.

The preference is for flowers with exposed nectar and most of the visits are to them in spite of the dominance of other classes. So that *exposed nectar as a determining condition*, is limited to a few visits of the most insignificant of hymenopterous pollinators. Even then it fails except when the flowers are social. Many visitors should probably be left out, being so minute as to be of doubtful value, even if all other guests were excluded.

Lower Hymenoptera.—Of 2360 visits of 335 species to 188 flowers, 47.8 per cent are to Mis, 37.0 to Pol, 62.9 to white, 95.5 to social flowers, 29.0 to Compositæ and 28.2 to Umbelliferæ. Pol shows 11.1 per cent of the flowers visited. Of 28 non-pollinating visits 19 are to Mas and 22 to red. Visits to red are 7.5 per cent compared with 18.8 for the Alps. Ten prefer Mas, 112 Mis, 206 Pol, 240 white and 89 yellow. After June the maximum changes from A 40.6 to B' 36.7. Yellow changes from 41.5 to 25.0.

Diptera.

Midaidæ.—Two species prefer Pol and white.

Nemestrinidæ.—The single species prefers Mas and red.

Bombyliidæ.—Of 370 visits of 28 species to 160 flowers, 45.6 per cent are to Mas, 31.6 to Mis, 38.3 to yellow and 50.8 to Compositæ. Of the flowers visited, 35.0 belong to Mas and 28.1 to yellow. Visits to red are 23.7 compared with 75.0 in the Alps. After June the maxima change from IIb 27.7 to B' 66.0, Mis 31.9 to Mas 58.0, white 52.9 to yellow 43.5.

Conopidæ.—Of 238 visits of 15 species to 115 flowers, 47 per cent are to Mis, 25.6 to Mas, 20.1 to Pol, 56.3 to white, 10.9 to Labiatæ, 14.2 to Umbelliferæ and 32.3 to Compositæ. Red shows 13.8 compared with 44.4 in the Alps. After June the maximum shifts from AB 29.9 to B' 43.6. Mas changes from 14.7 to 35.9, yellow from 35.2 to 25.3 and red from 9.8 to 19.0.

Syrphidæ.—Of 1165 visits of 86 species to 203 flowers, 51.5 per cent are to Mis, 20.0 to Pol, 58.8 to white, 33.9 to yellow, 24.4 to Compositæ and 17.8 to Umbelliferæ. Red shows 7.2, in the Alps 29.3. After June the maximum changes from AB 37.8 to B' 47.5. Mi changes from 22.2 to 7.8, Mas from 2.1 to 22.9, yellow from 39.2 to 29.0.

The importance of these flies as pollinators has been greatly exaggerated. The general habit of pollen-eating is shown from the fact that the proboscis is never modified so as to prevent it. In 104 visits of Syrphidæ to diclinous flowers 31.7 per cent were to pistillate, and 68.2 to staminate, flowers. This shows pretty decisively their preference for pollen. They make more non-pollinating visits than are made by all other flies together. Of 145 visits of this kind 50.3 per cent are to Ma and 42.7 to red.

The flowers showing the greatest number of Syrphidæ are *Sassafras variifolium* 19, *Salix cordata* 22, *Solidago canadensis* 22, *Pastinaca sativa* 26, *Aster ericoides villosus* 30, *Heracleum lanatum* 32.

Empididæ.—Of 162 visits of 24 species to 87 flowers, 48.1 per cent are to Mis, 25.3 to Pol, 60.4 to white, 31.4 to yellow, 12.3 to Roasceæ, 15.4 to Compositæ and 16.0 to Umbelliferæ. Pol shows 12.6 per cent of the flowers visited. Red shows 8 per cent of the visits, in the Alps 30.1. After June the maximum changes from A 38.5 to B' 57.5. The siphonate proboscis was evidently developed as a predaceous organ, but is also used for sucking nectar. *Parempis clausa* is evidently exclusively anthophilous. It flies 113 days after all of the other species have disappeared. Being 4 per cent of the species, it makes 27 per cent of the visits.

Stratiomyidæ.—Of 53 visits of 13 species to 36 flowers, 45.2 per cent are to Mis, 43.3 to Pol, 60.3 to white, 35.8 to yellow and 41.5 to Umbelliferæ. Red shows 3.7, in the Alps 40.0.

Tachinidæ.—Of 842 visits of 108 species to 158 flowers, 53.4 per cent are to Mis, 29.8 to Pol, 66.5 to white, 25.2 to Umbelliferæ and 33.9 to Compositæ. After June the maximum shifts from A 37.5 to B' 46.3. White changes from 59.3 to 70.1 and yellow from 37.5 to 26.0.

Other Calyptratæ.—Of 692 visits of 50 species to 140 flowers, 48.2 per cent are to Mis, 29.6 to Pol and 64.5 to white.

Of total Calyptratæ visits, 23 per cent are to Umbelliferæ and 25.5 to Compositæ.

Acalyptratæ.—Of 178 visits of 53 species to 59 flowers, 47.1 per cent are to Pol, 43.8 to Mis, 55.0 to white, 43.8 to yellow, 58.4 to Umbelliferæ and 12.3 to Compositæ.

Muscoidea.—Of 1712 visits of 211 species to 191 flowers, 50.3 per cent are to Mis, 31.6 to Pol, 64.3 to white, 31.7 to yellow, 26.6 to Umbelliferæ and 28.3 to Compositæ. Pol is 12 per cent of flowers visited. Red shows 3.9 per cent of the visits, to 14.1 in the Alps. They are probably more important to flowers than the Syrphidæ, since they are usually after nectar. Of the total fly visits 45.3 per cent are made by Muscoidea and 30.8 by Syrphidæ.

Tabanidæ, Scenopinidæ, Pipunculidæ, Leptidæ, Phoridæ.—Of 18 visits of 9 species to 13 flowers, 77.7 per cent are to Pol. 72.2 to white and 72.2 to Umbelliferæ.

Nematocera.—Of 44 visits of 15 species to 24 flowers, 50 per cent are to Pol, 56.8 to white, 43.1 to yellow and 50.0 to Umbelliferæ. These flies are usually associated with more efficient pollinators and often are so small that they can get the nectar without much probability of touching the anthers and stigmas.

Diptera.—Of 3775 visits of 403 species to 266 flowers, 48 per cent are to Mis, 25.4 to Pol, 59.3 to white, 32.9 to yellow, 21.8 to Umbelliferæ and 28.2 to Compositæ. Mis shows 31.9 per cent of the flowers, Pol 8.6 and white 46.9. One prefers Ma, six prefer Mi, 21 Mas, 158 Pol, 192 Mis, 9 red, 133 yellow, 253 white. Visits to red are 7.7, Alps 22.2, Low Germany 24.2, Berlin Garden 33.1. After June the maximum changes from A 35.4 to B' 48.1. Yellow changes from 37.7 to 28.3. Of 256 non-pollinating visits, 32.8 are to Ma, 21.0 to Mas, 17.0 to Pol and 38.6 to red.

Next to bees, flies visit more species of flowers and make more visits than any other anthophilous insects. Being 31.2 per cent of the species, they make 27 per cent of the visits, 36.8 per cent of the total visits to Pol. The total number of flowers visited is less than that for Bombidæ or Halictidæ. The flowers visited by 62 or more flies are *Solidago canadensis* 62, *Zizia aurea* 63, *Sium cicutæfolium* 71, *Cicuta maculata* 82, *Pastinaca sativa* 113, *Heracleum lanatum* 121, *Aster ericoides villosus* 121. The flowers showing the greatest number of siphonate flies are *Solidago canadensis* 16, *Boltonia asteroides* 18, *Bidens aristosa* 21, *Pycnanthemum flexuosum* 22, *Eryngium yuccifolium* 23 and *Aster ericoides villosus* 31.

The importance of flies as pollinators is greatly exaggerated. They are apt to show as the exclusive visitors in unfavorable weather, or in localities where the flora and insect fauna have been greatly disturbed. The proboscis is usually rather thick so that the pollen readily touches and adheres to it, but the more highly specialized for probing flowers it becomes, the less likely it is to extract the pollen. In the lists have been admitted flies which should probably be excluded on account of their small size, or ability to extract nectar or eat pollen without effecting pollination.

Some flies have taken possession of some non-social flowers which have become adapted to flesh-flies or minute flies. The flowers which the Diptera prefer, however, are highly specialized social flowers, usually with epigynous nectaries, 86.3 per cent of the visits being to social flowers.

Lepidoptera.

Sphingidæ.—Of 22 visits of 7 species to 15 flowers, 54.5 per cent are to Ma, 40.9 to Mas, 63.6 to red, 45.4 to Polemoniales and 13.6 to Labiatæ. In the Alps visits to red are 63.2.

Other Heterocera.—Of 106 visits of 21 species to 68 flowers, 47.1 per cent are to Mis, 31.1 to Mas, 10.3 to Pol, 48.1 to white, 34.9 to yellow and 57.5 to Compositæ. Red shows 16.9, in the Alps 58.6.

Rhopalocera.—Of 1065 visits of 67 species to 203 flowers, 43.6 per cent are to Mas, 24.3 to Mis, 38.3 to red, 11.0 to Labiatæ and 36.3 to Compositæ. In the Alps red shows 55.2.

Lepidoptera.—Of 1193 visits of 95 species to 211 flowers, 42.4 per cent are to Mas, 25.9 to Mis, 39.3 to white, 36.8 to red. In the Alps red shows 56.1, Berlin Garden 64.0, Low Germany 70.2. One prefers Mi, 7 Ma, 12 Pol, 22 Mis, 51 Mas, 46 red, 33 white, 16 yellow. Of 175 non-pollinating visits, 52.5 per cent are to Ma, 34.2 to Mas and 57.1 to red. Before July they prefer Mas and red; after June, Mas, Mis, Pol, white and red. The maximum changes from Hb 32.6 to B' 50.1. Visits to non-social flowers change from 48.2 to 7.2.

The structure of the proboscis seems to indicate that the butterflies not only had little, or nothing, to do with the origin of insect flowers but that they did not come into existence until after the highly specialized bee flowers had been developed. The moths are important visitors of few flowers and have influenced the development of few, except in the case of the Sphingidæ. Butterflies are large and correspond little with the variable sizes of flowers. Their proboscides average long, so that they are usually able to reach the nectar of the deepest bee flowers. Their relations to flowers are often that of nectar thieves. The proboscis is exceedingly slender, smooth and dry so that it often does not touch the pollen, or does not readily hold it. On flowers with exserted anthers and stigmas the butterflies are probably the most useful. But even in such cases they often insert their tongues into flowers whose anthers and stigmas they do not touch with their bodies. It is a regular thing for them to visit personate and papilionaceous flowers without any likelihood of touching the anthers. In slender tubed flowers with included anthers they may touch the anthers, but even here there is doubt about much pollen sticking to their tongues. There are probably no slender-tubed butterfly flowers from which bees are excluded and in which bees are not likely to be more useful. A bee's proboscis has from five to seven appendages wet with nectar or honey, and which get so covered with pollen that in mounting it is often necessary to wash the pollen out.

In the percentage of visits, 8.5, over species, 7.3, the Lepidoptera show a slight gain, but in 41 flowers whose visitors were taken as they came they lost in percentage of individuals.

Other Visitors.

Coleoptera.—Of 438 visits of 137 species to 113 flowers, 42.4 per cent are to Mis, 40.8 to Pol, 64.8 to white, 15.2 to Compositæ and 39.4 to Umbelliferæ. One prefers Mas, 48 Mis, 81 Pol, 46 yellow and 88 white. Visits to red are 5.2, in the Berlin Garden 16.9, Low Germany 18.3, Alps 23.2. Of 123 non-pollinating visits, 34.9 per cent are to Mis, 30.0 to Mas and 40.6 to yellow. After June the maximum changes from A 50.9 to B' 46.2.

The flowers showing the greatest number of beetles are *Pastinaca sativa* 42, *Aruncus sylvester* 33, *Cryptotænia canadensis* 19, *Sium cicutæfolium* 19.

Beetles seem to have developed anthophilous habits as a secondary matter, and were probably few on primitive flowers. Some have structures fitting them for obtaining nectar, as

Chauliognathus pennsylvanicus, which has maxillary lobes extensile by 4 or 5 mm, and makes more visits than any other beetle.

Beetles probably have produced no special flowers. They principally resort to social flowers with epigynous nectaries.

Hemiptera.—Of 113 visits of 21 species to 64 flowers, 47.7 per cent are to Mis, 30.9 to Pol, 52.2 to white, 38.0 to yellow, 34.5 to Compositæ and 30.9 to Umbelliferæ. Ten prefer Mis, eight Pol, 11 white and ten yellow. After June yellow changes from 47.1 to 29.0. The maximum shifts from B 39.6 to B' 50.0. The proboscis, though not developed for flower visits, is sometimes used to extract nectar.

The Hemiptera and Coleoptera form 12.2 per cent of the visitors observed, but make only 3.9 per cent of the visits.

Neuroptera.—*Chrysopa plorabunda,* found on some Umbelliferæ with exposed nectar, is not included in the tables.

Birds.—Of 29 visits made by the rubythroat, 82.7 per cent are to Ma, 55.1 to red, 17.2 to Personales, 13.7 to Labiatæ, 13.7 to Leguminosæ, 10.3 to Polemoniales. It picks out the most highly modified and brightest colored of the long-tongued bee flowers. The bird flowers belong to melittophilous groups and have been appropriated by the humming-birds.

Total Visitors.—Of 13971 visits made by 1288 visitors to 437 flowers, 39.8 per cent are to Mis, 20.4 to Mas, 18.7 to Pol, 51.3 to white, 31.7 to yellow, 28.9 to Compositæ and 15.9 to Umbelliferæ. Thirty-six prefer Mi, 44 Ma, 176 Mas, 471 Pol, 511 Mis, 126 red, 390 yellow and 755 white. After June visits to Mas change from 8.3 to 32.7, to yellow from 34.2 to 29.9, and the maximum changes from AB 26.8 to B' 44.6. Visits to red are 16.8 per cent, in the Alps 41.6.

Insects and Their Importance to Flowers.

Loew's Groups.—If the flower classes A, AB and Po are designated as allotropic, B and B' as hemitropic, and Hb, F and O as eutropic, and the insects are classed according to the kinds of flowers which they visit, it will be found that those which before July are eutropic, hemitropic or allotropic, are hemitropic after June. Really the highest specialized and latest developed flowers and insects are hemitropic.

Specialization for obtaining Nectar.—The rubythroat, the Lepidoptera, long-tongued bees and some siphonate flies can visit a great many flowers from which short-tongued bees are excluded. They are at some disadvantage on flowers with shallow nectar.

Müller (**3**,58) states that *Apis* and *Bombus* play by far the most important part in the fertilization of German indigenous flowers. Knuth (**2**,154) says: "Just as the pollen-collecting apparatus has reached its highest degree of development in *Apis* and *Bombus,* so also has the mouth of the bees become best adapted for rifling the nectar of flowers. It is therefore intelligible that bees belonging to these two genera play a far more important part than any other insects in the pollination of our indigenous flowers." When these bees are compared with other bees having a similar flight, the importance of the specialization of the proboscis and scopa is not so obvious. When 40 species of Halictidæ make nearly as many visits as 133 species of long-tongued bees, it is not on account of a more highly specialized tongue or scopa. The Halictidœ visit 14 more flowers and make 1123 more visits than the Bombinæ, 927 more than Bombinæ and *Apis* together. When *Apis* and *Bombus* make only 13.3 per cent of the visits recorded in Müller's *Fertilisation of flowers,* it is not easy to understand these statements regarding their importance in pollination.

Dependence on a Floral Diet.—The food of bees is almost exclusively from flowers. The fig chalcids and *Pronuba* are about the only insects which can compare with them. The importance to flowers of the nest-provisioning habit is shown by the fact that the nest-making bees average 23.4 visits, while the inquilines average 10.7. The females of the nest-makers average 20.6 visits, while the males average 10.3. The females of the inquilines average 8.8 and the males 8.0.

Number of Species.—On account of having more species, and in spite of a lower average number of visits, the flies and lower Hymenoptera surpass the Lepidoptera; the Halictidæ and Megachilidæ surpass the Bombidæ; the Andrenidæ surpass the Euceridæ; the Muscoidea surpass the Syrphidæ; the Syrphidæ and Bombyliidæ surpass the Conopidæ; the Eumenidæ surpass the Sphecidæ, Vespidæ and Scoliidæ; the Crabronidæ and Pompilidæ surpass the Vespidæ, Philanthidæ, Scoliidæ and Bembicidæ.

Average Number of Visits.—In spite of the fewer species, the bees surpass the flies in average number of visits. The Bombinæ surpass the Euceridæ, Megachilini, Nomadidæ, Osmiini or Epeolidæ which have more species. The Halictidæ make 1366 more visits than the Andrenidæ, although they have only five more species.

Length of Flight.—The high average for *Apis mellifera*, Bombinæ, Ceratinidæ, Halictidæ and Vespidæ is associated with the long flight, the most important condition determining the visits of bees. Bees flying all season are 23.3 per cent of the species and make 51.2 per cent of the bee visits.

Abundance.—Mere commonness is an important condition in determining the visits to flowers. Insects visiting 11 or more flowers are 27.1 per cent of the species and make 77.6 per cent of the visits. The bees, rubythroat and Lepidoptera are the only visitors which gain in percentage of visits over species. Bees gain in percentage of individuals over visits and all other insects lose.

The following insect groups make more than 139.7 visits, one per cent of the total:

Bees 6063 long-tongued 3061 short-tongued 3002.—Halictidæ 1951, Megachilidæ 786, Bombidæ 764, Andrenidæ 585, Euceridæ 521, Nomadidæ 272, Epeolidæ 198, Ceratinidæ 194, Prosopididæ 166, Panurgidæ 141, Colletidæ 140.

Flies 3775.—Muscoidea 1712, Syrphidæ 1165, Bombyliidæ 370, Conopidæ 238, Empididæ 162.

Lower Hymenoptera 2360, aculeate 2111, non-aculeate 249.—Eumenidæ 461, Sphecidæ 377, Crabronidæ 253, Pompilidæ 188, Vespidæ 182, Philanthidæ 182.

Lepidoptera 1195.—Rhopalocera 1065, Papilionidæ 324, Nymphalidæ 312, Hesperidæ 305.

Coleoptera 438.

Phenology of Anthophilous Insects.

Bees.

With a few exceptions bees are the only flower-visiting insects which are phenologically associated with flowers. Their presence implies the necessary presence of flowers. The composition of the bee fauna for the season or for particular parts of the season is determined by the presence of certain kinds of flowers.

Dasygastræ.

The bees forming the superfamily Trypetoidea differ decidedly from the long-tongued bees in general in forming an earlier maximum. They fly from March 21 to October 22 and have a maximum of 64.5 per cent July 4, 85.4 per cent flying in June. The Stelididæ, May 9—October 18, have a maximum of 83.3 per cent on June 14. The Megachilidæ, March 21—October 22, have a maximum of 69 per cent July 4, 85.7 per cent flying in June. The Osmiinæ, March 21—October 18, have a maximum of 75 per cent June 16, 90 per cent flying in June. The Megachilinæ, May 11—October 22, have a maximum of 95.4 per cent July 4.

Scopulipedes.

Apygidialia.—The Colletoidea, March 20—October 30, with a maximum of 54.1 per cent May 29-31, show 62.5 per cent flying in June. The Prosopididæ, April 20—October 11, show a maximum of 88.8 per cent May 15—June 9. The Colletidæ, March 20—October 30, show a maximum of 46.6 per cent June 21, 53.3 per cent flying in July and August.

The Ceratinoidea are represented by two Ceratinidæ, March—November ,and one of the Xylocopidæ, May 5—July 5.

The Apoidea, represented by Bombidæ and Apidæ, fly from March to November, with all, except one rare species, flying simultaneously June 22-28. The Bombidæ fly from March 15 to November 4. The females appear in March and April, the workers May—July, and the males in July and August. As far as pollination is concerned the maximum of the group is in August.

Pygidialia.—The Dasygastræ and Apygidialia form old and fragmentary groups characterized by distinct structural marks and by discontinuous geographical distribution. Together they make only 28.8 per cent of the indigenous bees. On the other hand the Pygidialia are 71.1 per cent of the species. They are more recent, more plastic, less distinctly separated into groups and of a more continuous geographical distribution.

The Halictoidea, March 17 to November, have a maximum of 91.3 per cent June 14-15, 93.1 per cent flying in June. The Halictidæ, March 17 to November, have a maximum of 94.6 per cent on June 14-15. Nineteen species have been observed in March and 21 in November. Some are so rare that their flight has not been made out, but it is likely that all are flying simultaneously from June until October. The Dufoureidæ are represented by *Halictoides marginatus*, August 27—October 3. The Nomiidæ are represented by *Paranomia nortonii*, June 26—September 9.

The Andrenoidea fly from March 17 to October 30, and have a maximum of 45.5 per cent May 11-13, 57.3 per cent flying in May. The percentage declines to 19.1 in July and rises again to 32.3 in August and September. The Andrenidæ, March 17—October 30, have a maximum of 60.7 per cent May 11-13, 70.5 per cent flying in May. Only one species is flying July 30—August 12, while six are flying simultaneously September 8-20.

All of the late ones are oligoleges of Compositæ and 44.4 per cent of the early ones are oligoleges of various flowers. *Andrena* and *Pterandrena,* a genus of Compositæ oligoleges, are both separated into early and late groups. The Panurgidæ have the most definite position of any of the dominant families of bees, May 28—October 29, all of them together August 30—September 3, 87.5 per cent being oligoleges. Of the oligoleges 78.5 per cent affect Compositæ. The Macropididæ are represented by *Macropis steironematis,* June 12—July 18.

The Anthophoroidea fly from April 8 to October 22, with a maximum of 58.9 per cent August 8-26, 66.6 per cent flying in July. The Euceridæ, April 8—October 22, have a maximum of 62.5 per cent August 8-28, 68.7 per cent flying in August. *Tetralonia* has a May maximum. All of the other Euceridæ complete their flight between June 13 and October 22, 76.9 per cent being simultaneous in August. Here the polyleges, oligoleges of Compositæ and other oligoleges have a very definite and similar position. The Anthophoridæ fly from April 8 to September 20. The Emphoridæ fly from June 24 to October 7.

Short-tongued Bees.—These fly from March 17 to November, and have a maximum of 58.6 May 18-31, 72.7 per cent flying in May.

Long-tongued Bees.—These fly from March 15 to November, and have a maximum of 48.6 per cent, July 13, 66.1 per cent flying in August.

Bees, Total.—These fly from March 15 to November and have a maximum of 47.2 per cent July 13.

Oligoleges.—That the oligolectic bees are associated in their time of flight with the blooming seasons of the flowers on which they depend is as evident as that the inquiline bees are phenologically associated with their hosts, or that other insects are associated with the time of the insects on which they are parasitic, or with the presence of the food on which their larvæ feed. This is more evident than the converse proposition that the blooming times are correlated with the flight of the oligoleges, for usually the flowers have other visitors which can effectually pollinate them. Sometimes the oligolege is of no particular use to the flower, so that the relation is quite one-sided. Usually the blooming season of a plant may be explained by the simple statement that it agrees with its relatives, all of which bloom about the same time.

The same statement, however, is true of the oligoleges. They resemble their relatives in time even more than the plants on which they depend. Evidently the groups to which the oligoleges belong were originally quite definitely located phenologically so that their members were in close competition, to avoid which there arose a diversification of food habits, some of the species becoming oligolectic and the others remaining polylectic. In some groups, however, the phenologically correlated relatives were oligoleges of related plants, like *Melissodes* and Compositæ. Here the diversification in food habits resulted in some of the species becoming polylectic. The food habits have evidently tended to restrict the oligoleges to the time of their food plants and to give the polyleges more latitude in the extension of the time. Consequently the flight of the oligoleges averages shorter than that of their related polyleges.

Inquilines.—The inquiline bees are phenologically associated with their hosts and have no direct relation to flowers. They visit the flowers most convenient to them. The Nomadidæ, inquilines of Andrenidæ, show evidences of having shortened their proboscides to suit the kinds of flowers which were most common where they were flying. Although they are long-tongued bees, their flower visits resemble those of their short-tongued hosts almost exactly.

Coelioxys consists of inquilines of Megachilini and the seasons are similar. *Psithyrus*, an inquiline of *Bombus*, has a similar flight.

The Sphecodinæ are evidently inquilines of other Halictidæ. With the exception of *Proteraner*, they resemble the other Halictidæ in the fact that the females appear first and the males later and that they fly all season. The same applies to *Paralictus* which evidently consists of inquilines of *Chloralictus*.

Among the Nomadidæ, some species of *Holonomada* may be inquilines of *Tetralonia* and *Melissodes*. In the Pasitidæ, *Holcopasites* is probably an inquiline of Panurgidæ. Of the Melectidæ *Bombomelecta thoracica* is evidently an inquiline of *Anthophora ursina* and *Melecta interrupta* of *Amegilla walshii*.

In the flight of the inquilines there is a marked correlation which often seems to determine the time. Thus *Alcidamea simplex* flies 85 days while its inquiline, *Microstelis lateralis*, flies 43 days. *Neotrypetes productus* flies 144 days while its inquiline, *Stelidium trypetinum*, flies 135 days.

But the phenological position is usually quite inveterate and hereditary, for the inquilines are usually related to their hosts. Ten species of *Triepeolus* are evidently mainly inquilines of Euceridæ. They fly from June 27 to October 21 while the Euceridæ fly from April 8 to October 22. Consequently *Triepeolus* only infests the late Euceridæ. So phenologically the species resemble their relatives more than they do the Euceridæ. One infests *Melitoma taurea*, one of the Emphoridæ. So it seems the genus is more apt to infest an unrelated host flying at the same time than it is to change time to follow the Euceridæ. Some of the early Euceridæ may be infested by *Holonomada*. *Colletes* flies from March 20 to October 30. Their inquilines, *Epeolus*, fly from May 29 to October 23. So there is at least one *Colletes* not infested by *Epeolus*, *C. inæqualis*, possibly infested by some *Nomada*. So that phenologically the Epeolidæ resemble one another more than they do the groups on which they are inquiline.

As in the case of oligoleges, the conclusion is reached that the phenological position is the oldest, most inveterate, and the inquiline habit later and determined by, rather than determining, the phenological position.

Other Visitors.

Lepidoptera.—The presence and time of flight of the Lepidoptera is determined by the occurence of their food plants. Usually they fly a long time and have more than one brood.

Naturally they occur throughout the flower-blooming season and are most abundant in summer when the most of plants are in vegetation. The butterflies form a long low curve, March 10—November 7, and have a maximum of 80.5 per cent July 7-22, 87 per cent flying in July. *Pronuba* is perhaps the only lepidopter whose season is correlated with, and indicates the presence of, particular kinds of flowers. Butterflies often have food plants which are not entomophilous. Given their food plants and long-tongued bee flowers, they could get along pretty well.

Diptera.—The Diptera fly from March 9 to November 6 and show a maximum of 59.2 per cent July 22-27, 67 per cent flying in June. The Nematocera, April 6—October 18, have a maximum of 50 per cent May 25—June 2, 90 per cent flying in May. The Stratiomyidæ, April 21—August 26, have a maximum of 70 per cent May 18-22, 80 per cent flying in May. The Empididæ, April 10—October 8, have a maximum of 72.2 per cent April 30—May 4, 88.8 per cent flying in May. The Syrphidæ, March 10—November 6, have a maximum of 67.5 per cent June 10-11, 80 per cent flying in May. The maximum of the lower Syrphidæ is May 12-15, while that of the higher is June 10-11. The Muscoidea, March 9—November 6, show a maximum of 69.2 per cent July 26-27. They are 51.6 per cent of the Diptera observed on flowers. The Bombyliidæ, March 21—October 29, have a maximum of 60.7 per cent August 21, 67.8 per cent flying in August. The Conopidæ, April 10—November 3, have a maximum of 76.9 per cent July 4—August 8, 84.6 per cent flying in August.

The flight of Diptera is evidently associated with that of the insects on which they are parasitic, or the presence of the plants, or other food, on which the larvæ feed. None have a primary relation to flowers. Their adaptations to flowers are only to such flowers as happened to be present during their flight. Not more than 18 per cent have siphonate proboscides.

Hymenoptera (ex. bees).—The lower Aculeata fly from March to November and have a maximum of 86.8 per cent July 25-27, 91.7 per cent flying in July and 90.6 per cent in

August. The total lower Hymenoptera have a maximum of 74.5 per cent July 22-27, 80 per cent flying in July and August. They are phenologically associated with their food plants or with the insects upon which they are parasitic or with which they provision their nests. Only the fig chalcids have an important relation to any flower.

Coleoptera.—The Coleoptera, March 21—November 6 have a maximum of 52.6 per cent June 9, 53.1 per cent flying in June.

Hemiptera.—The Hemiptera, April 7—October 23, have a maximum of 68.4 per cent June 28—July 8, 78.9 per cent flying in June.

Literature cited.

1. Knuth, P. Handbook of flower pollination. **1**: 1-382. (1906) Transl. of Handbuch der Blütenbiologie. 1898.
2. Müller, H. The fertilisation of flowers. (1883). Transl. of Befructung der Blumen. 1873.
3. Robertson, C. Synopsis of Panurgidæ. Psyche **29**; 159-73. 1922.

ON THE GENUS HALOBATES FROM JAPANESE AND FORMOSAN COASTS (HEMIPTERA: GERRIDÆ).

By Teiso Esaki.

Entomological Laboratory, Department of Agriculture, Kiushiu Imperial University, Fukuoka, Japan.

Of that well known pelagic genus of Hemiptera, *Halobates*, only two species have hitherto been recorded from the seas adjacent to Japanese islands. Recently, four more species, all apparently new, have come under my observation, thus giving in all six species to the Halobates-fauna of the same region.

Before describing these new species, it may be pointed out that the hind tarsus of this genus is two-jointed, instead of being one-jointed. The alleged one-jointedness of the hind tarsus has been considered as an important generic character of *Halobates* by many entomologists, except Dahl, who states that "Die Tarsen sind ebenfalls zweigliedrig" (Plank. Exped., Humboldt-Stiftung, Bd. 2, p. 2, 1893). The hind tarsi of all the species studied by me are two-jointed, as in all the other genera of the Family Gerridæ. This point is often difficult to make out, because of the fact that the joints are extremely slender and pubescent. In newly moulted specimens, however, the two-jointedness is readily recognizable.

Halobates apicalis sp. nov. (Fig. A).

Body ashy gray. Head pale yellowish brown, with a prominent longitudinal fascia on the vertex; frons with a black spot which is sometimes confluent with the fascia on the vertex. Eye moderately projected laterally, dark brown. Antenna with two basal joints pale yellowish brown and two apical joints black; first joint longer and thicker than others, with two blackish brown lines beneath; second joint about two-thirds as long as the first; fourth joint slightly shorter than the second, tapering toward the apex; jointlet between second and third joints pale yellowish brown, same between third and fourth joints black and much shorter than the former. Rostrum passing the anterior coxa, pale yellowish brown; apex of labrum of the same color; the line on the under surface of third and fourth joints entirely black. Pronotum pale yellowish brown with two large spots reaching the anterior margin, which is sinuate; posterior margin moderately so. Meso-and metanotum black with pale yellowish brown lateral sides; the central portion somewhat paler in the male; sternum pale yellowish brown, thickly pubescent. Anterior leg pale yellow; coxa and trochanter very short, the latter with an acute, apical bifurcate spine; femur thick especially so in the male, angularly projected interiorly at the base, inner surface black with minute and delicate dentation; tibia a little shorter than femur, with a distinct spine at the apex, blackish at the tip and on the inner surface; first tarsal joint very short, somewhat spherical in shape; second joint very long, about five times as long as the first, with the apical two-thirds black; claws brown, arising near the base of the second joint. Intermediate leg pale yellowish brown, with the inner margin of trochanter, outer margin and apex of femur, tibia and tarsus dark brown; tibia a little shorter and much thinner than femur, with a fringe of long hairs interiorly, except the basal one-fourth of the length; tarsus two-jointed, first joint a little longer than twice the length of the second, but not furnished with the fringe of hairs which is found in all other species of the genus, second joint with small claws near the apex. Posterior leg much shorter than the intermediate one, pale yellowish brown, with the apex of femur, of tibia and of tarsus dark brown; first tarsal joint about half the length of the second, which is furnished with small claws near the base. Abdomen black above, pale yellowish brown or pale grayish yellow below; sixth segment black with pale yellowish brown anterior margin, about as long as three preceding segments taken together. First male genital segment pale yellowish brown with somewhat greenish horn-like lateral processes beneath; second segment black above with brown posterior margin, pale yellowish brown below.

Female genital segments pale yellowish brown, posterior margin of the penultimate segment and the whole of the last segment black above.

Length of body: ♂3 mm., ♀ 3.5 mm.

Holotype, ♂, allotopotype, ♀, and many paratopotypes; Ampin near Tainan, South Formosa, Sept. 9, 1921, (Teiso Esaki).

This species is one of the smallest in the genus and is most readily distinguished from other species by the characteristic markings of the head, and by the absence of the fringe of long hairs on the first intermediate tarsal joint. It is somewhat allied to the species of the Genus *Metrocoris* in respect to the structure of anterior femur and tarsus, but the presence of the fringe of long hairs on the intermediate tibia, coloration and general aspect, as well as the marine habitat, make the species more rationally referable to *Halobates* than to *Metrocoris*.

This species is found on a small stream of salt water connecting a pond to the sea, and a large number of specimens swarm in a shaded surface of the stream.

Halobates shiranui sp. nov. (Fig. C).

Body ashy gray, short and broad. Head black with brown pubescence on lateral sides, vertex without markings; eye brown. Antenna black, first joint about as long as the third and fourth joints put together, third and fourth joints nearly equal in length. Rostrum black, reaching the anterior coxa. Pronotum black, anterior margin moderately sinuate, posterior margin very slightly so, distinct transverse impression at the middle of pronotum. Meso- and metanotum together almost as long as broad, swollen and black. Anterior leg black with brown coxa and trochanter; tibia nearly as long as femur; first tarsal joint joint very short, almost as long as thick, about one-fifth the length of the second joint; claws arising at the middle of the second joint. Intermediate and posterior legs black, femora tapering toward the apex; intermediate tibia a little shorter than femur; first tarsal joint about twice the length of the second;

posterior tibia nearly half as long as femur, tarsus about one-fourth as long as tibia. Abdomen black above, pale brown beneath.

Length of body: 4 mm.

Holotype, ♀, Masaru, near Saseho, Province of Hizen, Japan, on the coast of East China Sea, June 11, 1922 (Mr. Yanagiwara). Type in my collection.

The nearest ally of this species is *Halobates apicalis* n. sp., which is much smaller. These two species are separated from the rest of the genus in having very short first tarsal joint.

Halobates japonicus sp. nov. (Fig. B).

Body black, slightly suffused with ashy gray. Head black with two oblique brown spots near the posterior margin; eye moderately projected, brownish. Antenna black with the apex of the last joint brownish, not longer than the body, first joint subequal in length to the other three joints put together, second and fourth joints nearly equal, third joint much shorter than others. Rostrum black scarcely passing the anterior coxa. Pronotum black, moderately sinuate along anterior and posterior margins, somewhat elevated at the center. Meso- and metanotum black, moderately convex. Prosternum pale brown. Anterior leg black, coxa blackish brown, with pale brown apex; trochanter blackish brown, paler toward apex and base, with a small black spine at the apex; femur very thick in the male; tibia black with the inner surface more or less brownish, shorter than femur, the apical spine angular but not sharply pointed; tarsus black with the first joint shorter than the second, which is furnished with claws near the base. Intermediate and posterior legs black, femora gradually tapering toward the apex; tibiæ much shorter and thinner than femora. Intermediate tibia about two-thirds the length of femur, furnished with a fringe of long hairs along the apical two-thirds; first intermediate tarsal joint almost three times as long as the second, with a similar fringe of hairs. First posterior tarsal joint about three-fifth as long as the second, the latter with claws at the middle. Abdomen black, more or less suffused with brown. The first male genital segment black above with the lateral and posterior portions yellowish brown, dark brown beneath; the horn-like processes slender and very dark in color; second segment yellowish brown beneath.

Length of body: ♂ 5 mm., ♀ 5 mm.

Holotype, ♂, allotopotype, ♂, and paratopotypes: Aburatsubo creek near Misaki, Province of Sagami, Japan, July, 1921 (Teiso Esaki). Paratypes: the coast of the Province of Kii (Mr. Takeuchi), the coast of the Province of Tosa (Mr. Takenouchi). Types in my collection.

This species is found rapidly striding on calm water close to the shore near the head of Aburatsubo creek. A few probable examples of this species were observed by me on the Kagoshima Bay, the southernmost portion of Japan proper.

Although resembling *Halobates germanus* White, this species differs from it in its blackish coloration, much larger size, and in the structure of antenna.

Halobates germanus White.

Halobates germanus White, Chall. Rep., Zool., vol. 7, pt. 9, p. 50, pl. 1, fig. 6, 1883. Dahl, Plank, Exp., vol. 2, p. 7, 1893.

Distant, Fauna Brit. Ind., Rhyn., vol. 5, p. 152, 1910.

This species has hitherto been recorded from the following localities: "Celebes Sea," "between the Admiralty Islands and Japan," "Mare della China" (After White), "Andeman Sea" (After Distant). I have not yet found this species near either Japan or Formosa, but have in my collection four specimens of it from Papan, Johore, Malay Peninsula (Mr. Fukushima).

Halobates sericeus Eschscoltz.

Halobates sericeus Eschscholtz, Emtomogr., vol. i, p. 108, 1822. Burmeister, Handb. Entom., vol. 2, p. 209, 1835. Amyot et Serville, Hem., p. 412, 1843. White, Chall. Rep. Zool.,vol. 7, pt. 19, p. 47, 1883. Dahl, Plank. Exp., vol. 2, p. 7, 1893.

Oshanin, Verz. Palæ. Hem., vol. I, p. 500, 1908. Van Duzee, Cat. Amer. Hem., p. 432, 1917. Hungerford, Bull. Univ. Kansas, vol. 21, p. 116, 1919.

This species is widely distributed over the Pacific and Atlantic Oceans, and I have examined two specimens from Hawaii, kindly presented to me by Dr. S. Isshiki. Habita: "Many stations on the voyage from the Admiralty Islands to Japan, and from Japan to Honolulu" (White). Oshanin states that "In parte occidentali intertropicali oceani Pacifici, sub. 38 lat. bor. in vicinitate Japoniæ quoque investa species."

Halobates matsumurai sp. nov. (Fig. D).

Halobates sericeus Matsumura (nec Eschscholtz), Thaus. ins. Japan, Addit., vol. I, p. 27, pl. II, fig. 8, 1913.

Body ashy gray, very sericeus. Head with two brown oblique spots at the posterior margin; eye moderately projected, black. Antenna black with the apical half of the fourth joint brownish, not longer than the body, first joint nearly as long as the remaining three joints put together, second and fourth joints nearly equal in length, third joint shortest. Rostrum shiny black, reaching anterior coxa. Pronotum with moderately sinuate anterior and posterior margins. Anterior leg black; coxa, trochanter, and, in the female, the base of femur pale yellowish brown; femur very incrassate in the male; the apical projection of tibia somewhat acute; first tarsal joint much longer than the second, which is about two-thirds the length of the first and with claws near the base. Intermediate tibia about two-thirds the length of and much thinner than femur; first tarsal joint about four times as long as the second. Posterior tibia about half the length of femur; tarsus one-third of tibia, with the first joint shorter than the second. Body pale yellowish brown beneath. The first male genital segment black above with lateral and posterior portions brown; pale brown or gray beneath; the horn-like processes very slender and black; second segment pale brown beneath.

Length of body: ♂ 5 mm., ♀ 5.5 mm.

Holotype, ♂, allotopotype, ♀, and paratopotypes: the coast of Tansui, near Taihoku, Northern Formosa, Sept. 27, 1921 (Teiso Esaki). Paratypes: Takasago, Province of Harima, coast of the Inland Sea of Japan (Prof. S. Matsumura); Shimabara, Province of Hizen, coast of East China Sea (Mr. Yamasaki). Types in my collection.

This species is somewhat allied to *Halobates germanus* White but is much larger in size, more elongated, especially in the female, and has the first anterior tarsal joint much longer than the second.

Explanation of Plate V.

A1, *Halobates apicalis* n. sp. A2, antenna. A3, Anterior tarsus A4, Male genital segments, dorsal view.

B1, *Halobates japonicus* n. sp. B2, anterior tarsus. B3, antenna. B4, Male genital segments, dorsal view.

C1, *Halobates shiranui* n. sp. C2, anterior tarsus.

D1, *Halobates matsumurai* n. sp. D2, anterior tarsus. D3, antenna. D4, male genital segments, dorsal view.

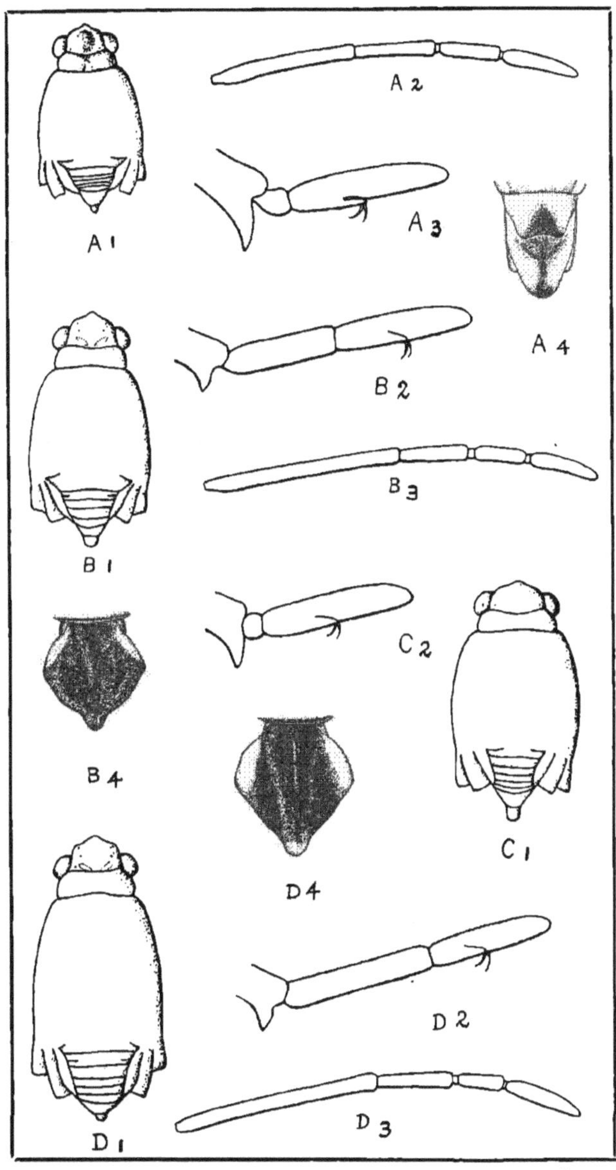

ESAKI—Halobates

PSYCHE

A JOURNAL OF ENTOMOLOGY

ESTABLISHED IN 1874

VOL. XXXI JUNE-AUGUST 1924 Nos. 3-4

CONTENTS

CAMBRIDGE ENTOMOLOGICAL CLUB

PSYCHE is published bi-monthly, the issues appearing in February, April, June, August, October and December. Subscription price, per year, payable in advance: $2.00 to subscribers in the United States, Canada or Mexico; foreign postage, 15 cents extra. Single copies, 40 cents.

Cheques and remittances should be addressed to Treasurer, Cambridge Entomological Club, Bussey Institution, Forest Hills, Boston 30, Mass.

Orders for back volumes, missing numbers, notices of change of address, etc., should be sent to Cambridge Entomological Club, Bussey Institution, Forest Hills, Boston, 30, Mass.

IMPORTANT NOTICE TO CONTRIBUTORS.

Manuscripts intended for publication, books intended for review, and other editorial matter, should be addressed to Professor C. T. Brues, Bussey Institution, Forest Hills, Boston, 30 Mass.

Authors contributing articles over 8 printed pages in length will be required to bear a part of the extra expense, for additional pages. This expense will be that of typesetting only, which is about $2.00 per page. The actual cost of preparing cuts for all illustrations must be borne by contributors; the expense for full page plates from line drawings is approximately $5.00 each, and for full page half-tones, $7.50 each: smaller sizes in proportion.

AUTHOR'S SEPARATES.

Reprints of articles may be secured by authors, if they are ordered before, or at the time proofs are received for corrections. The cost of these will be furnished by the Editor on application.

Entered as second-class mail matter at the Post Office at Boston, Mass. Acceptance for mailing at special rate of postage provided in Section 1103, Act of October 3, 1917, authorized on June 29, 1918.

PSYCHE

VOL. XXXI. JUNE-AUGUST 1924 Nos. 3-4

NORTH AMERICAN SPECIES OF THE SUBGENERA OPACIFRONS DUDA AND PTEREMIS RONDANI OF THE GENUS LEPTOCERA OLIVIER[1] (DIPTERA, BORBORIDÆ)

By Anthony Spuler.

Pullman, Washington.

Introduction.

The subgenus *Opacifrons* Duda is comparatively small and contains but a few North American species. In none of the species are the individuals abundant. Some of the species are represented by a single or a few specimens.

The subgenus *Pteremis* Rondani is represented by but three North American species. The characters in this subgenus are so striking that there is a question whether *Pteremis* should be classed as a subgenus as Dr. O. Duda has done, or whether it should be classed as a genus as was done by Rondani.

This paper is one of a series of papers on the North American species of the Family Borboridæ.

Opacifrons Duda.

Duda: Abahnd. Zool-botan. Ges. Wien., X. I. 28 (1918).

Frontal triangle opaque; preapical bristle usually absent; apical bristle always absent; hind tibiæ uniformly short hairy; first section of costa more or less densely short hairy; last section of third vein straight or gently curved like letter S; usually not more than three pairs of dorsocentral bristles, the anterior pair not convergent; posthumeral bristles usually absent; scutellum with four marginal bristles.

Genotype.—O. coxata Stenh. by present designation.

[1]Contribution from the Division of Entomology of the Agricultural Experiment Station, State College of Washington.

Species of Opacifrons Duda.

1. Preapical bristle present in the female, absent in the male.... 2
   Preapical bristle absent in both sexes.................... 4

2. Second section of costa distinctly longer than third.......... 3
   Second and third sections of costa equal or nearly so....... 5

3. Wings with dark infuscations along all veins with exception of last section of third; front with three silvery pollinose areas located as follows; one on each side and one directly in front of the ocellar tubercle; dorsocentral bristles in three pairs; acrostichal bristles distinct; halteres yellow Fig. 1.................................*grandis* n. sp.

   Wings clear; veins not so marked; front without such markings....................................... 4

4. Front, face and cheeks black; interfrontal bristles in four pairs, the anterior pair weak; orbital setulæ strong, as strong as the anterior pair of interfrontal bristles; wings clear; veins black; legs black; outer crossvein below apical third of last section of second vein; halteres yellow. Fig. 10.............................*sciaspidis* n. sp.

   Cheeks brownish yellow; legs brownish yellow; outer crossvein below middle of last section of second vein; smaller species. 1.5 mm.........................*cartagensis* Mall.

5. Lower front, anterior margin of epistome and anterior portions of cheeks yellowish; face fuscous; interfrontal bristles in three pairs, all three pairs cruciate; wings browned, veins blackish; notum opaque, brownish-black; acrostichal bristles distinct; halteres yellow. Fig. 6.*cœlobata* n. sp.

   Lower front opaque black; face and cheeks yellow; interfrontal bristles in four pairs, the upper and lower reduced, the middle two pairs cruciate; notum slightly to distinctly shining black; acrostichal bristles weak; wing veins pale; halteres fuscous. Fig. 8................*pellucida* n. sp.

6. Second section of costa longer than third; face, cheeks, and two spots on front slivery pollinose; notum glossy black; acrostichal setulæ very short; hind metatarsi one-half as long as second joint; abdomen piceous, hind margins of segments narrowly yellowish; halteres whitish. Fig. 4.................................*wheeleri* n. sp.

7. Lower front reddish; interfrontal bristles not cruciate, the lower pair weaker than the others; last section of third vein slightly curved up; face and cheeks black or grayish; second section of abdomen as long as the next two. Fig. 7..................................*coxata* Stenh.
Entire front black; face and cheeks yellow or with the posterior portion of cheeks blackish; lower two pairs of interfrontal bristles cruciate; second segment of abdomen but little longer than third. Fig. 9........*convexa* n. sp.

Limosina (Opacifrons) grandis n. sp. (Fig. 1.)

Subshining black. Front decidedly convex, opaque, almost twice as broad as deep; the divergent stripes velvety black; setigerous stripes and frontal triangle slightly silvery pollinose; vertex with a distinct silvery pollinose spot on each side and one directly in front of ocellar triangle; fronto-orbital bristles nearly uniform in size; upper two orbital setulæ bristle-like, as strong as the upper pair of interfrontal bristles; interfrontal setæ bristle-like, in three pairs, at right angles to the interfrontal rows; face gray dusted, slightly carinate; clypeus broadly visible from in front; cheeks silvery pollinose; at its narrowest point, one-third as high as eye; buccæ with a long upcurved outer bristle and three small setæ; oral margin with a row of long hairs; antennæ with third joint rounded, much larger than second and with minute whitish pubescence; arista three times antennal length with rather long pubescence. Mesonotum with three pairs of dorsocentral bristles in widely divergent rows; acrostichal setulæ strong, in eight rows between the anterior pair and in four rows between the posterior pair of dorsocentral bristles; scutellum triangular; marginal bristles bristles four;

pleuræ opaque black; sternopleuræ with as very strong posterior and a rather weak anterior bristle. Legs piceous; coxæ and trochanters silvery pollinose; knees fuscous; front femora with a row of long hairs on its anterior side, middle femora with a row of seven strong anterior preapical setæ; middle tibiæ with five extensor, two on basal third and three on apical third, and two flexor bristles, one at middle and one near apex; (preapical bristle absent in male) hind tibiæ without marcochætæ, hind metatarsi thickened, one-half as long as the much thinner second joint. Wings slightly browned, with heavy black markings along all veins with the exception of the third vein; veins black; costa ending slightly beyond third vein; first section short, ciliate, with two basal bristles, equal to third and three-fourths as long as second; penultimate sections of third and fourth veins subequal, one-third as long as last section of second vein and two and one-half times outer crossvein, third vein slightly bent forward, then backward and again forward on last section, and ending near wing-tip; fourth vein traceable to wing-margin, fifth vein produced a short distance beyond outer cross vein; discal cell broad at middle and narrowed at outer crossvein. Abdomen opaque, hairy, second segment a little longer than the others. Halteres yellow.

Length 4 mm.

Type.—Female; Portland, Oregon. Aug. 20, 1909. (Melander).

Paratypes.—Three specimens from Adna, Lake Cushman, and Quilcene, Wash. (Melander).

Leptocera (Opacifrons) sciaspidis n. sp. (Fig. 10).

Shining black; Front two times as broad as deep, slightly convex; setigerous stripes and frontal triangle slightly gray dusted, the divergent stripes velvety black; fronto-orbital bristles strong, widely divergent, the lower three-fourths as long as upper; orbital setulæ not extending above the upper fronto-orbital bristle, the upper three, bristle-like, the upper most setæ nearly as strong as the posterior pair of interfrontal bristles;

interfrontal bristles strong, in four pairs, the anterior pair reduced, the other three increasing in size anteriorly, with the third pair from above, cruciate; antennæ prominent, second joint with strong bristles, third joint oval, larger than second; arista two and one-half times antennal length, its pubescence short and dense; face concave in profile, slightly gray dusted; carina developed between the antennæ only; clypeus broadly visible from in front; cheeks gray dusted, one-fourth eye height; buccæ with a strong anterior upcurved bristle and three setæ; oral setulæ hair-like. Mesonotum with three distinct pairs of dorsocentral bristles, increasing in size posteriorly; acrostichal setulæ arranged in six rows between the anterior pair of dorsocentral bristles, the middle rows longer than the others; posthumerals absent; scutellum large, triangular, marginal bristles four, the posterior pair very long; upper sternopleuræ with two anterior setæ and a long posterior bristle. Legs with knees browned; front femora with five hair-like extensor and four preapical flexor bristles, middle femora with six preapical anterior bristles; middle tibiæ with five extensor, two before middle and two on apical third, and two flexor bristles, one at middle and one at near apex (preapical bristle absent in male); middle metatarsi with a flexor bristle at basal third and a number of apical bristles; hind tibiæ with a row of hair-like bristles on outer side; first and second joints of hind tarsi with a brush of stiff hairs beneath; hind metatarsi one-half as long as next joint. Abdomen broad, shorter than thorax; second segment one and one-half times as long as third; hypopygium moderately large and hairy. Wings slightly browned; second section of costa distinctly longer than third; first section weakly bristly and equal to third; penultimate section of third and fourth veins subequal and two times outer crossvein; last section of third vein nearly straight; fourth vein traceable to wing-margin; fifth vein produced but little beyond outer crossvein. Halteres white. Length: 2.5-3mm.

Type.—Female; Friday Harbor. June 25, 1909. (Melander)

Paratypes.—Fifty-one specimens of this species, distributed as follows:

Washington: Glenwood, Mt. Rainier, Husum, Friday Harbor, Olympia, Adna, Mt. Constitution, Kettle Falls, Roche Harbor, Wawawai, Nahcotta (Melander).

Idaho: Potlatch, Moscow, Juliaetta, Kendrick, (Melander); Troy (Cresson).

Leptocera (Opacifrons) cartagensis Malloch.

Malloch; Tran. Am. Ent. Soc. 40. 17 (1914). (*Leptocera*) Costa Rica.

Leptocera (Opacifrons) caelobata n. sp. (Fig. 6).

Opaque black. Front for the most part reddish, changing to brown or black toward occiput; bristles strong; fronto-orbitals divergent; the lower three-fourths as long as upper; orbital setulæ weak; interfrontal bristles in three pairs, the upper pair touching, the lower two pairs longer and cruciate; face and cheeks pale brown, with gray pollen; face concave in profile; cheek at vibrissal angle two-fifths as high as eye, buccal bristles in two pairs, the anterior pair quite strong; oral setæ long, hair-like; second joint of antennæ with strong apical bristles; third joint rounded; arista two times antennal length, microscopically pubescent. Mesonotum with three pairs of dorsocentral bristles; discal setulæ strong, middle acrostichals prominent, posterior pair bristle-like; scutellum triangular; disc bare, marginal bristle four; pleuræ with some grayish pollen; pleural sutures reddish, sternopleuræ with a single posterior bristle. Legs hairy, coxæ and trochanters fuscous; middle femora with six antero-apical bristles, the apical one very strong; middle tibiæ with five extensor bristles, a pair at basal third and three on apical third; hind metatarsi two-thirds as long as second joint. Wings infumated, veins black; costa produced to end of third vein, second section as long as third; basal section of third vein two times outer crossvein and a little longer than distance between crossveins, third vein straight on its last section, or slightly curved up at apex, ending near wing-tip, vein four faintly produced to wing-margin; vein five produced one-third distance from outer crossvein to wing-margin; discal cell broad. Abdomen cylindrical, very short, but little more than half as long as thorax; second segment as long as third. Halteres yellow. Length: 3 mm.

Type.—Male: Pullman, Wash. June 10, 1911. (Melander.)

Paratype.—A single specimen from Pateros, Wash. (Melander).

Leptocera (Opacifrons) pellucida n. sp. (Fig. 8.)

Opaque black. Front convex, two-thirds as broad as deep, slightly gray dusted except on the divergent stripes and lower orbital stripes; lower fronto-orbital bristle three-fourths as long as upper; orbital setulæ microscopic; interfrontal bristles in four pairs, the anterior and posterior pairs weak, the middle two pairs long and cruciate; interfrontal setulæ microscopic; face and cheeks yellow; face deeply concave in profile; anterior margin of epistome slightly projecting; clypeus not visible from in front; cheek at vibrissal angle one-fourth as high as eye; oral setulæ weak, hair-like; buccal setulæ in three pairs, the anterior pair stronger than the others, bristle-like; antennæ fuscous, third joint oval, equal in length to second; arista two and one-half times antennal length, pubescence microscopic. Mesonotum with three pairs of dorsocentral bristles, increasing in size posteriorly; discal setulæ in six rows between anterior pair and two rows between posterior pairs of dorsocentral bristles; scutellum triangular; marginal bristles four; pleuræ with gray pollen; pleural sutures reddish; sternopleuræ with a strong posterior bristle and two small anterior setæ. Legs brown; front femora with hair-like bristles; middle trochanter with a weak bristle; middle femora with five antero-preapical bristles, increasing in size apically, middle tibia with two pairs of extensor bristles, one on basal-fourth and one on apical fourth; hind metatarsi two-thirds as long as next joint. Wings hyaline; veins brown; costa extended slightly beyond third vein, second and third sections subequal; discal cell short; outer crossvein nearly as long as distance between crossveins; basal section of third vein less than one-half as long as last section of second vein and less than two times as long as second section of fourth vein; fourth vein not reaching wing-margin; fifth vein extending beyond outer crossvein. Abdomen as long as thorax, fuscous, margins of segments lighter; second segment one and one-half times third. Halteres fuscous.

Length: 2 mm.

Type.–. Male; Oroville, Wash. (Melander).

Paratypes..—Seven specimens from the following localities:

Washington: Oroville, Pullman (Melander).

British Columbia: Bear Lake (U. S. N. M.)

Leptocera (Opacifrons) wheeleri n. sp. (Fig. 4).

Front olivaceous black; ocellar triangle bordered on each side by a conspicuous lunate silvery-pollinose spot, lower frontal triangle depressed and with sloping sides, because of the sloping sides the depressed portion of the frontal triangle appears to have a different color than the rest of the front; bristles not very conspicuous; interfrontal bristles in five pairs, increasing in size anteriorly to middle pair, then decreasing, but not cruciate; face and cheeks silvery pollinose; face shallowly concave in profile; oral vibrissæ short; bucca with a distinct anterior bristle and a few posterior setæ; oral setulæ distinct; antennæ moderate in size, third joint with whitish pubescence; arista two and one-half times antennal length, microscopically pubescent. Thorax and scutellum glistening black with an opaque brownish pollinose stripe between the base of the wings and the humeri; dorsocentral bristles in four pairs; acrostichal setulæ very fine and short, arranged in eight rows between the anterior pair of dorsocentral bristles; scutellum trapezoidal, blunt at tip; marginal bristles four; pleuræ with the exception of the extreme upper portion, white-pollinose; upper sternopleuræ with a strong posterior bristle and minute anterior setæ. Legs black; tarsi brown; femora and tibiæ slightly gray dusted; all the bristles somewhat reduced; middle femora with a single preapical anterior setæ, middle tibiæ with four extensor, one on basal third, and two on apical fourth, and no flexor bristles, middle tarsi with a small seta on flexor surface near base; hind metatarsi as thick as tibiæ at apex and one-half as long as the much more slender second joint. Wings hyaline or but slightly yellowish; veins brown; costa extending slightly beyond third vein, second section one and one-fourth times as long as third; second vein ending beyond the outer crossvein; basal section of third vein one-third as long as the last section of second vein and nearly two times outer crossvein; last section of third vein gently curved, ending a little before wing-tip; fourth vein reaching margin of wing; fifth vein produced considerably beyond outer crossvein. Abdomen piceous, flat oval; hind margins of segments narrowly yellowish; second segment not much longer than third. Halteres whitish. Length: 2 mm.

Type.—Female; Austin, Texas; Oct. 29, 1899 (Melander).

Paratypes.—Two specimens from Illinois (Ill. Univ.)

Leptocera (Opacifrons) coxata Stenhammar (Fig. 7).

Stenhammar: Coprom. Scand. 396 (138) (1855). (*Limosina*).

Duda: Abhand. Zool.-Botan. Ges. Wien. X. I. 85 (1918). (*Limosina*).

Pusio Zetterstedt: Dipt. Scand. VI. 2496 (1847). (*Limosina*).

Pumilo Zetterstedt: Ins. Lapp. 771 (1838). (*Limosina*).

Septentrionalis Dahl: Berl. Sb. Ges. Natf. Freunder. (1909). (*Limosina*).

Nigricoris Dahl; Berl. Sb. Ges. Natf. Freunde. 375 (1909). (*Limosina*).

Forty seven specimens from the following localities:

Washington: Bellingham, Lake Whatcom, Nahcotta, Lake Cushman, Ilwaco, Granite Falls, Sultan, La Center, Tacoma,

Vancouver, Colby, Dungeness, Pt. Gamble (Melander).

Idaho: Lake Waha (Melander).

Oregon: Salem, Portland (Melander).

California: Berkeley, Muir Woods (Melander).; Stanford Univ. (Aldrich); Redwood City.

British Columbia: Abbotsford (Melander).

Leptocera (Opacifrons) convexa n. sp. (Fig. 9).

Opaque black. Front with fronto-orbital, the very narrow interfrontal stripes and the frontal triangle from lower ocelli to frontal lunule, slightly gray dusted, somewhat flat, two-thirds as long as broad; vertical and postorbital bristles moderate; fronto-orbital bristles divergent, the upper but little longer than the lower; orbital setulæ present, the upper two pairs quite distinct; interfrontal bristles in four pairs, the first from above, very weak, the second reaching the median line and the third and fourth pairs longer and cruciate; one pair of interfrontal setulæ present; face and cheeks yellow, pollinose; cheek black toward occiput, narrow, from mouth margin to lower margin of eye, equal to one-fourth eye-height; oral vibrissæ long; oral setulæ weak, in one pair; face concave in profile; epistome slightly projecting; clypeus very narrowly visible from in front; antennæ divergent, third joint rounded; arista three times antennal length, long pubescent. Mesonotum and scutellum grayish dusted; mesonotum with a single pair of dorsocentral bristles; acrostichal setulæ rather weak, arranged in six rows between the dorsocentrals, the posterior pair of middle acrostichals longer than the others; pleural sutures yellow to reddish; sternopleuræ with two bristles, the posterior longer than the anterior; scutellum quadrangular; disc with four nearly uniform bristles on margin. Legs hairy; coxæ, trochanters and tarsi infuscate; middle femora with a row of five anterior preapical bristles, the one nearest apex much the longest, middle tibiæ with no flexor and three extensor bristles arranged as follows: one at basal third, one at apical third, and one on apical fifth ,hind metatarsi three-fifths as long as second joint. Wings slightly browned; veins brown; costa ending beyond third vein, first and second sections black, second section three-fifths as long as third; last section of second vein two and one-half times as long as basal section of third vein; penultimate sections of third and fourth veins subequal and twice the length of the outer crossvein; last section of third vein straight and ending a little before wing-tip, last section of fourth vein evanescent and not reaching wing-margin; fifth vein traceable one-half way to wing-margin from outer crossvein. Abdomen cylindrical; second segment of abdomen one and one-fourth times as long as third; hypopygium large. Halteres with stem and tip of knob yellow. Length: 1 mm.

Type.—Male, Bovill, Idaho (Melander).

Paratypes.—Five specimens from the following localities:

Washington: Sultan, Mt. Constitution, Tacoma, (Melander).

Idaho: Priest Lake (Melander).

Pteremis Rondanis.

Rondani: Prodr. I. 124 (1856)., Coprom. Bull. Soc. Ent. Ital. XII 41 (1880).

Duda: Abhand. zool.-bot. Ges. Wien X. I. 28 (1918).

Head large, broader than thorax; wings rudimentary; costa extending considerably beyond third vein; outer crossvein absent; last section of third vein straight or but slightly curved up; preapical bristle present; middle tibiæ with a number of minute apical bristles, never with a single strong, apical bristle; middle metatarsal bristle absent.

Genotype.—*P. nivalis* Haliday.

Species of Pteremis Rondani.

1. Wings very short, not reaching beyond the second abdominal segment; second vein incomplete, not reaching costa; face and cheeks piceous, concave in profile; shining black species. Fig. 3 .... *parvipennis* n. sp.

   Wings longer, reaching the fourth abdominal segment......2

2. Front, face and cheeks entirely ferruginuous or yellowish; second section of costa less than one-half as long as third; halteres slightly reduced, fuscous. Fig. 5 .... *flavifrons* n. sp.

   Front, face and cheeks for the most part black; face slightly carinate, concave in profile; second section of costa a little shorter than third; halteres considerably shortened, yellow. Fig 2 .... *unica* n. sp.

Leptocera (**Pteremis**) **parvipennis** n. sp. (Fig. 3).

Shining black. Front almost twice as broad as deep; divergent stripes opaque; bristles of front and vertex moderately strong; interfrontal bristles in five pairs, the upper two and the lower pair very much reduced, the other two considerably longer but not cruciate; antennæ piceous; arista two and one-half times antennal length, with short dense pubescence; face and cheeks piceous; face carinate between the antennæ only; epistome curved up on anterior margin; clypeus broadly visible from in front; cheeks a little less than one-third as high as eye, when measured at vibrissal angle; vibrissæ strong. Mesonotum and scutellum with some brownish pollen; dorsocentral bristles in two pairs, the anterior pair rather weak; acrostichal setulæ few, in five irregular rows between the anterior pair of dorsocentral bristles; scutellum triangular with apex truncate; marginal bristles four, the posterior pair much longer than the others; pleuræ reddish below; upper sternopleuræ with a strong bristle. Legs with coxæ, trochanters, knees and tarsi reddish; front femora with some long hairs, middle tibiæ with two small extensor bristles on apical third; front and hind tarsal joints slightly thickened; hind metatarsi as thick as apex of tibiæ and two-thirds as long as next joint. Wings very short, not reaching beyond the second abdominal segment, brownish; veins heavy, piceous; costa ciliate its entire length and ending at third vein; second vein not reaching wing-margin and ending at a point opposite anterior crossvein; posterior crossvein absent. Abdomen very broad; dorsum hairy; segments equal. Halteres considerably reduced. Length 1.5 mm.

Type.—Female; Kukak Bay, Alaska. July 4, 1899, (Kincaid).

Paratype.—A single specimen from the same collection.

Limosina (Pteremis) flavifrons n. sp. (Fig. 5).

Shining black species with head almost entirely reddish yellow. Front rather flat, three-fourths as deep as broad; bristles black; vertical and occiputal bristles strong; interfrontal bristles very much reduced, in three pairs; antennæ widely divergent, slightly browned, second and third joints nearly equal; arista pubescent, three times as long as antennæ; face tuberculate between and below antennæ, slightly concave in profile near anterior margin; clypeus broadly visible from in front; cheeks one-third as high as eye when measured atvibrissal angle; oral vibrissæ well developed; buccal and oral setulæ minute; eyes piceous, two-thirds as wide as high. Mesonotum with two pairs of dorsocentral bristles, posterior pair of middle acrostichals longer than the others; scutellum trapezoidal; marginal bristles four; pleuræ opaque piceous; upper sternopleuræ with a rather distinct bristle. Legs piceous with front coxæ, front and middle trochanters, front femora and all tarsi ferruginous; front femora silghtly swollen; middle femora with a single preapical anterior bristle, middle tibiæ with three extensor, two on basal third and one on apical third; hind metatarsi but little thickened, two-thirds as long as next joint. Wings slightly smoky extending a little beyond the fourth abdominal segment; veins brown; costa setulose on first section, second section less than one-half as long as third; second vein reaching margin of wing at a point slightly anterior to the inner crossvein; basal section of third vein slightly longer than last section of second vein; inner crossvein very narrow; fourth vein produced a short distance beyond inner crossvein; outer crossvein absent; last section of third vein straight, ending at wing-tip. Abdomen longer than thorax; segments equal; dorsum minutely pubescent. Halteres fuscous, slightly reduced. Length: 1.25 mm.

Holotype.—Female: Falls Church, Virginia, Dec. 29, (Barber.) This specimen has been returned to the U. S. National Museum.

Leptocera (Pteremis) unica n. sp. (Fig. 2).

Subshining black. Front slightly reddish, much broader than deep; the divergent stripes, divided by the broad interfrontal stripes, opaque velvety black. (The poor condition of the head of this specimen makes it impossible to give the location of the bristles), third joint of antennæ reddish; face slightly carinate, concave in profile, with a slight reddish tinge; epistome curved up on its anterior margin; clypeus broadly visible from in front; cheeks at vibrissal angle, nearly one-half as high as eye; vibrissæ much reduced. Mesonotum with three pairs of dorsocentral bristles, the anterior two pairs very much reduced and rather indistinct; acrostichal bristles few, in five irregular rows between the anterior pair of dorsocentrals; scutellum triangular; disc bare; marginal bristles four; pleuræ reddish; upper sternopleuræ with a prominent bristle. Legs with coxæ, and trochanters yellowish; knees, apices of tibiæ and tarsi reddish; bristles of legs very much reduced; hind metatarsi thickened, two-fifths as long as next joint. Wings brownish, reaching to the middle of fourth abdominal segment; veins brown; costa ciliate for its entire length and ending at third vein, second section distinctly shorter than third; last section of second vein twice as long as basal section of third vein; inner crossvein narrow; outer crossvein absent. Abdomen glossy black, rather long and narrow, tapering posteriorly. Halteres considerably reduced, yellow. Length: 1.25 mm.

Holotype.—Female; Yellowstone National Park, Wyo. (U. S. N. M.)

This single specimen has been returned to the National Museum.

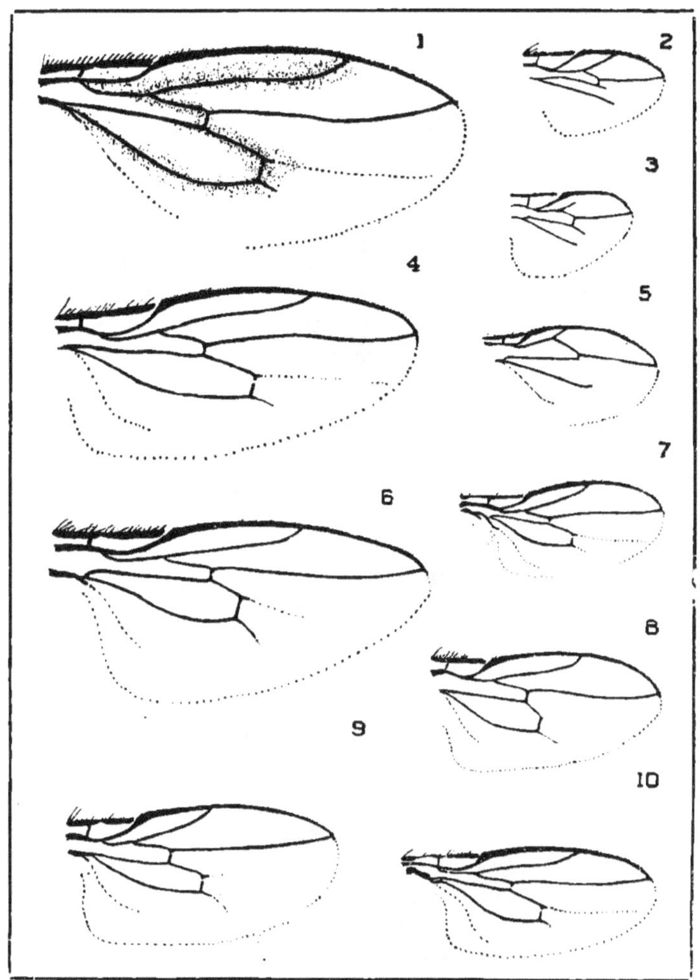

SPULER—OPACIFRONS AND PTEREMIS.

Fig. 1. *Opacifrons grandis* n. sp.; Fig. 2. *Pteremis unica* n. sp.; Fig. 3. *Pteremis parvipennis* n. sp.; Fig. 4. *Opacifrons wheeleri* n. sp.; Fig. 5. *Pteremis flavifrons* n. sp.; Fig. 6. *Opacifrons caelobata* n. sp.; Fig. 7. *Opacifrons coxata* Stenh.; Fig. 8. *Opacifrons pellucida* n. sp.; Fig. 9. *Opacifrons convexa* n. sp.; Fig. 10. *Opacifrons sciaspidis* n. sp.

A GYNANDROMORPH OF *TETRAMORIUM GUINEENSE* FABR.

By William Morton Wheeler.

Bussey Institution, Harvard University.

Mr. P. H. Timberlake has had the kindness to send me a very interesting gynandromorph of the common tropicopolitan ant, *Tetramorium guineense* Fabr., which was captured June 19th, 1923 by Mr. E. H. Bryan on Necker Island, some miles northwest of Honolulu. Unlike the previously recorded ant-gynandromorphs, this insect is a pure example of the antero-posterior type, the head being male, the remainder of the body female, with perfectly developed wings (Fig. 1a). I can detect no deviation in the structure of the head (Fig. 1b) from that of the normal male. The antennæ are perfectly developed and 10-jointed, and the details of the sculpture, pilosity and color of the normal male are accurately reproduced. The head of the normal female, shown in Fig. 1c, is, of course very different. The thorax, however, is precisely like that of the normal female, except that it is slightly less robust, with the mesonotum a little less flattened dorsally, and the metasternal spines are un developed. The thorax of the male *guineense* is very different from that of the female, since it lacks the epinotal spines as well as the metasternal spines, has a more convex mesonotum and mesosternum and the former has Mayrian furrows. The color is also darker and the surface much smoother and very differently sculptured from that of the female. The legs, petiole, post-petiole and gaster of the gynandromorph are precisely as in the normal female, even the sting, which is fully exserted, being of the same length and structure. The sculpture, pilosity and color are also as in the normal female, the thorax, legs and pedicel being yellowish ferruginous, the gaster very dark brown or blackish, with its extreme base and tip yellowish brown. There is every reason to assume that the internal reproductive organs are those of the normal female. The wings are whitish hyaline, with colorless veins and pterostigma, as in the normal female.

On looking over the specimens of *Tetramorium guineense* in my collection I find one male from Cagues, Porto Rico with an 11-jointed left antenna. The right antenna is broken so that the number of its joints cannot be ascertained. This and similar specimens, which one finds occasionally in Tetramorium and other ant-genera, are probably to be regarded as exhibiting "intersexual" rather than gynandromorphic traits since in the case mentioned the number of antennal joints is intermediate between the ten of the normal male and the twelve of the normal female.

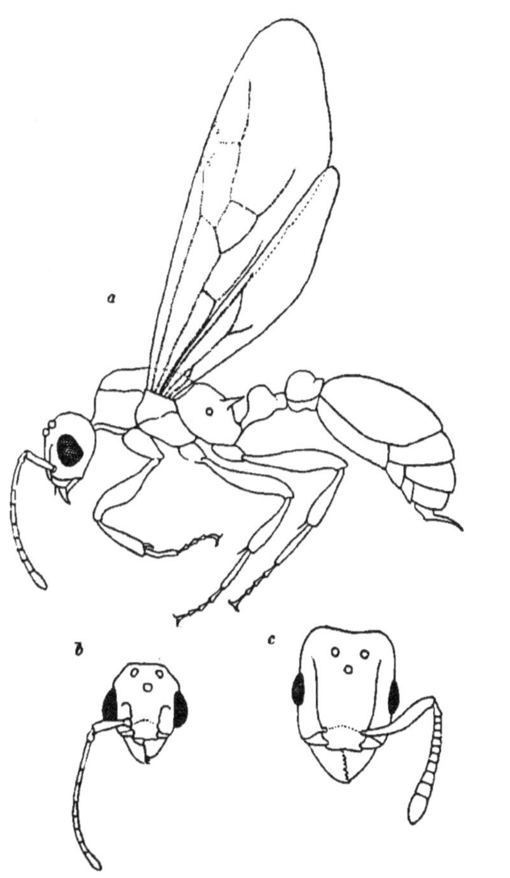

Fig. 1. Gynandromorph of *Tetramorium guineense* Fabr. a, lateral view; b, anterior view of head; c, head of normal female.

ATTACKS OF *VESPA COMMUNIS* DE SAUSSURE ON *HYPHANTRIA CUNEA* DRURY.

By M. T. Smulyan.

U. S. Bureau of Entomology, Melrose Highlands, Mass.

The wasp attacks reported here occured during September 1923, at Roycefield, N. J., and were made on fall webworm larvæ (*Hyphantria cunea* Drury) which had been collected in a number of localities for parasite study purposes. The wasps (*Vespa communis* De Saussure)[1] appeared, suddenly and in large numbers, as the first collection of the webworms was being examined out of doors, and they literally threw themselves upon the caterpillars, and their attacks were so persistent and savage that all efforts to drive them off, although it resulted in the death of many of them, were fruitless. The attacks began very early in the month, and they were continued at intervals—in connection with each out of door examination of the webworms—throughout the ten-day collecting period. Attacks upon the caterpillars were made also while they were in a more or less open, near-by shelter, where they had been placed in rearing trays, and the wasps exhibited the same degree of ferocity and voracity here. They attacked here not only at the feeding of the caterpillars, when the trays were uncovered, but throughout the greater part of the day—through the screen covers—whenever caterpillars appeared on the undersides of the latter; and they continued this, although in decreasing numbers, until the last week of September when following a two or three day period of cold weather they disappeared altogether.

The wasps, it should be added, apparently made no attempts to carry off the caterpillars. Nor, as far as could be seen, did they malax them. They would precipitate themselves upon them, pierce the integument with their mandibles, and consume the liquid and softer parts.

[1]Determined by Dr. J. Bequaert of the Harvard University Medical School, on the return of the writer to Melrose Highlands, Mass.

The wasps were not seen to attack insects prior to the attacks reported here, although individual workers were observed from time to time in the vicinity throughout the summer. But very likely they were at those times merely seeking food of vegetable character. The fondness of adult wasps for this type of food is well known of course, and their indifference to animal food at times of the abundance of the former has been noted.

The behavior of the wasps—aside from their apparent failure to carry off or to malaxate the caterpillars—may probably be explained on the ground of a shortage or dearth of food—both plant and animal—because of the lateness and dryness of the season; the summer of 1923 was exceedingly dry in New Jersey. The suggestion (which has been made) that the wasps' ferocity and rapid consumption of the liquid portions of the caterpillars were perhaps due to a desire for water—the fondness or need of wasps for water is also well known—is hardly satisfactory. First, there was available the water from the heavy dews; secondly, the wasps continued to seek the caterpillars in the rearing trays in the shelter, although in smaller numbers, during a two-day rain-storm. It was hunger, eivdently, rather than thirst which influenced the wasps.

The exact location of the wasp nest was not discovered.

NEW SPIDERS FROM SOUTHERN NEW ENGLAND.

J. H. EMERTON.

The following species of spiders have been found in the last few years in southern Massachusetts, Rhode Island and Connecticut. The *Grammonata* was at first considered a variety of *G. pictilis*, but has now been found in three different places, always with the same distinguishing characters. The *Ceratinopsis* is one of several species confused under the name of *C. nigriceps*. The *Euryopis* has been known for a long time, but has awaited description in the hope of finding females that might be referred to the same species. The *Theridion* and the *Lophocarenum* are described reluctantly from single specimens after careful search for more in the same localities.

Theridion terrestre n. sp.

3 mm. long, pale, with very distinct gray and black markings. The cephalothorax has a middle gray stripe as wide as the eyes in front, narrowing backward to the dorsal pit and widening again behind. The thoracic part is bordered by a narrow black line. The femora and tarsi have three gray rings. The abdomen

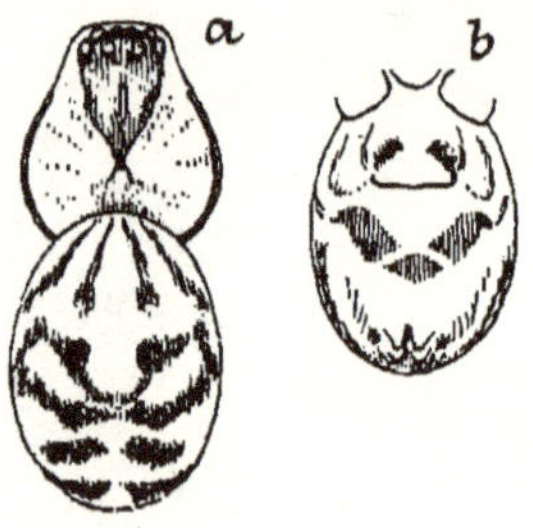

Fig. 1. *Theridion terrestre* n. sp.

has a complicated black pattern composed of two rows of spots in the middle, partly connected with two lateral rows in the anterior half. Fig 1a. On the under side there is a middle transverse marking composed of three gray spots, and there are indefinite gray marks along the sides. Fig. 1, b. The legs are long and slender, as usual in this genus, the fourth leg is 8 mm. long. The front legs, probably the longest, are broken off and lost.

One female only among weeds in an asparagus field. Holliston, Mass. N. Banks.

Ceratinopsis tarsalis n. sp.

Male 1.5 mm. long. Cephalothorax orange brown, black between the eyes. Abdomen and feet pale. The female is black around the eyes like the male, but does not have a sharply

Fig. 2. *Ceratinopsis tarsalis* n. sp.

defined black spot like *C. nigriceps*. The epigynum is distinctly different from that of *nigriceps* and resembles some of the *Lycosidæ*. Fig. 2b. The male palpus has the tibia larger and wider than in *nigriceps*. Fig. 2a. The outer edge of the tarsus is slightly thickened and there is a thicker ridge parallel with it. Fig. 2a.

Buttonwoods, near Providence, R. I., Monponsett, Middleboro, and Hyannis, Mass.

Grammonata capitata n. sp.

This resembles closely *G. pictilis*, and like it lives in trees. It is one-eighth smaller than *pictilis* and paler in color, the light spots of the abdomen running together so that in some specimens the whole back is pale except a middle gray mark. Fig. 3a. In the males the cephalothorax is slightly shorter and the hump on the head rises more abruptly behind. Fig. 3b. The male palpi and the epigynum cannot be distinguished from those of *pictilis*.

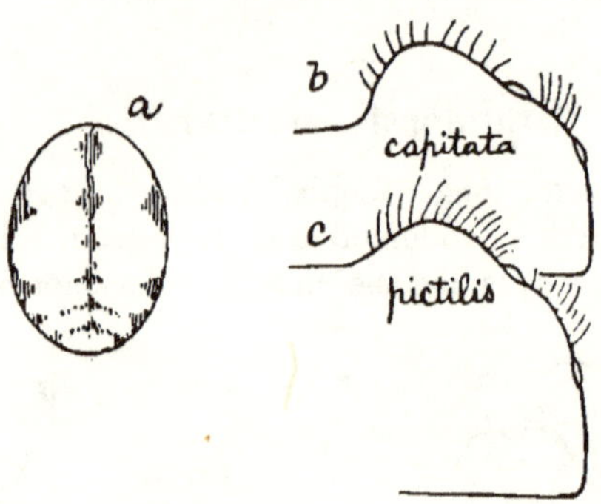

Fig. 3. *Grammonata capitata* n. sp.

Amston, Conn., Miss Bryant. Chatham, Mass. and Holliston, Mass. At Chatham both this species and *pictilis* have been found, but in localities a mile apart.

Euryopis spinigera Cambridge.

Biologia Centrali Americana, Arachnida, Vol. 1, page 146, plate 19, fig. 2.

Males only known, 1.5 to 2 mm. long, yellow brown with a darker thickened spot covering the back of the abdomen except the posterior end. Fig. 4a. On the under side of the abdomen are two large thickened spots, one covering the anterior end as far back as the spiracles and the other occupying the middle of the posterior half. Fig. 4b. Smaller thickened spots are scattered along the sides. The upper side of the abdomen is covered with scattered stiff hairs. Fig. 4a. The legs are short and without any markings. The cephalothorax is as wide as long and narrowed toward the head. The upper eyes as seen from above form a straight line. The lateral eyes of the front row nearly touch those of the upper row. The middle eyes are much lower and twice their diameter apart.

The male palpi have the patella and tibia very short, the tibia widened at the end covering the base of the tarsus. Fig. 4 c. d. The tarsus is oval and the palpal organ very simple with a short tube supported by a slightly longer and wider process. Fig. 4c.

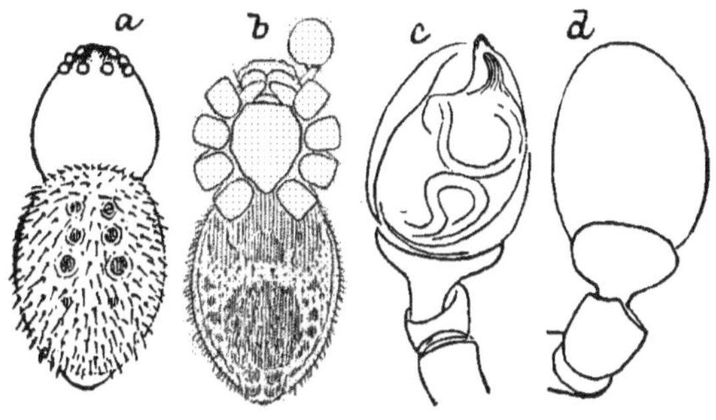

Fig. 4. *Euryopis spinigera* Camb.

Chatham, Mass., June 10, 1919. Riverhead, L. I., Sept., walking on railroad track, C. R. Crosby. Charleston, S. C., J. H. Emerton. The specimen described by Cambridge was from Guatemala.

Lophocarenum hortense n. sp.

A large and light colored species, 3 mm. long. Cephalothorax light orange brown, legs and palpi pale yellowish; abdomen yellowish white with fine gray hairs. The general appearance is like *L. domiciliarum*, Em. which has been found only once. The head is low and has very small grooves and shallow pits just behind the eyes. Fig. 5a. The male palpi have patella and tibia both short. The tibia is as wide as long and has only short projections on the front edge. Fig. 5b. The tarsus is short and almost round. The palpal organ is shown in Fig. 5c. The principal process has the end curved over in a double hook which nearly meets a sharp point branching from below.

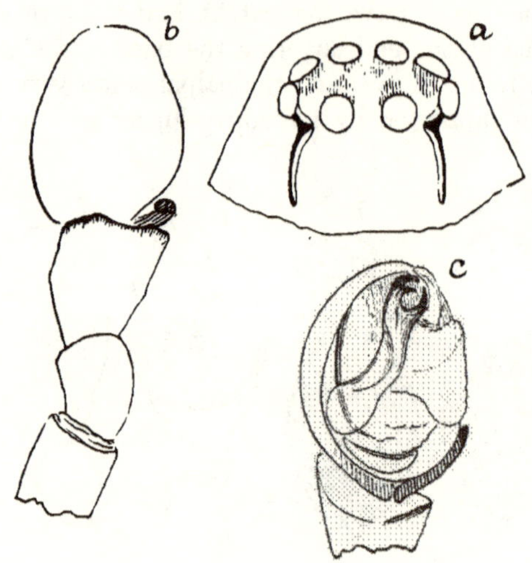

Fig. 5. *Lophocarenum hortense* n. sp.

One male only from weeds in an asparagus field, Holliston, Mass. N. Banks.

Clubiona agrestis n. sp.

4.5 mm. long. Cephalothorax 2 mm. long, the head a little more than half as wide as the thorax and only slightly darker in color. In general, it resembles *C. spiralis*, but is distinguished from it by the palpal characters. The tibia of the male palpus has two hooks on the outer side of about the same size. Fig. 6a.

The palpal organ has the hard process on the under side blunt with several short teeth on the inner side as shown in Fig. 6b.

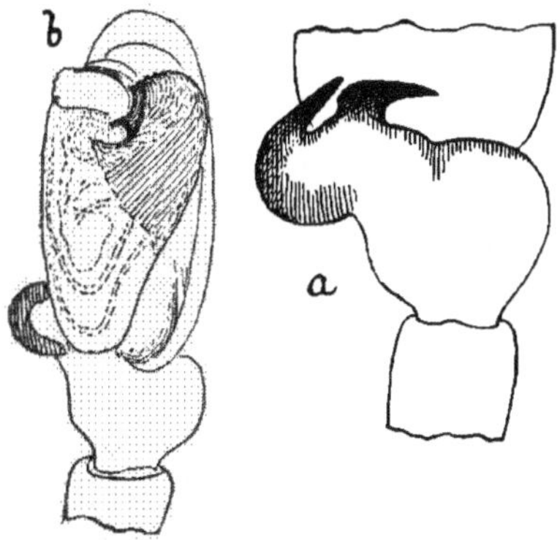

Fig. 6. *Clubiona agrestis* n. sp.

Holliston, Mass., June 17; one mature male and one just molted.

THE FAMILY POSITION OF GRAPHELYSIA (LEPIDOPTERA)

By Wm. T. M. Forbes.

Ithaca, New York.

Graphelysia Hampson (Annals and Magazine of Natural History (8) vol. 8, p. 408, 1911) was based on *Elysius strigillata* Rothschild, described as an Arctiid. Its position in the Arctiidæ has been unchallenged, and it appears in the Supplement to the Catalogue of Lepidoptera Phalænæ, vol. 2, page 337.

The Cornell Entomological Expedition of 1919-1920 captured two specimens, a female from Corumba, Matto Grosso, Brazil, Dec. 1919, and a male from Urucum, in the vicinity of Corumba, Dec. 23, making a considerable extension of the distribution, as the species was described from southern Peru.

The form is undoubtedly a *Noctuid*, not an Arctiid, as shown both by the venation and by the tympanum, which is of a type unknown in the Arctiidæ. It will find a place in the Acontianæ, as defined by Hampson, but is abundantly distinguished by the combination of conical front and stalked R_2 (vein 10); in fact it is not close to any known genus. The antenna is pectinate in both sexes, an extraordinary character in the quadrifid Noctuidæ, the frenulum hook of the male distinctly longer than wide, though far from having the slenderness typical of Acontianæ, the female frenulum of three strong bristles. At the base of the hind wing Sc is moderately thickened, and R is weak but free, fusing with Sc for a short distance only; M_2 is well developed, and distinctly cubital, though well separated from M_3 at the origin. On one side of the male specimen Sc and R though closely approximate are not actually fused, and M_2 arises from the middle of the end of the cell, though the other side, like the female, is normal. The tympanum is like no other form I have seen; without dissection it is not possible to make it out fully, but the alula is deeply fringed with loose hair, not forming the scaly cap frequent in the Acontianæ, the hood on the first segment of the abdomen is weakly developed, and encloses the spiracle as in other Acontianæ, and entirely unlike the deep subdorsal hood of the Arctiidæ, the tympanic membrane itself is high up and far back, practically on the level of the wing, and is not well set off from the articular membrane before it. The epimeron proper is unusually short and squarish, exaggerating a character found in other Acontianæ. The hind leg is also of an Acontiine type, being swollen and hairy, with end-spurs only, and with a swollen and somewhat flattened metatarsus.

Altogether the connection with the Acontiine Noctuidæ is unmistakable, though no genus known to me is at all close. The female does not differ in any striking way from the male.

SEX OF ADULT CECIDOMYIDÆ (OLIGARCES sp.) ARISING FROM LARVÆ PRODUCED BY PÆDOGENESIS.

REGINALD G. HARRIS.

Brown University.

Communicated from the Biological Laboratory, Cold Spring Harbor, Long Island.

The question of the sex of adult forms arising from parthenogenetically and pædogenetically produced individuals has called forth some debate and speculation, often in the absence of suitable date. Sturtevant (1923) summarized the evidence then available concerning some of the Chironomidæ and Cecidomyidæ in the following statements.

"Parthenogenesis has been described in the Chironomid genera Chironomus, Corynoneura, and Tanytarsus by Grimm (1870) Johannsen (1912), Goetghebuer (1913), Edwards (1919) and others. Eggs are produced in some cases by the larvæ, in others by the pupæ, and in still others by the imagines. In all cases in which imagines have been produced by parthenogenetic (including pædogenetic) lines, these have been females and have bred parthenogenetically if at all. Males are known to occur in these genera, and in one case even in a species that reproduces parthenogenetically; but in no case are males reported as arising from larvæ known to have been produced by parthenogenesis.

"The first case of parthenogenesis recorded among the Diptera was that of the Cicidomyiid, Miastor, discovered by Wagner (1863). In this case it is the larvæ that reproduce parthenogenetically. Imagines are often produced, but when they do appear both sexes are found (Meinert 1864, Wagner 1865, Kahle 1908). Kahle states that there is a significant excess of females, and Felt (1911) describes only the female, though he does not state that males were absent. It is not known whether the imagines breed at all, or not; Kahle states that he did not observe copulation. It does not appear to have been entirely proven that the males arise from larvæ that have been produced by pædogenesis, though most students of Miastor have apparently taken this for granted without making cultures from isolated larvæ."

This latter objection has been removed by the writer, who, in using *Miastor* and *Oligarces* as material for experimental work, has, for some time, made cultures from isolated larvæ, and maintained them on artificial culture media. The methods, and some of the results of this work have been reported already. A suitable method of cultivation of *Miastor metraloas* on an artificial culture medium was found (Harris 1923, 1, 2). This method was improved and simplified in later work on Oligarces (Harris 1923, 3). Both of these methods remove the possibility of contamination of the culture by other larvæ than those under observation. The data contained in this report are taken largely from the work on *Oligarces.*

Cultures of pædogenetic larvæ of *Oligarces*, if kept in darkness at a suitable temperature, are easily maintained in Petri dishes in the laboratory, on the following culture medium; 0.5 per cent malt extract, 2 per cent agar agar, 97.5 per cent water. Thus the difficulty of making cultures from isolated larvæ is greatly lessened. It may be said, however, that in making cultures from isolated pædogenetic larvæ it is advisable to take a mother larva containing nearly full term embryos, as cultures made from an individual larva are more liable to be unsuccessful than those in which several larvæ are present. By using a mother larva containing embryos about to be born, one is assured of starting a culture from an isolated larva, while, at the same time, providing the new colony, almost immediately, with several young larvæ with which to carry on the strain. Similar results may be obtained by freeing full term embryos from the skin of the mother larva by dissection in water on a microscope slide, and then transferring these young of an isolated mother to a new culture. Both of the foregoing methods are recommended as time-saving, and as productive of well established colonies.

I have previously reported (Harris 1923, 3, 1924, 1) that pupæ and adults can be produced at will in the laboratory by maintaining a crowded condition in the previous generation. Pupæ and adults produced in this way were used as material for the present study. These pupæ and adults arose in all cases from pædogenetic stock, taken in nature, and maintained on artificial culture medium in the laboratory. In no case are data given on cultures which did not pass at least one pædogenetic generation in the laboratory previous to the appearance of pupæ-larvæ. In some cases the data concern mass cultures, in other cases cultures which originated from an isolated pædogenetic mother larva.

It was found that the pupæ and adults which appeared in mass cultures, made from pædogenetic larvæ of pædogenetic origin, were as likely to be males as females. Thus in cultures B_{12} and C_{12} of 28 pupæ, chosen at random and sexed, 18 were males and 10 were females. In culture M79, of 2 adults, 1 was a male, 1 a female. A similar sex ratio was observed in culture MNO 340.

All of these cultures were originally made of varying numbers of isolated pædogenetic larvæ of known pædogenetic origin. Thus it is clear that male as well as female pupæ and adults arise from larvæ which have been produced by pædogenesis. Male pupæ, when dissected, were found to contain large numbers of sperms in the gonads, while in the female usually about four or five large eggs are visible in living specimens. It seems likely then that both males and females are functionally as well as morphologically different. Up to the present time, however, I have not attempted to obtain progeny from adults, and so cannot state whether or not copulation can be easily obtained in the laboratory.

Whether the number of males will be equal to or greater than the number of females, or *vice versa*, in a given culture, was shown to depend upon the type of stock which was selected in making the cultures, for it appears that in the same colony in nature certain pædogenetic larvæ belong to male producing strains, while other larvæ constitute female producing strains.

Thus in the eighth generation of material originally taken from a single colony in nature, and maintained in the Laboratory by the means already described, individual 4XX was segregated and transferred to a fresh culture made of the standard medium. In the third filial generation pupæ and adults appeared as a result of crowding in the previous generation (F_2). All of these pupæ and adults, 38 in number, which were sexed were females. In the fifth filial generation of the same strain, pupæ and adults again appeared under similar conditions, in three separate cultures. In culture M222, 26 pupæ and adults were sexed. All were females. This was equally true for the 23 individuals sexed in culture M223, and for the 59 individuals sexed in culture M224. Thus all of the 108 F_5 pupæ and adults which were sexed were females. It is apparent that the progenitor of this strain, individual 4XX, must have belonged to a female-producing strain, since all of the pupæ and adults produced by her offspring, both in the F_3 and F_5 generations, were females.

Conversely, at the same time, and under similar conditions, individuals of other strains of known pædogenetic origin, gave rise to male pupæ and imagines only. Thus in culture MN320 5 pupæ appeared; all were males. Similarly in culture $CO_2$3 five adults arose from an isolated pædogenetic mother of known pædogenetic origin. These five adults were males.

Male pupæ of *Miastor metraloas* appeared in a colony, maintained in decayed birch, wood in the laboratory in Paris (Prof. Maurice Caullery, Director) under crowded conditions in a tin box. Though these did not arise from larvæ all of which had been carefully segregated and examined, the fact that they appeared some two months after the material had been transferred to the laboratory makes it more than probable that they were produced by larvæ which had arisen pædogenetically from pædogenetic larvæ originally present in the material. This conclusion is further supported by the fact that all pædogenetic larvæ which were examined and segregated reproduced pædogenetically under similar conditions, about 2 weeks after birth. This would allow for four laboratory pædogenetic generations before the appearance of the male pupæ.

Table 1.

Sex of Imagines and Pupae produced by Paedogenetic Larvae of Known Paedogenetic Origin.

Culture	Pupae arose by	No. of ♀♀	No. of ♂♂	Total	Per Cent of ♂♂
		A.			
B_{12}, C_{12}	crowding	10	18	28	64.3
M79	crowding	1	1	2	50.0
MNO 340	crowding	1	1	2	50.0
	B. Female-producing strain.				
$4XXF_3$	crowding	38	0	38	0.0
$4XXF_5$ (M222)	crowding	26	0	26	0.0
$4XXF_5$ (M223)	crowding	23	0	23	0.0
$4XXF_5$ (M224)	crowding	59	0	59	0.0
$X8F_2$	crowding	1	0	1	0.0
	C. Male-producing strains.				
MN320	crowding	0	5	5	100.0
CO_2 3	CO_2	0	5	5	100.0

All cultures were maintained on the standard artificial culture medium, described earlier in this paper, under as nearly identical external conditions as possible, save culture $CO_2$3. The mother of the five imagines which appeared in this culture was treated with carbon dixoide at birth, and for some time subsequently, after which she was transferred to the standard medium employed in these studies. In all cases cultures were maintained in closed boxes in the same incubator, thus being exposed to similar conditions in respect to temperature, humidity, and light, as well as food. Thus the conclusion seems warranted that the observed sex-ratios are the expression of an internal mechanism, which, in the present instance in all probability, has not been greatly affected by external conditions (save possibly in the case of the strain produced by the pædogenetic mother larva which was treated with carbon dioxide.) Sufficient data are not yet at hand to warrant a statement concerning whether or not the carbon dioxide treatment changes the sex-ratio as in Cladocera (Banta 1923).

Summary.

Males as well as females arise from mass cultures of larvæ that have been produced by pædogenesis in *Oligarces sp.*

But males and females are not produced by the same individual, under normal conditions.

In the descendants of members of a colony taken from nature there were found to be two types of pædogenetic larvæ in respect to the sex of pupæ and adults which they produced, (1) male-producing, and (2) female-producing.

These two types of pædogenetic larvæ are not morphologically distinguishable.

The evidence indicates that the distinction is genetic, since it holds not only in the case of a given individual, but also, without observed exception, in its offspring through five generations of pædogenetic reproduction in two of which certain numbers of adult forms were produced.

Thus the potentiality for producing only males or only females seems to be inherited; there existing in the colony male-producing and female-producing strains.

LITERATURE.

Banta, A. M. and Brown L. A., 1923. Further control of sex in a species of Cladocera. Anat. Rec. Vol. 24, Abs. 144 p. 420.

Edwards, F. W. 1919. Some Parthenogenetic Chironomidæ. Ann. Mag. Nat. Hist. (9) 3; 222-228.

Felt, E. P. 1911. Miastor americana. An account of pedogenesis. New York State Mus. Bull. 147; 82-104.

Goetghebuer, M. 1913. Un cas de parthénogenèse observé chez un Diptère Tendipédide (*Corynoneura celeripes*). Bull. Acad. Roy. Belgique. 1913, 231-233.

Grimm, O. 1870. Die ungeschlechtliche Fortpflanzung einer Chironomus-Art und deren Entwicklung aus dem unbefruchteten Ei. Mem. Acad. Imp. Sci. St. Pétersbourg sér. 7, tome 15.

Harris, R. G. 1923, 1. Sur la culture des larves de Cecidomyides pædogenétiques (*Miastor*) en milieu artificiel. Comptes Rendus Soc. de Biol. Paris, Tome 88 p. 255-7.

Harris, R. G. 1923, 2. Occurence, Life-cycle, and Maintenance under Artificial Conditions of Miastor. Psyche Vol XXX. p. 95-101.

Harris, R. G. 1923, 3. Control of the Appearance of Pupa-larvæ in Pædogenetic Diptera. Proc. Nat. Acad. Sci. Washington, Vol. 9-407-413.

Harris, R. G. 1924, 1. Further Data on the Control of the Appearance of Pupa-larvæ in Pædogenetic Cecidomyidæ. (Oligarces sp.) in press.

Harris, R. G. 1924, 2. Reversal of Function in a Species of Oligarces (in press).

Johannsen, O. A. 1912. Parthenogenesis and Pædogenesis in Tanytarsus. Maine Agr. Exp. Sta. Bull. 187; 3-4.

Kahle, W. 1908. Die Padogenesis der Cecidomyiden. Zoologica, Bd. 21. Heft. 55. 80 pp., 6 plates.

Meinert, F. 1864. Weitere Erläuterungen über die von Prof. Nic. Wagner beschriebene Insectenlarven, welche sich durch Sprossenbildung vermehrt. Zeits. wiss. Zool. 14; 394-399.

Sturtevant, A. H. 1923. The Probable Occurence of Parthenogenesis in *Ochthiphila polstigmata*. (Diptera). Psyche vol. XXX 22-27.

Wagner, N. 1863. Beitrag zur Lehre von der Fortpflanzung der Insecten-larven. Zeits. wiss. Zool. 13. 513-527.

Wagner, N. 1865. Ueber die viviparen Gallmückenlarven. Zeits. wiss. Zool. 15, 106-107.

Acknowledgement is made to Dr. C. B. Davenport for facilities offered in connection with this work at the Department of Genetics of the Carnegie Institution of Washington at Cold Spring Harbor.

NEW AND UNRECORDED AMERICAN SPECIES OF THE FAMILY PHORIDÆ (DIPTERA)[1]

By Charles T. Brues.

The present short paper includes descriptions of three new species of Phoridæ of the genera Hypocera and Aphiochæta and records of the occurence in North America of two European species, *Gymnophora quartomollis* Schmitz and *Aphiochæta giraudii*. I am greatly indebted to Dr. C. F. Adams by whom two of the new species were collected, and who has graciously allowed the types to remain in the writer's collection.

Hypocera Lioy.

In this genus there is a group characterized by having the vertex semicircularly elevated and sharp above. The first species of this type to be described was *H. coronata* Becker from Europe, but several others have since been added. In the present collection made by Dr. Adams is another species from the United States. It may be distinguished from the other members of this group as follows:

1. Ocelli forming a distinct triangle, the lateral ones as far from the eye-margin as from the anterior ocellus, antennæ and palpi black......(Europe) *coronata* Becker.
   Ocelli forming a curved line, the lateral ones separated from the eye by only about their own diameter.........2
2. Third vein bare, except for a few bristly hairs near base; wings hyaline.................................3
   Third vein hairy for its entire length; wings tinged with brown......................(Europe) *ocellata* Schmitz.
3. Bristles near base of middle tibiæ opposite one another; forming a pair at the basal third; median bristles of lower frontal row nearer to one another than to the lateral bristle; tip of first vein midway between tip of costa and humeral cross-vein...............................4

[1]Contribution from the Entomological Laboratory of the Bussey Institution Harvard University, No. 238.

One of the bristles much nearer to the base of the tibia 5

4. Antennæ and palpi orange-yellow; third joint of male antenna fully as long as the width of the front; front tarsus of male greatly dilated, the second and third joints as broad as long. (North America) *johnsoni* Brues.

 Antennæ black, palpi yellow; third antennal joint of male considerably shorter than the width of the front; front tarsi of male less broadly dilated, the second and third joints decidedly longer than broad. (North America). *adamsi* sp. nov.

5. Front wider than high; bristles of middle tibia at basal third and basal fourth respectively; the middle row of frontal bristles curved upwards medially. (South) America)..............................*insperata* Brues.

 Front higher than wide; bristles of middle tibia at basal third and before middle respectively; middle row of frontal bristles straight. (Formosa).....*suspecta* Brues.

Hypocera adamsi sp. nov.

♂. Length 2.7 mm. Very robust; black, with only the palpi, front legs beyond the middle of the femora, and four posterior knees brownish yellow. Wings hyaline, venation dark brown. Front with a transverse carina below the median ocellus; above this highly polished and concave; ocellar bristles equidistant, the median pair larger and set midway between the ocellar carina and the upper margin of vertex; front below the carina shining, covered with sparse setigerous punctures; lateral bristles of lower row close to the eye, well above the median pair and farther from the median ones than the latter are from one another; upper row straight, its four bristles equidistant, the lateral one close to the eye; cheeks each with one long bristle. Antenna pyriform, the axis curved so that the top is slightly concave in profile; densely brown pilose; arista one-third longer than the third joint. Eyes not distinctly pilose; postocellar cilia strong, slightly longer above. Palpi small, compressed; with strong bristles, the apical one as long as the palpus. Thorax above and upper part of mesopleura very shining, clothed with fine recumbent bristly hairs which extend down on to the top of the pleura; sides of prothorax also hairy, with two bristles above the coxa and two very large ones below the spiracle. One pair of dorsocentral bristles; two scutellar bristles, the lateral ones reduced to hairs; posterior edge of mesonotum with six small bristles as long as the width of the scutellum. Abdomen above shining, faintly shagreened; sides sparsely clothed with recumbent hairs; second segment almost as long as the four following; sixth as long as the two preceding, clothed with sparse hairs. Legs very stout, the hind femora barely three times as long as wide; front tibia with a long bristle at the basal third, followed by a line of about eight small ones extending to the tip which bears two short spurs; middle tibia with a pair of large bristles at the basal third and two apical spurs, the longer one nearly half the length of the tibia; hind tibia with a single bristle externally just before the middle and with a pair externally at the tip in addition to the two subequal internally placed apical spurs; apex of tibia inwardly with four transverse combs of short bristles. Pleuræ shining, very finely shagreened. Costa extending barely beyond the middle of the wing; its cilia dense, but short, about twice as long as the thickness of the rather slender costal vein; humeral cross-vein distinct, but pale colored; mediastinal absent; first vein ending midway between the cross vein and tip of costa; third vein with several minute bristles at the base, but with no distinct hairs beyond (there are traces of a few minute hairs to be seen with the highest power of the binocular, but none like those seen in the species with this vein hairy); not widened apically; fourth vein originating well below the third, curved at base, straight beyond, ending at the wing tip; fifth and sixth complete, nearly straight; seventh obsolete.

♀. Length 3-3.2 mm. Essentially similar, except for the normal ovate antennæ, with the usual arista and slightly less elevated frontal margin.

Male type and four females paratypes collected by Dr. C. F. Adams at Atherton, Mo., October 4.

Gymnophora Macquart.

Quite recently Schmitz has distinguished four species of this genus from Europe (Jaarb. Naturhist. Genootsch. Limburg, for 1919, p. 132 1920). All of these have heretofore gone under the name of *Gymnophora arcuata* Meigen, as have also the North American members of the genus. On examining my collection in the light of Schmitz's paper, it is evident that the true *arcuata* does not occur in eastern North America, although I have a single male from Tacoma, Washington (A. L. Melander) which seems to be indistinguishable from a European specimen which according to Schmitz's description and figure is *arcuata*. Like many palæartic forms, it is probable that this one extends into the United States only along the Pacific Coast.

All other specimens, ranging from Kansas to Wisconsin and eastward are apparently *Gymnophora quartomollis* Schmitz (t. c., p. 133).

Aphiochaeta velutinipes sp. nov.

♀. Length 1.7 mm. Piceous, the abdomen above and the front almost black; humeri brown; the pleuræ becoming much lighter below till they are pale brown next to the coxæ, antennæ fuscous; palpi brownish yellow; legs pale brownish yellow on the coxæ but darker beyond, especially the four posterior pairs; wings hyaline, venation fuscous; halteres light brown. Front quadrate, with distinct ocellar tubercle and median frontal groove. Two pairs of proclinate bristles, the lower pair smaller and only two-thirds as far apart as the upper ones; lowest row of reclinate bristles forming a pair at each side of the front with the lateral bristle close to the eye and far above the inner one which is on a line with the lower post-antennal one, and half-way between it and the eye-margin; middle frontal row curved downwards medially, its median bristles farther from one another than from the lateral bristle which is very close to the eye; ocellar row of four. Antennæ small; arista conspicuously pubescent, one-third longer than the width of the front. Palpi of moderate size, with rather weak bristles. Mesonotum shining, with minute bristly hairs, longer behind and arranged in rather distinct longitudinal rows; one pair of dorsocentral bristles, scutellum broader than long, with four equally strong bristles. Propleura with a vertical band of bristly hairs below the spiracle, a long bristle above it and several bristles near the base of the coxa. Mesopleura bare. Second abdominal segment only one-third longer than the third, not bristly at the sides; fifth segment elongated. Fore tarsi not distinctly thickened, although not quite so slender as usual. Tibiæ finely hairy, but without trace of a dorsal seam or setulæ. Hind tibia with the dorsal surface somewhat expanded and flattened at the tip where it bears several transverse rows of minute comb-like setæ; hind metatarsus strongly spinose below. Costa long, extending distinctly beyond the middle of the wing, its cilia extremely minute and closely placed; first section almost as long as the second and third together; third two-fifths the length of the second; fourth vein strongly bent at the base, straight beyond; fifth with a sharp bend at the middle so that it runs parallel to the fourth; sixth straight; seventh curved, well removed from the margin. The light veins are all unusually thin and delicate.

Type from Atherton, Missouri, U. S. A., collected by Dr. C. F. Adams.

This species is extremely similar to *A. magnipalpis* Aldrich from the Lesser Antilles, and were it not for the peculiar chætotaxy of the front, I should be inclined to consider the two identical, especially as the fifth wing vein has the peculiar bend characteristic of *magnipalpis*. In the West Indian species the frontal bristles show the ordinary disposition, and the inner of the lowest reclinate row is not dropped below the post-antennals.

An examination of my series of *A. magnipalpis* has disclosed another species of this group, also with enlarged palpi in the male, but with normal wing venation. This is described below.

Aphiochaeta opaciventris sp. nov.

♂. Length 1.6 mm. Black, the mesonotum more or less piceous; pro- and mesopleuræ dark brown; front legs dilute piceous, other legs blackish brown. Wings hyaline, venation very dark; halteres black. Front distinctly broader than long; ocellar tubercle conspicuous; median groove poorly defined; four proclinate post-antennal bristles of nearly equal size; lower ones half as far apart as the upper which occupy one-fourth of the width of the front; inner bristle of lowest reclinate row on a level with the upper post-antennal and midway between it and the eye, lateral one considerably higher and close to the eye; upper row of four bristles strongly bowed downwards medially, the inner bristles separated by one-half the width of the front; ocellar row of four large bristles. Antennæ of moderate size, with the arista densely pubescent and one-half longer than the width of the front. Palpi greatly enlarged, as long as the height of the head and furnished below with very minute scattered bristles; in lateral view they are curved upwards and narrowed apically, less than one-sixth as thick as long; seen from below they curve outward anteriorly and are one-fourth as broad near the base as long. Mesonotum quite shining, sparsely hairy, the hairs more or less bristly behind; with one pair of dorsocentral bristles and several long bristles along the lateral margin. Scutellum slightly wider than long, its hind margin strongly arcuate and bearing four long, equal bristles, forming a pair near each lateral angle. Abdomen opaque, velvety black, the segments all of about equal length and without noticeable bristles along the sides. Hypopygium more or less globose, strongly asymetrical; nearly bare above, but conspicuously clothed with rather dense bristles below, on the left side and at apex; apical lamella small and with very inconspicuous bristly hairs. Propleura with a dense brush of bristles above, a close-set row along the posterior margin and several longer ones below near the base of the coxa. Mesopleura subshining, without bristles above. Legs quite slender, clothed with fine bristly hairs, but without cilia or setulæ on any of the tibiæ; hind tibiæ each with a single slender apical spur; inwardly near the tip with several very oblique rows of fine comb-like bristles; metatarsus below with five or six similar, nearly transverse rows. Anterior tarsi long and very slender. Costa slightly but distinctly more than half the wing-length, with short dense cilia;

first section barely longer than the other two together; third fully one third as long as the second and as long as the second vein; fourth vein feebly curved on basal half, straight beyond; fifth weakly sinuous on basal half, straight beyond, without a sharp bend before the middle, sixth and seventh nearly straight, the latter faint.

Type from Grenada, B. W. I. (Brues), 1910.

This species is at once distinguished from *A. magnipalpis* Aldrich from the same island, by the much more slender legs, opaque velvety black abdomen, normally curved fifth vein and by the complete absence of any cilia on the middle tibiæ. The palpi although similarly enlarged in the male, are more slender than in *magnipalpis*.

A. opaciventris does not closely resemble any European or North American species. Any of these which might be other wise confused with it have the fore tarsi enlarged.

Aphiochaeta giraudii Egger.

This European species has already been reported from North America by Mrs. Slosson on the basis of specimens determined by Coquillett. It appears that this identification was incorrect, however, and Malloch removed the species from the North American list in 1912.[1]

I have a male, however, collected by Mr. C. W. Johnson at Fort Kent, Maine which is undoubtedly this species. The only difference that I can detect is the shorter basal section of the costa which equals but is no longer than the second and third together. The specimen is rather large and has the second row of setulæ on the hind tibia well developed.

[1]Proc. U. S. Nat. Mus., vol. 43, p. 451.

SOME LIFE HISTORY NOTES ON THE BLACK WIDOW SPIDER *LATRODECTUS MACTANS*.[1]

By Phil Rau.

St. Louis, Mo.

This spider in livery of shining black decorated with bright red blotches, and called by Comstock the black widow spider, is often found in the vicinity of St. Louis under rocks and debris in sunny pastures. One specimen, with its round, white egg-case, was taken from her web high up in a corner of a barn on June 23, 1922.

In captivity she made four more of these egg-cases, on June 24, July 12, August 4 and August 15 respectively. After the making of each, her abdomen was shrunken to about half its former size, but it soon returned to normal proportions. Despite the fact that this individual had not access to the male, after its capture, the eggs in all five cocoons were fertile; this circumstance shows that it is not necessary for mating to precede each case of oviposition.

All the young in each cocoon emerged from one hole the size of a pin-head, probably made by the first restless spiderling The emerging young of two cocoons were counted; one gave forth 101, and the other 92 spiderlings. The young at emerging do not resemble the mother, whose color is black and red, but they are all of a medium shade of brown. While the young do not spin nests of any certain form, they do spin webs of criss-cross threads to which they cling. Fig. 1 shows a young spider (enlarged four times) clinging to these strands. In the glass cage in which they were kept, they almost always rested with the ventral surface of the body upwards, and with four or more legs holding on to the strands of criss-cross silk, as figured above.

While one seldom sees a nest of definite contour when one finds these adult spiders under stones, here confined in a large glass box (an unused aquarium), this spider made a large hollow

[1] Identified by Mr. J. H. Emerton.

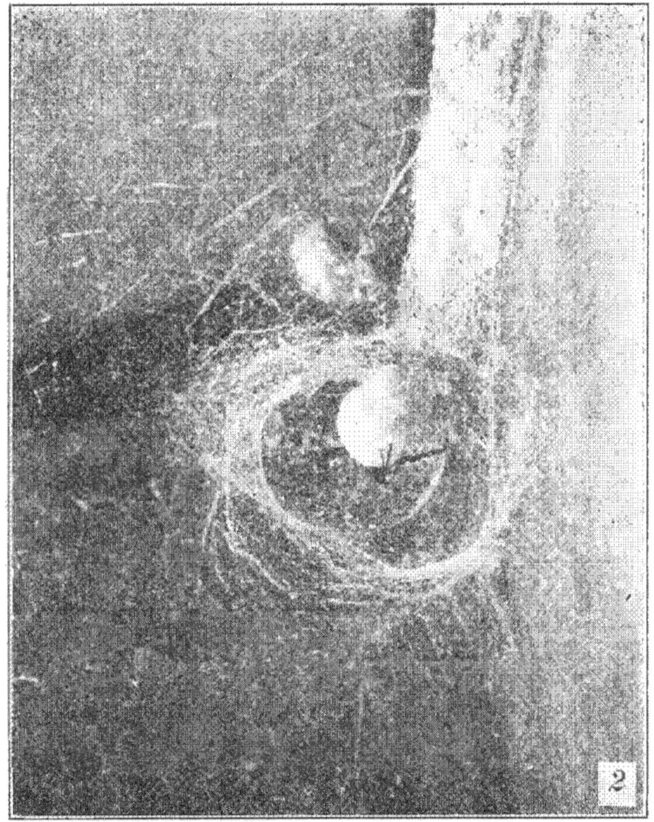

RAU—LIFE HISTORY OF LATRODECTUS.

nest in which she spent all of her time except when prowling. Here too she made the cocoons, and here they reposed until such a time as the mother chose to kick them out. Fig. 2. shows the nest, natural size, with two coccons, and the mother clinging to the lower one; just above is the larva of a mud-wasp which I dropped there for food. The spider was fed wasp larvæ of various species, white grub worms and grasshopper nymphs in this way, by dropping them on the web. The spider would always carry these morsels to the bottom of her cup-like den and spin a web around the food. The manoeuvers were always carried on at night, however. The young were less timid, and would feed upon the wasp larva at various times during the day. This was done by merely standing upon it and sucking out its juices. There was no evidence of the very young spiders covering the prey with web. The mother spider occasionally fetches the prey from some little distance and carries it into the nest. I once placed the quiescent prepupa of the mud-dauber on the floor of the cage three inches away; during the night she removed this to her nest. This shows not only that she can move loads as large as herself over and through her webby entanglements, but also that her prey need not be active to attract her attention.

The spider kept the nest very tidy, and carried out all the dried remains of her food that had accumulated. She did not do this every day, but occasionally when the accumulation of rubbish became conspicuous she turned in for the general housecleaning. I once arrived in time to see the latter part of one of these affairs at 6 a. m. This activity is also usually a night affair, but this time she did not finish until after day-break. Just as I arrived, she took up her last fragment, a dried grasshopper nymph, from the bottom of her lair, carried it by a circuitous route up to the rim of the hollow and cast it overboard where it dropped to the floor. She carried it in a queer fashion; with one hind leg she held it close to the tip of her abdomen while she slowly picked her way among the criss-cross threads of her web, until she reached a point from where it could be dropped below. All of the debris had been carried out during the night, and most of it had been carried some distance away. Most of the rubbish lay scattered at a distance of from eight to fifteen inches from the nest.

Her actions in regard to cleanliness appealed to me as commendable until I discovered that in her zeal she had also carried out and thrown away her own cocoon which she had just made; I wondered if she was not "throwing out the baby with the bath." Such a mental lapse or miscarriage of instinct caught my attention at once, and I watched for developments. But during the next few days, her behavior exhibited nothing short of maternal solicitude. As related above, in her early morning house-cleaning, she carried out the cocoon to a distance of eight inches, where it lay apparently discarded. The second morning thereafter I found the nest clean and the debris still scattered where she had dropped it. At 8 a. m. I dropped into the criss-cross webs above her den two wasp larvæ and a horse-fly, to tempt her appetite. At 9 p. m. the same day, I found the food items just where I had placed them, but to my astonishment, the cocoon that had lain on the floor eight inches away was now in the web, about two inches above her hollow nest, and the mother was clinging tenaceously to it. I promptly withdrew to avoid alarming her. My interpretation was that she was carrying the cocoon back to her den; an hour later when I again switched on the light, I found the cocoon nicely at rest on the bottom of the nest, and the mother clinging (I wish I dared say affectionately) to it. Her memory of her lost cocoon never failed her during the period of two and one-half days.

Quite likely the instinct-monger will interpret this behavior as a matter of accident; he will say that instinctively the spider carries food to the nest, and merely grabbed the cocoon in error. But I repeat that on top of the web were still entangled, three choice pieces of food that had remained untouched since morning, but she did not drag these nearby articles of food into her nest, but went afar and brought in the cocoon which she, in the heat of house-cleaning excitment, had discarded. Furthermore, let anyone who doubts the existence of maternal instinct here look at the picture and see the mother with all her legs entwined about this little ball, and ask him if he can imagine a spider clasping a food morsel in loving embrace for long hours at a time in this fashion; then he will know whether or not this mother herself knew the difference. He will agree with me that in the field of instincts, going in quest of food and taking care of the young arouse two distinct and remote responses. I therefore maintain that, with certain maternal instincts as a foundation, this mother spider, by the aid of associated memory, modified or enlarged certain inherent capacities to gain certain ends, although I doubt if she would have been able to recognize her own cocoon among others.

During the entire next day, whenever I visited the cage, this mother was clinging to her egg-case, and up to the last visit the food had not been removed from the webs where I had placed it. At dawn of the next day (July 30), I observed that the wasp larva was moved nearer to the den and was much reduced in size, and so shrivelled that I felt sure that the spider had drained its body juices during the night. Strange to relate, the cocoon was carried out again during the night, taken from the center of the hollow cup and hung in the webs an inch above the nest. The Spider seemed, however, to be almost playing with the egg-case, for at 10 o'clock the same night when I paid her a visit, it was again back in the hollow of her nest. On August 1, when it was next observed, the cocoon was again out on the open web, two inches above the nest; the next day it was still in the same position. On August 4, the fourth egg-case had been made; the mother tightly clung to this in the hollow of her nest, while the one referred to previously had not been moved.

The third cocoon, the one left outside the den, gave forth 92 young on August 13, after a period of incubation of 32 days. During the night this egg-case had once more been carried away and dropped several inches away from the web, but I have no way of knowing whether this was done before or after the hatching occured. An actual moult occurs in the young spiders before they emerge, for on opening a cocoon, one finds in addition to the empty egg shells the tiny shedding skins of the spiderlings.

The fifth and last egg-case was made on August 15. Just before the event, the opening of the hollow nest had been extended upward for about an inch. This mother died on August 25, ten days after completing her egg-case.

A second spider was taken on August 9, and died on September 20. Only fragmentary notes were made on this one. During this period she deposited four egg-cases, and all were found in a row in the corner of her cage among a tangled mass of threads that she made. While she had ample space, she made no elaborate or shapely nest as did the first.

This species is regarded as highly venomous, as are other species of this genus, and instances of fatalities are recorded by Warburton (Cambridge Natural History), Comstock (Spider Book), and Riley and Johannsen (Handbook of Medical Entomology). While the fact of its fatality to man is still in controversy, however, certain experiments carried on with mammals,[1] such as cats, dogs and guinea-pigs, show conclusively that this spider as well as others of the genus *Latrodectus* possesses a poison which paralyzes the heart and central nervous system.

[1]Handbook of Medical Entomology, p. 16. 1915.

CONCERNING THE AVAILABILITY OF CERTAIN TAXONOMIC CHARACTERS AND THEIR SIGNIFICANCE. (DIPTERA).[1]

By C. Howard Curran.

Ottawa, Ontario, Canada.

During the past year or more I have been engaged at various intervals in searching for new characters available in the classification of Diptera, and these efforts have resulted, in some cases, in the selection of characters which will evidently prove of value in due time. Mr. J. R. Malloch has pointed out that the Tachinidæ are readily separated from the remaining groups of the Muscoidea by the presence of a strong convexity beneath the scutellum. From an examination of various families I find that this development is limited to three of them. I would suggest that this portion of the anatomy be termed, for convenience, the "metascutellum."

In a paper now in the hands of the printer, I have pointed out that I consider the Syrphidæ more closely allied to the Stratiomyidæ than is generally supposed and also their evident relationship to the Calyptratæ. As the families Stratiomyidæ, Syrphidæ and Tachinidæ (inclusive of the Dexiidæ) are the three families known to me which possess a metascutellum, considerable confirmation of my previous conclusions has been secured. The possession of many characters in common by these three families would appear to indicate a much closer relationship than has heretofore been accorded them by taxonomists.

It appears that the Tachinidæ and Syrphidæ are both evolved from an ancestor more or less of the Stratiomyid type, the three families possibly having a common ancestor. At any rate it seems probable that the two first mentioned families originated within a reasonably short time of each other from common stock or very closely related forms.

[1]Contribution from the Division of Systematic Entomology, Entomological Branch, Dept. of Agric., Ottawa.

If we accept the foregoing suggestions as being more or less correct, several families—the Dolichopodidæ, Therevidæ, Asilidæ, Empididæ, and a few others, are left without indications of their origin, and it must be admitted that it is difficult to associate these families with any of those usually placed lower in the scale. However, there can be little doubt that these and allied families form a natural group and it is not difficult to trace true or fancied relationships from one family to the other. It may be necessary to eliminate the Tabanidæ from the line of direct descent and to consider for the present that they form a natural branch, therefore concluding that the Asilid group, through the Empididæ, are related to such forms as the Bibionidæ or even the Blepharoceridæ.

Malloch has recently pointed out that the Pyrgotinæ are evidently related to the Conopidæ, a view in which I concur. This indicates rather forcibly the relationship of the Pipunculidæ and Acalyptratæ.

If we consider the matter from the viewpoint of squamal[1] development, we find that the squamæ are large in the Tabanidæ, Stratiomyidæ, Syrphidæ, Muscoids and Tachinidæ, at least in so far as many members of these families are concerned. The exact value of this structure from the taxonomic point of view has not yet been determined. I am inclined to believe that it is a development more or less confined to robust species which are, or have been in the past, hoverers. Such a development seems to have been induced in flies which bred in liquid media, as the large squamæ have disappeared to a very large extent in those Syrphidæ which do not pass their early stages in such surroundings. If the squamæ have developed due to this habit, they must be looked upon merely as indicating habit and cannot be considered too seriously by the taxonomist.

Further, in connection with the squamæ, it should be pointed out that a character which is almost universal with the Stratiomyidæ occurs in the families enumerated in the preceding paragraph, but is not general. This is the presence of fine hairs or sparse pile on the upper surface of the lower squama, a character which is very evidently derived from the pubescence usually found, but which has disappeared in many Tachinidæ. These hairs are found in some Stratiomyidæ, *Syrphus* s. s., *Bombyliomyia* of the Tachinidæ, and several Calliphorid genera. Here again we have a character of doubtful value taxonomically, but one which might be considered to indicate relationship, and at the same time one which may be used to great advantage in the treatment of several genera.

It should be remembered that there are many characters not of true generic or family significance which are nevertheless of the greatest importance as aids in determination, and it seems advisable in very many cases to treat these as of generic importance merely for our convenience. If, by the use of such characters, we split up several genera, placing many of their representatives in a single genus, and eliminate other supposed genera, we are simplifying the determination of many species; it is surely advisable to use such a character. If our classification is such that genera are of but little assistance in the determination of species, or are not truly separable from each other, it is evident that we need a change in methods:—either that, or the elimination of genera entirely and the use of family names in a generic sense. A superabundance of genera is almost an equivalent of the foregoing condition. Perhaps the best example of this latter condition is to be found in the Tachinidæ where more than one thousand genera have been proposed, and at least half that number are recognized. It is not likely that more than one hundred genera should be recognized in this family if we are to have a classification of the maximum assistance in determination of the species. Characters being investigated at present indicate that several genera in the Tachinidæ and Dexiidæ can be lumped together to great advantage, or at any rate isolated into very distinct and easily recognized groups.

The above information is submitted in the hope that work along the lines indicated may be stimulated. There is much to be done but one must proceed carefully in dealing with a subject of this nature, taking pains not to overemphasize the value of such characters as have been enumerated, and to investigate as fully as possible before recording results.

DORATURA STYLATA BOHM IN MASSACHUSETTS

By Geo. W. Barber.

Cereal and Forage Insect Investigations, Bureau of Entomology, U. S. Department of Agriculture.

The discovery of *Doratura stylata* Bohm. in Massachusetts adds an interesting leafhopper to our constantly growing list of insect immigrants. During 1923 three specimens of this species have been taken as follows:

A brachypterous female, Marshfield, Mass., August 3.

A brachypterous male, Plymouth, Mass., August 1.

A macropterous female, Plymouth, Mass., September 11.

Specimens collected in Plymouth were taken by sweeping in a cranberry bog grown up to grass, the specimen from Marshfield by sweeping coarse grass in a fresh water marsh.

This species is adequately described and figured by Melichar 1896 (Cicadinen von Mittel-Europa, p. 210). It is apparently not uncommon both in continental Europe and in England. Buckton 1891 (Monograph of the British Cicadæ or Tettigidæ Vol. 2, p. 20) notes that the macropterous forms are extremely rare.

PROCEEDINGS OF THE CAMBRIDGE ENTOMOLOGICAL CLUB.

The meetings of the Club were resumed on September 11, 1923. Prof. Z. P. Metcalf of the North Carolina Agricultural Station who had spent the summer in Boston read a paper on "The Station Entomologist" from the various standpoints of the public, the profession and the entomologist himself.

A letter was read from Mr. Austin Clark, a former member who had been in the neighborhood of Boston part of the summer and had collected butterflies especially *Feniseca tarquinius* which was unusually abundant.

Mr. C. W. Johnson had investigated the 17-year Cicada on Cape Cod and found it abundant along the shore between Falmouth and Hyannis and northward to Bourne and Sandwich. It was also reported near Plymouth and down the Cape between Wellfleet and Truro. Its first appearance was about June 1 and mating and egg-laying continued from June 25 to the last of July. Mr. Metcalf showed young Cicadas which hatched from oak twigs brought from Cape Cod.

Mr. Johnson showed the mud nests of the wasp, *Ancistrocerus birenimaculatus* and a letter from Mr. Zeissig who had raised the wasps and numerous parasites which were exhibited.

Mr. Plath told about his summer's work on bumblebees of which he had 62 colonies under observation including two species not before found. Some of the nests were destroyed by a skunk which was caught and kept for some time in confinement and its habits in relation to the bees studied.

At the meeting of October 9 several members gave accounts of their summer work. Dr. Bequaert of the Department of Tropical Medicine of the Harvard Medical School spent part of the summer at Columbus, Ohio to study the collection of Tabanidæ of Prof. Hine. Field excursions were made in the neighborhood and a new Tabanus was found, allied to *T. longus*. A rare fossorial wasp, *Rhinopsis melanognatha* and a cyrtid fly *Acrocera subfasciata* were found on the bark of trees.

Mr. C. W. Johnson exhibited the tropical *Thysania zenobia* taken by J. D. Smith at Holbrook, Mass., September 9, the second one found in New England.

Mr. Johnson showed a fly from Mt. Desert which is probably the European *Spania nigra* which has a very variable venation.

Mr. J. H. Emerton gave an account of the summer collecting of spiders on the farm of Nathan Banks on Winthrop Pond in Holliston, Mass. Over 160 species were taken between April and October.

Mr. Plath showed some old nests of bumblebees which contained large numbers of larvæ of parasites. A nest had lately been found in the Arnold Arboretum four feet under ground with an entrance tunnel ten feet long. Thirty female bees were found hibernating in the earth near the mouth of the tunnel.

At the November meeting Prof. C. T. Brues read a paper on the triungulin larva of a meloid beetle from the Galapagos Islands. The peculiar mandibles were described which are modified for holding to the hairs of bees on which the larvæ are carried to the nest where they become parasites of the bee larvæ. The paper concluded with a review of the triungulins of Meloidæ and Stylops.

Prof. W. M. Wheeler followed with a paper on the planidium larvæ of various Hymenoptera and Diptera. Some brilliantly colored Chalcids were found in ant's nests where they grew up as parasites in the ant larvæ, having been brought into the nest in the planidium stage attached to adult ants. The complicated life histories of several species were described.

Mr. C. W. Johnson spoke of the European *Muscina pascuorum* which was so surprisingly abundant in the autumn of 1922. This year only a few were found in the fall and spring in Attleboro, Brookline, Walpole and Worcester. Specimens had been found in the fall and spring under loose bark indicating that the insects hibernate as adults in such places.

Dr. Jos. Bequaert reported an article in the Annals of the Natal Museum, So. Africa, October 1923 on the eating of small fishes by a spider of the genus Thalassius allied to our Salonedes. The paper is illustrated with photographs, one of which shows a spider in the act of catching a fish near the surface of the water.

Dr. Bequaert described a nest of wasps from Panama in which the paper cells were closed, not as usual by convex caps but by flat covers a little inside the mouth of the cell.

At the December meeting Prof. C. T. Brues gave an account of his last summer's automobile excursion from Boston to Yellowstone Park accompanied by Mrs. Brues and their son and daughter. A tent was carried and they camped at night throughout the trip. Their route was through Massachusetts, New York and Ohio to Chicago, thence to St. Paul, Minn., and the Bad Lands of North Dakota. At the Yellowstone Park they met Prof. A. L. Melander from the Washington State College and together visited the geysers, springs and lakes through the park giving special attention to the plants and insects of the hot springs in some of which dipterous larvæ were found at temperatures from 90° to 130°. Photographs were shown of the springs colored from nature by Mrs. Brues.

CAMBRIDGE ENTOMOLOGICAL CLUB

A regular meeting of the Club is held on the second Tuesday of each month (July, August and September excepted) at 7.45 p. m. at the Bussey Institution, Forest Hills, Boston. The Bussey Institution is one block from the Forest Hills station of both the elevated street cars and the N. Y., N. H. & H. R. R. Entomologists visiting Boston are cordially invited to attend.

PSYCHE

A JOURNAL OF ENTOMOLOGY

ESTABLISHED IN 1874

VOL. XXXI OCTOBER 1924 No. 5

CONTENTS

PSYCHE is published bi-monthly, the issues appearing in February, April, June, August, October and December. Subscription price, per year, payable in advance: $2.00 to subscribers in the United States, Canada or Mexico; foreign postage, 15 cents extra. Single copies, 40 cents.

Cheques and remittances should be addressed to Treasurer, Cambridge Entomological Club, Bussey Institution, Forest Hills, Boston 30, Mass.

Orders for back volumes, missing numbers, notices of change of address, etc., should be sent to Cambridge Entomological Club, Bussey Institution, Forest Hills, Boston, 30, Mass.

IMPORTANT NOTICE TO CONTRIBUTORS.

Manuscripts intended for publication, books intended for review, and other editorial matter, should be addressed to Professor C. T. Brues, Bussey Institution, Forest Hills, Boston, 30 Mass.

Authors contributing articles over 8 printed pages in length will be required to bear a part of the extra expense, for additional pages. This expense will be that of typesetting only, which is about $2.00 per page. The actual cost of preparing cuts for all illustrations must be borne by contributors; the expense for full page plates from line drawings is approximately $5.00 each, and for full page half-tones, $7.50 each: smaller sizes in proportion.

AUTHOR'S SEPARATES.

Reprints of articles may be secured by authors, if they are ordered before, or at the time proofs are received for corrections. The cost of these will be furnished by the Editor on application.

Entered as second-class mail matter at the Post Office at Boston, Mass. Acceptance for mailing at special rate of postage provided in Section 1103, Act of October 3, 1917, authorized on June 29, 1918.

PSYCHE

VOL. XXXI. OCTOBER 1924 No. 5

BIOLOGICAL NOTES ON *LETHOCERUS AMERICANUS* (LEIDY.)[1]

By William E. Hoffman.

University of Minnesota, St. Paul.

Although studied since 1847 when described by Leidy, very little has been written about the life history or habits of this "Electric-light Bug" or Giant Waterbug. This is rather surprising in view of the fact that its distribution is quite general and that it has been a favorite with biologists and naturalists for a long time, as evidenced by the many references to it in the literature. Its extreme voraciousness and the relation of this trait to fish culture is another reason for expecting that its life history might have been worked out.

In December of 1921 several specimens of this species were taken from their winter quarters by the writer. They were found near St. Paul in a small stream connecting two lakes. The water in this little stream of a hundred and fifty yards in length and about five yards in breadth, comes out of a long concrete conduit. As the water leaves the conduit it has considerable current but it becomes sluggish before it enters the lake. The current at this point, however, is sufficient to keep the water from freezing over during winter. The bugs were found under somewhat varying conditions. In the center of the stream they were found buried some five or six inches deep in the layer of disintergrated plant material forming the bed of the stream. The water at this point was over two feet deep. At the edge of the stream they were found among Typha roots. Here the water was but a few inches deep and the bugs were buried to a depth of

[1]Published with the approval of the Director as Paper No. 481 of the Journal Series of the Minnesota Agricultural Experiment Station.

two or three inches only. The bugs appeared to be dead when first taken but they soon responded to the warmth of the hands as shown by slight movements. They were placed in collecting cans and by the time we returned to the laboratory they were fairly active. Transferred to water of room temperature, in a short while they were as active as those taken during the warmer part of the year. They were kept in a glass vessel in the laboratory for a period of several months, but died before an aquarium suitable for the deposition of eggs was provided. During this period they received an occasional feed of small sunfish and small catfish.

On July first, 1923, a large Lethocerus nymph was secured from a small pond near University Farm campus. It was taken while dredging at the edge of a pond with a heavy water net. The nymph was feeding on a tadpole larger than itself and did not release its victim while it was being taken from the net and placed in a collecting can. In the laboratory it was placed in a glass vessel which was four inches deep and ten inches in diameter. This container was half filled with water and a little vegetation added. The nymph fed greedily upon beefsteak, grasshoppers, tadpoles, young frogs, young fish, flies and other things that were offered. On July fifth it molted. The cast skin measured dorsally as follows: Length along median line, 33 mm.; width of head across eyes, 6 mm.; width of posterior margin of prothorax, 10 mm.; width of posterior margin of metathorax, 14 mm.; width of abdomen across base of second segment, 16 mm. (widest portion of bug). Immediately upon molting it was of a very delicate yellow and green color and seemed quite frail. It was so translucent that it was easy to see what was going on within the bug. When observed a few hours later it had taken on the color it had previous to molting.

About seven hours after molting food was offered and it ate twelve large flies and two meadow grasshoppers. No doubt it it would have eaten more had they been offered. On the afternoon of the following day while out collecting, two tadpoles considerably larger than the nymph were secured, so one of these was offered. At the end of an hour nothing remained of the tadpole but the shriveled skin and some dark mud-like material in the digestive tract. The second tadpole was then offered to the bug with the same result. I was curious to know how much more it might eat but refrained from offering more food as I still had a vivid recollection of what happened to a number of Ranatra that were allowed to gorge themselves. These bugs had had no food for several weeks and then one evening offered all the flies they could eat. The next morning eleven of the thirteen water scorpions were dead. It was at first thought there might have been something toxic about the flies and later the experiment was tried again. This resulted in the death of all five bugs used in the test. Still later the same experiment was tried again, this time using cockroaches and damsel-fly nymphs. Again all the bugs died. This food ordinarily is very fine for these bugs so evidently it was the effect of a large amount of food being taken after a fast which caused death. When they have been fed more regularly no evil effect seems to occur, even though they have all they can possibly consume.

On the thirteenth of July a move was made to the State Fish Hatchery at St. Peter, where some lake studies were to be conducted. Some anxiety was felt about successfully transporting the Lethocerus nymph, but it made the trip apparently none the worse for the experience. The trip was made by Ford, and this insect along with nymphs and adults of more than a dozen species of waterbugs, came through without mishap. The distance was only eighty-five miles but the life histories were "packed up" for about fifteen hours. Before packing for the trip the water was drained from the life history jars, leaving the bugs upon the wet sand.

In its new home the Belostomid was fed mostly on young trout. Two 3½ inch trout were given every other day, with an occasional feed of grasshoppers, crickets and flies. It was fed trout principally, because the laboratory was located in a trout hatchery and trout became the most available food source. Every day the vegetation near the hatchery was "swept" for soft-bodied insects which were used as food for Velia, Microvelia, Gerrids, Nepa, Ranatra and other bugs in rearing. Grasshoppers and other large insects were often taken inadvertently and accordingly were given to the Lethocerus. The bug would refuse to take food the day following a meal of two sizeable trout. This rather surpised me for I had always supposed Lethocerus would kill because of a vicious nature, whether hungry or not.

Adults likewise would not kill food excepting when they were hungry enough to eat what they killed. The adults did not feed as often as did the nymphs. It would be expected that the adults would not require as much food as the growing nymphs but this may not be the only reason for their smaller food requirement. There may exist here a condition found in the family Nepidæ. Nepa adults caught afield consistently eat less than the adults reared in the laboratory. Two factors perhaps are responsible in part or altogether for this condition. The food may not suit them as well as what they secure in nature, and they were probably used to receiving food less frequently in nature.

On the twentieth of July the nymph died. Since there was no indication of any unusual condition in the breeding jar it is believed the bug was ready to undergo another molt. As is true of insects in general the period of ecdysis is a critical one for waterbugs. That this mortality occurs at molting time in nature was evidenced by an examination of dead Microvelia nymphs taken afield. Measurements of dead nymphs of the several instars were made and found to correspond with those of the reared specimens just previous to molting time. In addition to this specimens were often found in which the skin had already split. It would be hard to determine whether the death rate is higher with insects reared in captivity or with those reared in nature. Hungerford (1919) in discussing the biology of the water boatman *Palmacorixa buenoi* Abbot remarked, "Under laboratory conditions, molting appears to be a precarious process." I found that to be the case with Ranatra, and it is especially true of the later instars. A number of specimens of three different species of Ranatra were isolated for rearing purposes, not one of which reached maturity.

At death the Lethocerus measured as follows: (all measurements dorsal): Length along median line 45 mm.; width of head across eyes, 5.5 mm.; width of posterior margin of prothorax, 13.5 mm.; width across extremities of mesothoracic wing pads,

20 mm.; width of abdomen across base of second segment, a fraction more than 20 mm.

That this nymph was of the last instar there can be no doubt as it was practically as large as some of the smaller adult Lethocerus in my collection. A comparison of the size and shape of the wing pads with those of a fifth instar *Belostoma flumineum* Say strengthens the opinion that such is the case. In the following discussion the next to the last and the last nymphal stages will be referred to as the fourth and fifth respectively, but for reasons to be given below, this may not be the proper designation.

The shape of the fourth and fifth instar nymphs is noticeably different. The widest measurement of the thorax in the fourth stage is the width through the hind angles of the metanotum (tips of rudimentary wing pads), which flare out slightly, while the greatest thoracic width of the fifth stage nymph is across the mesothoracic wing pads at a distance of about three millimeters before their tips. In the fourth stage the greatest abdominal width is two millimeters more than the greatest thoracic width. The mesothoracic wing pads lack about 1 mm. extending to the hind angles of the metanotum. These angles are not yet differentiated into wing pads. In the fifth instar nymph the greatest abdominal width is equal to the width across the tips of the mesothoracic wing pads, which now extend slightly beyond the hind angles of the metanotum. In this stage the hind angles of the metanotum are clearly differentiated into wing pads. The greatest width of the bug is now across the thorax instead of the abdomen. Our attention has been called to the disappearance of one of the anterior tarsal claws during the last molt. Another difference between nymph and adult is that the nymph has a dense growth of hair on the ventral side of the abdomen, while the same region in the adult is glabrous and devoid of hair.

Weed (1897) figures the "Last stage of nymph." This undoubtedly is a drawing of a fourth stage nymph. It does not agree with the specimen before the writer, in that the shape of the wing pads is different. However, it could not possibly be a last nymphal stage.

Since Belostoma has five nymphal stages it would be expected that Lethocerus would likewise have that number. This, however, does not necessarily follow, for in the Nepidæ we have a different number of instars in the different genera, Ranatra and Curicta having five, while Nepa has but four. Roesel (1755) figured five nymphal stages for the European *Nepa cinera* L. If we can accept as authentic these notes on the biology of *N. cinera*, we have this difference in the number of instars occurring within the genus. This is known to be the case in the family Veliidæ, where in the genus Microvelia we have some species with five instars while others have only four.

Since the fifth instar is of fifteen or more days duration it is evident that the growing period, the period of great food consumption, extends over a considerable period. The progeny of one or two pairs of adults could do a great deal of damage in a fish pond during their developmental period. The fish culturists are surely justified in their denunciation of this form as a menace to young fish.

Literature is replete with references pertaining to the ferociousness of this bug. A very remakable account of Lethocerus attacking a fish was recently related to the writer by Professor J. R. Parker of the University of Montana. His statement follows: "some time in September 1923, Mr. C. A. Morton of Bozeman with his family was camped on a small creek near Ovando, Montana. Early in the morning Mr. Morton and another man went out along the creek to get some fish for breakfast. In clear, still water they saw a trout about ten or twelve inches in length and while watching the trout they noticed a giant waterbug lying aimlessly on the surface of the water, except for one leg which it appeared to be waving in a manner to attract the attenton of the fish. It appeared to be successful in this for the trout grabbed the waterbug by the leg that had been moving whereupon the bug raised up and sunk its beak into the top of the fish's head. The trout began to swim excitedly in circles and jumped clear of the water several times. It finally turned over on its back. Mr. Morton waded out into the water and caught the fish to which the bug was still attached by its beak. He carried the fish back to camp and the bug did not release its hold until half way there. Mr. Morton said there were so many skeletons of fish in this creek that they had hesitated to eat them, but after seeing this performance they no longer hesitated to eat them, thinking the waterbugs were the cause of the death of the fish. The stream was plentifully stocked with eastern brook trout and they had no trouble in getting a good string."

Lethocerus adults are strong fliers, and for this reason their distribution is quite general. Since these bugs are frequently taken at night it is likely they do most of their migrating at night. *Belostoma flumineum* Say, on the other hand is not taken at night. Leidy (1847) says both Lethocerus and Belostoma fly by night. In several years collecting the writer has never taken Belostoma at night although it has been taken on the wing during mid-day, far from any body of water.

Undoubtedly there is but one generation per year, although there is no assurance that the adults may not live over the second winter and lay eggs the second summer. If this were the case the potential damage of a pair of these bugs is indeed great. The writer would not be surprised to learn that many of the waterbugs produce eggs the second season. He now has specimens of *Velia watsoni* Drake which are over eighteen months old. These bugs produced eggs for a period of eight months last year and now after a winter rest of a few months, have again commenced laying eggs. There seems to be no reason why this species should not do the same in nature. It is true that in nature their food problem is not simple and enemies have to be reckoned with, but on the other hand they no doubt become inactive during the winter and perhaps age very little if any at this time. Those kept over winter in the laboratory (at room temperature) do not hibernate, consequently their greater activity probably shortens their lives. Further observations on this form are highly desirable.

The eggs of *Lethocerus americanus* Leidy have been searched for during the last two seasons but have not been found. The eggs of this species were first figured in 1868 (American Entomologist, Vol. I, pp. 61 and 62) as "The eggs of the Hellgrammite Fly." They were described as "oval, about the size of a radish seed, and of a pale color, with some dark markings. They are usually deposited in a squarish patch upon reeds and other aquatic plants overhanging the water." This was an unsigned article, presumably written by the editors, Benjamin D. Walsh and Charles V. Riley. Very much the same account was published in the Fifth Missouri Report by Dr. Riley. The same figure was used but this time it was turned upside down. Packard in his "Guide to the Study of Insects" also published the account accompanied by the figure. Weed (1889) tells of finding a mass of Lethocerus eggs while collecting on the outskirts of Lansing, Michigan, July 3, 1882. He says, "I found a mass of eggs,.. . . . . beneath a board lying at the water's edge. The eggs gave evidence of having been freshly laid, and beside them was a living *Belostoma americanum*." In this connection an observation made by Professor Parker of Montana is of interest. He found giant waterbugs guarding their eggs on the bank of a small slough. His statement follows: "This was on June 11, 1921, at Ronan, Montana. The eggs were stuck to the grassy bank about a foot above the water. The slough was premanent, being one of the hundreds of pot-holes which dot the Flathead Indian Reservation. As I approached the eggs the male started for the water but was captured. The female assumed a fighting attitude with the front pair of legs extended and ready for action. Whenever anything was brought near her she struck viciously at it. Finally she was allowed to grab a stick and hung so tenaciously to this that I was able to shake her off into a cyanide bottle. The eggs were taken to Bozeman and hatched in the laboratory on the 15th of June. The young nymphs lived for about two weeks and then died." The writer has examined one of the adults and determined it as *Lethocerus americanus* Leidy.

Literature Cited.

Hungerford, H. B. 1919. The Biology and Ecology of Aquatic and Semiaquatic Hemiptera. Kansas Univ. Sci. Bull., vol. XI, pp. 1-341, 1919. (p. 223, says molting under laboratory conditions appears to be a precarious process.)

Leidy, Joseph. 1847. History and Anatomy of the Hemipterous Genus Belostoma. Journ. Acad. Sci. Philadelphia, pp. 57-67, plate x.

Packard, A. S. 1889. Guide to the Study of Insects. Ninth edition, 1889, p. 607, fig. 598.

Riley, C. V. 1873. Fifth Annual Report on the Noxious, Beneficial and other Insects of the State of Missouri, pp. 142-145.

Roesel, A. J. 1775. Der monatlich herausgegebenen Insectenbelustigung, dritter Theil, etc.

Weed, Clarence M. 1889. Bull. Ohio Agric. Expt. Sta., Tech. Ser., vol. 1., pp. 4-17.

1897. Life Histories of American Insects, pp. 4-7. (Fig. 2 shows "last stage of nymph.")

NEW NORTHEASTERN DEXIINÆ (DIPTERÆ; TACHINIDÆ).

By Luther S. West.

Department of Entomology, Cornell University, Ithaca, N. Y.

The following preliminary descriptions are offered at the present time in order that the species names may be included by Mr. C. W. Johnson in his "List of New England Diptera" soon to be published. Full descriptions, which have been in manuscript for some time, will be published in the author's Monograph of Northeastern Tachinidæ, now in process of preparation.

Ptilodexia neotibialis n. sp.

Male: Front, at narrowest part, one and one-half times width of ocellar triangle. No orbitals. Antennæ nearly half as long as face. Facial carina small. Vibrissæ distinctly above oral margin, one or two bristles above each. Proboscis rather slender, nearly as long as head height. Palpi reddish-brown. Beard dense, light in color. Sides of face bearing coarse, dark hairs. Thorax black, sprinkled with gray pollen. Dorsal vittæ usually 5, all indistinct. Post-suturals 3, sternopleurals usually 3, one stout and several lesser pteropleurals. Wings hyaline, venation not distinctive. Legs black. Adbomen black, the sides reddish. Chætotaxy variable. First segment usually with one pair of marginals, second with two or three pairs of discals and one pair of marginals, third with two or three pairs of discals and a marginal row, fourth segment densely clothed with spines. Length 14 mm.

Female: Front, at narrowest part, as wide as either eye. Orbitals present. Bristles of abdomen usually as follows;—first segment without macrochætæ, second with a discal and a marginal pair, third with a discal pair and a marginal row, fourth with a discal row and a marginal row.

Described from eleven male and five female specimens

from the following localities; Colebrook, Conn., two males, one female, (W. M. Wheeler); Cohasset, Mass., Sept. 15, 1904, one male, (Owen Bryant); Riverhead, L. I., one male, July 30, 1922, (H. C. Huckett); one female, Sept. 15, 1913; North Dakota, one male; Selden, L. I., two males, Aug. 10, 1916 and Sept. 1, 1916, (W. T. Davis); Great Falls, Fairfax Co., Va., one male, Sept. 9, 1914, (W. Robinson); Cincinnati, O., one male, Sept. 11, 1900; Albany, N. Y., one female, July 4, 1900; Fire Island, N. Y., one female Sept. 7, 1922, (W. T. Davis); Bright Angel Trail, Gd. Can., Ariz., one male; Black Canon, Cimarron, Colo., one female, Sept. 13-15, 1918, (R. C. Shannon).

Holotype, from Colebrook, Conn., deposited at Boston Society of Natural History, Allotype, from Albany, N. Y., retained at Ithaca. Paratypes at Boston, Ithaca, and N. Y. State Museum, at Albany.

Rhynochodexia confusa n. sp.

Male: Eyes nearly contiguous. No orbitals. Antennæ nearly three fourths as long as face. Carina fairly conspicuous, of the narrow-keel type. Vibrissæ slightly above oral margin. Ridges bristly less than one fourth their height. Proboscis three-fifths head height. Palpi yellow. Beard scanty, light in color. Sides of face bare. Thorax black, sprinkled with gray pollen. Three or five dorsal vittæ. Post-suturals 3 or 4, sternopleurals 3, rarely 2 or 4, pteropleurals in a tuft. Wings hyaline, no costal spine, third vein with 4 or 5 small bristles at the base. Legs yellow to dark brown. Abdomen covered with grayish pollen, the mid-dorsal region usually darker. Bristles of abdomen usually as follows;—second segment with four discals and two stout and two lesser marginals, third with three pairs of discals and a row of marginals, fourth bristly over entire surface. Length 8.5 to 13 mm.

Female: Front two-thirds as wide as either eye. Orbitals present. Abdominal chætotaxy less dense, in allotype as follows; second segment with one discal and one marginal pair, third with a discal pair and a marginal row, fourth with a discal and a marginal row.

Described from a long series of both sexes from the following localities: Selden, L. I., Baiting Hollow, L. I., Washington, D. C., Poughkeepsie, N. Y., Wood's Hole, Mass., Ithaca, N. Y., Lake George, N. Y., Luzerne Co., Pa., Colebrook, Conn., Fire Island, N. Y., Albany, N. Y., Nelson Co., Va., Lake Placid, N. Y., Lakehurst, N. J., Riverhead, L. I., McLean, N. Y., Ridgewood, N. J., Chester, Mass., Rutland, Mass., Bolton Mt., Vt., Durham, N. H., Tiverton, R. I., Keene Valley, N. Y., Nassau, N. Y., Wells, N. Y., Duck Lake, N. Y., Freeville, N. Y., Storrs, Conn.; July to September.

Flies answering the above description have been passing in collections for *Ptilodexia harpasa* Walk. That species however, as I know it, has the parafacials hairy, though similar in many other respects to this species. I have before me a long series of each, and I feel confident that distinction on the basis of bare or hairy face is well warranted. More thorough study, involving the examination of genitalia, may disclose as fact, what I now suspect; namely, that *more* than two species are here involved. I am however confident that the holotype and allotype of *R. confusa* belong together, and therefore feel justified in publishing the above description at the present time.

Holotype, male, Selden, L. I., July 1, 1923, allotype female, Baiting Hollow, L. I., Aug. 12, 1923. Both at Ithaca. Paratypes at Albany, Boston Society of Natural History, and in the collections of Messrs. Davis and Huckett.

Ateloglossa wheeleri n. sp.

Male: Appearance similar to *Sarcophaga*. Front twice width of ocellar triangle. No orbitals. Antennæ brown, half as long as face. Carina large, protruding. Vibrissæ slightly above oral margin, three or four small bristles above each. Proboscis half the head height. Palpi wanting. Beard light colored. Sides of face bare. Thorax and abdomen black to grayish pollinose. Dorsal vittæ 5. Post-suturals 4, sternopleurals 3, 1 stout and several lesser pteropleurals. Wings hyaline, no costal spine, apical cell closed and ending just before wing tip. Squamæ translucent-brown. First abdominal segment without macrochætæ, second with one pair of marginals, third and fourth each with a marginal row. No abdominal discals. Length 8 mm.

Described from a single specimen collected by Professor W. M. Wheeler at Colebrook, Conn. Type is property of Boston Society of Natural History.

This species agrees with *A. cinera* Coq. in possessing marginal macrochætæ on the second abdominal segment, but differs in having the apical cell closed. It differs from *A. glabra* West MS in having the squamæ infuscated, and from *A. calyptrata* West MS in regard to the shape of the head, as well as in certain characters furnished by the bristles of the legs.

Arctophyto johnsoni n. sp.

Female: Appearance similar to *Sarcophaga*. Front as wide as either eye. Three pairs of orbitals. Antennæ yellow, half as long as face. Carina fairly large and conspicuous. Vibrissæ practically on level with oral margin. Facial ridges bristly on lowest fifth. Proboscis short and thick. Palpi yellow. Beard sparse, light colored. Thorax and abdomen dull grayish pollinose. Thoracic vittæ three, all indistinct. Post-suturals 4, sternopleurals 4, 1 stout pteropleural surrounded by a tuft of hairs. Wings hyaline, venation not distinctive. Legs dark, tibiæ tinged with yellow. First abdominal segment with one pair of marginals, second with a small pair of discals besides a marginal pair, third and fourth each with discals irregular, and a marginal row. Length 7 mm.

Described from a single specimen bearing the label Concord, Mass., Aug. 7, 1920. This specimen was loaned me by Mr. C. W. Johnson with the suggestion that it was probably "near *A. borealis* Coq." Type is property of Boston Society of Natural History.

Arctophyto regina n. sp.

Female: Similar to *A. johnsoni* but dffering in the following respects: Front, at the narrowest part distinctly one third wider than either eye. Frontal vitta nowhere wider than either side of front. Dorsal vittæ of thorax much more distinct, the two laterals much heavier than the median one. Sternopleurals three. Apical cell just closed in the margin; bend of fourth vein somewhat more angular. Length 8 mm.

Known only in the female. Described from a single specimen collected by Mr. C. W. Johnson from Brookline, Mass., Sept. 6, 1904. Type is property of Boston Society of Natural History.

Eutheresia montana n. sp

Male: Front twice width of ocellar triangle. No orbitals. Antennæ three-fifths as long as face, yellowish, the distal half darker. Arista short-plumose. Carina small and inconspicuous. Vibrissæ practically on level with oral margin. Facial ridges bristly nearly one-third their height. Proboscis one-third head height. Palpi yellow. Beard sparse, light colored. Eyes and sides of face bare. Thorax black, sprinkled with gray pollen, dorsal vittæ 5. Post-suturals 4, sternopleurals 2 or 3, 1 stout and several lesser pteropleurals. Wings hyaline, venation not distinctive. Legs dark brown to black. Abdomen black to reddish, sprinkled with gray pollen. First segment without macrochætæ, second with a marginal pair, third and fourth each with a marginal row. No abdominal discals. Length 8.5 mm.

Known only in the male. Described from a single specimen collected by A. P. Morse on Mount Mansfield, Vt., at an elevation of 4000 to 4450 feet, July 21, 1891. Specimen was secured from C. W. Johnson thru an exchange of material, and bore the designation *Eutheresiops* sp. That genus however is characterized as having hairy parafacials as well as hairy eyes, and cannot possibly be construed as including this species.Type at Ithaca.

Myiocera isolata n. sp.

Male: Head at vibrissæ as long as at base of antennæ, face about two-thirds height of head behind. No orbitals. Antennæ fully half as long as face. Carina very conspicuous, broad, high, protruding. Vibrissæ distinctly above oral margin. Facial ridges bristly one-sixth their height. Proboscis shorter than head. Palpi brown. Beard sparse, light colored. Sides of face bare. Thorax black, sprinkled with gray pollen. Dorsal vittæ 3, all heavy. Post-suturals 3, sternopleurals 3, several stout and several lesser pteropleurals. Wings hyaline, venation not distinctive. Squamæ yellowish. Legs black. Hind tibiæ irregularly ciliate. First two visible segments of abdomen black, third reddish, fourth yellow, all with sprinkling of gray pollen. First without macrochætæ, second with one pair of marginals, third with a few discals and a marginal row, fourth covered with heavy bristles. Length 11.5 mm.

Described from a single specimen taken at Hanover, N. H. July 4, 1908. Type is property of Boston Society of Natural History.

Myiocera novae-angliae n. sp.

Female: Head at vibrissæ slightly longer than at base of antennæ. Front nearly as wide as either eye. Three pairs of orbitals. Carina prominent. Vibrissæ slightly above oral margin. Facial ridges bristly nearly one-third their height. Proboscis two-thirds head height. Palpi yellow. Beard sparse, light colored. Sides of face bare. Thorax black, sprinkled with gray pollen. Dorsal vittæ three, all heavy. Post-suturals 4, sternopleurals 2 or 3, pteropleurals usually 2 besides several lesser hairs. Wings hyaline, venation not distinctive. Squamæ white. Hind tibiæ not ciliate. Abdomen nearly as broad as long, black, save for apical two-thirds of last segment, which is yellow, the whole covered with a uniform sprinkling of grayish pollen. First segment without macrochætæ, second with a marginal pair, third and fourth each with a marginal row. Length 9 mm.

Male differs from female as follows: Front, at narrowest part scarcely wider than ocellar triangle. No orbitals. Pollen of face more golden. Sternopleurals three or four. Squamæ a trifle infuscated. Abdomen more elongate. Fourth abdominal segment almost wholly reddish-yellow and with several discal macrochætæ besides the marginal row. Genital segments reddish.

Described from two specimens loaned the writer by Mr. C. W. Johnson. Holotype female, this specimen being in much the better condition; collected at Colebrook, Conn., by W. M. Wheeler. Allotype, male, collected by Mr. Johnson at Darien, Conn., June 16, 1909. Types are property of Boston Society of Natural History.

Myiocera protrudens n. sp.

Male: Large, robust flies. Head at vibrissæ as long as at base of antennæ. Face scarcely half height of head behind. Front twice width of ocellar triangle. No orbitals. Antennæ bright yellow, half as long as face or a little more. Carina very conspicuous, protruding between antennæ. Vibrissæ slightly above oral margin. Ridges bristly one-fifth their height. Proboscis about as long as head height. Palpi yellow. Thorax black sprinkled with gray pollen. Dorsal vittæ three, all heavy. Post-suturals 4, sternopleurals 3, 1 large and several lesser pteropleurals. Wings hyaline, venation not especially distinctive. Squamæ white. Legs black, hind tibiæ ciliate. Abdomen reddish black covered sparsely with grayish pollen. First segment without macrochætæ, second with or without a pair of marginals, third and fourth each with a marginal row. Length 14.5 mm.

Female differs from male as follows: Front, at narrowest part about as wide as either eye. Three pairs of orbitals. Ciliation of hind tibiæ not quite so even, nor extending quite so far. Described from one female and two male specimens, the first collected by Mr. C. W. Johnson from Sharon, Mass., Aug. 3, 1909. One of the males was collected by Mr. W. T. Davis from Newfoundland, N. J., July 6, 1908, the other is from Ringwood Hollow, near Ithaca, N. Y., July 5, 1920; collector unknown, probably M. D. Leonard.

Holotype male, (Ringwood specimen), retained at Ithaca. Allotype female, property of Boston Society of Natural History. Paratype in collection of W. T. Davis.

Dinera futilis n. sp. (Smith MS)

Male: Slender gadyish flies. Head at vibrissæ as long as at base of antennæ. Front to eye width as 10:19. No orbitals. Antennæ three-fourths as long as face. Carina prominent, bluntly keeled. Vibrissæ slightly above oral margin, one or two small bristles above each. Proboscis slender, as long as ventral length of head. Palpi pale yellow. Sides of face with a sparse covering of minute hairs. Thoracic vittæ two, indistinct. Post-suturals 3, (rarely 4), sternopleurals 3, 1 stout and several lesser pteropleurals. Wings hyaline, a pair of costal bristles present opposite termination of auxiliary vein. Apical cell varying from barely closed to open in the margin, ending just before wing tip. Legs yellow, certain joints brownish. First abdominal segment with a strong pair, a single bristle, a very weak pair, or no macrochætæ, second with a very stout pair, third and fourth each with a distinct marginal row. No abdominal discals. Tergites, except segment four, meeting in keel-like fashion on mid-ventral line. Length 6.5 mm.

Female differs as follows: Front, at narrowest part to eye-width as 17:13. Two pairs of orbitals. Parafacials sometimes more noticeably hairy. Inferior sternopleural sometimes lacking. Described from fifteen males and thirteen females from the following localities: Atco, N. J., one male, June 18, 1913; Brookings, S. D., one male, June 4, 1891; South West Harbor, Maine, one male, July 20, 1923 (Johnson); Needham, Mass., one male, Aug. 4, (A. P. Morse); Voorheesville, N. Y., one male, June 19, 1923 (M. D. Leonard); Baiting Hollow, L. I., two males, June 6, 1923, (H. C. Huckett), one male, Aug. 25, 1923 (H. C. H.); two females, July 29, 1923 (H. C. H.), one female, Aug. 29, 1923 (H. C. H.); Wading River, L. I., one male, Aug. 25, 1923 (H. C. H.); Intervale, N. H., one female, Sept. 4, 1707, (G. M. Allen); Ithaca, N. Y., one female, June 28, 1898, one female Aug. 4, 1885 (E. H. Sargent); Philadelphia, Pa., one female; Rochester Junction, N. Y., one female, July 24, 1914, (M. D. Leonard); Ft. Collins, Colo., one female; Wellesley, Mass., one female, (A. P. Morse); and six males and three females with no locality record. In addition to the above localities, Mr. Johnson informs me that he has specimens recorded from Hampden, Me., July 10 (C. W. J.); from Wonalancet, N. H., Sept. 13, (Cushman); Jackson, N. H., Sept. 25, (Bryant); from Pelham, N. H., Aug. 31; from Danvers, Springfield, Nantucket, Brookline, and Auburndale, Mass.; June 29-Sept. 14; from Kingston, R. I., July 19 (Barlow); and from Westville, Conn., June 20 (Britton).

Dinera futilis is a manuscript name of H. E. Smith's which has come into use in lists and other records although the species has never been described. I have been asked by Mr. Johnson and others to publish this description, which I am pleased to do, using of course, the name by which the species has already come to be known. Our species is exceedingly close to that known in Europe as *Dinera grisescens* Fall., of which I have before me five males and three females, obtained from the Vienna Museum. The only superficial difference appears to be in a tendency for the yellowish cast, on mid-ventral line and along posterior margins of abdominal segments one, two and three, on ventral side, to be somewhat more pronounced in the European than in the American form. The variation in chætotaxy is the same for both species, but being loath to pronounce them the same, I relaxed two males of each series in order to examine the genitalia. The inner forceps of both are fused, but there are certain other very appreciable differences, which surely warrant keeping the two species separate. The fused inner forceps in *futilis* exhibit a low, narrow carina, and are clothed with dark hairs at the base. In *grisescens* this structure is totally devoid of a carina, and bares only pale hairs at the base.

Holotype, male, from Atco, N. J., retained at Ithaca. Allotype, female, from Intervale, N. H., deposited at Boston Society of Natural History. Paratypes at Ithaca, Boston and Albany.

Note: It is the author's intention to arrange, eventually, for the deposition of certain paratypes at the U. S. National Museum in Washington.

NEW AND LITTLE-KNOWN CALYPTRATE DIPTERA FROM NEW ENGLAND.

By J. R. Malloch.

Biological Survey, Washington, D. C.

The first three species belong to the family Scatophagidæ, the others to the Muscidæ (=Anthomyiidæ auct.).

Microprosopa flavinervis sp. nov.

Male.—Head yellow, interfrontalia more rufous; ocellar triangle and upper half of occiput fuscous, gray pruinescent; second antennal segment and arista yellow, third antennal segment black; palpi whitish yellow; vibrissæ and genal bristles luteous; orbital, vertical, and ocellar bristles black. Thorax black, densely gray pruinescent. Abdomen tawny, fuscous dorsally on basal half. Legs, including coxæ, yellow. Wings yellowish, veins yellow. Halteres yellow.

Upper three orbital bristles nearer eye than lower three, the second and third curved forward and outward, the lower three incurved; arista almost bare; vibrissæ duplicated; eye a little longer than high, slightly pear-shaped, the narrow extremity in front. Dorsocentral bristles rather short, two pairs in front of suture; scutellum with four equal bristles. First and fourth visible tergites longer than second and third, fifth a little longer than fourth, not extending to margin on left side; sixth tergite as long as fifth; hypopygium large, occupying nearly half of length of venter; processes of fifth sternite robust, obtusely pointed. Fore and mid tibiae each with a fine median anterodorsal bristle; hind femur without distinct anteroventral bristles; hind tibia with one posterodorsal and one or two anterodorsal bristles.

Length, 5 mm.

Type and paratype, Auburndale, Mass., May.

Orthochaeta dissimilis sp. nov.

Male and female.—Black, shining, thorax and abdomen with distinct gray pruinescence, most dense on pleura. Head black, face and anterior portion of interfrontalia reddish; face, frons, and cheeks with white pruinescence; antennæ and proboscis black; palpi yellow. Thoracic dorsum rather indistinctly trivittate. Abdomen black or yellowish brown. Legs yellow, coxæ slightly brownish at bases. Wings clear, more yellowish basally, veins yellow. Calyptræ white. Halteres yellow.

Frons slightly over one third of the head width, narrowed anteriorly; each orbit with about eight bristles; antennæ nearly as long as face, third segment broad, its apex with an acute upper angle; arista nearly bare, second segment in male about twice as long as thick, third very much swollen at base, rapidly becoming slender apically; arista of female with second segment shorter than in male, the third swollen on its basal third; cheek not over one tenth as high as eye, with about six long marginal bristles; vibrissæ long, one bristle above it; proboscis slendee Thorax with the same bristles as the genotype, except that there are but two scutellars present. Fifth abdominal sternite of male with two long processes which are slightly tapered apically, their tips rounded. Fore femur with several bristles in a series on anterodorsal surface, the one nearest apex much stronger than the others; fore tibia with one posteroventral, two posterodorsal, and two anterodorsal bristles; mid and hind femora each with several widely spaced bristles on anterodorsal, anteroventral, and posteroventral surfaces; mid tibia with the following bristles: one anteroventral, two anterodorsal, two posterodorsal, and one posterior; hind tibia with one anteroventral, three posterodorsal and three anterodorsal bristles. Costa with short black spinules; last section of veins 3 and 4 nearly parallel.

Length, 7.5—8.5 mm.

Type, Algonquin, Ill., June 3, 1898. Paratypes, Urbana, Ill., May 7, 1907; Great Falls, Va., May 10, 1915; Norfolk, Ct., May 21, 1916; Columbus, Ohio, May 7, 1902; and four specimens from the Osten Sacken Collection in the Museum of Comparative Zoology, taken in 1874, without legible locality labels.

Scatophaga monticola sp. nov.

Male.—Similar to *furcata* Say in color, the third antennal segment fuscous, palpi yellow; dorsum of thorax with four pale brown vittæ; apices of abdominal tergites narrowly black; legs yellow, fore femora with a darker stripe on posterodorsal surface; wing veins clouded, the apices of veins 2, 3, and 4 rather faintly so, both cross-veins with spot-like clouds.

Arista bare; palpi dilated. Thorax with 2+3 dorsocentral bristles which are very distinct because of their strength and the scarcity of dorsal hairs; pteropleura and hypopleura bare. Processes of fifth sternite long, tapered to a rounded point, their basal width less than half as great as their length, no short spines evident. All femora and tibiæ with rather dense erect ventral hairs the length of which does not noticeably exceed the diameter of the parts upon which they are situated; fore tibia with two anterodorsal and one fine posterior bristle: mid and hind femora without distinct ventral bristles; mid tibia with two or three anterodorsal and posterodorsal bristles; hind tibia with three anterodorsal and posterodorsal bristles, the anteroventral bristles usually indistinguishable.

Female.—Similar to the male in color but slightly darker. Abdomen pointed. Legs less hairy, the hind femora usually with one or two anteroventral bristles apically.

Length, 7 mm.

Type, male, allotype, and one female paratype, Mt. Washington, N. H.

The fifth sternite in male is similar to Figure 22, pl. 14, in my paper on the Pribilof Island Diptera[1], which is unfortunately mislabeled *furcata* instead of *islandica* and so referred to in the text. Figure 21 represents the fifth sternite in *furcata*.

The description herein presented is drawn from specimens in the U. S. National Museum collected by Mrs. A. T. Slosson and labeled *S. bicolor* Walker. I am confident that Walker's species is a synonym of *furcata* Say. These specimens were brought to my attention by Dr. J. M. Aldrich. The bare arista,

[1]North Amer. Fauna, No. 46, U. S. Dept. of Agri., Biol. Surv. 1923.

pteropleura, and hypopleura distinguish the species from its allies.

Hylemyia sinuata sp. nov.

Male.—Black, shining, thorax uniformly gray pruinescent, abdomen with gray pruinescence on sides of tergites, the dorsocentral black vitta very broad. Legs black. Wings hyaline, fuscous at extreme bases, veins black. Calyptræ whitish. Halteres yellow.

Eyes separated by a little more than width across posterior ocelli; orbits narrow, setulose to above middle; interfrontalia with one or two pairs of cruciate bristles; parafacial at base of antennæ wider than third antennal segment, much narrowed below; cheek about as high as greatest width of parafacial, with a single series of bristles below; third antennal segment about 1.5 as long as second; arista subnude; proboscis normal. Presutural acrostichals uniserial, sparse, long; prealar over half as long as the bristle behind it; sternopleurals 1:2. Abdomen short and stout, hypopygium rather large; processes of fifth sternite long and slender, their length along inner margin as great as that of basal two segments of hind tarsus, the inner margin of each sinuate and furnished at middle with a fringe of dense, short, stiff hairs, apex on inner side with a few short, fine hairs, the outer margin with some long bristles. Fore tiabi with an anterodorsal and a posterior bristle; fore tarsus as long as tibia; mid femur with a few bristles on basal half of anteroventral and posteroventral surfaces; mid tibia with two anteroventral, anterodorsal, posterodorsal, and posteroventral bristles; hind femur with a complete series of anteroventral, and some shorter posteroventral bristles on basal half; hind tibia with three or four anteroventral, anterodorsal, and posterodorsal bristles, and a few posterior setulæ. Outer cross-vein of wing almost straight.

Length, 4 mm.

Type, Newton, Mass., May 15, 1920 (C. W. Johnson).

The peculiar processes of fifth sternite separate this species from any other in the genus known to me.

Hylemyia longipalpis sp. nov.

Male—Black, slightly shining, densely gray pruinescent, the abdomen with a slight bluish tinge. Anterior margin of frons and of parafacials reddish; orbits, parafacials, face, and cheeks with silvery pruinescence; antennæ and palpi black. Thorax indistinctly vittate. Abdomen with a black dorsocentral vitta which is dilated at anterior and posterior margin of each segment. Legs black. Wings hyaline. Calyptræ white. Halteres brownish yellow.

Eyes separated by about the distance between posterior ocelli; orbits almost obliterating interfrontalia in front of ocelli; orbital bristles extending to middle interfrontalia with a weak pair of cruciate bristles; parafacials at base of antennæ as wide as third antennal segment; slightly narrowed below; cheek as high as widest part of parafacial, armed as in *flavifrons*; third antennal segment on inner side subequal in length to second; arista swollen on basal fourth, almost bare; palpi longer than usual, slightly spatulate at apices. Thoracic dorsum with sparse, erect, long hairs; three pairs of acrostichals in front of suture; prealar about one third as long as the bristle behind it; sternopleurals 1:2. Abdomen depressed, narrow, the segments subequal; seventh tergite (fifth visible) with numerous long fine bristles; fifth sternite with the processes short, glossy and almost bare at apices. Fore tibia with several fine setulose hairs on posterior surface, the apical posterior bristle minute; fore tarsi compressed, as long as tibia; mid femur with a series of strong bristles on basal half of anteroventral and posteroventral surfaces and another series above the latter; mid tibia with two posterodorsal and posterior bristles; hind femur with very long bristles, which are rather closely placed, on anteroventral and posteroventral surfaces, the latter not extending to apex; hind tibia with three long bristles on posterodorsal surface, about 8 or 9 short anterodorsal and anteroventral setulæ, and some hairs on middle of posterior surface. Costal thorn minute.

Female.—Differs from the male in having the head with brownish pruinescence, the interfrontalia reddish, and the abdomen unmarked.

The frons is one third of the head-width, the cruciate interfrontals are long, the palpi more noticeably spatulate, and the legs much less bristly.

Length, 3.5—4 mm.

Type, male, and allotype, Waterville, Me., May 11, 1906. (*Hitchings*).

The male of this species is distinguished from any in the genus known to me by the form of the processes of fifth sternite, armature of fore tibia, hind tibia, and mid and hind femora.

It bears a resemblance to *bicaudata* Malloch in some characters but is easily separated by the femoral bristling.

Calythea Schnabl and Dzeidzicki

This genus I distinguished from Anthomyia by the presence of fine hairs on the upper margin of the hypopleura in front of the spiracle, but I find that in most of the European specimens of the genotype there are no hairs present and when there are any they are very sparse and difficult to distinguish. My statement was based upon an examination of specimens which had either been named by Stein or compared with those so named. Just recently I have had some European specimens given to me and after an exhaustive examination of these desire to amend the generic definition as follows: Hypopleura usually with some fine hairs on upper margin in front of spiracle, absent only in *albicincta* Fallen, and with some similar hairs at lower posterior angle; prosternum always with some fine marginal hairs; hind tibia with one long posterodorsal bristle beyond middle; lower calyptra protruded; propleura bare below humeral angle, but with a dense tuft of setulose hairs above fore coxa; scutellum with fine hairs below.

Calythea separata sp. nov.

Male.—Similar to *albicincta* Fallen in general color and habitus. Differs in having no fuscous spot surrounding the posterior notopleural bristle, the anterior margin of thoracic dorsum less obviously grayish, the gray stripes on posterior third of mesonotum much broader, that on line of intra-alar bristles more elongate, and the apex of scutellum more broadly gray.

Structurally this species differs from all others of the genus in having the antennæ separated at bases by a very noticeable rounded carina which is distinctly shining on upper part, and the epistome is much more produced, the anterior margin being almost in line with anterior margin of third antennal segment. Eyes subnude; arista almost bare. Hind femur usually with but two posteroventral bristles, one at base and the other near middle; posterodorsal bristle on hind tibia rather short.

Length, 3-4 mm.

Type, Buttonwoods, R. I., July 25, 1911. Paratype, Tiverton, R. I., July 31; Woodbury, N. J., June 27, 1896; Eastham, Mass., June 21, 1908 (C. W. Johnson); Potomac Run, Va., May 30, 1916, on *Chrysanthemum leucanthemum*; Chesapeake Beach, Md., September 19, 1915; Beltsville, Md., August 8, 1915 (W. L. McAtee); Denton, Texas, April 27 (C. R. Jones).

Stein has placed *micropteryx* Thomson, *anthracina* Bigot, and *monticola* Bigot as synonyms of *albicincta* Fallen and suggests the same relationship for *bidentata* Malloch. I have yet to see an authentic North American specimen of *albicintca*, my records and most if not all of those of Stein having reference to *micropteryx* Thomson, judging from what I know of the distribution of this species, which was described from California. It is highly probable that both the Bigot species are synonyms of this species also, but only an examination of the types will determine this. I have again examined the type of *bidentata* and consider that it is distinct from the other species, having a larger velvety brownish black frontal triangle, the orbits with denser bristles, the profile of the head different, and the dorsum of thorax and abdomen deep black, with only a very short whitish triangle on each side of the median line of each abdominal tergite. We have thus apparently three distinct species in North America, and from an examination of material which I was permitted to make in the U. S. National Museum by Dr. Aldrich I believe we have probably two others in South America and Mexico.

Spilogona Schnabl.

Spilogona will supplant Melanochelia Rondani as the generic name for the group dealt with under the last name in my paper in Canadian Entomologist, pages 61-64, 1921.

Spilogona argenticeps sp. nov.

Male.—Head black, entire frons, face, and cheeks densely white dusted, the two latter almost tomentose and silvery, back of head pale gray pruinescent. Thorax pale gray pruinescent, with three very faint dark vittæ; scutellum darker, more shining, and when seen from in front with the sides darker than the disc. Abdomen whitish gray pruinescent, first tergite largely black on disc, the next three each with a pair of large subtriangular black spots which extend almost the entire length of tergites and are distinctly separated in middle. Legs pitchy colored. Wings slightly grayish, veins brown, whitish at bases. Clyptræ white. Halteres yellowish white.

Frons a little less than one third of the head width, orbits not strikingly differentiated, narrowed posteriorally; ocellar bristles long; antennæ slender, third segment twice as long as second, its apex about one third from lower margin of face; arista pubescent; parafacial as wide as, cheek twice as high as width of third antennal segment; vibrissæ long; eyes much higher than long. Thorax with three pairs of postsutural dorsocentral bristles, the fine hairs very short and sparse; lower sternopleural bristle very weak. Abdomen narrowly ovate; hypopygium small, forceps much drawn out at apices (Fig. 1); fifth sternite not visible in type. Legs slender; fore tibia without a median posterior bristle; middle legs missing in type; hind femur with two or three fine setulæ near apex on antero-ventral surface, only one of these bristle-like; hind tibia with one anteroventral and two anterodorsal setulæ. Veins 3 and 4 slightly divergent at apices; outer cross-vein at a little less than its own length from apex of fifth vein; penultimate section of fourth vein less than half as long as ultimate section.

Length, 4 mm.

Type, Mt. Washington, N. H., August 8, 4000 feet.

This species is most nearly related to *caroli* Malloch to which it will run in my published key to the species already referred to. That species differs, however, in having the frons wider and, except for the orbits, black instead of white, the orbits with more numerous and stronger bristles, the legs stronger, and the fore tibia with a fine median posterior bristle.

The European species *pollinifrons* Stein, like *caroli*, has the cheek not higher than width of third antennal segment, and though the frons is white there is no anteroventral bristle on the hind femur, the last character being used as diagnostic in Stein's key to the European species.

Spilogona alticola Malloch.

This species is remarkably close to *contractifrons* Zetterstedt, to which it runs in all the keys to the European species which I have seen. To make certain of the specific status of the species I have dissected the male genitalia of both and present figures herein to illustrate their distinctions (Figs. 2 and 3). It is almost impossible to separate the species by the use of external characters. Staeger and Lundbeck have recorded *contractifrons* from Greenland but the records are probably erroneous.

Stein has recorded the closely related European species *baltica* Ringdahl as occurring in North America. The record should be confirmed by a comparison of the male genitalia of specimens from these continents before acceptance.

Spilogona novæ-angliæ Malloch

This species is very closely related to *brunneisquama* Zetterstedt (*armipes* Stein) which has been recorded from Washington State by Stein. I have dissected male specimens of both species and present figures of the hypopygia to show the specific distinctions (Figs. 4 and 5). Externally the species are almost the same and it is possible that Stein had *novæ-angliæ* and not *brunnesisquama* before him; an examination of his specimen is necessary to decide this, however.

Spilogona acuticornis Malloch.

This species is very closely related to *surda* Zetterstedt. It has, however, a distinct dorsocentral vitta between the spots on abdomen which is absent in *surda,* the frons is as wide as eye at middle as seen from in front, the apex of each process of fifth abdominal sternite is much more produced, and though, like *surda,* it has fine long bristly hairs on basal half of posteroventral surface of hind femur these are more numerous than in the latter and not in a single series. The crossveins of the wing are more widely separated than in *surda.*

One male, Machias, Me., July 17, 1909.

These notes are drawn from a comparison of the above specimen and an authentic male of *surda* sent to me along with *brunneisquama* and *contractifrons* by Mr. O. Ringdahl from Sweden.

Neohydrotæa, gen. nov.

Generic characters: Male.—Eyes bare, barrowly separated; arista distinctly pubescent on basal half; cheek narrow, with many marginal bristles, and 1 strong upwardly curved bristle about one third from anterior extremity. Prealar bristle strong, over half as long as the one behind it; sternopleura with lower posterior bristle distinct, but not nearly as long as the upper; hypopleura and pteropleura bare. Fore femora with a flattened, slightly excavated area at apex on ventral surface, basad of which on the antero-ventral surface the bristles are short and stout, no stout thorn present. In other respects as Hydrotæa.

Genotype, the following species.

Neohydrotæa hirtipes, sp. nov.

Male.—Black, shining. Head black, face and orbits with silvery pruinescence; antennæ black, third joint reddish at base on inner side; palpi brown. Thoracic dorsum with whitish pruinescence, most distinct, in the form of a broad vitta, on acrostichal area; viewed from behind the dorsum has a quadrivittate appearance. Abdomen with a slender black dorso-central stripe and very faint dark checkering, the surface with yellowish gray pruinescence. Legs yellow, fore coxæ brownish, mid and hind coxæ brownish, all trochanters, and the tarsi fuscous. Wings yellowish, noticeably so basally. Calyptra and halteres yellow.

Eyes at narrowest part of frons separated by a little more than width across posterior ocelli; antennæ not extending to lower margin of face, third joint twice as long as second; cheek about one eighth as high as eye. One pair of long widely separated acrostichals just in front of suture, the remainder of acrostichal area proximad of suture with 6 to 8 series of setulose hairs; 3 pairs of post-sutural dorsocentrals. Abdomen elongate ovate; fifth sternite with a groad rounded posterior excision, the lateral extremities slightly recurved ventrad as in Hydrotæa; hypopygium retracted, glossy black. Fore femur with a series of stout bristles on postero-ventral surface which is duplicated beyond middle, and on apical third the bristles become longer, more slender, and dense; antero-ventral surface with very short bristles up to beginning of the preapical excavation; fore tibia with black shaggy hairs on the entire length of postero-ventral surface, which are most dense near base; mid femur with several very long bristles on basal half of anterior surface; the ventral surface with a few widely placed bristles; mid tibia with three posterior bristles; hind femur with 5 or 6 long bristles on apical fourth of antero-ventral surface; hind tibia with apical half of ventral surface furnished with dense black hairs which are longer and bristly on antero-ventral surface; antero-dorsal surface with short hairs and 2 or 3 weak bristles; postero-dorsal surface with 2 or 3 bristles, the upper one straight; apex of tibia with 2 or 3 bristles, one of which on ventral surface is long and curved; tarsi long and slender. Outer cross-vein oblique, curved; veins 3 and 4 convergent apically.

Length, 8 mm.

Type locality, Chester, Mass., July 25, 1913 (C. W. Johnson).

The only allied North American species which has yellow legs is *succedens* Stein, but this has the prealar bristle absent and the abdomen largely yellow. *H. succedens* appears to be a true Hydrotæa.

The type has a weak setulose hair near base of auxiliary vein on right wing and a similar setula on first vein near the same place on left wing. These setulæ are evidently abnormal and are not given in the description as either generic or specific characters.

Explanation of Plate IX.

Hypopygial Characters of Males of Spilogona.

Fig. 1, *argenticeps*, apex of superior hypopygial claspers.
" 2, *alticola*, a, fifth sternite; b, left half of hypopygium; c, lateral view of internal parts of hypopygium; d, cephalic view of base of apical parts of same.
" 3, *contractifrons*, same as above.
" 4, *novæ-angliæ*, a, fifth sternite; b, hypopygium from behind, c, lateral view of internal parts of hypopygium; d, front view of left half of last.
" 5, *brunneisquama*, letters same as in above but b shows apex only of superior hypopygial claspers.

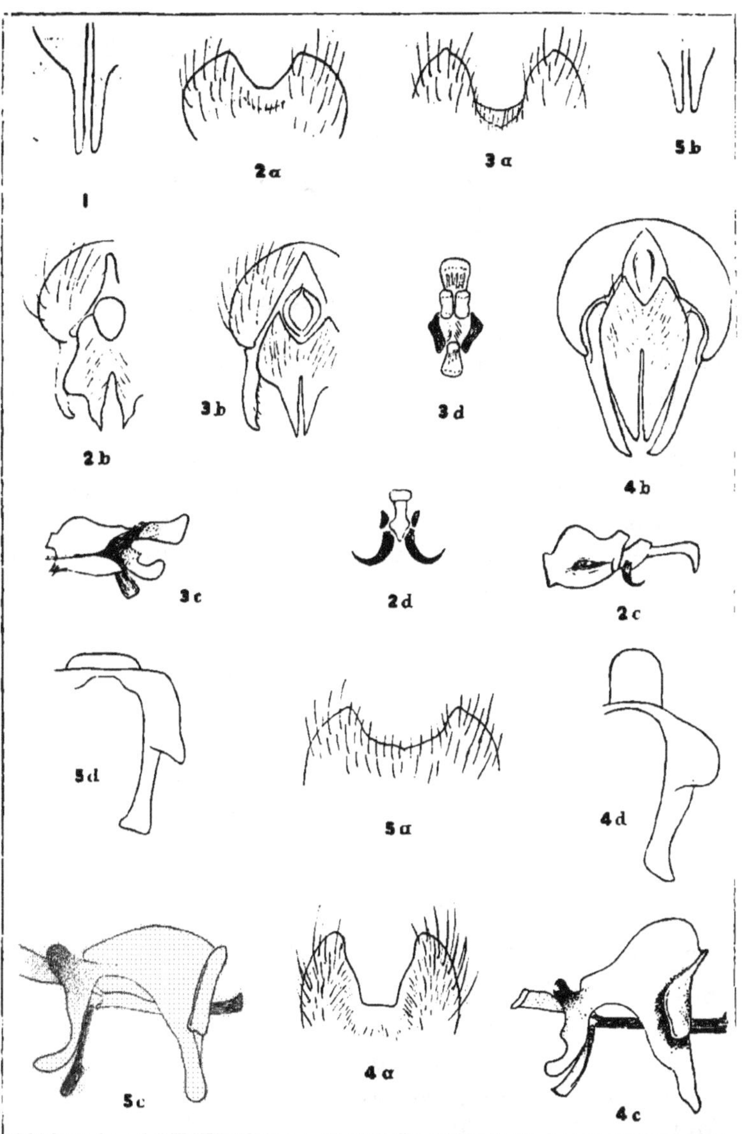

MALLOCH—HYPOPYGIAL CHARACTERS OF SPILOGONA.

ADDITIONS TO THE PHORIDÆ OF FORMOSA (DIPTERA)[1]

BY CHARLES T. BRUES.

In 1911[2] the present writer published a list of the Phoridæ of Formosa, based on collections made by Mr. Hans Sauter during the years 1907 and 1908. Several years later, in 1911 and 1912 the same collector obtained an additional extensive series which are dealt with in the present paper. The material here considered, like the previous series was loaned from the collections of the Hungarian National Museum by my good friend the late Dr. K. Kertész and the types have been returned to the museum. The first collection contained twenty species, all but one undescribed at that time. The present one includes fifteen species of which eight are new and seven have been previously described; of the latter one is the widespread *Aphiochæta picta* Lehm., another a species known from Java and seven were described from Formosa in my previous paper.

Thirty species are therefore at present known to occur in Formosa, distributed in the following genera: Dohrniphora (4), Hypocera (1), Conicera (1), Aphiochæta (21), Phalacrotophora (1), Mallochina (1), and Puliciphora (1). Becker has reported the occurence of *Aphiochæta flava* Fall., *A. lutea* Meig. and *A. pulicaria* Fall., and described *Aphiochæta fasciventris* which is not recognizable from his description. His *Phora bicolorata* is a synonym of the first species listed below.

Dorniphora egregia Brues.

Ann. Mus. Hungarici, vol. 9, p. 534 (1911). (Phora).

Becker, Suppl. Entom., No. 3, p. 88 (1914) (*Phora bicolorata*).

Brues, Journ. New York Entom. Soc., vol. 23, p. 184 (1915).

This is evidently a common species as there are nine specimens from Kaukau (April, July and August) and Taihorin (May, July, August). It occurs also in Java. The proboscis of

[1]Contributions from the Entomological Laboratory of the Bussey Institution Harvard University, No. 239.

[2]The Phoridae of Formosa. Ann. Mus. Nat. Hungarici, vol. 9, pp. 530-535, 19 figs. (1911).

the female is strongly chitinized, twice as long as the head-height, stout and geniculate at the middle.

The chætotoxy of the hind tibiæ is variable; in one male the hind tibia bears a bristle at the basal third and one beyond the middle, and in two of the females there is still another at the basal sixth; a single bristle just beyond the basal third is the most common arrangement. The front and mesonotum are sometimes reddish and the hind legs may be entirely yellowish.

Dohrniphora conventa Brues.

Ann. Mus. Nat. Hungarici, vol. 9, p. 535 (1911) (*Phora*)

A long series of over sixty specimens representing both sexes are in the present collection. They are from Taihoku and Anping, taken during April and May.

Dohrniphora mordax Brues.

Ann. Mus. Nat. Hungarici, vol. 9, p. 531 (1911).

A series of nearly sixty specimens of this species was obtained at Anping during May "from a box with papers, etc. which had been eaten by termites and containing also a rat's nest." From this it is probable that this form like several of its congeners develops in decaying animal matter.

Phalacrotophora Enderlein

Phalacrotophora punctifrons sp. nov.

♀. Length 2-2.7 mm. Fulvous yellow, mesonotum darker and pleuræ lighter below; palpi and legs testaceous; front piceous, yellowish near the lower margin; abdomen yellowish black at apex with a black spot at each side of the second segment and a brown one at the side of the third; first, second and third segments with a brown streak across the hind margin, except at the sides. Wings strongly tinged with yellow, the heavy veins light brown, light veins darker brown. Front slightly more than twice as high as broad. Four proclinate bristles of nearly equal size; upper pair occupying one-third the width of the front, lower pair one-sixth; inner bristle of next row near the eye-margin and well above the post-antennals, inner bristle very close to the eye and but little below the middle of the front; upper row with the lateral bristle very close to the eye, the inner bristle considerably higher, all bristles equidistant; ocellar row of four strong bristles. Ocellar tubercle and median frontal groove distinct; vertex slightly elevated, sharp above. Front covered with sparse, rather strong setigerous punctures. Antennæ small, nearly round, well retracted within their cavities; arista bare, as long as the eye; palpi small, with rather short bristles. Postocular cilia strong, larger near the middle of the eye; cheek with two stout bristles and a series of smaller ones between these and the antennæ. Mesonotum subshining, clothed with minute silky black hairs; two widely separated dorsocentral bristles with several long black hairs between them. Scutellum large, semicircular, with two very strong marginal bristles and a weak hair at each corner. Propleura with three bristles near the coxa, three weaker ones above and a few hairs between. Mesopleura above hairy like the mesonotum, with one stout bristle almost as long as the eye at the lower hind angle of the hairy area. Sides of second segment with a brush of stiff, bristly hairs; third segment with a few scattered black hairs behind, especially at the sides. Fourth segment soft and membranous, very pale; following darker, but still weakly chitinized; last segment narrow, tubular, black, with longitudinally striated chitinous covering. Legs rather stout, the hind pair especially so. Front tibiæ with a single line of close-set setulæ, their tarsi slender; middle tibia with a series of strong setulæ on each side of the seam, the outer row absent, however, on the apical third; hind tibiæ also with two rows, the inner one slightly stronger, with about ten bristles, and the outer one with only eight as it does not extend quite to the tip of the tibia. Hind metatarsus not noticeably thickened. Costa extending barely beyond the middle of the wing, not thickened, its cilia short and densely placed; first section one-fourth longer than the other two together; third one-third as long as the second; second vein leaving the third at a very acute angle; third vein nearly straight, lying near to the costa; fourth vein arising at the fork, bent at the base, straight beyond; fifth bent just before the middle, but scarcely sinuate; seventh long, nearly straight.

Type and four paratypes from Tainan, Formosa, April.

This is a typical member of the genus with the long narrow front and biseriately setulose middle and hind tibiæ. Two species of Aphiochæta known from Formosa, *A. atriclava* Brues and *A. flaviclava* may be distinguished at once by the shorter front. From *Phalaczotophora jacobsoni* Brues described from Java the present species differs most conspicuously by having the front punctate, not smooth and polished.

Aphiochæta Brues.

As in other parts of the world where Phoridæ have been collected, this genus is represented by more species than all the other genera of the family combined, and on account of the large number of Formosan species, a key has been included to facilitate their identification.

Key to the Formosan Species of Aphiochæta.

1. Hind tibia with only a single row of setæ, placed just inside the posterior edge. . . . . .2.
   Hind tibiæ with a series of setæ, sometimes only on the basal half, just outside the edge, in addition to the inner series . . . . 19.
2. Mesopleura bare . . . . .3.
   Mesopleura above with a patch of bristly hairs which sometimes includes also a large bristle. . . . . 16.
3. Scutellum with two bristles. . . . . .4.
   Scutellum with four equal, or nearly equal bristles.. . . . . . 14.
4. Costa about half as long as the wing or longer . . . . .5.
   Costa very short, about one-third as long as the wing *pygmæa* Zett.

5. Front much shortened, twice as broad as high; four proclinate bristles of equal size. . . . .*curtifrons* Brues.
   Front quadrate, or with the lower proclinate bristles weaker than the upper pair. . . . . 6.
6. Halteres black, much darker than the mesonotum.. . . . . . .7.
   Halteres pale, much lighter than the mesonotum. . . . . . . 10.
7. Costal vein extending far beyond the middle of the wing; fourth vein curved forward at both base and apex; wings distinctly infuscated. . . . .*chipensis* Brues
   Costal vein not noticeably more than half the wing-length 8.
8. Four well developed proclinate bristles, setulæ of hind tibiæ well developed. . . . . 9.
   Only two proclinate bristles, the lower pair reduced to fine hairs, hind tibiæ obsoletely setulose. . . . .*meracula* Brues.
9. Costal bristles extremely minute; setulæ of hind tibiæ rather small . . . .*meijerei* Brues.
   Costal bristles larger, but rather short; setulæ of hind tibiæ long. . . . .*sauteri* Brues.
10. First section of costa longer than the second. . . . . 11.
    Second section of costa longer than the first... . . . . 13.
11. Wings hyaline; front about as wide as high; second vein nearly perpendicular to the costa. . . . . .*nana* Brues.
    Wings distinctly infuscated; front wider than high. . . . . 12.
12. Costal cilia very short and densely placed; abdominal tergites normal. . . . .*formosana* sp. nov.
    Costal cilia long and rather closely placed; third tergite reduced in female. . . . .*pedicellata* sp. nov.
13. Middle row of frontal bristles forming a straight transverse row; thorax piceous; hind legs very slender. *recta* Brues.
    Middle row of frontal bristles strongly curved downwards medially; thorax yellowish brown; legs moderately stout. *curva* Brues.
14. Costal vein less than two fifths as long as the wing. *insulana* Brues.
    Costal vein extending to the middle of the wing. . . . . 15.

15. Four proclinate bristles on the front; second vein entering the costa almost at a right angle; costa extending di- tinctly beyond middle of wing. . . . . *trivialis* Brues.
 Only two proclinate bristles; fork of third vein very acute; costa extending just to the middle of the wing.
 brunnicans sp. nov.
16. Scutellum with four bristles; halteres yellow. *ochracea* Brues.
 Scutellum with only two bristles; halteres black. . . . . . 17.
17. Costa about half as long as the wing. . . . . 18.
 Costa only two-fifths as long as the wing. *breviuscula* sp. nov.
18. One of the mesopleural bristles greatly enlarged; wing broad especially at base. . . . . *æmula* Brues.
 Mesopleura with the bristly hairs all small; wing long and quite narrow. . . . . *simplicior* Brues.
19. Four scutellar bristles; mesopleura bare. . . . . *picta* Lehm.
 Two scutellar bristles; mesopleura above with bristly hairs and one large bristle. . . . . 20.
20. Halteres pale. . . . . 21.
 Halteres black; mesonotum yellowish brown. *articlava* Brues
21. Front one-third higher than broad; wings hyaline; costa half as long as the wing. . . . . *flaviclava* Brues
 Front quadrate; wings distinctly yellowish; costa extend- ing well beyond the middle of the wing. *lanceolata* sp. nov.

Aphiochæta meijerei Brues.

Journ. New York Entom. Soc., vol. 23, p. 189 (1915).

This species was described from Java. There are six spe- cimens representing both sexes from Formosa, collected at Anping during April, 1912, and at Tainan during April, May and June, 1912. The female does not differ essentially from the male from which the species was described.

The setæ of the hind tibiæ form a single row just inside the posterior edge, but those of the middle tibiæ are disposed in two rows, one on each side of the hair-seam.

Aphiochæta formosana sp. nov.

♂. Length 1.7-2.1 mm. Head and thorax brown, the front blackened, except at the edges and upper corners; abdomen black, dull yellow on the base of the first segment; segments one to six with dull yellow posterior margins, wider on four and five which have the middle portion brown; antennæ rufous, with the tip of the third joint black; palpi yellow; pleuræ dark brown above, lighter below; legs yellowish brown, the hind femora blackened at tips. Wings with a decided brownish tinge especially around the margins; venation deep brown; halteres pale brown, concolorous with the lower part of the pleuræ. Front distinctly wider than high; four postantennal bristles, the lower pair much weaker and closer together than the upper pair which occupy one-fifth the width of the front; inner bristle of lowest reclinate row on a level with the upper proclinate bristle and midway between it and the eye, the outer bristle well above it and less than half as far from the eye. Upper postocular cilium much enlarged, the others all strong and well-developed; cheek with a pair of strong bristles and a line of small ones extending to the antenna. Palpi with very strong bristles at tips. Antennæ rather small; arista stout, pubescent, as long as the head-height. Mesonotum distinctly shining, with one pair of dorsocentral bristles; scutellum nearly as long as wide, with only two bristles, placed near the margin. Propleura with several minute bristles above and several larger ones below. Mesopleura bare. Second segment of abdomen with a conspicuous tuft of bristles at the sides, much longer than the third; third to sixth gradually growing shorter. A marginal row of short bristly hairs on segments two to five; sixth with similar ones on the disc. Hypopygium small, shining, with fine bristly hairs below. Apical lamella large, orange yellow, sparsely hairy, with the two apical bristles small. Front tarsi slightly thickened, the second and following joints each but little more than twice as long as thick, the first three together as long as the tibia. Middle tibia with a row of very weak cilia inside the posterior edge; hind pair with a stronger series of about 10-12 cilia, longest near the middle of the tibia where they are slightly longer than half the width of the tibia. Wings rather narrow, especially toward the tip, the costa and third vein not at all thickened apically, unusually far apart toward the base; costa just half the length of the wing with very short and densely placed cilia; first section as long as the second and third together; third one-third as long as the second; second vein very oblique, the cell narrow; fourth vein faintly curved near base, straight beyond; fifth and sixth each bisinuate, nearly parallel on the basal half and strongly divergent apically; seventh almost straight. In one wing the fourth vein is furcate near the tip where it gives off an oblique forwardly directed branch, an abnormality which I have never seen in any other Phorid.

Type, four paratype males and one female all from Taihoku, Formosa, May 1912 (Sauter).

In Lundbeck's table of European species (Diptera Danica, Pt. 6, p. 212) this runs to *A. uliginosa* Wood, from which it differ by the brownish wings and extremely short costal cilia. The thorax is also much lighter colored than in the European species. It is not very similar to any described oriental species.

The female is essentially like the male, with the front tarsi equally thickened; the costa is slightly, but quite distinctly longer than half the length of the wing.

Aphiochæta pedicellata sp. nov.

♀. Length 2.0 mm. Thorax dull ferruginous, the mesonotum fuscous; legs dark brownish yellow; front black, whitish pollinose; abdomen piceous or black, the fourth segment with a yellowish stripe on each side of the median line; antennæ rufopiceous; palpi dark yellow. Wings distinctly tinged with brown, venation clear yellowish brown. Halteres light yellow. Front broad, fully one-half wider than high; its bristles strong, more nearly perpendicular to the surface of the front than usual; four postantennal bristles, the lower pair considerably smaller and not much more approximate than the upper which are separated by one-fourth the width of the front; inner bristle of lowest reclinate row midway between the upper proclinate bristle and on a level with it; lateral one but little higher, close to the eye;

upper row forming a nearly straight line, its bristles equidistant with the lateral one close to the eye; ocellar tubercle and median frontal groove distinct. Antennæ small, round; arista strongly pubescent, one-fourth longer than the head height. Palpi rather large, with strong marginal bristles near tips. Cheeks each with three strong downwardly directed macrochætæ and a series of smaller bristles extending to the base of the antenna. Mesonotum rather long, highly convex; one pair of dorsocentral bristles set as far apart as the lateral corners of the scutellum. Scutellum nearly twice as broad as long, with two marginal bristles, but no trace of a second pair. Propleura with a tuft of small bristles above, several more below near the coxa and a series of minute ones between, along its posterior margin. Mesopleura entirely bare. Abdomen with some short hairs at the sides of the second and third segments, but without distinct lateral tufts; first three tergites completely chitinized; fourth with a short basal chitinized band and a very narrow median stalk-like chitinized strip, but with the sides entirely membranous; segments five and six chitinized as usual (these may be the sixth and seventh if two segments are included in the structure described above as the fourth, which I think may possibly be the case); next segment short and very narrow, pale; last narrow, tubular, black. Legs rather slender; fore tarsi slightly, but distinctly thickened, the second and following joints but little more than twice as long as broad. Cilia of hind tibia in a single row, rather delicate, the larger ones near the middle of the tibia about two thirds as long as its width; internally at the tip the hind tibia bears three comb-like transverse rows of minute bristles. Costa extending to distinctly beyond the middle of the wing, its bristles long and rather closely placed; first section barely longer than the second; third nearly half as long as the second (22:19:9); fork of third vein not very acute, the cell rather large; fourth vein strongly curved near base, more weakly so beyond, recurved at the extreme base; fifth nearly straight; sixth weakly bisinuate, seventh faintly curved.

Type from Taihorin, Formosa, July, 1911 (Sauter).

This is a very distinct species, resembling the Formosan *A. curtifrons* Brues, from which it differs by the long costal cilia.

Th ereduction of the abdominal tergites is somewhat similar to that of several European species, a character formerly overlooked, but recently described by Lundbeck and Schmitz.

Aphiochæta insulana Brues.

Ann. Mus. Nat. Hungarici, vol. 9, p. 542 (1911).

There are upwards of 150 females from Anping, Formosa, April to June, 1912. The species varies greatly in size, ranging from 1.4 to fully 2 mm. in length.

This species resembles *A. curtineura* Brues from the Philippines, but there are four strong scutellar bristles, instead of two and the mesopleura is bare; the propleura bears a large, conspicuous bristle at its posterior angle just below the spiracle.

Six males in the collection, also from Anping, possibly represent the other sex of this species. They are much darker with the thorax fuscous and the legs dull brown. The abdomen is black, with narrow apical whitish bands at the apices of all the tergites. The scutellum bears only two bristles. If these should prove to be the male, the species must be like a few other members of the genus dimorphic, the males having two and the females four scutellar bristles.

Aphiochæta brunnicans sp. nov.

♀. Length 2 mm. Thorax above brownish yellow; front piceous, somewhat lighter below; abdomen black, with very narrow pale posterior borders on segments 1 to 4; antennæ piceous; palpi pale yellow; pleuræ fuscous, much paler below; legs light brownish yellow, tips of hind femora blackened; halteres pale brownish; wings distinctly tinged with brownish yellow, the venation fuscous, the discal veins heavy. Front quadrate or barely wider than high; ocellar tubercle and median groove present. Only two proclinate postantennal bristles, but these are large and strong, set half as far from one another as from the eye-margin; inner bristle of lowest reclinate row on a level with the proclinate bristle and midway between it and the eye-margin, the outer bristle close to the eye and only slightly higher than the inner one; middle row of four equidistant bristles, the lateral ones very close to the eye and set distinctly higher than the middle ones; ocellar row of four bristles, uppermost postocular cilium very much enlarged, directed upward and inward, lower cilia somewhat enlarged; cheek with a pair of macrochætæ; a series of four strong bristles between them and the base of the antennæ; antennæ of moderate size, with a stout pubescent arista as long as the head-height. Palpi rather large, closely and strongly bristled. Mesonotum quite shining; with a bristle above the spiracle and two dorsocentral macrochætæ; scutellum nearly twice as wide as long, with four large bristles behind, the lateral pair distinctly smaller, but still well developed. Propleura bristly above, along the posterior margin, and with three rather strong bristles just above the coxa. Mesopleura bare. Abdomen with segments two to six of nearly equal length, the second. at the sides with a very noticeable tuft of bristles; sixth at the tip with a fringe of bristly hairs; all tergites fully chitinized Legs moderately stout, but not thickened; anterior tarsi slender middle tibiæ with a series of extremely minute cilia just inside the posterior edge; hind tibia with a similar series of rather small cilia which are stronger near the middle and weaker at base and apex. Costa extending just to the middle of the wing, with rather short, very closely placed cilia; first section slightly longer than the other two together; second three times as long as the third, the second vein leaving the third at a very acute angle, so that the lower side of the cell is twice as long as the upper; fourth vein curved at the base, but almost straight beyond, originating distinctly beyond the fork of the third vein; fourth and fifth very slightly sinuous; seventh faintly curved; wing large and rather narrow. Halteres brownish yellow.

Type from Tiahoku, Formosa, April 1912 (Sauter).

This species resembles *A. humeralis* Zett, but differs in the weak cilia of the hind tibia, very much higher front and non-thickened costa. From *A. rubricornis* Schmitz it differs by the absence of the lower postantennal bristles, weaker cilia of the hind tibiæ and in the course of the fourth vein. From *A. errata* Wood it differs by the longer first costal division and absence of a distinct intraalar bristle. Among the previously known Formosan species it resembles *trivialis* Brues most closely, but differs conspicuously in color and wing venation.

Aphiochæta ochracea Brues.

Ann. Mus. Nat. Hungarici, vol. 9, p. 543 (1911).

There is an additional female from Taihoku, April 1912 (Sauter). This specimen differs from the type, which was from Takao, in having the abdomen generally blackened above, but I can find no structural differences.

Aphiochæta breviuscula sp. nov.

♂. Length 1.3 mm. Dark brown or piceous, the head and abdomen darker, almost black, and the pleuræ lighter below; legs yellowish brown, the hind pair much infuscated and the front pair much lighter; antennæ piceous; palpi pale yellow; apical lamella of hypopygium yellowish brown; halteres very dark brown or black. Wings hyaline, veins piceous, the thin veins very distinct. Front very slightly higher than broad, with the ocellar tubercle and median frontal line distinct. Four proclinate post-antennal bristles of very nearly equal size; upper pair more than twice as far apart as the median ones, midway between the median line and the eye margin and on a level with the inner bristle of the row above; outer bristle of lowest reclinate row next to the eye, the inner one well below it and twice as far from it as from the eye-margin; upper frontal row of four equidistant bristles with the lateral ones very close to the eye, curved downwards medially; median pair of the ocellar row very large, two-thirds as long as the height of the front. Cheek with three stout bristles. Antennæ small; arista densely pubescent, one-fourth longer than the front. Palpi of moderate size, with rather strong bristles. Mesonotum quite shining, closely and finely hairy over its entire surface. One pair of dorsocentral bristles, without any smaller bristles between them. Scutellum twice as broad as long, with one pair of very large bristles, much stronger than the dorsocentrals, but with no trace of the second pair. Second abdominal segment slightly lengthened; third to sixth of equal length; dorsum and sides without hairs or bristles, except for some small hairs on the sixth segment. Hypopygium smooth, without bristles; apical lamella of moderate size, with two upturned bristly hairs at tip; when well extruded the hypopygium shows two large ventral hook-shaped pieces and one or two long slender curved bristles below and above near the base. Propleura with several stout bristles just above the coxa and one very small one above near the spiracle; mesopleura with a patch of bristly hairs above and one very large backwardly directed bristle at the lower posterior corner of the bristly area. Wing rather broad, evenly oval. Costa two-fifths as long as the wing, closely ciliate, the cilia short at base, but apically somewhat longer than the second costal division; first division one and one-half times as long as the other two together; second barely longer than the third; second vein rising abruptly to the costa; third vein very widely separated from the costa at the base; fourth vein weakly and evenly curved, recurved at extreme tip; fifth weakly bisinuate, ending as far from the wing tip as the fourth; sixth strongly bisinuate; seventh curved, long. Front legs with the tarsi thickened, the metatarsus nearly as thick as the tibia; middle tibia with six or seven very small setæ on basal three fourths; hind tibia with a series of about eleven, very minute basally but longer beyond the middle of the tibia; hair-seam along the posterior edge curved outwards toward the tip.

Female essentially like the male, but larger, 1.5 mm. in length; dorsal abdominal plates, including that of the third segment of full width.

Male type and five paratypes and two females from Anping, Formosa (Sauter) collected during April and May 1912.

On account of the bisetose scutellum, very short costa and bristly mesopleura with one large bristle this species is close to three European species described by Wood. From *A. hirsuta* it differs by the pale palpi; from *A. spinata* by the long costal cilia and shorter first section of costa; and from *A. pectoralis* by the pale palpi. These species are widely separated in Wood's tables, but Lundbeck has grouped them together with a few other European species on the basis of the two scutellar bristles, very short costa and the enlarged bristle with a patch of small ones on the mesopleura above.

Aphiochæta simplicior sp. nov.

♂. Length 1.9 mm. Black, the lateral margins of the mesonotum fuscous; pleuræ fuscous above, yellowish brown below; front legs light brownish yellow; middle and hind ones much darker, fuscous, with the posterior surface of the tibiæ almost black; palpi and terminal lamella of hypopygium honey yellow or brownish. Wings strongly tinged with brown, venation piceous. Halteres black. Front about one-fourth wider than long; four post antennal bristles, all large, but the upper considerably stronger and placed unusually far above the lower ones; upper pair separated by a little more than one-third of the width of the front, the lower pair half as far apart; bristles of lowest reclinate row rather close together at the side of the front, their bases indicating a line 45° from the vertical; lateral one on a level with the upper postantennal and very close to the eye; next row above of four equidistant bristles forming a line that curves slightly downward at the middle; ocellar row large and strong like the others; ocellar tubercle and median frontal groove well developed, the surface of the front slightly pollinose. Antennæ rather large, oval; arista slightly longer than the head height, very thinly pubescent. Palpi with long stout bristles apically. Cheeks each with three strong downwardly directed bristles and a row of short ones between these and the antenna. Mesonotum rather shining, almost bare in front; highly convex; one pair of dorsocentral bristles, with irregular bristly hairs between them. Scutellum rather long, scarcely twice as broad as long, with two large marginal bristles and two microscopic hairs. Propleura with four bristly hairs above and four longer ones below, but with none between these. Mesopleura above with a patch of bristly hairs, but without any greatly enlarged bristles although those near the posterior margin are distinctly larger. Abdomen with the second and sixth segments slightly lengthened; second with a very inconspicuous tuft of minute bristles laterally, otherwise the first four segments are practically bare; fifth and sixth with scattered fine bristly hairs. Hypopygium small, almost bare. Wings long and quite narrow; costa extending to barely beyond the middle, the costa and second vein close together; costal cilia closely placed and rather short, about three times as long as the thickness of the costa; first section as long as the second and third together, the third fully half as long as the second; fork of third vein acute; fourth vein gently and evenly curved, with recurved tip; fifth almost straight; sixth very weakly sinuate; seventh gently curved. Legs rather slender; front tarsi not thickened. Middle tibia with delicate but distinct setulæ; those of the hind tibiæ rather strong, in a single line just inside the seam; hind metatarsi conspicuously spinose beneath.

Type from Taihoku, Formosa, April 1912 (Sauter).

This species resembles the Formosan *A. canaliculata* Brues in the mesopleuræ and wings, but differs by the different proportions of the costal divisions and much shorter costal cilia. Among the European species it will run to *A. armata* Wood in Lundbeck's table (Diptera Danica, pt. 6, p. 219) from which it differs by the brown wings, darker palpi, shorter first costal division, and concealed ventral process of hypopygium.

Aphiochæta picta Lehmann.

A single female of this species from Kankau, July 1912, considerably extends the range of this species which is already known from Europe, North America and southern Africa.

Aphiochæta lanceolata sp. nov.[1]

♀. Length 1.5 mm. Head, thorax and legs in great part brown; abdomen black. Front yellowish below, infuscated above, the ocellar triangle black; antennæ deep yellow, darker at apex; palpi pale yellow; mesonotum fuscous, lighter behind and yellowish on the sides behind the wings. Pleuræ and four posterior coxæ light fuscous; front legs yellowish, middle ones more brown and hind ones darkened beyond the base of the femur; wings distinctly yellowish, venation light brown. Front quadrate; median line and ocellar tubercle distinct; four large postantennal bristles, the lower ones slender, close together; upper ones widely separated, as far from the median line as from the eye-margin, well above the lower ones and on a level with the inner bristle of the lower reclinate row which is close to the eye margin and directly below the lateral bristle; next row of four equidistant and distinctly bowed downward medially. Antennæ small, arista nearly bare, scarcely one half longer than than the head-height. Palpi with strong bristles below. Cheeks each with two downwardly directed bristles and a row of several smaller ones extending toward the antenna. Mesonotum subshining, with one pair of dorsocentral bristles and a strong bristle at the lateral margin just anterior to them; scutellum one-half broader than long, with only two bristles. Propleura with a few scattered minute hairs and three bristles at the base of the anterior coxa; mesopleura finely bristly above, with one large backwardly directed bristle inserted at the upper posterior angle. Abdomen with the third segment elongated, one-half longer than the second which has a small tuft of long bristles at the sides; fourth segment not abbreviated; ovipositor pale yellowish. Anterior tibiæ without setulæ, their tarsi slender; middle tibiæ weakly setulose inside the seam and with a row of setulæ outside the seam on the basal half; posterior ones similiar, but the setulæ are moderately strong in both rows, numbering seven or eight and being over half as long as the width of the tibia. Wings very narrow; costal vein extending well beyond the middle, with very short and fine, closely placed bristles; first section as long as the second and third together, the third nearly half as long as the second. Third vein running nearly parallel to the costa, but approaching it more rapidly beyond the fork which forms a very acute angle; fourth vein curved only at the base, ending no nearer to the wing-tip than the fifth; fifth, sixth and seventh nearly straight. Halteres yellowish white.

Type from Taihorin, Formosa, July 1911 (Sauter).

This species is related to *A. ciliata* Zett and the several similar palæarctic species, and especially to *A. flavescens* Wood, from which it differs at once in having the fourth abdominal segment of normal size in the female. From all the members of this group it may be separated by the presence of the second series of setæ on the hind tibia.

Mallochina sauteri sp. nov.

♂. Length 1.0 mm. Black, slightly brownish on the pleuræ and the sides of the mesonotum in front; legs brownish yellow, the hind pair considerably darker; palpi pale yellow; antennæ brownish basally, but black at tips; dorsal lamella of hypopygium fuscous. Wings hyaline, heavy veins dark brown, light veins very delicate; halteres piceous. Front quadrate or slightly higher than broad, with three transverse rows of four bristles each and four post-antennal bristles. Upper post-antennals occupying one-third the width of the front; lower ones smaller and closer together; bristles of lower reclinate row forming a pair at each lower angle of the front, the inner one on a level with the upper post-antennal and almost directly below the outer bristle, although not quite so close to the eye; upper row slightly curved downwards medially, its bristles equidistant; ocellar row as usual; ocellar tubercle and median frontal groove present. Antennæ of moderate size; arista nearly bare, as long as the head-height. Palpi small, with the usual bristles of moderate size; cheeks each with a pair of very large bristles. Mesonotum distinctly shining, with one pair of small, widely separated dorsocentral bristles close to the posterior margin. Scutellum twice as broad as long with a single pair of very long bristles. Propleura with two minute bristles just above the coxa; mesopleura hairy above, with one or two small bristles at the lower posterior corner of the patch of hairs. Abdomen with the fifth segment slightly elongated; upper surface bare, no hairs at the sides of the second segment. Hypopygium minutely bristly at the sides and below. Legs slender, the front tarsi somewhat stouter than usual, but not greatly thickened, the metatarsus much narrower than the tibia. Middle and hind tibiæ with distinct hair-seam along the upper edge, and with a single row of extremely delicate setulæ. Single spur of middle tibia more than half as long as the metatarsus; spur of hind tibia much shorter. Costa barely, but distinctly less than half the length of the wing; cilia rather short and sparse, with about 15 in each of the two rows. First section of costa almost twice as long as the second; first vein unusually slender; second not forked at tip, slightly thickened on its apical half, fourth vein gently and evenly curved, fifth and sixth weakly bisinuate; seventh nearly straight.

Type and paratype from Anping, Formosa, April 1912. Named in honor of Mr. H. Sauter whose vast collection of insects from Formosa have enormously increased our knowledge of its fauna. A third specimen (Anping, May 1912) without head probably belongs here also.

This species is closely related to *M. exempta* Becker, the type and only species of Mallochina. It differs in the quadrate front, more slender front tarsi, longer costa and comparatively longer first costal division.

ON THE ANT-GENUS CHRYSAPACE CRAWLEY.

By William Morton Wheeler.

Bussey Institution, Harvard University.

Very recently Mr. W. C. Crawley has described a beautifully sculptured Ponerine ant from Sumatra as *Chrysapace jacobsoni* gen. et sp. nov. (Ann. Mag. Nat. Hist. (9) 13, 1924, p. 380). Among a lot of Formicidæ generously sent me by Dr. K. W. Dammerman of the Buitenzorg Museum I find a specimen of this same insect, which was taken by Karny at Wai Lima, Lampong, Southern Sumatra, Nov. 12, 1921. It agrees in all respects with Crawley's description and figure and awaited description in my collection under the label "*Cerapachys mirandus* sp. nov." Crawley's description of the sculpture is somewhat incomplete. In my specimen, which like his possesses three small, closely approximated ocelli and is therefore apparently an ergatomorphic female, the ventral surface of the post-petiole is very regularly, transversely costate and the sternites of the second, third and fourth gastric segments, which are exposed, have their basal surfaces developed as very finely striated stridulatory organs and their apical borders pitted, or cribrate.

Crawley calls attention to the affinities of this insect with *Cerapachys* F. Smith and *Phyracaces* Emery but decides to make it the type of a distinct genus. In my opinion the matter is not quite so simple. In the Ponerinæ of the "Genera Insectorum" (1911) Emery recognized *Cerapachys* and *Phyracaces* as independent genera, the differences being that in the former the worker and female have the terminal antennal joint enlarged to form a distinct club and the petiole and postpetiole non-marginate on the sides, whereas, in the latter the terminal antennal joint is not enlarged to form a club but tapers to a blunt point and the sides of the petiole and sometimes also of the postpetiole are marginate. Crawley's genus is clearly intermediate in that the body is that of a *Cerapachys* s. str. while the antennæ are those of a *Phyracaces*. The peculiar sculpture cannot be regarded as a generic character and the narrowness of the petiole and postpetiole recurs in the East Indian *Cerapachys antennatus* F. Smith, which happens to be the type of the genus.

Emery seems to have regarded the non-clavate antennæ and margination of the petiole as more important characters than the number of antennal joints since he made *Phyracaces* an independent genus and separated *Cerapachys* into four subgenera on this character, namely *Cerapachys* sens. str. with 12, *Parasyscia* with 11, *Oöceræa* with 10 and *Syscia* with 9 joints. But the finding of an intermediate form like *Chrysapace* brings us face to face with a dilemma. Either we must raise all the subgenera mentioned to generic rank and retain *Chrysapace* and *Phyracaces* as independent genera or we must reduce these two genera to subgeneric rank under *Cerapachys*. The "splitters" will probably adopt the former, the "lumpers" the latter alternative. Should the lumpers carry the day the specific name of Crawley's species will have to be changed, because Forel had previously described a *Cerapachys jacobsoni* from Java (Notes Leyden Mus. 34, 1912, p. 103). In that case I suggest that the Sumatran ant be called *Cerapachys* (*Chrysapace*) *crawleyi* nom. nov. It is, however, not improbable that we shall do more splitting in the Cerapachyinæ in the near future. The subfamily is proving to be more extensive than we had supposed. Mr. James Clark and I have recently brought to light quite a number of species of *Eusphinctus* and *Phyracaces* in Australia and there are several diverse, undescribed species of *Cerapachys* and *Phyracaces* from the East Indies in my collection. The sexual phases, larvæ and pupæ of the great majority of Cerapachyinæ are quite unknown. A knowledge of these phases and stages will probably aid materially in a final revision of the genera and subgenera of the subfamily.

BRIEF DIAGNOSES OF SOME DIPTERA OCCURRING IN NEW ENGLAND.

By C. H. Curran.

Department of Agriculture, Ottawa, Canada.

The following very brief descriptions, enumerating the salient points in the detailed descriptions of several species, of Diptera are given herewith in order that the names may be included in Mr. Johnson's forthcoming list of the Diptera of the New England States. The detailed descriptions will be found in a contribution to a monograph of the Syrphidæ and a revision of the genus *Rhaphium* prepared by the writer.

Microdon pseudoglobosus new species.

Brownish and reddish, with darkened wings; third antennal joint of almost equal width throughout and a little shorter than the first two combined; ocellar triangle small, equillateral; apex of scutellum with a wide even concavity the broad points moderately projecting. Hind basitarsi of ♂ greatly swollen. Length, 7 to 8 mm.

♂, Lucaston, N. J., Sept. 14, 1917, (Daecke); ♂ same locality, June 27, 1902; ♀, Hammonton, N. J., Sept. 6, 1902; ♀, Da Costa, N. J., July 1, 1905; ♂, Cape May, N. J., July 8, (Viereck); ♂, Aweme, Manitoba, Aug. 11, 1920, (Robertson); Chittenden, Vt., Aug. 15 (Bequaert), and specimens mentioned in detailed description.

Microdon conflictus new species.

Chiefly brownish, the abdomen sometimes partly reddish; wings largely dark brown; third antennal joint but little longer than the first; ocellar triangle small, wider than long; apex of scutellum with moderately wide, deep concavity, the broad points long; hind basitarsi of ♂ greatly swollen. Length, 9 to 11 mm. Much darker than the preceding, the wings more heavily clouded.

♂, Great Falls Va., June 22: ♀, Lawrence, Kans., June 18, (Curran); ♀, N. J.; ♂, Washington, Mass.; ♂, Bar Harbor, Maine, (Johnson), and those mentioned in detailed description.

Microdon ocellaris new species.

Hind basitarsi not unusually swollen. Eyes with sparse, microscopic hairs (rarely extremely difficult to see); color metallic dark green, densely punctured, the reflection not vivid; pile of head whitish to pale yellowish; of body yellowish, or greyish white; third antennal joint shorter than the first; ocellar triangle much broader than long; vertex considerably swollen; apex of scutellum with widely separated, strong spines, much as in *tristis*. Length 12 to 15 mm.

♀ Linglestown, Pa., June 14, (Champlain); ♂, Lyme, Conn., Aug. 30, 1911, (Champlain); ♂, Lyme, June 1, 1918; 2♂, Linglestown, June 3, 1919; ♂, Lyme, April 30, 1911, (all Champlain); 2♀, Darien, Conn., June 12, 1915, (Johnson); 2 ♀, Newton, Mass., May; ♂, Framingham, Mass., (Frost).

Microdon manitobensis new species.

Eyes bare; hind basitarsi not unusually swollen; first antennal joint as long as the following two; ocellar triangle a little wider than long; head and thorax yellow pilose, the latter usually with more than the posterior half bright tawny pilose, the scuttellum almost invariably so; spines of scutellum small, moderately separated. Length, 11 to 13 mm. Nearest *cothurnatus* but more robust, the tawny pile on scutellum and structural characters distinguishing it.

Fifteen specimens of both sexes, Megantic, Que., June, (Curran); Capens, Me., July 15, Oquossoc, Me., July 2 and Southwest Harbor, Me., June 22, (Johnson); 2♂2♀, Elmboro, Sask., (Jewsbury); 2♂, Ottawa, Ont., June, (Curran); several specimens, Manitoba, (Hunter). Not rare about large ant hills.

Cerioides proxima new species.

Differs from *abbreviata* Loew as follows: There is no small roundish or oval yellow spot at the outer end of the thoracal suture; the black surrounding the antennal pedicel is angulate on either side above, not rounded; the abdomen is a little more narrowed at the base.

Female, Guelph. Ont., June 8, 1923, (Curran); ♂, Orono, Me., June 26, 1917; ♂, Agr. Exp. Sta., Orono, June 16, 1915, (both Metcalf); ♂ ♀, Metagamon, Me., July 4, 1901; Bennington, Vt., June 18 (Johnson); 2♂4♀, Megantic, Que., June 12-21, 1623, (Curran); 2♀, Ottawa, Ont., May; ♀, Boucher, Saks.; ♀, Vernon, B. C., July, 2, (Ruhmann).

The genus Rhaphium as here used, includes Porphyrops and Xiphandrium.

Rhaphium subarmatum new species.

Allied to (*Leucostola*) *slossonæ* Johns. but the posterior tibiæ are wholly black; face silvery white, beard white; third antennal joint acute, three times as long as wide. Length, 6 to 6.5 mm.

♂♀, Oromocto, N. B., July 9, 1913, (A. B. Baird); 2♀, Franconia, N. H., 5♂1♀, same data as type pair; , ♀ Gornish, N. B., July 11, 1913.

Rhaphium gracilis new species.

Face and beard white; front bright green legs chiefly yellow, the posterior tibiæ and tarsi brown; outer genital lamellæ triangular, broad, jagged apically, the inner ones very slender, long; middle coxæ with black apical spine; arista shorter than the long, ribbon-like third antennal joint. Length, 5.5 mm.

3♂, 1♀, Beverly, Mass., May and June, (Riley Collection).

NOTES ON *PIESMA CINEREA* SAY.

By Geo. W. Barber.

Cereal and Forage Insect Investigations, U. S. Bureau of Entomology.

During the summer of 1922 *Piesma cinerea* Say was found to be very plentiful in certain sections near Boston, Mass. In Medford a plot of "Love-lies-bleeding" (*Amaranthus caudatus* L) was completely destroyed, the leaves curling and falling and even the buds of the partly grown plants being destroyed. "Prince's feather" (*Amaranthus hybridus* L., form *hypochondriacus* Robinson) and the wild *Amaranthus retroflexus* L. were also

Fig. 1. Adults of *Piesma cinerea* Say.

attacked, altho injury was not observed except for some curling of the leaves. During July, August and September all stages of the insect were found in the field.

The eggs were deposited on the under surface of the leaves where they lay on their sides, very often parallel to and near the veins, particularly the larger ones. They usually were deposited singly but in some instances there were twenty or more on a single leaf.

The nymphs fed on the under surface of the leaves, the resulting curling furnishing protection to them. New adults were usually of a light cream color tinged with green, but soon became darker altho there was considerable variation, some remaining light, others becoming fuscous or with dark irregular patches.

The Egg.

Length .72 mm.; width .25 mm. Color uniformly light yellow; cylindrical, sides parallel; chorion bearing some 10

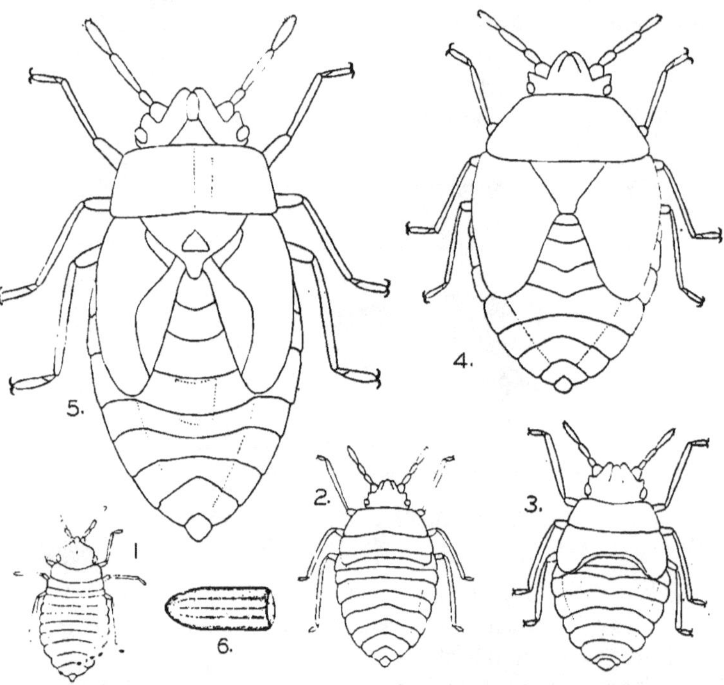

Fig. 2. Immature stages of *Piesma cinerea* Say. 1-5, first to fifth instar nymphs; 6, egg.

longitudinal ridges but little raised from the surface, the interspaces broader; end distant from the cap narrowed for about a fourth of the length into a bluntly rounding cone; scarcely narrowed to the cap which is flat, the edge bearing five very minute hemispherical chorial processes evenly spaced.

The First Instar Nymph.

Length .74 mm; width .35 mm. Color light yellow, eyes red, antennæ apically and tip of the beak somewhat brownish; body subdepressed, the sides nearly parallel; head nearly as long as wide, the protuberances before the eyes scarcely developed; antennæ as long as the head and prothorax together; eyes moderately prominent; beak reaches the middle coxæ; posterior edge of the prothorax not wider than the anterior; abdomen but little wider than the prothorax, the edges somewhat flattened; head and thorax finely and sparsely punctured.

The Second Instar Nymph.

Length .87 mm; width .53 mm. Color uniformly light yellow with a faint tinge of green; head a little wider than long, the protuberances before the eyes faintly developed; antennæ as long as the head and prothorax; thorax wider than the head, the posterior edge somewhat wider than the anterior; abdomen widest at the second segment, a little wider than the thorax, the edges flattened; head and prothorax sparsely punctate.

The Third Instar Nymph.

Length 1.16 mm; width .66 mm. Uniformly light yellow with a tinge of green, paler at the margins; head wider than long, the protuberances before the eyes bluntly developed; thorax wider than the head, the wing pads nearly attaining the anterior edge of the third abdominal segment; prothorax two and a half times as wide as long; antennæ minutely ciliate apically.

The Fourth Instar Nymph.

Length 1.75 mm; width .91 mm. Light yellow with a decided tinge of green; head wider than long, the protuberances before the eyes well developed; antennæ nearly the length of the head and prothorax, ciliate apically; prothorax nearly twice as wide as long, posterior edge nearly twice the length of the anterior; wing pads attain the fifth abdominal segment; scutellum moderately prominent; abdomen widest at the second segment, edges thin; body sparsely punctate.

The Fifth Instar Nymph.

Length 2.5 mm; width 1.1 mm. Color light with green markings; antennæ with a brown tinge apically; prothorax with a light green area each side; abdomen light green, the edges and a quadrate area centrally placed on the third and fourth segments light, the quadrate area bordered with brown; head twice as wide as long, the protuberances before the eyes strongly developed; antennæ as long as the head and prothorax, ciliate at the apex; head narrowed behind the eyes; beak scarcely reaching the middle coxæ; prothorax rectangular, two and a half times as wide as long, the posterior margin but little longer than the anterior, marked with a faint ridge each side of the median line; scutellum prominent, triangular, wider than long; wing pads nearly reach the fifth abdominal segment; abdomen somewhat wider than the thorax, widest at the second segment; body coarsely and sparsely punctate.

NOTES ON *PIESMA CINEREA* SAY IN NEW JERSEY (HEMIPTERA).

By Harry B. Weiss and Ralph B. Lott.

New Brunswick, N. J.

This species occurs throughout New Jersey being locally common, and according to Smith (Insects of New Jersey) on horse-chestnut, under the bark of Platanus, etc. It has been mentioned frequently in literature but very little has been recorded concerning its various food plants and life history. Parshley (Canadian Entom. Feb. 1917, p. 47) mentions its occurrence in ocean drift at Beach Bluff, Mass., on June 21. Osborn and Drake (Bull. 8, vol. 11, no. 4, p. 219) state that it is common throughout Ohio under the bark of sycamore and horse-chestnut during the winter. Summers (Bull. Agric. Exp. Sta. Tennessee, vol. 4, no. 3, p. 90, 1891) has observed it "so abundant on the young leaves and flowers of grape as to do considerable damage." In the recently published "Hemiptera of Connecticut" it is listed from several localities and the statement is made that it is rather rare in the northeast. Parshley in his "Fauna of New England, Hemiptera-Heteroptera" (Occas. Papers Boston Soc. Nat. Hist., vol. 7, p. 53) gives localities in Massachusetts, Rhode Island and Connecticut. In the "Insects of Florida" by Barber (Bull. American Mus. Nat. Hist., vol. 33, Art. xxxi, pp. 495-535. 1914) it is listed from a single locality. Van Duzee (Cat. Hemip. America north of Mexico) lists it from Ontario, New York, Pennsylvania, North Carolina, Florida, Ohio, Illinois, Kansas, Colorado and California and McAtee (Bull. Brooklyn Entom. Soc., vol. 14, p. 86, 1919) summarizes its distribution as a transcontinental species by giving its range as from the state of Washington, Ontario and Massachusetts south to Texas, Florida and to Linares and Tampico, Mexico.

From the foregoing it is evident that the species is common and widely distributed. In New Jersey we have found it feeding on the flower heads of rush (*Scirpus atrovirens*) at Monmouth Junction, June 17, Bound Brook, August 9 and at Dayton, August 1, Riverton, August 9 and Moorestown, July 25 feeding on *Amaranthus retroflexus* L., a weed commonly known as red root or pink root and sometimes very plentiful in cultivated orchards and fields.

At Moorestown, New Jersey, on July 25, where most of our observations were made, many plants of *Amaranthus retroflexus* were observed to be heavily infested with all nymphal stages and adults. Many eggs were present also. The upper leaf surfaces were mottled and spotted with white and some entire plants were almost white from top to bottom due to the combined attacks of hundreds of nymphs and adults. The injury appeared to be most severe at the tips of the plants and here the flowers and young, tender leaves hung limp and white. Eggs and empty egg shells were quite plentiful on this date. Some leaves carried as many as 18 or 20 eggs, anywhere on the lower surface and some of the flower heads were full of eggs. A few eggs were found on the upper leaf surfaces close to and parallel with the main ribs and side veins, sometimes in the axils of the veins. Others were found attached to the portions of the leaves between the side veins.

The pearly-white eggs appear to be deposited singly and fastened lightly to the leaf tissue and sides of the ribs and veins. The nymphs inhabit the lower leaf surfaces and flower heads, but the adults may occur on any portion of the plant. The nymphs are green or greenish with white markings and their color blends with that of the injured leaves. Whereas at Moorestown on July 25, many eggs and all stages were present, adults and last stage nymphs greatly outnumbered the other forms. It appeared at that time as if a new brook of adults had just gotten under way. Later in the season or on August 30, quite a few adults were present, a very few last stage nymphs and a very few eggs. Many of the adults appeared in to copulation on the flower heads.

Adult. This was described by Say (Complete Writings vol. 1, p. 349) as follows.

"*T. cinerea*—Not dilated, hemelytra with six or seven marginal spots.

Inhabits United States.

Body gray; not dilated on the margin; with much dilated punctures; head deeply bifid at tip and with a short robust spine between the eye and antennæ, basal joint spherical, abruptly smaller at base, second joint not longer than the first and less dilated; thorax with four elevated lines, obsolete behind; anterior lateral margin a little dilated; hemelytra covered, like the thorax with dilated approximate punctures, and having on the lateral margin a series of six or seven black spots; beneath grayish, more or less varied with brown; venter brownish, with spots or lines of grayish. Length to tip of hemelytra more than one-tenth of an inch. In form much resembling *T. cardui* F. It is not uncommon."

The coloration of the adult is variable and the color varieties grade into each other with one exception, this being the variety *inornata* described by McAtee (Bull. Brooklyn Entom. Soc., vol. 14, 1919) and said by him to be distinct and always separable.

MORE NOTES ON FUNGUS INSECTS AND THEIR HOSTS.[1]

By Harry B. Weiss.

New Brunswick, N. J.

Recently, Dr. George W. Martin sent me several species of beetles which he had collected on fungi in the neighborhood of Iowa City, Iowa, and they proved to be *Hister lecontei* Mars., on *Mutinus elegans*, August 11 (probably not feeding on the fungus); *Mycetophagus punctatus* Say feeding on *Polyporus radicatus*, August 11; *Mycotretus pulchra* Say on *Russula irrescens*, July 4; *Diaperis maculata* Oliv., on *Polyporus spraguei*, July and *Phenolia grossa* Fab., on *Polyporus sulphureus*, July 9.

In the Pennsylvania Department of Forestry Bulletin No. 12 (1915) Studhalter and Ruggles writing under the title, "Insects as Carriers of the Chestnut Blight Fungus" review the more important publications dealing with insects which have been considered accountable for the spread of fungi or bacteria which are saprophytic or parasitic upon plants and from their own observations, found that nineteen out of fifty-two insects collected in the field were carrying spores of *Endothia parasitica*. They concluded that some insects carried a large number of spores of the chestnut blight especially the beetle *Leptostylus macula*.

In the order Collembola, Folsom (Proc. U. S. Nat. Mus. vol. 50, p. 493) records *Achorutes armatus* Nic., as occuring commonly on agarics and on *Boletus, Polyporus, Morchella*, etc., and *Xenylla welchi* Folsom (Proc. U. S. Nat. Mus. vol. 50, p. 497) on mushroom beds in a greenhouse at Manhattan, Kansas. Alexander and McAtee (Proc. U. S. Nat. Mus. vol. 58, p. 413) state that *Limnobia triocellata* O. S., (Diptera, *Tipulidæ*) was reared from *Clytocybe* sp., and *Boletus felleus* on Plummer's Island.

Upon looking into the European literature for records of fungus insects one finds as in American literature, a general

[1]For other papers on fungus insects see Proc. Biol. Soc. Washington, vol. 33 pp. 1-20; vol. 34, pp. 59-62; pp. 85-88; pp. 167-172; vol. 35, pp. 125-128; Canadian Ent., Sept. 1922, pp. 198-199; Sept. 1923, pp. 199-201; merican Natural vol. 54, pp. 443-447.

absence of definite information concerning the specific identities of the hosts. In Calwer's Kaferbuch (1916) many species are recorded as occurring in "Locherpilzen, Wiedenschwammen, Blatterschwammen, Schleimpilzen, Buchenschwammen, Birnbaumschwammen, Staubpilzen, Schwammen, Pilzen," etc., which terms furnish little or no clue to the identity of the host. However some fifteen European species of beetles were coupled with definite host records and these are as follows:—*Agathidium seminulum* L., on *Trichia cinnaberina* (p. 289); *Saprinus lautus* Er., in faulendem *Agaricus* (p. 315); *Pocadius ferrugineus* F., in *Bovistus* (p. 439); *Mycetophagus atomarius* F., in *Sphæria deusta* (p. 500); *Sphindus dubius* Gyll., larvæ in *Reticularia hortensis*, *Lycogala miniata* (p. 502); *Asphidiphorus orbiculatus* Gyll., in Bovisten (p. 502); *Cis boleti* F., in *Polyporus versicolor*, *Boletus* sp. (p. 504); *Cis rugulosus* Mell., in *Polyporus unicolor* (p. 504); *Cis micans* F., in *Lenzites betulinus* (p. 504); *Cicones variegatus* Hellw., on *Sphæria deusta* (p. 513); *Endomychus coccineus* L., in Bovisten (p. 529); *Tetratoma Baudueri* Perr., in *Pleurotus ostreatus* (p. 771); *Hallomenus binotatus* Quens., in *Polyporus maximus* (p. 772); *H. axillaris* Ill., on *Lenzites quercicola* (p. 772); *Hypulus sericea* Sturn., in *Polyporus abietinus* (p. 775); *Diaperis boleti* L., in *Lentinus degener* (p. 807).

REMARKS ON THE PHYLOGENY AND INTERRELATIONSHIPS OF NEMATOCEROUS DIPTERA

By G. C. Crampton, Ph. D.

Massachusetts Agricultural College, Amherst, Mass.

During the course of an anatomical study of the Nematocerous Diptera, undertaken at the suggestion of Dr. C. P. Alexander, a number of interesting and important points concerning the interrelationships of these most primitive representatives of the order Diptera, were brought to light, and I would present herewith a brief resumé of the principal features suggested by this study. The accompanying diagram of the lines of

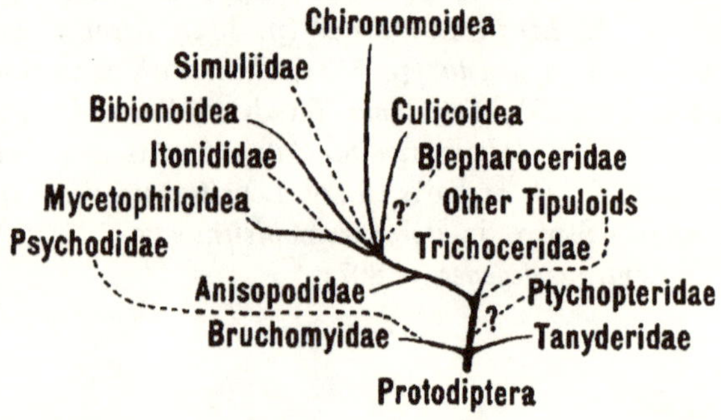

Fig. 1. Lines of descent of the Nematocerous Diptera.

descent of the Nematocerous Diptera will serve to illustrate the interrelationships here indicated.

Among the most primitive Diptera known, are the Tanyderidæ and Bruchomyidæ. Alexander, 1920, lists the Bruchomyidæ as a subfamily (Bruchómyinæ) of the Tipuloid family Tanyderidæ, but it seems preferable to raise them to family rank, since they differ from the Tanyderidæ in many important features.

The immediate ancestors of the Bruchomyidæ and Tanydreidæ evidently had a common origin—possibly in a Protodipteran stem represented by such forms as *Austropsyche*, etc., described by Tillyard, 1919.

The Bruchomyidæ are very like the ancestors of the Psychodidæ, which branched off from the Bruchomyid stem to follow their own isolated path of development. On account of the isolated character of the Psychodidæ, which differ from both the Tipuloid Nematocera (Pronematocera) and non-Tipuloid Nematocera (Eunematocera) the Psychodidæ and their ancestral types, the Bruchomyidæ, might possibly be grouped together as Paranematocera, composed of the superfamily Psychodoidea but this point is of no particular importance in the present discussion.

The Tanyderidæ are among the most primitive of the Tipuloid Nematocera, and have departed but little from the ancestral Dipteran stock, but they have developed modifications of their own, and it would be impossible to derive the rest of the Tipuloid Nematocera from this family alone, although it is possible that the Tipuloid family Ptychopteridæ branched off from the ancestral Tanyderid stem, as shown in Fig. 1.

The Tipuloid subfamily Trichocerinæ of Alexander, is here raised to family rank, because the Trichoceridæ differ markedly from the Anisopodidæ (Rhyphidæ) in which family they have usually been placed. On the other hand, the Trichoceridæ are very like the ancestors of the Anisopodidæ, and apparently had a common origin with the Anisopodidæ, from which common origin they have departed less than the Anisopodidæ have. The ancestors of the Trichoceridæ arose from the common stem giving rise to the Bruchomyidæ and Tanyderidæ, and it would be impossible to derive the Trichocerids from any known Bruchomyid or Tanyderid. The rest of the Tipuloid Nematocera are of no particular interest in the study of the lines of development of the non-Tipuloid Nematocera, and need not be further considered here.

The Anisopodidæ (Ryphidæ) furnish the "key" group in tracing the phylogeny of the non-Tipuloid Nematocera, and it is a question as to whether the Anisopodidæ are still to be considered as true Tipuloid Nematocera, or whether they have progressed far enough toward the non-Tipuloid Nematocera to be classed with the latter. At any rate, the Anisopodidæ are extremely close to the actual ancestors of the non-Tipuloid Nematocera, which were possibly of some "post-Anisopodid," but "pre-Mycetophilid" type intermediate between the Anisopodidæ and Mycetophilidæ.

The Mycetophiloidea (i. e. Mycetophilidæ, Mycetobiidæ, Sciaridæ, etc.) arose from the Anisopodidæ themselves, or from forms extremely like the Anisopodidæ, and it is extremely difficult to determine whether to group such annectant types as the Mycetobiidæ with the Mycetophilidæ, or with the Anisopodidæ. I have raised the subfamily Mycetobiinæ of Edwards, to the rank of a family, and have placed it among the Mycetophiloidea next to the Mycetophilidæ, rather than to include the Mycetobiinæ in the family Anisopodidæ as Edwards does.

The Sciaridæ are rather primitive Mycetophiloids worthy of family rank, but I do not think that Malloch is justified in raising the Mycetophilid subfamily Platyurinæ to family rank, and there is even some question of the advisability of raising the Bolitophilinæ to family rank.

The Itonididæ (Cecidomyidæ) might be included among the Mycetophiloidea. At any rate, they arose from the Anisopodid-like ancestors of the Mycetophiloids, and their line of development parallels that of the Mycetophiloidea remarkably closely, so that there can be no doubt that their closest relatives are the Mycetophiloids.

The Bibionoidea include the Bibionidæ, Scatopsidæ, etc., and the Simuliidæ may possibly be grouped in this superfamily also. The Bibionoidea are very closely related to the Mycetophiloidea, and apparently arose from the Anisopodid-like ancestors of the Mycetophiloidea.

The genus *Hesperinus* (and *Hesperodes* also) has been much shuffled about, having been placed in the family Bibionidæ by some, in the family Mycetophilidæ by others, and *Hesperinus* has even been placed in a separate family, the Pachyneuridæ, by certain European entomologists. *Hesperinus*, however, is so closely related to the Bibionid genus *Plecia*, that if *Plecia* is retained in the family Bibionidæ, then *Hesperinus* must be retained in the Bibionidæ also.

The Simuliidæ are extremely closely related to the Chironomoid family Ceratopogonidæ, and apparently represent a connecting group annectant between the Chironomoidea and Bibionoidea, with some suggestions of affinities with the Culicoidea. The Simuliidæ apparently branched off at or near the base of the Bibionoid stem.

The Chironomoidea include the Chironomidæ and Ceratopogonidæ, and possibly the Thaumaleidæ (Orphnephilidæ) also. The Ceratopogonidæ branched off from the base of the Chironomoid stem, and have retained many characters suggestive of affinities with the Simuliidæ and with the Culicoidea also. The Chironomoidea are so closely related to the Culicoidea that it might be preferable to include them in the superfamily Culicoidea, but for the sake of convenience, the Chironomoidea have been treated as a distinct superfamily in the phylogenetic tree shown in Fig. 1.

The Culicoidea include the Dixidæ, Culicidæ, and Chaoborídæ, the latter being usually regarded as a Culicid subfamily, the Chaoborinæ (Corethrinæ). The Dixidæ appear to be very close to the ancestral stock from which the Culicidæ and Chaoboridæ were derived. The Culicoidea and their close relatives, the Chironomoidea, were apparently derived from ancestors very closely allied to the Anisopodid-like ancestors of the Bibionoidea and Mycetophiloidea, so that these Anisopodid-like forms were the types from which the Mycetophiloids, Bibionoids, Chironomoids and Culicoids were derived.

The Blepharoceroidea, containing the single family Blepharoceridæ, represent an extremely isolated "compact" group whose affinities are very difficult to determine. Of the three Blepharocerid subfamilies Edwardsininæ, Blepharocerinæ, and Deuterophlebinæ, the Edwardsininæ, represented by the genus *Edwardsina*, are the most primitive; but even with the help of *Edwardsina*, it is practically impossible to determine the closest affinities of the Blepharoceridæ, for despite *Edwardsina's* primitiveness, it is extremely isolated, and is not approached at all closely by any Nematocera I have seen. I find in the Blepharoceridæ some slight indications of affinities with the Bibionoidea, and also some slight suggestions of resemblances to the Chironomoidea and Culicoidea. The mouthparts of *Edwardsina* resemble those of the Tanyderidæ, and Dr. Alexander finds suggestions of affinities with the Tanyderids in the wings of *Edwardsina*; but the other structures of Edwardsina show no marked resemblance to the Tanyderids, so that it is preferable to group the Blepharocerids with the non-Tipuloid Nematocera provisionally, leaving the matter of their closer affinities until more data on the subject is available.

In brief, the Culicoidea, Chironomoidea, Bibionoidea and Mycetophiloidea were apparently descended from Anisopodid-like ancestors, which in turn lead to the ancestral Trichoceridæ. These were derived from ancestors like those of the Bruchomyidæ and Tanyderidæ, which sprang from the common Protodipteran stem, represented by such forms as the fossil Protodipteron *Austropsyche*. The latter is extremely Mecopteroid in nature, and beyond a doubt the Protodiptera arose from the Mecoptera themselves, or from the immediate ancestors of the Mecoptera, and the Trichoptera also arose from the same stock. These lines of development are joined by those of the Hymenoptera and Neuroptera as we trace them back to their ultimate source in the Protorthoptera, or in the common Protorthopteran-Protoblattid stem from which the insects above the Palædicyoptera (i. e., the "Neopterygota") were derived. These in turn lead to the Palæodictyoptera, and the Palæodictyoptera together with the Odonotoids and Ephemeroids (*i. e.*, the "Archipterygota"), were apparently derived from the Lepismatoid ancestors of the Pterygota in general.

A NEW BEE FROM OREGON.

By T. D. A. Cockerell.

University of Colorado.

Halictoides crassipes sp. nov.

♂. Length about 10.5 mm; black, with much long brownish-black hair, becoming paler on tubercles and sides of metathorax, and some white hair along hind margin of posterior tibiæ; tegulæ dark brown; wings dilute fuliginous. Closely related to *H. maurus* (Cresson), to which it exactly runs in my table in Ent. News, Feb. 1916, but easily separated thus: larger; lower margin of clypeus concave: flagellum considerably longer, and bright ferruginous beneath; second cubital cell much longer, more produced apically, and receiving first recurrent nervure near base; wings browner; hind femora much more massive. The fifth abdominal segment presents a broad emarginate shining ferruginous plate.

Albany, Oregon (*Holleman*; Peabody Academy). Type in Museum of Comparative Zoology, Harvard University.

Halictoides is a Holarctic genus which is much better represented in North America than in the Old World. Even in the Old World, most of the species are Asiatic, coming from Turkestan, Mongolia and China. The closely allied *Dufourea*[1] is confined to the Old World, extending from China to Egypt and Spain, with one species (*D. calidula* Ckll) in tropical Africa. Friese has described a species from Mongolia. We may surmise that *Halictoides* had its origin in America, *Dufourea* in the Palæarctic region. In addition to the characters of venation and antennæ cited by authors to distinguish *Dufourea* from *Halictoides*, the following peculiarities of the mouth-parts may be used to separate the type species of *Halictoides* from *Dufourea*.

[1]*Dufourea* Lapeletier, 1841; not *Dufouria* Desvoidy, 1830.

1. *Halictoides dentiventris* Nyl. Labial palpi with first joint longer than the other three together, second shortest; maxillary palpi with first two joints stout, galea reaching to about middle of fourth joint.
2. *Dufourea vulgaris* Schenck. Labial palpi with first joint about as long as 2+3; maxillary palpi with first three joints stout, galea reaching a little beyond middle of third.

However *Halictoides paradoxus* Morawitz (Switzerland) has the first joint of labial palpi thickened beyond the middle (as in the Californian *H. virgatus* Ckll), and not nearly so long in proportion to second as in *H. dentiventris*. It has the first four joints of maxillary palpi stout, the galea reaching about middle of third.

H. virgatus has the second joint of labial palpi very long, nearly as long as first, thus differing conspicuously from *H. paradoxus*. In *H. virgatus* the mandibles are simple; in *H. campanulæ* Ckll., *H. tinsleyi* Ckll., *Dufourea vulgaris*, etc., and they have a conspicuous inner tooth. The labrum of *H. campanulæ* is much shorter in proportion to its width than in *H. virgatus*, and also differs in having prominent lateral corners. The general outcome of these and other studies is that *Halictoides* can be taken in a broad sense as including very diverse forms; or it can be divided into numerous genera, for which quite a series of names is already available. Probably the best method is to treat the divisions as subgenera; accordingly *H. paradoxus* may be taken as the type of a new subgenus *Cephalictoides*, nov., most obviously differing from *Parahalictoides* in the shape of the head. For other details see Ann. Mag. Nat. Hist., Dec. 1899, p. 420.

PROCEEDINGS OF THE CAMBRIDGE ENTOMOLOGICAL CLUB.

The annual meeting was held January 8, 1924. The secretary's report showed that 10 meetings were held during the year with average attendance of 14.5 continuing the gradual decrease since 1920 when it was 22.5. Two members were elected and the whole number of members is 73. The editor's report showed that volume 30 of Psyche just completed contains 235 pages. During the war the number was reduced to 139 pages in 1918 since which there has been a gradual increase. The following officers were elected, President C. T. Brues, Vice President R. Heber Howe, Secretary J. H. Emerton, Treasurer Fred H. Walker, Editor C. T. Brues. Executive Committee A. P. Morse, S. W. Denton, S. M. Dohanian.

Mr. A. P. Morse retiring from the presidency read a paper on Insect Music in English Literature.

This meeting being the 50th anniversary of the founding of the Club, J. H. Emerton one of the original members read a paper on its early history which is published in Psyche for February 1924. W. L. W. Field followed with an account of the Harris Club which was organized in Boston in 1899 and merged with the Cambridge Club in 1903.

At the meeting of February 12, Mr. C. W. Johnson explained his system of noting localities in New England where insects have been collected. The area is divided into some thirty districts numbered serially beginning at the north. In cataloguing only the numbers are used or where a district has to be divided the number with a letter added.

At the meeting of March 11, Prof. Brues read a paper on certain Phoridæ, minute Diptera many of them without wings. Originally found in the tropics, several species of this type have later been discovered in northern localities and on snow in winter. Prof. W. M. Wheeler read a paper on the Bullhorn Acacias which have enormous thorns in pairs at the base of the leaves. Ants perforate these thorns while they are green, eat out the pith and use them as habitations. See Psyche April 1924. Mr. J. H.

Emerton showed by maps the distribution of several northern New England Spiders.

At the April meeting Prof. Wheeler read a paper on Dipterous larvæ, allied to Microdon, found in ants' nests in Panama and British Guiana. Mr. Emerton showed lantern photographs of the tracks of insects on sand at the Ipswich sand-dunes. Dr. Smulyan read a paper on the eating caterpillars of the "fall web-worm" by yellow-jacket wasps. See Psyche June-August 1924.

At the meeting of May 13 Prof. Brues read a paper on the Insects of the warm springs of Yellowstone Park. Prof. Wheeler showed an ant *Tetramorium guineense* in which the head has all the characters of a male and the rest of the body those of a female. See Psyche June-August 1924. Mr. C. W. Johnson read a list of the families of Diptera of New England now amounting to 3170 species.

A special meeting of the Club was held on Tuesday evening May 27, 1924 to meet Mr. E. A. Schwarz now of the National Museum at Washington who was one of the original members of the Club. Refreshments were served and reminiscences of early members discussed.

At the meeting of June 10, 1924 Dr. Joseph Bequaert told about a visit to Honduras to investigate the midges at a station of the United Fruit Co. Dr. Bequaert made observations on the mosquitoes, Tabanidæ and other insects. With this meeting the Club adjourned for the summer.

J. H. Emerton,
Secretary.

PSYCHE

A JOURNAL OF ENTOMOLOGY

ESTABLISHED IN 1874

VOL. XXXI DECEMBER, 1924 No. 6

CONTENTS

CAMBRIDGE ENTOMOLOGICAL CLUB

PSYCHE is published bi-monthly, the issues appearing in February, April, June, August, October and December. Subscription price, per year, payable in advance: $2.00 to subscribers in the United States, Canada or Mexico; foreign postage, 15 cents extra. Single copies, 40 cents.

Cheques and remittances should be addressed to Treasurer, Cambridge Entomological Club, Bussey Institution, Forest Hills, Boston 30, Mass.

Orders for back volumes, missing numbers, notices of change of address, etc., should be sent to Cambridge Entomological Club, Bussey Institution, Forest Hills, Boston, 30, Mass.

IMPORTANT NOTICE TO CONTRIBUTORS.

Manuscripts intended for publication, books intended for review, and other editorial matter, should be addressed to Professor C. T. Brues, Bussey Institution, Forest Hills, Boston, 30 Mass.

Authors contributing articles over 8 printed pages in length will be required to bear a part of the extra expense, for additional pages. This expense will be that of typesetting only, which is about $2.00 per page. The actual cost of preparing cuts for all illustrations must be borne by contributors; the expense for full page plates from line drawings is approximately $5.00 each, and for full page half-tones, $7.50 each: smaller sizes in proportion.

AUTHOR'S SEPARATES.

Reprints of articles may be secured by authors, if they are ordered before, or at the time proofs are received for corrections. The cost of these will be furnished by the Editor on application.

Entered as second-class mail matter at the Post Office at Boston, Mass. Acceptance or mailing at special rate of postage provided in Section 1103, Act of October 3, 1917, authorized on June 29, 1918.

PSYCHE

VOL. XXXI. DECEMBER 1924 No. 6

SOME NOTES ON CERCYON, WITH DESCRIPTIONS OF THREE NEW SPECIES.

BY H. C. FALL.

Tyngsboro, Mass.

Some recent correspondence with Mr. Chas. Liebeck of Philadelphia has led to a critical exmaination of certain of our species of Cercyon, the results of which it seems desirable to make known.

More than half (14 out of 25) of the Cercyons recorded in the Leng List are more or less common European species, and in most cases the identity of the North American and European forms can scarcely be questioned. Some exceptions however have been noted. Specimens carefully compared by Mr. Liebeck and found to be identical with the *melanocephalus* and *lugubris* of the Horn collection have been sent me for examination. These, on comparison with the best European descriptions and with authentic European representatives of the species in my collection, prove conclusively that the *melanocephalus* and *lugubris* of the Horn Synopsis[1] are not the true European species of these names.

In the *melanocephalus* of Horn the palpi are said to be entirely pale. In the true *melanocephalus* they are black or dark brown. Ganglbauer, in his Käfer von Mitteleuropa, IV, p. 278, observes this fact and remarks in a foot note that *C. melanocephalus* Horn=*nanus* Melsh and can not be the *melanocephalus* of Linnæus. The intimation here that the species should be known as *nanus* Melsh is of course based on the published American synonymy. In the Crotch List of 1873, and the Henshaw List of 1885, both *melanocephalus* L. and *nanus* Melsh appear.

[1]Trans. Am. Ent. Soc., XVII, Oct. 1890.

In Horn's paper of 1890 *nanus* is set down without remark as a synonym of *melanocephalus* but on what grounds it is impossible to say. There is not now a single discoverable example of any of Melsheimer's species of Cercyon either in the Melsheimer or Le Conte Collections. It is understood that Le Conte was free to transfer to his own Collection anything he wished from the Melsheimer Collection, and he himself has somewhere stated that he possessed the authentic types of Melsheimer, Haldemann and Ziegler. There are now in the Le Conte Collection specimens bearing name labels (in Le Conte's hand) of three of the Melsheimer species—*maculatus*, *mundus* and *minusculus*—but nothing bearing the name *nanus* Mels. So far as discoverable there is nothing in the label, type of pin or style of mount, to indicate that any of these specimens came from the Melsheimer collection; if any such there are they must have been remounted by Le Conte.

It follows that in the case of *nanus* at least, there is no recourse but the original description, and this I do not hesitate to say does not agree with the *melanocephalus* of Horn. Melsheimer's diagnosis is rather brief but he describes his insect as "deep glossy black" and remarks that the antennæ are piceous. *Melanocephalus* Horn is on the other hand rather dull in lustre, the elytra, as in the true *melanocephalus* and *pygmœus*, rufous or yellowish with a scutellar triangular black cloud which may spread over the greater part of the disk but never involving the entire lateral and apical margins; furthermore the antennæ are pale.

Fortunately however there is no need to consider *nanus* in this connection, for a careful study of descriptions convinces me that Horn's *melanocephalus* is really another of the European species—*terminatus* Marsh—which has hitherto not been recognised in our fauna. This is of the same type and a close ally of *melanocephalus* and *pygmœus*, differing from the former in the smaller size, entirely pale palpi and antennæ, and the absence of the metasternal line extending obliquely forward to the front angles. The specimens sent by Liebeck as agreeing with Horn's *melanocephalus* all possess precisely these characters, and fit in all other respects Ganglbauer's description of *terminatus*.†

In passing it may be well to say that Horn is in error in saying that *pygmæus* may be distinguished from *melanocephalus* by its pale epipleura. The Epipleura are normally blackish in all three of the species here mentioned, which may be readily separated as follows.

Metasternal area extended by an oblique line toward the anterior angle.

Size much larger—2.2 to 3 mm., palpi blackish. . . . . *melanocephalus*

Size much smaller, always less than 2 mm., palpi yellowish to brownish, the terminal joint darker. . . . . *pygmæus*.

Metasternum without oblique line extending forward from the central area; antennæ and palpi pale; length about 2 mm. *terminatus*.

Although I have seen no native specimens, it is by no means unlikely that *melanocephalus* L. may have been found or may yet occur in America.

Cercyon opacellus new species.

This is the species described as *lugubris* Payk. in the Horn Synopsis, but the two seem to me quite certainly distinct, nor am I able to identify our North American form with any other European species. In *lugubris* Payk. the head and prothorax are strongly shining, the surface polished without trace of alutaceous sculpture, the elytra alutaceous and conspicuously dull. In our species the entire upper surface is always finely alutaceous, the head and thorax scarcely more shining than the elytra; the form is also appreciably more convex. Horn's description is entirely characteristic and need not be repeated. Whether the true *lugubris* Payk. (*convexiusculus* Steph.) really occurs with us I am unable to say. I have as yet seen no American examples.

†Since writing the above I have received from Mr. Arrow of the British Museum a specimen of *terminatus* carefully compared by him with Marsham's type, which completely substantiates my conclusions.

Cercyon minusculus Melsh.

In Horn's synopsis of the genus this species of Melsheimer is for the first time relegated to synonymy and declared to be the same as the European *granarius* Erichs. Careful comparisons by Mr. Liebeck with the series of four specimens (Mass., Pa., D. C.) in the Horn collection upon which his conclusions were based, and by myself with the series of *minusculus*, so labelled, in the Le Conte collection shows them to be identical. These and all examples of the very considerable series in the collections of Mr. Liebeck and myself agree in the strikingly deep and sharply impressed elytral striæ, especially toward the apex. A European specimen of *granarius* in my own collection has the elytra much less deeply striate and the interspaces very finely punctulate, whereas in *minusculus* the punctures of the interspaces are much more distinct and scarcely at all finer than those of the prothorax. *Granarius* and *minusculus* are indeed closely allied, but so far as the evidence at hand goes I consider their identity unlikely, or at least unproven.

Cercyon connivens new species.

A small species of the *lugubris—granarius—minusculus* type. Form rather broadly oval, slightly attenuate behind, very strongly convex, black, the sides of the prothorax very narrowly tinged with rufous, the elytra with a sharply defined apical pale space which extends froward along the outer margins to about the middle. Head and thorax polished, densely moderately finely punctate, elytra finely alutaceous and duller, a little more shining however along the suture, the striæ impressed and entire, a little deeper at sides and apex; interspaces spârsely punctulate, the punctures finer than those of the prothorax but quite distinct. Beneath piceous or rufopiceous, legs and antennæ reddish brown, palpi a little paler; meso—and metasternal plates very densely and unusually coarsely punctate

Length 1.6 to 2 mm.; width 1. to 1.3 mm.

Of this species I have seen a considerable series from Camden, Gloucester and Anglesea, New Jérsey, mostly collected by

Mr. Liebeck and a single specimen from Wakefield, Mass. taken by myself. One of the Camden specimens is selected as the type; it bears date "xi-23."

From *minusculus* the present species differs in being less broadly obtusely rounded behind; from both *minusculus* and *granarius* by the sharply limited apical pale area and the distinctly alutaceous surface sculpture of the elytra; from *opacellus* by the non-alutaceous head and thorax, and distinctly punctate elytral interspaces, and from all allied forms by the more coarsely densely punctured sternal areas.

C. connivens is really by its polished head and thorax and alutaceous elytra more nearly allied to *lugubris* than to any of the above mentioned species, and perhaps most closely of all to *subsulcatus* Ray of the European fauna. The latter however is said to have the elytral interspaces not or scarcely detectably punctate, which statement is not properly applicable to our species.

Cercyon californicus new species.

Oval, a little attenuate posteriorly, form nearly as in *tristis* but slightly less convex. Black, prothorax with either the entire side margin or (typically) with only a spot at the front angles paler; Elytra with a distinctly limited pale area which extends forward along the side margins at least to the middle, and often quite to the base. Head and thorax distinctly alutaceous, finely numerously punctate; elytra visibly but as a rule somewhat less distinctly alutaceous than the thorax, striæ fine and very lightly impressed, becoming obsolete just before the apex; interspaces sparsely punctulate, the punctures generally a little finer than those of the prothorax; eighth interspace uniserially punctured. Body beneath piceous, the epipleura paler in those examples in which the pale color of the apex extends forward to the humeri; legs reddish brown to piceous brown; palpi brown with the last joint darker; antennæ rufotestaceous, the club piceous. Mesosternal area evenly oval, twice as long as wide, rather coarsely punctured; metasternal area more finely sparsely punctate.

Length 1.8 to 2.4 mm.; width 1 to 1.3 mm.

California—Elsinore Lake 8-22-17 (type); Pomona; San Diego; San Francisco. All collected by the writer. Although slightly less convex than most species of Horn's category "13" this species by all essential characters belong there and should stand next to *tristis*, from which and all others of the group it differs by having the prothorax more noticeably alutaceous than the elytra. In one example from Pomona the alutaceous sculpture is equally developed over the entire surface.

The species belonging to Horn's category "13" (except the very distinct *navicularis*) may with advantage be retabulated as follows:

Entire upper surface alucateous.
- Alutaceous sculpture equally developed on thorax and elytra; form shorter and more convex (Eastern U. S.). *opacellus*.
- Alutaceous sculpture as a rule a little more distinct on the thorax; size a little larger, form evidently less convex (California). . . . . *californicus*.

Head and thorax polished, elytra distinctly alutaceous.
- Elytral striæ extremely fine, scarcely impressed, obsolete toward the apex. . . . . *tristis*.
- Elytral striæ entire.
  - Elytral interspaces very finely to scarcely visibly punctulate.
    - Striæ fine. . . . . *lugubris*.
    - Striæ much stronger. *subsulcatus*.
  - Elytral interspaces distinctly punctate, striæ well impressed. . . . . *connivens*.

Entire surface shining and with at most but feeble traces of alutaceous sculpture on the elytra.
- Elytral apex with sharply defined pale area. . . . . *floridanus*.
- Elytral apex at most only diffusely and obscurely paler, often scarcely at all so.
  - Elytral striæ fine, the interspaces much more finely punctate than the prothorax. . . . . *granarius*.
  - Elytral striæ sharply and deeply impressed, the punctures of the interspaces nearly as coarse as those of the thorax . . . . *minusculus*.

Cercyon maculatus Melsh.

Analis Horn nec Paykull., *indistinctus* Horn.

The *C. maculatus* of Melsheimer is given in Horn's synopsis as a synonym of *analis* Payk. The species which Horn thus describes is undoubtedly Melsheimer's *maculatus* as accepted by Le Conte but is an entirely different thing from Paykull's *analis.* The latter is a narrower, blacker, more attenuate species, resembling more in general aspect the species of the *lugubris* group than it does *maculatus* and allies. According to the books *analis* constitutes the subgenus Paracercyon Seidl., differing from all other European species in having the metasternum angularly emarginate between the middle coxæ for the reception of the point of the mesosternal plate. Mr. Liebeck writes me that there are three examples of the true *analis* (Phila. Neck) in the Horn series of *analis* but he is of the opinion that these have been added since the Horn Revision.

The characters upon which *indistinctus* Horn was founded, viz —the color of the elytral apex and the punctuation of the eighth interspace, are variable and lie within the limits of variation of *maculatus.* Specimens identical with the type series of *indistinctus* have been sent me by Mr. Liebeck and I do not hesitate to confirm his opinion to this effect.

HOW A BEETLE FOLDS ITS WINGS

Wm. T. M. Forbes.

Cornell University, Ithaca, N. Y.

When I was a boy in high school I became interested in insects, and started a collection. Having no adviser to misguide me I carefully pinned all my beetles through the scutellum and spread them like butterflies, which made a curious-looking collection, but developed in me an interest in the wings of beetles that has not yet faded. The title of this paper is one of the first questions that I asked, and one of the many to which I found no answer. The present answer is merely a hint, but I think, correct so far as it goes.

The first suggestion one would make, and I think the one that has been hinted at in the literature, is that the beetle wing is in its resting position straight and stiff, like that of any other insect, and that the beetle folds it and packs it away with the help, perhaps of its hind legs, perhaps of the tip of its abdomen. I think this answer is partly correct, most nearly so in such Clavicorns as the Nitidulidæ and Coccinellidæ, where when the wing is released it snaps open ready for flight. But in the more familiar of the larger beetles, such as the Adephaga and Serricornia, it will be found that the natural condition of the wing is folded, completely or almost completely, and the question arises how the wing is opened, and what holds it stiff for flight. The present paper aims at answering this question.

Serricornia.

Let us take a beetle of somewhat simple type of folding,—the Lampyrid, *Telephorus* (figs. 1-3). Remove the elytron and pull forward on the costa of the wing. We will find the wing swings out from the body as a folded bundle until it is almost in the flying position, while the anal area unfolds. Finally the anal area is completely unfolded and a strain comes on the disc of the wing. Then suddenly the fanlike fold in the middle of the wing opens, and at the same moment the apex unfolds and flattens out. Now let us see the possible mechanism.

Represent the principal lines of stiffness in the wing by heavy solid bars, as in figure 3: A, B, C, D, E. As A is drawn away from E the part of the wing lying between them will first unfold like a fan, and soon become tense. I have represented the lines along which the tension is most important by chain-lines on the diagram: A1-B1, A2-B2, B2-C, C-D, D-E. The flattening of the basal part of the wing is obvious enough; but the reason why the apex opens is not so plain. Now let us represent the principal lines of stiffness in each folded area of the apex of the wing in the same way as the basal ones. There are four of these areas, but one is so supported by the surrounding ones that it will be seen to need no support, and a glance at the chitinizations in the wing-substance shows that in fact it has none. The other three may be represented by the bars K, N and S. Take K. The inner half of it lies between the bars A and B, in such a way that it lies in taut, flat membrane. So any tendency to bend it up or down will draw on the lines of tension A1-B1 and A2-B2, which will elastically support it. A working model can be easily made by looping two rubber bands on two fingers, and then running a match through the two bands (fig. 8). N is supported in exactly the same way. Then the tips of K and N in turn develop a third line of tension (K-N), which, with the help of A2-B2 supports S in a similar manner. It can be seen that the small folds in the middle of the wing are supported by the tension between A and B, and so have no structural value. In fact the arrangement of these folds varies a good deal in detail among forms that have essentially this manner of folding, being considerably more complex in the Elateridæ, and especially the Hydrophilidæ, and somewhat simplified in such forms as Cebrio and many Buprestidæ. These variations are of considerable value in throwing light on relationships, but do not affect the mechanics. In the same way the fourth of the outer areas, below S, (which we may call T) is supported by the tension between S and the apex of N, and needs no structural support of its own. In sum the support of the unfolded wing is due first to the fanlike arrangement of the supports which run from the base, and the tension which muscles in the base put on the first and last of them (A and the body behind E), and secondly that in the outer part each succeeding series of supports overlaps the apex of the preceding, and is held flat by the tension between members of the preceding series. So all folds in the outer part of the wing should necessarily be chevronlike, zigzagging between the apices of an inner, and the bases of an outer series of supports. We find this arrangement very general, not only in the other Serricorns, but even in such aberrant things as the Staphylinidæ; but in the Adephaga a further specialization comes into play.

Adephaga.

I have chosen *Cicindela sexguttata* (figs. 3-7) as a fair example of the Adephaga. In general it is typical of the terrestrial Adephagous series, but differs from most Carabidæ in having a strong apical portion of vein R4+5, supporting the outer part of the wing along the line lettered M in the diagram. So the details of conditions in the apex will not be duplicated outside of the Cicindelidæ, through the central part of the wing is as in the true Carabids.

Conditions in the base of the wing are exactly as in the Lampyrid, so far as the mechanics is concerned. (The fan-like fold in the vicinity of M has a different relation to the veins and is probably homologous not to the one so conspicuous in the Lampyrids, but to another below it which appears in many other Polyphaga.) When we come to the principal fold we find that there is no definite chevron-like arrangement that could explain the stiffness of that part, as in the Lampyrid, but that the folds across all the principal veins lie in a straight line. On examining the wing it is found that the stiffness of the outer part of the wing in flying position is wholly due to the curiously constructed costal margin (formed of the fused veins C, Sc and R1) This is rather a flat ribbon than a normal vein, and is also ribbed transversely on its front edge, so that it bends easily from front to back, but is very stiff against any vertical pressure.

Looking at the diagrams (figs. 6 and 7) A, B, D, and E are as in Telephorus. C is also represented by veins, but is not needed to explain the unfolding of the wing. Next comes F. This bar in the diagram represents an insignificant-looking, but in fact very important sclerite which the tracheation shows to be a fragment of vein Rs. It is thrown into a horizontal position and supported by the tension between A and B, exactly as in the Lampyrid. The fragment of vein M represented by bar G is also apparently of some use, though as it is crossed by one of the folds it must be flexible, and is resistent only to compression. It no doubt helps to fix the bases of M and N. The outer part of the wing is held flat in a curious way. E as already stated can be bent back, but not up or down, on account of its peculiar structure; and it is attached at its outer end to a large area supported by a complex of strong veins (HILKJ). This area is only kept from bending up or down by the support of E, and is kept forward by the support of the tip of F, which articulates with it and pushes against it, as can be demonstrated by cutting E and F in turn. The tip of J may also get some support from the tip of G, which will help keep the whole area from bending down obliquely by twisting X. Altogether the whole area seems very weakly supported, but I can find no other factor. HILKJ, in turn, supports the entire posterior part of the wing by tension in the direction indicated by chain-lines on the diagram. This pull has to act against a strong spring-like action of the root of O, which tends to fold up the wing, and it seems surprising that the bracing of H by F is strong enough to do it. The apex of the wing is supported by S in relation to I and M, and by T in relation to M and S, in much the same way as S is supported by K and N in the Lampyrid.

Other Adephaga show a great deal of variation, especially in the outer part of the wing; but I believe the relation between X, F and H, to stiffen the outer part of the wing, is functional in all.

It will be interesting to compare other beetles with these two principal types of folding, and especially to find if any other mechanism is made use of. As I said at the start, I have a strong suspicion that in the various Clavicorn groups there are still other methods of folding, and some seem to make use of the feet. But careful observation of living specimens will be necessary to settle the matter. I hope this paper will attract some good observers to a very interesting problem.

PSYCHE, 1924 VOL. 31, PLATE 9

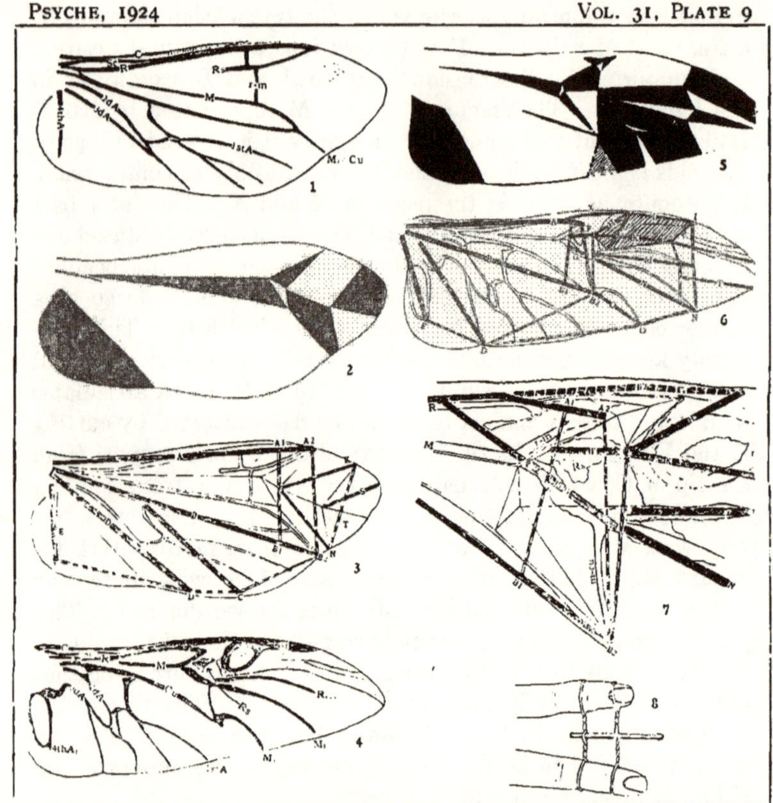

FORBES—WING FOLDING IN BEETLES

EXPLANATION OF PLATE 9.

1. *Telephorus* species (Lampyridæ). Venation.
2. Same. Folding pattern. (Areas reversed in folding black).
3. Same. Mechanics of folding. (Lines of stiffness are represented by heavy solid lines, lines of tension by chain-lines).
4. *Cicindela sexguttata* (Cicindelidæ). Venation.
5. Same. Folding pattern.
6. Same. Mechanics of folding.
7. Central costal part of fig. 6, more enlarged.
8. Method of stiffening apical part of wing, illustrated by a model.

ON THE SYSTEMATIC POSITION OF THE FAMILY TERMITAPHIDIDÆ (HEMIPTERA, HETEROPTERA), WITH A DESCRIPTION OF A NEW GENUS AND SPECIES FROM PANAMA.

BY J. G. MYERS[1].

RELATIONSHIPS OF THE FAMILY, TERMITAPHIDIDAE (nom. nov.)

In 1902 Wasmann erected the genus, *Termitaphis*, on a peculiar termitophile which he called *Termitaphis circumvallata*, and which he considered an aberrant aphid. Silvestri, describing two additional species in 1911, recognized that the genus was not even homopterous and established for it the new family Termitocoridæ, which he placed in the sub-order, Heteroptera. In 1914 a further species was described in a preliminary manner by Mjöberg, while in 1921 Silvestri recorded from India a fifth species of the genus. These references were all listed in the Zoological Record under the family, Aphididæ, and apparently received no attention from heteropterists. The list of species was brought up to eight by Morrison in 1923. Such in brief is the history of the genus.

The writer is indebted to Dr. W. M. Wheeler for the opportunity to study and describe a ninth species collected at Panama and to offer some suggestions on the relationships of the family to other heteroptera. Mr. Harold Morrison had also received specimens of the same insect from Panama, and was about to describe it but has very generously turned over his material to me.

The Rev. E. Wasmann most kindly sent for comparison the unique specimen of the type of the genus. Thanks are due also to Dr. W. M. Mann for bringing this valuable type from Europe. Previous workers have invariably referred their material to the type-genus, but Wasmann's type shows that it is decidedly not congeneric. A new genus, *Termitaradus*, is therefore erected here for the Panama species and its allies, which

[1]Contributions from the Entomological Laboratory of the Bussey Institution, Harvard University, no. 243.

undoubtedly include all species described subsequently to *T. circumvallata.*

None of the previous workers on these insects has made any suggestion as to the position of the family in the Heteroptera. Nor have the heteropterists themselves given the matter any attention although the very detailed and entirely adequate descriptions and figures of Silvestri and of Morrison were all that could be desired in the absence of actual specimens.

Silvestri's family name must be changed in accordance with the International Rules, which state that the family name must be derived from that of the type-genus. *Termitaphis* Wasm. was the original genus, and was used by Silvestri as the type-genus. The genus, *Termitocoris* apparently does not exist. The family name must therefore be Termitaphididæ. Dr. Wheeler drew my attention to this point.

Superficially the insects of this family are remarkably distinct from all other Heteroptera. This unique appearance is in keeping with a habitat shared, so far as known, by no other members of the sub-order. All the species collected have been found in the nests of termites, and such characters as are entirely peculiar to the family may be tentatively explained as results of adaptation to the termitophilous habit.

Reuter's (1912) Bemerkungen über mein neues Heteropterensystem was taken as the latest authoritative and comprehensive review of heteropterous taxonomy.

In following the key to families and also in comparing the separate diagnoses of Reuter's series and superfamilies, it was found that the *Termitaphididæ* were best placed in or near the series *Phlœobiotica,* a group established to contain the two families of bark-bugs, the Aradidæ and the Dysodiidæ, of which the latter is now by most authorities, e. g. Parshley, 1921, considered a sub-family of the former.

Reuter's diagnosis of this series is as follows (1912, p. 32).—

Unguiculi semper aroliis destituti. *Caput horizontale, inter antennas longe prolongatum,* utrinque tuberculo antennifero plerumque acuto instructum, bucculis sulcum rostralem formantibus. *Ocelli desunt. Rostrum quadri-articulatum,* sed articulo primo minutissimo, aegre distinguendo. *Antennæ capite plerumque longiores, quadriarticulatæ, sæpe crassæ.* Hemielytra c clavo, corio et membrana composita. Clavus apicem versus sensim angustatus, apicem scutelli nunquam superans. Membrana venis nonnullis irregularibus et anastomosantibus vel raro his tota destituta. *Meso-et metapleura simplicia. Coxæ posticæ rotatoriæ. Tarsi biarticulati.* Corpus superne et inferne deplanatum.

The characters italicized are those which are clearly exhibited also by the *Termitaphididæ*. The widest divergence lies in the wing characters, both pairs of wings being completely absent in the latter genus. But presence or absence of wings was never even a family character and there are Aradids with both pairs missing. There is therefore a strong presumption that the Termitaphididæ are related to the Aradidæ. The presumption is rendered almost a certainty by three other considerations now to be examined in some detail.

Reuter (1912) laid considerable emphasis on the presence or absence of arolia as a taxonomic character. The Aradidæ are said to possess no arolia and it was largely on this account that Reuter was unable to agree with Kirkaldy and with Bergroth that the Aradidæ exhibit marked affinity with the Pentatomoids. The Termitaphididæ on the other hand are furnished with very well-developed arolia shown clearly in Silvestri's excellent figures (1911, 1921). Whether this deficiency should be taken to indicate lack of affinity between the *Termitaphids* and the Aradids is questionable, since it is doubtful whether these organs afford such good taxonomic characters as has been supposed. In fact Reuter, who used their presence or absence so largely, has himself shown (1912) that they are probably of directly adaptive origin, varying apparently with the habitat even in genera of the same family. In the present case however no decision as to the importance of the arolia is essential to the argument since the Aradid genus, *Ctenoneurus* Bergroth, (Dysodiinæ, Mezirinæ) possesses arolia as well-developed as those of *Termitaphis*, or as those of any of Reuter's aroliate families—Miridæ, Pentatomidæ etc. The arolia of *Ctenoneurus hochstetteri* (Mayr) are shown in figure 9. This constitutes the first supplementary proof of the relationship of *Termitaphis* to the Aradidæ. Similar structures occur in certain species of the genera *Aradus*, *Dysodius* and *Isodermus*.

Incidentally the term "arolium" is used in general insect morphology and in hemipteran taxonomy with several different meanings which urgently need elucidation. Crampton (1923) applies the name primarily to the undivided pad-like structure between the claws of Orthoptera, e. g. *Periplaneta*. Further he mentions that the arolium in certain Hymenoptera and Homotera may be partially divided or faintly marked off into two lateral portions. There is no reference in Crampton's paper to the fact that in Heteroptera the arolium is always divided and in fact is referred to by taxonomists only in the plural. As illustrative of the most exact use of the term in Hemipterology, figure 11 shows the arolia of a Mirid after Knight (1923). The same drawing shows also the *pseudarolia* which in many Mirids are greatly developed and perhaps take the place of the true arolia which are reduced to mere bristles. Knight's arolia arise as shown in the figure truly between the claws and are probably homologous with the undivided arolium described by Crampton. But in Pentatomids, Coreids, some Aradids and in *Termitaphididæ*, the present writer finds that the arolia do not arise between the claws, but each from the base of the corresponding claw as shown in figures 7, 9 and 12. In these families it would seem that the so-called arolia are really homologous with the pseudarolia of the Miridæ, while the true Mirid arolia are represented by bristles between the claws as shown in the Pentatomid, *Euschistus* (fig. 12) and in a *Termitaphid* in Silvestri's drawings. Organs evidently exactly homologous with the so-called arolia of *Euschistus*, *Ctenoneurus* and *Termitaphis* are described and figured in the Coreid, *Anasa*, by Tower (1913) as *pulvilli*.

Whether the appendages figured in *Termitataradus* and in *Ctenoneurus* constitute true or pseudarolia or pulvilli does not affect the question of relationship since they are obviously homologous structures in the two genera.

In 1920 Spooner for the first time recorded a peculiar condition in the Aradid head in which the rostral setæ, instead of proceeding more or less directly cephalad and then caudad to enter the labial trough or rostrum, are coiled several times, like a watch-spring, in a semi-circular sheath formed by the tylus. The setæ are thus extremely long. That such an extraordinary condition should previously have escaped the notice of hemipterists is probably the result of the heavy chitinisation and black coloration of the head, which renders this structure entirely invisible in the untreated insect. The present writer noticed the setal coil independently in 1920 in the newly hatched nymph of *Ctenoneurus*, in which the coil shows as a dark mass against the soft white nymphal tissues. This arrangement of the trophi is present in an almost identical condition in the *Termitaphididæ* and constitutes the second supplementary proof of the relationship of these interesting termitophiles with the Aradids. To these two families alone of the Heteroptera are the coiled setæ apparently confined.

Here we meet the difficulty that the feeding-habits of Aradidæ and even more so of the Termitaphididæ are very little known. It seems likely that the insects of both families suck the sap of trees or the moisture of dead wood and of fungi. Obviously only liquid nutriment could be taken up by such mouthparts.

The first important character in which the *Termitaphididæ* appear to differ from the Aradidæ lies in the extraordinary development of laminæ on the margin of the body, round every portion of the periphery. These laminæ are furnished with stout outwardly directed bristles and with peculiar *flabella*, so named by Morrison. In some Aradids there is a lobulate expansion of the flattened lateral margin of the body. Such lobes are conspicuous in the imago of *Dysodius lunatus* (Fabr.) of which Dr. Nathan Banks has shown me specimens from Panama. In addition, Dr. Wheeler collected at Barro Colorado Island, Canal Zone, Panama, a single *Dysodius* nymph, probably referable to *D. lunatus*. This nymph, which is apparently in the third stadium, shows the marginal lobes very well-developed and offering striking points of resemblance to those of *Termitaphis*. There are twelve rounded lobes on each side of the body, not including projections of the head. The first is pro-, the second meso- and the third and fourth together metathoracic, while the rest pertain to the abdomen. Every lobe (fig. 10) is furnished with an irregular series of long conical processes, evidently hollow and provided with a rather thick but elongate distal flagellum usually more or less curved. The flagella are very liable to be broken off, particularly from processes near the apices of the lobes; and many are missing in the nymph under study. In the pinned imago of *Dysodius lunatus* no trace of the flagella is discernible, but in alcohol specimens examined later they are as well-marked as in the nymph. In the nymph there is thus a striking similarity to *Termitaphis* in the essential features of the marginal lobes. The number and distribution of the lobes themselves, their division into lobules or processes, the presence on every lobule of an easily detachable solid appendage arising apparently at the base of the lobule and running through or beneath its axis to protrude beyond its apex—in all these particulars there is practical agreement between the two genera. These constitute a third group of facts which may reasonably be considered to support the hypothesis of relationship between the *Termitaphididae* and the Aradidæ. The most striking superficial difference lies in the fact that the lobes in *Dysodius* are widely separated and thus fail to form such a continuous peripheral margin as in the *Termitaphididæ*. In the *Dysodius* nymph the conical processes with flagella are present also on the margin and projections of the head, and on the segments of the antennæ. The metanotum is provided with two lateral lobes instead of one as in *Termitaphis* and allies.

It seems probable that marginal laminæ in *Termitaradus* constitute a defensive apparatus enabling the insect to withdraw all its appendages under cover. For such withdrawal the form and articulation of the peculiar antennæ are especially adapted. Were the laminæ closely appressed to the substratum there would remain no unprotected part of the whole periphery. A similar development of lateral laminæ is frequent in myrmecophiles and termitophiles, notably in the larva of *Microdon* and in certain beetles and Myriapoda. In the termitophilous millipedes of the genera *Leuritus* Chamberlin and *Gasatomus* Chamberlin the general form of the body segments with their lateral lobes is strikingly reminiscent of the condition in *Termitaradus*

Wasmann (e. g. 1911, pp. 228-230) recognises this type of lateral lamination of body segments coupled with flattening of the ventral surface, as a direct adaptation to termitophily or myrmecophily—as a protection against the owners of the nests in which these arthropods live. It is a modified form of the adaptive type which he designates "der Trutztypus." All the specimens of *Termitaphididae* so far known have been collected in company with termites or in their nests.

The total absence of eyes and ocelli in *Termitaphids* is probably correlated with life in the gloomy recesses of the termite nest. The Aradids, themselves living in a cryptozoic habitat, have advanced a stage in this direction in that ocelli are lacking. The absence of wings in *Termitaphids* is similarly explicable. The peculiar structure of the antennæ, by which a superficially cryptocerate condition has been achieved, has been explained as a provision for tucking these organs under the cephalic laminæ. The antennæ are inserted very near the lateral margin and are folded in towards the rostrum.

The chief remaining morphological distinction between the *Termitaphids* and the Aradids lies in the structure of the rostrum and related parts. The head itself differs considerably. In the former it is more flattened and exhibits on side margins and fore-border a remarkable lamination with division into two main lobes on each side. This condition could perhaps be derived from that of a typical Aradid by an antero-lateral extension and lamination on each side of the tylus, so that the latter instead of forming the anterior projection of the head as in most Aradids, came to lie at the posterior end of a deep incision extending caudad from the anterior margin of the head.

So far as the rostrum is concerned the Aradids show a condition which has been described as apparantly three-segmented but really four-segmented. As a matter of fact, in *Ctenoneurus* at least, (fig. 8) the second segment is peculiarly constricted where it lies between the buccülæ, but four distinct segments are easily discernible. In *Termitaphids* the bucculæ form no appreciable sulcus for the rostrum. Wasmann described and figured the rostrum of *Termitaphis* as three-segmented and such it decidedly appears to be to all but the most searching examination. Silvestri, however, in all his work characterizes it as four-segmented and shows four very distinct segments in his figures. Such distinctness is certainly in error. The second segment, reckoning on this basis, is very indistinctly articulated and the present writer is by no means sure that it constitutes a true segment. (Figs. 2, 3).

The dorsal pores described and figured by Morrison are unlike anything known in other Heteroptera. Possibly, however, this worker's technique would reveal similar structures in other families.

To sum up it would appear that the Termitaphididae may be regarded as Aradoids specialized, in some respects degeneratively (absence of wings, eyes, ocelli and rostral sulcus), in others additionally (lateral lamination and armature and folded antennæ in *Termitaradus;* physogastry in *Termitaphis*), for a life of termitophily.

The diagnosis of the series Phlœobiotica (=superfamily Aradoidea) as set out by Reuter in 1912 and quoted above, may be modified as follows to include the Termitaphididæ.—

Arolia present or absent; head horizontal, much prolonged between the antennæ or else furnished with an acute antenniferous tubercle; a rostral sulcus formed by the bucculæ present or absent; ocelli absent; rostrum 4-segmented, often thickened. Hemielytra when present formed of clavus, corium and membrane; clavus narrowed towards the apex and never reaching beyond apex of scutellum. Membrane with some irregular and anastomosing veins or rarely completely destitute of venation. Meso-and meta-pleura always simple. Posterior coxæ rotatory. Tarsi 2-segmented. Body except in *Termitaphis* flattened above and below.

This series and superfamily comprises two families distinguished as follows.—

Tylus forming anterior projection of head; bucculæ forming a rostral sulcus; margin of body more or less simple or furnished with well separated irregular lobes. . . . . *Aradidæ* (Spin.)

Tylus at end of a deep incision extending caudally from anterior margin of head; bucculæ forming no appreciable rostral sulcus; margin of body furnished with lobes, separate or fused, which form a practically continuous lamina encircling the whole.

Termitaphididæ (n. n.)

As regards the position of the series Phlœobiotica, the discovery of arolia or similar structures in the Aradid, *Ctenoneurus*, is a further indication that Bergroth is correct in considering it nearest related to the Pentatomoids. Reuter was impressed by the fact that the eggs of Pentatomoids and of Coreoids are operculate, the embryo being furnished with a peculiar egg-burster for forcing up this lid; while the ova of Aradids, according to Heidemann, lack lids entirely and resemble more those of Lygæids. The operculum and correlated egg-burster are, however, by no means universal in the Pentatomoids, since they are totally lacking in the New Zealand Acanthosomatine genera, *Oncacontias* Breddin and *Rhopalimorpha* Mayr. The writer's notes on these insects are now in the press. In addition, observations now being carried out on certain North American Coreoids indicate a lack of these structures in this superfamily also. Since the above was written I have seen Barber's (Psyche, 1923) description of the egg of *aradus 4-lineatus*, which has a distinct cap and chorial processes.

Biology of Termitaphididae.

Very little is known under this heading. All the recorded specimens have been collected in association with termites, of which the following species have been identified. The hosts of Dr. Wheeler's Panama examples were kindly determined by Mr. Banks, those of the other Panama material by Dr. Snyder.—

Termitaphis circumvallata Wasm.,	
Amitermes foreli Wasm.,	Colombia.
Termitaradus mexicana (Silvestri),	
Leucotermes tenuis (Hag.),	Mexico.
T. subafra Silv.,. . *Rhinotermes putorius* Sjöst.	Africa.
T. australiensis (Mjöb.),	
Coptotermes sp.,	Australia.
T. annandalei (Silv.),. . *Coptotermes heimi* Wasm.,	India.
T. guianæ (Morr.),	
Leucotermes crinitus (Emerson),	British Guiana.
T. trinidadensis (Morr.),. . . *L. tenuis* (Hag.),	Trinidad.

T. insularis (Morr.),........	*L. tenuis* (Hag.),	Trinidad.
T. panamensis n. sp.,.....	*L. tenuis* (Hag.), *L. convexinotatus* Snyder	Panama.

In view of the additional species which have been brought to light within recent years coincident probably with intensified study of termites and of termitophiles, it would be premature to say much about distribution of the family. At present Central America seems to be the centre of greatest abundance but this may be due to greater collecting in the region. The distribution is certainly however practically circumtropical. In many respects it resembles that of *Peripatus* (sens. lat.) and may, as in the case of that genus indicate considerable antiquity as Mjöberg has suggested.

Habitat notes of the previously described species are scanty in the extreme. Of *T. mexicana*, Silvestri (1911) writes "in cuniculis nidi *Leucotermes tenuis* (Hag.)." When describing *T. annandalei* the same writer states "in nido *Coptotermes Heimi* Wasm., in trunco arboris (*Ficus bengalensis*) emortui et super solui sistentis exempla nonnulla Dr. N. Annandale legit." Mjöberg found a number of examples of his Queensland species "under bark of dead eucalyptus trunks in the colonies of a white ant (*Coptotermes* sp.) in the open forest country."

Dr. Wheeler found the Panama specimens within a termite nest (*Leucotermes convexinotatus* Snyder) the Termitaphids themselves being close to the cambium of the tree trunk from which they might probably have extracted nourishment. They were running about fairly actively.

What little is known of its habitat therefore seems to suggest that *Termitaphids* may have the same feeding habits as the Aradidæ.

What advantage they derive from living in the termite nest is uncertain. *Termitaradus* is probably protected from the termites themselves by its lateral laminæ and their armature. *Termitaphis* exhibits a certain degree of physogastry, a well-known feature of termitophiles and one which might indicate this genus as the more specialized of the two, though in the structure of the body margin it is intermediate between the Aradids and *Termitaradus*.

Dr. Wheeler suggests they may extract nourishment from either the nest material or the contained debris. Wasmann (1902) considers *Termitaphis* and *Termitococcus* Silvestri as affording the only known cases of trophobiosis among termites. Of *Termitococcus* nothing has been reported since the original description. As regards *Termitaradus* the peculiar dorsal pores discovered by Morrison may possibly secrete some material attractive to the termites, but only field observations can decide this point.

Most of the species of the family have been described from females alone. Males are now known of *Termitaradus annandalei*, *T. guianæ* (?), and *T. panamensis* sp. n. Silvestri has given good figures of the male genitalia. Nymphs have been found of *T. annandalei* and of *T. panamensis* only. Silvestri has figured the outline of the body of the ultimate and second (?) instars in *T. annandalei*. Both these instars have one lateral lobe on each side of the body more than in the imago (female) the numbers being 14 and 13 respectively. The same difference is observable in *T. panamensis*, between all female nymphs examined and the common 13-lobe type of female adult. Silvestri considers the additional lobe in the nymph to belong to the metathorax but to the present writer it seems to correspond exactly to the extra lobe present in the adult females of some of the species and shown by Morrison to pertain to the mesothorax. The reduction of lobes has gone furthest in *T. insularis* (Morr.) in which the female possesses only twelve, the number present in the males of those species in which both sexes are known.

TAXONOMY.

An examination of the unique and beautifully preserved type of *Termitaphis circumvallata* Wasm. shows it to be a female, of a different genus from all later described species. Wasmann's figures (1902) express these divergences quite clearly. It is a very different-looking insect with a swollen egg-shaped body surrounded by an incurved and upcurved dorso-lateral, segmentally-divided lamina almost meeting on the anterior half of of the body and showing the structure described in the key below. Some of the Panama material showed an upward curling of the laminæ in alcohol, but the condition thus artificially produced was not even superficially similar to that in *Termitaphis.* The Panama species is strongly flattened above and below, both in alcohol specimens and in life (Professor Wheeler), whereas Termitaphis would be rotund even were the laminæ removed entirely. A new genus is therefore erected for the Panama species and for all other species described since *T. circumvallata.* The Panama material was used as the genotype as it is the best known to me.

Silvestri's family diagnosis (1911, p. 232) may be modified by deletion of the phrase "corpus valde depressum," and by changing his statement regarding stigmata to read as follows: stigmata 9, of which two are thoracic. and seven abdominal.

The two genera may be separated as follows: *Termitaphis,* Wasm. (1902, p. 105); Body egg-shaped, surrounded by a strongly incurved and upcurved, dorso-lateral segmentally divided lamina, the edges of which are further divided into distinct, often quite distantly separated lobules each with a long fine almost smooth flagellum.

Type, *T. circumvallata* Wasm.

Termitaradus, gen nov., Entire body strongly flattened above and below and surrounded by a flat lateral segmentally divided lamina the margin of which is crenulate forming short non-separated lobules, each provided with a short, circular, clavate or lanceolate flabellum with serrate edges.

Type, *T. panamensis,* sp. nov.

In addition, the tylus, covering the setal coil, is in *Termitaphis* strongly protuberant, while in the other genus it shares the general flattening of the body. In the structure of the rostrum, antennæ, legs and last ventral segments of the female the two genera are similar.

To Wasmann's original description of *T. circumvallata* may be added the following: marginal lamina on each side divided into 13 lobes (Wasmann did not count the minute 8th abdominal), bearing lobules as follows: 6, 3 (head), 9 (prothorax), 7 (mesothorax), 7-8 (metathorax), 8-10, 8-9, 9-10, 8-9, 7, 6, 5, 3 (the 8 abdominal segments). There are thus fewer head lobules than in any other species of the family and more than the average of abdominal lobules. The flagella seem to me in most cases longer than figured by Wasmann. Both in the distinct separation of the marginal lobules and in the length and flagellate appearance of their appendages *Termitaphis* is clearly intermediate between the Aradid nymph described above and *Termitaradus*. The swollen form of the body is however very un-Aradoid, and may be best explained as an instance of termitophilic physogastry.

THE SPECIES OF TERMITARADUS.

Eight species, including the new one described below may be referred to this genus. Of these, one, namely *T. australiensis* (Mjöb.) is quite inadequately described and its relationships at present obscure.

The important characters in the genus appear to be the form and average number of the flabella. It is therefore unfortunate that these peculiar structures are so easily detached. In their absence however, their number can be ascertained by counting the lobules in which they arise. The *number* of the lobes, at least in those species which show 13 or 14 on each side seems less reliable. One would of course have been inclined to regard the presence or absence of an additional lobe as a character at least of specific importance, but the following considerations have led the writer to reject it as such.—

It is a single meristic character, and such are known to vary intraspecifically.

Nymphs in species in which the adult female is 13-lobed (*T. annandalei* and the normal 13-lobed Panama form) show the extra lobe clearly developed.

Specimens taken together in the case of three separate lots include a mixture of 13-lobe and 14-lobe examples.

The specimens in these lots agree exactly in all other characters.

The males taken with these lots are all identical and all show 12 lobes, as does also the male of the typically 13-lobed *T. annandalei.*

The 14-lobed specimens have the lobes distributed as follows in the manner indicated by Morrison.—2 to the head, one to the prothorax, 2 to the mesothorax, one to the metathorax and eight to the abdomen. Silvestri differs from this interpretation in considering the extra lobe (which by the way may be easily distinguished by its smaller size) to belong to the metathorax in *annandalei* nymphs, and to the prothorax in the 14-lobed adults, while Morrison assigns it to the mesothorax. The writer agreed with Silvestri but a rigorous combined examination by Mr. Morrison and himself of material treated in different ways has led to the conviction that Morrison's interpretation is correct.

The males differ from the females in that none of the abdominal segments after the seventh are furnished with lobes or form part of the marginal lamina. In number of flabella on head, thorax and segments 1 to 7 of the abdomen they agree with the corresponding female except that there is a tendency towards an average of one more flabellum in the abdominal segments.

The following table shows the number of lobules and their flabella on one half of the body in the seven adequately known species, in the females only. The thirteen-lobed form of the Panama species has been taken as typical and the description founded on it alone. Should future work show that the fourteen-lobed form is specifically distinct there need then be no confusion.—

	mexicana	*subrafra*	*annandalei*	*guianæ*	*trinidadensis*	*insularis*	*panamensis*
Head	7 4	7 3	8 3	7 3	7 3	7 3	7–8 3
Prothorax	9	12	10	9–10	8	10–11	10
Mesothorax	{4 {5	{4 {5	6–7	{4 {4	{4 {4	}11	5
Metathorax	5	5	6–7	4–5	3–4		5
1st abdominal	7	7	7–8	5–6	4	6	6
2nd "	7	7	8–10	6	4	7–8	6–7
3rd "	7	7	8–10	6–7	4	6–7	6–7
4th "	7	7	8–10	6–7	4	7	6–7
5th "	7	7	8–10	6	4	7	6–7
6th "	7	7	8–10	6	4	6	6
7th "	4	4	5	4	4	4	4
8th "	2	2	2	3	3	3	3

Key to the females of the seven adequately described species.

a Only 12 lobes to body margin on each side. . . . . *T. insularis* Morr.

aa 13-14 lobes to body margin on each side.

b Lobules of 2nd to 6th abdominal lobes not more than four. . . *T. trinidadensis* Morr.

bb Lobules of 2nd to 6th abdominal lobes six or more.

c Flabella short and rounded, at most hardly more than twice as long as broad.

d 8th abdominal lobe with two lobules; anterior abdom. segments with normally 7 or more lobules on each margin.

e Lobules of 2nd to 6th abdom. lobes not more than 7; flabella rounded. . . . . *T. mexicana* Silvestri.

ee Lobules of 2nd to 6th abdom. lobes 8 or more; flabella short clavate. . . . . *T. annandalei* Silvestri.

dd 8th abdominal lobe with 3 lobules; anterior abdom. segments with normally 6 or fewer lobules on each margin. *T. guianæ* Morr.

cc Flabella elongate, much more than twice as long as broad

f Flabella lanceolate, very acute at apex; 8th abdominal lobe with 3 lobules . . . . *T. panamensis* sp. n.

ff Flabella subcylindrical, rounded at apex or at most very obtusely pointed; 8th abdom. lobe with 2 lobules. *T. subafra* Silvestri.

Termitaradus panamensis sp. nov.

Male, female: Colour of alcohol specimens pale yellowish. Very similar save in details, to the Indian *T. annandalei* Silv., from which it differs in the smaller number of lobules on the marginal lobes, and in the shape of the flabella, which are elongate and lanceolate, the broadest part being nearer base than apex, the apex itself being very sharply pointed. The dorsal surface of the body is minutely papillated, marked into innumerable polygonal areas (chiefly irregular hexagons) by lines of slightly larger papillæ, and supplied with numerous pores. The tibial comb is similar to that described and figured by

Morrison in *T. guianæ*. The male genital segments differ from those of *T. annandalei*, especially in the caudal margin of the seventh abdominal segment, (mesad of the marginal lamina, see Silvestri, 1921, fig. III, 4) which is far less sinuate in the present species.

Length: male, 2.35; female, 2.40 mm.

Holotype (a slide mount) Type Cat. No. 27855 U. S. National Museum.

Allotype (slide mount, 13-lobed form). U. S. National Museum.

Paratypes in U. S. Nat. Mus. and in colls. Dr. W. M. Wheeler and Museum of Comparative Zoology.

Described from eight lots, with data as follows.—

5 males and 3 females, Barro Colorado Id., C. Z., Panama, 20th June, 1924, W. M. Wheeler. No. 510 (in nest of *Leucotermes convexinotatus* Snyder);

2 females, same locality, 21st Feb., 1924, T. E. Snyder. (in nest of *Leucotermes tenuis* Hag.)

3 females, same locality, 6th June, 1923, Zetek-Malino coll. (with *Leucotermes tenuis* on soft dry wood on ground) Z.2081

10 females, 2 males and 4 nymphs, near Fort San Lorenzo, C. Z., Panama, 14th June, 1923, J. Zetek, Z.2128A. (on soft wood of tree-stump);

3 females and two nymphs, same locality and date, J. Zetek, Z.2132A. (with *Leucotermes tenuis*);

1 female (Z.2171): In moist very soft rotting log on ground, Rio Acjeta, C. Z., Panama, Aug. 19th, 1923. With *L. tenuis* and *Cornitermes acignathus* Silv. J. Zetek coll.

1 female (Z.2263 S): In branch on ground, hard wet wood, Sweetwater, Fort Sherman, C. Z., Sept. 7th, 1923. With *L. tenuis*. Zetek-Malino coll.

3 females and one nymph (Z.2264 A) in pieces of branches on ground, hard wood. Other data as Z.2263 S.

Termitaradus guianae (Morr.)

Among the material kindly lent by the U. S. Bureau of Entomology through the courtesy of Mr. Morrison, were six females and one male from Rio Frio, Colombia, collected by Dr. W. M. Mann in February, 1924. These have been referred provisionally to *T. guianæ.* The male has twelve marginal lobes on each side, while five of the females have thirteen and the sixth shows fourteen. These seem all conspecific in spite of the divergence in the number of lobes. In this connection reasons have been adduced above for rejecting this character as specific among thirteen—and fourteen-lobed forms. Unfortunately the flabella are almost entirely lacking in the seven specimens, but the few that remain (fig. 13.) are identical in shape with those figures by Morrison in *T. guianæ.* Moreover the number of lobules in the respective lobes corresponds very closely with that in *T. guianæ*, the chief differences being as follows:

Number of lobules	*T. guianæ*	Colombian material
2nd lobe of mesothorax	4	5–6
2nd abdominal lobe	6	7
5th abdominal lobe	6	7

The variation in the considerable series of *T. panamensis* examined supports the suggestion that these differences come well within the range of intraspecific variability. In any case they seem an insufficient basis for specific rank.

In conclusion the writer would express his deep indebtedness to Professor W. M. Wheeler, Professor C. T. Brues and Mr. Nathan Banks for references to and loan of literature and for much helpful advice; and to Mr. Harold Morrison not only for turning over the task of describing his new species but also for much time, and patient work in demonstrating the interpretation of the segmentation.

Literature Cited.

CRAMPTON, G. C. 1923. Preliminary note on the terminology applied to the parts of an insect's leg. *Canad. Entom.* vol. 55, no. 6, pp. 126-132, Pl. 3.

KNIGHT, H. H., 1923. Miridæ: in, Hemiptera of Connecticut *Conn. State Geol. and Nat. Hist. Survey, Bull.* 34.

MJÖBERG, E., 1914. Preliminary description of a new representative of the family Termitocoridæ.
Ent. Tidskr., Uppsala, vol. 35, pp. 98-99, 2 figs.

MORRISON, H., 1923. Three apparently new species of *Termitaphis*. *Zoologica*, vol. 3, no. 20, pp. 403-408, Pl. 24.

PARSHLEY, H. M., 1921. Essay on the American species of *Aradus*. *Trans. Am. Ent. Soc.*; vol. 47, pp. 1-106, Pl. 1-7.

REUTER, O. M., 1912. Bemerkungen über mein neues Heteropterensystem.
Ofv. Finsk. Vet.-Soc. Forh., 54, A, no. 6, pp. 1-62.

SILVESTRI, F., 1911. Sulla posizione sistematica del genere *Termitaphis* Wasm. (Hemiptera) con descrizione di due specie nuove.
Portici Boll. Lab. Zool., vol. 5, pp. 231-236.

ibid., 1920. Contribuzione alla conoscenza dei Termitidi e Termitofili dell'Africa occidentale. *Op. cit.*, vol. 14, pp. 265-319.
(includes just a copy of the description and figures of *T. subafra* from Silvestri, 1911).

ibid., 1921. A new species of *Termitaphis* (Hemiptera-Heteroptera) from India. *Rec. Ind. Mus.*, Calcutta, vol. 22, pp. 71-74, 3 text-figs.

SPOONER, C. S., 1920. A note on the mouth parts of Aradidæ *Ann. Ent. Soc. Am.*, vol. 13, pp. 121-122, 1 text-fig.

TOWER, D. G., 1913. The external anatomy of the squash bug, *Anasa tristis* DeG. *Ann. Ent. Soc. Am.* vol. 6, pp. 427-441, Pl. 55-58.

WASMANN, E., 1902. Species novæ insectorum termitophilarum ex America meridionali.
Tijdschr. v. Ent., vol. 45, pp. 75-107; *Termitaphis*, p. 105, Pl. 9, fig. 7, 7a-c.

ibid., 1904. Res. Swed. Zool. Exped. to Egypt and White Nile, 1901; no. 13. Termitophilen aus dem Sudan. Pp. 1-21 taf. 1. Upsala.

ibid., 1911. Die Ameisen und ihre Gäste.
1st Congr. Int. d'Ent. Bruxelles, 1910.Pp. 209-234, Pl. 12-17.

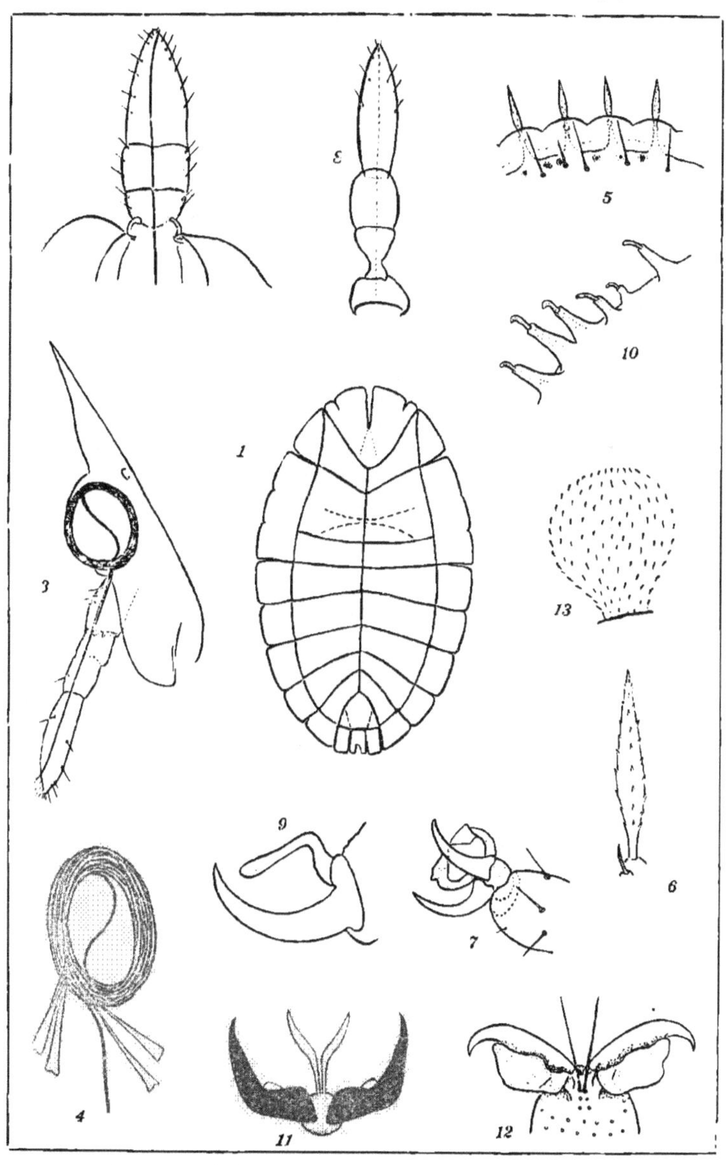

MYERS—TERMITAPHIDIDÆ.

Figures.

1. *Termitaradus panamensis* sp. nov. Outline of body of female showing lobes and sutures.
2. Do. Rostrum projecting from body and viewed from behind.
3. Do. Lateral view of head showing rostrum, setal coil and insertion of left antenna.
4. Do. Setal coil, semi-lateral view.
5. Do. Portion of marginal lobe (pronotum, dorsal).
6. Do. Flabellum much enlarged.
7. Do. Tip of tarsus showing claws and arolia.
8. *Ctenoneurus hochstetteri* (Mayr). Rostrum.
9. Do. One claw and its associated arolium.
10. *Dysodius* sp., nymph. Portion of marginal lobe (pronotum, dorsal).
11. *Lygus vanduzeei* Knt. Claws, arolia and pseudarolia (after Knight).
12. *Euschistus variolarius* (Pal. de Beauv.). Tip of tarsus from below. The small circles are insertions of long spines. The arolia are united to the claws only at the base.
13. *Termitaradus guianæ* (Morr.) (Colombian specimen). Flabellum.

THE IMPORTANCE OF WINTER MORTALITY IN THE NATURAL CONTROL OF THE EUROPEAN CORN BORER IN NEW ENGLAND.[1]

By George W. Barber.

Cereal and Forage Insect Investigations, Bureau of Entomology, United States Department of Agriculture.

Among the factors that limit the spread and occurrence of an injurious insect in numbers sufficient to cause injury to crops, the ability of a species to withstand the rigors of winter occupies an important place, particularly in colder climates. If an insect is unable to pass successfully through this troublesome period of the year, it probably will rarely become a pest of first importance, although by means of annual migration it may occur frequently in some numbers. Such a condition is found, for example, in the case of the corn earworm (*Heliothis obsoleta* Fab.) which as far as our knowledge goes cannot successfully winter in New England or other northern sections of the United States. However, this insect appears nearly every summer in numbers ranging from a mere trace to serious abundance in such areas, and as the writer has shown, (Jour. Agri. Res. 1924, XXVII p. 65) it became a pest of importance in New England in 1921. The accepted explanation of this phenomenon is that the moths of this insect migrate northward each spring and summer, arriving in larger numbers some years than in others, and in the case of favorable growing seasons, possibly pass through a partial second generation, in which case injury is most noticeable.

It may happen in the case of another species that a large number of individuals may perish in the overwintering stage, more dying during severe winters than during mild winters. This too may result in the species becoming injurious during some seasons and unimportant during others following a high or low rate of mortality during the preceding winter.

Investigations of the European corn borer (*Pyrausta nu-*

[1]Contribution from the Bureau of Entomology, U. S. Department of Agriculture in cooperation with the Entomological Laboratory of the Bussey Institution, Harvard University, (Bussey Institution No. 242.)

bilalis Hübn.) in the New England area have been conducted for several years to determine the importance of winter mortality as a limiting factor in the spread and injurious occurrence of this insect. It has been found that the spread of the insect has been greatest along the coast of New England and least inland from

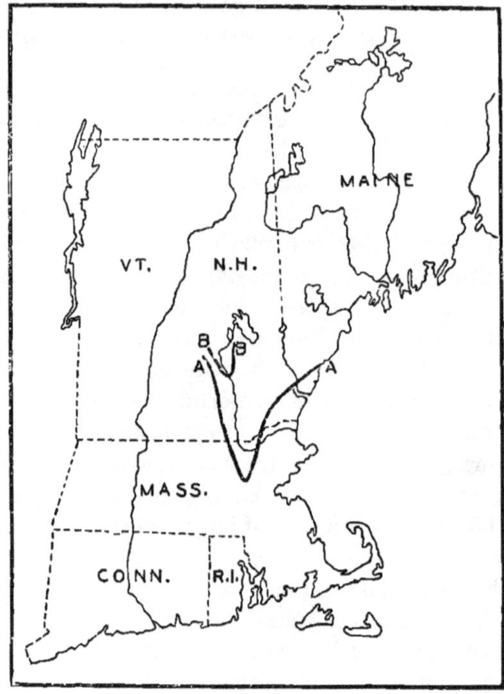

Fig. 1. Map showing the southern extent of the area of high winter mortality of the European corn borer in New England during the winters of 1922-1923 (AA) 1923-1925 (BB).

the sea. This condition may be due in part to an ability of the overwintering larvæ to survive more successfully along the coastal region where the winter temperatures due to the moderating effect of the ocean are less severe than farther inland where such a moderating effect is less noticeable. On the other hand no such condition may exist, and the more rapid spread along the coast may be the result of other causes.

In the following account of winter mortality of the European corn borer, information has been obtained in two ways. Field counts of larvæ in the spring have usually been made in localities where the insect occurs abundantly and in host plants that have remained undisturbed. Over much of the area now infested in New England, however, the insect occurs in insufficient numbers to permit such counts in numbers large enough for accuracy. In this case experiments were placed in the field in representative localities in the fall after activity of the insect had ceased and collected in the spring before activity was resumed. In the studies of the results obtained in this work, the conditions found to exist in the spring of 1922, 1923 and 1924 may be considered separately.

Observations in the spring of 1922.

During the spring of 1922 observations of winter mortality were confined to host plants that had passed the winter undis-

TABLE No. 1.

WINTER MORTALITY FOUND IN THE SPRING OF 1922 IN SEVERAL HOST PLANTS THAT HAD PASSED THE WINTER UNDISTURBED.

Host Plant	No. of localities	Total No. larvae examin-ed	No. larvae dead	Aver. % winter mor-tality	Greatest % winter mor-tality for any locality	Least % winter mor-tality for any locality
Sweet Corn.......	9	901	100	11.1%	16%	6.2%
Cocklebur (Xanthium sp.)....	5	644	33	5.1%	7%	2%
Barnyard Grass (*Echinochloa crus-galli* (L). Beauv).	4	273	30	10.9%	13%	10%
Smartweed (Polygonum sp.)...	2	150	4	2.7%	4%	0%
Beggar-ticks (Bidens sp.).......	2	210	16	7.6%	8%	0%
Pigweed (*Amaranthus retroflexus* L.).............	2	200	42	21%	27%	15%
Lamb's quarters (*Chenopodium album* L.)..........	1	100	8	8%	....	....

turbed. These observations were in corn and certain other host plants in which the insect occurs abundantly. The observations were also confined to that section of New England where the insect occurred in large numbers, an area bounded by Marblehead, Mass., on the north, Arlington, Mass. on the west and Quincy, Mass. on the south. The results of these observations are shown in Table I.

For all these localities and in all host plants the average winter mortality was 9.4 per cent, being highest in pigweed (*Amaranthus retroflexus* L.) and least in Cocklebur, (*Xanthium* sp.) and Smartweed (*Polygonum* sp.).

TABLE No. 2.

WINTER MORTALITY FOUND IN THE SPRING OF 1923 IN VARIOUS HOST PLANTS.

Host Plant	Number of Collections	Number of localities	Total number of larvae	Number larvae dead	Mean per cent larvae dead	Highest per cent dead-in any collection	Lowest per cent dead, in any collection
Sweet Corn........	50	20	5,150	415	8%	24.5%	1%
Beggar-ticks (Bidens sp.)............	9	7	800	66	8.2%	19%	0%
Pigweed (*Amaranthus retroflexus* L.).	9	5	850	119	14%	24%	7%
Horseweed (*Erigeron canadensis* L.)....	1	1	100	9	9%	......	...
Cocklebur (Xanthium sp.)..........	10	6	1,050	67	6.4%	15%	1%
Barnyard grass (*Echinochloa crusgalli* (L.) Beauv.)....	8	5	750	72	9.6%	20%	4%
Smartweed (Polygonum sp.).........	7	5	650	43	6.6%	18%	0%
Dahlia (Dahlia sp.)..	4	2	400	26	6.5%	12%	3%
Prince's feather (*Polygonum orientale* L.)..............	1	1	50	2	4%	......	...
Hemp (*Cannabis sativa* L.)..........	2	1	200	9	4.5%	7%	2%
Flase ragweed (*Iva xanthifolia* Nutt.).	1	1	100	17	17%	......	...

Observations in the spring of 1923.

Investigations of winter mortality during the spring of 1923 were of two distinct sorts; first, observations of the winter mortality in host plants that had remained undisturbed through the winter and second, observations of the winter mortality in corn stalks placed in representative localities the previous fall for the purpose of obtaining information on this subject.

In Table 2 the results of the observations of winter mortality in host plants that had remained undisturbed during the winter are shown. The highest rate of winter mortality was found in pigweed (*Amaranthus retroflexus* L.) and false ragweed (*Iva xanthifolia* Nutt.); the least mortality in prince's feather (*Polyfonum orientale* L.) and hemp (*Cannabis sativa* L.). These examinations were confined to localities within the heavily infested area of Massachusetts as were the corresponding observations of the preceding spring. The average winter mortality for all localities and host plants was found to be 8.3 per cent.

In table 3 winter mortality is compared in corn stalks that had passed the winter in various conditions. Here mortality appears to have been highest in corn stubble and lowest in corn that was piled up in the fall and passed the winter in this condition.

TABLE No. 3.

WINTER MORTALITY IN CORN STALKS THAT PASSED THE WINTER IN SEVERAL CONDITIONS.

Condition of corn stalks	Number of collections	Number of localities	Total number of larvae	Number of larvae dead	Mean per cent of larvae dead	Greatest winter mortality, in any collection	Least winter mortality, in any collection
Standing stalks.....	25	19	2450	186	7.6%	14%	1%
Stalks lying on surface of soil.......	12	10	1300	101	7.8%	13%	3%
Stalks placed in piles in the fall........	5	3	500	26	5.2%	12%	1%
Corn stubble.......	8	6	900	100	11.1%	24.5%	2%

None of the localities summarized in tables 2 and 3 were far enough inland to show any marked difference in winter mortality that might be associated with any climatic factor. In fact all these localities are in a very small area, somewhat larger than the area covered by the examinations of the previous year but confined to the heavily infested regions for the reason previously stated.

The experimental work, on the other hand, shows very clear differences in winter mortality. An experiment was placed in the late fall of 1922 in each of twenty localities representing all sections infested by this insect at that time. These experiments were placed in the field in November, 1922, after activity of the insect had ceased and were recovered in April, 1923, before spring activity began. Migration of larvæ from the corn stalks was for this reason limited to a few individuals. Each experiment consisted of ten stakes to each of which were fastened six infested stalks. The findings in the spring of 1923 may be best shown in the following table.

TABLE No. 4.

WINTER MORTALITY FOUND IN THE EXPERIMENTAL MATERIAL IN THE SPRING OF 1923.

Locality	Date placed in field	Date re-covered	Total number of larvae re-covered	Number of larvae dead	Per cent of winter mortality	Average per cent of winter mortality in group
Bristol, N. H.	11-8-22	4-26-23	1307	307	41.9	
Farmington, N. H.	11-7-22	4-25-23	1341	559	41.7	35.5
Wells, Me.	11-7-22	4-25-23	1132	507	44.8	
Tyngsboro, Mass.	11-8-22	4-14-23	990	161	16.3	22.6
Concord, Mass.	11-4-22	4-10-23	854	256	29.8	
Methuen, Mass.	11-2-22	4-14-23	1014	52	5.1	
Worcester, Mass.	10-26-22	4-11-23	1222	34	2.8	
Walpole, Mass.	11-6-22	4-11-23	661	32	4.8	3.9
Quincy, Mass.	11-4-22	4-11-23	944	31	3.3	
Manomet, Mass.	10-30-22	4-6-23	1081	14	1.3	
Wareham, Mass.	11-1-22	4-8-23	1066	10	.9	
Falmouth, Mass.	10-31-22	4-7-23	1135	13	1.1	.88
Harwich, Mass.	11-1-22	4-6-23	909	9	1.	
Wellfleet, Mass.	10-31-22	4-7-23	1106	1	.09	

Several of the experiments placed in the field and recovered are not shown in this table because birds removed such a large number of the larvæ from the stalks that too few remained from which to draw conclusions. However, several areas stand out rather distinctly as showing considerable difference in the extent of winter mortality. First, an area represented by three stations in southern New Hampshire and Maine where winter mortality averaged 35.5 per cent; second, two localities in Massachusetts in inland river valleys where winter mortality averaged 22.6 per cent; third, four localities in eastern Massachusetts where mortality averaged 3.8 per cent; and fourth, five stations on Cape Cod where winter mortality averaged only .88 per cent.

Observations in the spring of 1924

In the fall of 1923 a series of experiments similar to those described for the previous year were placed in the field in the infested area of New England. As in the former instance the experiments were placed in the field in the fall after activity of the larvæ had ceased and they were recovered in the spring before activity commenced so that the loss through larval migration was expected to be limited to a few individuals. Each experiment consisted of four stakes to each of which were attached five infested corn stalks. The stations, 50 in number, were chosen in an attempt to represent the whole infested area in as fair a manner as possible. Using Arlington, Mass., as a center, these stations were run out in lines as far as the infestation was known to exist to the northeast, the north, the north by northwest, the northwest, the west, the southwest, the south and the southeast. On these stations 47 were recovered in good condition, 16 of which exhibited considerable feeding by birds. The average winter mortality of these 16 stations which were all located in Massachusetts was 1.7 per cent of the total number of larvæ recovered. The extent of winter mortality is shown in table 5. In this table the stations are grouped in three main divisions similar to those into which the area seemed to be naturally divided the previous spring.

TABLE No. 5.

EXTENT OF WINTER MORTALITY IN EXPERIMENTS EXAMINED IN THE SPRING OF 1923.

Maine and New Hampshire		Eastern Massachusetts		Cape Cod	
Per cent of winter mortality	Number of stations	Per cent of winter mortality	Number of stations	Per cent of winter mortality	Number of stations
1%	1	0%	2	0%	1
3 to 4%	3	less than 1%	7	less than 1%	1
4 to 5%	2	1 to 2%	2	1 to 2%	3
7 to 8%	2	2 to 3%	8	2 to 3%	1
8 to 9%	1	3 to 4%	3		
9%	1	4 to 5%	2		
24%	1	5 to 6%	3		
39%	1	6 to 7%	1		
		7 to 8%	1		
Average mortality 9.3% Average mortality omitting the two highest 5.4%		Average mortality 2.6%		Average mortality 1.3%	

Although the mortality was not nearly as extensive as it had been during the preceding winter, the same general conditions are noted; that is, a relatively higher rate of mortality at stations in Maine and New Hampshire and an extremely low rate on Cape Cod. Only two stations showed an important mortality—Concord, N. H. (39 per cent) and Bristol, N. H. (24 per cent). Why these stations should have shown extensive winter mortality while other stations in the same region did not, is a point not clearly understood. They were in more exposed locations, however, and may not have benefited by snow protection to so great an extent as the other stations.

The following table exhibits the protecting influence of snow as found in an experiment overwintering in Wells, Maine and examined April 28, 1923.

TABLE No. 6.

THE EFFECT OF SNOW PROTECTION ON THE EXTENT OF WINTER MORTALITY.

	Sweet Corn (24 stalks)			Longfellow flint corn (29 stalks)		
	Total No. of larvae	Number dead	% of winter mortality	Total No. of larvae	Number dead	% of winter mortality
Top foot of stalks........	130	67	51%	92	55	60%
Middle section of stalks...	435	190	43%	223	92	41%
Bottom foot of stalks.....	68	13	19%	49	13	26.5%

It is believed that the top of these stalks was exposed most of the winter, that the middle sections were exposed some of the time during the winter months and that the bottom foot was covered with snow during the whole period of severe winter weather.

Since it has been shown that the variation in winter mortality of this insect has been quite marked during the two winters, 1922-1923 and 1923-1924, it may be useful to examine the temperatures of the area covered by experiments during these winters. The extent of the area infested by this insect in New England is only some 80 miles east and west and about 175 miles north ands outh, while the extent of the injurious occurrence is only a small portion of this area. This is indeed a small area in which to study climatic conditions, but on the other hand, these conditions will be shown to be quite variable. There is considerable difference between the conditions on Cape Cod and the winter climate of the hills of Central New Hampshire where much more variable winter temperatures are experienced.

In tables 7 and 8 certain figures are presented for 15 localities throughout this larger area. These are divided into groups to correspond with the main sections of the area into which the results of the study of winter mortality seem to fall. Five localities represent the conditions of southern Maine and New Hampshire; three localities, the river valleys of northeastern Massachusetts; five localities, eastern Massachusetts and two localities

TABLE

SYNOPSIS OF WINTER TEMPERATURES

Locality	Elevation in feet	Precipitation (Total)	Minimum temperature	Date of minimum temp.	No. days minimum below 32°
Portland, Me	99	19.19	-8	Feb. 17	116
Plymouth, N. H.	500	10.47	-21	Dec. 20	117
Franklin, N. H.	440	11.06	-23	Jan. 7	118
Concord, N. H.	350	7.96	-14	Feb. 18	116
Durham, N. H.	88	12.27	-10	Dec. 20	112
Lawrence, Mass.	51	16.80	-13	Feb. 17	113
Lowell, Mass.	100	13.53	-18	Feb. 18	115
Concord, Mass.	139	14.79	-13	Feb. 17	108
Rockport, Mass.	25	12.33*	-4	Feb. 17	106
Fitchburg, Mass.	550	14.29	-9	Feb. 17	113
Worcester, Mass.	518	10.46	-3	Feb. 17	114
Boston, Mass.	124	10.06	2	Feb. 17	100
Fall River, Mass.	200	17.51	1	Feb. 24	104
Plymouth, Mass.	50	14.15	-2	Feb. 17	115
Provincetown, Mass.	40	15.95	8	Feb. 17 Mr. 29	99

*Record for March Missing.

TABLE

SYNOPSIS OF WINTER TEMPERATURE

Locality	Elevation in feet	Precipitation (Total)	Minimum temp.	Date of minimum temp.	No. days minimum below 32°
Portland, Me.	99	12.81	-18	Jan. 27	97
Plymouth, N. H.	500	11.26	-19	Jan. 27	110
Franklin, N. H.	440	9.67	-28	Jan. 28	114
Concord, N. H.	350	9.03	-18	Jan. 27	100
Durham, N. H.	88	12.95	-18	Jan. 27	101
Lawrence, Mass.	51	14.50	-14	Jan. 27	98
Lowell, Mass.	100	15.01	-18	Jan. 27	111
Concord, Mass.	139	13.40	-10	Jan. 27	105
Rockport, Mass.	25	13.15	-10	Jan. 27	84
Fitchburg, Mass.	550	11.49	-16	Jan. 27	99
Worcester, Mass.	518	11.20	-9	Jan. 27	100
Boston, Mass.	124	12.91	-6	Jan. 27	75
Fall River, Mass.	200	17.84	-2	Jan. 27	86
Plymouth. Mass.	50	11.39*	-3	Jan. 27	96
Provincetown, Mass.	40	13.25	2	Jan. 27	78

*Records for December Missing.

No. 7.

DECEMBER 1, 1922 TO MARCH 31, 1923.

No. days minimum below 0°	Total amount temp. below 32°	Total amount temp. below 0°	Greatest range in a 24 hr. period	Average daily range	Detail of greatest range in a 24 hr. period	Winter mortality averaged in groups	Number of localities
9	2204	33	38	15.3	36 to −2		
29	2826	235	39	19.	44 to 5	33.5%	3
34	2980	300	51	23.2	33 to −18		
19	2399	106	45	18.5	35 to −10		
13	2269	66	44	18.9	35 to −9		
9	2084	68	48	19.3	36 to −12		
25	2404	201	46	22.6	36 to −10	22.6%	2
23	2366	141	49	20.4	37 to −12		
1	1359	4	33	14.8	41 to 8		
12	1999	39	42	18	36 to −6		
4	1718	7	31	13.2	35 to 4	3.9%	4
0	1347	0	37	14.7	42 to 5		
0	1410	0	37	15.5	42 to 5		
2	1701	3	36	17.5	54 to 18	.88%	5
0	987	0	24	11.9	36 to 12		

No. 8.

DECEMBER 1, 1923 TO MARCH 31, 1924.

No. days minimum below 0°	Total amount of temp. below 32°	Total amount of temo. below 0°	Greatest range in a 24 hr. period	Average daily range	Detail of greatest range in a 24 hr. period	Winter mortality averaged by groups	Number of localities
5	1430	55	48	14.5	36 to −12		
11	2052	83	38	16.1	38 to 0		
22	2296	175	53	21.2	39 to −14	9. %	12
9	1677	65	40	17.3	45 to 5		
3	1624	31	39	17.6	43 to 4		
6	1407	27	41	18	40 to −1		
10	1711	49	38	21.6	38 to 0		
8	1558	35	37	19.1	41 to 4		
1	940	10	35	15.3	45 to 10		
4	1409	32	39	17.7	59 to 20	2.6%	29
4	1241	17	34	14.2	28 to −6		
					55 to 21		
2	806	9	37	13.8	37 to 0		
1	892	2	25	14.4	25 to 0		
					33 to 8		
					37 to 12		
2	1126	4	32	16.8	42 to 10	1.3%	6
0	710	0	33	13.	45 to 12		

represent Cape Cod. The information contained in these tables has been computed from records of the United States Weather Bureau and information is restricted to localities for which this Bureau obtained detailed records during the periods covered by this study. The records were mostly of maximum and minimum daily temperatures, columns headed "total amount of temperature below 32 degrees" and "total amount of temperature below 0 degrees" being obtained by adding minimum temperatures experienced at each locality. The information contained in these tables is presented as comparisons between different localities and as a comparison of the two winters. They are not intended to show that any one set of factors explains the variation in winter mortality that was found in the several localities where experiments were placed.

Several interesting points may be noticed in a study of these tables; 1, the moderating effect of the sea is shown in those stations that are located on the sea coast *i. e.*, Portland, Me., Rockport, Boston, Plymouth and Provincetown, Mass. 2. In all localities the fact that the winter of 1922-1923 was severe in comparison to the mild winter of 1923-1924, is clearly indicated. The mortality rate for each winter is for the most part readily compared with this difference in severity. 3. A distinct correlation is shown for the winter of 1922-1923 between high percentages of mortality and winter severity.

It does not appear that a slow westward spread of this insect in New England is to be accounted for by winter mortality except that barriers of high mortality may in severe winters appear, such as was represented by Concord, Mass. during the severe winter of 1922-1923 when mortality there was found to be 30 per cent. Worcester, Mass., the station located farthest west in the experiments of 1922-1923 showed 2.8 per cent of mortality (table 4) and in the experiments of 1923-1924 the average winter mortality of the six stations located farthest west in Massachusetts was but 3.6 per cent.

To the north, however, it does seem that the insect may be entering territory in which it will suffer annual winter mortality sufficient to keep its numbers below that which would allow serious injury to crops, at least in certain areas. In Merriam's map of Life Zones of the United States (1910-Check-List of North American Birds, 3d ed., rev.; also published in separate form, Biol. Survey, U. S. Dept. Agr.) the Boreal region is shown to extend southward into central New Hampshire in the shape of a long arm. It is interesting to note that the experiments placed in Bristol, N. H. in the fall of 1922 showed the following spring 22 per cent of winter mortality and the material placed in the same location a year later and examined in April of 1924 showed winter mortality of 24 per cent. This town is located within the southern point of the boreal region referred to above and is the only locality that showed considerable winter mortality during each of the two years. Furthermore, the only other locality that showed a high percentage of mortality during the winter 1923-1924 (Concord, N. H. with 39 per cent of mortality) lies just without the southern edge of this region. This is the only area in New England where infestation by this insect is known to approach the boreal zone as portrayed in the map referred to. The information is not sufficient to warrant a prediction as to whether this insect would thrive in the Boreal zone, but it may be highly suggestive of a condition that may eventually be found to exist.

Summary.

The studies recorded in this paper were undertaken to determine what importance winter mortality played in the natural control of the European corn borer in New England. Examinations of several host plants of this insect in the spring of 1922 and the spring of 1923 showed that mortality was greatest in pigweed (*Amaranthus retroflexus* L.) and barnyard grass (*Echinochloa crusgalli* (L.) Beauv.), the mortality in pigweed averaging 21 per cent in 1922 and 14 per cent in 1923, while in barnyard grass 10.9 per cent were found dead in 1922 and 9.6 per cent perished in 1923. The average mortality in all host plants and localities was 9.4 per cent in 1922 and 8.3 per cent in 1923. All of these examinations were made in the heavily infested area of the New England infestation, bounded by Marblehead, Mass., on the north, Arlington, Mass., on the west and Quincy, Mass., on the south.

In the fall of 1922 and again in the fall of 1923 experiments consisting of corn stalks tied to stakes were set out in 20 localities the first year and 50 localities the second year, throughout the area known to be infested by this insect in New England. The results obtained by the examination of these experiments in the spring of 1923 and the spring of 1924 showed somewhat greater mortality during the winter of 1922-1923 than during the winter of 1923-1924. Winter mortality was found to be greater in localities farther north than in localities in the southern part of the infested area. Thus on Cape Cod, 5 localities averaged 0.88 per cent of mortality in the spring of 1923 and 6 localities averaged 1.3 per cent of mortality in the spring of 1924: In the remainder of the infested area in Massachusetts, 4 localities not in river valleys averaged 3.9 per cent of mortality, and 2 localities in river valleys averaged 22.6 per cent of mortality in the spring of 1923, while 29 localities averaged 2.6 per cent of mortality in the spring of 1924. In the infested area of Maine and New Hampshire 3 localities averaged 33.5 per cent of mortality in the spring of 1923 while 12 localities averaged 9.3 per cent of mortality in the spring of 1924.

From a study of winter weather of 15 localities representing the entire invested area, no one factor alone seems to be responsible for winter mortality, but the extent of mortality seems to be associated with winter severity. While winter mortality seems to be of minor importance in the area infested by the European corn borer in New England at the present time, areas of rather high mortality have appeared, and these must play some part in limiting the advance and increase of the infestation in such localities.

ON SOME NEW PHLŒOTHRIPIDÆ (THYSANOPTERA) FROM THE TRANSVAAL

By J. Douglas Hood,

University of Rochester.

The new species described below constitute only a very small part of a collection of Thysanoptera made in the Transvaal by Mr. Jacobus C. Faure, Professor of Entomology in the Transvaal University College, at Pretoria. The descriptions were prepared early in 1924, before I learned that Mr. Faure had himself decided to work up the Thysanoptera of Southern Africa, and while I was engaged in special studies of the genera to which they belong. It is to be hoped that Mr. Faure will soon publish his interesting observations on the group.

Compsothrips recticeps sp. nov.

Female (apterous).—Length about 2.9 mm. Color nearly black, with posterior margin of pterothorax, first abdominal segment, sides of second segment, and a pair of lateral blotches on fifth segment, white; trochanters, and hind coxæ, brown; antennæ nearly black, excepting apical portion of segment 2, which is brownish yellow, and segment 3, which is brownish yellow and heavily shaded with blackish brown near base and at apex; subhypodermal pigmentation purple.

Head 2.3 times as long as wide, broadest across eyes, surface nearly smooth, lightly reticulate at base; cheeks nearly parallel in anterior three-fifths, slightly converging posteriorly; anterior prolongation of head with sides slightly converging anteriorly; vertex flattened, sloping downward, and with a slight median ridge in lower portions; frontal costa slightly concave; three pairs of short, knobbed bristles on head, the anterior pair longest and situated near anterior angles of eyes, the middle pair just in front of posterior margins of eyes, the posterior pair well down on cheeks and somewhat more than twice their length behind eyes. Eyes protruding, less than one-fourth as long as head and less than one-half as wide as their interval. Ocelli wanting. Antennæ about one and one-third times as long as head; segment 3 about equal to 1 and 2 together and 1.4 times the length of 4; 4-7 prolonged ventrally[1] at apex, 4 and 7 only slightly; all bristles and sense cones particularly short and weak. Mouth cone shorter than its width at base, about reaching middle of prosternum, broadly rounded at apex, tip of labrum not attaining that of labium.

Prothorax less than one-half as long as head and (inclusive of coxæ) about 1.6 times as wide as long, surface nearly smooth, with sides and the abruptly declivous posterior margin lightly subreticulate; midlaterals minute, all other bristles present, brownish yellow, knobbed and about equal to postoculars and coxals. Pterothorax very small, decidedly narrower than prothorax; mesoscutum transversely striate with anastomozing lines, becoming subreticulate at sides; metascutum subreticulate at sides and base, rather closely longitudinally striate elsewhere. Wings wanting. Legs long and slender, with femora and tibiæ (particularly those of posterior legs) arcuate; fore tarsi armed with a long, stout tooth.

Abdomen broad and heavy, fully 1.5 times as wide as prothorax. Tube less than half as long as head and about twice as long as basal width, which is twice the apical. Bristles nearly colorless, long, nearly pointed; terminal bristles brownish, about 0.7 as long as tube.

Measurements of holotype (♀): Length 2.90 mm.; head, length 0.593 mm., width (across eyes) 0.257 mm., width at base 0.204 mm.; eyes, length 0.128 mm., width 0.060 mm., interval 0.135 mm.; prothorax, length 0.255 mm., width (inclusive of coxæ) 0.408 mm.; pterothorax, width 0.330 mm.; abdomen, width 0.638 mm.; tube, length 0.249 mm., width at base 0.126 mm., at apex 0.061 mm.

Antennal segments:	1	2	3	4	5	6	7	8
Length (μ)	84	90	170	119	115	102	63	60
Width (μ)	57	43	44	45	41	38	31	20

Total length of antenna 0.80 mm.

[1]Several genera of Phlœothripidæ have certain of the intermediate antennal segments prolonged in this way, and the teeth so formed are set with a series of short, sensory bristles. Various entomologists have described these teeth as being situated on the *dorsal* surface of the antennæ, whereas they are clearly *ventral* in position.

Described from 2 females taken by Mr. J. C. Faure at Duivelskloof, Transvaal, December 7, 1918, "on grass" (No. 407).

The coloration of the antennæ and body associate this species with *C. albosignatus* (Reuter) from which it differs most conspicuously in the much shorter third antennal segment and the shape of the head.

Stictothrips gen. nov.

(*Stiktos*, spotted; *thrips* a wood worm)

Depressed; roughened, non-shining and mottled above; glabrous beneath. Head not elongate, rounded but not swollen behind eyes, narrowed at base; cheeks with several prominent funnel-shaped bristles; vertex with a cup-like depression or groove, with the anterior ocellus at its upper edge. Eyes large, rounded and closely facetted, dorsal extent much greater than ventral. Fore femora not enlarged nor toothed; fore tarsi armed in both sexes. Wings of fore pair broad at base, abruptly constricted at basal two-fifths, apical three-fifths narrow, parallel-sided, delicately but distinctly reticulate, without median vein. Abdomen with a broad dorsal furrow for the reception of the wings. All prominent body bristles fan-shaped. Terminal bristles shorter than tube, pointed.

Genotype: *Phlœothrips maculatus* Hood.

Closest to *Neurothrips*, even to the general plan of coloration and the habits of the two known species, but separable by the absence of the median vein of the wing, the less swollen cheeks, and the short terminal bristles.

Stictothrips faurei sp. nov.

Female (macropterous).—Length about 1.6 mm. Color (to naked eye or as seen under hand lens) pale yellowish brown, intricately mottled with white and brown, with head, pterothorax, and tube dark brown, and appendages annulate with blackish brown. Under 16 mm. objective, the color appears paler—more nearly brownish yellow; head pale brown, vertex yellow, a narrow, median brown streak on dorsum of head behind eyes, and a small, white, lateral spot at extreme base, cheeks narrowly edged with brown; antennæ straw-yellow, with segments 4, 6 and 8 dark blackish brown, except pedicel and apex of 4 and pedicel of 6, which are yellow, and outer surface of 1, inner and outer surfaces of 2, pedicel of 3, and sides and apical portion of 7, which are shaded with brown; prothorax pale straw-yellow, anterior plate at hind angles brown, posterior plate white, coxæ and ventral plates brown; pterothorax with sides brown and darkest posteriorly, dorsum paler, brownish yellow; mesoscutum with anterior angle white and a dark brown blotch on posterior margin at middle; metascutum with a pair of tooth-like dark brown blotches directed posteriorly, their points paler, and nearly or quite touching; legs pale yellowish, with tarsi nearly black, tibiæ broadly ringed with dark brown just before middle, and femora with a dark brown blotch on inner, and one on outer, surface; wings colorless or lightly clouded with yellowish; segment 1 of abdomen yellowish, with a median, pale brown blotch, and with the pair of small plates at base dark brown; remaining segments (excepting 8-10) with a pale brown blotch at middle, with a white one on either side, followed by a dark brown one (much the largest on segment 2), and at extreme lateral margins, by a small pale brown one, the area in front of the latter white, all blotches becoming less distinct on the more posterior segments; segment 8 with two pairs of small brown spots, arranged in a transverse row, the outer pair involving the stigmata; 9 with two pairs of small brown spots, arranged in two longitudinal rows; tube dark blackish brown apically and at sides of base, remainder pale yellow.

Head about 1.1 times as long as wide, broadest behind eyes, converging to base, the latter about 0.8 the greatest width, dorsal and ventral surfaces lightly reticulate (not clearly visible in all specimens), cheeks minutely serrate and set with about five pairs of transparent, trumpet-shaped bristles; vertex with a cup-shaped depression, the anterior ocellus located on upper margin of cup and directed forward; sides of head in front of eyes produced anteriorly to form a pair of strong teeth slightly overhanging outer margin of first antennal segment. Eyes large and rounded, very closely facetted, prolonged posteriorly on dorsal surface of the head.[1] Ocelli exactly equidistant, pigment red. Antennæ almost exactly as figured in the original description of the genotype, but more slender (see measurements) and without infundibuliform bristles at base of segment 2 and apex of segment 3; sense cones as in figure of that species. Mouth cone acute, about attaining posterior margin of prosternum, labrum acutely pointed.

Prothorax somewhat more than half as long as head and (inclusive of coxæ) nearly 2.4 times as wide as long, surface finely granulate; all usual bristles present, broadly dilated, fan-like, so transparent as to be easily overlooked; posterior plate at hind angles with two bristles, instead of one, the posterior bristle the largest on prothorax. Pterothorax wider than prothorax, sides subparallel for half their length, then roundly converging to base of abdomen. Wings of fore pair sharply constricted near middle, where there is a short median thickening; basal portion without fringe on anterior margin, but with about 8 minute hairs in outer portion of posterior margin; distal portion of wing rather sparsely fringed, without accessory hairs; entire wing roughened and lightly but distinctly reticulate; subbasal bristles set close to base of wing, minute, expanded. Legs short, fore and hind femora swollen, fore tarsi with a long, slender, hooked tooth; leg bristles mostly expanded apically.

Abdomen distinctly broader than prothorax. Tube nearly two-thirds as long as head, unusually slender, more than three times as long as basal width which is hardly twice the apical, slightly widened at base, sides slightly converging apically. Bristles broad, nearly clavate, almost transparent, the latero-ventral pair on segment 9 longer and pointed; terminal bristles yellowish, hardly twice as long as tube.

Measurements of holotype (♀): Length 1.55 mm.; head, length 0.252 mm., width 0.221 mm., width at base 0.182 mm.;

[1]In the original description of *S. maculatus* (Hood), Entomological News, XX, 1909, p. 250, the eyes are said to be reniform, and are so shown in the figure given on page 251. As the wings of the unique type had not been spread, and as the coloration was so dark as to make difficult any detailed study of the chitinous exoskeleton, the writer ventured to clear the specimen in potassium hydroxide and remount it; and subsequent study shows the eyes to be broadly rounded posteriorly, and not at all reniform. Only the type is known.

eyes, length 0.111 mm., width 0.065 mm., interval 0.084 mm.; prothorax, length 0.135 mm., width (inclusive of coxæ) 0.323 mm.; pterothorax, width 0.350 mm.; abdomen, width 0.540 mm.; tube, length 0.161 mm., width at base 0.050 mm., at apex 0.029 mm.

Antennal segments:	1	2	3	4	5	6	7	8
Length (μ)	48	69	78	61	57	51	44	39
Width (μ)	30	32	28	31	28	26	21	11

Total length of antenna 0.45 mm.

Male (macropterous).—Apparently similar to female in all respects, excepting for the smaller size and slenderer form.

Described from 11 females and 7 males taken by Mr. J. C. Faure at Malelane, Transvaal, December 12, 1918, "on pawpaw tree trunk" (No. 403).

A particularly beautiful species, quite distinct from its North American congener, and one which I take pleasure in naming after its discoverer.

Plectrothrips atactus sp. nov.

Female (brachypterous).—Length about 1.8 mm. Color pale brownish yellow, shaded with blackish brown on front margin of head, cheeks, posterior margin of prothorax, mesothorax (particularly at sides) and second abdominal segment; tube with a reddish cast; legs and antennæ yellow; no subhypodermal pigmentation except the three, bright-red, ocellar spots.

Head smooth above, roughened at sides, 1.2 times as long as wide, broadest midway between eyes and base of head, cheeks rounded; postocular bristles pointed, much shorter than eyes, almost lateral in position; other cephalic bristles minute. Eyes moderately small, hardly one-third as long as head and about 0.4 as wide as their interval. Ocelli situated far forward, the anterior one almost between bases of antennæ, the posterior pair very widely separated, situated close to anterior angles of eyes. Antennæ of structure normal to the genus[1], except that

[1]See Hood, Ins. Insc. Menstr., Vol. IV, 1916, Pl. 1, fig. 4.

segment 8 is more slender than usual and distinctly the longest in entire antenna, and segment 6 has no long sense cone on the outer surface at apex. Mouth cone shorter than wide, broadly rounded at apex.

Prothorax smooth, about equal in length to head and (inclusive of coxæ) about twice as wide as long, notum not attaining lateral margins, median thickening distinct; one pair of pointed bristles at posterior angles, somewhat longer than postoculars and subequal to coxals; other bristles minute. Pterothorax about as wide as prothorax. Wings short and scale-like. Legs short and stout; fore tibiæ not toothed on inner surface of apex; middle and hind tibiæ with the usual long stout spines; fore tarsus with a long, curved tooth.

Abdomen of normal structure; tube 0.7 as long as head and about twice as wide at base as at apex, sides slightly concave, apex slightly constricted. Bristles long and pointed; terminal bristles much shorter than tube.

Measurements of holotype (♀): Length 1.83 mm.; head, length 0.230 mm., width 0.191 mm.; eyes, length 0.070 mm., width 0.039 mm., interval 0.096 mm.; postocular bristles, length 0.057 mm.; prothorax, length 0.198 mm., width (inclusive of coxæ) 0.390 mm.; pterothorax, width 0.390 mm.; abdomen, greatest width 0.456 mm.; tube, length 0.165 mm., width at base 0.086 mm., at apex 0.046 mm.

Antennal segments:	1	2	3	4	5	6	7	8
Length (μ)	49	63	58	60	56	55	55	67
Width (μ)	44	43	43	44	36	31	24	14

Total length of antenna 0.46 mm.

Male (brachypterous).—Similar to female except for the somewhat smaller size, slenderer abdomen, and the more enlarged prothorax and fore legs. Ninth abdominal tergite slightly prolonged at middle of posterior margin to form a thin, semicircular plate overlying the tube.

Described from 20 females and 5 males taken by Mr. J. C. Faure at Boksburg, Transvaal, April 21, 1914, "under dead Eucalyptus bark" (No. 401).

The long terminal segment of the antenna and the absence of the usual sense cone from the outer surface of the sixth antennal segment should serve to distinguish this species. The structure of the 9th abdominal tergite of the male is interesting. The same process occurs in *P. antennatus* Hood but is lacking in *P. pallipes* Hood.

Trichothrips transvaalensis sp. nov.

Female, forma brachyptera.—Length about 1.7 mm. Color brown, with pterothorax somewhat lighter and head yellow; femora concolorous with body, except fore pair, which are yellow apically; tibiæ paler than femora, mid and hind pairs shaded with brown; tarsi yellow; tube brown, paler at extreme base and in apical half; antennæ dark blackish brown, excepting segments 1, 2 and 3, which are pale brown, with base of 1, apex of 2 and pedicel of 3 pale yellow; subhypodermal pigmentation red.

Head slightly longer than broad, widest at middle of cheeks, abruptly rounded to eyes and slightly converging to base of head; occipital region faintly subreticulate and with the usual bristles on cheeks rather stout and prominent; postocular bristles less than half as long as head, pointed. Eyes small, directed forward, less than one-fourth the length of the head, and about five-eights as wide as their interval. Ocelli usually wanting, but sometimes minute and barely visible, in which case the anterior one is situated well down toward antennæ, and the posterior ones opposite middle of eyes. Antennæ distinctly more than twice the length of the head; segment 1 tapering to apex; 2 much longer and narrower than 1; 3 the longest, subconical; 4-8 successively shorter and narrower; 8 lanceolate, pedicellate, pedicel somewhat dilated at base; sense cones: 3, 1-2; 4, 2-2; 5, 1-1+1; 6, 1-1+1; 7 with one on dorsum near apex. Mouth cone reaching nearly across prosternum, semicircularly rounded at apex, tip of labrum about attaining that of labium.

Prothorax nearly 0.9 as long as head and (inclusive of coxæ) about twice as wide as long; anterior marginal and anterior angular bristles about half as long as postoculars; others long, pointed, midlaterals and inner pair at posterior angles about as long as postoculars, the other pair shorter but longer than coxals.

Pterothorax about as wide as prothorax, sides almost parallel. Wings minute. Fore tarsus with a moderately long, stout tooth.

Abdomen broad, 1.4 times as wide as prothorax. Tube about 0.8 as long as head, about twice as long as basal width, and distinctly more than twice as broad at base as at apex. Bristles long and pointed, those on the ninth segment somewhat shorter, subequal to terminal bristles, two-thirds as long as tube.

Measurements of holotype (♀): Length about 1.74 mm.; head, length 0.228 mm., greatest width 0.209 mm., width at base 0.188 mm.; eyes, length 0.052 mm., width 0.018 mm., interval 0.081 mm.; postocular bristles, length 0.090 mm.; prothorax, length 0.200 mm., width (inclusive of coxæ) 0.408 mm.; pterothorax, width 0.413 mm.; abdomen, width 0.573 mm.; tube, length 0.180 mm., width at base 0.091 mm., at apex 0. 043 mm.

Antennal segments:	1	2	3	4	5	6	7	8
Length (μ)	54	67	78	71	66	62	51	48
Width (μ)	45	32	35	34	31	30	26	18

Total length of antenna 0.50 mm.

Female, forma macroptera.—Head concolorous with body, instead of yellow; eyes much larger, rounded, their width nearly equal to their interval; ocelli large, the anterior one situated in front of eyes and overhanging; pterothorax broader than prothorax; wings broad, colorless, fore pair with 8 or 9 accessory hairs on posterior margin; outer subbasal bristle on fore wings short and pointed, others three times as long and capitate.

Male (brachypterous).—Only slightly smaller than female and quite similar in general structure; fore femora greatly swollen, tarsal tooth much stronger, nearly triangular.

Described from 30 females and 20 males, taken by Mr. J. C. Faure at Johannesburg, Transvaal, April 21, 1914, under dead Eucalyptus bark (No. 404).

A true *Trichothrips*, with the terminal antennal segment pedicellate. Separable from its congeners by the coloration, the rather long third antennal segment, and the details of chætotaxy.

THE IDENTITY OF LEPTOFŒNUS F. SMITH AND PELECINELLA WESTWOOD (HYMENOPTERA).

By Charles T. Brues.

Bussey Institution, Harvard University.

In 1862 Frederick Smith[1] described as Leptofœnus a peculiar Hymenopterous insect of doubtful affinities which he says unites some of the characters of Fœnus (Gasteruption), Megischus and Pelecinus). A recent examination of this paper led me to compare his description with a specimen of the remarkable chalcid-fly Pelecinella, and I find that the two are undoubtedly synonomous. As the Leptofœnus (1862) antedates Westwood's Pelecinella (1868), Smith's name must take precedence.

These insects are now generally conceded to form a part of the family Cleonymidæ although they constitute a very aberrant group represented, so far as is known, only in the neotropical region from Brazil to Panamá

Subfamily Leptofoeninæ Handlirsch.
Genus Leptofoenus Smith.

Type: *L. peleciniformis* Smith

1862 F. Smith, Trans. Entom. Soc. London (3) vol. 1, p. 43 ♀ (*Leptofœnus*)

1868 Westwood, Trans. Entom. Soc. London, Proc., p. XXXVI (*Pelecinella*)

1874 Westwood, Thesaur. Entom. Oxon., p. 142 Pl. XXVI, fig. 8 (*Pelecinella*)

1889 Schletterer. Berliner Entom. Zeits., vol. 33, p. 239 (*Leptofœnus*)

1895 Ashmead, Proc. Enton. Soc. Washington, vol. 3, p. 232 (*Pelecinella*)

1902 Dalla Torre, Catalogus Hymenopterorum, vol. 3, p. 1075 (*Pelecinella*).

1903 Szépligeti, Ann. Mus. Nat. Hungarici, vol. 1, p. 365 (*Leptofœnus*).

[1]Trans. Entom. Soc. London, (3), vol. 1.

1904 Ashmead, Mem. Carnegie Mus. Pittsburgh, vol. 1, p. 285, p. 384, p. 486 (*Pelecinella*)
1909 Schmiedeknecht. Genera Insectorum, fasc. 97, p. 150 (*Pelecinella*)
1910 Kieffer, Evaniidæ, Das Tierreich, Lief. 30, p. 410 (*Leptofœnus*)
1912 Viereck, Bull. U. S. Nat. Mus., No. 83, p. 84 (*Leptofœnus*).
1915 Brues, Psyche, vol. 22, p. (*Pelecinella*)
1923 Gahan & Fagan, Bull. U. S. Nat. Mus., No. 124, p. 112 (*Pelecinella*)
1924 Handlirsch, Schröder's Handbuch der Entomologie, vol. 3, p. 744 (*Leptofœnus*); p. 764 (*Pelecinella*)

As already stated Smith ('62) did not locate his genus Leptofœnus in any family, and as his remarks concerning it preclude its association with the Chalcidoidea, Westwood ('68) placed his Pelecinella there without suspecting its identity. Schletterer ('89) quoted Smith's description and speculated concerning the relationships of Leptofœnus, but made no attempt to locate it in any family. Ashmead ('95) transferred Pelecinella to the family Cleonymidæ, considering it better placed there than in the Torymidæ (Callimonidæ) where Westwood had first ('68) placed it, or in the Perilampidæ where it is located in Westwood's "Thesaurus." Since then no one has seen fit to suggest relationship with any other Chalcidoids. Kieffer ('10) includes Leptofœnus in the Evaniidœ where it is placed at the end of the subfamily Aulacinæ. Finally Handlirsch ('24) has erected a new family for Leptofœnus, placing it between the Stephanidæ and Megalyridœ, and in the same volume he includes Pelecinella as the tribe Pelecinellini of the subfamily Cleonyminæ of the Chalcididæ, not suspecting any relationship between the two genera.

The checkered taxonomic career of Leptofœnus thus illustrates well the great difficulty which attends the allocation of aberrant insects on the basis of descriptions.

The five described species of Leptofœnus are all very closely similar although differing strikingly in color. The type species, *L. peleciniformis* Smith seems to be most closely similar to *L. ashmeadi* Brues from Brazil, although undoubtedly distinct.

Since this was written I have seen a specimen of Leptofœnus from Panama. This is a female found by Prof. W. M. Wheeler on Barro Colorado Island in the Canal Zone, where it was seen in company with several others on the bark of a felled Cordia tree. Contrary to expectations, however, this is evidently not Smith's species, but appears to be a variety of *L. westwoodi* Ashmead described originally from Brazil. It differs conspicuously from the latter in color, lacking the rufous markings which are replaced by black, but agrees so well otherwise that I believe it to be only a well marked color variety of that species.

NOTES ON THE GENUS NECTARINA SHUCKARD. (VESPIDÆ).

BY CEDRIC DOVER.

British Museum (Natural History), London, England.

The following notes are based on material in the British Museum (Natural History).

Nectarina championi sp. nov.

Female: head black, remotely punctured, covered with very short golden pubescence; genæ yellow, the yellow extending on to the occiput just behind the middle of each posterior ocellus; eyes dark greenish-bronze with golden iridescence; antennæ mostly ochraceous, lighter on the underside, flagellum on outerside, except the three apical joints, brownish-black;

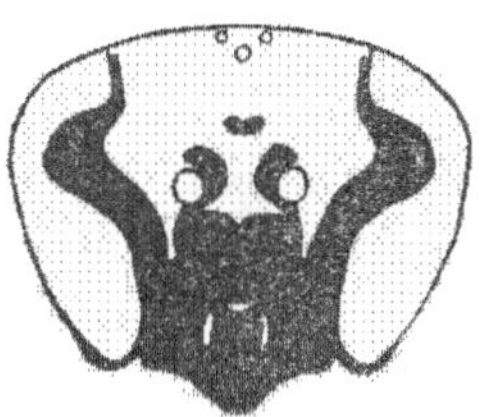

Fig. 1. *Nectarina championi* sp. nov. Front view of head; yellow markings indicated in black.

clypeus yellow, usually with two, short, longitudinal indefinitely shaped, brownish markings, convex, broader than long, posterior margin emarginate, anterior margin acutely prolonged; supra-clypeal area with a band of yellow, posteriorly notched with black in the middle; two more or less rounded yellow markings on the frons adjacent to the base of the antennæ and a small transverse yellow marking above these; mandibles yellow; pronotum yellow with short golden brown hairs arising from minute punctures; mesonotum black, sparsely, but regularly and finely, pitted, with a longitudinal median carina anteriorly, and two, yellow curved-in stripes extending across it longitudinally on each side of this carina; scutellum yellow, pitted, having a rather coarse appearance, broadly grooved down the middle; post-scutellum yellow, slightly narrower than scutellum, sides parallel, anterior margin transverse, posterior margin rounded, shining and almost impunctate; median segment yellow, much broader than long, broadly and shallowly excavated down the middle, more or less impunctate, with comparatively long golden-brown hairs on the sides; abdomen ochraceous-brown, posterior margin of second segment, and succeeding segments, ochraceous, the first two segments with hairs arising from fine punctures, which lie along them closely longitudinally adpressed, giving them a finely striated appearance; succeeding segments very closely punctate with short golden hairs arising from them; legs ochraceous; with short golden pubescence on the tibiæ and tarsi; wings iridescent-hyaline, nervures brown; tegulæ ochraceous.

Length: 6 millimetres.

Habitat: David, Chiriqui, Panama (*G. C. Champion*).

Holotype and twenty-eight paratypes in the British Museum.

The small size and ochraceous color of this species makes it so distinct from the other species of the genus known to me that it is unnecessary to institute a comparison.

Nectarina scutellaris Fabr.

Additional records: Corcovada, Rio de Janeiro (*G. E. Bryant*, 10. v. 12); Guaruja, Ilha Santo Amaro (*G. E. Bryant*, 9. iv. 12); Santarem; Sao Paulo; Issororo, British Guiana (*G. E. Bodkin*, Jan. 1912).

Nectarina azteca Suass.

In the British Museum from the following Mexican localities: Oojaca; Amula, Guerrero, 6000 feet; Hacienda de la Imagen, 6000 feet; Tierra Colorada, Guerrero, 2000 feet; Rincon; Acapulco; Etat de Puebla, Jehuacan.

Nectarina augusti Sauss.

Additional records: Parintins, Lower Amazon (*E. E. Austen*, 4. xi. 96); La Guayra, Venezuela, 1-200 feet (*G. B. Longstaff*, 20. xii. 06).

Meade-Waldo (A. M. N. H. ser. 8, vii, p. 112, 1911) gives *Chartergus amazonicus* Cam. specific rank, but as Ducke has shown (Ann. Mus. Nat. Hung., viii, p. 481, 1910) Cameron's insect is a synonym of *N. augusti* Sauss.

Nectarina bilineolata var. **smithii** Sauss.

Additional records: El Reposo, 8000 feet (*G. C. Champion*); S. Geronimo (*G. C. Champion*); Parintins, Lower Amazon (*E. E. Austen*, 4 xi96); "West Indies" (*E. F. Becher*).

Nectarina lecheguana var. **velutina** Spin.

The following localities for this form appear to be worth recording: Oojaca; Mazatlan; Xucumantlan, Guerrero, 7500 feet; Acaguizotla, Guerrero, 3500 feet; Tepetlapa, Guerrero, 3000 feet; Chilpancingo, Guerrero, 4600 feet; Rincon, 2800 feet; S. Geronimo; Orizaba; Atoyac; Bugaba, Panama; Teapa, Tabasco; V. de Chiriqui, 25-4000 feet; Chontales, Nicaragua; Issororo (*C. B. Williams*, July, 1916); Sta. Catharina; Puerto Bertoni, Paraguay. Mr. G. E. Bryant has taken the typical form at Estancia Biscacheras near Santa Elena, Entre Rios (25, 8, 12). Cameron's *Chartergus centralis* is a synonym of this form, as is also his *aztecus*, needlessly renamed *cameroni* by Meade-Waldo (*loc. cit.*), as Ducke had already established its identity (*loc. cit.*).

THE MALE OF THE PARTHENOGENETIC MAY-FLY, *AMELETUS LUDENS.*

By James G. Needham.

Cornell University, Ithaca, N. Y.

This paper is to record the capture of a single adult male specimen of *Ameletus ludens* and to describe it. This sex has been sought diligently for more than a dozen years by a number of competent students of the Ephemerida, and many hundreds of nymphs have been reared in a vain effort to obtain it. Females are common enough at Ithaca, N. Y. The nymphs live in the pools of the rapid brooks that run down East Hill into Cayuga Lake. They poise gracefully on submerged twigs, or dart rapidly about over the sandy bottom, and are easily collected in April and May. Dr. W. A. Clemens found a single male sub-imago and took it into the laboratory but it died before its final moulting (Canad. Ent. 54: 77-78, 1922). On June 9, 1924, Dr. O. A. Johannsen captured a single adult male in flight by the side of Vanishing Brook near his home on Cornell Heights, and turned it over to me for study.

The nymph of this species was briefly described and beautifully figured by Eaton in his Monograph (Trans. Linn. Soc. Lond. (2) 3: 204, pl. 49) in 1885: it was doubtfully (and, as we now know, incorrectly) referred to the genus Chirotenetes, whose nymph was then unknown. The specimen had been collected in 1874 by Mr. Hubbard at Trenton Falls, N. Y. Female sub-imagos taken by Mr. D. B. Young in transformation at Newport, N. Y. were described by me in 1905 (N. Y. State Mus. Bull. 86: 36).

Males of the other species of Ameletus, all of which come from the Rocky Mountains or farther westward, are well known. The search for the male of this species was begun by Miss Anna H. Morgan. In 1911 she described the adult female (Ann. Ent. Soc. Amer. 4: 118) and gave a detailed report of rearings of scores of nymphs taken at Ithaca, N. Y., all of which were females. She first pointed out that here is a case of probable parthenogenesis. Two years later she described and figured the curiously sculptured egg (Ann. Ent. Soc. Amer. 6: 400, Pl. 52, fig. 59, 1913); and she continued to rear the nymphs without finding a single male. I have myself, also, reared scores of nymphs—all females. Clemens examined hundreds of nymphs and found them all females. He demonstrated parthenogenesis by taking the eggs of these females, reared in isolation from males and unmated, and hatching them. He found the period of incubation to be five months (l. c., p. 78).

I have recently come upon this same marked tendency toward parthogenesis in the genus Ephemerella. In the course of a biological survey of the Lloyd-Cornell Reservation near McLean, N. Y., made during the past summer, two species of this genus were collected, and the commoner one was represented only by females. Hundreds of nymphs were collected by Mr. C. K. Sibley and myself, and scores of these were reared in cages, and only females were found. As a nymph this species has long been known. I described and figured it in 1905 (as *Ephemerella sp.* N. Y. State Museum Bull. 86:45, Pl. 10). It is widely distributed in New York State. Since no males are to be had and there is no present prospect of obtaining materials for more adequately characterizing the species, it might as well bear a name, so I propose the name *Ephemerella feminina* for it. I note that Dodds, in describing a similar Ephemerella nymph from Colorado (Trans. Amer. Ent. Soc. 49:99, 1923), says of it "About thirty nymphs of this species in our collection include no males."

Little is known as yet concerning unusual life cycles in the Ephemerida. The ovo-viviparous habit of the European *Chlœon dipterum* has long been known (See Lestage, Larves aquatiques des Insectes d'Europe, Vol. I, p. 250, 1921). Recently Miss Helen E. Murphy, on dissecting out the eggs from the ovaries of a female of a South American Callibætis, discovered them to contain well grown embryos; wherefore, we named this new species *Callibœtis viviparus* (Lloyd Library Bull. 24: 50, Pl. XII, fig. 154, 1924). It is probable than much remains to be discovered on more complete studies of the life histories of the group.

Cytologists who gather females of *Ameletus ludens* for the study of chromosome behavior in development need to be reminded that it is not necessarily and exclusively parthenogenetic.

The male may be described as follows:—

Ameletus ludens Needham.

Adult male: Length of body 8.5 mm.; tails 10.5 mm. additional; fore wing 9 mm.; fore leg 12 mm.

Head blackish, including the small lower division of the compound eyes. The large subspherical upper division of the eyes is honey yellow. Antennæ black.

The dorsum of the thorax is brown, with only small peripheral yellow markings around the humeri and on the metanotum. On the latter a pair of divergent pale marks is followed by a yellow U-mark in the rear upon the crest. In a side view the dorsum shines by reflected light with a golden metallic lustre. The thorax is black beneath except for narrow areas around the leg bases. The abdomen is brownish above, varied with paler on the middle segments at the ends. Beneath, the abdomen is whitish on the basal half. Middle and hind legs are brown; the fore legs, blackish, with one claw somewhat paler. Wings hyaline, with all venation black except at the extreme base. Tails blackish, becoming a little paler apically. Forceps black, tawny at the base, with extremely short basal segment, subequal terminal segments and the second segment much exceeding in length the other three taken together.

This is the smallest known species of the genus. Its nearest allied species is *Ameletus velox* Dodds (Trans. Amer. Ent. Soc. 49: 105, Pl. 8, fig. 17, 1923). The male genitalia differ from those of that species in the following points: the basal segment of the forceps is much shorter, being wider than long; the second segment is less cylindric, being constricted at its basal third and widened toward both ends; between the two triangular lobes of the plate beneath the penes there is a broadly rounded median notch; and the penes themselves are shorter and less incurved at the tips.

The unique male specimen is in the Cornell University collection.

NOTE ON THE HABITS OF *SPHENOPHORUS PONTEDERIÆ* CHTTN.

By D. H. Blake.

Bureau of Entomology, Washington, D. C.

In late August of 1924 the ponds of eastern Massachusetts were very low and in some instances dry because of a long drought. In two ponds in Stoughton and Easton beds of pickerel weed (*Pontederia cordata* L.) outside water level were brown and dying, while other plants nearby, although not any more supplied with pond water than the dying ones, were apparently healthy. Investigation showed that the dead patches of plants were heavily infested with larvæ, pupæ, and newly emerged adults of *Sphenophorus pontederiæ* Chttn. The thick rootstocks were completely hollowed out and rotten, and each plant contained several larvæ or pupæ. So disintegrated were these plants that when one took hold of the leaves and stalks they separated at once from the rootstock. The larvæ were most frequently found tunneling the rootstocks, but when they became mature they generally bored up into the flowering stem an inch or two above the earth to pupate.

In several stalks a dipterous puparium was found beside the remains of the larva, plainly a parasite of *Sphenophorus*. The adult fly that emerged has been identified by Dr. J. M. Aldrich as *Lixophaga variabilis* Coq. This parasite, closely allied to the parasite (*Lixophaga diatrææ* Tns.) of the sugar-cane borer (*Diatræa saccharalis* Fab.) has been reared in one instance, according to Dr. Aldrich, from *Lixus scrobicollis* Lec. at Dallas, Tex. In another case a carabid larva was found feeding on a pupa. Several carabid and staphylinid beetles also occurred suspiciously near the infested plants.

PROCEEDINGS OF THE CAMBRIDGE ENTOMOLOGICAL CLUB.

The meetings of the Club were resumed September 9, 1924. Mr. O. E. Plath who has studied the habits of bumblebees for several seasons reported many new observations made during the past summer.

Prof. W. M. Wheeler gave an account of the Barro Colorado biological reservation on an island in the Panama canal where he had spent part of the summer in company with Mr. Banks and Prof. Parker.

At the meeting of October 14, Dr. Joseph Bequaert told about his recent excursion to the Amazon river on the expedition conducted by Hamilton Rice, with several medical companions. Much of the country was under water but at Manaos and other landing places many interesting studies were made. Dr. Bequaert showed a dipterous parasite of a land-snail and a termite that excavates its nest in healthy and growing trees.

Mr. C. W. Johnson spoke of the large number of Diptera of several species on the salt-marshes and beaches of Gloucester, Mass.

Mr. A. P. Morse showed ends of branches of the blue spruce enlarged by the aphid, *Chermes cooleyi.*

At the meeting November 11, Mr. J. G. Myers gave an account of some little known Hemiptera from Panama. One of these lives in webs of spiders hanging among the outer threads like the guest spider Argyrodes. Mr. R. L. Schwarz spoke of a small moth from Texas (Meskea) which lives on plants of the mallow-family in gall-like enlargements of the stem. Mr. A. P. Morse exhibited the wingless female of the moth *Erannis tiliaris* of the linden tree and thirty males showing great variation in markings of the wings.

At the meeting of December 9, Mr. C. R. Kellogg of the Agricultural College at Foochow, China gave a lecture on the cultivation of silk in China which is still largely carried on by small farmers in the most primitive way. Mr. Kellogg is studying improved methods by which disease and parasites are reduced and larger yields obtained. Models of the common hand reel and many other implements used in sericulture were shown and some cocoons unwound.

Mr. A. P. Morse exhibited a dried chimney-swift from which the finer parts of the feathers had been entirely eaten away leaving only the quills. This was thought to be the work of Anthrenus.

TP pp315-16 removed

placed in front of v.

Binding Unit..

PSYCHE

INDEX TO VOL. XXXI, 1924.

INDEX TO AUTHORS.

INDEX TO SUBJECTS

All new genera, new species and new names are printed in Small Capital Letters.

www.ingramcontent.com/pod-product-compliance
Lightning Source LLC
Chambersburg PA
CBHW022124020426
42334CB00015B/751

* 9 7 8 3 7 4 1 1 7 8 1 5 3 *